UNDERSTANDING

University of Liverpool

For conc

MACMILLAN TEXTS IN ECONOMICS

This series presents a new generation of economics textbooks from Macmillan developed in conjunction with a panel of distinguished editorial advisers:

David Greenaway, Professor of Economics, University of Nottingham
Gordon Hughes, Professor of Political Economy, University of Edinburgh
David Pearce, Professor of Economics, University College London
David Ulph, Professor of Economics, University College London

Published
Understanding the UK Economy (3rd edition): edited by Peter Curwen
Business Economics: Paul R. Ferguson, Glenys J. Ferguson and R. Rothschild
International Finance: Keith Pilbeam
The Economics of the Labour Market: David Sapsford and Zafiris Tzannatos

Future Macmillan Texts in Economics cover the core compulsory and optional courses in economics at first-degree level and will include:

Public Sector Economics: Stephen Bailey
Financial Economics: Kevin Dowd
Environmental Economics: Nick Hanley, Ben White and Jason Shogren
Development Economics: Ian Livingstone
Econometrics: Ian D. McAvinchey
International Trade: Mia Mikic
Macroeconomics: Eric Pentecost

UNDERSTANDING THE UK ECONOMY

Third Edition

Edited by

Peter Curwen

Contributors

David Gowland and Stephen James
Keith Hartley and Nick Hooper
Paul Marshall

MACMILLAN

First edition 1990
Reprinted 1990
Second edition 1992
Third edition 1994

Published by
THE MACMILLAN PRESS LTD
Houndmills, Basingstoke, Hampshire RG21 2XS
and London
Companies and representatives
throughout the world

ISBN 0–333–61526–3

A catalogue record for this book is available
from the British Library.

Copy-edited and typeset by Povey–Edmondson
Okehampton and Rochdale, England

Printed in Great Britain by The Bath Press, Avon

Series Standing Order (Macmillan Texts in Economics)

If you would like to receive future titles in this series as they are published, you can make use
of our standing order facility. To place a standing order please contact your bookseller or, in
case of difficulty, write to us at the address below with your name and address and the name
of the series. Please state with which title you wish to begin your standing order. (If you live
outside the United Kingdom we may not have the rights for your area, in which case we will
forward your order to the publisher concerned.)

Customer Services Department, Macmillan Distribution Ltd,
Houndmills, Basingstoke, Hampshire, RG21 2XS, England

To Benjamin and Alexandra

Contents

List of Figures

List of Tables

List of Abbreviations

ACT	Advance Corporation Tax	EEA	Exchange Equalisation Account
AD	Aggregate Demand	EEC	European Economic Community
AFBD	Association of Futures Brokers and Dealers	EER	Effective Exchange Rate
		EFF	Extended Fund Facility
AMS	Aggregate Measure of Support	EFL	External Financing Limit
APC	Average Propensity to Consume	EFTPOS	Electronic Funds Transfer at Point of Sale
AS	Aggregate Supply		
ATM	Automated Teller Machine	EMCF	European Monetary Co-operation Fund
BBC	British Broadcasting Corporation		
BES	Business Expansion Scheme	EMI	European Monetary Institute
BIS	Bank for International Settlements	EMS	European Monetary System
BoP	Balance of Payments	EMTNs	Euromedium-term Notes
BTEC	Business and Technician Education Council	EMU	Economic and Monetary Union
		EPU	European Political Union
CAP	Common Agricultural Polcy	ERI	Effective Exchange Rate Index
CBI	Confederation of British Industry	ERM	Exchange Rate Mechanism
CCC	Competition and Credit Control	ESCB	European System of Central Banks
CD	Certificate of Deposit	ET	Employment Training
CET	Common External Tariff	EU	European Union
CFSP	Common Foreign and Security Policy	FES	Family Expenditure Survey
CGT	Capital Gains Tax	FIMBRA	Financial Intermediaries, Managers and Brokers Regulatory Association
CR	Concentration Ratio		
CSE	Consumer Subsidy Equivalent	FIS	Family Income Supplement
CSO	Central Statistical Office	FMI	Financial Management Initiative
CTT	Capital Transfer Tax	FRN	Floating-rate Note
DCE	Domestic Credit Expansion	FSBR	Financial Statement and Budget Report
DHSS	Department of Health and Social Security		
		GAB	General Agreements to Borrow
DIB	Defence Industrial Base	GATT	General Agreement on Tariffs and Trade
DM	Deutsche Mark		
DTI	Department of Trade and Industry	GCSE	General Certificate in Secondary Education
EAGGF	European Agricultural Guarantee and Guidance Fund		
		GDFCF	Gross Domestic Fixed Capital Formation
EAP	Enlarged Access Policy		
EAS	Enterprise Allowance Scheme	GDP	Gross Domestic Product
EC	European Community	GEMM	Gilt-edged Market-maker
ECB	European Central Bank	GGE	General Government Expenditure
ECU	European Currency Unit	GNP	Gross National Product
EDI	Electronic Data Interchange	HBAI	Households Below Average Income

HMSO	Her Majesty's Stationery Office	NDP	Net Domestic Product
IBELs	Interest-bearing Eligible Liabilities	NHS	National Health Service
ICCs	Industrial and Commercial Companies	NI	National Income
		NICs	National Insurance Contributions
IDC	Industrial Development Certificate	NIESR	National Institute for Economic and Social Research
IFA	Independent Financial Adviser		
IFS	Institute for Fiscal Studies	NNP	Net National Product
IGA	Inter-governmental Agreement	NSB	National Savings Bank
IGC	Inter-governmental Conference	OECD	Organisation for Economic Co-operation and Development
ILO	International Labour Office		
IMF	International Monetary Fund	OFGAS	Office of Gas Supply
IMRO	Investment Management Regulatory Organisation	OFT	Office of Fair Trading
		OFTEL	Office of Telecommunications
IPD	Interest, Profits and Dividends	OMO	Open-market Operation
IPR	Intellectual Property Right	OPEC	Organisation of Petroleum Exporting Countries
ISDA	International Swap Dealers Association		
		OTC	Over the Counter
JA	Jobseeker's Allowance	PAYE	Pay As You Earn
LA	Local Authority	PDI	Personal Disposable Income
LASFE	Local Authority Self-financed Expenditure	PEP	Personal Equity Plan
		PIA	Personal Investment Authority
LAUTRO	Life Assurance and Unit Trust Regulatory Organisation	PIBS	Permanent Interest Bearing Shares
		PPP	Purchasing Power Parity
LDC	Less Developed Country	PPS	Perpetual Preferred Stock
LDMA	London Discount Market Association	PRT	Petroleum Revenue Tax
LFS	Labour Force Survey	PSBR	Public Sector Borrowing Requirement
LIBOR	London Inter-bank Offered Rate	PSDR	Public Sector Debt Repayment
LIF	Low Income Families	PSE	Producer Subsidy Equivalent
LIFFE	London International Financial Futures Exchange	R&D	Research and Development
		RDG	Regional Development Grant
LSE	London Stock Exchange	REG	Regional Enterprise Grant
LTOM	London Traded Options Market	RER	Real Exchange Rate
MCA	Monetary Compensatory Amount	RPI	Retail Prices Index
MFA	Multi-fibre Arrangement	RPIX	Underlying Retail Prices Index
MIPs	Mortgage Interest Payments	RPM	Resale Price Maintenance
MIRAS	Mortgage-interest Relief at Source	RSA	Regional Selective Assistance
MLR	Minimum Lending Rate	SB	Supplementary Benefit
MMC	Monopolies and Mergers Commission	SDR	Special Drawing Right
		SEA	Single European Act
MoD	Ministry of Defence	SEAQ	Stock Exchange Automated Quotation
MPW	Marginal Propensity to Withdraw		
MSC	Manpower Services Commission	SEM	Single European Market
MTFS	Medium Term Financial Strategy	SERPS	State Earnings Related Pension Scheme
MTN	Multilateral Trade Negotiations		
NAIRU	Non-accelerating Inflation Rate of Unemployment	SFA	The Securities and Futures Authority
		SFF	Supplementary Financing Facility
NBFI	Non-bank Financial Intermediaries	SIB	Securities and Investments Board
NCT	New Control Total	SMU	Support Measurement Unit

SRO	Self Regulatory Organisation	YTS	Youth Training Scheme
TB	Treasury Bill		
TDI	Total Domestic Income		
TEC	Training and Enterprise Council	Countries are abbreviated in tables and figures in	
TESSA	Tax Exempt Special Savings Account	accordance with the originals. The following ab-	
TFE	Total Final Expenditure	breviations are used:	
TPI	Tax and Price Index		
TRS	Transitional Reduction Scheme	Belgium	B
TSA	The Securities Association	Denmark	DK
TSB	Trustee Savings Bank	France	F or FR
UAA	Utilised Agricultural Area	Greece	GR
USM	Unlisted Securities Market	Ireland	IRL
VAT	Value Added Tax	Italy	I or IT
VER	Voluntary Export Restraint	Luxembourg	L
VSTF	Very-short-term Financing	Netherlands	NL
WIRS	Workplace Industrial Relations	Portugal	P
	Survey	Spain	S or E
YES	Youth Employment Subsidy	United Kingdom	UK
YOP	Youth Opportunity Programme	West Germany	FRG or WG or D

Preface to the First Edition

We very much hope that the justification for writing a book of this kind is self-evident. If this is not the case, then we simply wish to point out that economic literacy remains at far too low a level in the UK. In seeking to enhance this literacy we like to think that this book will be of interest to a very wide-ranging audience, but we recognise that, in practice, almost all those who read it will be studying a parallel course in economic principles, either at A-level or as undergraduates, or will already be acquainted with economic issues either through their work or their reading of the financial press. We hope that the book is sufficiently challenging to interest readers who are already conversant with economics, but not so challenging as to prevent readers who are not conversant with economic theory from following the discussion.

We have tried to strike an acceptable balance between **analysis** and **description**. It is obviously necessary, in a book of this kind, to describe how the UK functions at the present time, and also how it has functioned in the past where this has been different. It is, however, unilluminating simply to explain what is done in policy terms without simultaneously explaining why, and the reasons why are also to be found in the book where appropriate. It should be noted that the kinds of models to be found in textbooks may often fail to explain why many policies are being pursued, because the real world may be evolving very rapidly and be using fairly crude rules of thumb whilst coming to terms with these changes. It is accordingly our intention to concentrate upon the real world, and to give short shrift to textbook models which cannot shed much light upon it.

Most readers familiar with economics will have been taught the subject as a succession of separate boxes labelled 'employment', 'inflation', and so on. There is, as a consequence, a preference for applications to be organised into similar boxes, to be dipped into one by one as appropriate. We do not care for this approach because, first, it fails to emphasise the **fundamental linkages** between the various parts of the economy; secondly, it fails to deliver a satisfactory **historical perspective**; and thirdly, it permits the authors covering the content of separate boxes to offer a **subjective interpretation** of events which conflicts with that to be found in other boxes. Rather oddly, some books consider this latter point to be a virtue, and express distaste for the imposition of monolithic structures. Our view is that this is very much a vice, and indicative of lack of editorial control. This book is accordingly approached from precisely the opposite viewpoint – namely, that individual authors should work to a carefully predetermined structure and that stylistic differences should be kept to a minimum. In particular, each author has been asked to set out the pros and cons of every policy debate without prejudice. This does not mean that the authors do not have strong preferences concerning the conduct of policy, nor indeed that they have refrained from expressing them, but rather that they do not seek to persuade by omitting to mention what the counter-arguments are.

The issue concerning the need to provide a framework which integrates individual sections has been difficult to resolve. One innovative feature in this respect is the introductory chapter which seeks to provide both a philosophical basis and an historical perspective for all that follows. A second innovation is to set the discussion of fiscal and monetary policy at the end of the book, in Chapter 12, so that it draws together the macroeconomic threads from previous chapters, with Chapter 11 doing the same for the microeconomic threads. The early chapters presume least prior knowledge, but when necessary they are extensively cross-referenced to later points in the text where the missing information is to be found. Issues which can be broadly be said to concern welfare have been allocated a chapter of their own (Chapter 10), rather than ignored altogether or dispersed in brief and unrelated sections throughout the text.

Certain themes inevitably appear under several chapter headings – for example, the development of the Single European Market (SEM). Generally speaking they are left dispersed, but cross-referenced to other parts of the book where the same themes recur. However, in certain cases – for example, agriculture – it has made more sense to collect the themes together under one heading in order to avoid duplication and the loss of continuity in the discussion. For these reasons, the structure of the book may at first sight appear unusual, but we firmly believe that it does, in fact, make better sense than the structures to be found in other texts, and we leave it to the readers to judge for themselves (and hopefully to let us know their opinions on the matter in due course).

While the book is essentially about the UK economy, it has a stronger international flavour than is commonly associated with books on this topic. This reflects a whole host of developments, such as the SEM and deregulation in general, which are making it increasingly inappropriate to view policy within the physical confines of the UK alone. Since this is very much a feature of ongoing policy we have deliberately set up our discussion so that it offers clear pointers towards the future, and we have chosen to compensate for this by saying much less than is usual about the more distant past.

In our opinion the election of the current government was a significant watershed in policy terms, for reasons set out in the Introduction. Each chapter is accordingly structured to say relatively little about the period before 1969; to provide a fairly detailed review of the decade 1969–79; and to focus primarily upon the decade 1979–89 and especially upon how it has compared with the decade which preceded it.

All this places great demands upon the handling of data. We have tried to introduce as much data as possible, and to locate it all within the appro-priate context rather than relegate it to appendices. Equally, we recognise that tabular material can be boring – and, at times, a poor means of communication – so where appropriate other methods of presentation have been used. A point to be emphasised is that data are expressed in the form normally used by government and reported in the media. Thus, for example, the Public Sector Borrowing Requirement (PSBR) is not simply stated as an absolute number but as a percentage of gross domestic product (GDP). Much of the data is adjusted for inflation, and whenever space permits the comparable data for other countries are also included.

The contributors to this book (other than the editor) have been chosen because they are knowledgeable in their fields. However, too much knowledge can be a vice as well as a virtue when it comes down to the need to compress a great deal of information into a small space, and the authors are commended to you not so much because they are 'specialists' but because they have proved in their previously published work that they have the facility to communicate to the target audience for this book. We hope that it makes enjoyable reading. No doubt you will let us know if that is not the case. One way or the other the editor is more than happy to accept ultimate responsibility for the entire finished product, although individual authors are responsible only for the chapters which bear their name.

Finally I would like to thank Gordon Hughes and the other five anonymous reviewers for their thorough dissection of the text in its varying stages of completion. There is a myth – propagated, one suspects, by those who write only short articles – that textbooks are not refereed adequately, but that has been far from the reality in this particular case. Whilst some suggestions for improvements have been set aside for this edition, it is anticipated that they will be incorporated in the second edition.

Any restructuring of the text in subsequent editions will be determined entirely by the suggestions of users, and these are accordingly welcomed by the editor.

PETER CURWEN

Preface to the Second Edition

Armed with reviews and a large number of questionnaires completed by teachers, we have set out to revise the text significantly for this second edition. While not every suggestion for improvement has been adopted on this occasion, we are already considering how best to manage the book's evolutionary path.

It is important to begin by clearing up one particular misunderstanding. Although it is hoped that many readers will be able to enjoy the text without having previously learned economics in a formal way, we anticipated that most readers would use this book in conjunction with a basic text on economic theory, thereby allowing us to concentrate upon its applications in the real world. The text contains such models as are essential to assist both the general reader and students of economics who are reading ahead of their main text to understand the issues which we address, which can be very complicated, but it is simply impractical to try to combine detailed theory and applications in a single text.

We have attempted to keep the text as up to date as is humanly possible. To this end we have introduced a large amount of new data, particularly in the form of Figures, whilst removing a much smaller amount which appeared in the first edition. We believe that this database provides a truly comprehensive overview of the workings of the UK economy. In recognition of recent developments we have included a good deal of additional material on the European Community, and have sought wherever possible to draw comparisons between the performance of the UK and other member states.

The editor has chosen in this edition to take over responsibility for writing all of the first nine chapters in the book, two of which have been divided compared to the first edition as a result of the addition of much new material. This should ensure greater uniformity of approach, and also ease the burden of revision for future editions. The new material is generally intended to introduce developments which have taken place over the past two years, but completely new sections have also been added where it was thought that they would enhance the discussion in a material way. For example, there is a new section devoted to the housing market in Chapter 3, which is accompanied by a fuller discussion of the link between wealth, consumption and saving, and Chapter 2 contains a completely new version of the overall model of the economy.

It is hoped that these, and other, improvements have enhanced the usefulness of the text for a wide variety of readers. As before, the text has been thoroughly reviewed in draft form in order to ensure that this is so, and we would like to thank the reviewers for their extensive and helpful comments.

PETER CURWEN

Preface to the Third Edition

Only two years have passed since the publication of the second edition, but events have, as ever, refused to stand still, necessitating some significant revisions to parts of the text. Looking back at what was written two years ago, the analysis appears to have held up well and we see no need to retract anything of substance, but there can be no doubt that two years of recession oblige us to rethink the probable course of the UK economy during the rest of the decade.

When the second edition was at final proof stage it proved necessary to insert a substantial section relating to the Maastricht Treaty. At the time it was assumed that it would be signed and sealed before 1992 was out, with member states if anything moving closer together in the narrow band of the Exchange Rate Mechanism (ERM). In the event, the outcome has been rather different, so this edition contains a good deal of analysis of what went wrong and where it is taking the UK.

In this, and other respects which reflect, for example, the official creation of the SEM on 1 January 1992, the text is increasingly seeking to examine the role of the UK as part of a wider political/economic system. Nevertheless, the UK has recently been affected by the consequences of some of its own peculiar structures, and of these the housing market is clearly the most prominent. For this reason, the discussion of the role of the housing market has been greatly extended in this edition.

In most other respects the primary task has been, as usual, to update the database so that it provides a meaningful picture of the current state of the economy; in effect, that prevailing at the end of 1992 or some months into 1993, but any significant turns in events at the end of 1993 have also been integrated into the text. We therefore trust that this new edition will continue to provide teachers and students alike with an invaluable insight into the workings of the UK economy.

One final change of practice needs to be noted. Whereas in previous editions we referred to the European Community (EC), throughout this edition we refer to the European Union (EU), or occasionally simply to the Community, in line with current practice in the majority of governmental and media commentary. In practice, insofar as the terms EC and EU relate to the subject matter of this book, they can be treated as interchangeable.

PETER CURWEN

Acknowledgements

The authors and publishers wish to thank the following for permission to use copyright material:

Bank of England for Tables 3.8, 3.10, 3.12, 4.2, 4.3, 4.7, 6.3, 8.12 and Figures 2.8, 2.10, 2,11, 2.12, 3.3, 3.5, 3.8, 3.9, 3.11, 3.25, 3.27, 4.3, 4.5, 4.6, 4.7, 5.11, 6.4, 6.8, 6.12, 6.13, 6.14, 6.15, 12.1.

Barclays Bank for Table 12.6 and Figures 3.26, 12.3.

Confederation of British Industry for Figures 3.10 and 9.2.

The Controller of Her Majesty's Stationery Office for Tables 2.1, 2.2, 2.3, 2.4, 2.5, 2.6, 2.7, 2.8, 3.1, 3.2, 3.3, 3.4, 3.5, 3.9, 3.11, 5.1, 5.2, 5.4, 5.5, 5.7, 5.8, 5.9, 5.11, 5.12, 6.1, 6.2, 6.4, 6.5, 6.6, 6.7, 6.8, 7.6, 7.17, 8.1, 8.2, 8.3, 8.4, 8.5, 8.6, 8.7, 8.8, 8.9, 8.10, 9.1, 9.3, 9.5, 9.6, 10.1, 10.2, 10.3, 10.4, 10.5, 10.6, 10.7, 11.1, 11.2, 11.5, 11.8, 11.9, 12.1, 12.3, 12.4, 12.7; and Figures 2.5, 2.6, 2.7, 2.9, 3.1, 3.2, 3.4, 3.6, 3.13, 3.15, 3.16, 3.17, 3.18, 3.19, 3.20, 3.21, 3.22, 3.23, 3.24, 5.1, 5.2, 5.3, 5.4, 5.5, 5.6, 5.7, 5.10, 5.12, 6.1, 6.2, 6.3, 6.5, 6.6, 6.9, 6.11, 7.1, 8.1, 8.2, 8.5, 8.6, 8.7, 8.9, 8.10, 8.11, 8.12, 8.13, 8.14, 9.1, 9.3, 9.4, 9.5, 10.4.

Council of Mortgage Lenders for Table 4.6.

Financial Times for Table 7.15 and Figures 4.2, 4.4, 4.10, 7.8, 8.3.

Information Division, HM Treasury, for Table 3.6 and Figure 3.14.

Institute for Fiscal Studies for Tables 10.8, 10.11 and Figure 10.3.

Noel Alexander Associates for Tables 4.5 and 4.9.

Office for Official Publications of the European Communities for Tables 5.3, 5.13, 7.12, 7.16, 10.12, 10.13 and Figures 10.5, 10.6, 10.7.

The Economist for Figures 4.1, 4.9, 6.7, 8.4.

Every effort has been made to trace all the copyright-holders, but if any have been inadvertently overlooked the publishers will be pleased to make the necessary arrangement at the first opportunity.

■ Chapter 1 ■

History and Politics

Peter Curwen

■ *1.1* Introduction

Our purpose in this chapter is to set the scene for the detailed analysis of the UK economy which is the subject matter of this book.

Economics has become increasingly technical, in an attempt to build ever more sophisticated models which tend to lose touch with the behaviour of economic agents in the real world. This, in its turn, has tended to detract from the need to study the historical and political context within which policy making actually takes place. This book, however, is entirely about the real world, and therefore requires the reader to have at least a rudimentary understanding of economic history and political systems. This chapter sets out to provide this understanding and may, therefore, readily be omitted by those already well versed in these fields.

Economic ideas, in common with those in many other disciplines, tend to pass through the successive phases of **revolution** and **evolution**. The revolutionary phases are often associated with a particular event, such as the publication of a book, although the seeds of the ideas may have been sown a great many years earlier and be awaiting the ideal moment for germination. Furthermore, it is not altogether easy to pinpoint when a revolution is set in motion since there is inevitably a great deal of inertia before revolutionary ideas gain widespread acceptance. The

subsequent discussion is concerned primarily with the Keynesian and monetarist revolutions. The former is generally associated with the publication of the *General Theory* in 1936, but for our purposes is more sensibly seen in policy terms as underpinning the significant changes which took place between 1944 and 1949. The monetarist revolution flowered during the 1970s and came of age in the UK during the early years of the period of Conservative rule commencing in 1979, and it is partly for this reason that 1979 is treated as the watershed year for the text as a whole.

The evolutionary phase of Keynesianism lasted broadly from 1950 to 1970, at which point events (discussed below) conspired to bring about its steady decline prior to its official replacement by monetarism. Monetarism, on the other hand, barely had the chance to evolve at all before significant aspects were consigned to virtual oblivion, leaving the UK in a kind of polcy limbo: part-monetarist, part-Keynesian and part whatever seemed to be a good idea at the time to deal with short-term problems.

It is important to appreciate, to begin with, that there two quite divergent ways of looking at those economic models which are put into practice. The first, clearly enunciated by Keynes himself and generally favoured by the intellectual circles in which he moved, is that the ideas of economists and political philosophers are the **driving force behind the implementation of policy**. Support for

1

this viewpoint can be found in the influential doctrine of **laissez-faire** during the nineteenth century, and subsequently in the writings of Keynes himself. The opposing doctrine is that economists have a barely detectable influence on society as a whole, since the popularity of particular ideas ultimately depends upon their compatibility with economic and political circumstances at the time. In other words, the broad direction in which economic policy moves is determined by the ways in which **interest groups in society respond to changing economic opportunities**, and economic models are chosen because they lend intellectual support to the behaviour of those groups.

The debate between these two schools of thought will, naturally, never be satisfactorily resolved because it is hard to see how either case can be 'proved' to everyone's satisfaction. An interesting current illustration of this debate relates to the case of privatisation, where it is possible to argue, on the one hand, that the policy was adopted as a result of ear-bending in influential Conservative circles by the Institute of Economic Affairs and other like-minded groups and, on the other, that once the decision had been taken to reduce the role of government and to cut public expenditure, asset sales were simply one available means to achieve these goals.

A variety of economic models is analysed in the chapters which follow. However, it is at best unhelpful simply to model the economy at a specific point in time as though it can be divorced from the historical and political context which shaped it over a period of many decades. Indeed, it is possible to argue that many of the key influences moulding the way the economy behaves today have their origins well back in the nineteenth century, but a shortage of space does not permit us to examine these other than in a fairly cursory way.

■ 1.2 The Neo-classical World

At the end of the nineteenth century the **forces of the market place** still largely held sway over economic life. Certainly, government had been taking on board ever wider responsiblities which needed to be financed through taxation, but macroeconomic management of the kind practised after 1945 was incompatible with the prevailing 'neo-classical' orthodoxy.

This held true, for example, with respect to unemployment. The mechanisation of argriculture at the turn of the century forced large numbers of people off the land and into towns and cities. There were, understandably, difficulties in absorbing this inflow of labour into the industrial workforce, and the prevailing orthodoxy therefore needed to explain the adjustment process whereby the level of employment would be restored to equilibrium. The line taken by the neo-classical school was that, in a competitive market system such as characterised the UK economy at the time, the **equilibrium condition was one of full employment**. In other words, any imbalances between the supply of, and demand for, a factor of production such as labour could only be temporary, since any imbalance between the two would automatically trigger forces in the market place which would bring them back into balance. The forces in question were **changes in relative prices**, such that if there was excess demand for a factor of production its price (its wage in the case of labour) would be driven upwards until the point was reached at which potential purchasers would be induced to switch over from demanding the new, relatively expensive, factor of production, to others which in the process had become relatively cheap. Likewise, the price of a factor of production in excess supply would be driven steadily downwards, until a level was reached at which all that was being supplied at that price level was purchased.

Given its resurgence in the modern context of **supply-side economics**, it is important to appreciate what interpretation this line of argument placed upon the concept of full employment. What the neo-classical model was effectively saying was that if the market for labour was left to its own devices, a wage rate would be established such that anyone who was willing to work would have a job to go to, and employment would in that sense be permanently 'full'. By implication, all unemployment could be treated as **voluntary** because the individuals in question must either be unwilling to work at **any** wage rate, or willing to work, but only at a wage rate higher than that which the market was prepared to pay. There would always be enough potential jobs to employ everyone willing to work; it was simply a question of finding the market-clearing wage. However, if some individuals chose not to accept that wage, then clearly they were preventing the market from functioning smoothly, in which case they were themselves the **cause** of the problem of unemployment. Since they were the cause, and a cure was readily available were they willing to accept a reduction in their target wage rate, it could not by implication be anyone else's responsibility to deal with unemployment. Hence there was no need for governments to intervene in the labour market.

1.2.1 Real and Money Magnitudes

Within the neo-classical model a crucial distinction was made between **real** and **money** magnitudes. The total **volume** of labour – or of any other factor of production – in employment at any one time was regarded as a real magnitude, governed by the price of one factor relative to that of others. If all other things remained equal, and if a unit of labour cost £1 whilst a unit of machinery cost £2, then labour was half the price of capital and would be employed in preference to capital. This would be wholly unaffected by a doubling of the **general price level**, with the prices above rising to £2 and £4 repectively, since labour would remain one-half of the price of capital per unit employed, and indeed this would hold true were prices in general to rise by a multiple of 100 or 1000 times. The **volume** of labour would remain constant while the monetary **value** of labour used would vary enormously.

It followed that there was no direct link between the general level of prices and the level of employment. Nevertheless, there had to be a reason why the general price level showed considerable volatility over time, and the reason was

called the **Quantity Theory of Money**. The original, or 'old' version of the Quantity Theory was formulated within the context of a monetary system called the gold standard. This meant that the total amount of money available was directly related to the available stock of gold, originally on a one-to-one basis; but, subsequent to the widespread adoption of the principle of credit creation, it was in a fixed proportionate relationship. Hence, if more gold was put into circulation, but no more real goods and services, prices in general would be driven upwards in order to ensure that the available stock of money would remain just sufficient, **and no more**, to purchase the available stock of goods and services. This applied equally well in reverse, with prices falling when the output of goods and services increased but no new supply of gold became available.

1.2.2 Mass Unemployment

The return of the labour force from active military duty after 1918 coincided with a sharp downturn in economic activity resulting from a combination of matters such as an overvalued exchange rate, ageing tecnology and increased world-wide competition. Industries such as coal mining suffered badly. Motive power was switching from coal to oil, and deep-mining in Britain was very expensive compared to the costs of newly-opened mines elsewhere. The coal-mine owners sought to resolve the problem by forcing their coal miners to take a reduction in their wages. However, the miners resisted, going on strike in 1921 and triggering the General Strike of 1926. They were ultimately defeated (hindered, in part, by the lack of a welfare system to fall back on in hard times), but many mines were nevertheless forced to shut down. This was paralleled in other industries and, as a result, there was widespread unemployment in the UK at a time when other economies were booming.

Although the depression which began in the UK in 1919 was by no means typical (the overvalued currency was a critical fator not found elsewhere), it did provide food for thought for many economists brought up in the neo-classical orthodoxy, amongst them John Maynard Keynes. The neo-classical model was steadily amended and refined, and within Keynes's *Treatise on Money*, published in 1930, one can detect a distinct step forward along the evolutionary path of the existing orthodoxy at precisely the point in history when events conspired to expose the model's inadequacies, for in 1929 there occurred the Wall Street Crash.

Unfortunately, the response of most governments after the Great Crash was to do all the wrong things. In particular, America rapidly introduced an era of trade protectionism to which other countries responded in kind, with the result that the total volume of world trade fell sharply. It has also been argued by writers such as Milton Friedman that the American Federal Reserve System deliberately engineered a shortage of liquidity, thereby making it very difficult for debtors to obtain the money they needed to settle their debts. Irrespective of the causes, the effects were straightforward enough. Unemployment rose sharply throughout the Western world, the impact falling particularly upon towns and regions overdependent upon traditional industries such as shipbuilding.

In the face of mass unemployment the neo-classical orthodoxy effectively broke down. To argue that millions of people could be got back to work simply by lowering the wage rate, thereby restoring equilibrium in the labour market, seemed futile in the extreme; but on the subject of what else could be done the model was largely silent. The time was at last ripe for the seed of revolution to grow.

■ 1.3 The Keynesian Revolution

This revolution is associated with the work of Keynes, and in particular with the ideas expressed in the *General Theory of Employment, Interest and Money*, published in 1936. The *General Theory* is a book of baffling obscurity; some argue this obscurity was deliberate in order to get the central, simpler propositions accepted while the arguments raged about interpreting the com-

plexities. The standard textbook version essentially dates back to the model introduced after the Second World War, and it is certainly only fair to argue that Keynes himself, who died in 1946, would have made significant alterations to his text had he lived longer. Nevertheless there can be little dispute about his main lines of attack upon the neo-classical orthodoxy.

In the *General Theory*, Keynes set out to demonstrate that the level of national income (NI) – and hence effectively of output and employment – was determined by the **interaction of changes in both real and monetary variables**, and also that there was a direct link between decisions taken by **individual households and firms** and the effect upon the **economy as a whole**. The cornerstone of Keynes's work was the rejection of the reasoning which led in the neo-classical model to the automatic restoration of full employment, the creation of an alternative theory which in the general case would generate less than full employment, and the use of that theory to explain how unemployment could be cured.

One of the main innovations of the Keynesian model was its stress upon the role of **expectations in the face of uncertainty**. Keynes felt that decisions with respect to the expansion or curtailment of output were to a considerable degree dependant upon the prevailing set of expectations about the future held by households and firms. In the event, for example, that firms in general did not expect an early recovery from a period of recession, their natural reaction would be to hold back from producing output which they did not expect to be able to sell, and to lay off workers whom they could no longer gainfully employ. The consequence of such a policy would be a significant reduction in the amount of money which households had to spend since, insofar as it existed, State assistance was not as rewarding as full-time employment. The consequent cut-back in consumption spending would adversely affect retail outlets, which in turn would reduce orders from wholesalers, and the latter would cut back orders from manufacturers.

The curtailment of output and employment undertaken in the expectation of the fall in demand for goods and services would thus itself create the expected circumstances of reduced consumption. In other words, expectations have an in-built tendency to be **self-fulfilling**, and in so doing they inevitably help to generate a further set of **similar expectations**. The confirmation of a firm's expectations that it would not be able to sell what it produced would thus probably cause the firm to curtail output and employment still further. The link between decisions taken by households and firms, and their consequences for the economy as a whole were, therefore, plain to see.

This line of reasoning tended to imply that the level of employment was affected by the prevailing set of expectations. But there seemed little enough reason to suppose that the prevailing state of expectations would always be such as to secure full employment. The neo-classical model argued that full employment could always be restored by reducing the wage rate. But suppose the wage rate was indeed to fall as it recommended. The result would logically be a reduction in the amount of money available for current consumption, which in turn would lead inevitably to a reduction in sales and profits. The Keynesian model argued that firms would respond by **cutting** output and employment. Since this was exactly the opposite conclusion to that postulated in the neo-classical model, the inevitable conclusion was that full employment could not, in fact, be restored through changes in relative prices.

The one undisputed fact of the early 1930s was that the Great Crash and its aftermath had resulted in depressed expectations. It was not that the firms did not want to expand on an individual basis, but if one firm produced more output, created new jobs and paid out more in wages at a time when other firms did not follow suit, then almost all of the extra wages would be spent on the output of other firms rather than that of the firm paying out the wages, thereby inevitably driving it into bankruptcy. Of course, if all firms chose to expand simultaneously there would be enough extra wages in circulation to keep them all in business, but that could only happen if their expectations were simultaneously to improve, and in the climate of the 1930s that was simply not going to happen.

It followed logically from this that full employment could be restored if either households unilaterally decided to spend more money – for example, by running down accumulated savings – or firms decided to invest in more capital machinery. But if neither group was willing to behave in this way, the necessary improvement in the climate of expectations would have to be engineered by some other party. Clearly, the only other party capable of achieving this was the **government**.

The implication was that full employment could be restored only if the government created a demand for goods and services. This, however, flew straight in the face of the neo-classical orthodoxy and, somewhat curiously, given the part played by Keynes in this tale, the UK Government was particularly disinclined to accept the need for increased government spending.

□ 1.3.1 A Matter of Debt

What other objections, apart from a simple-minded belief in the neo-classical model, were there to increased government spending? The answer was that increased spending not covered by increased taxation meant that the indebtedness of the government would have to increase. In general, public expenditure was not expected, unlike private investment, to be self-financing over time. Hence balancing the fiscal books was held to be the soundest way to behave.

In advocating government spending in excess of tax revenue, Keynes was not, however, suggesting that borrowing to get the economy on the move again was to be regarded as anything other than a temporary measure. The idea was that once public spending and the consequent increase in income and employment had generated more optimistic expectations, the simultaneous expansion of private sector organisations would once again be restored as the driving force behind economic activity, thereby allowing the government to cut back its own operations and to use revenue from the newly-expanded tax base to redeem at least part of the outstanding debt.

In fairness to Keynes, it should be said that his view of the world was one in which a group of public-spirited intellectuals would operate economic policy with wisdom, discretion and foresight. His was not a world of fiscal profligacy; debt was perfectly sensible so long as there was an intention to repay, to balance the books over the longer haul. But spending other people's money proved to be more enjoyable than spending one's own, especially as it helped to keep politicians in elected office, so acceptance of the belief that there was nothing particularly immoral about debt **per se** was turned around and used in evidence against him. Politicians in office all agreed that debt **ought** to be repaid, but they could not see any political advantage in doing so, especially as the interest payments might fall due during another political party's period in office.

In practice, it is probably fair to argue that it was the Second World War, rather than the *General Theory*, which accounted for the demise of neo-classicism in the UK. Elsewhere the Nazis in Germany were behaving in a thoroughly Keynesian way by the mid-1930s, and the New Deal was implemented in the USA, albeit with far less effect because the desire to help the disadvantaged had to compete with the desire not to run budget deficits. However, unemployment remained extremely high in the UK, especially on a regional basis (thereby providing further 'evidence' of labour market inflexibility), until the government was forced, despite itself, to re-arm. Even then it was well into 1941, the second year of the War, before all of the unemployed could be absorbed into 'productive' work.

□ 1.3.2 *The New Order Cometh*

By the end of the Second World War the Keynesian revolution had inexorably entered into its 'orthodoxy' phase, common to all advanced Western economies for roughly 25 years. Not surprisingly, the sacrifices of the war years served to speed up enormously the process of social change. Under no circumstances was there to be a re-run of the 1930s, which meant that a clear priority had to be given to the eradication of

unemployment. On the whole, the expectation was that, once the economy was restored to a peacetime footing, there would be considerable problems in switching the labour force into civilian occupations. The concept of **full** employment was not, therefore, an immediate objective. The *White Paper on Employment* in 1944 talked in terms of something less ambitious, but for once the reality was an improvement upon the expectation. Naturally, the initial period of postwar reconstruction was bound to generate exceptionally high levels of demand in the short term. But the maintenance of demand in the longer term would obviously require the government to play a more active role via **demand management**, which would have the characteristics established in the Keynesian model: namely, short-term, counter-cyclical fiscal policy. Monetary policy would also need to be short-term and counter-cyclical, but would have little to do bar keeping down the interest rate in order to cheapen the cost of borrowing for investment.

However, the Keynesian revolution was not simply an issue of macroeconomic objectives and instruments: it was an era in which voters turned away from markets, which were perceived as **efficient** but **inequitable**, in order to create a fairer and more just society. Although Churchill, who had led the wartime government, was a Conservative, there was nevertheless a massive swing towards the Labour Party, which by that time had almost completely displaced the Liberals. The era of the **Welfare State** had arrived.

■ 1.4 Efficiency versus Equity

The postwar years have been characterised by contradictions within the processes of macroeconomic control, but one must not lose sight of the underlying debate about the role of market mechanisms. The Keynesian model effectively discarded the view that a modern advanced economy could be left to its own devices, and ushered in the era of the **mixed economy**. But there are clearly an enormous variety of ways in which one can draw boundaries between private and public sectors, and a great deal therefore hinges on the balance between **efficiency and equity at the microeconomic level**. At the end of the day there are very few goods and services that cannot be supplied efficiently by the market mechanism, in the sense of maximising output for given inputs; but the amounts of goods and services produced, and their allocation between households, may be considered inequitable from a wider social perspective. One may naturally respond by arguing that concentration upon the issue of equity does not of itself necessitate any conflict with the objective of maximum efficiency, and indeed it is clear that the introduction of the Welfare State presupposed that no serious conflict would occur.

However, efficiency in the market is dependent upon the profit motive, and the profit motive has accordingly to be subjugated to the wider **public interest** if equity issues are to be given greater priority. This line of argument can best be clarified by a concrete example. Before the Second World War the health service largely required payment to be made at the point of consumption. Its size, therefore, depended upon people's willingness and ability to pay, but insofar as there was a demand for the service it could be provided very efficiently. The National Health Service (NHS) was introduced because this level of provision was felt to be both inadequate and inequitable, but equity – or so it was thought – could be maximised only by providing health care free at the point of consumption. Theoretically, there was no reason why this expanded provision could not be delivered as efficiently as before, but logically this would be true only if the motivation towards efficiency was generated as strongly by the pursuit of the public interest as by the pursuit of profit. At the time this was taken for granted, because it was felt that there was a consensus within society that the public interest should transcend private interests. In setting up the NHS, in expanding education and welfare services and in taking industries into private ownership, very little thought was thus given to the issue of objectives and how best to achieve them.

In retrospect this was, at best, unfortunate, but it reflected the widely held view at the time that a transfer of ownership from private to public sector would be sufficient to guarantee an improvement in performance. For example, there was bound to be a better relationship between managers and workers in an industry once it had been transferred to public ownership, since the owners would no longer be seeking to squeeze every drop of profit out of the workers. There would be no more General Strikes and no more trouble in the coal industry (the long-term future of which would now be assured). Regrettably, hardly anyone observed that the coal miners themselves had no greater personal stake in the industry post-nationalisation than had existed previously. Indeed, if anything, they had even less of a stake since wages and jobs were no longer directly related to the profitability of the industry. It would thus be in their personal interest to try to raise their wages even if it resulted in the industry making losses. They might well prefer not to take this action because, for example, there was a government in power which had their wholehearted support. But if another, less appealing, government took power, or if the economic environment became so problematic that any government would be forced to try to control wages, then confrontation would almost inevitably occur. In such a situation it would be vital for someone to re-establish control, whether management or ultimately government. Yet to **re-establish** control there needed to be an **effective** system of control established in the first place, which even a cursory glance at the statutes governing the nationalised industries or the NHS demonstrates not to have been the case.

A further aspect of the **efficiency versus equity** debate to which insufficient attention is paid relates to the distributions of income and wealth, and their implications for tax regimes. So far we have discussed the Keynesian orthodoxy largely from the expenditure side, but if public spending is to rise appreciably then it will be necessary to raise taxes, in which case one needs to stress the issue of **whom or what to tax**, and how onerously the individual taxes are to be applied. Once one starts out with the premise that a greater degree of equity is needed, it follows logically that the primary purpose of taxation, other than simply to finance expenditure, is to **redistribute**. This requires a strong element of progressivity to be present, most obviously in the income tax and wealth tax schedules. But this in turn has implications for efficiency, since it affects the incentives to work and to take risks.

One further point is worth emphasising at this stage, before we return to the historical narrative. No matter what macroeconomic control system is adopted, it must send out both explicit and implicit signals at a microeconomic level. In a market system the signals are primarily in the form of **changing prices,** and this will remain true of many goods and services which are publicly provided even though the prices in question are not market prices. The **absence** of a price – as in the provision of health care – sends out an equally strong signal. When one compares different societies with roughly equal wealth, one should **expect** to find different consumption patterns. This is because a good may be taxed or subsidised in one society where in the other society it is not. If, for example, mortgages and pension contributions are subject to tax relief, one should hardly be surprised to discover that the most popular forms of wealth are houses and pensions.

To summarise this part of the argument, what we are saying is that the macroeconomic model, whether Keynesian or otherwise, requires one to look deeply into its microeconomic implications, and this is why in later chapters we will be looking at tax regimes, industrial policy, welfare provision and other related matters.

▌ 1.5 Employment, Trade and Inflation

As we have indicated above, the primary focus of the Keynesian model was upon the level of unemployment. However, it followed logically that if there was insufficient demand for private sector goods and services, and a consequent falling-off in the level of employment, then the new jobs created by public spending in order to maintain full employment would tend to be in the public sector:

that is, in central and local government and the nationalised industries. And if the prevailing orthodoxy held that any shortcomings in the operations of private sector bodies needed to be remedied by government in order to promote the cause of **social justice** (and sometimes **efficiency**), then the mix of the mixed economy was logically going to become weighted increasingly towards the public sector and away from the private sector. But the Keynesian model did not of itself imply a significant long-term shift, since public expenditure was meant to come to the fore only during recessions. When the economy was booming it could even be necessary for the public sector to be cut back in order to dampen down excess demand in the private sector.

So why did the upsurge in public spending happen in every major European economy? One obvious reason was that elected politicians saw themselves as elected to change things for the better, and this was bound to cost money. Furthermore, a consensus about the desirability of improving equity and welfare was incompatible with sharp cuts in public spending, since no element of such spending could be cut without causing someone somewhere to lose his or her job. Yet if the government could not bring itself to make meaningful cuts, the political opposition had little choice, if it wanted to get elected, other than to differentiate its product by promising to spend even more, and to resist any cuts which were on the agenda.

This argument had particular implications for employment policy. In principle, the objective of giving everyone a job could be fulfilled independently of locational issues. In other words, if an industry shut down in the North and another simultaneously expanded in the South, full employment could be maintained by moving the redundant workers to the new location. However, this inevitably meant both short-term hardship for those required to move and probably long-term decline in the areas where firms shut down. In countries such as West Germany these consequences did not trouble politicians overmuch, but in the UK they were considered to be unacceptable, and steps were taken, even by Conservative governments ostensibly dedicated to free-market principles, to prevent them (through, for example, the rescue of lame-duck industries).

The according of primacy to the objective of full employment also created other kinds of difficulty. The maintainance of high levels of demand in order to sustain full employment had implications for other important policy objectives, in particular for inflation and for the external trading position as reflected in the balance of payments (BoP). The existence of inflation and of deficits in the BoP needed to be examined from the point of view both of cause and of cure. Unfortunately, the Keynesian model had nothing useful to say about inflation because it had been formulated during an historical period when prices were tending to fall rather than to rise, and there seemed to be no obvious reason in theory why the demand for labour could not be expanded to absorb the available supply without bidding up its price.

Nevertheless, inflation did exist throughout the 1950s and 1960s, albeit at a fairly modest level, so in many ways the simplest thing was to do very little about it and to hope that it would go away. Every now and again prices would rise unusually sharply, and something would need to be done about it, but on the whole there were more important things to worry about. In particular, high levels of demand tended to be associated with high levels of imports, the more so as the UK became increasingly unable to compete internationally with respect to her manufactured goods.

Now, a BoP deficit can be dealt with in a number of different ways:

a the **domestic economy can be deflated** (expenditure reducing) so that there is less demand to spill over into imports;
b the **price of imports can be raised**, and that of exports lowered, via an alteration in the exchange rate (expenditure switching);
c artificial retraints on trade **can be introduced, such as tariffs and quotas on imports or subsidies to exports**.

In the event the remedy mentioned in c was available on only a short-term emergency basis,

because the UK was a member of the GATT (General Agreement on Tariffs and Trade) which required free trade to be pursued whenever possible. Solution **b** was available within the terms and conditions of the adjustable-peg exchange rate regime introduced in 1944 at Bretton Woods. Unfortunately, it was considered to be a sign of failure for a country to lower its exchange rate, and so it was a policy to be avoided except as a last resort for fear that the government so doing would lose votes. But this left only solution **a**, although its implementation meant that the level of aggregate demand (AD) would have to be cut back, thereby adversely affecting output and employment.

Given the higher priority assigned to full employment than to the external balance, this could obviously be tolerated only for the minimum period compatible with restoring the BoP into better shape, whereupon demand would need to be expanded again in order to restore full employment. However, since this procedure had done nothing to deal with the underlying causes of the problem – namely an uncompetitive economy – but only with its symptoms in the form of a BoP deficit, the symptoms were obviously going to recur once the economy was back at full employment again. A succession of periods of demand expansion to create jobs followed by demand reduction to control imports thus became the dominant characteristic, known as **stop–go**, of UK economic policy during the 1950s and 1960s.

1.5.1 *Fiscal versus Monetary Policy*

As we have indicated, the level of AD was largely manipulated via **fiscal means**, and monetary policy had relatively little to do. However, its assigned role (namely, low interest rates to foster investment) was somewhat incompatible with a world in which inflation was a persistent phenomenon, since rising prices implied the need to **raise interest rates to deter consumption financed by credit**.

In the USA during the late 1950s, Professor Milton Friedman at Chicago University and others began publishing material which indicated that the **money supply** was the all-important aggregate on which the authorities would have to concentrate their attention if they wished to have any meaningful control over economic activity. Friedman argued, in particular, that the role of monetary policy during the Great Depression had been widely misunderstood. The orthodox version of events held that the US monetary authorities had pursued aggressively expansionary monetary policies between 1929 and 1933, but that these policies had proved ineffectual. Friedman, on the other hand, contended that the monetary authorities had pursued highly **deflationary** policies. According to his research, the quantity of money in the USA fell by one-third during the course of the Depression, thereby providing clear evidence that monetary policy was extremely effective in regulating the level of economic actitvity, rather than the reverse.

At the heart of Friedman's work lay the **New Quantity Theory** which represented a modernised version of the neo-classical model, linking the money supply to **money national income** (the volume of (real) output at current prices). In his model, most commonly known as **Monetarism**, real output resulted from decisions taken primarily by households and firms in the private sector, and could not be adjusted by demand management. Since real magnitudes were ultimately unaffected by the supply of money, the latter **was directly linked only to the rate of inflation**, and became its **primary cause**.

However, the fact was that in trying to elevate inflation to become the primary focus of economic policy, Friedman's time had not yet arrived, particularly where the UK was concerned, although his ideas caught on more quickly elsewhere. Just as the Keynesian revolution had to wait for the neo-classical orthodoxy to break down in the face of mass unemployment, so the monetarist revolution had to wait for a breakdown of the Keynesian orthodoxy. But for the moment at least, the Keynesian façade seemed impregnable. Quite simply, in an atmosphere of

you've never had it so good, one does not seriously question the view that the prevailing orthodoxy had helped to bring this about. True, the UK economy had grown slowly by comparison with most other comparable countries, but growth was rapid by comparison with previous periods in the UK. True, there were periodic BoP crises which deflected the economy, and inflation was also ever-present. But jobs were freely available for those who wanted to work, and most people's standard of living was rising steadily. It was not a time for revolution, even in ideas.

The issue of inflation remained largely ignored, both in academic and political circles. This passive view of the problem was reinforced when, in 1957, A. W. Phillips published an article discussing what henceforth became universally known as the **Phillips Curve**. The Phillips Curve suggested that inflation need not be considered as an independent problem, but its real importance lay in the fact that up until that point in time the Keynesian model had contained no theory of inflation. Given that inflation was treated with rather more indifference than it merited, this missing link had not prevented the model from operating to most people's satisfaction. Nevertheless, the apparent message of the Phillips Curve that there was a **predictable trade-off** between employment and inflation (thereby offering, in effect, a **menu of choices** between combinations of employment and inflation) appeared greatly to simplify economic policy. The government simply had to choose the particular **level of aggregate demand** which would generate the **target level of employment**, and a predetermined amount of inflation would simultaneously be generated. The price level could, therefore, be regulated to a lowly place in the pecking order of economic objectives, since in choosing the target value for the primary objective one could not be thrown off course by an unforeseen rate of inflation as one could by the balance of payments.

Unfortunately, at the end of the 1960s the situation began to deteriorate alarmingly. The rate of inflation began to rise sharply, and to register a value well above what had been predicted on the basis of the Phillips Curve. At first the authorities understandably treated this as an aberration, arguing that the original relationship between unemployment and inflation would shortly be restored. But when employment was allowed to rise slightly to help rein back inflation, it did not have the desired effect, and a new phenomenon appeared which became known as **stagflation**: namely, rising prices at the same time as rising unemployment. This phenomenon clearly needed to be explained within the context of the Keynesian model, but the model was found wanting. After 25 years its Achilles' heel had been exposed.

By a quirk of history, it was precisely at this point in time, at the beginning of the 1970s, that the exchange rate mechanisms introduced at Bretton Woods also began to break down, to the point at which the UK felt obliged, in 1972, to move over to a **floating rate** (albeit a **managed** one). This meant that BoP crises could now be dealt with via the exchange rate rather than via deflation (given the political will to accept currency depreciation), and thus allowed more freedom for demand to be managed in order to maintain full employment. But raising demand at a time when inflation was roaring ahead was not really a sensible option, and the quadrupling of oil prices by the Organisation of Petroleum Exporting Countries (OPEC) helped send the inflation rate soaring to 24 per cent in 1975, as well as causing significant damage to the balance of payments. The Labour Government in power at the time was unable to cope with these pressures, particularly as foreign currency reserves were inadquate for the purpose, and turned for help to the International Monetary Fund (IMF), a body which was sympathetic to the monetarist doctrines now coming into vogue. The price exacted in return for assistance was that the UK economy would have to be subjected to a dose of monetarism, with tight control over the money supply and a tight fiscal policy keeping demand in check.

It was rather ironic that a Labour Government should be the **first to apply monetarist doctrines**, since its underlying philosophy was hardly right-wing. Nevertheless, it was as much imposition as choice at the time (or at least that was how the government excused its behaviour) and an inevitable effect was what, from the government's point of view, was a highly undesirable further upturn in unemployment. Indeed, the attempt to impose fiscal discipline, and to control inflation via a prices and incomes policy, ultimately led to the **winter of discontent** and to the government's downfall. It was replaced in 1979 by the first Thatcher Government which, unlike its predecessor, **deliberately chose** to make a version of monetarism the key plank of UK economic policy.

1.6 The Brief Reign of Monetarism

As previously indicated, the Keynesian orthodoxy collapsed in the face of a persistent rate of inflation well above the rate predicted by the Phillips Curve, and into the vacuum created by the failure of the model stepped the **monetarist revolution**. It is important to remember that monetarism was a reworking of the neo-classical model rather than a totally new approach, and that it was **not invented after 1970**. As with the Keynesian model, it had been advocated for many years prior to that, but few people were altogether persuaded by it. In particular, it must be borne in mind that its underlying philosophy placed particular emphasis upon **markets**, and played down very heavily the role of government as prime mover in the economy.

It would be fair to argue that the Conservative Government under Edward Heath was sympathetic to the doctrine of the free market, but at the end of the day it did not have the conviction to let markets have their head. Indeed, it is an interesting aspect of the Heath Government that it took Rolls-Royce and British Leyland **into** public ownership rather than let them be destroyed by the forces of the market, thereby demonstrating that expediency was often a stronger factor than polemic in political manifestos. The Thatcher Government was different in that it set out determinedly to apply monetarism as a philosophy, relying heavily upon the evidence that the lax monetary policy introduced during the Heath Government's term of office had been responsible for the inflationary boom of the early 1970s. However, what the Thatcher Government did not at first realise was just how difficult this was going to be. Because monetarism is about markets, it is clearly much more than simply a statement about the money supply and the macro-economy, and in that respect it becomes difficult to form a judgement as to its success or failure since some parts of the philosophy may work quite well whereas others may need to be discarded as unworkable. Whether what remains at the end of this process is still monetarism is, therefore, highly debatable, and we need to shed some light on this issue below.

Viewed in terms of macroeconomic policy monetarism is fairly straightforward. It contends that the price level is the most important economic objective because real variables, such as employment, can best be stimulated in the context of a non-inflationary environment. However, whereas zero (or near-zero) rates of inflation assist in the generation of employment through their positive impact upon the prospects of the private sector, demand management is either self-defeating (because public spending simply displaces private spending: 'crowding out') or a recipe for accelerating inflation. The only way to control the price level is via the money supply. Hence it follows that the growth of the money supply should be geared to the expected growth rate of real output, which thereby makes it possible to buy any extra output at the **existing** level of prices. The balance of payments can be left to its own devices by allowing the exchange rate to float freely, thereby ensuring a tendency for it to self-equilibrate.

However, certain points follow logically from the above. First, governments must resist the temptation to create money by **spending more than they earn** and thereby creating a borrowing requirement, so fiscal policy must be viewed from the point of view of its consequences for the money supply. Fiscal conservatism means balancing government spending against taxation but, since markets are much better at determining what people want to consume than the bureau-

crats in local and central government, public spending must be kept under tight control. This in turn will permit taxes to be cut, which will leave more of their incomes in people's pockets and provide the incentive for them to work harder, thereby generating economic growth. This growth will eventually provide new jobs in areas of the economy where there is genuine private demand, represented by direct spending by consumers, rather than an artificial demand generated by government spending designed, for example, to keep technologically backward and internationally uncompetitive industries in business.

This approach is generally known as **supply-side economics** because it rests upon the assumption that **supply must be created before demand** if there is to be non-inflationary growth within the economy (see Chapter 3 for a fuller discussion of these matters). At the microeconomic level, the philosophy has far-reaching effects. Individual households and firms must be made to stand on their own feet, to succeed or fail as the market for what they provide dictates. Those who fail may need to be helped by the government within reason, but not to the point at which failure seems to be a soft option. In particular, employment is dependent upon the forces of the market. Jobs may need to be preserved by workers taking wage cuts and/or retraining, or they may need to move to where the work is (possibly on their bicycles). If institutions such as trade unions are less than keen about these developments then their power to prevent them must be destroyed, and that applies to professional bodies as well as to craft unions.

Not surprisingly, these doctrines seem firmly rooted in the neo-classical orthodoxy where the individual is responsible for his or her own predicament, and it is not the job of government to provide relief. In other words, the postwar swing from efficiency to equity must be put into reverse gear. Efficiency is once again to be king, and those who are productive will be allowed to enjoy the fruits of their labour. To be rich is no longer socially unacceptable; to be poor is unnecessary, so poverty must be pushed back into decent obscurity.

1.7 The Thatcher Years, 1970–90

At a good many points in the body of the text we will have cause to note that the Thatcher years in office are open to a variety of interpretations. Mrs Thatcher was not afraid of controversy, and the very fact that she sought to revitalise the economy by attacking those groups which she felt had traditionally held back progress was bound to engender very strong feelings among those affected by her decisions. Some controversies were driven by theoretical considerations: for example, the renewed debate about the theoretical underpinnings of both the Keynesian and monetarist models. Others were concerned with the use and alleged abuse of statistical data generated both by the government and by other sources. Yet others had to do with her style of government.

On the theoretical front we have already referred to the debate between demand-siders and supply-siders, but there has also been a reinterpretation of the Keynesian model in order to make it more compatible with the observed phenomena of the 1970s and the 1980s. The adherents of this approach are usually known as new, neo- or radical Keynesians. In addition, there has arisen a school of thought known as 'New Classical Economics', which has much in common with monetarism but which differs with respect to, for example, the role of expectations (see **p. 481**). It is fair to say that most economists take an eclectic view of the proceedings, accepting parts, but not all, of any one viewpoint. However, one consequence is that the government receives conflicting advice, particularly where it is sought internally from the likes of the Treasury as well as from outsiders such as the 'seven wise men', and it has become increasingly difficult to divine which model – if any – of the economy it is trying to implement. Accepting for the moment that economic policy may, therefore, be driven as often by short-term expediency as by the logic of a specific model, it is nevertheless desirable to provide a brief summary of recent experience.

One unchanging point of reference, explored fully in Chapter 10, has been the priority accorded to the **control of inflation**. In the early Thatcher years this was seen as the task assigned to the money supply, but that has now altered insofar as control of the money supply is widely (but not universally) seen as a failure. Indeed, the government itself declared, in June 1989, that it no longer intended even to compile the money supply measure, known as M3, favoured during the early 1980s. For some time now the government has relied upon the **interest rate** as its primary means of regulating demand, a policy which, as is noted at many points in this text, has met with mixed success, although it may anyway be argued that there is no unanimity about the meaning of the term 'success'. For example, it is possible to argue simultaneously that the UK's growth record during the 1980s was good because it remained high by international standards for many years, and that it was bad because the level of output barely rose above the level achieved at the time the government first took office. Equally, the inflation rate did fall to well below 5 per cent at one stage during the 1980s, the soaring money supply notwithstanding, and it is currently comfortably below that figure, but it has never shown any sign of getting down to zero and until very recently has remained fairly consistently above that of some of the UK's main competitors.

The Thatcher Government certainly achieved its aim of fiscal conservatism for a period during the late 1980s, turning the inherited borrowing requirement into a debt repayment. However, there remains a body of opinion which believes that such behaviour was inappropriate (see the discussion concerning the repayment of debt in Chapter 10), and it is significant to note that this did not result from the intended reduction in government spending combined with a lesser reduction in taxation. Rather, in absolute terms, even after allowing for inflation, government spending rose in almost every year, with tax revenue rising even faster in the mid-1980s due to the phenomenon known as **fiscal drag** (all of which matters are discussed in detail in Chapter 4). The fiscal position has also deteriorated sharply in the early 1990s.

The **exchange rate**, in particular, presents ambiguities. The one certainty is that it was never permitted to float as freely as it should in a basic monetarist model, which allows the advocates of such a model to contend that it has never been properly tested. There was an increasingly acrimonious debate about whether the UK should become a fully committed member of the European Monetary System (EMS: see Chapter 6) and indeed, more widely, about the UK's role in Europe, particularly in relation to the Maastricht Treaty.

At the microeconomic level there was a real attempt to deregulate markets and to transfer assets from the public to the private sector; in fact, the UK is generally acknowledged to be the world leader in privatisation, although Americans might remark that it would have been better not to have created so many areas that needed to be deregulated in the first place. However, asset sales were likened in some quarters to 'selling the family silver', and it is also the case that some of the worst rigidities (such as are manifested in the housing market) were not addressed at all successfully. Indeed, for many the overriding impression given by the Thatcher Government was its interventionist and centralising stance in a wide variety of markets, and particularly in relation to the local authorities (LAs). At heart this reflects one of the most awkward realities of economic life: namely, the fact that, since free markets are subject to abuse, the more free the markets are supposed to be the more they need to be regulated. This issue is addressed at various points in the text (for example, with respect to financial markets in Chapter 4), and particularly in Chapter 11.

At the macroeconomic level, as already indicated, the Thatcher Government came to suffer from a shortage of instruments to control the economy, and hence it came to overuse – and arguably abuse – those that were favoured. Here again it is much easier to explain where the government went wrong than to provide a convincing alternative approach.

As has been noted above, the Keynesian model broke down in the face of exceptionally high levels of inflation. It can just as easily be argued, however, that the most telling indictment of monetarism was its failure to reduce unemployment to acceptable levels. The fact that during the Keynesian orthodoxy governments chose to live with permanently rising prices, and that during the monetarist orthodoxy they chose to live with heavy unemployment, may be put down to the forces of democracy (at the end of the day the electorate must vote for one particular party), but even democracy can be made to mean all things to all men, and it is possible to argue that votes are not so much cast in favour of policy packages as against alternatives which are viewed as wholly unacceptable. Some reflections on political processess are contained in the section which follows, and also in Chapter 11. For the moment, it is necessary only to note that the movement away from any kind of established orthodoxy and towards what may best be termed pragmatism may be the only way forward. As will constantly be reiterated in the course of the text, the world's economies are evolving very rapidly, and the model of last year's behaviour may provide a poor guide to the current year, let alone to the future. In the UK, the Keynesian orthodoxy lasted for three decades, whereas the monetarist experiment lasted for well under one decade. For the moment revolution is unfashionable and evolution is the name of the game.

The UK has a relatively new political leader in the guise of John Major. Unlike his predecessor he is no visionary, and he has shown, as in relation to the exchange rate, not merely a tolerance for U-turns in policy but a regrettable tendency to claim credit for the very consequences which he had previously been trying hard to avoid. Attempts to persuade commentators that there is a consistent set of policies worthy of the term 'Majorism' have been greeted with amused disbelief. Partly for this reason the future path of the economy is extremely hard to forecast, but then the Treasury already knows this to its cost.

■ *1.8* The Political Context

It is a reasonable expectation of a so-called 'democracy' that its citizens will consider it to be their right – and possibly their duty – to exhort the government to adopt this or that economic strategy. However, what they often fail to appreciate is that in order to deliver economic policies one must first create a **political system** with that end in mind and, since there are many ways of devising such a system, its precise form is ultimately of great consequence. One simple point to make in this context is to ask whether the 'Thatcher revolution' would have occurred in any of the other major industrial countries had it not occurred in the UK. The answer must be a firm negative, because it was critically dependent upon the political context of the UK. In retrospect, there can be no doubt that Mrs Thatcher had a more profound impact than President Reagan. However, as we shall argue below, the odds were stacked in her favour before she began.

A crucial – though by no means unique – feature of the UK political system is that it involves a race to be 'first past the post' between a very small number of very strong contenders, and a number of 'also-rans'. Each constituency race produces a single Member of Parliament (MP) who may well fail to be supported by a majority of those casting their vote, let alone of those eligible to vote. Hence this system permits of a government being formed by a political party irrespective of whether it has been supported by more voters than any other alternative party, let alone all other parties in aggregate, and once a government has been formed the level of electoral support is normally a non-issue until the electoral term is over.

On occasion, the combination of a stong Opposition party and the also-rans may muster enough MPs to outvote the government, but here again the key issue is that this rarely happens in practice, and that even when it does the Opposition parties are generally less than fully united in their political goals. The style of political debate is inevitably highly adversarial, but this should not be allowed to conceal the key point that, when the fire and fury has died down and the vote is taken, **a government with an absolute majority of MPs is always the official winner provided its own MPs vote with it.**

Clearly, this system delivers extraordinary powers to a majority government. Constitutionally, the monarchy has no power of veto, and neither does the House of Lords (the upper chamber) which can only debate and recommend. A simple majority of one seat in the House of Commons is thus sufficient (provided, of course, every MP is available to vote) to permit the government to steamroller through any legislation that it wishes, irrespective of whether or not it was mentioned in the campaign manifesto issued to voters.

In principle, individual MPs can refuse to vote in accord with their party line, but the rules disallowing the use of private monies to 'buy votes' effectively mean that an MP who rejects a 'three-line whip' can expect to lose the support of the party machine and later, if not sooner, lose his or her seat. It follows that, especially when a party has a small overall majority, MPs habitually toe the line rather than bring down the government provided it makes some concessions to those whose consciences are troubling them.

As a consequence, backbench MPs normally have little effective power over economic policy, whereas a small section amongst them, appointed to the Cabinet, have a great deal. Furthermore, a prime minister, elected from within the ranks of MPs and hence inseparable from the party in power, can exercise exceptional power by using the threat of dismissal from the Cabinet to force recalcitrant members to do what he or she wishes.

This ability to steamroller policy through Parliament is both a virtue and a vice. It obviously permits of very strong government, and there can be no doubt that voters prefer a government with a clear sense of purpose and a determination to put it into practice, to one which is constantly vulnerable to losing on a vote of confidence. But such power can easily be abused, and it follows that if the Opposition cannot bring a government to heel, that task must fall to the government's own backbenchers. It is slightly ironic, therefore, that the latter can do little unless the government's majority is small, but where that is the case and backbenchers are willing to put their careers on the line on a point of principle, they can cause endless problems for their own party. We will have much to say about this in the context of the vote on the Maastricht Treaty in Chapter 7.

□ *1.8.1 Other Political Systems*

We will return subsequently to comment upon the performance of government in the UK, but first it is salutary to compare the above analysis to political systems elsewhere. In the USA, which has a two-main-parties, first-past-the-post system, the President is not, however, the leader of the party in power in the House of Representatives (often called 'the House'), but elected independently, and may well belong to the other party. If the House is unsympathetic he may, therefore, find it very difficult to get his Bills enacted. He, in his turn, has considerable power to veto Bills emanating from the House, so one rebuff may well be repaid in kind. The upper chamber (the Senate) is a powerful body in its own right, and may well be controlled by the opposite party to the House. A President, House and Senate (which together constitute the Congress) may periodically, though by no means invariably, belong to the same party, but this does not guarantee complete cooperation. This is partly because election is as much a function of the wealth and prestige of the individual as of the party machine, and hence individual Representatives and Senators quite frequently vote against their own party line. All this prevents the accumulation of too much power in too few hands, as was precisely the original intention, but it is not exactly designed to deliver priorities, such as cuts in government spending, since every politician in an area adversely affected by such cuts will automatically vote against the strategy, irrespective of party.

In continental Europe there is **proportional representation** (seats allocated in proportion to votes cast). This effectively prevents any one party from getting an absolute majority over all others, which on the face of it should lead to weak govenment. On the other hand it follows that, as a general rule, a coalition must reach agreement on priorities which are common to all parties if it wishes to avoid government by crisis, and the important policies may, therefore, get carried out with all-party support even when there is fundamental disagreement about other matters. The obvious drawback is that these shared prio-rities invariably sit somewhere near the political centre, and if voters are unhappy about that they can express their disapproval only by voting for someone or something on the extreme of the political spectrum (fascist or communist). As has also been demonstrated in Italy very recently, there is some tendency for corruption to creep in by way of payment for political favours.

If, on the other hand, the UK government thinks that the electorate want, for example, privatisation or a poll tax, then they can be delivered by the system. Critics complain that this is all very well and good, but that it enables the government to deliver such policies **irrespective of whether** they are wanted by the electorate.

Nevertheless, it must never be forgotten that governments are by no means all-powerful, and may be forced to take involuntary actions. This may arise simply because the UK is not a particularly big player on the world stage and cannot therefore be insulated from the forces which buffet the world economy. No matter how healthy the underlying economy, the UK cannot expect to grow much – if at all – at a time when other advanced economies are sliding into recession. More generally, the government may find itself in a losing battle with the forces of the market place. The government may, for example, wish to see the exchange rate rise, but if the foreign exchange market wishes to see the exchange rate fall that may well prove to be the ultimate outcome.

To sum up this brief discussion, the overall picture with respect to the UK is that it has a political system with enormous potential power to direct economic policy. The system could result in enormous swings in the direction of policy as each successive government seeks to undo what its predecessor has done, but this does not necessarily happen because many priorities are shared, and the external enviroment may not permit it. It should, finally, be remembered that for a government to spend its time in office removing its predecessor's legislation from the statute book is not merely very unconstructive, but may leave little time to enact new policies. In any event, many policies which the political system requires the Opposition party to oppose may privately be approved of, and others may simply be too expensive to implement. For example, no future government could possibly afford to repurchase the shares of privatised companies even if, as is unlikely, they were prepared to devote scarce parliamentary time to that end.

■ *Chapter 2* ■

The Macroeconomy: 1

Peter Curwen

■ 2.1 Introduction

In the course of this book we will be examining a great many facets of the aggregate enonomy. Certain of these require detailed consideration, and hence have an entire chapter given over to their analysis. Others, however, require less detailed treatment, and it is our primary purpose in this and the subsequent chapters to bring them together at the earliest stage in the overall discussion. Although this necessarily means that these chapters are less cohesive than those which follow, they are essential pieces of the complete macroeconomic jigsaw puzzle. Indeed, one of the primary purposes of these chapters is to provide an overview of the entire jigsaw which must, of necessity, be put together in accordance with the picture on the lid. Unfortunately, as we shall soon dicover, the picture on the lid is out of focus, so we can never be entirely sure that each piece is in its proper place!

The schematic figues which follow may well appear complex at first sight, especially to those with no prior experience of modelling the economic system of the UK. Nevertheless, it is worth observing that the 'Treasury' model which the government uses for forecasting purposes contains literally hundreds of equations, and there will, no doubt, be a number of readers who feel that our schematics are too simplistic. The only sensible response to such a criticism is to point out that the recent record of both the Treasury and most other models in forecasting such variables as the level of unemployment and the rate of inflation has been less than inspiring, so it is debatable whether there is any correlation between accuracy and the number of variables in the model. The obvious reason for recent difficulties in forecasting is that the behaviour of economic agents (such as households and firms) is constantly evolving, while forecasts are generally based upon measures of behaviour in past periods.

In the sections which follow we will be making use of the conventional distinction between **instruments**, **targets** and **objectives** of policy. It should, however, be noted that these will be treated in a more flexible manner than is the custom in introductory textbooks. The evolution of the UK economy over the past decade has turned many relationships upon their head, and engendered much controversy about the linkages – and especially the causality implied by these linkages – between different parts of the economic system. For example, it is clear that under certain circumstances both the interest rate and the exchange rate can be used as instruments (that is, as levers which, when pulled, set in train a sequence of changes in other variables, acting as intermediate targets, which ultimately cause changes in policy objectives).

However, interest rates and exchange rates are closely inter-related, as discussed below, so it is evident that one must be regarded as the instrument and the other as the target. Which is which depends upon how one sets up the system, so it is possible to argue that 'one model's instrument is another model's target'.

■ 2.2 The Internal Sector

The internal sector is modelled in **Figure 2.1**. It is essentially a Keynesian version of the model, with the alternative version operating via the money supply (this is discussed separately below). There are three objectives in the model; the rate of economic growth, the level of employment and the rate of inflation. The route to all of these

Figure 2.1 *The Internal Sector: Demand*

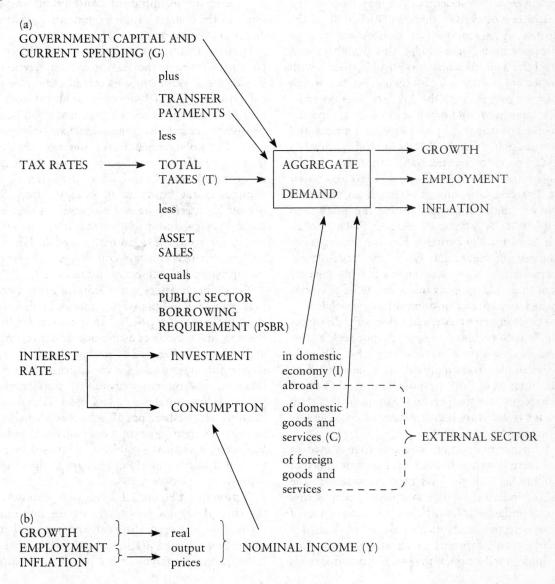

objectives passes through the box marked 'aggregate demand'.

It is accordingly important to consider whether an increase or decrease in aggregate demand (AD) will cause all three objectives to move simultaneously in the desired direction. Unhappily, this is not the case in practice. Whereas an increase in AD can be expected to increase the level of employment, at least in the short term, it almost always also causes the rate of inflation to rise (the Phillips Curve relationship: see **pp. 82–3**).

Clearly, therefore, there are **trade-offs** between objectives in the model. Now it may be observed that, if one objective can be satisfied only at the expense of a second when a single pathway is followed through the model, this drawback can largely be avoided where it is possible to deal with the second objective by following a route which does not pass through the AD box. It is possible, for example, to hold down prices during a period of buoyant demand by recourse to a prices and incomes policy (see **p. 484**). Regrettably, this has never proved to be successful other than in the short term, and while it is possible to argue that the Thatcher Government operated an unofficial policy in the public sector during the 1980s, and that Mr Major is doing so currently, such a policy does not officially exist and has as a consequence been left off **Figure 2.1**. Given the trade-off between objectives, it is necessary for the government to decide upon a **rank ordering** of priorities – which objective is most important, which least – and to determine the **desired value** for each objective. It is to be noted that we do not seek at this juncture to specify what these might be. Whereas, for example, oversimplified arguments tend to talk in terms of 'full' employment, we do not do so here because the precise meaning of this term has for many years been a matter of considerable controversy (see **p. 303**).

A further reservation is in order. It is evident that there is a consensus about the desirability of maintaining a 'high' level of employment in the UK, as indeed there is about maintaining a low rate of inflation. Nevertheless, the attainment of these objectives can often prove to be less of a benefit than it appears to be at first sight. For example, a reduction in the price of raw materials

which are imported represents 'good news' for a manufacturing nation such as the UK, since it helps to hold down costs, and hence inflation. It follows, however, that it must be very damaging to less-developed nations which export those materials. Such countries may subsequently prove unable to repay their international debts, which may partly be owed to the UK government and partly to UK banks (see **pp. 00**). Thus, if there is a default on the debt, any initial benefits derived from lower import prices are partly or wholly wiped out by subsequent losses. Such considerations are, for example, of considerable importance in the context of the Common Agricultural Policy (CAP: see **pp. 271–81**).

Figure 2.1 indicates that there are a variety of pathways through the AD box. In a Keynesian world, the government concentrates upon its fiscal position $(G - T)$ since it has direct control over its own spending whereas it can influence consumption and investment decisions only indirectly. Particular expenditures and tax rates are thus the preferred instruments of policy, but it is to be noted that C and I are also affected by changes in the structure of interest rates. The use of the interest rate is a monetary rather than a fiscal policy, and it follows that both monetary and fiscal policies are normally used in tandem, although there is constant controversy concerning the optimum balance between the two.

Two other matters are worthy of note. In the first place, the internal sector cannot be divorced from the external sector, which is analysed below. Possible linkages via consumption and investment are indicated in **Figure 2.1**. Second, the PSBR is an important magnitude which is created by the formula: government expenditure **plus** transfer payments **less** total taxes **less** asset sales (for a detailed analysis, see **pp. 177–9**). It is accordingly possible to treat it as an aspect of fiscal policy. However, it is also possible, as discussed below, to treat it in the context of changes in the money supply.

Section (b) of **Figure 2.1** serves two purposes. In the first place, it serves to clarify the important distinction between the **real** and **nominal** approaches to measuring economic activity. Growth and employment are physical measures, expressed as volumes, which are 'real' in the sense that they are measured independently of the prices at which they are sold. When a volume measure is multiplied by current prices it is converted into a money value, its 'nominal' counterpart. Hence the value of economic activity at current prices, or nominal income, changes because more activity (growth) is taking place at unchanged prices, or because the same activity is taking place at higher prices, or because both output and prices are changing simultaneously.

Second, section (b) of **Figure 2.1** serves to remind the reader of the feedback mechanisms which are ever-present in the model. As shown by the final upward-pointing arrow, the level of consumption is itself determined in large part by the level of nominal income. Hence, when the level of consumption changes, it changes the level of nominal income as shown by the pathway through **Figure 2.1**, which in turn causes the level of consumption to change, which subsequently causes the level of nominal income to change and so forth (the multiplier mechanism, as set out below).

2.3 Money Supply and the Supply Side

As discussed in Chapter 1, the prevailing view that the UK economy is driven by demand in accordance with the Keynesian model became very unfashionable during the late 1970s, and was replaced by the view that the regulation of demand would more appropriately be conducted via control of the money supply. The controversy this engendered is set out fully in Chapter 12, and need not concern us in detail here. What we do need to bear in mind is that a primary objective of economic policy during the 1980s was to reduce inflation, and that it was argued that this could best be achieved via a restrictive policy towards money supply growth.

This is illustrated in **Figure 2.2** where the direct link runs from AD to inflation, whereas the links from AD to growth and employment are shown as broken lines indicating that AD was not, in general, being manipulated in order to affect these

Figure 2.2 *Money Supply and the Supply Side*

variables. Given the perceived direct link between the money supply and AD it is evident that the money supply now becomes an intermediate target of policy. As such, it needs to be regulated via policy instruments such as open market operations, or other instruments such as credit controls or monetary base control (see **p. 489**). It is, however, also determined in part by the size of the PSBR insofar as this has implications for the way in which it is financed – that is, whether the method of financing creates new money or transfers existing money between the private sector, banks and government.

In other words, the fiscal stance that determines the PSBR has some bearing upon the money supply, as has the rate of interest which represents the cost of issuing or redeeming government securities (for example, via an open-market operation or OMO). A sharp change in the size of the PSBR necessitates an adjustment to the structure of interest rates. When the interest rate changes, it either attracts or deters a flow of short-term international capital ('hot money'). This, in turn, affects the money supply, since if international capital flows into the UK then foreign borrowers must first convert it into sterling, whereas if it flows out then UK residents must first turn sterling into foreign currencies. Both flows necessarily affect the amount of sterling held in the UK, although it is possible to neutralise any inflows by converting them into holdings of government securities (**sterilisation**).

The obvious difficulty with this approach to policy making is that there is no longer a direct link between **aggregate demand** and **growth/employment**. Hence these objectives must be regulated by instruments on the **supply side** of the economy: that is, via the box marked aggregate supply (see **pp. 91–2**).

It should be noted that, once the primary purpose of managing aggregate demand is to restrain prices, it is possible to achieve this objective using **any** form of demand management, whether fiscal or monetary. In this respect, therefore, the box marked aggregate supply (AS) can just as easily be superimposed upon **Figure 2.1**, although it should be borne in mind that the general thrust of the Keynesian model is to enlarge AD, whereas its

role would have to switch to restraining AD if the objective was the control of inflation.

■ 2.4 The External Sector

Let us now turn to the external sector, which is illustrated in **Figure 2.3**. This part of the model introduces additional complications, since it is evident that all kinds of external difficulties can arise if policy is directed exclusively at resolving internal problems. We can begin by noting that AD is increased by exports of goods and services, and reduced by imports of goods and services which form part of aggregate consumption in the internal sector. In this respect exports can be subsidised, as in the case of agriculture, as a component of a fiscal policy, whereas imports can be altered via the use of tariffs and quotas (which are not marked in **Figure 2.3** as they are currently of little significance, but see the discussion of the GATT on **pp. 266–70**).

More significantly, given international agreements to restrict subsidies and tariffs, both imports and exports can be affected by alterations in the **exchange rate**, which itself responds to imbalances in trade flows. However, the use of this instrument was severely constrained during the period when the UK was a member of the ERM of the EMS (see **pp. 246–7**), and at that time the exchange rate was more appropriately thought of as an **objective** rather than as an **instrument** of policy.

This can be clarified as follows. Consumption spending rises in the UK, creating additional demand of which part leaks out into imports. In order to purchase these it is necessary to change sterling into the currency of the seller, which causes the exchange rate to fall against that currency. It is a matter of necessity, from a book-keeping perspective, that the balance of payments accounts sum to zero (see **p. 189**), so a current account deficit must be exactly counterbalanced by a net inflow of capital. For the most part, this inflow will need to be attracted in the short term by offering attractive rates of interest compared to those prevailing in other major financial centres, so a worsening current account

Figure 2.3   *The External Sector*

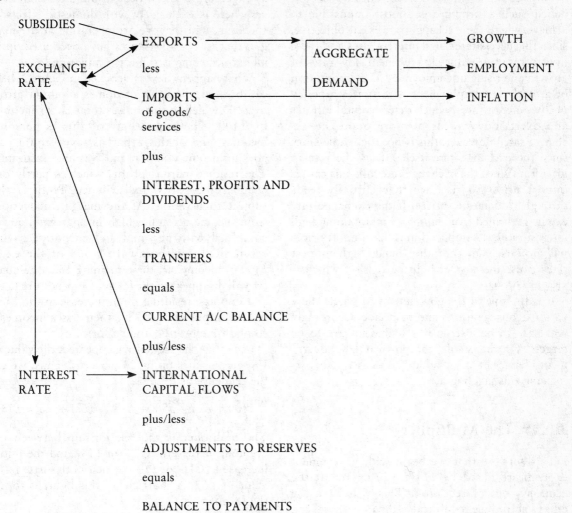

deficit will result in an increase in interest rates in the UK.

As a consequence of the capital inflow the exchange rate is prevented from falling (or, in the context of the ERM from breaching any lower limit permitted for sterling). This lower limit accordingly represents the minimum value for the objective while the change in the interest rate which prevented it from being breached represents the instrument.

Where there are no set bounds for the exchange rate, as is currently the case in principle (although the government appears to wish to see it rise rather than fall, even though trading conditions are difficult), the exchange rate reverts back to its status as instrument with a view to promoting exports and restraining imports. This allows the interest rate to continue to be used as an instrument, but with a view to controlling domestic demand rather than capital flows. Insofar as the interest rate can be relieved of its role in the external sector, it removes one of the major dilemmas of economic policy, namely how to achieve a structure of interest rates that is simultaneously appropriate for both internal and external equilibrium.

For a country with an ongoing current account deficit such a structure is almost impossible to achieve where the exchange rate is an objective, since this necessitates high interest rates and these in turn result in reduced investment, low rates of growth and rising unemployment. The promotion of growth and employment necessitates a policy of low interest rates, which deters capital inflows and exerts downwards pressure upon the exchange rate. However, this is not the whole story since the exchange rate itself affects the rate of inflation. When the exchange rate falls this causes import prices to rise, which eventually feeds through to domestic prices. If the exchange rate can be prevented from falling by maintaining high interest rates, the implication is that import prices will not rise. On the other hand, high interest rates cause the cost of housing to rise, which is also inflationary!

It is the role of the government to juggle these various considerations and to decide accordingly what are to be instruments and what are to be targets. On the whole, the postwar UK governments have not been notably successful in performing this juggling act.

■ 2.5 The Multiplier

Let us suppose that we begin with government expenditure raised by £133 in order to lift the economy out of recession. This will have the effect, according to official estimates, of raising GDP in the UK by roughly £100 because some of this initial expenditure will leak out into imports and some will immediately return to the Treasury as expenditure taxes. Bear in mind that our concern here is exclusively with **domestic** effects of spending, and that we are operating **at the margin**: that is, tax allowances have been used up so all extra income is subject to taxation.

What happens next is depicted in **Figure 2.4**. As can be seen, the value of domestic output grows by £100 which in turn raises total factor incomes by £100. The major part of this is personal incomes, and of this a part is saved and a part goes in income taxation and National Insurance. The residual part is profit, which is partly distributed and partly undistributed. Profit is also subject to taxation. At the margin, deductions from income are quite high in aggregate, and if combined with personal and corporate saving result in the withdrawal of £68 of the extra £100 of income. Of the remaining £32, one-quarter will disappear in the form of expenditure taxes and imports, resulting in an increase in the value of UK output of £24. This then raises incomes a second time by £24, and so forth.

Each time the sequence is repeated, the value of UK output goes up by 24 per cent. Thus, we get the sequence as follows:

$$£100 + £24 + £5.8 + £1.4 + £0.3 + \ldots = £132$$

The **multiplier** is the relationship between the **eventual increase** in GDP of £132 and the **initial increase** in GDP of £100, which in this case has a value of 1.32. A short cut to this figure is to use the formula:

$$\text{Multiplier} = 1 \div \text{the marginal propensity to}$$
$$\text{withdraw (MPW)}$$

Figure 2.4   *The Multiplier*

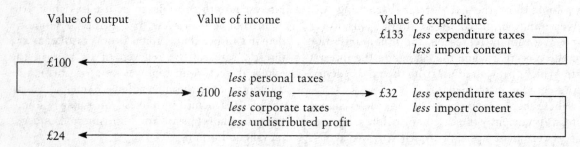

The MPW is a technical term for the marginal rate of deductions of all kinds in one full circuit of **Figure 2.4**, and is thus equal in this case to 76 per cent: hence $1/0.76 = 1.32$.

The above is a much simplified version of the full multiplier equation expressed in the Treasury and other econometric models. Nevertheless, it is sufficiently accurate to bring out the basic point that the UK fiscal multiplier is actually much smaller than is popularly supposed.

◼ 2.6 Crunchy Numbers

In what follows there is a great amount of data which, wherever possible, is the most up-to-date available as at October 1993. Much of this data comes from the Central Statistical Office (CSO). Over the past decade, CSO statistics have become less reliable, primarily because the abolition of exchange controls has made it much more difficult to keep track of money moving in and out of the UK, because statisticians have failed to keep pace with the shift from manufacturing to services and because the government has reduced the range of numbers it collects, partly to save money and partly to ease the burden of paperwork for business.

As a result, the current figures published each month or quarter are subject to significant errors. In many cases, the practice is to insert a 'balancing item', which means that the money is known to exist, but for the time being (and perhaps for ever) it cannot be attributed to any particular category in a set of accounts. As time passes, missing money tends to turn up and it becomes possible to attribute balancing item money to specific categories. Hence, if we look back to 1979 we have a very good idea what was happening at the time, but we do not know very accurately what is happening right now even though that is precisely what we need to know if we are to manage the economy intelligently.

No doubt, by the time the next edition of this book comes out, the data in this edition will have been substantially revised, and it may be an interesting exercise for readers to look back to the previous edition and compare the data for the

years up to 1991. Above all else, the reader should treat almost all of the monthly data reported in the media with great caution since it is habitually inaccurate or distorted by non-recurrent items. Unfortunately, financial markets tend to be driven by the latest data, but the reader is advised to take a more sanguine view.

◼ 2.7 Introduction to National Income Accounting

It is possible to use some simple NI accounting to bring out a proposition of considerable importance to our later discussion. As a matter of definition, total spending on domestic goods and services (E) must consist of private sector final consumption (C) plus private sector investment (including houses) (I) plus government spending (G) plus spending on domestic goods by foreigners (exports (X)) less spending on imports (M). Thus:

$$E = C + I + G + X - M$$

In its turn, C is assumed to take place out of net-of-tax income $(Y - T)$, and income that is not spent must, by definition, be saved (S). Thus:

$$C = Y - T - S$$

But Y and E are simply two alternative ways of measuring economic activity, as demonstrated in the sections which follow. Thus:

$E = Y$, and hence by substitution

$$Y = [Y - T - S] + I + G + X - M$$

Thus:

$$Y - Y + T + S - G - X + M = I$$

Cancelling the Ys and rearranging the other elements gives

$$S + [T - G] + [M - X] = I$$

In other words, **investment** in the UK economy must be **financed** either by domestic savings (S), a budget surplus $(T - G)$ or by running a BoP deficit $(M - X)$. In the latter case this arises because the counterpart to such a deficit is an **inflow of capital** of equal size.

One element of this equation may appear to be puzzling, namely the assertion that a budget surplus can finance investment. Let us assume that the external sector is in balance $(X = M)$. If we also assume that savings are zero $(Y = C + T)$, then some of the claims on income are transferred to the government in the form of taxes, and the only way in which the above equation can balance, which it must as a matter of definition, is if the government does not use up all of its claims on income (that is, T is greater than G) but makes some of them available for investment purposes.

■ 2.8 The National Accounts

□ 2.8.1 The Basic Building Blocks

The concept of 'aggregate economic activity' is clearly of fundamental importance for our understanding of how the economy works. Before any action is taken, the government needs to know what state the economy is in, and it needs to know restrospectively what difference was made by undertaking a particular course of action. In order to do these things we need a set of national accounts, and this is provided by the CSO. It appears each year as the *UK National Accounts*, known as the 'Blue Book', which is published each September.

During the period between Blue Books the CSO produces either monthly or quarterly data which appear in a variety of publications such as *Economic Trends*, the *Monthly Digest of Statistics* and *Financial Statistics*, and there are also periodic press releases. Unfortunately, the data appear under a wide array of definitions, so there is no choice but to explain below what all the terms mean that the reader may come across in his or her reading, even though it may seem at times that they are infinite in number.

As with any system of accounts, the Blue Book records flows of money. The value of a transaction can be approached in one of three ways, namely: the amount of money that the buyer gives up in

order to obtain a good or service (**expenditure**); the amount of money received by the seller (the value of **output** or **product**); and the amount of money received in various forms by all those who contributed to the value of the end-product (**income**). These three figures must be equal **by definition**, since there is clearly only one sum of money involved in any given transaction.

If the value of all transactions is aggregated together we get the variable known as Gross Domestic Product (GDP). This accordingly comes in three variants, namely GDP(E) where 'E' stands for expenditure; GDP(O) where 'O' stands for output; and GDP(I) where 'I' stands for income. It is important to bear in mind that the accounts are ultimately concerned with **final products**: for example, the sale of a desk in a shop to an end-user. However, there are a string of transactions prior to the final sales which might, for example, run as follows: raw materials sold to producer of semi-finished product; semi-finished product sold to producer of the finished product; finished product from factory sold to wholesaler, sold from wholesaler to retailer and sold from retailer to customer. It would be seriously misleading to add together all of these transactions and to call them 'economic activity' since there would be elements of double, triple, quadruple and so on counting involved. It is necessary, therefore, to use a **value-added** principle in counting. Beyond the raw material stage we add only the value added by each further stage **en route** to the end-user. In other words, we take the value of a transaction and **subtract** from it the value of the immediately preceding transaction in the above-mentioned sequence.

What we end up with is the value of the final transaction at the price ruling at the time it takes place. This is known as the **nominal** or **money** value of the transaction. However, if precisely the same transaction takes place at a different point in time it is possible that the value of the transaction will be different because there has been a change in the price. In other words, the value of economic activity can go up over time because **more** goods and services are being sold at **constant** prices; because the **same number** of goods and services are being sold at **higher** prices; because **slightly**

more goods and services are being sold at **slightly higher** prices; and so forth. In order to isolate the change in the **volume** of sales it is necessary to strip away the effect of rising prices by **deflating** the nominal value such that it leaves us with an inflation-adjusted magnitude. This so-called **real** value is thus measured in **constant-price** terms. It is necessary to select a base year for this purpose, which for most variables in this book is currently 1985 but for the Blue Book is 1990.

Measuring changes in the volume of output over time is a critical matter since this is the concept known as **economic growth**. Obviously, therefore, the particular sequence of prices used to deflate money GDP is of some importance but, as we will discover below, there are many price indices which could be used for this purpose, and the reader must be careful to check which deflator is being used if data are to be truly compatible.

It is also the case that GDP and other measures of economic activity can be recorded in several ways. GDP at market prices is final output valued at the **market prices** at which it is sold. This is usually a greater magnitude than the sum of production costs (value added) because the government levies taxes such as value added tax (VAT) at the point of sale. In some cases the rate of VAT is zero, so no differences will arise, and in some cases market prices are reduced below production costs because of subsidies paid by the government to producers. Hence we also need to take account of GDP **at factor cost**, which is equal to GDP at **market prices** minus total **indirect taxes** and plus **subsidies**. In the national accounts, the sum of indirect taxes and subsidies is termed **Net Indirect Taxes**.

GDP, as the name suggests, is concerned solely with measuring the monetary flows generated by economic activity within the boundaries of the UK. However, UK residents may receive income from abroad, and there may be flows of money to foreigners as a result of domestic UK economic activity. GDP thus needs to be adjusted if it is to measure the total income available to UK citizens, which is called **Gross National Product** (GNP) and which is equal to GDP **plus net property income from abroad**.

Account must also be taken of the fact that part of the UK's stock of physical capital is used up over the course of a year. Buildings and machines may wear out through use (depreciation) or they may become outmoded by a technologically superior product and hence fall in value even though physically intact (obsolescence). **Capital consumption** of these kinds must be replaced if the economy is to maintain its capacity to produce. When capital consumption is deducted from economic activity measured **gross** the residual is termed **net**, and GNP thereby becomes **Net National Product** (NNP), whereas GDP becomes **Net Domestic Product** (NDP). These net figures express the value of resources generated in the course of a year which can be used either for consumption or to renew the stock of physical capital via investment. When NNP is expressed at factor cost it is customary to call it **National Income** (NI).

As noted previously, all three measures of economic activity must be equal by definition. However, in practice, for each measure there are data limitations and measurement difficulties such that the estimates never do coincide exactly despite their conceptual equivalence. For this reason, the CSO produces a definitive estimate known as GDP(A) where 'A' stands for average. For the period since the latest base year, GDP(A) is the unweighted arithmetic average of GDP(E), GDP(O) and GDP(I). If each of the measures of GDP is subtracted from GDP(A) it gives rise to a **statistical discrepancy** which is itemised in the accounts in order to bring all of the individual definitions into line.

No matter how accurately economic activity is measured, it is necessarily a flawed measure insofar as it can only take account of transactions where a monetary flow is recorded: in other words, market-based activities. Where a transaction occurs, but no monetary flow is thereby generated, the transaction will not appear in the national accounts. Thus, for example, the accounts ignore the activities of housewives, all do-it-yourself and all voluntary work. In the case of all illegal activity, and also where, for example, someone employed in the official economy is 'moonlighting', there actually is a monetary flow when a transaction occurs, but it is not declared to the authorities and hence does not appear in the national accounts. Such unrecorded flows are called the **black economy**. Hence, the national accounts understate substantially the true value of all economic activity, but provided the unrecorded part remains roughly the same proportion of the total then the rate of growth of recorded activity will still be correct. Problems could arise, however, if, for example, reductions in tax rates caused unofficial activity to appear in the official market and to become recorded, since this would give the impression that growth had accelerated when in reality it remained unchanged.

2.8.2 Measures at Market Prices: Effects of Introducing the Community Charge

GDP estimates for the years 1989–92 are affected by the abolition of domestic rates and the introduction of the Community Charge, commencing in Scotland in April 1989. In the national accounts, domestic rates are classified as a tax on expenditure on housing services, and are therefore included in consumers' expenditure at market prices. However, the Community Charge, until its demise in April 1993, is classified as a separate category of transfer, which is treated as a deduction from income in calculating personal disposable income (PDI). It follows that the Community Charge is not part of consumers' expenditure. Estimates of consumers' expenditure and of GDP at current market prices from 1989 to 1992 are, therefore, marginally lower than they would have been if the Community Charge had not replaced domestic rates. GDP at current factor cost is unaffected. Estimates at constant 1985 prices of consumers' expenditure and GDP are also unaffected (see **Economic Trends**, August 1989).

☐ 2.8.3 The Expenditure Approach

The calculation of GDP, GNP and NI using the expenditure approach involves the measurement of all categories of expenditure in the economy. The sum of consumers' expenditure, investment (called gross domestic fixed capital formation – GDFCF – in the national accounts), additions to work in progress and general government final consumption is equal to **Total Domestic Expenditure**. If exports of goods and services is added to this we arrive at **Total Final Expenditure** (TFE). However, not all of this expenditure is upon domestically produced goods and services, so in order to arrive at GDP it is necessary subsequently to deduct expenditure on imports.

It is conventional to value expenditure at the prices actually paid, which yields an estimate of GDP at market prices. If indirect taxes are subsequently deducted and subsidies added in, the end-result becomes GDP at factor cost. The further addition of net property income from abroad results in GNP **at factor cost**. Finally, the deduction of estimated capital consumption results in **NNP** at factor cost, which is known as **National Income (expenditure-based)**. These relationships are set out for 1992 in **Table 2.1**.

☐ 2.8.4 The Income Approach

Table 2.2 shows the alternative way of calculating 1992 GDP and NI in terms of income. **Total Domestic Income** (TDI) is the sum of all incomes from employment, incomes from self-employment, gross trading profits of companies, the gross trading surplus of public corporations and general government enterprises, rent and other (imputed) incomes. If the nominal increase in the value of stocks of raw materials and products is subtracted from TDI the residual becomes GDP (income-based), and measures the income arising from economic activity during the year in question.

In order to reconcile the income-based measure of GDP with that based upon expenditure, a statistical adjustment or residual error term is added, as noted previously. The resultant figure is measured at factor cost because it is literally a method of deriving GDP through the summation of incomes paid to factors of production. Further adjustments in order to calculate GNP, NNP and

Table 2.1 *National Product Expenditure-based, at Current Prices (£ bn)*

	Consumers, expenditure	382.7
plus	General government final consumption	132.4
plus	Investment expenditure	
	of which:	90.9
	Gross domestic fixed capital formation (92.9)	
	Value of physical increase in stocks and work in progress (−2.0)	
equals	Total domestic expenditure	606.0
plus	Exports of goods and services	139.8
minus	Imports of goods and services	−149.2
equals	Gross domestic product (GDP) at market prices:	596.6
minus	Taxes on expenditure	−87.7
plus	Subsidies	6.1
equals	Gross domestic product (GDP) at factor cost:	515.0
plus	Net property income from abroad:	5.8
equals	Gross national product (GNP) at factor cost:	520.8
minus	Capital consumption:	−64.0
equals	Net national product (NNP) at factor cost or national income (expenditure estimate)	456.8
plus	Statistical discrepancy (expenditure adjustment)	−0.4
equals	Net national product (NNP) at factor cost or national income (average estimate)	456.4

Source: UK National Accounts Blue Book (CSO, 1993), Table 1.2; UK Economic Accounts.

NI are exactly the same as for the expenditure-based estimate.

Tables 2.1 and **2.2** contain Blue Book estimates for 1992 which, when measured at current market prices, was worth £596.6 billion (thousand million). Much the largest share, at 64 per cent of GDP, consisted of consumers' expenditure. To this we need to add government expenditure (22 per cent) and investment expenditure (15 per cent) in order to arrive at the share of GDP which is 'domestic'. The contribution of the external sector is counted net (−1.7 per cent) as the difference between exports (23.3 per cent) and imports (−25.0 per cent).

GDP at factor cost was valued at £515 billion after adjusting for the net impact of expenditure

taxes and subsidies of £81.6 billion. Net indirect taxes thus accounted for 13.7 per cent of GDP at market prices.

The transition to GNP at factor cost requires the addition to GDP of net property income from abroad of £5.8 billion. In turn, GNP is reduced to NNP by the subtraction of £64 billion of capital consumption. This is the expenditure estimate of NI which can be converted to the 'average' estimate through the statistical discrepancy or expenditure adjustment.

GDP at factor cost only can also be calculated using the income approach in **Table 2.2**. TDI before deducting stock appreciation amounted to £516.6 billion, of which the largest share (66.3 per cent) consisted of income from employ-

Table 2.2   *1992 GDP Income-based at Current Factor Cost (£ bn)*

Factor Incomes		
Income from employment		341.0
Income from self-employment		58.1
Gross trading profits of companies[1,2]		64.6
Gross trading surplus of public corporations and general enterprises		1.9
Rent		46.8
Imputed charge for consumption of non-trading capital		4.2
Total domestic income[2]		516.6
minus	Stock appreciation	−2.2
equals	GDP (income-based)	514.4
plus	Statistical discrepancy (income adjustment)	0.2
equals	GDP, at factor cost, average estimate	514.6
plus	Net property income from abroad	5.8
minus	Capital consumption	−64.0
equals	NNP at factor cost or national income (average estimate)	456.4

Notes:
[1] Before providing for (deducting) stock appreciation.
[2] Before providing for (deducting) capital consumption.
Source: UK National Accounts Blue Book (CSO, 1993), Table 1.4.

ment, valued at £341 billion. After subtraction of £2.2 billion of stock appreciation from TDI we get an estimate of 1992 GDP at factor cost. This is fractionally different from the equivalent figure using the expenditure approach, so a statistical discrepancy or income adjustment of £0.2 billion is needed to produce the estimated GDP(A) of £514.6 billion. The addition of net property income from abroad and the subtraction of capital consumption from GDP(A) produces the same figure for national income as in **Table 2.1**.

□ 2.8.5 *The Output Approach*

As output has to be produced before either incomes are paid out or those incomes are spent, the calculation of output is the first of the various estimates of economic activity to be published. It is customary to publish data on GDP(O) on a provisional basis, at quarterly intervals roughly three weeks after the end of the relevant quarter. Data are derived from estimates of physical output and survey returns from producers, and are subject to considerable revision, partly in the light of subsequent and more detailed estimates of income and expenditure.

It is not customary to express output data in money terms, but rather as a series of index numbers, as in **Table 2.3**, which contains not only the series for GDP(O) spanning the period 1979–92 (omitting 1982–3) but also the series for various sub-categories of GDP(O). In the left-hand column the total output in 1990 is assigned

Table 2.3 *GDP at Constant Factor Cost: Output Based Measure, Index Numbers of Output by Sector (1990 = 100)*

	1990 weight in total output	1979	1980	1981	1984	1985	1986	1987	1988	1989	1990	1991	1992
Agriculture, forestry and fishing	19	71.3	79.2	81.2	100.6	95.3	95.5	93.5	92.1	96.7	100.0	103.9	106.0
Energy and water supply	22	80.4	80.0	81.9	71.3	86.5	95.1	97.6	97.7	97.3	100.0	105.9	105.4
Manufacturing	237	90.6	82.8	77.7	82.2	84.5	85.6	89.6	95.9	100.2	100.0	94.7	93.9
Total production	281	87.2	81.5	78.9	83.4	88.0	90.1	93.7	98.2	100.3	100.0	96.0	95.6
Construction	72	69.4	65.6	60.5	72.8	73.0	76.0	84.9	92.3	97.6	100.0	92.1	87.1
Services: Distribution hotels, etc.	142	75.6	70.9	69.9	78.0	81.3	85.8	91.4	96.9	100.8	100.0	95.3	93.9
Transport and communication	84	73.4	72.0	72.2	77.2	80.3	83.7	89.6	94.2	99.1	100.0	97.3	98.6
Other	402	76.7	78.3	79.2	85.5	87.7	90.9	94.0	98.0	98.8	100.0	100.3	100.5
Total services	628	76.1	75.8	76.0	82.7	85.2	88.8	92.8	97.2	99.3	100.0	98.8	98.7
GDP (output based)[1]	1000	78.5	76.9	76.0	81.9	85.2	88.6	92.7	97.3	99.4	100.0	97.7	97.2

Note:
[1] Adjusted for the statistical discrepancy this yields the index of the output of goods and services.
Source: UK National Accounts Blue Book (CSO, 1993), Table 1.6.

a weight of 1000, and each sub-category or part thereof is assigned a proportion of the total weight according to the proportion of GDP(O) that it contributed in 1990. Thus it can be seen that the service sectors, with a weight of 628, accounted for 62.8 per cent of 1990 GDP(O), whereas the production industries accounted for 28.1 per cent. This is not all that unusual for a major advanced economy where the service sectors no longer commonly constitute less than 50 per cent of output.

It can be seen from **Table 2.3** that the service sectors rode out the 1980–81 recession without much difficulty, although distribution was hit fairly hard as one might have expected. In contrast, both manufacturing and construction fell back heavily. Interestingly, the 'other services' sector grew at the same rate as manufacturing from 1981 onwards, despite their sharply contrasting experiences during 1979–81, and construction grew at the same rapid rate as transport and communications.

From 1985 to 1990 there was a boom in construction, and distribution and transport also grew unusually rapidly. Manufacturing (which peaked in 1989) and other services also performed creditably. It can also be seen that the agriculture, forestry and fishing sector barely affects total output, although it has a disproportionate effect upon policy making. It performed poorly from 1984 to 1988, but has subsequently done much better.

It is obviously possible to put a value upon the output of a given year, as is done for 1992 in **Table 2.4**. This has to be done on a **value-added** basis, as noted earlier, and this in turn requires that the data be collected on a factor cost basis which is recorded net of stock appreciation but before deducting capital consumption.

The level of disaggregation in **Table 2.4** is greater than in **Table 2.3**. Both contain a composite category for the energy and water supply industries, which in 1992 was worth £13.7 billion. This can be compared with agriculture, forestry and fishing with its much smaller net output of £9.3 billion. In fact, this comparison is deceptive because energy and water are mostly sold in the free market whereas agricultural pro-

Table 2.4   *UK GDP by Industry,[1] 1992 (£ bn)*

Industry Category	Net Output
Agriculture, forestry and fishing	9.3
Energy and water supply	13.7
Mining/quarrying	9.9
Manufacturing	114.7
Construction	32.0
Distribution, hotels and catering; repairs	72.5
Transport and communication	41.6
Banking, finance, insurance, business services and leasing[2]	84.7
Ownership of dwellings (rent)	37.1
Public administration, national defence and compulsory social security	36.6
Education and health services	52.5
Other services	32.9
Total	537.5
Adjustment for financial services[3]	−23.1
GDP (income-based)	514.4
Statistical discrepancy (income component)	0.2
GDP at factor cost (average estimate)	514.6

Notes:
[1] The contribution of each industry to the GDP (its value-added), net of stock appreciation but before providing for (deducting) capital consumption.
[2] Including net interest receipts by financial companies.
[3] The same as net interest receipts by financial companies.

Source: UK National Accounts Blue Book (CSO, 1993), Tables 2.1 and 2.2.

Table 2.5   *GDP, Growth of Output by Sector, 1980–92*

	(1) 1992 Weight in Total Output[1]	(2) Percentage Change from 1980 to 1992	(3) Contribution to Change in Output 1980 to 1992 ((1) × (2))	(4) Percentage Share of Total Change
Agriculture, forestry and fishing	1.9	33.8	64.2	2.4
Production	28.1	17.3	486.1	18.1
Construction	7.2	32.8	236.2	8.8
Services	62.8	30.2	1896.6	70.7
Total Index of Output	100.0	26.8	2683.1	100.0

Note:
[1] Expressed as % of total weights in Table 2.3.

Source: UK National Accounts Blue Book (CSO, 1993), Table 1.6.

ducts are heavily subsidised, so the real contribution of the agricultural sector is much less than it appears to be on the basis of **Table 2.4**.

The contribution of financial services to GDP(A) is brought out clearly in **Table 2.4**. The figure of £84.7 billion includes net interest receipts which need to be subtracted lower down **Table 2.4** because they do not contribute directly to net output. On a grossed-up basis, the gap between the contributions of financial services and manufacturing is no longer all that large, and it can be expected to narrow further in due course.

Table 2.5 serves to emphasise yet further the evolving nature of the UK economy. As can be seen in column (2), construction and services substantially outgrew production during the period 1980–92, with agriculture, forestry and fishing also performing well (but only at the beginning and end of the period). After adjusting for the relative importance of the various sectors, as signified by column (1), it is possible to calculate, in column (4), the percentage share of the total change in output between 1980 and 1992 contributed by each sector. As can be seen, the services sector played a dominant role, with the production industries lagging far behind.

2.8.6 *Real National Income, 1979–92*

The purpose of this section is to examine briefly real NI data spanning the full term of Conservative rule. This is presented in **Table 2.6**. **Table 2.6** culminates with an index of GDP(A) at factor cost. As can be seen, real GDP(A) fell back during 1980–81. It regained its 1979 level in 1983, and significant gains were made in every year from 1982 to 1989 with a further small gain in 1990. It suffered a severe setback in 1991 and a modest one in 1992, prior to a modest (forecast) improvement in 1993.

Overall, therefore, GDP imroved during eight of the ten years comprising the 1980s, and the overall improvement, even allowing for the prior recession, was roughly 20 per cent. Some leeway has subsequently been lost, but the UK is significantly wealthier overall than it was when Mrs Thatcher was first elected. The main driving force was clearly real consumption, although real investment performed very creditably from 1981 to 1989. In contrast, general government final consumption was very subdued, demonstrating

Table 2.6   *UK Real Domestic Product by Category of Expenditure at 1990,[1] 1972–92 (£ bn)*

	1979	1980	1981	1985	1986	1987	1988	1989	1990	1991	1992	1993[2]
Consumers' expenditure	247.2	247.2	247.4	276.8	295.6	311.2	334.6	345.4	347.5	340.0	340.0	346.0
General government final consumption	99.3	101.0	101.3	105.2	106.9	107.9	108.6	110.1	112.9	115.8	116.0	114.0
Gross domestic fixed capital formation	75.8	71.8	64.9	81.6	83.7	92.3	104.7	110.5	106.8	96.2	95.2	96.0
Value of increase in stocks and work in progress	5.4	−5.5	−5.2	1.3	1.2	1.7	5.5	3.7	−1.1	−4.7	−1.7	−2.0
Exports of goods and services	95.1	94.9	94.2	109.2	114.0	120.6	121.2	126.8	133.3	132.0	135.5	139.0
Imports of goods and services	−89.7	−86.5	−84.0	−106.0	−113.3	−122.1	−137.4	−147.6	−148.3	−140.2	−148.3	−151.0
GDP (expenditure-based) at market prices	433.4	423.5	418.0	468.1	488.1	511.6	537.2	548.9	551.1	539.1	536.7	542.0
Statistical discrepancy	−0.5	−1.4	−2.4	–	–	–	–	–	–	−0.4	−0.4	–
GDP (average estimate) at market prices	–	–	–	–	–	–	–	–	–	–	–	–
Factor cost adjustment	−56.9	−55.3	−54.1	−60.3	−63.9	−67.8	−71.5	−72.7	−72.2	−71.0	−70.6	−72.0
GDP at factor cost	376.0	368.2	361.1	407.8	424.2	443.8	465.7	476.2	478.9	467.7	465.7	470.0
Index of GDP at factor cost, 1990 = 100	78.5	76.9	75.4	85.2	88.6	92.7	97.2	99.4	100.0	97.7	97.2	98.1

Notes:
[1] For the years before 1983, totals differ from the sum of their components.
[2] Forecast.

Source: UK National Accounts Blue Book (CSO, 1993), Table 1.3; *Economic Trends.*

that the 1980s were years in which the government largely turned its back on Keynesian demand management.

☐ 2.8.7 Exports and Imports

Our discussion in this section is essentially concerned with matters internal to the UK, but it is worth picking up from **Table 2.6** a few pointers to the subject matter of Chapter 7 on international trade. As can be seen, the volume of exports remained almost static during the 1980–81 recession, in which respect it must be remembered that export demand is determined by spending power in other economies which did not collapse anything like as steeply as in the UK at this time. Furthermore, North Sea oil moved into excess supply and the UK was able to become a net exporter.

The effects of the recession on UK demand are clearly seen when one examines the real value of imports, which fell during 1980 and 1981. However, by 1983 imports had regained all of the lost ground as the economy moved out of recession. In 1984 export and import demand were in approximate balance, and continued to be so until 1987, after which the growth of imports easily outstripped that of exports, although the devaluation of September 1992 is expected to improve the situation slightly in 1993. Nevertheless, one of the most remarked-upon features of the 1990–92 recession, which differed from prior experience, was the fact that import demand was as high in 1992 as in 1990.

2.9 Sectoral Surpluses and Deficits

Although this text is concerned primarily with the period since 1979, it can be illuminating to examine certain longer-term trends. This is true, for example, in the case of sectoral surpluses and deficits. There are basically four of these, covering the personal, public, overseas and company sectors, although there is also a variant of the latter which covers only those companies deemed to be industrial and commercial (ICCs). The overseas sector account tracks the direction in which money flows, and hence is a mirror image of the current account surplus or deficit. In other words, a deficit on the current account of the balance of payments shows up as a sectoral surplus because money flows in to finance it and vice versa.

It is for this reason that, starting in 1970, the modest deficit of the **overseas sector** at the time turned rapidly into a sizeable surplus at the time of the first oil price rise, only to settle back to zero at the end of the decade. At the beginning of the 1980s, on the back of North Sea oil, it dropped sharply into deficit, only to rise back to zero by the mid–1980s and to rise further to a substantial surplus which peaked in 1989, as shown in **Figure 2.5**. For the past two years it has remained in surplus, but at somewhat reduced levels which reflect the prevailing recessionary conditions.

At the beginning of the 1970s the **public sector** was in surplus, but by the mid–1970s it had collapsed back into massive deficit. Subsequently the situation improved somewhat, although substantial deficits remained the order of the day until 1985. During the years which followed, as we will discover in detail in Chapter 4, the fiscal position improved dramatically but, as shown in **Figure 2.5** the past three years have seen the customary deficit reappear in no uncertain fashion.

Throughout the entire period, the **personal sector** exhibited an almost exactly opposite pattern. It remained in surplus from 1972 to 1986, although from 1981 to 1988 the trend was almost continuously downwards, amounting in all to a change of nearly 10 per cent of GDP. The opposite turnaround for the public sector, commencing in 1975, was actually larger than this, but took longer to be achieved, and like that sector the personal sector has recently moved significantly into reverse gear as shown in **Figure 2.5**. We will be discussing this pattern in detail in the sections which follow.

From 1970 to 1982 the **ICC** sector balance exhibited relatively little variability, oscillating regularly from a small positive to a small nega-

Figure 2.5   *Financial Surplus/Deficit,[1] by Sector (£ bn Quarterly, 1988–93)*

Note:
[1] This balance is equal to saving *plus* capital transfers *less* GDFCF *less* increase in value of stocks and work in progress.

Source: Economic Trends, Table 35.

tive percentage of GDP. However, in 1982 it rose to 4.4 per cent of GDP, and in 1983 began a decline which accelerated after 1986. By 1989 the total turnaround represented 10 per cent of GDP but, as shown in **Figure 2.5**, this sector has spent the past three years repairing its balance sheets and has succeeded in eliminating its deficit during 1993. The overall **company** sector has generally moved in line, with non-ICC companies faring badly in 1991, although in 1990 and 1992 they produced a modest surplus.

The various sectoral lines converged in 1986, which had not happened since the early 1970s. At that time the collapse of the public sector's financial position was mirrored by a major upturn for the personal and, temporarily, the overseas sector. However, in 1986 every sector was, most unusually, in the throes of a massive uni-directional movement, from an early 1980s surplus into deficit or vice versa. This sequence came to an end in 1988–89, and a pattern has reappeared remarkably similar to that seen after the lines previously converged in the early 1970s. That begs the question whether this is another case of history repeating itself, but it will be some time before we can discern roughly how long it is going to take before the personal and public sector lines come back into equivalence.

In the sections which follow we will be examining the company and personal sector in more detail. However, the discussion of the public and overseas sectors is more sensibly held over to the later chapters dedicated to fiscal policy and trade respectively.

☐ 2.9.1 Company Sector

The most remarkable feature of the period 1986–89 was the collapse in the financial health of the company sector, with an almost equally remarkable improvement since then which has yet to run its full course. In 1989 as a whole (**Figure 2.5** plots quarterly data) ICCs ran up a deficit of £22.7 billion, a threefold increase on 1988, which was followed by a £19.9 billion deficit in 1990. Surprisingly, however, this was not reflected in the balance sheets of most large corporations, which

were sufficiently strong to be able to sustain dividend growth. In fact, large companies continued to pay out dividends well in excess of what was warranted by their income growth, a policy which makes some sense as a smoothing device through the economic cycle but which obviously causes short-term problems. As the Bank of England noted at the time, the ratio of dividends to post-tax profits reached 'an almost unprecedented' 62 per cent in the final quarter of 1989. Needless to say, this strategy has been significantly reversed in recent years, and the current reporting season (1993) has seen cut-backs in dividend payments; too late, perhaps, in certain cases to save companies from the hands of the receivers.

In 1987 the ICCs' net borrowing requirement stood at £23.6 billion, whereas it had risen to £49.9 billion in 1988 and to £53.8 billion in 1989 (see *Economic Trends*, Table 38). During these two years investment abroad was running at a level in excess of £10 billion per year but, more notably, investment in UK company securities soared from £5.3 billion in 1987 (the year of the crash) to £14.5 billion in 1988 and £17.9 billion in 1989. Once the acquisition of financial assets is added in, the resultant gross borrowing requirement roughly trebled between 1987 and 1989.

It is almost facile to argue that this trend clearly could not be sustained in the face of a deepening recession commencing in 1990. This shows up in the data, although there are the usual caveats which arise because account has to be taken of an often large and variable balancing item (unidentified flows), and of an expansion in the size of the ICC sector as a result of privatisation. Furthermore, it is possible to argue that the onset of the deficit reflected the confidence of the sector rather than the reverse. Fixed investment rose from £32.2 billion in 1987 to £43.5 billion in 1988 and to £54.9 billion in 1990, since when it has declined a little. ICCs seemed to be quite happy to finance this by bank and other borrowing, which had soared to £70 billion by 1989, thereby raising noticeably their 'gearing' (ratio of debt to equity).

Obviously, it had become difficult to raise much finance via an issue of ordinary shares in the aftermath of the 1987 crash, but ICCs do not seem to have taken much account of the possibility (probability?) that interest rates might rise and cause the interest charges on their borrowing to become overburdensome. Another interesting feature of this period, which we will discuss further in Chapter 3, is that increasing reliance was placed upon innovatory financial instruments, such as interest rate swaps. Further features of the late 1980s were the sharp upturn in the acquisition of UK company securities, which indicated much increased activity in the merger/takeover market, and the high level of overseas investment, especially in the USA, which greatly exceeded the acquisition of ICCs by foreign companies at this time. It is notable that 80 per cent of all takeover bids in 1989 were conducted in cash, which understandably made it necessary to resort to bank borrowing.

The net borrowing requirement peaked at £18.8 billion in the third quarter of 1989. Since then, apart from the £15.3 billion recorded in the final quarter of 1990 following on from an unusually small quarterly total, the quarterly figures have mostly fallen below £10 billion, and on several occasions below £5 billion. Although other forms of borrowing have remained buoyant, it is especially notable that bank borrowing fell to £19.9 billion in 1990 and to **minus** £0.9 billion in 1991 and **minus** £1.9 billion in 1992. Equally, investment in UK company securities fell to a negligible

£2.3 billion in 1990, reflecting the demise of the mega-bid, and has subsequently shown no signs of returning anywhere near to late 1980s levels. Investment abroad has also collapsed, bottoming out at £0.5 billion in 1990 and showing only modest growth beyond that point. In other words, the corporate sector has well and truly battened down the hatches, and concentrated wholeheartedly upon restoring battered balance sheets. For the most part this has been a successful strategy, although company failures have remained a regular feature of 1993.

□ 2.9.2 Personal Sector

It is of great interest to examine why the personal sector moved from a position of surplus to a position of deficit late in 1987 and back into surplus at the end of 1990. As noted above, the decline in the financial surplus of the personal sector commenced at the beginning of the 1980s, so it is the experience of the past three years which stands in sharp contrast to that of the first decade of Conservative rule. In order to clarify what happened we need to refer to **Table 2.7**, which identifies the major changes since 1986.

As usual, a key element relates to the housing market. The table shows that the build-up of debt primarily took the form of loans for house pur-

Table 2.7   *Personal Sector: Financial Account, Main Changes 1986–92 (£ bn)*

	1986	1987	1988	1989	1990	1991	1992
Loans for house purchase	−27.0	−29.4	−40.1	−34.1	−32.6	−26.1	−18.0
UK company securities	−6.8	−6.5	−12.4	−19.8	−7.8	−2.7	+3.6
Sterling bank lending	−5.2	−8.8	−13.0	−13.2	−8.1	−2.3	−0.7
Unit trust units	+20	+3.4	−0.1	+0.9	+0.0	+0.9	−0.1
Deposits with building societies	+11.8	+13.6	+20.2	+17.6	+18.0	+17.3	+10.6
Sterling bank sight deposits	+7.3	+7.4	+8.6	+11.0	+8.5	+5.5	+3.1
Sterling bank time deposits	+1.1	+0.3	+8.0	+10.2	+8.0	+0.6	+2.6
British Government securities	+1.8	+1.7	−1.8	−2.2	−1.0	+1.3	+2.5
Life assurance and pension funds	+21.0	+20.0	+20.0	+26.5	+25.9	+24.5	+22.6
Balancing item	−8.6	−9.3	−8.0	−4.5	−8.5	−9.6	−5.7

Source: Financial Statistics, Table 1.11.

chase, which peaked at an astonishing £40 billion in 1988 at a time when house prices were rising rapidly. The recent price falls have gone hand-in-hand with a massive reduction in such loans, on a scale which has dwarfed most of what has happened elsewhere in the account. However, there has also been a massive movement out of direct holdings of company securities, most notably in the two years following the 1987 crash. While this has now reversed itself, it is evident that, privatisation issues notwithstanding, the personal sector has lost its enthusiasm for direct holdings of equity.

On the other hand, it has continued to pump massive amounts of money into life assurance and pension funds, which means that the sector has an ever-larger but increasingly less direct interest in the stock market. However, until very recently, sectoral investment in unit trusts struggled to regain its pre–1987 momentum. The period from 1987 to 1990 also witnessed a run-down in personal holdings of government securities, although this partly reflected the paucity of supply as a result of repayments of the national debt. The debt is once again rising rapidly, so personal holdings have begun to follow suit, particularly since the government expressly targeted the sector for such sales in 1993.

Very large sums of money have been lodged in building society accounts, partly as a result of liquidating other assets. Such accounts are interest-bearing, as for the moment are bank accounts of various kinds which in aggregate were roughly as popular in the late 1980s. As interest rates have declined in recent months, so the attraction of such accounts has declined, and this has begun to show up in **Table 2.7** in 1992.

Overall, therefore, the picture until 1992 was one of the personal sector maintaining its liquidity, cutting back on mortgage debt and, as shown by the data on bank lending, cutting back hugely on its loans from banks at high rates of interest. This was a recipe for prolonged recession, but there are a few 'green shoots' evident in the data for 1992 and in that for the first half of 1993, so we will probably see the personal sector surplus heading back towards balance by the end of the year.

■ *2.10* Income and Wealth

In the light of the above comments, and before proceeding any further, it is important to clear up a misunderstanding that, to judge by their utterances over the years, is particularly prevalent among politicians but which is also made too little of in introductory textbooks; this concerns the distinction between the concepts of **income** and **wealth** (see also Chapter 9). Income is a **flow**: that is, it appears in a series of instalments over time (for example, weekly, monthly or yearly). Most income is **earned**, and consists primarily of payments in return for labour inputs (that is, wages and salaries as shown in **Table 2.2**). However, it may also be **unearned**, in the form, for example, of rent, interest and dividends. Some also appears as transfer payments (for instance, payments to the unemployed).

Wealth, on the other hand, is a **stock**, and is measured at a particular point in time. Wealth may either be **physical**, taking the form of assets which can be handled (for example, a house or its contents or **financial** (for example, cash in the bank or building society, stocks and shares). It must be counted net of liabilities: a person's wealth tied up in a house is equal to the current market value of the property less any outstanding mortgage.

This is less straightforward than it looks. In the first place, it is evident that income can be converted into wealth via the act of **saving**, and for most people their wealth originates in setting aside some part of their income flow. However, where a person takes out a repayment mortgage, for example, part of the monthly outgoing is a payment of interest while another part is a repayment of capital. The latter part therefore constitutes an addition to that person's wealth, although in practice most people tend to think of mortgage payments as spending rather than saving. Equally, wealth can create a flow of unearned income, either because a property which is let out produces rent, a bank account yields interest or a share yields a dividend.

Further ambiguities arise where, for example, a person buys a car. Strictly speaking a car is a form of physical wealth, but unlike a house it can be expected to self-destruct within, say, fifteen years (although a 'classic' car is an exception), and hence tends to be viewed by purchasers as a form of expenditure. The same may be said of clothing and household appliances, and the key issue is ultimately how the Inland Revenue view such assets for tax purposes since some kind of arbitrary decision has to be made for official purposes.

Trickier problems arise in respect of pension rights. Employees' contributions to a pension fund are often deducted at source, and are effectively a form of compulsory saving in order to acquire a stock of wealth which the employee cannot access prior to retirement, subsequent to which there is generally a lump-sum payment followed by a flow of unearned income in the form of a pension which continues for an indeterminate number of years. For this latter reason it is extremely difficult to say how much wealth any single individual has tied up in a pension right.

Trickier still is human capital. In effect, if a person borrows money to finance his or her education, then the knowledge gained is a form of wealth that can generally be expected to result in a flow of income in future years which exceeds what would have been available in the absence of that knowledge. Thus the loan finances the creation of wealth which subsequently generates incremental income that can be used to repay the loan.

For these and other reasons, hardly anyone has any real idea how much wealth he or she owns, though people are obviously well informed about their incomes. Interestingly, when one considers the widespread usage of the term **rich**, the word could equally well apply to a person who has a huge income and no assets as to a person who has virtually no income but a great deal of wealth (for example, a widow on a pension living in a big house free of mortgage). These usages are by no means interchangeable, as politicians constantly need reminding, and this not merely causes endless problems for tax/benefit policy, as in the case of local taxation, but there is an issue of wider significance because it becomes unclear to what extent spending decisions are driven by considera-

tions of income and/or wealth. Given that housing constitutes such a large part of most people's stock of wealth, it follows that the state of the housing market is closely tied to patterns of spending in the modern economy. In effect, as discussed below, wealth provides the collateral security that facilitates overconsumption: failing all else, if debt piles up as a result of overindulgence with credit cards, it is generally possible to sell off property and settle debts with the proceeds before a new property is acquired.

■ 2.11 The Housing Market

It has become increasingly apparent over the past decade that the workings of the housing market play an extremely important role in the conduct of economic policy. The liberalisation of financial markets in the early 1980s led to much increased competition between banks, building societies and other intermediaries to make loans secured against housing. These, the banks belatedly discovered, were much less risky than lending to sovereign states.

The effects of liberalisation were to weaken prudential controls in the housing market. Prior to the 1980s owner-occupation was subsidised, first of all insofar as tax relief was given on mortgage interest payments (up to a loan limit of £25 000 which, in the mid–1970s, bought a splendid house anywhere outside London), and second because houses were not subject to capital gains tax (CGT). Not surprisingly, owner-occupation was very popular, as shown in **Figure 2.6**. However, most of the money provided in the mortgage market originated in retail (High Street) deposits in building society branches, and there were accordingly periodic famines and few feasts. As a result, mortgages were rationed and this made it almost impossible for borrowers to overextend themselves. Large deposits were required, and a loan of 2.5 times income, or even less, was the norm.

Once capital controls were dismantled in 1979, and wholesale finance became available in a more competitive market, prospective borrowers found

Figure 2.6 *Stock of Dwellings by Tenure, UK, 1963–92*

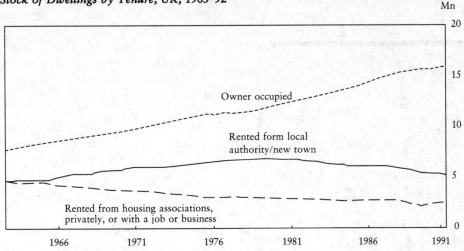

Source: Department of the Environment.

The UK Housing Market

If we compare the housing market and the housing finance system in the UK with those of other advanced economies, several features stand out (see also *Bank of England Quarterly Bulletin*, February 1991, pp. 56–66). These features have become less prominent over the past two years as the housing market has adjusted to its difficult trading conditions and problems of bad debts.

- Mortgage lending is relatively long-term
- Unusually small deposits are required
- Income multipliers are relatively high
- The private rental sector is relatively regulated
- House prices on average run further ahead of retail prices
- Personal savings are relatively low
- Mortgage debt is high relative to GDP
- Equity withdrawal via a remortgage is relatively easy

- Mortgages are subsidised, which is uncommon
- There is relatively little tax on capital gains

The US housing market bears the closest resemblance to that of the UK, but things are quite different in Germany and Japan. In the latter countries, for example, it is not customary to lend more than 60 per cent of the value of a property, so it is not surprising that their inhabitants save much more than their counterparts in the UK, who expect to borrow at least 90 per cent of a new property.

In the case of Japan, the high rate of savings also reflects an acute shortage of building land which results in such high property prices that first-time buyers are frequently unable to enter the market until they are relatively old, if at all. It is also a demonstrable proposition that countries such as Japan, Germany and France, with the least developed systems of housing finance, have the highest personal saving ratios.

Figure 2.7   *Total Cost of Mortgage Interest Tax Relief,[1] UK*

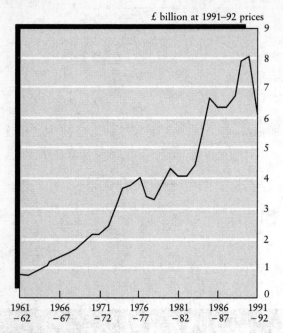

£ billion at 1991–92 prices

1961 1966 1971 1976 1981 1986 1991
−62 −67 −72 −77 −82 −87 −92

Note:
[1] Includes expenditure on option mortgage scheme.
Source: Social Trends, 23 (1993 edn), Chart 8.22.

Figure 2.8   *Personal Sector: Income and Capital Gearing*

Per cent

Housing market[1]

Capital gearing[2]

Income gearing[3]

1975 77 79 81 83 85 87 89 91

Notes:
[1] Stock of lending to persons for house purchase as a proportion of the value of owner-occupied housing shock.
[2] Borrowing from banks and building societies as a proportion of personal sector financial and physical assets.
[3] Ratio of interest payments to income.
Source: Compiled from the *Bank of England Quarterly Bulletin.*

it progressively easier to demand reduced deposits and much higher income multiples (generally taking into account second incomes as well). As a result total mortgage debt in Britain, already high in 1982 (at 32 per cent of GDP) soared to 60 per cent of GDP by 1990, by far the highest ratio of the major economies. Only in the USA, where all mortgage debt is tax-deductible, did anything like such a surge take place. In Germany, by way of contrast, where home loans cannot exceed 60 per cent of the value of a property and where interest payments attract no tax relief, mortgage debt actually fell as a proportion of GDP.

The owner-occupied stock of dwellings shown in **Figure 2.6** represented 67 per cent of the total stock by 1992, at the expense both of the public and private rental sectors. As it happens, this was not an unusually high proportion in that it was only slightly higher than in the USA, Japan and Canada, and below that in Ireland, Spain and Italy, but it was becoming increasing burden-

some in terms of mortgage interest tax relief, as shown in **Figure 2.7**. Just as importantly, the strong demand for owner-occupied houses drove up house prices, at times so rapidly that they outstripped retail prices by a comfortable margin. The period to 1989 could truly be said to be

Figure 2.9 *House Transactions*

Source: *Economic Trends*, Table 43.

characterised by the phenomenon of **asset price inflation.**

Beyond the middle of the decade the slackening of prudential controls quite simply got out of hand. Not merely did 100 per cent mortgages become commonplace (although a building society was typically only responsible for the first 80 per cent and an insurance company for the rest), but sums in excess of the buying price were happily advanced on the grounds that house prices would rapidly catch up. The Department of the Environment calculated in 1989 that 36 per cent of first-time buyers had mortgages in excess of the value of their property. The effects of this can be seen in a number of ways, of which the most significant is shown as **Figure 2.8.**

Figure 2.8 illustrates two aspects of the personal sector's capital gearing. The first of these covers bank and building society lending as a proportion of total assets, which roughly doubled in the course of the 1980s. As the economy moved out of recession in 1983, real PDI began to grow

Figure 2.10 *Real and Nominal House Price Growth*

Department of Environment house price index and RPI

Source: Compiled from the *Bank of England Quarterly Bulletin*.

Figure 2.11   *House Price: Earnings Ratio*

Department of Environment house price index and average earnings

Source: Compiled from the *Bank of England Quarterly Bulletin*.

rapidly, and this provided the leverage for house-holds to opt for owner-occupancy and to attempt to move up the housing ladder by borrowing ever-larger sums. The number of house transactions began to rise inexorably towards 2 million per year, as shown in **Figure 2.9**, but there were also more people chasing each property which drove up prices. This can be seen in **Figure 2.8** as a sharp increase in the value of the owner-occupied hous-ing stock represented by lending rather than paid-up capital.

There was a parallel increase in income gearing, which measures the ratio of interest payments to income. However, the real explosion did not take place until 1987, at which time house prices began to rise so rapidly that they eventually doubled in nominal terms throughout almost all of the UK, although the process effectively rolled out of London and the South-East towards other areas. This can be seen in **Figure 2.10**, which illustrates nominal and real house price growth. The nom-inal increase in 1987–88 was about the same as in 1979–80, and somewhat less than in 1973–74, but these were periods of much higher general infla-

tion such that real house prices in 1987–88 rose faster than at any time other than in 1973–74.

The effects show up in **Figure 2.8** as a dramatic rise in the housing market capital gearing line, but more notably in the income gearing line because interest rates rose sharply in belated recognition of the fallout from this enormous increase in personal wealth. We have already noted in our previous discussion of consumption that the surge in wealth, and effectively in collateral, appears to have triggered overconsumption and an asso-ciated collapse in saving, leading to the appear-ance of a huge personal sector financial deficit. This also reflected the phenomenon of **equity withdrawal**. The sale of inherited houses to re-lease cash was nothing new, but it was progres-sively dawning on householders that the con-stantly rising value of their homes was providing a cushion of equity between the market price and the outstanding mortgage which could be released by taking out a second mortgage. This desire to release liquidity was happily met by an endless stream of financial intermediaries which could not envisage the possibility of losing money since, after all, nominal house prices had never been known to fall.

As a result, even more liquidity was released in addition to that released via inheritance, and yet more was released because when people moved house, they typically did not reinvest all of their untaxed capital gains net of expenses, but rather increased their mortgages to reflect their higher incomes and pocketed the difference in cash.

This phenomenon was very important because it provided the wherewithal for a very high level of consumption (particularly, as it happens, of imports), much of it associated with housing. This level of consumption was not sustainable in relation to net incomes, but the ready provision of credit combined with increased collateral in the form of property relieved most households of the worry traditionally associated with high levels of indebtedness. In this respect there was a link with the interest rate since that determined the servicing cost of the increased debt, and an important consideration at the time was that, as shown in **Figure 12.3**, interest rates were on a downwards trend from 1985 onwards, and had been brought down to an exceptionally low level

in nominal terms in the aftermath of the stock market crash of October 1987.

Cheap mortgages naturally fuelled the desire to buy houses, and this can be seen clearly in **Figure 2.11** which plots the relationship between house prices and earnings. This relationship has a 'norm' to which it can be expected to revert in the medium term, although recent reductions in the tax subsidy may have lowered the norm relative to the period pre–1979. The data suggest that this norm was traditionally in the region of 3.0 to 3.5, with a current equivalent of 2.5 to 3.0. The peak value in 1989 was approaching 5.5 and, with hindsight, it is obvious that this was unsustainable. However, the more interesting phenomenon was the extraordinary collapse which began in 1989 and which has just about run out of steam in mid–1993.

A major contributory factor, as shown in **Figure 12.3**, was the doubling of the nominal interest rate from 7.5 to 15 per cent, since this hugely increased mortgage repayments as a proportion of net income. This shows up in respect of the income gearing line in **Figure 2.8** which rose to almost 14 per cent, over twice the level prevailing

Figure 2.12 *Percentage Deviation of Regional House Prices from the National Average Since 1983*

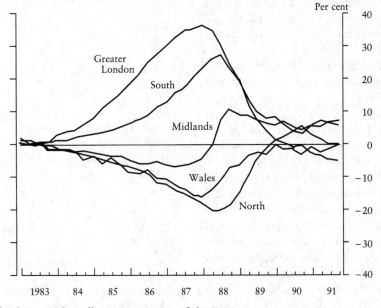

Source: Bank of England Quarterly Bulletin, Department of the Environment.

even in the early 1980s let alone the 1970s. In this context it has to be said that the interest rate is a rather blunt weapon as an instrument for domestic demand management. Raising interest rates is unlikely to deter consumption unless it forces up monthly mortgage repayments to the point at which householders' pips squeak loudly, and even that may act with a lagged effect because so many mortgages are currently readjusted only once a year. It also has to be said that the use of penal interest rates to regulate new mortgage borrowing serves to punish all other debtors at the same time.

The collapse in the housing market was indeed dramatic. At the end of 1989 the housing stock was worth close to £1000 billion, but one year later £100 billion of this had evaporated and this reduction has been continuing until very recently. It is nevertheless worth noting that the debt secured on property is worth several hundred million pounds less than the value of that property even at its current much reduced level.

The situation after 1989 can be viewed from a variety of perspectives, as in **Figures 2.8, 2.9** and **2.10**. **Figure 2.9** shows that the number of house transactions fell back in 1992 to half the level prevailing in 1989. It is, however, **Figure 2.10** which illustrates the most extraordinary aspect of what happened, namely the unprecedented fall in **nominal** house prices. Furthermore, this fall was neither modest nor short-lived, as nominal prices have yet to regain their 1989 levels. It is also notable that real house prices fell by a much lesser amount than in 1975.

We have already observed that the surge in house prices rolled outwards from London. It is unsurprising, therefore, that the effects were somewhat dampened by the time the outermost regions of the UK were reached. At the time this was perceived as something of a misfortune in these areas, but the subsequent impact of the collapse in demand was also disproportionately felt in those regions where the rises had been largest, and was of much less consequence elsewhere. This can be seen most clearly in **Figure 2.12**, which expresses regional variations in house prices relative to the UK average. At the end of 1987 the gap between London and the North had

become enormous, in the process making it financially impossible for anyone to move in a southerly direction. By the end of 1990 regional house prices had converged back to roughly the relative relationship previously seen in 1984. The nominal reductions this implied in London, and especially in East Anglia, were commonly of the order of 30 per cent, although as a consequence much property was withdrawn from the market to await better times.

For most households the combination of an increasingly expensive mortgage and, for those who had entered the market when prices were at their highest in 1988–89, a house worth less than was owed to the mortgagee, was basically an

Table 2.8 *Mortgage Lenders:[1] Number of Mortgages, Arrears and Possessions, UK (thousands)*

| | Number of mortgages | Loans in arrears at end-period | | Properties taken into possession in period |
		By 6–12 months	By over 12 months	
1971	4506	17.6	..	2.8
1976	5322	16.0	..	5.0
1980	6210	15.5	..	3.5
1981	6336	21.5	..	4.9
1982	6518	27.4	5.5	6.9
1983	6846	29.4	7.5	8.4
1984	7313	48.3	9.5	12.4
1985	7717	57.1	13.1	19.3
1986	8138	52.1	13.0	24.1
1987	8283	55.5	15.0	26.4
1988	8564	42.8	10.3	18.5
1989	9125	66.8	13.8	15.8
1990	9415	123.1	36.1	43.9
1991	9815	183.6	91.7	75.5
1992[1]	9840	205.0	147.0	68.5

Note:
[1] Council of Mortgage Lenders estimates as at 31 December in each year. Estimates only cover members of the Council, but these account for more than 90 per cent of all mortgages outstanding.
Source: CSO.

inconvenience which forced a cut-back in consumption. They paid their monthly instalments and stayed put. For many, however, the situation was the recipe for disaster. If they could not afford the monthly repayments (which 800 000 were unable to do in June 1993), perhaps as a result of unemployment, the arrears mounted up very quickly. This can be seen in **Table 2.8** which indicates that the number of loans in arrears by 6–12 months tripled between 1989 and 1992, and the number in arrears by over 12 months rose more than tenfold during the same period, although this reflected in part the reduction in interest rates over the period since it takes more months to repay an outstanding balance when the monthly instalment falls. On the other hand, many mortgagors had their arrears 'capitalised', thereby causing the arrears to disappear. Unsurprisingly, faced with the possibility that some mortgagors

were unlikely to be able to repay anything of significance for the foreseeable future, most lenders opted for repossession, with the number of cases tripling in 1990 alone.

As noted, provided there is an ability to pay mortgage instalments, the fact that a property is worth less than the outstanding mortgage is not of itself a problem for the householder. However, on a sufficient scale it is a problem for the economy because of the immobility it engenders, given a reluctance on the part of lenders to permit negative equity to be transferred from one property to another. **Figure 2.13** provides the Bank of England's 1992 estimates of the overall position in respect of negative equity, including various projections through 1993. These figures may appear to be fearsomely large, but by March 1993 the Bank had revised the total upwards to 1.8 million on the grounds that house prices had continued to

Figure 2.13   *The Evolution and Possible Development of Negative Equity*

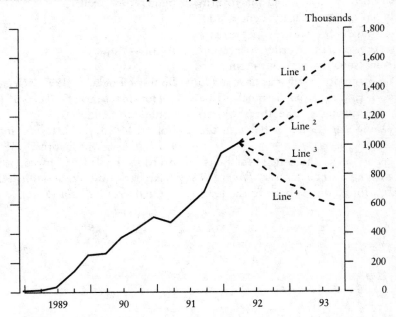

[1]   One per cent per quarter fall in prices in all regions to the fourth quarter of 1993.
[2]   One per cent per quarter rise in prices in all regions to the fourth quarter of 1993.
[3]   One per cent per quarter fall in the South, similar rise in the rest of the country.
[4]   One per cent per quarter rise in the South, similar fall in the rest of the country.

Source: Bank of England Quarterly Bulletin (August 1992).

fall sharply in the interim. Total negative equity was estimated to be of the order of £12 billion, with one in three households with mortgages in the South-East suffering from negative equity. The Council of Mortgage Lenders has always disputed these figures (see letter in the *Financial Times*, 11 June 1992) and the exact truth will probably never be known.

The government understandably felt under pressure to relieve these problems, but had no desire to do so in a manner that would once again run the risk of setting off the spiral of rising house prices and overconsumption. In November 1991, for example, a scheme was launched to make empty repossessed houses available to the homeless through housing associations. This was followed by a scheme to allow householders threatened by repossession to remain in their homes while paying rent rather than a mortgage. In December 1991, home-buyers were given an eight-month holiday from stamp duty on properties worth up to £250 000, and the government agreed to pay social security benefits designed to cover mortgage interest payments (MIPs) direct to the lenders in order to prevent householders from 'squandering' the money on other things. These and other schemes have made little progress so far, and neither is much to be expected from the raising of the threshold to £60 000 before stamp duty becomes liable in the Spring 1993 Budget.

Affordability is no longer the issue in the housing market. According to the *Financial Times* (14 November 1992) affordability is back to the level of the early 1970s. The main problem is one of confidence. This is slowly returning, but there is unlikely to be any sharp upturn in house prices either in 1993 or 1994, if only because supply will rise initially to meet demand. Meanwhile the number of repossessions is forecast at 64 000 for 1993 and 59 000 for 1994. This is somewhat less than in previous years, but fewer repossessions tends to mean an associated increase in arrears. Householders are unlikely ever to forget completely the lesson that nominal house prices can fall as well as rise, and mortgagees are likely to remain scarred by their experience of repossession for the foreseeable future. It is also worth noting that Personal Equity Plans (PEPs) and TESSAs (Tax Exempt Special Savings Account) currently provide alternative ways of accumulating tax-relieved assets, so housing is likely to be seen increasingly in terms of its value in use rather than its value as an investment. Precisely what this implies for the conduct of economic policy remains to be seen.

Bibliography

Bank of England (1992) 'Negative Equity in the Housing Market', *Bank of England Quarterly Bulletin* (August).

Boleat, M. *et al.* (1991) *The State of the Economy 1991* (London: Institute of Economic Affairs).

Breedon, F. and M. Joyce (1992) 'House Prices, Arrears and Possessions', *Bank of England Quarterly Bulletin* (May).

■ *Chapter 3* ■

The Macroeconomy: 2

Peter Curwen

■ 3.1 Personal Income, Consumption and Saving

☐ *3.1.1 Consumption Rules OK?*

Before we turn to analyse the database a few introductory words are in order. Consumption holds the key to the behaviour of the UK economy. Adam Smith, who should be mentioned in all self-respecting books on political economy, knew all about this two centuries ago. 'Consumption is the sole end and purpose of all production', he wrote in *The Wealth of Nations*. Elsewhere, he noted that England was 'a nation that is governed by shopkeepers'. Perhaps what he should have said is that England is a nation of **shoppers**. The British do not habitually take to the streets to protest, or indeed to vote in local elections. They know that, irrespective of who governs them, the shops will be full, and that they can express their position in society through what they buy. It should not be forgotten that Britain has an amazingly efficient system of retail distribution; just compare it with that of Japan, a country which is more efficient at **making** things but hopelessly inefficient at **distributing** them (it even has a law preventing the spread of depart-

ment stores). However, the Japanese are hardly likely to agree with Adam Smith's assertion that 'The interest of the producers ought to be attended to, only so far as it may be necessary for promoting that of the consumer.'

If readers have seen old newspapers they will know that their primary function was to spread information about what was on offer. It is, therefore, hardly surprising that the demand side of the economy came to dominate economic thought, as in the work of Keynes, rather than the supply side. When Macmillan expressed the opinion that the British had 'never had it so good', he was being deadly serious: governments are elected in Britain by looking after the interests of consumers. What consumers want is low interest rates, rising real incomes and house prices but not rising prices elsewhere in the economy. That so many people are unemployed seems to have had remarkably little effect upon voting patterns since 1979.

It has not traditionally been especially difficult for the government to generate the urge among consumers to go shopping, as Chancellor Lawson discovered in the late 1980s. Neither is it normally easy to destroy their confidence to the extent that they lose the desire to shop. However, it can be done, as recent experience testifies. In the sections which follow we will have much more to say on these matters.

☐ *3.1.2 Personal Income*

Personal income consists of wages and salaries, employers' **national insurance contributions** (NICs), current grants from general government and other personal income. In total these constitute much the largest element of NI. However, the term 'personal' is somewhat ambiguous in that it refers not merely to individuals but to incorporated businesses, private non-profit-making bodies and life assurance and pension funds. The latter three elements are largely excluded in data for 'household' incomes, but in making this distinction there are particular difficulties with, for example, the earnings of entrepreneurs who are, in effect, both individual person and business rolled into one. Measured at current prices, personal income has risen continuously since 1979, and its annual rate of growth has averaged roughly 10 per cent.

Personal income net of income taxes, social security contributions and transfer payments is called **personal disposable income** (PDI). While PDI is understandably more volatile than pre-tax income given that tax regimes can be altered at specified points in time, the longer-term trends are very similar and exhibit an almost identical rate of growth. The individual components of pre-tax personal income can mostly be measured quite accurately (+/− 3 per cent or less) and the same is true for income tax and social security contributions. However, the subtraction of the latter from the former inevitably renders PDI less accurate than either (+/− between 3 and 10 per cent).

Figure 3.1 plots PDI in real (inflation-adjusted) terms from 1980 to 1993. As can be seen, it started to rise quite rapidly as the economy came out of recession in 1982, and slowed down abruptly at the onset of the current recession, since when it has remained more or less constant. It is evident that in terms of their spending power, most people in the UK did very well during the Thatcher years.

Figure 3.1   *Personal Income, 1980–93, Quarterly at 1985 Prices*

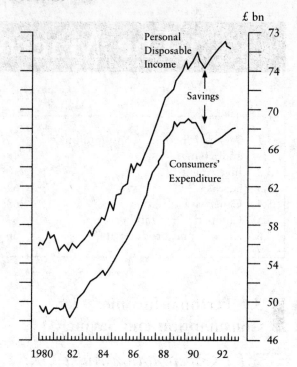

Source: *Economic Trends*, Table 4.

☐ *3.1.3 Consumers' Expenditure*

Consumers' expenditure represents the consumption not merely of households but of the other non-household parts of the personal sector. Nevertheless, household consumption constitutes 90 per cent of the total, and it is reasonable to treat one as a close approximation of the other. Consumers' expenditure is plotted in real terms in **Figure 3.1**, where the quarterly data are seasonally adjusted. This is necessary because consumption always surges in the final quarter of each year due to Christmas shopping, and the unadjusted data give the false impression that this heralds an ongoing upturn in expenditure.

As can be seen, consumers' expenditure rose even more rapidly than PDI during the second half of the 1980s, in the process squeezing the residual (which represents savings). However, it came to a standstill before the recession really set in, only to collapse back at the end of the decade, in the process driving many companies to the wall. More recently it has stabilised and, while there is obviously some desire for it to start growing again, there are reservations which result from the fact that even in the recession an excessive amount of consumption took the form of imported products.

Figure 3.2 breaks consumption down into a number of selected categories on an inflation-adjusted basis. Between 1971 and 1993 total real consumers' expenditure rose by roughly 70 per cent. Despite this, tobacco consumption fell by some 20 per cent and beer consumption fell slightly. Expenditure on food rose very slightly in real terms, which is not unexpected given that people do not tend to eat all that much more as they get richer, especially if it is fashionable to be slim. On the other hand, real expenditure on durable goods rose sharply during the 1980s such that at the end of the decade 98 per cent of households had a television (91 per cent colour); 84 per cent a washing machine; 77 per cent a deep freeze; 85 per cent a telephone; 53 per cent a video; and so forth. From the mid-1980s onwards real consumption of services also began to soar

and, given that the market for durable goods must eventually reach saturation (although some households have a television for every adult and every child), services are likely to provide the fastest-growing sector in the 1990s overall even though they temporarily stalled in the recession.

Table 3.1 indicates how these trends have affected the spending patterns of UK households. Food has become proportionately much less important (the CAP notwithstanding), and there have been proportionate reductions in alcohol, tobacco, clothing and fuel and power (despite those rising gas and electricity bills which have begun to show up in recent data). Transport has become more important, but it is the somewhat catch-all 'other goods and services' where the increase is most marked. The practice of eating out has become much more common, but the biggest change of all since the mid-1970s has been the practice of taking foreign holidays.

It is also worth noting that attention in the media is addressed to trends in **retail sales** as a guide to trends in consumers' expenditure, since the former are published on a provisional basis much earlier than the latter. However, it must be borne in mind that, for example, whilst food

Figure 3.2 *Consumers' Expenditure at Constant Prices, by Selected Item, UK, 1974–93*

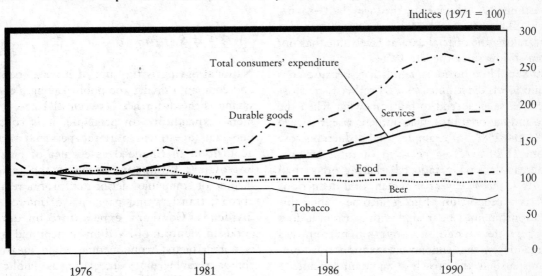

Indices (1971 = 100)

Source: Economic Trends, Table 5.

Table 3.1   *Share of Total Household Expenditure at Current Prices, UK*

	1976	1981	1985	1987	1989	1990	1991	1992
Food	19.2	16.3	14.4	13.2	12.2	12.4	12.4	12.1
Alcoholic Drink	7.6	7.3	7.4	6.7	6.2	6.4	6.6	6.6
Tobacco	4.1	3.6	3.3	2.9	2.6	2.6	2.7	2.7
Clothing and footwear	7.7	6.7	7.0	6.8	6.2	6.1	5.9	5.7
Housing	13.6	14.9	15.4	15.2	15.3	14.0	14.5	15.4
Fuel and power	4.7	5.1	4.9	4.2	3.6	3.6	4.0	3.9
Household goods and services	7.6	6.9	6.7	6.7	6.7	6.4	6.4	6.5
Transport and communication	15.4	17.2	17.4	17.9	18.6	18.5	17.6	17.3
Recreation, entertainment and education	9.2	9.4	9.4	9.4	9.6	9.9	9.8	10.1
Other goods, services and adjustments	10.8	12.5	14.1	17.0	19.0	20.1	20.1	19.7
Total	100.0	100.0	100.0	100.0	100.0	100.0	100.0	100.0

Source: UK National Accounts Blue Book (CSO, 1993), Table 4.7.

represents 12–13 per cent of consumers' expenditure, it represents roughly 40 per cent of retail sales which exclude energy, rent and rates and other services. Hence, in the short term, retail sales may prove a very unreliable guide to trends in the larger aggregate.

As can be seen from **Table 3.2**, PDI is, by definition, either **consumed** or **saved**. The proportion saved (the **saving ratio**) is specified in **Table 3.2**, and it follows that the proportion consumed, known technically as the **average propensity to consume** (APC), is given by the formula '1−saving ratio'. This has recently fallen below 90 per cent but, taking the official data at face value, has not been so low since the late 1970s.

It should be borne in mind that, because consumption is determined by PDI rather than gross income, savings tend to fall somewhat when the tax and national insurance burdens rise. Between 1983 and 1987, for example, total deductions rose from 21.20 to 21.45 per cent of total income, whereas the saving ratio fell sharply other than in 1984, the only year in which total deductions fell as a proportion of gross income. While this relationship must be treated with caution, it does suggest that when the government removes demand from the economy via taxation, consumption steps into the breach to maintain demand.

During the late 1980s, consumers' expenditure rose faster than PDI. It appears to have been the case that consumers not merely spent the whole of their PDI but borrowed in order to finance yet more consumption. As the subsequent discussion on saving indicates, such behaviour may not repeat itself for a long time to come, but the former Chancellor, in his Spring 1993 Budget, announced that taxes would rise sharply commencing in the 1994–95 financial year, so it will be interesting to see whether consumption is maintained under those circumstances by running down savings.

☐ *3.1.4 Saving*

National Saving is the sum of private (personal and company) saving and public saving. **Personal saving** is the difference between PDI and consumers' expenditure. In principle, it is equal to personal investment plus the personal sector's acquisition of financial assets net of personal borrowing. **Company saving** is the residual income of companies net of tax, profits remitted abroad, transfers and payments of interest and dividends. Company expenditure on durable goods in the form of fixed investment and stocks is **not** deducted from income when measuring company saving, but depreciation is. **Public saving** is the difference between the public sector's current receipts and current expenditure, and is

Table 3.2 *Personal Income, Expenditure and Saving, 1985–92 (£ bn)*

	1985	1986	1987	1988	1989	1990	1991	1992
Wages and salaries	169.1	183.9	200.4	223.8	248.5	274.9	288.8	299.4
Employers' contributions	26.5	27.6	29.4	31.9	34.4	36.9	40.4	43.6
Current grants	46.8	50.9	52.5	54.1	56.8	62.0	72.1	82.6
Other personal income	62.6	69.7	78.9	92.9	103.9	115.7	116.6	124.7
Total personal income	305.0	332.1	361.2	402.7	443.6	489.5	517.9	550.3
Less deductions:	37.7	40.8	43.4	48.3	53.6	61.5	63.6	64.9
Taxes on income	24.2	26.2	28.6	32.1	32.9	34.7	36.4	37.5
Social security contributions	1.7	1.9	2.1	2.4	2.4	2.6	2.6	2.7
Community charge	–	–	–	–	0.6	8.6	8.1	7.9
Personal disposable income (PDI)	241.4	263.2	287.1	319.9	354.1	382.1	407.2	437.3
Less consumers' expenditure	217.9	241.9	267.5	302.1	330.5	350.4	367.5	386.6
Balance: personal saving	23.5	21.3	19.6	17.8	23.6	31.7	39.7	50.7
Saving ratio %[1]	9.7	8.1	6.8	5.6	6.6	8.3	9.7	11.6

Note:
[1] Saving as % of PDI.

Source: Monthly Digest of Statistics, Table 1.5.

broadly equivalent to public sector net investment **less** public sector borrowing (or **plus** public sector debt repayment).

The discussion of saving in the media is concerned primarily with the personal sector although, as we will note later, this is somewhat misguided. Unfortunately, personal sector saving is a very unreliable statistic (potentially up to 20 per cent inaccurate in either direction) as it is the difference between two somewhat inaccurate figures for PDI and consumers' expenditure respectively. Furthermore, the distinction between consumption expenditure on durable goods and saving can be a fine one. Whereas, for example, the purchase of a car is treated as current consumption in the statistics, many purchasers would see the accumulation of a deposit and the repayment of the residual purchase price as an act of **saving**. On occasion, the CSO redefines consumption as saving (for example, expenditure on do-it-yourself goods in 1984), and more generally the saving ratio tends to be retrospectively adjusted in

each year's Blue Book. The ratios recorded during the 1970s have in recent years accordingly been much reduced with, for example, a downgrading of each of the previous seven years ratios by almost 1 per cent in the 1987 Blue Book.

A further consideration obscures the meaning of saving, namely that whereas personal payments into a private pension fund are counted as saving, contributions to the government's pension and social security schemes are not. Obviously, if the latter were not deducted from gross income, both PDI and the saving ratio (including such payments) would be considerably larger. Finally, as noted earlier, it is evident that whereas interest payments on a mortgage constitute consumption, that part of the monthly repayment which expunges part of the capital owed to the lender must transfer wealth to the borrower, and in that sense is clearly an act of saving.

In many ways it is surprising that the saving ratio is treated with the reverence it is accorded in the media. As shown in Cullison (1990), the official saving ratio in the USA, which is even lower than in the UK, is widely regarded as a nonsense, with estimates of the true rate varying from twice the official rate to an astonishing six times the official rate.

As noted in *Barclays Bank Review* (February 1990, p.17) the ratio derived from identified financial transactions is almost twice as high as the official ratio. When it comes to saving, therefore, the most sensible approach is, as usual, to take a long-term series defined on a consistent basis, so that there is a clear view of the trend even if not of the absolute magnitudes.

Figure 3.3 illustrates the official net saving ratio from 1985 to 1990. It is interesting to note that after a surge in 1960, it moved steadily upwards, on average, until 1980, peaking at this time at roughly 15 per cent. From 1980 to 1988 it was more or less downhill all the way, with the ratio bottoming out in 1988 at less than 5 per cent. Since then the onset of recession has witnessed a steady, quite rapid climb back to 12 per cent, a pattern heavily reminiscent of the early 1960s. This raises the issue as to what could reasonably be seen as a 'normal' rate of saving. It is probably sensible in this context to regard the situation in 1980 as an aberration, with the 'normal' pattern

being in the region of 10 per cent, which was regained at the end of the decade.

It is evident that there is at least one big difference between the 1980–81 recession and that of 1990–92, namely the saving ratio at the commencement of each period. This is unsurprising when one considers the changes in the personal sector's balance sheet during the 1980s. As we have noted, net wealth is much higher in relation to income compared to a decade ago and, more importantly, the personal sector is loaded up with liabilities which, being financial, are not subject to asset price inflation.

Figure 3.4 shows that between 1982 and the end of 1989 total credit outstanding (in addition to mortgage liabilities) in Great Britain rose in money terms from £16 billion to £40 billion, and to well over £30 billion in inflation-adjusted terms. Possibly for the first time ever, the personal sector found itself with more debts than assets at

Figure 3.4   *Consumer Credit, Amount Outstanding, Great Britain, 1982–90 (£ bn)*

Note:
[1] Real terms figures are the cash figures adjusted to 1982Q1 price levels by excluding the effect of general inflation as measured by the RPI.

Source: CSO.

Figure 3.3   *The Personal Saving Ratio, 1958–93 (%)*

Source: Bank of England Quarterly Bulletin.

floating interest rates (in mid-1990, net floating-rate liabilities represented 15 per cent of disposable income).

Table 3.3 disaggregates the problem up to the end of 1992. During the period 1984–90 total credit outstanding rose by 136 per cent. There was little variability in the sources of credit. The building societies were allowed to enter the market through a change in the law, but had very little impact. The main loss of market share affected retailers as more and more customers switched to national credit cards, but their absolute level of business remained high.

In money terms total credit remained static for the following two years, implying a modest reduction in real terms. However, this disguises somewhat the fact that the balance between new borrowing and repayment of debt had begun to alter significantly, as shown in **Figure 3.5**. By the middle of 1992 there was actually a net repayment of debt, albeit briefly, which may not seem altogether strange until one puts it into the context of the rampant consumerism of the previous decade. Just how dramatic the turnaround has been is well illustrated by the data on retail sales, as shown in **Figure 3.6**. To say that the 'shop till you drop' philosophy had gone out of fashion would clearly be an understatement.

Figure 3.5 *New Borrowing, Net of Repayments*

Source: Bank of England Quarterly Bulletin.

3.1.5 Why the Saving Ratio Varies over Time

At this juncture it may be useful to pull together the strands of the previous discussion in order to analyse why the saving ratio may vary over time. It is useful to start with the relationship between inflation and consumption/saving behaviour.

Table 3.3 *Composition of Consumer Credit, UK, 1984–92 (% and £ bn)*

	1984	1985	1986	1987	1988	1989	1990	1991	1992
Bank credit card lending	14.8	15.7	17.2	16.6	15.8	15.0	17.1	18.2	18.7
Bank loans[1]	63.2	62.1	61.6	62.7	64.8	65.9	64.0	62.9	62.7
Finance houses[2]	9.9	10.7	11.9	11.9	10.9	10.8	10.4	10.3	9.5
Insurance companies	3.1	2.7	2.6	2.2	2.3	2.2	2.3	2.5	2.7
Retailers	9.0	8.4	6.6	6.6	5.6	4.9	4.7	4.7	5.0
Building societies	0.0	0.0	0.0	0.2	0.6	1.2	1.5	1.4	1.4
Credit outstanding at the end of year (= 100%) (£ bn)	22.3	26.1	30.2	36.2	42.5	48.4	52.6	53.6	52.9

Notes:
[1] Banks and all other institutions authorised to take deposits under the Banking Act 1987.
[2] Finance houses and other credit companies.
Source: Financial Statistics, Table 9.3.

Figure 3.6   *UK Retail Sales*

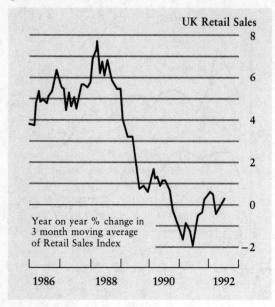

Source: CSO.

The traditional view was that once people came to realise that the value of money would be adversely affected by inflation, they would rush out to spend it as quickly as possible. This view was broadly supported by behaviour during the overseas hyper-inflations of the prewar period, but the relatively modest price rises manifested in the UK since 1970 appear to have stimulated more mixed behaviour, with the saving ratio rising during the high (by UK standards) inflation of the 1970s, then falling with inflation in the 1980s. There are a number of ways of explaining this, and their relative merits are unlikely ever to be satisfactorily distinguished since they are, in any event, significantly interdependent.

For example, if a person sets out to maintain the **real**, rather than the **nominal** value of his or her savings, he or she will be obliged to increase the nominal value of those savings at the same rate as prices are rising. Furthermore, since high rates of inflation generally go hand in hand with rising unemployment, people who fear that they may lose their jobs may try to build up a pool of savings in order to cushion their potential loss of income. Equally, if prices of consumer goods are

rising so rapidly that people feel that they will never be able to afford to buy them, they may decide to give up trying to do so and save instead.

The role of interest rates in all of this is hard to divine. Since interest rates, in nominal terms, tend to rise with inflation, the sacrifice in terms of interest forgone when buying consumer goods must itself be rising. However, the real rate of interest was negative during the mid–1970s at a time of very high nominal rates, and positive in the mid–1980s at a time of much lower nominal rates. One could accordingly have expected savings to be higher rather than lower in the later period (assuming, of course, that savers were not suffering in the 1970s from **money illusion**: the illusion that nominal and real rates are the same). In fact, correlating savings against real rates of interest appears to indicate a rather weak relationship. This may, in turn, reflect the fact that financial deregulation has made it increasingly easy for people to borrow, and hence the principle that one has to save before one buys a costly item (even a house) has steadily been eroded. Rather perversely at first sight, people may continue to put increasingly large sums of money into life assurance and pension funds and simultaneously borrow to finance current consumption. Savings are defined net of borrowing, so increased borrowing reduces the saving ratio. However, the borrower is unlikely to view borrowing as dissaving. Indeed, pension fund contributions may well be compulsory rather than voluntary, and hence be dismissed as having no direct bearing on decisions about current consumption. In 1980, after adjusting for contributions to life insurance and pension funds, the personal sector still placed 30 per cent of its savings on a discretionary basis, whereas by 1986 this latter figure had become negative.

A broader view of these factors may be termed the **wealth effect**. Over the long haul – and indeed in most individual years – the value of property has tended to rise faster than prices in general. Equally, the value of company shares has easily outstripped inflation over the past decade, and more recently, though not previously, post-tax rates of interest have also outstripped inflation. As a result, people who own assets (currently, in practice, the majority of households) will tend to feel wealthier as time passes, and hence feel less need to convert current income into wealth via saving. This will also reflect the increased probability of inheritance.

One could also reasonably expect consumers to smooth their spending over the business cycle, maintaining it in recessions while boosting it very modestly in booms. This would cause saving to be pro-cyclical, falling in recessions and rising in booms. Unfortunately, this does not accord with UK experience since, as we have already noted, the saving ratio was extremely high in 1980–81 and rose sharply during the recent recession after falling right back during the mid–1980s boom.

This ties in with our previous point, since it is clear that the period of falling house prices, both in nominal as well as real terms, during the early 1990s must have affected people's perceptions about their wealth and the long-term security provided by their assets. As a result they evidently chose to save much more to provide security against the possibility of rainier days ahead. This was also supported by several other factors. For example, the sharp rise in unemployment at the end of the 1980s introduced an added element of uncertainty, more especially because it struck not only at the relatively unskilled in the North but at the relatively skilled in the South, where house prices were falling most rapidly. A further consideration was the dawning realisation that with so many people living to a grand old age, and needing to be looked after at enormous expense in nursing homes, inheritances could melt away to nothing much at all. Finally, it is important to remember that the saving ratio is calculated net of liabilities, and there was a sharp contrast between the huge growth in liabilities in the mid-1980s and the much reduced level of borrowing commencing at the end of the decade. In effect, it was as much a case of people borrowing less as of people saving more, in response to the factors described above.

A final factor relates to the **age structure of the population**. The bulk of savings are accumulated by people between the ages of 45 and 65. Younger people have heavy outgoings incurred in setting up homes and raising families, whereas the elderly earn little and may need to eat into past savings, as noted above. The high birth rate immediately after the Second World War has produced an exceptionally large generation which is now entering its period of high savings, and this is likely to buoy up savings during the 1990s.

All the above inevitably sows the seeds of doubt about our ability to forecast trends in savings. Nevertheless, it is also important not to interpret saving purely within the context of the personal sector. The Bank of England, utilising a somewhat different approach to the calculation of savings from that used previously, has aggregated the savings of the personal sector, company sector and public sector, all expressed as a percentage of GDP at factor cost. From this it would appear that the decline in personal saving was offset by an increase in company saving from 1979 to 1988, whereas the saving of the public sector remained consistently negative until 1987. As a result, total savings at current prices showed a remarkable degree of stability from 1980 to 1988. Since that time, as noted earlier, the public sector has returned to deficit but the personal sector has moved the other way, so the tendency for there to be offsetting trends has continued.

Adjusting the data for inflation has no effect upon this general proposition, although it affects the sectoral shares quite noticeably. This arises because, when inflation is rapid, a sector with positive net assets has an artificially increased income and saving rate, and vice versa. As a result, the conventional national accounts misallocate savings among sectors when inflation is high. The high nominal saving ratio of the personal sector in 1979 was thus in reality negative after adjusting for inflation, and the 1986 nominal 1 per cent was much the same in real terms as the nominal 16 per cent in 1980. On the other hand, the real saving of the company sector was almost invariably slightly higher than its nominal saving. In the case of the public sector the real saving ratio was positive, but rapidly declining, between 1979 and 1982, and negative thereafter.

Given the evident constancy of national savings the government has been somewhat ambivalent about the necessity of offering incentives to savers, although pressure from the media was such as to induce a 'Savers' Budget' in 1990. It is somewhat ironic that the government has subsequently found it difficult to induce people to go out and **spend** in more recent times as an antidote to recession.

■ 3.2 Investment

□ 3.2.1 Investment Defined

The term **investment** is used by the general public to refer to the acquisition of certain physical and financial assets. For our purposes, however, the purchase of an asset such as a painting or putting money into a building society account must be regarded as an act of **saving**. When we refer to investment, we mean that an addition has been made to the stock of productive capital machinery known as **fixed capital formation**. The existence of this capital stock is what enables the economy to produce output both in the current and in future periods.

Total investment, or **Gross Domestic Fixed Capital Formation** (GDFCF), consists of **replacement** investment and **net** investment. Replacement investment is simply that investment needed to make good any reductions in the capital stock due to depreciation and obsolescence. Net investment is any investment over and above that needed to keep the capital stock constant, and hence results in an increase in that stock. In general, net investment is the driving force behind economic growth and improved productivity. Nevertheless, this can be attributed in part to replacement investment insofar as this is technically superior to the capital stock which is being replaced.

Table 3.4 sets out the path of GDFCF as a proportion of GDP over the period from 1979 to 1992, but omitting certain intermediate years. In absolute terms the growth of GDFCF during the period up to 1989 was superficially impressive, but the economy was growing rapidly during part of this period and this renders much of this improvement illusory when taken in relation to the growth in real GDP. Only in 1988 did the ratio of GDFCF to GDP rise noticeably above that

ruling in 1977, and it has once again fallen back to levels customary in the late 1970s and mid-1980s.

Investment in **physical assets** can take a wide variety of forms. Officially these are categorised as private dwellings, other building and work, vehicles, ships and aircraft and plant and machinery. The first of these is the odd man out because a house used for personal rather than business purposes cannot contribute to output, although the money spent on its purchase clearly contributes to AD. Hence it is sensible to concentrate upon the ratio relating GDFCF **minus** expenditure on dwellings to GDP, which constitutes the second row of **Table 3.4**. Here the picture is more promising. In 1984 the ratio rose back to the level prevailing during the late 1970s, and subsequently moved upwards to peak in 1989 at 16.3 per cent. Since then it has only fallen back to the level of 1988, and should rise back to its peak in 1993.

Other notable features of **Table 3.4** are the comparative buoyancy of general government investment in recent years, and the declining importance of the public corporations. However, private sector investment also ended the decade well above its starting level, and it would appear to be the case overall that investment has been surprisingly resistant to recession, which bodes well for the recovery phase of the cycle. On the other hand, it must be recognised that technological progress has become so rapid that simple maintenance of the real level of GDFCF is insufficient to sustain the UK's ability to compete. It will be necessary, when the recession finally ends, to do rather better than to return to the level of real GDFCF prevailing in 1989 if the level of investment is to be seen as sufficient to ensure real growth in future years.

□ 3.2.2 The Pattern of Investment

The pattern of investment is revealed in the lower rows of **Table 3.4** and the whole of **Table 3.5**. What was discovered in **Table 3.4** was the dominant role played by private sector investment, and **Table 3.5**, which divides total GDFCF into its component parts, indicates the destination of

Table 3.4   *Investment (GDFCF) by Type of Asset and by Sector as % of GDP, at Market Prices, 1979–92[1]*

	1979	1980	1981	1983	1984	1985	1987	1988	1989	1990	1991	1992
GDFCF as % of GDP	17.2	16.5	15.0	15.8	16.9	16.9	17.4	19.0	20.0	19.2	17.7	17.7
GDFCF excluding dwellings as % of GDP	13.1	12.7	12.0	12.3	13.2	13.6	13.9	15.2	16.3	16.0	15.0	15.1
Private sector of investment as % of GDP	12.3	12.0	11.3	11.6	12.8	13.5	14.3	16.3	16.8	16.0	14.6	14.3
General government invest- ment as % of GDP	2.2	2.0	1.4	1.8	1.9	1.9	1.8	1.6	2.0	2.4	2.3	2.6
Public corporation invest- ment as % of GDP	2.6	2.6	2.4	2.5	2.2	1.6	1.1	1.1	1.1	1.0	0.8	0.9
Stocks and work in progress as % of GDP	1.0	−1.0	−1.0	0.4	0.3	0.2	0.3	1.0	0.6	−0.3	−0.8	−0.3

Note:
[1] For the years before 1983, totals may not equal the sum of their components, because of the method used in rebasing to 1985 prices.

Source: Economic Trends, Annual Supplement (1993); *Economic Trends*, Table 9, Table 3.

Table 3.5   *Investment by Type of Asset as % of GDFCF, 1979–92[1]*

	1979	1980	1981	1983	1984	1985	1987	1988	1989	1990	1991	1992
Investment in dwellings as % of GDFCF	23.7	23.3	21.1	22.9	21.6	19.6	19.9	20.1	18.4	16.9	15.0	14.7
Investment in other new buildings and work as % of GDFCF	28.7	28.7	30.8	31.1	31.3	30.2	32.0	32.1	31.7	33.7	36.6	36.2
Investment in plant and machinery as % of GDFCF	34.9	36.9	37.9	36.3	36.6	39.5	38.3	38.6	40.5	40.7	40.6	41.5
Investment in vehicles, ships and aircraft	13.3	11.8	10.1	9.7	10.5	10.7	9.8	9.2	9.4	8.7	7.8	7.6

Note:
[1] For the years before 1983, totals may not equal the sum of their components, because of the method used in rebasing the original data to 1985 prices.

Source: UK National Accounts Blue Book (CSO, 1993), Table 13.1; Monthly *Digest of Statistics*, Table 1.8.

that investment over the period beginning in 1979. Initially, investment in plant and machinery was the dominant sector, and had indeed risen from 32 per cent in 1977. In 1985 it surged to almost 40 per cent, which could be seen as a positive factor for the economy since this category of investment contributes most to economic growth. In that respect the subsequent decline was a disappointment, although the ratio rose above 40 per cent in 1989 and has remained almost constant ever since. Unfortunately, elsewhere in the G7 investment was biased more heavily towards plant and machinery than in the UK, and this is likely to prove detrimental to the UK in the longer term. The slight rise in 1992 may indicate a further upwards trend in the UK, but this is unlikely because of the factors affecting housing noted below.

In the light of our previous discussion on housing, the decline in the ratio of investment in dwellings to GDP may come as something of a surprise. However, if this is broken down into private and public sector the picture is quite different. In real terms, for example, public sector investment in dwellings remained remarkably constant from 1984 to 1989, and hence declined quite rapidly in relation to a fast-growing GDP.

Private investment, on the other hand, was 20 per cent higher in real terms in 1989 compared to 1984, and over the decade as a whole some £100 billion was invested in private dwellings, representing 40 per cent of total investment in plant and machinery. It would doubtless have been better for the economy if the balance had been more in favour of the latter. As it happens, that is what occurred after 1989 as falling nominal house prices eroded the desirability of house purchase at a time when the public sector was also running in low gear. The pick-up in demand for private housing in 1993 is almost certain to show up as an increased share of GDFCF either in 1993 or 1994.

Interpretation of recent trends is obviously clouded by the difficulty in determining whether the recession truly is over, and in forecasting the future rate of growth. Fluctuations in the level of investment have a considerable impact upon the business cycle. Over time, the level of investment determines the rate of growth of the capital stock, and this is a major determinant of the rate of growth of real income. **Figure 3.7** shows that during the 1980s the UK grew on average at the same rate as France and West Germany, but needed two percentage points less investment to do so. While this does not provide a full excuse for having such a low level of investment by international standards, it does suggest that the UK's performance has converged upon that of other major EU economies.

It is often argued, with some justice, that the quality of investment is a critical issue. For this reason, UK investment has been viewed as of questionable value because much more of it has traditionally been devoted to the defence industries compared to Japan and West Germany, and these industries have not been viewed as particularly beneficial for growth, exports and jobs. Equally, the poor performance of parts of the nuclear industry in which huge sums were invested, and the money wasted on prestige products such as Concorde, have provided ammunition for critics of British investment performance. Nevertheless, the 1980s do not appear to conform to this stereotype, and it would appear that investment in, for example, West Germany was overall rather less efficient.

Government policy has had some part to play in this turnaround. Fiscal policy changes no longer make it worthwhile for companies to invest mainly to save tax rather than to enhance the capital stock and improve efficiency. In addition, the low level of corporation tax helps to make the UK a particularly attractive destination for investment by foreigners, and such investment tends to be highly efficient and productive. On the other hand, a problem still remains in that pension funds, the major shareholders in the UK, continue to exert pressure for distribution of dividends at times when it would be preferable for at least a part of this money to be retained for reinvestment.

☐ 3.2.3 Business Investment

Business investment is investment which takes place in the trading sector of the economy. This necessarily excludes private investment in dwellings, and also in practice excludes general government investment. On the other hand, it includes

Figure 3.7 *Growth Rates and Investment Ratios, OECD, 1979–90*

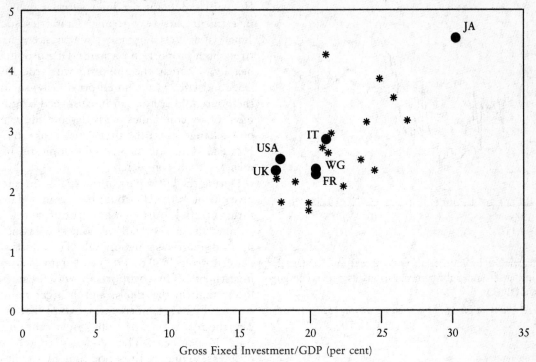

Source: Organisation for Economic Co-operation and Development (OECD).

the public corporations (but not NHS Trust hospitals), and in particular nationalised industries, which supply goods and services in the same way as private corporations.

A sub-category within business investment is **manufacturing** investment. Business investment currently accounts for roughly two thirds of GDFCF, and manufacturing investment for roughly one quarter of business investment. As is customary, the longer-term trend is best represented by expressing business investment as a percentage of GDP, as seen in **Figure 3.8**.

During the 1970s business investment adjusted for inflation was fairly static, and this resulted in a steady decline in the ratio to GDP from 1975 onwards because GDP was growing. Investment fell back so sharply in 1980–81 that the ratio worsened despite falling GDP, but equally surged faster than GDP from 1982 to 1985, causing the ratio to rise. During 1986–87 business investment

did not keep up with GDP even though it was itself at record levels in real terms, but as GDP growth fell away at the end of the decade the continued growth of investment caused the ratio to climb above 15 per cent, well above the trend line. Unsurprisingly, this could not last for long, and the forecast trend is currently for a gradual decline towards the longer-term trend level.

The short surge in the mid-1980s resulted from the bringing forward of investment to avoid changes in the tax system intended to discourage forms of investment undertaken primarily in order to obtain tax breaks. The longer surge at the end of the decade suggested that the message was at last getting through to business that sustained investment is a pre-condition for sustained growth and, while investment has fallen back during the recession, it remains noticeably higher than during the previous recession. This is especially important given that the urge to drive

Figure 3.8   *Business Investment[1] as % of GDP*

Note:

[1] Investment by industrial, commerical and financial companies and public corporations as a percentage of GDP (O).

Source: Bank of England Quarterly Bulletin; FSBR, 1993–94, Chart 3.11.

growth via domestic consumption expenditure has gone out of fashion.

Manufacturing investment accounted for roughly one-third of business investment in the period to 1970. Subsequently it fell back to its current level of one-quarter. The void was filled by investment in financial services and, to a far lesser degree, investment in retail and wholesale distribution, and from the late 1980s onwards there was a surge in investment in the energy and water sectors subsequent to their privatisation. There is an element of deception in the substantial switchover from manufacturing to service sector investment, insofar as manufacturing companies tended increasingly to sub-contract maintenance, finance, recruitment, training and other services. Nevertheless, it is evident that the UK has a comparative advantage in the provision of services (at least until competitors catch up) rather than in the provision of manufactures, although it would be highly inadvisable for this to induce overinvestment in services and underinvestment in manufacturing.

☐ 3.2.4 Saving and Investment

Up until the 1980s the link between saving and investment was very strong. Countries such as Japan and West Germany, which saved a relatively high proportion of their GDP, also invested heavily, whereas the opposite was true for the USA and UK. As we noted previously, saving by the household sector can be absorbed by government or by companies overseas, and the removal of exchange controls after 1979 broke the link between domestic saving and domestic investment, but not completely.

During the latter part of the 1980s, the surge in investment in the UK could be accommodated by international borrowing without being constrained by a shortfall of domestic saving, but most domestic saving in OECD countries (61 per cent from 1980 to 1987) ended up as domestic investment. This proportion was 30 per cent lower than in the 1960s, and a larger reduction was felt by EC member states, except that in their case the reduction was from 74 per cent down to only 36 per cent. The tendency to rely upon overseas saving is thus not limited to the UK, although the UK is certainly more vulnerable than most to any shortfall in overseas saving given the inadequate level of domestic saving.

■ 3.3 Stocks

Fixed investment does not include investment in stocks or inventories. The scale of investment in stocks is small in comparison with GDFCF. Nevertheless, it is important both because it reflects changes in the level of demand and also because it causes such changes to occur.

Although stocks play no part in the provision of services, they are clearly vital in overcoming imbalances between the supply of demand for raw materials and semi-finished and finished manufactures. When sales rise relative to production this causes stocks to be run down, which acts as a signal to producers to increase output if the increased demand is expected to continue. Conversely, a rise in stocks relative to production, unless it is planned by producers in anticipation of a higher level of future sales, signals a reduction in demand and the need to cut back production if demand is expected to remain low. As the economy slides into recession, producers cut back severely and rely upon their cushion of stocks to meet demand. Destocking accordingly speeds up the rate of decline of output, and this phenomenon is very clear in the major postwar recessions, with destocking cutting output by over 3 per cent in 1974–75 and by 2.5 per cent in 1980 alone. However, the reduction was much milder in 1990, as destocking only appears to have continued for one year (mid-1989 to mid-1990) compared to all of 1980 and half of 1981, and to all of both 1974 and 1975. The reason for this is that there was relatively little stockbuilding in the pre-recession period.

If GDP is growing erratically then this will cause the accumulation or run-down of stocks to be erratic in its turn, and this will then feed through to cause further erratic movements of GDP. This pattern is clearly seen during the 1970s, and can usefully be analysed in terms of the **stock:output ratio**.

During the 1970s, as shown in **Figure 3.9**, the stock:output ratios for both the manufacturing and retail sectors exhibited a procession of peaks and troughs, culminating in an exceptionally high peak at the end of the decade. In the period 1976–79 stockbuilding was positive, encouraged by negative real interest rates and a tax regime favourable towards stockholding. However, when in 1980 real interest rates rose sharply and demand collapsed, stocks were reduced sharply in order to maintain cash flow. The reduction in tax relief on stocks in 1981, combined with high real rates of interest and improvements in stock-control methods throughout the decade, served to stabilise stockbuilding at a modest positive rate which, given the rather faster rise in GDP, triggered a decline in the stock:output ratio which has yet to come to an end in the case of manufacturing, although, as shown in **Figure 3.9**, the retail sector responded to growth in consumer demand after 1985 by restocking at a rapid pace.

Overall, at the equivalent of roughly three months' output, UK stockholding remained higher in 1991 than was customary for its major

Figure 3.9 *Stock: Output Ratio*

Source: Bank of England Quarterly Bulletin.

competitors, although there was only so much fat left to trim. It would appear that improved information systems have enabled firms to recognise that stocks were building up at an early stage as the recession took hold, and that they were able to cut back on their orders in good time. However, this process itself exerted a depressive effect upon GDP growth, and there can be no doubt that a sharp upturn in stockbuilding in the manufacturing sector is a necessary pre-condition if growth is to be resumed at the rate of the late 1980s. Regrettably, destocking accelerated in the first quarter of 1993.

■ 3.4 Capacity Utilisation

Figure 3.10 is based on the responses to the Confederation of British Industry (CBI) survey of business conditions and expectations. It shows the percentage of firms answering 'No' to the question: 'Is your present level of output below your capacity output level?' The degree of capacity utilisation revealed by the answers to this question provides a very good indication of the strength of AD in the economy. In 1979, 50 per cent of firms surveyed reported full capacity working. This represented the highest negative response since the 1970–73 boom, as shown in **Figure 3.10**, although it hardly suggested an economy working flat out. The rapid decline in the

Figure 3.10   *Capacity Utilisation (%)*

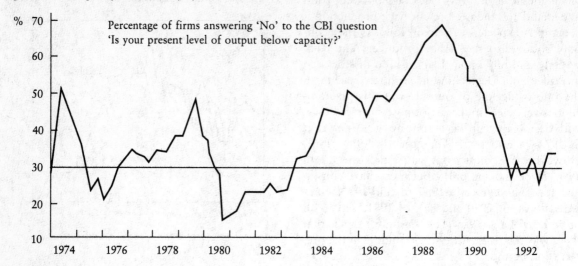

Percentage of firms answering 'No' to the CBI question
'Is your present level of output below capacity?'

Source: CBI.

degree of capacity utilisation in 1980 was the sharpest recorded in any single year from 1970 to date, and also the lowest absolute level of capacity utilisation (85 per cent of firms reported below-capacity output).

By 1985 capacity working had regained the 1979 level, and this was followed by further growth of demand which produced the highest level of capacity utilisation, at 70 per cent, since 1970. The level of capacity utilisation in 1988 indicated a very high level of AD in the economy, and hence the likelihood of both increasing inflationary pressure and a worsening balance of trade deficit.

These duly materialised, with inflation rising just as it had after the previous cycle peaks in 1973 and 1979. It is possible to argue that improvements in management and on the supply side generally made it possible to run the economy nearer to capacity during the 1980s compared to previous decades without causing the economy to boil over, but the situation in 1988 was unsustainable on any measure, as indeed it had been in 1979 at a time when there was even less slack in the labour market than in 1988.

The downturn in 1979–80 was short but severe. The more recent downturn was more gradual but longer-lasting, with the response rate in **Figure 3.10** falling back from 70 per cent to 30 per cent prior to levelling off at the end of 1991. Since that time the economy has been 'bouncing along the bottom', but the emergence of 'green shoots' in 1993 should see the level of capacity utilisation picking up quite rapidly as it did in 1983. There appears to be plenty of headroom for non-inflationary growth but, the depreciation of the exchange rate notwithstanding, it will be a struggle to switch spare capacity into export markets in the face of the depressed conditions elsewhere in the EC.

■ 3.5 Company Profitability

Figure 3.11 presents a long-term view of companies' pre-tax profitability, adjusted also to take account of the North Sea oil sector after the mid-1970s. The profitability of all ICCs sagged fairly continuously from 1962 to 1970, and as can be seen it fell abruptly from 1973 to 1975 as costs rose sharply as a consequence of rising oil and other commodity prices. From this point on there was nowhere to go but up, although not for long as there was a further sharp downturn after 1978 which, in the case of non-oil ICCs, depressed profitability below even the level prevailing in the mid-1970s.

The excellent profitability of the oil sector produced a somewhat better result for ICCs as a whole, and as the economy grew rapidly out of the recession profitability grew alongside GDP. The improved climate for profits in turn fostered investment even though borrowing costs remained high, and additional investment helped to sustain profitability. By the late 1980s the situation appeared to be much healthier than it had been for two decades, but the onset of recession caused profitability to slump once again during 1990.

For ICCs as a whole the reduction in profitability in 1990–91 was as severe as in 1980–81, although the non-oil sector did not perform significantly worse this time around. As a result, profitability did not fall back as much as might have been expected, before beginning to rise again in 1992.

It is not particularly easy to interpret the overall picture. One of the main thrusts of the Thatcher government was to improve the workings of the economy, as discussed below. This included reductions in corporate taxation and the removal of distortions in the tax system that encouraged investment for short-term financial gain rather than for the long term. The power of organised labour was also eroded. Despite these changes profitability fell back after 1989 in a similar manner to that in previous recessions, so these measures either had a limited impact upon profitability or they were offset by other supply-side problems which were as yet unaddressed. Certainly, the endemic problem of productivity gains showing up as increases in real wages rather than as rising profits continues to cause concern, although the fact that the rate of return stabilised in 1992 must be attributed, at least in part, to the containment of labour costs earlier in the recession.

The fact that profitability did not ultimately fall back to the levels seen during the 1980–81 recession can be attributed first to the fact that levels of, and growth in, productivity were much higher

Figure 3.11 *Companies' Real Rates of Return on Capital, Pre-tax, 1970–92*

Source: Bank of England Quarterly Bulletin (August 1993), Chart 5.6.

Figure 3.12   *Net Operating Surplus as a Proportion of the Net Capital Stock: Business Sector*

Source: OECD, *Economic Outlook*.

entering the 1990s recession than a decade earlier; second, to the fact that UK industry was more competitive than in the early 1980s; and third, to the fact that UK export markets were stronger and capacity utilisation higher (*Bank of England*, 1993, p. 362).

Profitability in the UK has been consistently poor by the standards of comparable economies, as shown in **Figure 3.12**, although the data may exert a downwards bias in the case of the UK (Bank of England, 1992, p. 300). Nevertheless, the relatively rapid growth of UK profitability in the mid-1980s served to reduce the gap for a while, although this shows up more clearly for manufacturing rather than for business as a whole. The gap appears to have opened up again in recent years, but the onset of growth in the UK at a time of recession elsewhere in the Community should see it close down somewhat in 1993–94.

■ 3.6 Growth and Productivity

For a country to grow richer, it must first of all grow. In other words, it is the increase in the volume of goods and services (real GDP) which economic growth represents that underpins the improvement in a country's standard of living over time. It should be observed that there are quite a number of qualifications to be made when linking growth to living standards: for example, if the extra goods and services are all exported, domestic consumption will not be affected, and the fruits of growth may not be distributed at all equally such that some individuals may become worse off even when the economy is growing rapidly. Nevertheless, provided population growth does not outstrip economic growth – fortunately not the case in advanced societies – the only certain way for individuals to become steadily richer is for economic growth to be the rule rather than the exception.

It must also be remembered that growth is **compound**. In other words, if there is 10 per cent growth for three years, the index of real GDP will not rise in the sequence 100: 110: 120: 130 but in the sequence 100: 110: 121: 133. Whereas this makes little difference in any single year, it makes an enormous difference over several decades. At 10 per cent compound, real GDP doubles in 7.5

years, triples four years later and is four times as large less than three years after that. At a growth rate of 5 per cent it takes 33 years to raise real GDP by a factor of 5, whereas at a growth rate of 10 per cent it takes only 17 years.

This is why Japanese growth rates have traditionally been regarded with envy, but a word of caution is nevertheless necessary. If GDP is initially very low, high growth rates make little absolute difference. Thus, if a country with a GDP of £10 billion doubles its GDP, the absolute difference is only equivalent to a 10 per cent growth rate for a country with an initial GDP of £100 billion. By and large, mature advanced economies do not, therefore, grow at all rapidly. Now that Japan falls into this category, it also struggles to grow noticeably faster than comparable large economies. The key issue about growth is, accordingly, not why the UK grows slowly but why it has traditionally grown **more slowly** than comparable economies.

It is important to emphasise that the UK economy does grow in the majority of years, and hence that in the aggregate the citizens of the UK have become progressively better off, both in terms of income and wealth. For whatever reason, some critics like to refer to the 'good old days' of the 1960s or 1970s, but although growth may at the time have been relatively rapid by recent standards, households were, on average, considerably less well off than today. The fact that some households have become worse off does not imply that this is true **on average**, and it is an issue of income and wealth distribution (to be addressed in Chapter 10) rather than an issue of growth (or lack of it).

In order for real GDP to grow year on year we strictly need only to keep increasing the size of the labour force and to maintain output per person employed at a constant level. However, if the labour force is not growing at all rapidly, what is needed is to make each worker more **productive**. Productivity is thus of crucial importance, and it is in respect of **productivity** that a 'miracle' is alleged to have taken place in the UK during the 1980s.

Did it? The first difficulty is deciding exactly what the word 'productivity' means. As indicated above, most of the discussion centres around **labour** productivity as measured by **output per person employed** (or output per head). It can also be measured as output per person hour, although this produces an almost identical trend in practice. One could also refer to output per unit of **capital**, or capital productivity, but the most commonly utilised alternative is known as **total factor productivity** which is defined as output per unit of average input, where average input is a weighted average of capital (roughly 30 per cent) and labour (roughly 70 per cent), and where account is taken not merely of increases in the quantity of capital and labour but of improvements in quality, reductions in inefficiency and better techniques. Labour productivity, for example, can be responsive to changes in the quality of the capital stock, to the way work is organised and to the industrial relations climate. With such caveats in mind, what is the overall picture?

☐ 3.6.1 Long-term Growth

It is useful to begin by taking a long-term perspective, as is done in Figure 3.13 which presents the data on an annualised basis from 1956, including an official forecast to 1996. This is reworked on a different basis in **Figure 3.14**, where the data have been used to calculate overlapping six-year period growth rates, rather than annual growth rates, in order to facilitate comparison with the high-growth period in the mid-1980s (here taken as 1981–87). **Figure 3.14** shows that during the 1950s and 1960s successive six-year periods had annual growth rates contained largely in the 2.5 to 3.5 per cent range. Nevertheless, the sharp improvements in the mid-1960s and late 1960s, and then again in 1973, are of particular interest in relation to the period post-1985, both in terms of the fact that they were short-lived and that each peaked at a successively lower level. Essentially, it was downhill all the way from 1965 to 1985, spanning the term of office of several governments of quite different political hues. The strength of the upturn after 1985 is comparable only to that during the early postwar recovery

Figure 3.13   *GDP (Annual Charge)*

Source: CSO.

Figure 3.14   *Average Growth for Six-year Periods, 1949–54 to 1983–87 (%)*

Source: Treasury Economic Progress Report, 196 (June 1988).

phase, but its starting point was a far lower rate of growth than at any point during the intervening period.

Taking the period 1960–87 as a whole, the UK's performance was poor by comparison with other advanced economies with the exception of the USA. During most of the 1960s it was worse even than that of the USA, although it was quite good compared to previous decades and better than the two subsequent decades. The downwards trend from 1974 to 1979 was by no means unique to the UK as 'shocks' such as oil price rises affected other advanced economies to much the same extent, but that simply meant that the UK continued to grow relatively slowly (although the USA did even worse).

The big difference occurred after 1981 since the UK started to grow strongly whereas other advanced economies, with the exception of Japan, continued to perform badly by their own standards. As a result, the UK shot up the growth league. Nevertheless, the previous long period of relatively slow growth had placed the UK in the invidious position of getting progressively wealthier at a time when many comparable countries were becoming wealthier than the UK. Even in 1966, only the USA had a higher level of GDP per head. At that time Japan was a long way behind, but by 1980 Japan had joined the increasingly long list of countries with a higher GDP per head than the UK. After two decades of falling behind, it obviously needed more than a short burst of relatively rapid growth for the UK to recover all of the lost ground. Nevertheless, at least the fatalistic view commonly voiced during the 1970s (that the process of relative decline was irreversible) had been shown to be demonstrably false.

☐ 3.6.2 Productivity

Table 3.6 is concerned with labour productivity over the period 1960–88, divided into three sub-periods and covering manufacturing industry as well as the whole economy. The most notable feature is the significant reduction in productivity during the 1970s compared to the 1960s, and the rather modest improvement during the bulk of the 1980s. Once again, the poor performance of the UK compared to the other major economies during the 1960s is plain to see, especially with respect to manufacturing. During the 1970s the general level of performance was much inferior, but the UK nevertheless managed to fall even further behind in manufacturing. In the words of Crafts (1993, p. 49):

In sum, the evidence is that a good deal of the relatively slow growth of the UK during [1950–73] was due to an environment which permitted or even encouraged the survival of the ineffi-

Table 3.6 *Output Per Person Employed, Average Annual Percentage Changes*

Whole Economy	1960–70	1970–80	1980–88
UK	2.4	1.3	2.5
US	2.0	0.4	1.2
Japan	8.9	3.8	2.9
Germany	4.4	2.8	1.8
France	4.6	2.8	2.0
Italy	6.3	2.6	2.0
Canada	2.4	1.5	1.4
G7 average	3.5	1.7	1.8

UK data from CSO. Other countries' data from OECD except 1988 which are calculated from national GNP or GDP figures and OECD employment estimates.

Manufacturing Industry	1960–70	1970–80	1980–88
UK	3.0	1.6	5.2
US	3.5	3.0	4.0
Japan	8.8	5.3	3.1
Germany	4.1	2.9	2.2
France	5.4	3.2	3.1
Italy	5.4	3.0	3.5
Canada	3.4	3.0	3.6
G7 average	4.5	3.3	3.6

UK data from CSO. Other countries' data from OECD, except France and Italy which use IMF employment data. 1988 data for France and Italy cover first three quarters only.

Source: CSO, OECD, IMF; Reproduced from *Treasury Economic Progress Report*, 201 (April 1989).

cient and created a situation where the bargaining power of those seeking to block productivity-enhancing change was often considerable.

Figure 3.15 illustrates the relationship between output and labour productivity during the period 1975 to 1986, based upon 1980 = 100. **Figure 3.15** brings out very clearly the contrast between the 1970s and the 1980s. In the manufacturing sector,

Figure 3.15 *Output and Productivity,[1] UK, 1975–86 (1980=100)*

Note:
[1] Seasonally adjusted.

Source: Employment Gazette.

real output hobbled along during the second half of the 1970s, with productivity following an almost identical trend but below that of output. The sheer inefficiency of labour use in manufacturing is scarcely credible in the light of the more recent discovery that UK workers are not necessarily bone idle by choice but can be motivated to

work as productively as the Germans and Japanese.

The situation for the rest of the economy was scarcely much better. However, the effects of the 1980–81 recession are interesting in that, as discussed in Chapter 7, output and employment collapsed in manufacturing but not in the rest of

Figure 3.16 *Output and Productivity,[1] UK, 1985–93 (1985 = 100)*

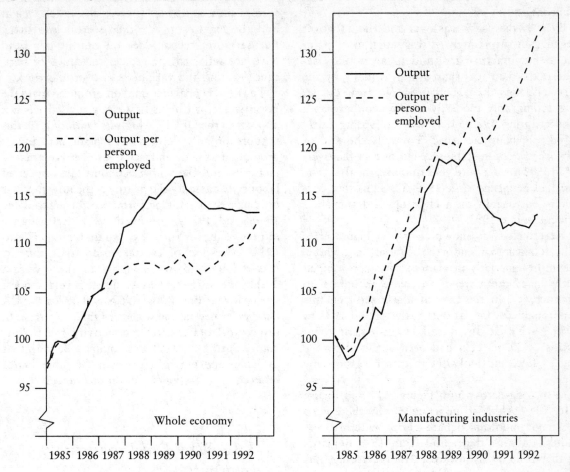

Note:
[1] Seasonally adjusted.
Source: Employment Gazette.

the economy. Indeed, employment in manufacturing collapsed so fast that productivity responded quite quickly and was back to its pre-recession level during 1981. Output in manufacturing barely budged from its nadir until 1983, and was still well below its pre-recession level even in 1986.

Elsewhere in the economy the situation was less serious in that the fall in output was short-lived, but it still took several years for output to regain its pre-recession level because few jobs had been shed and productivity growth was consequently sluggish. Not so in manufacturing. With hundreds

of thousands of jobs lost, productivity took off at a rate which previously would have come to a grinding halt in no time at all. However, on this occasion it did not falter, as shown in **Figure 3.16** (which is based upon 1985 = 100). As can be seen, from 1985 to the end of 1988 output in manufacturing rose by 20 per cent. Unemployment had ceased to grow much by 1985, and began to fall in 1986, so labour productivity only just kept ahead of output during this period. Elsewhere in the economy output continued to grow steadily, albeit much more slowly than in manufacturing, and as employment picked up the consequence was that labour productivity ceased to grow at all from the end of 1986.

By 1989 the party was over and the hangover began. Not surprisingly, it was much more painful in manufacturing although, as noted elsewhere, the pain was shared more equally by the service sectors than in 1980–81. Whereas output was falling only modestly in the economy as a whole during 1989–91, it was collapsing fairly rapidly in manufacturing. Towards the end of 1991 the situation stabilised, but output fell overall in 1992 for the third year running, the first time this had happened since 1930–32. Signs that output is once again on a clear upward trend are evident in mid-1993.

Nevertheless, as shown clearly in **Figure 3.16**, the fall in employment in the economy as a whole, but more especially in manufacturing, combined with these output trends to create an upturn in productivity. In the case of manufacturing this was roughly as fast as during the period 1985 to 1989, such that an overall improvement of in excess of 30 per cent had been achieved by the end of 1992 and looks set to continue for some time.

In looking across both **Figure 3.15** and **Figure 3.16** it is possible to understand why there is so much acrimonious debate about whether one should examine the period from 1979 onwards or that from 1981 onwards. Manufacturing output, for example, is roughly 12 per cent above its 1985 level, and is therefore only slightly above the level prevailing in 1979. On the other hand, it is comfortably above the level prevailing in 1981. In other words, a peak to trough (1979–91) perspective can be made to provide a severe indictment of government policy towards the manufacturing sector. On the other hand, a trough to peak (1981–88) perspective can be used to support the resurrection of UK manufacturing hypothesis, which can be supported even more satisfactorily when the data on output per person employed are used.

It may be noted that, both within the manufacturing sector and elsewhere in the economy, the performance of different sub-sectors has been very variable. This may have resulted in an understatement of productivity. The weights are based on 1985, which means that the shrinkage of sectors such as textiles is given too much weight and the expansion of other sectors too little. Furthermore, recent data on output per head have not reflected the greater incidence of part-time working and variations in overtime work.

The OECD provides data on productivity in the business sector (this is frequently revised when it appears in the OECD *Economic Outlook*). As this is more broadly defined than manufacturing, it provides a kind of halfway house between manufacturing and the whole economy. In respect of **labour** productivity the picture is the now familiar one, namely a poor performance throughout the 1960s and 1970s, followed by a performance improved upon only by Japan from 1979 to 1988. In respect of **capital** productivity the UK was the only major economy to show a gain during the 1979–88 period, albeit a very modest one, whereas during the 1960s and 1970s the UK had performed in line with the OECD average. In respect of **total factor productivity** the performance during 1979–88 was comparable with that of Japan and much better than the other major economies, with the exception of France.

3.6.3 Why Did Productivity Improve?

It is widely accepted that the recovery had little or nothing to do with investment. One alternative possibility is that improvements in productivity are related to plant closures. If the effect of the 1980–81 recession was to close down a large proportion of the least-efficient plants in the UK, then that alone could account for much of the subsequent improvement in productivity as output became increasingly concentrated in efficient plants (and utilised the most-efficient workers). Unfortunately, the evidence on this topic is ambiguous. A reasonable interpretation would appear to be that the rate of scrapping of the capital stock accelerated sharply at the beginning of the 1980s, and continued at levels some 50 per cent higher than in previous years.

This sounds impressive, but given that scrapping accounted previously for roughly 2 per cent of the capital stock each year, the acceleration accounted for only roughly 1 per cent extra each year for possibly six years. This additional 6 per cent of scrapped capital would indeed have boosted productivity, but not significantly, especially when account is taken of the fact that during the 1980–81 recession plant closures were not concentrated among the least-productive plants, but involved many larger plants with above-average productivity.

It is more plausible to argue that the shock effect of the 1980–81 recession, both for management and workers, accounts for the productivity gains of the 1980s. During the 1970s, labour was hoarded and hence productivity was repressed. The effect of North Sea oil upon the exchange rate, rendering UK companies increasingly uncompetitive, effectively forced them to improve productivity or go under, and this caused over 2 million workers eventually to lose their jobs. The government's deflationary policies, its attack upon restrictive labour practices and the withdrawal of many subsidies combined to force a reappraisal of work organisation that rapidly paid dividends. It is, however, slightly ironic that the government never intended the recession to be so severe, yet if it had been as mild as elsewhere in Europe the transformation of UK productivity would almost certainly not have occurred.

This line of argument also implies, however, that the easy productivity gains have been realised, and that unless there are continuing high levels of investment and training there will be severe difficulties in engineering a second productivity 'miracle' during the mid-1990s. In this context there is the performance of manufacturing output to consider. As can be seen in **Table 3.7**, the productivity improvement in the UK up to 1987 was, according to the OECD, entirely the effect of labour shedding whereas in the USA, and especially in Japan, it reflected primarily increases in output. Only in West Germany was the situation at all comparable to that in the UK, although the critical difference, as ever, shows up in the final column. In the UK, the productivity gains

Table 3.7 *Manufacturing Industry, 1979–87*

| | Output per Worker | % Change in | | |
		Employment	Output	Real Earnings[1]
USA	29.8	−6.3	21.6	−3.9
Japan	52.2	6.7	62.4	13.4
W. Germany	16.5	−7.5	7.6	10.4
UK	37.8	−27.5	0.0	25.8

Note:
[1] Hourly earnings deflated by consumer price index.
Source: OECD.

reappeared as higher real earnings. In the USA real earnings actually fell, and in Japan they absorbed only one-quarter of productivity gains.

A rerun of this phenomenon clearly offers no long-term solution to the UK's problems. As shown in **Figure 3.16**, the situation improved a good deal between 1986 and 1990, with manufacturing output growing rapidly. However, the onset of recession has produced a pattern very similar to that of 1980–81. The prognosis for the mid-1990s is nevertheless better than for 1982–85 in two respects. In the first place, overseas investors in the form of, for example, Japanese car-makers, have demonstrated that they can achieve levels of output and productivity comparable to best practice overseas. Second, there is little expectation of another dramatic surge in real earnings. Nevertheless, a rapid expansion in manufacturing output is a pre-condition for catching up some of the ground lost in the past, and while the exchange rate is more competitive than in 1992, the recession in other major markets bar the USA (where there are nevertheless some signs of faltering in mid-1993), as shown in **Table 3.8**, indicates that the path ahead will not be smooth. It is fashionable to be pessimistic rather than the reverse, especially in the light of the UK's relatively small manufacturing sector. However, the USA, which has an even smaller manufacturing sector in relation to GDP, produces not merely twice as much net output per manufacturing worker as the UK but almost half as much again as Japan and Germany, so all is not yet lost.

Table 3.8   *GDP/GNP Growth in the Major Six (Percentage Changes on Previous Year)*

	1990	1991	1992	Forecast 1993
United States	0.8	−1.2	2.1	3.0
Canada	−0.5	−1.7	0.9	3.4
Japan	4.8	4.1	1.5	0.5
Western Germany	5.3	3.8	1.1	−1.5
France	2.3	0.6	1.2	0.4
Italy	2.2	1.4	1.0	0.2
Major six	2.3	0.9	1.7	1.4
United Kingdom	0.6	−2.5	−0.5	1.25[1]
EC12	2.8	1.3	0.6	−0.3

Note:
[1] FSBR forecast.

Source: Bank of England Quarterly Bulletin (May 1993).

■ 3.7 Inflation

Since the late 1940s the UK economy has experienced a succession of severe macroeconomic problems punctuated by short periods of more favourable economic performance. The same problems have recurred, often simultaneously, although at particular times one has tended to be dominant. These problems have encompassed a low or non-existent growth rate, high unemployment, persistent inflation, balance of trade deficits and fiscal deficits. Since the early 1970s the dominant problem has most frequently been that of persistent inflation, since even when – as is true currently – inflation is low and set to remain that way for a while, there is little confidence that this will remain the case for very long.

In 1975, at the height of the oil crisis, the annualised rate of inflation exceeded 24 per cent, a higher rate than at any other time this century and one rarely seen in other advanced economies. That was an experience which no-one wishes to repeat, and the period since 1979 has been dominated by the desire to prevent not merely its recurrence but even the recurrence of double-digit inflation. In this respect it is fair to say that West Germany has been even more concerned about the problem than the UK, but then the Germans suffered a hyperinflation which put the British experience of the 1970s in the shade.

☐ 3.7.1 Measurement of Inflation

The term inflation refers to a rise in the general level of prices in the economy, or in an average measure of prices in the economy, rather than to the behaviour of the price of an individual good or service. Inflation becomes a serious problem when the general level of prices rises **persistently** and unpredictably. The rate of inflation is calculated using an index of the general price level, or some other relevant concept of prices, and the index is constructed as a **weighted average** of the relevant prices. The issue of relevant prices highlights the fact that different groups of people are interested in the behaviour of different sets of prices; for example, a manufacturer will be concerned about the rate of increase of fuel and raw materials, while a consumer will be more interested in retail prices. For this reason the CSO publishes several different price indices or measures of inflation.

The most widely used of these is the **Retail Prices Index** (RPI), which is published by the Department of Employment. This is a weighted average of prices for a basket of 600 goods and services consumed by a 'typical' household. The total weights of 1000 are distributed so as to reflect the pattern of spending as revealed by the Family Expenditure Survey (FES), and a new set of weights is introduced at the beginning of each year (see *Employment Gazette*, June 1992, pp. 304–6). Over time the weights assigned to different groups of goods and services can vary considerably, and it is also necessary periodically to alter the main categories of weights in order to reflect major changes in spending patterns. In January 1987 a significant amendment was made to the categories, which had been in force since 1974, in order to take account of such items as holiday expenditure and the cost of financial services. The most recent amendments were, in February 1993, the inclusion of foreign holidays and, in April 1993, the replacement of the Community Charge by the Council Tax.

Figure 3.17 *Structure of the RPI*

Source: CSO.

The three largest categories in May 1993, as shown in **Figure 3.17**, were housing (172), motoring expenditure(143) and non-seasonal food (130). The largest single weighting was MIPs (48). These weights exclude the spending of high income earners and of pensioner households, the latter having their own independent RPI which is used in order, for example, to index-link pensions.

The RPI for the period since 1975, based upon 1985 = 100, is shown in **Table 3.9**. However, inflation is commonly expressed as a rate of change, which is set out on an annual basis in the brackets. Thus, for example, the annual rate for calendar 1992 can be calculated from **Table 3.9** by the formula 146.4 **less** 141.1 **divided by** 141.1 **times** 100 per cent, which equals 3.7 per cent. When this is repeated on a monthly basis the resulting pattern is as shown in **Figure 3.18**. It is especially interesting to note the pattern described by the sequence **abc** and by **adefgh**. **Abc** is virtually a linear sequence, and while **adefg** is curvilinear it, like **abc**, is constantly downward sloping. This would suggest that inflation has been on a downward path since the first oil shock in 1974, the sharp upturns in 1979–80 and 1988–90 notwithstanding. The very low rates over the past year would appear to be compatible with this pattern rather than an anomaly.

The RPI measures only the prices of final goods and services. It thus excludes the prices of intermediate products, but includes the effects of alterations in indirect taxes and in excise duties. There are obviously other ways of going about the measurement of inflation, and a number of other measures in common usage are set out in

Table 3.9. The **Tax** and **Price Index** (TPI) has been published since August 1979. The general idea was to take account of changes in income taxes and NICs which were expected to fall, thereby leaving households with more real spending power than appeared to be the case after adjusting gross incomes for changes in the RPI. This was expected to exert downward pressure on wage demands. However, as it turned out the TPI promptly rose more rapidly than the RPI as a result of the 1980 Budget, and was put into abeyance, a position it has continued to occupy ever since, although the TPI has risen somewhat more slowly than the RPI since April 1983. The **Producer Price Index**, previously known as the Wholesale Price Index, is divided into an index covering the prices of materials and fuel and an index covering the prices of home sales of manufactured products ('factory gate' prices). These

Table 3.9   *Assorted Price Indices (1985 = 100)*

Year	General Index of Retail Prices		Tax and Price Index		Producer Price Index				GDP Deflator[1]	
					Materials and Fuel		Manufactured (Home Sales)			
1975	36.1	$(24.1)^2$	37.7	$(25.3)^2$	40.0	$(11.7)^2$	37.9	$(23.1)^2$	37.6	$(27.6)^2$
1976	42.1	(16.5)	45.0	(19.4)	49.9	(24.7)	44.0	(16.1)	42.9	(14.1)
1977	48.8	(15.7)	51.6	(14.7)	57.5	(15.2)	52.0	(18.2)	48.2	(12.4)
1978	52.8	(8.2)	53.1	(2.9)	59.6	(3.7)	57.1	(9.8)	53.9	(11.8)
1979	59.9	(13.4)	59.5	(12.1)	67.3	(12.9)	63.3	(10.8)	60.8	(12.8)
1980	70.7	(18.0)	69.8	(17.3)	73.0	(8.4)	72.2	(14.1)	72.3	(18.9)
1981	79.1	(11.9)	80.1	(14.8)	79.7	(9.2)	79.1	(9.6)	79.9	(10.5)
1982	85.9	(8.6)	88.0	(9.9)	85.5	(7.3)	85.2	(7.7)	85.2	(6.6)
1983	89.8	(4.6)	91.5	(4.0)	91.4	(6.9)	89.8	(5.4)	90.1	(5.8)
1984	94.3	(5.0)	95.0	(3.8)	98.9	(8.2)	95.0	(5.8)	94.5	(4.9)
1985	100.0	(6.1)	100.0	(5.3)	100.0	(1.1)	100.0	(5.3)	100.0	(8.0)
1986	103.4	(3.4)	101.9	(1.9)	92.4	(−7.6)	104.3	(4.3)	102.6	(2.6)
1987	107.7	(4.2)	104.5	(2.6)	95.3	(3.1)	103.3	(−1.0)	107.8	(5.1)
1988	113.0	(4.9)	107.6	(2.9)	98.4	(3.2)	113.2	(9.6)	114.8	(6.5)
1989	121.8	(7.8)	115.2	(7.1)	104.0	(5.7)	119.0	(5.1)	123.7	(7.8)
1990	133.3	(9.5)	124.7	(8.2)	103.8	(−0.2)	126.0	(5.9)	133.6	(8.0)
1991	141.1	(5.9)	131.4	(5.4)	102.6	(−1.2)	133.0	(5.6)	141.7	(6.2)
1992	146.4	(3.7)	136.4	(3.8)	103.0	(0.4)	138.0	(3.8)	147.9	(4.4)

Notes:
[1] GDP at current factor cost ÷ GDP at constant factor cost.
[2] Figures in brackets represent the percentage change from the previous year.

Source: Employment Gazette; Economic Trends; Monthly Digest of Statistics.

Figure 3.18   *RPI (%)*

Source: Employment Gazette.

indices respond to inflationary pressures earlier than the RPI, and hence can be useful in providing prior warning of an upsurge in retail prices. As shown in **Table 3.9**, the RPI shadows factory gate prices fairly closely in most years, whereas the index for materials and fuel is relatively volatile and is the more likely to show reductions. A combination of falling input prices and rising output prices is evidence of a sharp rise in profit margins.

Although these are the only price indices which are widely reported, much of the adjustment from nominal to real magnitudes is done using so-called 'price deflators'. The best-known of these is the index of total home costs, commonly referred to as the **'implicit' price deflator**, which is also recorded in **Table 3.9**. This index measures the change of all prices in the economy as

reflected in changes in the cost of producing all of the components of GDP.

As with so many other things, data on inflation must be treated with caution because, for exmaple, inadequate account is taken of **changes in quality over time**. Companies are constantly turning out goods that are lighter, faster, more energy-efficient and more reliable than their predecessors. For example, one can buy a video for much the same price as five years ago even though it will have many additional features. Basic office computers keep falling in price, but simultaneously become more powerful. A plane ride to the Costa Del Sol may appear to be an unchanging commodity but, as any passenger will know, modern jets are faster and more comfortable than those they replace. In recent times there has also been a shift from traditional retailers to discount stores, and from national brands to cheaper private-label goods.

All the main measures of inflation tell much the same story in the longer term, but monthly and quarterly data can deviate quite appreciably (which is why one should not pay too much attention to them). Since the recorded figures for short-term inflation do have a significant impact upon financial markets, there is political capital to be made out of the exclusion from the RPI of any components which are rising undesirably fast from the government's point of view. In this respect, for example, controversy has surrounded the treatment of housing costs in the RPI.

The key point to bear in mind is that inflation can be **persistent** only if something is persistently causing prices to rise: in other words, it is **recurrent**. Wages, for example, tend to rise continuously. Interest rates, or rates of tax, on the other hand, tend to change on a periodic, one-off basis. Because the RPI is a rolling twelve-month index, an increase in, say, VAT in June 1993 will appear in the index (June 1993 − June 1992 ÷ June 1992) but not in the corresponding index for the previous month, and will therefore cause the RPI to rise in June 1993. However, in June 1994, assuming VAT remains **unchanged**, the 1993 increase in VAT will have shifted in the formula (June 1994 − June 1993 ÷ June 1993) in such a way as to cause the RPI to **fall** in June 1994. In effect, the RPI is as much dependent upon what happened to prices a year previously as upon what happens in the current month. Because of the formula it means, for example, that a series of interest rate reductions will cause the RPI to fall back very sharply, but the effect will wear off a year later unless they fall further in the interim, which logically cannot go on for ever.

As noted previously, housing constitutes the biggest single element in the RPI, and can therefore have a significant distorting effect in the short term. As can be seen in **Figure 3.19**, this did not happen prior to 1988, but became very important subsequently, especially when, on the advice of

Figure 3.19   *Housing, Selected Components of the RPI (January 1987 = 100)*

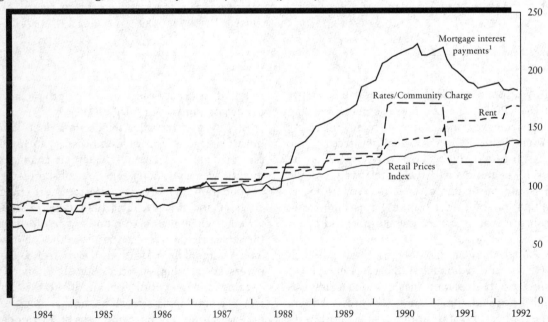

Note:
[1] Mortgage interest payments included in the RPI as a proxy for owner-occupiers' shelter costs.
Source: Social Trends, 23 (1993 edn), Chart 8.15.

the Retail Prices Index Advisory Committee, the Community Charge was substituted for domestic rates in the RPI at the time the Charge was introduced. From the beginning of 1986 to June 1990, the RPI rose by 32 per cent, whereas the rent index rose by 45 per cent and the rates/Community Charge index rose by 95 per cent (mostly between March and April 1990). The index of MIPs rose by 132 per cent over the same period, and in every month from May 1988 to June 1990, due partly to increasing mortgage balances related to house price inflation.

These developments sparked off a furious debate about the 'proper' way to measure inflation (and brought about the publication of an extensive report on inflation in each edition of the **Bank of England Quarterly Bulletin**). As a result, it has become customary to distinguish the official **headline** and **underlying** RPIs from others proposed by non-governmental sources. However, it is possible to devise a variety of underlying rates, depending upon what is excluded from the headline RPI. The exclusion which defines the underlying rate as officially published is MIPs, thereby generating the index known as RPIX, but to this may be added local taxation and/or petrol and/or VAT and/or excise duties (generating so-called **core** rates which tend, in practice, to follow the same trend as the underlying rate).

The point of the exercise is to strip out those factors in the headline rate which can potentially cause sharp one-off effects capable of disguising the underlying trend. If all one-off factors are excluded one is left primarily with wage effects: in other words, underlying inflation cannot be reduced to zero unless wages, on average, more or less stop rising. An additional rationale for stripping out MIPs is that if it becomes necessary to raise interest rates in order to restrain inflationary pressures, this has the perverse short-term effect of raising the headline rate of inflation.

The relationship between the headline rate and the underlying rate, which is illustrated in **Figure 3.20** spanning 1987–93, is obviously dependent upon these one-off effects. From 1987 to 1990 these essentially had the effect of boosting the headline rate because of sharp rises in interest

rates and local taxation. The basic rate of VAT was raised in April 1991, but this coincided with a steady downwards trend in interest rates, as noted previously, and with reductions in local taxation and nominal oil prices. As a consequence, the headline rate fell below the underlying rate in mid-1991, and has remained below it ever since. This is slightly ironic because, when the opposite relationship was commonplace, it was argued that wage negotiations should be tied to the underlying rate on the grounds that companies should not be expected to compensate workers for changes external to the corporate sector, such as higher interest rates.

In the month to January 1993, the underlying rate fell by 0.5 per cent, the biggest fall since the CSO started records in 1975. Little wonder, then, that many commentators take the view that inflation has been permanently tamed. History might suggest otherwise, but what it does suggest is that the government's recent over(?)emphasis upon inflation as the ultimate objective of its macroeconomic strategy may need to be reconsidered (in particular by Kenneth Clarke, the new Chancellor). In the UK since 1945, no government has been re-elected after raising the rate of inflation significantly during its term of office. However, given the fact that so many people remain fearful of losing their jobs in 1993, it might seem to be appropriate for attention to be diverted, albeit temporarily, to creating jobs even at the expense of a modest increase in inflation.

The government's current target is to keep the underlying rate within a 0 to 4 per cent band, which leaves a little leeway for the time being, but it would seem sensible to remain at the top of this band rather than try to bring the rate down further. If we assume that quality improvements are roughly equivalent to a 2 per cent reduction in prices then 2 per cent recorded inflation is anyway tantamount to price stability. It should also be taken into account that zero inflation does not permit nominal interest rates to fall below the rate of inflation – that is, for real interest rates to become negative as might be desired when emerging from recession – since this would imply lenders paying borrowers to borrow. Nevertheless, this is not to suggest that an underlying rate

Figure 3.20   *Official Measures of Inflation, 1987–93 (%)*[1]

Note:
[1] Increase in prices on a year earlier.
Source: Employment Gazette, CSO.

much, if at all, **above** 4 per cent is desirable, since the drawbacks are severe in terms of lost growth and jobs in the long term (as noted in *The Economist*, 1992).

☐ 3.7.2 International Perspectives

It is understandable that, in addressing the problem of inflation, individual countries tend to judge their performance either against a norm based upon historical experience or, less frequently, against an ideal set well below that norm. As a result, relatively little attention is paid to what is happening in other advanced economies even though, logically, some of the forces operating to raise prices in the UK will be operating in exactly the same way elsewhere. In other words, in judging just how much attention should be paid to the problem of inflation relative to, say, unemployment, it is useful to know how inflation-prone the UK really is by international standards.

Figure 3.21 *Change in Consumer Prices, EU Comparison, 1981–91*

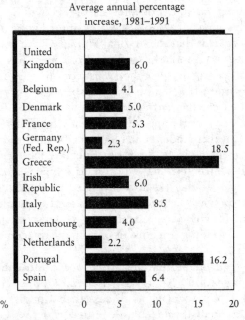

Average annual percentage increase, 1981–1991

United Kingdom 6.0
Belgium 4.1
Denmark 5.0
France 5.3
Germany (Fed. Rep.) 2.3
Greece 18.5
Irish Republic 6.0
Italy 8.5
Luxembourg 4.0
Netherlands 2.2
Portugal 16.2
Spain 6.4

Source: Social Trends, 23 (1993 edn), Chart 6.11.

Such an issue is best addressed by recourse to the standardised data produced by the OECD, and these will be illustrated in **Figures 3.20** and **3.21**. **Figure 3.20** produces data on inflation for the 12 EU member states during the period 1981–91. As can be seen, the UK fared a bit worse than average, but whereas the media are prone to make invidious comparisons with West Germany (as was) and the Netherlands, one can see that the Greeks, Portuguese and Italians are inclined to think we have the problem under reasonable control.

The span of years in question is somewhat unflattering because of the UK's much improved recent record, so **Figure 3.22** is set up to span a longer period and to concentrate upon the UK's main competitors. Here, the picture is in many ways less pleasing since the UK spent much of the 1980s suffering a worse rate of inflation than all bar Italy. Nevertheless, there are clear similarities in the long-term trends for individual countries. All six countries had a rising rate of inflation from 1966 to 1972, although the UK was the worst performer. All then suffered a significant increase in the rate of inflation, peaking in 1975, followed by a period of high but declining rates which, with the exception of the USA, lasted for several years only to turn up to a further peak in 1980.

The factor common to the experience of every country in the 1970s was the behaviour of the price of **crude oil**. In real terms, this rose by a factor of four in 1974 as a consequence of the formation of the OPEC cartel (known as the first 'oil shock'). The fact that the real price of oil subsequently held steady for nearly five years largely explains why inflation rates began to fall in oil-importing countries (which at that time included the UK). In 1979 there was a second 'oil shock' which was proportionately less severe but nevertheless quite sufficient to trigger an upturn in inflation throughout the world, as shown in **Figure 3.22**. Combined with increases in the prices of other commodity imports, the effects were quite severe, but once again the real price of oil stabilised, after falling sharply in 1985 due to the collapse of OPEC, at a level somewhat below that of the late 1970s, and apart from a

Figure 3.22   *Consumer Price Indices, Selected Countries, 1978–93 (%)*

Note:
[1] Forecast.

Source: OECD *Main Economic Indicators*; *Employment Gazette*.

sharp blip at the time of the Gulf War it has shown no further tendency to rise.

The sharp drop in 1985 helped to pull down the inflation rate worldwide, as shown in **Figure 3.22**, with all countries converging for the first time in over a decade. It is interesting to note that France and Italy were converging **down** to the UK rate which had fallen back extremely sharply in the 1980–81 recession. In the period post–1986 the UK once again performed badly, but since the most recent peak in 1990 it has converged rapidly on rates elsewhere. In fact, the comparison is somewhat unflattering since the rate in 1993 has remained below that forecast by the OECD, and the situation is deteriorating rapidly in Germany.

☐ *3.7.3 Analytic Considerations*

We do not propose, in the sections that follow, to go into a detailed analysis of inflation. In the first place, we have yet to investigate such matters as unemployment and trade deficits, and it is more sensible to bring everything together in Chapter

12. Second, it is simply not the purpose of this book to replicate the abstractions of more theoretical texts. We do not, therefore, intend to conduct an in-depth analysis of Phillips Curves at this point. If, however, we examine **Figure 3.23** it is evident that the original Phillips Curve trade-off between inflation and unemployment has not been seen again since the 1960s. For our purposes, the interesting empirical question is why the sequence unwound as it did from 1980 to 1986, and why, after improving markedly from 1986 to 1988, it then underwent a loop very similar to that commencing in 1978 but on a much reduced scale (and which may have begun to happen again). Because at this juncture we have yet to discuss concepts such as the 'natural' rate of unemployment (discussed in Chapter 9), we must accordingly conduct the discussion in fairly general terms.

It is evident that inflation is a **multi-causal phenomenon**. No doubt monetary policy has had a part to play, as discussed in Chapter 12. Undoubtedly, trade union militancy is a factor which must, at times, be taken into account,

Figure 3.23 *The Phillips Curve*

Note:
[1] Author's estimate.
Source: Employment Gazette.

and the external sector (the subject of Chapter 6) cannot be ignored. It seems to the author (though others may disagree), that there is no reason to believe that the UK is inherently more inflation-prone than other countries, and that this opinion is supported by the evidence, discussed below, of the UK's inflation record during the past decade.

However, what cannot be disputed is that in the early postwar period the UK was uncompetitive. Attempts to deal with this problem were legion, but generally unsuccessful, in part because of the resistance of the workforce which was highly unionised compared to competitor countries. In good part, the pressure to introduce reforms floundered because governments of all political persuasions were locked into the belief that they had to maintain full employment. This meant running the economy with high levels of demand, since this was adjudged an easier way to keep people in jobs than by increasing supply. However, it is evident that expanding demand in the face of fixed supply is an excellent recipe for the creation of inflationary pressure.

Some of this excess demand usually leaks out into the external sector, and results in BoP crises. In effect, these provide an alternative manifestation of an inflationary crisis, and hence are unlikely to disappear without triggering a resurgence of inflation unless something has been done to control the latter in the meantime. Certainly, the traditional expedient of lowering the exchange rate simply served initially to raise import prices, and fed through into domestic inflation as companies adjusted their prices to take account of increased costs. This process represented 'cost-push' rather than 'demand-pull' pressures, as textbooks were wont to label them.

Cost-push pressures also arise if either wages rise **independently** of demand or companies increase their profit margins **independently** of demand. In either case, the key issue is whether the government is willing to **validate these pressures** by recourse to an accommodating fiscal and monetary stance. During the heyday of the Keynesian model, governments were rarely willing to tolerate cuts in output and jobs and, if at all, only in the short term. Starting in the period after 1976, but more notably after 1979, governments adopted a tougher stance. Such an about-turn in policy may at first be treated with scepticism, but if adhered to the message will eventually get through, as it did during 1980–81. Nevertheless, it was far costlier than expected – or intended – in terms of the number of workers who lost their jobs in the process of persuading employers and employees that the government meant business.

Inflationary pressures which arise from other sources are more problematic. If, say, the prices of imported commodities rise, then the standard of living of UK residents must necessarily decline. If the labour market is competitive this will result in a reduction in wages, keeping total costs, and hence prices, unchanged. However, wages will probably not fall, in which case there is renewed inflationary pressure, and either the government reins back demand and uses job losses to suppress inflation or it accommodates the pressure and prices escalate. In the latter case, the tough stance is merely delayed in practice since the government will be forced to act once the inflationary pressure becomes severe.

The inflationary pressure described here is cost-push – that is, it occurs on the supply side of the economy – but its effects are clearly dependent upon the demand-side response by government. Given the above, it is a touch unfortunate that the UK government changed its stance from tough to accommodating during the so-called 'Lawson boom' in the latter part of the 1980s. Nevertheless, this permits us to adopt an optimistic view about future developments since the government appears to have learned from this experience (though for how long?).

One further point needs emphasising very strongly. It is clearly fallacious to argue that inflation cannot be reduced unless the economy stops growing, or that growth cannot be resumed until inflation is suppressed. As the data below show clearly, periods of rapid productivity growth are periods when unit costs rise very little, if at all, in the high-growth sectors (predominantly manufacturing). Where inflation emerges is in those sectors where productivity growth is low or non-existent, but which obtain

roughly the same increase in wages on grounds of 'comparability'. Nevertheless, it is clearly impractical and inequitable to lock all of the gains from productivity within the manufacturing sector.

What the government must guard against are attempts by workers to protect themselves against any erosion in their standards of living which arises for **external reasons** such as higher oil prices. As we remarked earlier, there is scant sympathy in the UK for the view that when imported commodities go up in price this often represents the only means by which workers in much poorer societies can improve **their** standard of living.

☐ *3.7.4 Inflation Since 1980*

It is possible to analyse what has happened since 1980 in the manufacturing sector by reference to **Table 3.10**. As can be seen, the ongoing rise in labour costs, which has always been a characteristic of the UK economy, has in every year since 1981 been compensated by some improvement in productivity, most obviously in the periods when the economy was emerging from recession. As a result, at least in manufacturing, unit labour costs have rarely contributed significantly to any rise in output prices. 1993 is set to be very similar to 1983, judging by the fall in unit costs throughout 1993 so far.

Since the early 1980s input prices have also rarely fed through to the shops to any significant degree. Their influence was particularly benign in 1990–91, but the depreciation of sterling in October 1992 began to show up in the final quarter, and this is likely to become a significant factor during 1993. Bought-in services have been a more significant influence since 1988, responding to the growth in employment opportunities, but the effects of the recession have begun to show up clearly in the data for 1992 because job losses have been severe in the services sector.

During the mid-1980s a major contributory factor was clearly domestic profit margins. These rose exceptionally sharply in 1986, although this was evidently a one-off phenomenon. It has been argued that manufacturing companies basically

Table 3.10 *Contributions[1] to Output Prices in Manufacturing[2] from Changes in Cost Components (%)*

	Labour productivity (increase−) (1)	Labour costs (2)	Unit labour costs $(3)=(1+2)^3$	Input prices (4)	Bought-in services[4] (5)	Margins (residual) $(6)=$ $(7-(3+4+5))^3$	Output prices (7)
1980	1.7	7.3	9.9	3.8	5.2	−3.5	15.4
1981	−1.9	6.4	4.4	2.9	2.8	−2.7	7.5
1982	−3.0	4.4	1.3	2.3	1.1	2.2	6.9
1983	−3.6	3.7	0.1	2.6	0.9	1.8	5.4
1984	−2.7	3.5	0.8	3.0	1.1	0.3	5.2
1985	−1.6	3.5	1.9	1.0	1.1	1.7	5.7
1986	−1.7	3.1	1.5	−3.4	0.8	5.3	4.1
1987	−3.0	3.4	0.3	1.7	0.8	1.6	4.4
1988	−2.7	3.6	0.8	1.6	2.0	0.4	4.8
1989	−1.9	3.7	1.8	1.8	2.2	−0.4	5.4
1990	−0.3	4.1	3.8	−0.3	2.3	0.2	6.0
1991	−0.7	3.5	2.9	−0.7	2.5	0.4	4.9
1992	−2.1	2.7	0.5	−0.7	1.2	1.2	2.3
1993Q2	−3.2	2.4	−0.8	1.4	−0.2	2.0	2.3

Notes:
[1] Calculated for each component as the twelve-month growth rate scaled by weights derived from 1984 input–output tables as follows:

unit labour costs   0.44
input prices   0.33
bought-in services   0.22

[2] Excluding food, drink and tobacco.
[3] Figures may not add up to totals because of rounding.
[4] Proxied by unit labour costs in the service sector.

Source: Bank of England Quarterly Bulletin (August 1993) p. 319 and (November 1993) p. 438.

apply a mark-up to their expected long-run costs, which does explain the rise in margins in 1986 when oil-related import prices fell sharply, but the relationship is much more ambiguous in other years. It is evident that, whereas companies were constrained in their ability to put up their prices because of competitive pressures in the early 1980s, they felt able to take advantage of their improved competitiveness in subsequent years. It is also evident that, as spare capacity was used up, there was a tendency to take advantage of the shortage of supply by raising margins.

Margins in manufacturing have understandably suffered during the recession, and there appears to be some evidence that UK companies have begun to emulate their Japanese and German rivals in their willingness to cut margins in order to maintain competitiveness. Profit margins were so poor in the early 1980s that it is hard to castigate companies for taking advantage of the window of opportunity to restore them in later years. The fact that margins fell throughout 1992 is thus a good omen, given that so much of the manufacturing sector sells in competitive international markets. With Japan and Germany sliding headlong into recession, the need is to remain competitive and not merely take advantage of the sterling depreciation; in particular, to raise productivity and reduce unit labour costs.

The fact that these rose so far during 1990 and 1991 is troubling, although this was more a case of poor productivity than of excessively high wage costs by 1980s' standards. This shows up in **Table 3.11**, where the trend is similar to that in **Table 3.10**. **Table 3.11** also illustrates the point that the record across the economy as a whole has been inferior to that in manufacturing where most (measurable) productivity gains are located. In most advanced countries, Japan excepted, service-sector inflation has traditionally exceeded inflation in manufacturing. As previously noted, the prices of, for example, electrical goods may actually fall, but this is most unusual in respect of services. Service-sector inflation is relatively high for five reasons: because wages roughly keep pace with those in manufacturing but productivity growth is slower; because services cannot be stockpiled leading to price reductions in order to clear stocks; because as incomes rise, consumers demand improved services; because consumers are less likely to switch doctors than tins of beans; and, in particular, because most services are protected from the forces of international competition. For these reasons the objective of zero inflation is more meaningful when applied to the manufacturing sector rather than to the service sector.

Table 3.11 *Index of Wage Costs Per Unit of Output[1] (%)*

	Manufacturing	Whole economy
1980	22.3	21.7
1981	9.3	9.4
1982	4.4	5.2
1983	0.4	3.5
1984	3.1	5.9
1985	5.8	5.4
1986	4.0	4.6
1987	1.8	4.5
1988	2.5	7.1
1989	4.5	9.5
1990	7.8	10.1
1991	6.5	7.5
1992	1.5	4.1

Note:
[1] % change from a year earlier.
Source: Employment Gazette, Table 5.8.

Table 3.12 *Unit Labour Costs in Manufacturing (Percentage Change on Previous Year)*

	1990	1991	1992	Forecast 1993
United States	0.6	1.6	−0.6	−3.3
Canada	1.9	−3.6	1.3	0.5
Japan	2.5	3.5	8.4	0.5
Western Germany	3.5	5.5	5.6	9.8
France	3.1	3.5	3.3	2.4
Italy	9.2	12.5	4.4	0.7
Major six	2.2	3.2	2.9	0.5
United Kingdom	7.7	6.6	1.6	−1.5[1]

Note:
[1] FSBR forecast.
Source: Bank of England Quarterly Bulletin (May 1993).

These factors are clearly not confined to the UK, and **Table 3.12** brings out the point that the UK's record was much worse than the average for the major six economies in 1990 and 1991, but considerably better in 1992 and, almost certainly, in 1993. The deterioration in Japan and West Germany, the latter set to continue throughout 1993, is especially noteworthy.

It is particularly interesting to examine the path of earnings, which is shown for manufacturing industries in Great Britain over the past decade in **Figure 3.24**. The pattern for the whole economy is, in practice, very similar, albeit set mostly at a somewhat lower level. The apparently uniform upper limit for the data throughout the period can be contrasted with what happened previously. The average earnings index fell progressively from a starting point of 15 per cent in the 12-month period ending in January 1981 to just under 10 per cent in the 12-month period ending in January 1983. At this point the index stabilised, and that for the whole economy remained absolutely constant at 7.5 per cent for nearly three years. Starting in mid-1987, the latter index climbed to a new equilibrium in the 9–10 per cent band where it remained until the Spring of 1991. Meanwhile, the manufacturing earnings index fluctuated remarkably little. Indeed, given

Figure 3.24 *Earnings and Output per Head: Manufacturing Industries – Increases over Previous Year, Great Britain (%)*

Source: *Employment Gazette.*

the rapid growth in the economy, its consistency was quite remarkable and, for that matter, much remarked upon.

However, this rapid growth did affect wages and salaries per unit of output which, given the consistency of earnings, effectively presented a mirror image of the trend in output per head, as can clearly be seen in **Figure 3.24**. The exceptionally strong growth in output per head, which emerged from negative territory in 1980, came to a halt at the end of 1983, and was followed by a decline lasting two years. However, within the space of one year the situation had so reversed itself as to cause wages and salaries per unit of output to fall briefly below zero. They stayed comfortably below 5 per cent until 1989, at which point output per head fell sharply, itself entering negative territory in 1990, by which time wages and salaries per head had touched 10 per cent for the first time in a decade.

At this juncture, concerns resurfaced about **stagflation** (rising prices in conjunction with rising unemployment). Given that competitor countries were keeping a tight grip on their unit labour costs at the time, the fear was increasingly voiced that there would be a rerun of the late 1970s. However, events have turned out very differently, as shown in **Figure 3.24**. There are, in practice, three key determinants of wage inflation, namely the rate of price inflation, the level and rate of change of unemployment and the level of profits. Since the end of 1990 these have affected pay negotiations in such a way as to achieve something not seen for almost a decade, a fall in the average earnings index; and one, note, that **began almost exactly where the previous one finished off.**

Since 1990 the rate of price inflation has progressively fallen, as previously noted. From 1990 to the end of 1992 unemployment continued to rise, and although it dropped a little in recent months, no-one is yet persuaded that this will be a permanent trend. Finally, profitability has been poor, although the prognosis for 1993 is rather better. Underlying earnings can accordingly be expected to rise only modestly during the rest of

Figure 3.25   *Output Gap: Deterministic Trend Measure*

Per cent

Source: *Bank of England Quarterly Bulletin* (May 1993).

1993, especially as the government is playing tough in respect of public sector pay.

This, in turn should help to suppress price inflation, especially when taken in conjunction with the existence of a negative **output gap** (the gap between actual output and the level of output consistent with a constant rate of inflation) as shown in **Figure 3.25** (but see *Bank of England Quarterly Bulletin* (May 1993) p. 167 for a discussion of alternative estimates). The main fear in the short term is that the depreciation of sterling in October 1992 will feed through into higher shop prices, although there is little evidence of this so far. There is also the rise in VAT on domestic fuel to contend with in 1994. Nevertheless, the Bank of England, at least, expects the underlying rate to remain under 4 per cent until the end of 1994.

■ *3.8* Credit Crunch

A **credit crunch** exists when financial intermediaries, and especially banks, become unwilling to lend to the private sector. They may try to widen the gap between the interest rate at which they borrow and the rate at which they lend, as was

generally the case throughout the 1990–92 recession. For example, in early 1991 there were four reductions in base rates, but the overdraft rate to personal customers went up. Alternatively, they may toughen the criteria to be met before a loan is sanctioned. If crunch becomes crisis, lending may dry up altogether.

In **Figure 3.26** the left-hand triangle represents a credit crunch, whereas the full figure represents a financial crisis. In the heyday of Keynesian demand management the expansionary phase of the business cycle was set off via a loosening of fiscal policy. This did not happen during the 1980s, however, when as previously noted the upswing was based primarily upon the free availability of credit. This was similar to what happened in the nineteenth century when there were a series of booms and recessions driven by the behaviour of the financial markets. A credit crunch presupposes a prior boom based upon credit. The indebtedness of the personal and company sectors grows sharply and bank lending becomes directed increasingly towards more speculative types of activity, such as junk bond financed management buy-outs and property development, where returns are potentially very high.

When the slow-down inevitably arrives, there is a rash of company failures which in turn damages the banks' balance sheets when the loans are written off. This causes the banks' credit ratings to be lowered and hence raises the cost of finance. The banks respond not merely by raising the cost of their other lending in order to recover their own higher costs, but also by widening the spread between borrowing and lending rates. They also dispose of their collateral when payments secured by that collateral cease to be made, and shut down companies which in better times they would have been willing to tide over a bad patch. This may cause their credit rating to be downgraded yet further.

The step from credit crunch to financial crisis requires that depositors become afraid that their deposits will be put at risk by the banks' problems and consequently withdraw their funds, thereby precipitating a run on the banks. In practice, deposit insurance can be expected to prevent this

Figure 3.26 *Financial Crisis and Credit Crunch*

Source: Adapted from Barclays Bank Review (November 1990).

later step, especially if combined with assurances by the authorities that they will maintain the liquidity of the system.

It is accordingly more appropriate to ask whether there is currently a credit crunch in the UK. In practice, the banks appear to have withstood the recession reasonably well, and their share prices indicate that the financial markets take a positive view of their prospects. As indicated above, this is because they have pulled in their horns and taken a very tough line with companies that have borne the brunt of the recession. The banks have consequently been much criticised in the media for their apparent indifference to the suffering of both entrepreneurs and mortgagees in difficulties because they have lost their jobs, but they have taken the view that someone (other than, of course, their top management) must bear the brunt of banks' mistakes in the credit boom of the late 1980s.

Corporate failures have risen extremely sharply in recent years, although to some extent this reflects a high rate of company formations dur-

ing the mid-1980s. There are a number of different sources of data on this issue, such as Dun & Bradstreet and the British Chambers of Commerce, but the data tell a uniform story despite the use of different definitions, as is illustrated in Figure 3.27.

Company insolvencies rose steadily from 1980 to 1986, by which time the overall number had roughly doubled. They then fell back sharply to the level of 1982 between 1986 and 1988 and, after marking time in 1989, they began to rise very sharply in 1990. This possibly arose because the introduction of wrongful trading provisions aimed at protecting creditors in the Insolvency Act of 1986 may have led some firms to opt for insolvency earlier than in the 1980–81 recession, but it has also to be recognised that the number of small firms had grown significantly during the 1980s. The 1992 figure was roughly three times that of 1989, but there appears to have been a fairly sharp downturn in the two quarters before 1993's first quarter (*Bank of England Quarterly Bulletin*, August 1993).

Figure 3.27   *Company Insolvencies*

Source: Bank of England Quarterly Bulletin (February 1993).

The rate of increase, at roughly 65 per cent, was highest in 1991, but it still registered a 30 per cent rise in 1992 despite the odd 'green shoot'. Of particular interest is the fact that recent failures have been located primarily in the South-East outside London, Scotland and the South-West, indicating a high failure rate among companies formed in the late 1980s boom.

It should be borne in mind that new company formation in the UK has indeed been a 'growth industry' throughout the 1980s, and that company formations have always outnumbered failures, although the ratio of six to one in 1988 had fallen to two to one by 1992. In that year the number of new companies formed in Great Britain was 107 375, down from a peak of 130 478 in 1989. There is evidently still a strong urge to behave entrepreneurially, although this reflects in part a response to the loss of jobs during the 1980s.

The relatively unhelpful attitude of the banks, which they would presumably prefer to regard as more realistic, will probably hold back growth in company formation, but with the failure rate

falling back from its peak it is very unlikely that failures will come to outnumber new formations. It would accordingly appear reasonable to conclude that a credit crunch has been averted for the time being, although for a time, until interest rates began to fall appreciably, it looked to be a close-run thing.

■ 3.9 Is There a Business Cycle?

During the Vietnam War era of 1961–69, the US economy grew continuously for 106 months compared to the average in previous expansions of 35 months. Before turning down in 1990, the US economy logged up over 90 months of expansion, the longest ever in peacetime. It would appear to be the case that expansions have become longer and downswings shorter and shallower: the average US downswing now seems to last less than a year. Evidence from Britain, Japan and Germany suggests that the severity of cyclical swings has been much reduced since 1975.

There may be a number of reasons for the relative stability of the cycle (see *The Economist*, 9 June 1990, p. 85).

1 Manufactured products exhibit a strong cyclical effect, in good part because of variability in investment and stocks. Services, however, are less volatile, partly because they cannot be stored. Advanced economies have switched progressively from manufacturing to the provision of services.
2 Government spending, which acts counter-cyclically, has grown as a proportion of GDP. Automatic stabilisers have also become more important.
3 Stock-control methods have become more sophisticated, so stockbuilding has less impact upon the cycle.
4 Improved financial management, as manifested after the October 1987 crash, has tended to avert panic responses to severe malfunctions in the world economy which serve only to make the problem worse.

In respect of the long expansion of the 1980s, it would appear that this was assisted by the modest levels of inflation endured by most countries compared to the 1970s. Governments tend to respond to a sharp rise in prices by pressing on the monetary brake, and this has frequently brought an upswing to a grinding halt during past cycles. In addition, the collapse of the oil price in 1986 gave a boost to the major advanced economies just as the expansion was running out of steam.

One of the curiosities of the current cycle is that there no longer appears to be a synchronised cycle for all major economies. Both the USA and UK relapsed into recession in the middle of 1990, at a time when Japan and Germany (on the back of reunification) were still buoyant. As a result, international trade did not collapse and the world economy as a whole remained comparatively prosperous for such a late phase in a major expansion.

Subsequently, the situation reversed itself, with first the USA, having adopted a very low interest rate policy, and more recently the UK, pulling off the bottom and beginning, in a halting manner, to grow again at precisely the time when Japan and most of the EU were suffering sharp reductions in output. The fallout from this unsynchronised behaviour has been severe, not least in terms of displacing governments in many major economies. The strains within the EU have resulted both in devaluations and in countries such as the UK departing from the ERM altogether. In particular, as will be discussed in Chapter 7, there has been a resurgence of protectionist sentiment which bodes ill for the future.

It is difficult to know whether the major economies will move back into line again once growth is restored everywhere in due course. The world economy performs badly when the major economies are pulling in opposite directions, not least because it produces widely divergent views about the appropriate path for interest rates and exchange rates. Unfortunately, the disappearance of a regular business cycle suggests that synchronised behaviour may be more difficult to promote in the future.

■ *3.10* Supply-side Economics

During the long period of Keynesian orthodoxy it was widely accepted both that government intervention was desirable of itself and also that the purpose of macroeconomic intervention was primarily to maintain demand during recessions in order to boost output and employment. In terms of a standard economic model, this is best viewed as a shift to the right of the AD curve. However, it follows that if prices are to remain stable (as measured in aggregate by a price index), then AS must increase in line with AD. In a recession, with machinery and men lying idle, this seems a reasonable proposition, but in practice it is open to a number of objections. In the first place, the labour supply may be inflexible because it is geographically located in a different place from where the demand is being created. Alternatively, it may possess skills which are unsuitable, or no skills at all. It is possible to argue that regional policy can resolve the former difficulty by moving work to the workers, although this may prove to be both inefficient and expensive, but the latter problem is likely to be much more intractable. Equally, there is the issue of 'crowding out', whereby government spending may to a greater or lesser degree simply displace private sector spending.

However, if AS is inflexible, then a surge in AD is almost certainly going to create excess demand and hence drive up prices, thereby generating the kind of trade-off between employment and inflation enshrined in the Phillips Curve. Faced with this phenomenon, the logical response might be to try to suppress the inflationary pressure while maintaining high levels of AD, in which case inflation cannot be suppressed by reducing AD itself. This suggests that a prices and incomes policy should be used in order to prevent, by law, the onset of both price and wage inflation, but given that this does nothing of itself to reduce the excess demand, it is unlikely to have lasting effects (see **p. 484**).

This being so, logic suggests that if output and employment are to be fostered without creating inflationary pressures, then the model must be made to work the other way around: that is, by holding AD in check in order to prevent it spilling over into higher prices, while at the same time increasing AS. Indeed, if AS increases while AD remains constant, then not only do output and employment rise, but downwards pressure is also exerted on prices. It may, of course, be argued that AD cannot be held down so easily in the face of rising AS (at least, not in the context of the UK economy), but so long as supply moves first and demand does no more than keep pace with it, rising output and employment are compatible with stable prices. It is possible to set some of the subsequent discussion in the context of this simple model. In particular, monetarism can best be viewed as an attempt to **rein back aggregate demand** after 1979 **in order to control inflation** while supply-side economics got on with the task of **creating output and jobs**. It is clear that both needed to work in tandem, or alternatively that some other mechanism for reining in demand such as **high interest rates** be introduced instead of money supply control.

The Achilles' heel of such an approach is straightforward: if demand moves ahead of supply, which could most easily happen when supply runs up against capacity constraints, then rising output and employment will be accompanied by rising prices; and if prices rise too quickly demand may have to be reined in so sharply that a recession is caused. The issue of whether demand can be adequately reined in is discussed in detail in Chapter 12. For the moment, the concern is to address how a supply-side policy has been introduced in the UK since 1979.

It is important to appreciate that AS is dependent upon supply at a microeconomic level. The bottom line is that individuals must be given **incentives to work harder and more productively** and to behave in an **entrepreneurial manner**. This can happen only if markets are allowed to work as freely as possible; hence the main task of government is to create an environment in which effort is rewarded rather than to take decisions on behalf of individuals. From this it follows that governments should reduce their share of total expenditure and reform the fiscal system so that the total tax burden is reduced and disincentive effects are kept to a minimum.

Lower tax rates encourage saving, investment, work effort and risk-taking. Consumption, leisure, the use of tax shelters and the black economy cease to be as attractive as before. As supply increases in response, the consequent rising incomes, profits and wealth provide an increase in the tax base which returns to the Treasury revenue lost as a consequence of the tax rate reductions. Savings also rise, thereby providing additional funds for investment.

At least, that is the theory. It is often objected that work effort and saving are unresponsive at best to reductions in tax rates. Furthermore, the 'substitution effect' will come into play whereby, if it is possible to earn a given net-of-tax sum with less work effort once tax rates are lowered, then less work will be done. However, whereas this could be true for individuals, it cannot be true in the aggregate since if everyone worked less hard, total output and incomes would fall and people would have to work harder to restore their pre-tax incomes to their previous level.

The effect upon work effort may be difficult to measure directly. One way in which workers have traditionally responded to what they perceive as an insufficient net-of-tax reward for work effort has been to work more slowly, absent themselves, take longer vacations and move jobs more frequently. In other words, it may be that the supply-side effects will show up as much in the **quality of work** as in the number of hours worked.

It is, however, slightly ironic that, at least in the medium term, it is incumbent upon the government to take a great deal of (often legislative) action in order to get the supply side of the economy to work. Thus, for example, the failure of the private sector to deal adequately with the training of the labour force has left the government with much of the responsibility for improving the quality of the labour supply. Equally, deregulation of markets has generally brought regulation hard on its heels. There is a wide range of governmental initiatives which may reasonably be considered as supply-side policies, and it is not possible to comment on all of these in detail, but it should be noted that some, for example, are directed at removing the **unemployment trap** (that is, the tendency for certain people to find themselves no better off financially when in employment than when out of employment); some at encouraging workers to price themselves back into jobs, mainly by curbing the power of trade unions to push up wages; some to improve the quality of the labour force; some to deregulate markets; and some to transfer activity back from the unofficial (black) economy to the official economy.

It is extremely difficult to judge whether these policies have been successful, as few unambiguous econometric studies have as yet been published. Obviously, such indicators as the rate of growth offer some support for the efficacy of supply-side measures, and there is widespread agreement that the labour market works rather better than it did ten years ago. However, whether cuts in tax rates have achieved anything is at best open to doubt, particularly since the aggregate tax burden remains rather high.

Appendix: Say's Law, the Laffer Curve and the Gutman Effect
Say's Law

Supply-side economics has its roots in the work of J. B. Say (1767–1832), who is best-known for coining the expression **supply creates its own demand**, an opinion shared by many neo-classical economists. Say's basic argument was that if there was an increase in the numbers of those seeking work, then competition among the suppliers of labour would drive down the real wage to the point at which employers would be willing to buy any available labour that had not already chosen to be self-employed. In the process of using these labour inputs to make products, payments would have to be made for both labour and other inputs in the form of interest, dividends and profits. The value of output is thus exactly matched by an equal amount of factor payments sufficient to buy everything which has been produced. Hence supply creates its own demand.

During the Keynesian orthodoxy Say's Law came to be held in low esteem once it became widely accepted that there could be a deficiency of effective demand (see discussion in the introduction). Say's Law came back into fashion along with the Quantity Theory when a solution was sought to the problem of 'stagflation'.

The Laffer Curve

The Curve, associated with the work of A. Laffer in the mid-1970s, but which can be traced back to the ideas of Adam Smith (1776) among others, correlates tax rates with tax revenue. The Curve begins with zero revenue at a zero rate of tax, rises to a peak at some positive rate of less than 100 per cent (which can be determined only empirically) and subsides back to zero revenue at a tax rate of 100 per cent. This latter point is supposed to be the consequence of the total disincentive effect of such a tax rate, although it seems extremely implausible once one accepts that most tax revenue is returned to workers as benefits of one kind or another.

However, the key issue is that if tax rates are raised continuously then eventually tax revenue will begin to fall, which implies the need to keep the rate below the threshold rate that triggers the fall in revenue. It follows logically that if tax rates start above this threshold then lowering them will increase tax revenue. Just what is going to happen if tax rates are lowered when they are already below the threshold is somewhat less clear-cut, but the benefits are likely to be rather greater if tax-deductible allowances (such as mortgage interest relief) are simultaneously phased out. In the case of the UK there is considerable disagreement about the exact shape of the Laffer Curve.

■ The Gutman Effect

This phenomeneon, named after P. Gutman, essentially arises when reductions in the rate of tax induce transactions occurring previously in the black economy, and hence generating no tax revenue, to re-enter the official economy because the possibility of fines or imprisonment is no longer warranted given the relatively small deduction in tax if transactions are declared to the tax authorities. Hence, the tax base is widened if tax rates are reduced and tax revenue rises accordingly. This effect will operate in conjunction with the Laffer Curve.

Bibliography

Bank of England (1992 and 1993) 'Company Profitability and Finance', *Bank of England Quarterly Bulletin* (August).

Blackaby, D. and L. Hunt (1990) 'An Assessment of the UK's Productivity Record in the 1980s: Has There Been a "Miracle"?' *Economics* (Autumn).

Boleat, M. *et al.* (1991) *The State of the Economy 1991* (London: Institute of Economic Affairs).

Chrystal, A. (1992) 'The Fall and Rise of Saving', *National Westminster Bank Quarterly Review* (February).

Crafts, N. (1993) *Can De-Industrialisation Seriously Damage Your Wealth?* (London: Institute of Economic Affairs).

Craven, B. and R. Gausden (1991) 'How Best to Measure Inflation? The UK and Europe', *The Royal Bank of Scotland Review* (June).

Cullison, W. (1990) 'Is Saving Too Low in the United States?', *Economic Review* (May/June).

Eltis, W. (1991) 'United Kingdom Investment and Finance', Chapter 3 in M. Boleat *et al.*, *The State of the Economy 1991* (London: Institute of Economic Affairs).

Eltis, W., D. Fraser, and M. Ricketts (1992) 'The Lessons from the Superior Economic Performance of Germany and Japan', *National Westminster Bank Quarterly Review* (February).

Feinstein, C. and R. Mathews (1990) 'The Growth of Output and Productivity in the UK: the 1980s as a Phase of the Post-war Period', *National Institute Economic Review* (August).

Feldstein, M. and P. Baccheta (1989) 'National Saving and International Investment', *National Bureau of Economic Research, Working Paper*, 3164.

Gilbert, C. (1990) 'Primary Commodity Prices and Inflation', *Oxford Review of Economic Policy* (Winter).

Layard, R. and S. Nickell (1989) 'The Thatcher Miracle?', *American Economic Review, Papers and Proceedings* (May).

Lee, C. and W. Robinson (1990) 'The Fall in the Savings Ratio: the Role of Housing', *Fiscal Studies* (February).

Lipsey, R. and I. Kravis (1987) 'Is the US a Spendthrift Nation?', *National Bureau of Economic Research, Working Paper* 2274.

Muellbauer, J. (1991) 'Productivity and Competitiveness', *Oxford Review of Economic Policy*, 7 (3).

Nickell, S. (1990) 'Inflation and the UK Labour Market', *Oxford Review of Economic Policy* (Winter).

Oulton, N. (1990) 'Labour Productivity in UK Manufacturing in the 1970s and in the 1980s', *National Institute Economic Review* (May).

Roberts, P. (1989) 'Supply-side Economics', Chapter 3 in J. M. Buchanan *et al.* (eds), *Rea-*

ganomics and After (London: Institute of Economic Affairs).

The Economist (1992) 'Zero Inflation', 7 November.

van Ark, B. (1992) 'Comparative Productivity in British and American Manufacturing', *National Institute Economic Review* (November).

■ Chapter 4 ■

The Financial System

Peter Curwen

■ 4.1 Financial Intermediation

In a primitive economic world those who have saved part of their income and who wish to **on-lend their savings** (the ultimate lenders), will meet together with those who wish to **borrow** for various reasons (the ultimate borrowers) and arrange a mutually agreeable price for the transfer of funds between them. However, in a sophisticated world such transfers are beset with difficulties; the lenders and borrowers may be geographically dispersed, the amounts which lenders wish to make available may not match the amounts which borrowers wish to borrow and the term to maturity of funds on offer may not match borrowers' requirements. In principle, the price charged for transfers of funds – **the interest rate** – can be adjusted to overcome most of these difficulties, but in many cases a mutually agreeable interest rate will not be forthcoming, and the transfers will not take place even though lenders wish to lend and borrowers wish to borrow. Financial intermediaries are needed to overcome this problem.

Any lender who has decided to hold a portfolio of financial assets has to balance a number of considerations in deciding which assets to hold. In the first place, he or she is concerned with the risk element in the loan, which arises either because he or she may need cash prior to an asset's redemption date or because even if an asset can be redeemed before maturity this may involve a partial loss. Furthermore, if relatively small sums are involved, these can generally be turned into only one or two different types of asset, thereby preventing the lender from holding a sufficiently diversified portfolio of assets to protect against a particularly bad performance or outright default by one type of asset held. Second, the lender is unlikely to want to lend for long periods, partly because it constrains the ability to spend as the opportunity arises. Finally, the individual lender is unlikely to be well-informed. It may prove a time-consuming and expensive process to find a borrower willing to match the characteristics of the loan, and indeed the lender may ultimately fail to do so.

It is equally true that potential borrowers may be unable to find lenders willing and able to match their requirements, which generally include a desire to borrow for long periods of time. At the end of the day these considerations, combined with the fact that the lender obviously wants to maximise the interest rate whilst the borrower wants to minimise it, severely constrain the volume of funds transferred directly between individuals.

It is also necessary to take account of **liquidity considerations**. Liquidity is concerned primarily with the speed with which any financial instrument can be turned into cash, or wholly liquid, form. But it is also important that the value of the instrument is preserved in the process. It is possible to sell most financial instruments in the open market for cash, but there is no guarantee that the exact face-value of the instrument will be repaid to its holder unless it is held to maturity. If it is sold prior to maturity, then its face-value will be determined by the face-value of newly-issued instruments having the same characteristics with respect, for example, to yield, maturity and risk. An early sale of any instrument may thus result in either a capital gain or a capital loss. Conventionally, any instrument issued with an original life-span of no more than 91 days is considered to be liquid, and this term also applies to any instrument which, irrespective of its original term to maturity, has less that 91 days left to maturity.

These matters can be addressed by an intermediary. The **law of large numbers** operates such that, whereas some liablilities to depositors need to be kept in cash or near-cash form to meet daily cash withdrawals, the rest can be on-lent to borrowers as long-term lending. As a consequence, the intermediary, unlike an individual, can create a balance sheet with its liablilities in relatively liquid forms and its assets (representing its claims on those to whom it lends) in relatively illiquid forms. Because it handles large numbers of loans, an intermediary must expect some borrowers to default. However, such defaults are very unlikely to put the intermediary at risk of going out of business. Hence, whereas the ultimate lender, in lending directly to one or a few individuals, faces the possibilty of a total default, he or she generally runs the risk of losing no more than a small proportion of his or her funds if the intermediary they are deposited with gets into difficulties. Furthermore, the rate of interest can be adjusted to take account of different degrees of risk when lending to different intermediaries.

It is important to note from this discussion that when funds are deposited with an intermediary the money is not, in the majority of cases, on-lent in exactly the same form to the ultimate borrower. Instead, the process of **funds transformation** takes place whereby the intermediary creates liabilities, in the form of claims against itself by the ultimate lender, having different characteristics to its assets in the form of its own claims against the ultimate borrowers. Sometimes one intermediary may on-lend to another, with the result that funds transformation takes place on more than one occasion as funds flow through the financial system, and in the process the ultimate lender becomes increasingly separated from the ultimate borrower.

In summary, the process of intermediation is as beneficial to lenders as it is to borrowers. On the one hand, as discussed above, lenders face a reduced risk; they can withdraw their money on demand or by giving relatively short periods of notice; they have to choose between only a small number of intermediaries; and they effectively obtain a share in a much more diversified portfolio than they could hold as individuals. On the other hand, the borrower knows where to go to get funds, and there are more funds available.

One final point which should be noted is that, whereas in principle the use of an intermediary might be expected to cause interest rates paid to depositors to fall and those charged to borrowers to rise (since the intermediary exists to make a profit by selling its services), this may well not happen in practice. The depositor faces a reduced risk of default, and therefore should accept a lower reward for the risk-taking element of the loan, so that even after adding the intermediary's mark-up the cost to the borrower may be lower than for a direct transfer from the ultimate lender.

4.2 Classifying Financial Intermediaries

The range of financial intermediaries in the UK is unusually varied. The first task, is, therefore, to determine the most coherent way to arrange them in classes for further analysis. There are two main considerations here. In the first place, monetary controls operate through intermediaries, and it would seem helpful to divide up intermediaries into those that are affected by controls (particularly over the money supply) and those that are not. In this respect, it was traditionally argued that intermediaries which can create credit (**banks**) should be distinguished from those which cannot create credit (**non-banks**).

The second consideration is that it is necessary to lay down in law what, for example, is or is not a bank so that appropriate prudential supervision can be exercised by the Bank of England (see discussion of the Banking Act 1987 below). Historically, these considerations did not create particular difficulties, but the 1980s witnessed much blurring of traditional distinctions between intermediaries, partly as a result of attempts to regulate particular institutions in the pursuit of money supply control. In September 1983 the Bank of England introduced a new classification system for banks which created three categories of **British bank**. The first category comprises the **retail banks**, as listed below. The second, categorised as **other British banks**, comprises primarily the subsidiaries of the clearing banks, while the third category comprises the **British merchant banks**. All other banks are categorised as **overseas banks**.

The banks can also be divided into those which conduct business primarily in the **retail** market – that is, branch banks handling vast numbers of small accounts – and those which conduct **wholesale** business, involving small numbers of very large transactions. The retail banks are mostly British, whereas the wholesale banks are mostly foreign. Most banks fall partly into both categories, so their classification is determined by their predominant form of business. The **discount houses** retain a separate classification.

However, many intermediaries are not banks as defined above. Whereas these can be lumped together as **non-bank financial intermediaries** (NBFI), some closely resemble banks in that they take in deposits, often via branch networks, while others conduct their business in quite different ways. The box below shows the full classification.

We now need to examine, albeit briefly, the individual components of the UK financial sector. At the heart of the sector lies the Bank of England, so we will start by discussing its role, subsequently moving on to look at the banks,

Banks	
Retail banks:	London clearing banks (5)
	Scottish clearing banks (3)
	Northern Ireland banks (4)
	Abbey National plc
	TSB Bank plc
	Co-operative Bank plc
	Yorkshire Bank plc
	Girobank plc
	Bank of England Banking Department
Wholesale banks:	Other British banks
	British Merchant banks
	Overseas banks
Discount houses	
Non-bank financial intermediates	
Other deposit-takers:	Building societies
	National Savings Bank
	Finance houses
Other NBFI:	Insurance companies
	Pension funds
	Investment trusts
	Unit trusts

both retail and wholesale, and the NBFI. We will then examine the capital market where equities and bonds are traded, before completing the discussion with an overview of how the sector has evolved in recent years and the changes that can be expected to take place in the near future.

■ 4.3 The Bank of England

The Bank of England (the Bank) is the central bank of the UK. It started life as a joint stock company in 1694, and in return for a large loan to the government was put in a privileged position which enabled it to become the largest private bank. It was subsequently authorised to hold the gold reserves of the banking system. In 1844 note-issuing powers were terminated other than via the Bank, which gradually became a monopoly supplier (other than in Scotland and Northern Ireland). It also increasingly stood prepared to maintain liquidity in the banking system. While not technically a public sector body until the passing of the Bank of England Act 1946, it had long been under the control of the Treasury (Chancellor of the Exchequer). It still retains today the residual part of its private sector clientele. It is managed by a Court of Directors, headed by the Governor, who are appointed by the Crown.

Since 1844 the Bank's balance sheet has been somewhat artificially divided into two halves, namely the **Issue Department** which is concerned with the issue of notes by the Bank, and the **Banking Department** which is concerned with everything else. Issue Department liabilities consist of notes in circulation, and its assets consist of an equivalent amount of government and other securities. Banking Department liabilities consist of public deposits (accounts of the government), bankers' deposits and reserves and other accounts. Bankers' deposits are either **operational** and used for inter-bank clearing, to equalise cashflows between banks and the government or to pay for the purchase of notes and coins, or **non-operational** cash-ratio deposits to comply with banking regulatory requirements. Banking Department assets consist of government securities, advances and other accounts, and premises, equipment and other securities which are primarily in the form of commercial bills.

4.3.1 Functions of the Bank of England

The Bank performs a wide variety of functions. It:

a   is reponsible for the issue of notes and coins;
b   acts as banker to the central government;
c   acts as banker to the banking sector;
d   manages the Exchange Equalisation Account (EEA);
e   advises the government on, and on behalf of the government carries out, its monetary policy;
f   supervises the banking sector.

These days, notes and coins are the proverbial 'small change' of the financial system, and are produced to meet demand rather than to implement policy. As banker to the government the Bank handles the daily net balances of government departments, financing them when they show a deficit and converting any surplus into repayments of debt. The balance sheet item 'public deposits' is normally kept as small as possible in order to minimise the need to issue – and pay interest on – new national debt. The Bank is responsible not only for debt transactions that arise in the present period, but also for managing all the outstanding debt from previous periods. This requires a continuous stream of transactions in both the bill market and in the market for longer-dated government securities, known as **gilt-edged** (or gilts for short). Most government debt instruments can be freely traded on the Stock Exchange and money markets, and can therefore be controlled for policy purposes in the manner set out below.

All clearing banks keep an account at the Bank through which pass the daily transfers of funds between public deposits and the accounts of the banks' customers, and also the daily transfers of funds from one bank to another for bank clearing purposes (plus the occasional purchase of notes and coins). These transfers utilise the bankers' operational balances at the Bank, which do not need to be particularly large as all daily cash flows are netted out.

The **Exchange Equalisation Account** contains the UK's gold and foreign currency reserves. These reserves are used periodically for intervention purposes in order to maintain the value of the exchange rate for sterling in accordance with the wishes of the government. If sterling is considered to be too high the Bank will sell sterling and buy foreign currencies. Sterling required for this purpose is obtained from the National Loans Fund which forms part of the public deposits. The Bank accordingly needs to keep accounts with a large number of overseas central banks.

Altogether, the Bank operates in three separate markets: **gilt-edged**, **discount** and **foreign exchange**. These operations collectively constitute the government's **monetary policy**. The Bank has always had the right to use its expertise to give advice to the government concerning the conduct of monetary policy, but it is nevertheless only the **government's agent,** and it is the Chancellor of the Exchequer, acting via the Treasury, who has ultimate responsibility for such policy. Confusion may arise in this respect because it is inevitably reported in the news that the Bank has taken particular actions in the gilt-edged or currency markets, but in so doing it is simply following instructions. Market interventions are, however, best performed at particular times and on a particular scale, and the Bank has considerable discretion in this respect since the Chancellor cannot be expected personally to keep the markets under continuous scrutiny.

The Bank has an important role to play in the gilt-edged market. The Bank also not merely issues gilts on behalf of the government, but underwrites the issues in that any unsold gilts are bought-in by the Issue Department for future resale. It buys and sells on a daily basis in order to ensure that there is a receptive market for large-scale holders of gilts, especially insurance companies and pension funds that may wish to adjust their portfolios. The Bank's operations also inevitably affect gilt-edged prices, and hence long-term interest rates. Until recently this was considered of great importance, because sales of gilts reduce the liquidity of the private sector and hence help to control the money supply.

The final, but increasingly vital, role of the Bank is to **supervise the banking sector** (and indirectly, in practice, other financial intermediaries). With such vast sums at stake confidence is all-important, and it is the Bank's job to set the rules and ensure fair play. It was not customary to question the Bank's ability to achieve this in the banking sector, although recent events such as the BCCI scandal have cast a cloud over the Bank's reputation in this respect. However, the increasing sophistication and diversity of non-banking activity did oblige the Bank to permit other regulatory bodies to take over some of its reponsibilities, for example the Securities and Investments Board (SIB) under the terms of the Financial Services Act 1986 (see **pp. 134**).

Banking supervision was first formalised under the Banking Act 1979 which allowed the Bank to authorise recognised banks and licensed deposit takers (which offered a narrower range of services). However, the collapse of Johnson Matthey Bankers in September 1984 set in train a reappraisal which resulted in the passing of the **Banking Act 1987,** which now treats all banks as a uniform category. In order for a bank to be authorised, it is required in particular that every director, controller and manager shall be a fit and proper person to hold that position; that the business of the bank be conducted prudently, especially in respect of capital adequacy, liquidity, and bad and doubtful debt provision; that proper systems of accounting and control are maintained; and that net assets are at least ECU (European Currency Unit) 5 million. If necessary, required standards can be adjusted in individual cases. The Bank can object to takeovers and mergers involving banks. The Bank must be notified if a bank becomes overexposed (borrowing in excess of 10 per cent of bank capital) to an individual borrower. A Board of Banking Supervision has been set up to give guidance on the development of the supervisory system.

In May 1993 it was revealed that the Bank had been clandestinely supervising a lifeboat operation at the end of 1991, which cost it £115 million in indemnities and subsidies given to bigger banks to persuade them to lend to a few small (unnamed) banks in difficulties. It was public knowledge that the Bank had cleared up the mess surrounding the National Mortgage Bank, had stepped in to save City Merchants Bank and had actively intervened when the local authorities withdrew funds from smaller banks during the fallout from the BCCI affair. Nevertheless, the fact that some 40 small banks had been in difficulties, and that perhaps five had to be saved from bankruptcy, came as something of a surprise to the financial markets.

Traditionally, monetary policy was heavily dependent upon **liquidity ratio controls.** This is no longer the case, and since 1982 no such controls have been enforced by the Bank. Individual banks are expected to maintain what they themselves consider to be a prudent level of liquidity, but the Bank requires that banks maintain systems for keeping proper checks on liquidity, and reserves the right to check up that this is the case.

In 1988 the Bank issued a consultative paper which contained a new set of tough proposals concerning bank liquidity. However, banks objected to being told what type of assets they had to hold, particularly since the Bank wanted them to include low-yielding Treasury bills. In addition, foreign banks complained that they were already subject to liquidity controls in their home countries. As a result, the Bank dropped the proposals in April 1990 on the grounds that the banking system was too diverse to be subjected to a common liquidity regime, and that the EC might soon be proposing its own regime.

The **Financial Services Act 1986** also led to a more formal regulation of the wholesale money markets. To become an approved institution a bank must pass a 'fit and proper' test covering ability to manage and capital adequacy, and agreement to abide by the 'London Code of Conduct'. The Bank also runs the scheme which insures depositors against the failure of an authorised bank.

In October 1990 the Bank issued a set of procedures which it wished banks to adopt when dealing with companies in a liquidity crisis. In particular, it encouraged creditor banks 'jointly [to] ensure that [a troubled company] has sufficient liquidity to continue trading until a considered view of its prospects can be reached'. The Bank was, however, at pains to emphasise that its purpose was to remind banks of traditional procedures rather than to recommence the policies of intervention forsaken during the 1980s.

4.3.2 Should the Bank be Independent?

As noted previously, the Bank is essentially an arm of government, and as such is one of the least independent central banks in the developed world. In recent months many voices have been raised in favour of granting more independence to the Bank. Such independence has two dimensions, namely political and economic. Political independence denotes that decisions can be made without interference by the government, and by implication that appointments to the governing board are not politically motivated. Economic independence denotes that monetary policy can be executed without fear of offsetting behaviour by the government.

The main justification for independence is that it will provide credibility to programmes for restraining inflation. This is linked to the Maastricht Treaty provisions for full monetary union (see **pp. 253-4**) which require that a European Central Bank (ECB) be set up that is constitutionally independent of member states and legally obliged to maintain price stability within the EU. Given the necessity for the ECB to operate via national central banks, it follows that they must themselves be independent prior to a member state embracing full monetary union.

At the time of writing the UK has withdrawn from the ERM and opted out of any formal obligation to proceed to full monetary union, hence there is considerable reluctance on the part of the government to loosen the apron strings which tie the Bank to the Treasury. The government is aware, for example, that this would remove any possibility of using inflation as a surrogate tax to supplement revenue when the borrowing requirement becomes excessive.

Alesina (1989) ranked central banks according to an index of independence, taking into account characteristics such as the formal institutional relationship between the government and the central bank, the presence of government officials on the bank's board and the existence of rules forcing the central bank automatically to print money to finance budget deficits. The study demonstrated that over the period 1973 to 1986 the least independent central banks were in Italy and Spain, whereas the most independent were in Switzerland and West Germany. Britain was included amongst those central banks with only a modicum of independence. Subsequent work has examined the relationship between independence, inflation and unemployment, as shown in **Figure 4.1**.

As can be seen, there was a close correlation between the index of independence and the rate of inflation, although this has weakened since 1988 which suggests that independence is by no means

Figure 4.1 *Central Bank Independence and Inflation/Unemployment*

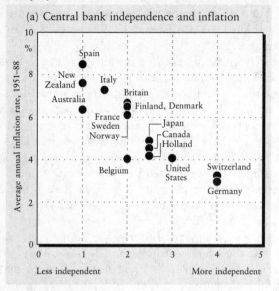

(a) Central bank independence and inflation

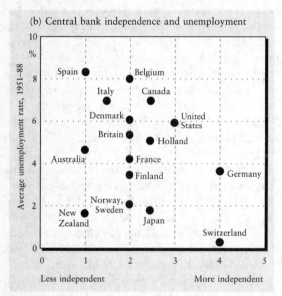

(b) Central bank independence and unemployment

Source: *The Economist*, 25 January 1992.

a necessary condition for success in suppressing inflation (as in respect of the UK and France). Furthermore, unemployment tended to be associated with highly independent banks, but the overall correlation was much weaker as was the case for the link between independence and growth. This suggests that inflation is affected

by expectations as to whether the central bank means what is says when it adopts a tough anti-inflationary stance, or whether it is expected to be told to relax its stance by politicians anxious to protect jobs. Given the position of Britain in **Figure 4.1**, it is understandable that there is a credibility problem in respect of monetary policy. The government's view is currently that the high level of home ownership makes changes in interest rates too sensitive an issue to be divorced from government control, and Blake and Westaway (1993) argue that there is little benefit in having an avowedly independent bank that is continuously at odds with the government's own policies.

■ 4.4 Banks in the UK

As previously discussed, there are two ways in which the banking sector can usefully be divided up for analytic purposes: namely, British/overseas and retail/wholesale. **Table 4.1**, parts (**a**) and (**b**), sheds considerable light on why these distinctions are useful. As shown in part (**a**), the total deposit liabilities of banks in the UK at the end of 1992 were £1 398 billion. Of this total, over £1 285 billion was recorded separately, either as sterling or foreign currency liabilities, whereas the rest was in a mixture of currencies. To those unfamiliar with the Eurocurrency markets (discussed below), it may come as a surprise to note that roughly 59 per cent of the £1 285 billion was in the form of non-sterling deposits.

The proportions are in practice somewhat variable, because they are a snapshot of the picture on one particular day which may be unrepresentative of the days which both precede and follow it. One reason for this is that wholesale banking tends to **respond to demand**: in other words, if there is a potential borrower for a very large sum of foreign currency at a particular point in time, the wholesale banks will go out and attract deposits of the same magnitude. One must also bear in mind that the valuation of foreign currency deposits varies according to movements in the exchange rate. It is thus quite possible to find the ratio between sterling and non-sterling deposits registering a much lower order of magnitude.

Table 4.1   (a) Banks in UK,[1] Deposit Liabilities at 30 December 1992

	Sterling deposit liabilities (a)		Foreign currency deposit liabilities (b)		Total deposit liabilities
	£ bn	%[2]	£ bn	%	£ bn[3]
Retail banks	318.2	75.9	100.8	24.1	492.0
British merchant banks[4]	33.3	62.9	19.6	37.1	61.6
Other British banks	31.6	80.2	7.8	19.8	49.5
American banks	13.0	14.4	77.5	85.6	93.4
Japanese banks	33.1	14.5	195.3	85.5	232.2
Other overseas banks[5]	100.4	22.1	354.4	77.9	469.5
Total	529.6	41.2	755.4	58.8	1398.2

Notes:
[1] As a result of the changes in the monetary sector culminating in the conversion of the Abbey National Building Society into a bank on 12 July 1989, the term 'monetary sector' was replaced by 'banks in the United Kingdom' or simply 'banks'.
[2] Expressed as percentage of (a) + (b) only.
[3] Including items in suspense and transmission, capital and other funds.
[4] Members of British Merchant Banking and Securities Houses Association (formerly the Accepting Houses Committee).
[5] Including consortium banks listed separately prior to August 1987.
Source: Calculations based on Bank of England data.

(b)

	% Banks in the UK sterling deposits	% Banks in the UK foreign currency deposits	% Banks in the UK total deposits[1]
Retail banks	60.1	13.3	32.6
Wholesale banks	39.9	86.7	67.4
British banks	72.3	17.0	39.8
Overseas banks	27.7	83.0	60.2

Note:
[1] Excluding items in suspense and transmission, capital and other funds.
Source: Calculations based on Bank of England data.

This ratio disguises the fact that the retail banks, which are primarily British banks with branch networks, conduct much more of their business in sterling than the wholesale banks. As shown in part (b) of **Table 4.1**, sterling deposits were fairly equally divided between retail and wholesale banks, whereas the latter took nearly 87 per cent of foreign currency deposits in the UK. Since the wholesale banks are mostly subsidiaries of foreign banks, it follows that the latter must take in the majority of all deposits and, as shown in **Table 4.1(b)**, the proportion was roughly 67 per cent of the total. Here again, the distinction between British banks taking in most of the sterling deposits, and overseas banks taking in an even bigger proportion of the foreign currency deposits, is particularly notable.

☐ 4.4.1 Retail Banks

The retail banks comprise primarily the clearing banks in England and Scotland and the Northern Ireland banks. There are also the TSB Bank, Abbey National, Yorkshire Bank, Co-op Bank and the Girobank which provide very similar services. The odd man out is the Bank of England Banking Department, which gets included in the statistics despite its quite different role (discussed above).

The typical retail bank is a clearing bank which provides services to individuals and firms through a branch network. The traditional side of the business is represented by current (sight) and deposit (time) accounts, provision of cheque books, clearing of cheques, overdraft facilities and personal loans, small currency transactions and a wide range of financial advice. In the 1980s there has been considerable innovation in the way that traditional services are provided, such as cheque-guarantee cards, automated teller machines (ATMs), Eurocheques and, most recently, new lines of business have been developed such as large-scale mortgage lending, managed unit trusts and share-dealing services.

All retail banks publish balance sheets to a set pattern, and their combined balance sheet as at 31 December 1992 is set out in **Table 4.2**. Retail banks do an increasing amount of wholesale business, as discussed below, but this is not distinguished separately in the balance sheet. The balance sheet ultimately represents a trade-off between a number of contradictory forces. On the one hand, retail banks are, with minor exceptions, obliged to make profits for shareholders, and high rates of return can be earned only by lending for longish periods of time and by taking a certain amount of risk. On the other hand, account holders constantly require cash to be made available, and other low-return assets may need to be held either for prudential reasons in order to avoid a possible loss of confidence by

depositors, or because it is so required by the Bank of England.

The balance sheet, both liabilities and assets, is divided into sterling and foreign currency categories. **Sterling deposits** are heavily dominated by the sight and time deposits of individuals and companies in the UK. Traditionally, the latter paid interest while the former did not, but sight deposits remained in the majority because they offered instant access whereas time deposits required notice of withdrawal. However, factors such as the provision of interest-bearing instant-access accounts by building societies eventually persuaded large numbers of depositors that only minimum sums should be kept in bank current accounts, and the banks were forced to respond by offering to forgo charges on such accounts provided, typically, they were kept in credit. As a result, time deposits lost their appeal, and sight deposits once again became equally popular.

In 1987 the Midland Bank introduced a **Vector account** which paid interest on accounts held in credit, but attracted few customers because interest earned was largely offset by account charges. The decision by Lloyds Bank in October 1988 to offer all of its customers an interest-bearing current account came as a considerable surprise, but once the Midland, Barclays, Royal Bank of Scotland and TSB Bank followed suit, this process became unstoppable. Indeed, in January 1989, Barclays went one stage further by abolishing charges for transactions on current accounts such as standing orders and cheques. The distinction between sight and time deposits will eventually appear to be no more than an historical anachronism, especially when it is borne in mind that the retail banks' wholesale business largely comprises interest-bearing sight deposits.

Wholesale deposits (listed as UK banks) have recently risen well above **deposits from overseas in sterling**, which are currently in decline. Wholesale deposits have fixed terms to maturity varying from days to years, and are paid a market-determined rate of interest which may therefore differ considerably from interest rates paid to individuals. Whereas wholesale deposits are still fairly modest, it must be recognised that there is intense competition for retail deposits and the retail

Table 4.2   *Retail Banks: Balance Sheet*

	31/12/88 (£ mn)	31/12/90 (£ mn)	31/12/92 (£ mn)
Sterling Liabilities			
Notes Issued	1 407	1 678	2 084
Deposits: UK banks	20 165	27 830	31 383
UK public sector	4 185	4 550	4 233
UK private sector	137 362	218 053[5]	237 471
Overseas	17 609	26 730	22 386
Certificates of deposit[1]	11 965	21 354	22 732
Other Currency Liabilities			
Deposits: UK banks	6 373	6 903	11 268
Other UK	6 883	10 371	15 402
Overseas	26 437	37 346	60 419
Certificates of deposit[1]	3 549	6 690	13 666
Sterling and Other Currencies[2]	47 038	64 609	70 965
TOTAL LIABILITIES[3]	282 974	426 114	492 009
Sterling Assets			
Notes and Coins	3 375	3 926	4 293
Balances with Bank of England[4]	749	1 032	829
Market loans: Secured money with LDMA	5 220	7 375	4 947
Other UK banks	17 639	31 748	43 743
UK banks CDs	4 201	8 469	9 161
UK local authorities	738	226	297
Overseas	3 573	5 258	7 265
Bills: Treasury bills	1 502	2 469	1 762
Eligible local authority bills	388	31	24
Eligible bank bills	6 060	10 064	7 997
Other	137	150	217
Advances: UK public sector	702	527	348
UK private sector	147 920	234 239[5]	248 871
Overseas	5 284	4 599	2 380
Banking Dept. leading to central government (net)	956	1 657	1 227
Investments: British government stocks	3 547	3 226	2 571
Others	5 122	10 785	17 839
Other Currency Assets			
Market loans and advances: UK banks	10 007	9 395	16 911
UK bank CDs	178	736	729
UK public sector	–	18	2 575
UK private sector	7 648	10 980	12 541
Overseas	30 391	38 020	53 437
Bills	436	1 153	3 540
Investments	6 198	11 675	20 499
Miscellaneous (all currencies)	20 999	28 355	28 016
TOTAL ASSETS	282 974	426 114	492 009

Notes:
[1] And other short-term paper issued.
[2] Items in suspense and transmission, capital and other funds.
[3] Of which eligible liabilities amounted to £160 billion at end-1988; £249 billion at end-1990; £258 billion at end-1992.
[4] Including cash ratio deposits.
[5] These figures were affected significantly by the reclassification of existing business with Abbey National Group at 1 July 1989. This added roughly £30 billion to UK private sector sterling deposits, sterling advances and eligible liabilities.

Source: Bank of England.

banks, like all other intermediaries, can no longer rely on a sufficiently large inflow of retail deposits to meet their needs for on-lending particularly in, for example, the mortgage market.

Certificates of Deposit (CDs) are fixed-term deposits that are exchanged for a certificate issued by the bank which can be traded in the open market. Hence, although the deposit itself cannot be withdrawn before maturity, the original depositor can get at the cash much earlier by selling his or her CD, although he or she may well be obliged to sell it for less than its face value if interest rates have risen.

The large item, **sterling and other currencies**, includes items in suspense because, for example, of uncertainty about ownership, items being transferred between accounts and finally the capital injected into the banks by shareholders **plus** liabilities to bond holders. It is also the custom to itemise 'eligible' liabilities. These comprise all sterling deposits from non-bank sources with an original maturity of no more than two years; net inter-bank lending in sterling; sterling CDs issued **less** sterling CDs held; any net deposit liabilities in sterling to overseas offices; and any net liabilities in currencies other than sterling **less** 60 per cent of the net value of transit items. Eligible liabilities were first introduced in 1971 for the purposes of monetary control, and since August 1981 all banks with eligible liabilities in excess of £10 million must hold 0.35 per cent of their eligible liabilities in the form of non-interest-bearing balances at the Bank of England. Although these were originally intended to operate as a cash-ratio monetary control mechanism, they currently serve only to provide the Bank of England with a free source of income to pay for its functions as the central bank.

Overall, the preponderance of instant-access or short-notice deposits means that retail bank liabilities are exceptionally liquid, and this inevitably has to be reflected in their asset portfolios. The liquid assets category includes, first, notes and coins (till money) plus balances at the Bank of England which are partly involuntary to finance the Bank, and partly voluntary to facilitate inter-bank clearing. Sterling market loans represent short-term money market lending, whether (a)

to the discount houses, (b) to the inter-bank market, (c) to another bank in return for that bank's CD, (d) to local authorities, or (e) to overseas individuals and banks.

Of these, inter-bank lending is by far the most important, although it is only in recent years that it has become so dominant. It represents transfers from banks which temporarily have an excess of liquidity to those which are temporarily short of funds (an especially useful practice in the days when monetary controls operated on bank liquidity, although this is no longer of any relevance). There is a speculative element, insofar as any bank which expects interest rates to rise can borrow for long periods in the hope that the money can be on-lent for an initial short period at current interest rates, and then re-lent subsequently for successive periods at higher rates, thereby earning a speculative profit. If interest rates are expected to fall, successful speculation would require the bank to borrow short, and subsequently to re-borrow more cheaply, while lending long at current rates.

Eligible bank bills are also prominent in the balance sheet. An eligible bill is one which the Bank of England will buy, via the discount houses, in order to make good a shortfall of cash in the banking sector. Only the bills issued by private companies, called **commercial bills**, which have been 'accepted' (guaranteed to be redeemed at face value) by major banks that fulfil specified requirements laid down by the Bank of England acquire the status of eligible bank bills. The government's own bills (Treasury bills) are obviously also eligible, as are certain bills issued by local authorities.

It is worth noting that when a bank buys a bill it is not redeemed at face value plus interest by its issuer, but rather the bank buys the bill at a discount to its face value and when it matures its issuer redeems it at face value. The difference between the price paid and the face value can then be divided by the price paid in order to convert the discount into a conventional rate of interest. Any discounted bill can be rediscounted any number of times: that is, it can be resold at a different price to another party who subsequently is paid the bill's face value if it is held to maturity. By rediscounting bills a bank can, therefore, hold a portfolio of bills some part of which matures on any given day of the year.

The bulk of bank lending to private individuals and firms is represented by UK **private sector advances**. Public sector advances are normally insignificant because lending to the government and local authorities is largely via discounting their bills, money market loans and the purchase of long-dated government securities (gilt-edged). Private sector advances are linked to bank base rates where modest sums are involved, but large loans are commonly linked to the central money market interest rate, known as the **London Inter-bank Offered Rate** (LIBOR). It is important also to note that traditionally the pattern of private sector sterling deposits and advances was one where the deposits of individuals were recycled into loans to firms. In 1978, individuals deposited three times as much as they borrowed. By 1988 these deposits had trebled, but their borrowing had risen nearly tenfold, and marginally exceeded these deposits. Since 1983 they have borrowed more than firms in aggregate.

Banking Department lending to central government represents the net contribution to the retail banking sector of the Banking Department of the Bank of England. As it retains certain long-standing private individual accounts these do need to be itemised as retail bank assets, but the major part, which represents transactions with government departments, is something of an anachronism in the balance sheet. This item is quite often negative, which simply means that government departments have more money on deposit than they are borrowing at that point in time.

Foreign currency assets are almost entirely in the form of inter-bank lending within the UK and of lending to overseas residents, companies and especially banks. It may finally be noted that the fixed assets of retail banks, in the form primarily of property, are not separately itemised because of their relatively modest value.

In conclusion, we may note that the pattern of the retail banks' balance sheet is constantly evolving. In particular, the difficulty of attracting adequate retail funds has driven banks into the wholesale markets where interest rates are linked to LIBOR, and this has to be balanced by increased LIBOR-linked lending. The problem is accentuated by the need to pay interest on sight deposits which were traditionally a free source of funds. Furthermore, the retail banks are obliged to hold some non-interest earning assets in the form of bankers' balances. These factors, combined with a very expensive branch network and with severe losses on many of their loans have understandably made considerable inroads into their profitability, and they have increasingly seen the solution as a movement away from traditional banking services and towards other financial services – that is, banks as financial supermarkets.

☐ 4.4.2 Retail Banks in Transition

Retail banks have acquired an unenviable reputation for losing money. It all began when they decided that sovereign states would not default on their debts. Unfortunately, the rulers of many of these states decided that they could do as they pleased, which in many cases was not to repay. Then the banks decided that property lending must be sound because it was secured by real assets, which in many cases subsequently proved to be unsaleable except at bargain basement prices. Then they advanced money for highly-leveraged management buy-outs in the expectation that the junk bonds (very high yielding but risky) they obtained in return would indeed yield a high return once the company taken over was broken up and resold. In many cases, they were wrong again (see **4.4.5** below).

So then they decided to engage in devices to abolish risk such as swaps (discussed below), only to discover that they **shifted risk** – in the case of LA swaps, on to themselves – but they did not **abolish** it. Finally, they decided to create financial services empires by buying estate agency chains – just in time for the housing market to collapse – and insurance companies. Whereas it is theoretically possible to make a loss in the life and pensions business if too many customers die at the wrong time or surrender their policies, if expenses go out of the control or if investment returns deteriorate, it had always been difficult to do so in the past. Nevertheless, the TSB paid £227 million for Target Life in August 1987, only to end up selling it for a loss in excess of £200 million to Equity and Law in January 1991. It then followed this up by shutting down its centralised mortgage lending arm, Mortgage Express (the third largest of its kind established in 1986), in April 1991 because it was unsaleable.

The TSB experience was not all that unusual, and the losses sustained in estate agency were by no means confined to banks. In March 1993 Abbey National put its 355 branch Cornerstone network, in which it had invested £226 million since 1987, up for sale for roughly £35 million. It remained unsold in September. Meanwhile TSB admitted to huge losses on its chain, as did Lloyds in respect of its Black Horse Agencies.

The consequences were fairly predictable in that the banks had to slash their branch networks and their staff. Overall, some 13 000 banking jobs were shed in 1990, 26 000 in 1991 and 30 000 in 1992. Another 30 000 are expected to disappear in 1993. In 1987 the big four banks had 10 300 branches, but will be left with roughly 8500 at the end of 1993. This process is likely to continue since the UK remains 'overbanked' by international standards. For example, there is one branch per 1400 people in Britain compared with one per 2200 in France and one per 3000 in Italy.

Banks are also having to rethink their global strategies. As retail banks have discovered, often to their cost, banking remains largely a domestic business, and cultural, tax and regulatory obstacles have so far prevented the creation of a single market in the EU despite the directives discussed below. The banks' attitude to their US operations has been particularly ambivalent. At the end of the 1980s such large losses were being sustained that withdrawal was the key concern, with Barclays completing its withdrawal in May 1992. However, with bad debts mounting up at home, US subsidiaries have once again begun to look attractive.

There is plenty of fat still to be trimmed in banking. The Halifax Building Society, for example, has far fewer branches and employees per customer than the retail banks. Furthermore, the banks' tribulations are creating more problems for the future. The retail banks have mostly been downgraded from AAA status by the main credit-rating agencies, and as a result their borrowing costs have risen. More importantly, many blue-chip companies now have a higher rating, and hence can save money by going directly to the money markets rather than by operating through the banks.

Over the past year the reputation of the banks has been damaged by a stream of adverse publicity, related in particular to accusations that they have profited from falling base rates by failing to pass on the benefits to small-business customers. A Bank of England study published in January 1993 refuted these claims, but was widely regarded as a whitewash. The banks' greatest concern currently is whether to reintroduce charges on accounts in credit (some 60–70 per cent of the total). In June 1993 National Westminster introduced penal charges on current account holders who overdraw substantially without authority, thereby temporarily opting to penalise their most unprofitable customers. However, with banks allegedly losing money on 80 per cent of their current accounts, the burning issue is whether they are willing to court further unpopularity in order to restore their finances.

4.4.3 Basel (Basle) Capital Convergence Accord

In July 1988 the Governors of the Group of Ten central banks signed the Basel Capital Convergence Accord, thereby making banking the first industry to be regulated on a world-wide basis. The central purpose of the Accord (which is not, however, legally binding) is to force all international banks to comply with minimum capital requirements, and thereby to **ensure fair competition between them**. So far the Accord only covers credit risk but, while it is true that non-repayment of domestic and international loans has been the biggest risk faced by banks, other sources of risk, such as those associated with exchange rate and interest rate variability, need to be added to the

Accord and are currently under discussion, as noted below.

The Accord essentially lays down a definition of **capital** and a formula for working out how much of it banks must have, depending upon the **riskiness** of their assets. The definition was complicated by different practices in different countries, but needed to identify capital **permanently available to meet losses**. In the UK, banks are financed with both equity and debt, but German banks have very little of the latter. Equally, US banks issue 'perpetual preferred stock' (PPS) which is neither one nor the other. In the event, a compromise was reached whereby **at least 50 per cent** of capital must be tier 1 or 'core' capital, comprising equity, disclosed reserves and PPS (but only if it is non-cumulative, meaning that failure to pay dividends in one year must not create an obligation to make them up in later years). Tier 2 includes long-term debt and other debt instruments.

The other complication concerned the 'risk weighting' of assets. Risk assets comprise all bank assets, including off-balance sheet commitments, weighted according to their riskiness. The UK, as a full member of the OECD, is deemed to be a low-risk borrower, as are other OECD members (with the possible exception of Turkey) plus Saudi Arabia. Bank lending to other countries is deemed to be at greater risk. All commercial lending is deemed to be at equal risk, irrespective of the size of the borrowing company, in order to avoid vast numbers of individual decisions about credit-worthiness.

Every bank had until 1991 or early 1993 to meet its minimum '**risk asset ratio**', which could be imposed at a level higher than that of the Accord if individual countries so wished. The Accord itself requires that capital must be equivalent to at least 8 per cent **of a bank's risk-weighted assets**, together with a minimum tier 1 ratio of 4 per cent. These ratios are sometimes known as the BIS (Bank for International Settlements) ratios. The Bank of England decided, however, not to leave matters to chance and to a last-minute cleaning-up of banks' balance sheets, and accordingly announced in November 1988 that UK banks would have to meet the Accord stipulations by the end of 1989, well in advance of most other signatories.

In practice, UK banks have had little difficulty in meeting their ratios via retained earnings and modest rights issues, as shown in **Figure 4.2**. Oddly enough, it is the big Japanese city (commercial) banks which have got problems. At the end of the 1980s, 9 out of the biggest 10 banks in the world and 23 out of the biggest 30 were Japanese. Several were bigger, in market capitalisation terms, than the entire British banking industry. They were permitted to count 45 per cent of the investment gains on shareholdings as capital, and the booming Tokyo Stock Market was viewed as an effective guarantor that their ratios would be easy to safeguard. The enormous fall in the Nikkei index during 1990 proved how vulnerable they were in reality.

There is still room for improvement in implementing the ratio. It is argued that the necessity to retain capital equal to 8 per cent of commercial loans compared to zero for cash, 10 per cent for Treasury bills and 20 per cent for gilts has undesirably distorted lending away from the former category. It is also alleged that it makes little sense to treat all commercial loans as equally risky since this may incline banks to divert scarce capital away from blue-chip companies to others where the capital is, in reality, much more at risk. Also, the fact that loans secured on residential property require only half as much capital as commercial loans will inevitably make it harder to suppress asset price inflation.

At the end of April 1993 the Basel Committee recommended that from January 1994 banks should set aside less capital when they have arrangements with other banks for netting out liabilities. It also recommended that, commencing in 1997, banks should set aside extra capital to cover the market risks they run in respect of operations in derivatives markets. It may be difficult to get this proposal accepted as it will put bank ratios under further pressure.

☐ *4.4.4 Directives*

As with other parts of the financial system the banks have had to come to terms with a stream of EU directives. A first step was taken in 1977 with

Figure 4.2   *Bank Capital Ratios*

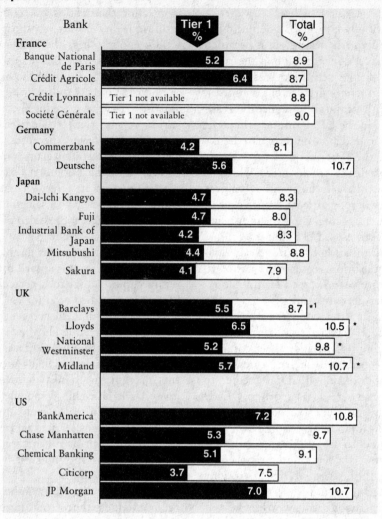

Bank	Tier 1 %	Total %
France		
Banque National de Paris	5.2	8.9
Crédit Agricole	6.4	8.7
Crédit Lyonnais	Tier 1 not available	8.8
Société Générale	Tier 1 not available	9.0
Germany		
Commerzbank	4.2	8.1
Deutsche	5.6	10.7
Japan		
Dai-Ichi Kangyo	4.7	8.3
Fuji	4.7	8.0
Industrial Bank of Japan	4.2	8.3
Mitsubishi	4.4	8.8
Sakura	4.1	7.9
UK		
Barclays	5.5	8.7 [*1]
Lloyds	6.5	10.5 [*]
National Westminster	5.2	9.8 [*]
Midland	5.7	10.7 [*]
US		
BankAmerica	7.2	10.8
Chase Manhatten	5.3	9.7
Chemical Banking	5.1	9.1
Citicorp	3.7	7.5
JP Morgan	7.0	10.7

Tier 1: – ordinary shares
– non-cumulative
  preference shares
– retained earnings

Tier 2: upper Tier 2 – perpetual subordinated
  debt
lower Tier 2 – subordinated debt
  – provisions[2]
  – hidden reserves[2]
  – other reserves[2]

Notes:
[1] 1991 unless *1992.
[2] Depends on national interpretation.
Source: Financial Times, 31 December 1992, updated.

the adoption of the **First Banking Co-ordination Directive** which required all 'credit institutions' to be authorised and monitored. The **Second Banking Co-ordination Directive** followed in 1989, and came into force on 1 January 1993. This provided a passport for credit institutions to supply certain services throughout the EU once authorised in the home state.

On 3 January 1991, the Bank of England adopted two directives which govern banks' capital and the size of their balance sheets. The directives also affect building societies, but in that case implementation is the reponsibility of the Building Societies Commission. The **Solvency Ratio Directive** lays down a formula for calculating how large a balance sheet a credit institution can run, based on the riskiness of its assets and the size of its capital. It sets a minimum ratio of capital to assets of 8 per cent. The **Own Funds Directive** states how a credit institution's capital is to be calculated. These directives came into force on 1 January 1993. The two directives were essentially a reiteration of the Basel capital adequacy provisions, and hence did not require major policy changes since the banks were already operating under the Basel provisions.

The **Large Exposures Directive** is to come into effect on 1 January 1994, and will harmonise the rules which cover the exposures of credit institutions to individual borrowers or groups of connected clients.

4.4.5 International and Domestic Bad Debts

The analysis of the international debt problem is more appropriately left to Chapter 6. At this juncture it is appropriate simply to clarify the previous reference to its impact on banking practice. It was clear by the early 1980s that a good deal of the money lent to less developed countries (LDCs) would never be repaid even if these countries did not officially renege on their debts (see **pp. 230–3**). However, banks which had become heavily involved in this lending – possibly because of the fanciful idea that sovereign country debt is more secure than lending to households and firms, but also because it gives a measure of status to a bank to be the banker to a sovereign state – were unwilling to write the debt off their balance sheets for fear that it would expose their inadequate capital structure. Initially, the common practice was to convert short-term loans into long-term loans, and to set aside some of the profits earned on other business into a reserve fund to cover international bad debts. Where possible, the capital base of a bank was replenished by an additional issue of equity, and it was possible to offset some losses against tax liabilities.

In 1987 the international banks, following the example set in America, decided to bite the bullet and write a significant part of the debt off their balance sheet. Nevertheless, it remained understandably difficult for banks to raise new capital in the markets, especially in the aftermath of the October 1987 crash. In 1989, Lloyds' cover for problem country debts was raised to 47 per cent, well above that for the other three which stood at between 31 and 22 per cent in 1988. Since that time all the banks have seen fit to make additional provisions, so that there will be no further need to make major provisions against defaulting sovereign debt.

Unfortunately, as previously mentioned, there are plenty of other non-performing loans to take its place. They stem primarily from increased participation in highly-leveraged transactions and increased exposure to the property sector. These appeared to be commercially sound in the boom conditions of the late 1980s, but rebounded on the banks with the arrival of high interest rates and recession. This can be seen in **Figure 4.3**, which covers the period to 1991. **Table 4.3** extends the provisions for most major banks into 1992, and also indicates the variable performance during that financial year, with Barclays notably registering its first ever pre-tax loss.

4.4.6 Wholesale Banks

As shown in **Table 4.1(a)**, at the end of 1992 the total deposit liabilities of the wholesale banks amounted to some £906 billion, of which some £794 billion was held at overseas banks. Collectively, therefore, wholesale banks greatly outweigh retail banks, but as there are 600 or so such banks currently in operation in the UK, their individual portfolios are on average much smaller than those of the typical retail bank.

Figure 4.3 *Provisions and Write-offs in Large British Banks*[1]

Note:
[1] Barclays, Lloyds, Midland, National Westminster, Bank of Scotland, Royal Bank of Scotland, Standard Chartered, TSB.

Source: Bank of England Quarterly Bulletin.

Table 4.3 *Bank Results, 1992.*

	Pretax profits (£mn)		Dividend (P)		Debt Provisions (£mn)	
	1992	1991	1992	1991	1992	1991
Barclays	−242	533	15.15	21.16	2554	1758
Abbey National	564	618	11.5	10.5	322	158
Lloyds	801	625	18.4	16.7	736	918
HSBC (Midland)	178	36	Not quoted		676	903
NatWest	405	110	17.5	17.5	1903	1875
TSB	43	−47	6.4	6.4	597	654
Bank of Scotland	125	141	4.6	4.4	372	257

Source: Company Reports.

Wholesale banks concern themselves with small numbers of large-scale transactions. Deposits of less than £100 000 are unlikely to be accepted, and these deposits are often parcelled up into even larger loans. Deposits are not normally withdrawable on demand, so there is no need to keep anything like the same degree of cash and near-cash reserves as retail banks. Furthermore, it is possible to supplement liquidity by borrowing in the inter-bank market or through issuing certificates of deposit. Because each deposit is in a specific currency (mostly non-sterling – see **pp. 126–8** for a discussion of the Eurocurrency markets), and the depositor can specify the term to maturity, wholesale banks need to find borrowers who want the same currencies for as near as possible the same periods of time. A perfect match between assets and liabilities is, however, rarely possible because of the preference among lenders to lend for periods of time which are shorter than the periods over which borrowers prefer to borrow, and there are obvious problems in matching currencies. The characteristic transaction of a wholesale bank is, therefore, quite different from that of a retail bank, but this has led to the main retail banks setting up wholesale banking subsidiaries in order to diversify their pattern of business, so there are in practice more links between the two banking sectors than may at first seem apparent.

British Merchant Banks

The British merchant banks are distinguished from other British wholesale banks by virtue of their membership of the British Merchant Banking and Securities Houses Association. Their former name of 'accepting houses' arose from the traditional practice of 'accepting' commercial bills, which effectively guarantees repayment in full upon maturity and hence both makes the bills easier to market and reduces the discount which needs to be offered. Some bills are retained for their own portfolios, but this type of agency business is no longer all that important.

Currently banking activity is almost entirely wholesale rather than retail. The total deposit liabilities are modest by wholesale banking standards, and are generally divided between sterling and foreign currencies in approximately a 60:40 ratio. Both deposits originating overseas and from the inter-bank markets (UK banking sector) have become increasingly prominent. Assets are correspondingly distributed, with the bulk of sterling assets in the form of loans to the UK inter-bank market and advances to UK borrowers, and the greater part of foreign currency assets in the form of lending abroad, especially to foreign banks. Lending to non-bank customers is relatively unimportant and, as indicated above, very little cash is held.

British merchant banks are also significant providers of financial services. Many undertake reponsibilty for all the administrative aspects of issuing new equity; provide a wide range of banking services for companies and some wealthy individuals; act as management consultants with respect to, for example, mergers and takeovers; and provide portfolio management services for pension funds and, in certain cases, unit trusts and investment trusts.

Other British Banks

The typical other British bank, so categorised because whereas it is registered in the UK it does most of its business with overseas clients, is considerably smaller than the typical British merchant bank. Of the 200 or more such banks, the core group comprises long-standing institutions originally set up to facilitate retail banking in British colonies. This has understandably not been a a growth area for some time, and this category now includes a number of the smaller UK banks which offer a restricted range of services, including some which, although not officially merchant banks, provide almost identical services. Since the Banking Act 1979 took them within its provisions, many former finance houses have also operated in this category, competing directly with organisations listed separately under the heading.

The total deposit liabilities of other British banks are no longer greater than those of the British merchant banks, and there are considerable similarities in the respective balance sheets.

Other British banks do not, however, hold many acceptances.

☐ *4.4.7 Overseas Banks*

A number of American and European banks have had a London office for many decades in order to provide services for their customers while in the UK. However, the number of overseas banks has grown enormously over the past two decades, initially as a result of the growth of Eurocurrency markets, and more recently as a result of financial deregulation.

As shown in **Table 4.4**, there were 494 overseas banks in London in 1992, a gain of roughly 100 since 1981. The invasion was originally spearheaded by American banks, although their numbers peaked in 1982 and are now fewer than those of Japanese banks which have more than doubled since 1980, with departures commencing only in 1990.

As shown in **Table 4.1**(a), whereas the American banks alone still have deposit liabilities of £93 billion, equal to over 85 per cent of the combined liabilities of British merchant banks and other British banks, this represents only 40 per cent of the liabilities of the Japanese banks, which are mostly comparative newcomers to London. The Japanese banks in 1988 had deposit liabilities virtually equal to those of the retail banks and it was thought that they would soon overtake them, but in the event the sterling liabilities of the retail banks shot up as did deposits at other (non-American) overseas banks. The latter currently exceed the deposits of Japanese banks by a wide margin. As **Table 4.4** indicates, this has resulted from the huge influx of European banks (82 net between 1979 and 1989), with a significant surge after the Single European Act in 1986.

The Eurocurrency markets are discussed separately below, and it is necessary to note at this stage only that the enormous growth in **international money** (for example, dollars traded outside America) was particularly centred in London, so all the important overseas banks necessarily had to open an office there to participate on any scale in these markets. American banks, in particular,

Table 4.4   Foreign Banks in London

	US			Europe			Japan			Arab			Others			Summary		
	Total	Out	In	Total	Out	In	Total	Out	In	Total	Out	In	Total	Out	In	Total	Out	In
1980	71	2	1	141	3	21	24	0	0	19	0	1	128	3	12	383	8	35
1981	73	1	3	147	2	8	25	0	1	23	0	4	131	5	8	399	8	24
1982	77	0	4	153	0	6	29	0	4	26	0	3	144	1	14	429	1	31
1983	76	2	1	165	3	15	31	0	2	28	0	2	145	2	3	445	7	23
1984	75	1	0	168	6	9	35	0	4	35	0	7	146	2	3	459	9	23
1985	70	7	2	169	0	1	38	0	3	34	2	1	143	5	2	454	14	9
1986	68	3	1	184	3	18	40	0	2	34	2	2	136	8	1	462	16	24
1987	64	5	1	190	5	11	46	0	6	33	1	0	131	6	1	464	17	19
1988	59	8	3	201	5	16	50	0	4	36	1	4	132	3	4	478	17	31
1989	57	4	2	204	6	9	50	0	0	35	1	0	136	1	5	482	12	16
1990	53	4	0	207	10	13	51	2	3	34	1	0	133	6	3	478[1]	23	19
1991	49	5	1	209	8	10	54	1	4	36	0	2	146	1	14	494	15	31
1992	45	5	1	202	12	5	52	2	0	40	1	5	155	2	11	494	22	22
Total		47	20		63	142		5	33		9	31		45	81		169[2]	307

Notes:
[1] Comparable figures for Paris and Frankfurt were 277 and 247 respectively.
[2] Many of these departments were due to mergers of foreign banks.

Source: Noel Alexander Associates.

were drawn to London by a desire to avoid the much tighter regulations in their domestic markets. Because American and Japanese banks have been at the forefront of developments in electronic banking, they have been particularly well placed to take advantage of the recent deregulation of financial services, and their recent movement into, for example, the mortgage market has had profound effects upon traditional practices in the UK. No doubt overseas banks will steadily encroach upon other areas of business, such as corporate finance, and given that their deposits are backed by the vastly greater assets of the parent companies, they look set to play an increasingly dominant role.

As shown in **Table 4.2** (a), the overseas banks do the vast bulk of their business in **foreign currencies**. Their deposits, unsurprisingly, largely come from overseas, and mostly from parent organisations. Around one-third of their sterling deposits also come from overseas, and most of what remains is borrowed in the UK inter-bank markets which also provide over 15 per cent of foreign currency deposits. On the assets side of the balance sheet there are minimal amounts of cash and balances held at the Bank of England, but massive amounts of foreign currency lending to overseas residents, a great deal of which is routed via overseas banks. Inter-bank lending is very important, both in sterling and foreign currencies. As with other categories of wholesale banks, almost exactly the same amount is borrowed from the inter-bank markets as is lent to them. Apart from the modest net effect of retail bank operations in the inter-bank markets, it is simply a matter of definition that total lending must be equal to total borrowing, and the very large sums being transferred represent either portfolio adjustments by individual banks (for example, adjustment of maturity profiles) or simply opportunities which individual banks have to borrow from other banks with no immediate customers and to on-lend at a profit. Because wholesale banking is in aggregate so much larger than retail banking, the small proportion of assets held in sterling still represents a far from modest amount of lending. Whereas they are clearly more than happy to compete for sterling business in the

UK, they do not as yet show any real interest in operating outside London, and this is why one gets the impression, even in the largest provincial cities, that the UK retail banks are the only major banking intermediaries.

☐ *4.4.8 The Discount Market*

The discount market is a money market, the membership of which was until recently restricted to the eight discount houses which were members of the London Discount Market Association (LDMA), of which seven currently remain in business. The nature of their business can be clearly seen in the LDMA balance sheet which consists almost exclusively of sterling liabilities in the form of funds borrowed 'at call' (recallable without notice) and overnight. These funds, as we have seen, represent the most liquid asset except for cash itself in the retail banks' balance sheet. On the assets side of the balance sheet are to be found very little bar sterling-denominated short-term assets.

The functions of the discount market are to make a market in bills of all kinds, to give the banking sector a means by which they can replenish their cash holdings virtually on demand and to assist in the financing of short-term trade debts through the purchase of discounted commercial bills from banks and their customers. The discount houses are also committed to tender for the whole of every issue of Treasury Bills (TBs) in order to guarantee that government departments can pay their way, but they can be outbid, and indeed holdings of TBs have fallen to quite modest levels.

The LDMA, in essence, exists to maintain liquidity in the financial system. There are vast amounts of short-term instruments in existence, and the LDMA effectively guarantees that they can be bought and sold freely, thereby greatly reducing the need for cash holdings. At the end of daily cheque clearing, for example, some banks will have cash surpluses which can earn interest, albeit at very low rates, by being placed in the discount market, while the others can find on the spot the cash which is needed to settle deficits.

The discount market also has an important role to play in the conduct of monetary policy. Every day, money flows between government departments and the clearing banks via accounts held at the Bank of England. On any given day this may result in a very large net cash flow in one direction or the other. If government departments have drawn heavily on cash held at the clearing banks, the banks will have to go immediately to the discount market to replenish their cash holdings. With cash in short supply, short-term interest rates will have to rise rapidly to attract sufficient cash into the market. Conversely, if the clearing banks are flush with cash, which is then deposited in the discount market, the LDMA will have to bid for short-term assets, causing their prices to rise and their yields to fall.

If short-term interest rates become very volatile, this will quickly be transmitted to longer-term interest rates and to the exchange rate. In order to avoid this, the Bank of England stands ready to smooth cash flows between government departments and the clearing banks. If the banks have too much cash the Bank will mop it up by selling eligible bills to the LDMA, and if there are cash shortages the Bank will buy eligible bills in return for cash. This is called an OMO. While it is the case that the Bank of England is willing on occasion to deal directly with financial intermediaries other than the LDMA, it is formally the case that only the LDMA may go to the Bank for funds when they cannot be obtained from any other source.

An OMO in the discount market therefore provides the means whereby the Bank can influence short-term interest rates. Since August 1981 the procedure has been as follows. When cash is in short supply the Bank will invite the LDMA to sell eligible bills. If their selling price is acceptable to the Bank it will buy the bills and relieve the cash shortage. However, if the price is unacceptable, it will ask the LDMA to re-offer at a different price, thereby raising or lowering the interest rate as appropriate. The same procedure can be used if the Bank offers to sell eligible bills in order to mop up surplus cash.

If the Bank was, exceptionally, to refuse to buy bills at any price offered by the discount houses, then it would leave them with no option but to ask for a 'lender-of-last-resort' loan from the Bank, and the Bank would be able to charge any interest rate that it wished as a condition for making the cash available. The significance of this procedure is that the money markets cannot know for certain, in advance of the Bank's reponse to an offer to buy or sell eligible bills, what the Bank's views are about the appropriate level for short-term interest rates. The money markets are constantly nudging short-term interest rates up and down, but the Bank can signal its desire either to see these rate movements go beyond the limits set by the market, or the restoration of rates previously prevailing. By behaving in this way the Bank does not seek to dominate the markets on a continuous basis, as was the practice throughout most of the period prior to 1981, but rather to give clear guidance to the markets as and when it is considered to be appropriate.

4.5 Non-bank Financial Intermediaries

☐ 4.5.1 Building Societies

The building societies began life as terminating societies, which lasted as long as it took to build houses for all of the members. Over time they became permanent, and came to monopolise a particular form of financial service. Modern societies are **mutual organisations**, which bring together the generally modest savings of large numbers of individuals and parcel them up into a much smaller number of mortgages. Savers' accounts are known as **shares** and **deposits**. Shareholders do not, however, share in a society's profits, but by virtue of being society members can vote at annual general meetings on such issues as conversion to banking status (see below). Interest rates are slightly lower on deposit accounts, which have the balancing advantage of priority in repayment if a society goes bankrupt. This is not generally thought to be much of a risk, so there are understandably several times as many shareholders as depositors.

Table 4.5 *Building Society Statistics (End-year)*

	1960	1970	1975	1980	1985	1990[1]	1991[1]	1992[1]
Number of societies	726	481	382	273	167	117	110	105
Number of branches	N/A	2016	3375	5684	6926	6055	5921	5765
Number of shareholders (mn)	3.9	10.3	17.9	30.6	40.0	37.0	37.9	37.5
Number of depositors (mn)	0.6	0.6	0.7	0.9	2.1	4.3	4.7	3.9
Number of borrowers (mn)	2.4	3.7	4.4	5.4	6.7	6.7	7.0	7.1
Number of advances in year (mn)	0.4	0.6	0.8	0.9	1.7	1.4	1.5	1.2
Volume of advances in year (£ bn)	0.6	2.0	4.9	9.5	26.5	43.1	43.0	35.0

Note:
[1] Excluding Abbey National plc.
Source: Housing Finance (formerly the *BSA Bulletin*) (August 1993).

During the 1970s the societies faced little competition from the banks, which thought mortgage lending to be too long-term; they did not enjoy the composite tax rate arrangement which cheapened the cost of funds to societies; they had, unlike the societies, to build a profit margin into the interest rate charged; and they had their aggregate lending constrained by monetary controls. The societies chose to avoid competition amongst themselves by operating an **interest rate cartel**, and mortgage lending was heavily constrained by the inflow of retail funds in the absence of access to wholesale markets.

None of these considerations any longer apply. Building societies both compete amongst themselves for business, and are under attack not merely from the 'clearing' banks, but also from the foreign banks and the mortgage corporations which keep down costs by having no branch network. When funds were in short supply, large-scale borrowing attracted an interest rate penalty. Currently, the larger the loan the cheaper it tends to be, as funds from the wholesale markets appear to be almost limitless. Faced with bank encroachment upon their traditional business, the societies have responded by encroaching on the business of the banks.

Table 4.5 provides an interesting historical snapshot of the building society sector. The number of societies has dropped dramatically since 1960, and although the rate of reduction has necessarily slowed down, the process of merger is still continuing. Assets are thus concentrated in the hands of a relatively small number of societies, many of which are huge by historical standards. As the number of societies shrank so they snapped up sites in every High Street in the land, a process which peaked in the mid-1980s when there were twice as many branches as a decade earlier. This process is now beginning to reverse itself as societies seek to economise on their operations, but the biggest reduction in 1989 resulted from the transfer of Abbey National's branches to the banking sector.

This also cut back the number of shareholders which peaked at 44 million in 1988. This is rather astonishing given the size of the population, but many people hold accounts at several societies. In a given year only a fraction of these accounts are active, and many lie dormant for years on end, but the number of active accounts has nevertheless risen sharply since the passing of the Building Societies Act 1986. The number of borrowers has grown more steadily (adjusting for Abbey National), but whereas the amount borrowed only rose by a factor of less than 5 during the highly inflationary 1970s because inflows to societies were limited, it trebled during the first half of the 1980s alone in the face of much tougher competition from other lenders. This reflected much sharper increases in house prices than in retail prices in general, together with an enormous influx of money into the mortgage market. Had it not been for the exclusion of Abbey National, the sums advanced would probably have doubled again by the end of the decade.

Not surprisingly, this was financed mainly from share and deposit account liabilities. These stood at £50 billion in 1980, and at the time this represented over 90 per cent of total liabilities. By 1988 deposit liabilities stood at £151 billion, but even so this represented less than 80 per cent of the total.

This is accounted for by the fact that in 1979 wholesale borrowing from the money markets was non-existent, yet in 1992 a total of £47.6 billion was being borrowed, representing some 18 per cent of the total. One can anticipate the continuance of this reduction in reliance upon retail deposits into the future.

The asset side of the balance sheet is dominated by mortgage lending (see **Table 4.6**), the traditional business of the societies. In future years we are going to see the long-term effects of the relaxed personal lending rules set out in the Building Societies Act 1986. Immediately after the Act there was a portfolio adjustment. Over £1 billion of LA investments were sold off and, after a significant build up of British government securities between 1980 and 1983, these were also heavily depleted between 1986 and 1989.

The liquidity of the societies is hard to explain. The Chief Registrar of Friendly Societies used to require that cash plus investments be maintained at a minimum of 7.5 per cent of total assets. As the balance sheet shows, it is the custom for the societies to keep well in excess of that amount. Historically, it was just about possible to argue that, if inflows dried up, commitments to mortgage lending could be maintained by running down these reserves but, with wholesale funding now freely available, that hardly any longer seems necessary.

Building Societies Act 1986

As most deposits are effectively withdrawable upon demand, whereas mortgages are mostly granted for 25 years, the **liquidity mismatch** between assets and liabilities is very striking. However, the average life of a mortgage is in reality only 7 years (which partly explains the belated

Table 4.6   *Building Societies, Assets and Liabilities, 1992, Quarter 4*[1]

	£ mn	%
Assets		
Commercial[2]	220 026	82.7
Cash and bank deposits	28 352	10.7
British government stock	3 738	1.4
Other investments	3 430	1.3
Other assets	4 631	1.7
Other public sector debt	5 949	2.2
Total	266 126	100.0
Liabilities		
Shares and deposits	190 831	71.7
Wholesale	47 548	17.9
Other liabilities and reserves	27 747	10.4
Total	266 126	100.0

Notes:
[1] From July 1989 figures exclude Abbey National plc.
[2] Of which 207 587 are Class 1 assets, namely advances to individuals secured on land for the residential use of the borrower which must also be first charges on the property.

Source: Bank of England Quarterly Bulletin, Table 5.2.

enthusiasm for mortgage lending by the banking sector); there is a constant inflow of capital and interest repayments; very little bad debt; and almost all borrowing and lending is at floating interest rates, so there is always a margin between them to cover expenses and leave room for profit.

The Building Societies Act 1986 has operated since January 1987, and has subsequently been amended to relax its rules which, while allowing societies to move some way from their traditional business both in terms of methods of raising finance and of disposal of funds, are nevertheless regarded as overly restrictive.

For example, the original 20 per cent limit on the amount of funding to be raised from wholesale sources was doubled with effect from 1 January 1988. The Building Societies Commission sets a lower limit for each individual society, thought currently to average 30 per cent. Some societies have pressed for the 40 per cent limit to be raised, and the Commission is currently considering permitting selected societies to securitise (that is, to fund mortgages by issuing bonds).

One of the most important new powers gained by societies in the 1986 Act was the ability to undertake limited unsecured lending. Three classes of commercial asset were introduced. Up to 7.5 per cent of commercial assets can be in the form of class 3 assets (unsecured advances, investment in land and investment subsidiaries), but only provided societies have commercial assets in excess of £100 million. This has permitted qualifying societies to issue credit cards, to provide overdrafts and to provide unsecured loans for non-housing-related purposes. Once again, societies have not used these powers all that fully so far but that has reflected the buoyancy of mortgage lending, and societies chafe against the restrictions.

The review of building society powers completed in June 1988 resulted in their being able to offer a wide range of banking and housing-related services; to take up to a 100 per cent stake in life assurance companies and up to a 15 per cent stake in general insurance companies; to undertake fund management; and to take up to 100 per cent stakes in stockbrokers.

There was also a provision in the Act for designating bodies with wide powers in which societies may invest which has been used on several occasions. From 1 July 1989, appropriate mortgage companies were designated as suitable for investment or support by a society. These may buy, administer or sell the existing mortgage books of other lenders as well as making mortgage loans on their own account. Furthermore, since 1 January 1988, societies have been permitted to establish subsidiaries to operate in other EU member states.

With some societies eager to expand their range of financial services even faster than the rate at which the rules evolved, the issue inevitably arose as to whether any of them might wish to convert to banking status. The government adopted a neutral stance, and introduced draft rules governing conversion on 28 July 1988. The Abbey National, the second largest society, obtained the necessary majority to convert in April 1989. Support for conversion by Abbey members was so high that other societies were thought to be almost certain to follow suit. In the event, however, no other society has yet followed the Abbey's example, in good part because they are now permitted to do so many new things under their own relaxed rules. Perhaps this is just as well, because they have not shown themselves to be particularly astute in expanding into new spheres of operation. This is especially true in respect of their acquisition of estate agency chains.

As building societies cannot easily issue shares, they have to raise capital by increasing their retained earnings which makes it difficult to finance acquisitions and other forms of expansion. Legislation was accordingly introduced in June 1991 permitting societies to issue **Permanent Interest Bearing Shares** (PIBs) which, like non-voting shares, would yield interest rather than dividends, and the Leeds Permanent made the first issue only a few days later.

Nevertheless, the fact that societies do not have to distribute dividends to shareholders has been highly beneficial in recent times when, like the banks, they have had to make provisions for bad loans. In practice, the societies rarely commit themselves to provide more than 80 per cent of the value of a property in the form of a mortgage, leaving the residual part to be provided by an insurance company via a mortgage indemnity policy, but house prices have fallen so far in some instances that societies have suffered losses. When the insurance companies responded to their own losses by raising their charges, the societies successfully pressed the government in April 1993 to accede them the right to set up their own insurance companies.

On those occasions when bad debts have appeared to threaten the viability of smaller societies, their larger brethren have been happy to step in and take them over, thereby expanding their branch networks and market shares. Whereas such mergers can be expected to continue, bad debts have discouraged demutualisation which would make societies answerable for such debts to shareholders.

The societies are going through a patchy time on account of the collapse of the housing market, and in 1992 their net inflow of savings amounted only to £295 million, compared to £5 billion in each of the previous five years. 1993 has shown some improvement, but the market remains very competitive.

Cross-border Activity

The implementation of the Single European Market (SEM) has made little progress with respect to the integration of housing finance systems in the EU. Levels of owner-occupancy are highly variable in member states, and the legal procedures, institutions and financial instruments are often incompatible. As a result, the creation of a mortgage directive is unlikely to be realised. However, the Second Banking Coordination Directive, published at the end of 1988, permitted mortgage lenders to operate outside their home country in the same way as they operate at home.

The 'mutual recognition of techniques' has so far failed to lead to a plethora of cross-border activity. Part of the difficulty lay in the need to establish a subsidiary elsewhere in the EU before conducting business there, and UK legislation will have to be amended before funds can be transmitted through societies' UK branches. The most active society in recent times has been the Woolwich, which established an Italian subsidiary at the end of 1990. More recently, in June 1993, the Bradford & Bingley was the first society to announce plans to set up in Germany, but the biggest society, the Halifax, does not intend to open its first European office until the end of 1993.

☐ 4.5.2 Insurance Companies

The business of life insurance is often conducted by large composite insurers which also cover general risks such as damage to house and car. Our concern here is primarily with **life insurance**, which may also be provided by specialist insurance companies. The business of life insurance has little to do with liquidity. The commonest form of policy is where the individual makes regular monthly payments which entitle him or her to a lump sum at a specific future date (an **endowment**). If the endowment is 'with profits', then bonuses will be added in line with the profitability of the company. If the policy holder dies before the policy matures, then a lump sum will be paid to the next-of-kin or specified beneficiary.

An endowment may alternatively be purchased via a single, large, lump-sum down-payment. Special forms of endowment are increasingly linked to mortgages, either 'low cost' endowments or mortgage protection policies which simply guarantee to repay the outstanding mortgage upon the death of the mortgagee (term insurance). Unit-linked endowments are also increasingly available, with several companies giving up traditional endowments altogether because of their difficulty in maintaining bonuses, and indeed there is the now customary proliferation of new forms of life insurance in this exceptionally competitive market. Endowments can be, and frequently are, cashed in before maturity, although this generally results in a repayment of less than the total amount paid in, since insurance brokers are frequently paid the first year's premium as a fee for arranging the endowment.

Life insurance companies hold roughly half of their long-term assets in the form of UK and overseas equities, and the rest mostly comprises gilts and UK land, property and ground rents. Equities are even more prominent in the assets structure of pension funds, because fixed-yield assets would not keep pace with commitments to make payments based upon rapidly-rising incomes. These institutions clearly, therefore, play a dominant role in the equity and gilt-edged markets.

Like the commercial banks, the insurance companies are often less than astute investors on behalf of their policy holders. In May 1991, for example, the Prudential Corporation decided that it was 'emotionally unsuited' to being a residential estate agent, and completed the sale of its 500-branch operation which it had built up at a total cost of £338 million. Total receipts from branch sales were £30 million. General Accident did equally badly with its ill-fated acquisition of its New Zealand subsidiary, NZI Corporation.

The life insurance companies have cause to be very grateful for the decision to introduce personal pensions, discussed below, since it provided them with a huge source of new business. It is to be expected that they have learned their lesson from the 1980s: namely, that it is not easy to cross-sell life insurance and other similar policies with the products of other types of financial intermediary.

The advent of the SEM has not been favourable for UK insurers. Whereas they have been discouraged from investing elsewhere in the EU by relatively tough regulatory regimes, their relatively well-capitalised German and French equivalents have moved into the UK market and eroded their market share.

Lloyd's of London

The cornerstone of the UK's insurance market is Lloyd's of London. Traditionally, one had to be very rich to join a syndicate and become a 'name' since 'names' were subject to 'unlimited liability'. From 1967 to 1987 Lloyd's made substantial profits; the risk attached to unlimited liability seemed of little account. As a result, large numbers of modestly wealthy middle-class individuals signed up as 'names'. However, this proved to be a case of very bad timing.

Lloyd's is very slow to declare its results because syndicates cannot close their accounts for any year in whch there are unknown oustanding claims. Heavy and unremitting pollution claims from the USA, together with a series of severe natural disasters and events such as the explosion on the Piper Alpha platform in the North Sea, have plunged Lloyd's into the red since 1988 to an extent that can ultimately only be guessed at. Losses for the 1990 year, announced in June 1993, amounted to £2.9 billion, the largest ever. Many outstanding claims relate to policies written decades ago to cover pollution and diseases unforeseeable at the time (such as asbestosis). As a result a 'name' may ultimately be liable for hundreds of times the original investment.

Unsurprisingly, many 'names' are now taking legal action, claiming that Lloyd's was lax in its regulation of the market and that they are victims of negligence. In its turn, Lloyd's has instigated wide-ranging reviews of its procedures, to include the issue of 'unlimited liability', but these have failed to satisfy a large proportion of the 'names' who are technically bankrupt. The market has recently been opened to corporate capital with limited liability.

Pension Schemes

A **pension** cannot be paid out to anyone other than the person in whose name the monthly payments are made, irrespective of who pays the premiums, or in part to anyone other than his or her spouse or children upon the death of the pensioner. Most pension schemes involve payments both by the individual and the company he or she works for. Until recently, this has meant that if the individual moved jobs the pension in the old job would be frozen until retirement, and the individual would have to start up a new one with the new employer. In certain circumstances, however, pensions are now 'portable' between jobs. The self-employed must buy personal pensions for themselves, and it is now possible for individuals to top up existing pension rights by buying additional personal pensions.

Pension, or superannuation, funds make payments for as long as a pensioner lives after reaching pensionable age. In certain cases these payments were index-linked before 1990. Thus, while life insurance is primarily a means of buying protection (for dependents) in the event of early death, a pension fund exists to cover the risk of living too long without an income. The popularity of life insurance and pension funds has traditionally been fostered by the existence of tax concessions both to individuals and to companies. Tax relief on life insurance premiums was, however, discontinued in the 1985 Budget.

The State Earnings Related Pension Scheme (SERPS) was once compulsory for all, and financed, at least in principle, by NICs. In 1985 the decision was taken to allow people to opt out by contracting a personal pension for themselves. This was expected to reduce the burden on the National Insurance Fund, although this was to be more than offset by the 5.8 per cent NICs' rebate, the special incentive of 2 per cent of relevant earnings payable until April 1993 and tax relief on the employee's part of the rebate. It is estimated that at least 50 per cent of personal pension plans are financed in this way, and high rates of surrender and high expense ratios among intermediaries have caused the government to announce a restructuring of the rebate system in April 1996.

It was estimated that 500 000 people would immediately take out personal pensions, with numbers eventually peaking at 1.75 million, but by April 1990 approximately, 4 million personal pensions had been taken out. As a result, the net cost to the Exchequer was estimated by the comptroller and auditor-general to reach an eventual figure of £5.9 billion at April 1988 prices (when the new pensions were first introduced). In 1990–91 the net cost was estimated at £1.8 billion, equivalent to a 1.5p rise in the rate of income tax.

During 1993 the government began increasingly to hint at two ways of reducing the burden of state pensions as the population ages over the next two decades. The projections are set out in **Figure 4.4**. The first was to target the basic state pension at those who need it most, and the second was to raise the age for women at which it

becomes payable. In the event a common retirement age of 65 was announced in Autumn 1993 with a long implementation lag.

By tying state pension increases to prices rather than earnings in 1988, the projected cost of state pensions in 2030 will be 'only' £34.7 billion and less thereafter. Unfortunately, this will be insufficient to provide even a minimal standard of living for the retired. The debate over pensions is therefore far from resolved, not least because it remains wholly unclear why everyone should be expected to retire at precisely the same age.

☐ 4.5.3 Unit Trusts

Direct investment in equities has never been popular among individuals in the UK. This is partly because it is not possible to obtain a diversified porfolio of shares if there is only a modest amount of capital to invest. Unit trusts and investment trusts pool the savings of large numbers of individuals, and by giving them a share in a diversified portfolio of assets this reduces the risk element in equity-related saving. Nevertheless, as with any equity-linked portfolios, those of trusts can fall heavily in value when the Stock Exchange is depressed.

In the case of unit trusts there is a legally binding trust deed. A trustee, normally a large financial intermediary, holds the trust's assets on behalf of unit holders, and the trust is independently managed by another company within the terms of the trust deed. Units can be bought and sold only with the trust itself. New units are created as desired, and old ones eliminated when units are sold back to the trust. The trust repays such units by disposing of investments. There has recently been considerable dispute about the rules for calculating the purchase and sale price of units, and it is permissible for a unit trust to refuse to repurchase under specified circumstances.

The period from 1980 to 1987 was a very successful one for unit trusts. The value of annual gross sales soared from little more than £1 billion to in excess of £15 billion in 1987 and, although there was a good deal of repurchasing,

Figure 4.4 *UK Pensions: Social Security Cost if Benefits are Linked to RPI*

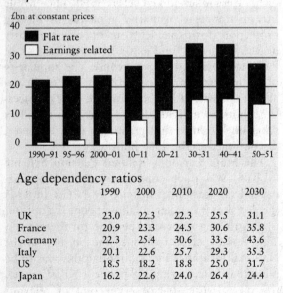

£bn at constant prices

- ■ Flat rate
- □ Earnings related

Age dependency ratios

	1990	2000	2010	2020	2030
UK	23.0	22.3	22.3	25.5	31.1
France	20.9	23.3	24.5	30.6	35.8
Germany	22.3	25.4	30.6	33.5	43.6
Italy	20.1	22.6	25.7	29.3	35.3
US	18.5	18.2	18.8	25.0	31.7
Japan	16.2	22.6	24.0	26.4	24.4

Source: Financial Times, 28 June 1993.

net investment was significantly positive in every year; total unit trust funds rose to roughly £40 billion. In 1985 there were 2.5 million holdings, but by 1987 this had increased to 5 million holdings. Annual net investment has remained positive until the present day, although it was close to zero in 1990 and 1992. From its 1987 peak the number of unit holders fell continuously to a total of 4.35 million by the end of 1992. The introduction of unit trust PEPs, together with a sharp reduction in interest rates which enhanced the attractiveness of equity-linked investments, have led to a revival in holdings which totalled 4.68 million in August 1993. Funds under management have risen to a record £78.8 billion.

As shown in **Table 4.7**, by the end of March 1993 most categories of funds were comfortably above their levels five years previously. This was not, however, such good news for investors since 6 per cent front-end sales charges plus 1 per cent annual charges ate into capital gains and the bid/offer spread amounted on average to a further 6 per cent of the price. When the government lifted controls on charges in 1979, it was in the expectation that competition would drive them down, whereas in practice they are currently often twice as high over a twenty-year period.

With three times as many trusts in existence compared to a decade ago, the customer is under-standably rather bewildered. The number of management companies has nevertheless fallen, but as there is a clear advantage for larger groups in terms of costs there are likely to be ongoing mergers among management companies.

☐ 4.5.4 Investment Trusts

Investment trusts are much the smallest class of NBFI in terms of assets. They operate rather differently from unit trusts in that they are public companies rather than legal trusts, and sell shares in the trust itself. The money received is then invested in other equities and securities. Their own shares are quoted in the Stock Exchange and can be fully traded.

☐ 4.5.5 National Savings Bank (NSB)

The NSB, which had its origins in the need for wartime financing and which is now under the control of the Department of National Savings, is important primarily as a route for channeling private sector savings directly into the hands of the government. In this way the PSBR can be financed without the need to issue an equivalent amount of marketable debt instruments. National Savings were unpopular in the decades prior to 1975, but it has subsequently been possible to widen their appeal by deliberately making them attractive compared to deposits at banks and building societies. This is done primarily either through index-linking, which guarantees that a specified real rate of interest, adjusted for inflation, is earned, or through a reduction in the tax burden to be borne by such savings.

☐ 4.5.6 Finance Houses

The finance houses are no longer of much importance in the financial system because there has been a tendency for the largest houses to convert into banks, included statistically in the 'other

Table 4.7 *Unit Trust Index*[1]

	Index 28.03.93	1 year ago	2 years ago	5 years ago
UK Equity	249.9	201.5	210.3	171.2
International	230.2	189.6	177.2	138.6
North America	218.1	172.3	137.9	99.6
Europe	308.0	270.2	260.4	177.2
Japan	231.1	184.1	229.9	210.2
Australia	162.2	141.7	117.2	116.3
Far East	275.1	211.4	198.4	144.3
Av. of all trusts	242.3	195.6	194.7	155.5

Note:
[1] Unweighted and based on 2 January 1985 = 100. Net income has been reinvested.

Source: Micropal.

British banks' category. Funds are raised in the wholesale markets and by issuing bills. They are used to provide loans to individuals (to be repaid in instalments) and to private companies, together with leasing finance whereby a finance house buys a machine or factory and leases it to a company. This type of business is also done by retail banks, but many finance houses have special relationships with large manufacturers and retail chains.

■ 4.6 Money Markets

□ 4.6.1 A Brief History

We have already referred, when discussing individual groups of financial intermediaries, to the existence of money markets, and it is now necessary to say something about these markets in general, and specifically about those of them not previously mentioned.

The movement of huge sums of short-term funds around the financial system is historically a relatively new phenomenon. Up until the early 1960s, organisations acquired short-term funds either from the commercial banks in the form of overdrafts and loans, or as trade credit from suppliers. The banks' ability to lend was itself determined largely by the value of retail deposits, and they did not compete amongst themselves as their interest rates were uniformly linked to the central Bank Rate. Furthermore, direct controls on lending were frequently imposed by the Bank of England.

However, commencing in the early 1960s, large amounts of dollars began to be deposited in London (see discussion of Eurocurrency markets below), and these deposits were totally independent of the existing banking system. They could, therefore, be handled by any institution willing to make a sufficiently attractive offer to depositors, and they could be dealt with flexibly because they did not fall within the compass of existing monetary controls. As a result, large numbers of foreign banks came to London, each intent on grabbing as big a share of the business as possible, and this in turn meant that competition for deposits was so intensive as to exclude the possibility of interest rate cartels. Once in the UK, they also began to compete for sterling deposits, previously the exclusive preserve of the UK banks, which were obliged to match their interest rates.

The Bank of England acknowledged the desirability of competition on an equal footing between institutions when it introduced the Competition and Credit Control (CCC) document in 1971. This detached bank interest rates from Bank Rate, which was abolished, and allowed each bank to set its own **base rate**. The replacement of Bank Rate by the market-determined **Minimum Lending Rate** (MLR) was, however, more apparent than real in practice, as the government found it increasingly difficult to forgo the use of the interest rate as a major instrument of monetary control. Furthermore, base rates have tended to fall back into line. However, this disguises the fact that whereas retail banking is still operated as a virtual cartel, wholesale banking is not. If one has a large sum of money to sell then it can be offered around to the highest bidder. One interesting consequence is that **asset management** (whereby, as discussed above, financial intermediaries and especially banks must maintain part of their asset portfolio in liquid forms) becomes matched by **liability management** (whereby liquidity can be supplemented via borrowing in the money markets). Precisely the same argument applies for governments and commercial organisations. Cash, which does not earn interest, can no longer be left lying idle, even overnight. It is hardly surprising, therefore, that retail banking, where small accounts are handled at considerable expense, is increasingly viewed as simply a means whereby a captive audience is acquired for the sale of profitable financial services, and the primary concerns of liquidity, risk and profitability are juggled in the money markets.

□ 4.6.2 Types of Money Market

The primary money market is the **discount market**. This has already been discussed, and nothing further needs to be added at this juncture. In addition to the discount market there are currently six other significant sterling money markets known, collectively, as the **'parallel' or secondary markets**. These are the inter-bank market; the certificate of deposit market; the sterling commercial paper market; the local authority market; the finance house market; and the inter-company market. They are called 'sterling markets' to distinguish them from the Eurocurrency market discussed below.

The inter-bank market has also been mentioned previously. It is the largest parallel market and, as the name indicates, is the market in which **banks lend to one another**. After a period of rapid growth it went into a sharp decline in 1991, partly as a reflection of concerns about the credit quality of banks and partly as a result of the growth of derivatives markets. Having started in 1955, the local authority market is the oldest of the five, and is where local authorities issue their own debt instruments which are sold to banks and other investors. Loans are unsecured, so the reputation of the borrower is all-important. Until recently local authorities, with their right to levy local taxes, were regarded as low-risk borrowers, but the dubious practices of certain authorities have altered that somewhat. The inter-company market, which began in 1969, is where **large companies lend directly** to one another. It is a low-key affair because there are alternative ways to lend with security at much the same rates of interest. The finance house market is also fairly insignificant because of the transfer of many of the largest houses to the banking sector. The sterling CD market, started in 1968, consists of a **primary** market in which new CDs are issued, and a **secondary** market in which they are subsequently bought and sold, thereby enhancing their liquidity and hence desirability. The market has grown rapidly, but it is totally dwarfed by the foreign currency CD market.

It is not always possible to distinguish to which market a particular transaction should be assigned, since many types of intermediary operate in several of them simultaneously. Supervision is accordingly exercised largely over participants' banking activities although, as discussed above, the Bank of England is involved in the discount market on a daily basis. In the parallel sterling markets **supervision is light**. Participants are ex-pected to join the Sterling Brokers Association and adhere to the Bank's issued code of practice. The Bank also checks on the various instruments issued to ensure that they are of the highest quality. This lightness of touch has provided a suitable environment for rapid growth, but the Bank must occasionally wonder why it fosters markets which make its monetary controls much harder to implement.

4.6.3 Financial Futures and Options

So far, we have been exclusively concerned with transactions involving a current payment in exchange for the current delivery of some kind of asset, such as a share or bond. However, a large number of contracts involve either the delivery of an asset at some **future date** in exchange for a payment made **in the present**, or the purchase of the right to buy or sell (or to decline to buy or sell) an asset at some **future date** at a price **agreed when taking out the option**. The former are traded on the London International Financial Futures and Options Exchange (LIFFE/LTOM) and are known as **financial futures**, and might involve, for example, a contract to buy an amount of gilts in three months' time at a current price which reflects the expectations of the parties to the contract about the future trend of interest rates. Currencies can also be traded in this way. The latter are also traded on LIFFE/LTOM and are known as **traded options** (as distinct from the similar but less-commonly purchased **traditional** options). These involve the outlay of a modest sum today for the rights to buy or sell in the future at an agreed price, known as 'calls' and 'puts' respectively. If the market price moves in such a way as, for example, to rise above the agreed price for a call option, then the option will be enforced by the buyer. Where the writer of the option (the seller) does not have the asset to hand it will have to be purchased in the market and immediately resold at a loss (which is partly offset because the seller has received the price of the option in cash). If, however, the market price has fallen below the price agreed at the time of buying the option (in other words, the asset can be bought more cheaply in the open market) then the option will be allowed to lapse, and the writer of the option gets to keep the money paid for the option **less** trading costs.

Financial futures and traded options clearly involve risks for both buyer and seller. Almost invariably, **one must gain at the expense of the other**. However, there is a sound rationale behind this kind of behaviour. When a buyer agrees to buy an asset at some future date he or she runs the risk that it could have been bought more cheaply in the future compared to the present. On the other hand, the buyer avoids the risk that he or she would have had to pay well above the agreed price. Traded options are thus a mechanism for **financial leverage**. In other words, in return for the down-payment of a modest sum, a buyer of call options is guaranteed the chance to make a profit by buying and instantly reselling a very expensive portfolio of assets which the buyer could not have afforded to pay for in full at the time of buying the option. Equally, the most he or she can lose is the total cost of the options should he or she decline to take them up, even if the price of the asset has fallen disastrously in the meantime.

Traded options also provide a hedge against share movements which would be disadvantageous to a shareholder. Thus, for example, a shareholder whose shares have risen sharply in value can protect at least part of the capital gain by taking out an option conferring the right to sell the shares at a price of his or her choosing. If this happens to be the current share price then the maximum loss is the cost of taking out the options **plus** trading costs, irrespective of how much the shares subsequently fall in value.

It was intended that in March 1991 LIFFE and LTOM would merge, with the International Petroleum Exchange, the London Metal Exchange and the London Commodity Exchange (until 1 July 1993 known as the FOX) eventually joining LIFFE/LTOM to form an overall exchange capable of challenging the pre-eminent position of Chicago. So far, however, little progress has been made with this scheme although LIFFE/LTOM did eventually merge in March 1992.

Figure 4.5   *Aggregate Turnover on the London Derivatives Exchanges*

Average number of contracts per day ('000s)

Source: Bank of England Quarterly Bulletin (Nov 93) p. 476.

LIFFE is the dominant partner in LIFFE/LTOM which itself accounts for two-thirds of aggregate turnover on the derivative exchanges, as shown in **Figure 4.5**. The 1990 Budget was a big boost for trading in derivatives because it permitted institutions to avoid paying tax on any of their transactions without having to prove that they were not 'trading' in the market. Turnover soared in 1991 and 1992 and amounted to 72 million contracts in the latter year as traders grappled with volatile market conditions. There has been even more volatility in 1993 and turnover will be correspondingly much higher. The largest contracts are still traded using 'open outcry' on the Stock Exchange floor, but there has been some movement towards screen-based trading. This may help to bring back retail clients who constitute only 30 per cent of business compared to 70 per cent in Chicago, but fees remain high and it is the usual Catch 22 situation in which fees cannot come down until trading volume picks up, but trading volume will not pick up until fees come down.

☐ *4.6.4 Eurocurrency Markets*

The size of the Eurocurrency markets in the UK, as indicated in **Table 4.1 (p. 103)**, is much larger than one might expect. The stock of outstanding Eurobonds alone is currently worth $1320 billion. Eurocurrency transactions are **wholesale** borrowing and lending in a currency other than that of the country in which the transactions take place. Thus Eurosterling can be transacted anywhere other than in the UK, and Eurodollars anywhere other than in the USA and so forth. The term 'Eurocurrency' is, therefore, something of a misnomer since it can involve non-European currencies and be transacted outside Europe. It arose because, as previously stated, the markets began with dollars deposited in Europe. At present London is the biggest Eurocurrency market, accounting for approximately 20 per cent of all transactions by value.

There is normally a lower limit of $1 million set for each transaction, and also often an upper limit since loans are unsecured, whereas much of the lending is very short-term loans in the form of Eurocommercial paper (the total market for which rose from $4 billion in early 1986 to $45 billion in early 1988), and especially of Eurobonds which are largely fixed-interest securities or floating-rate notes (FRNs) denominated in a Eurocurrency. FRNs are attached to LIBOR in the UK, and may be convertible to equity. They are issued by multinational firms, foreign governments, LAs and public corporations. There is also a great deal of inter-bank lending. Eurobonds are not usually traded on the Stock Exchange, but rather certain international banks and security houses 'make a market'. There are sufficient market-makers to ensure that Eurobonds can be freely traded at competitive prices.

Consequences

The Eurocurrency markets have, as noted above, been an important source of funds for inter-bank lending. This has had the effect of bringing together banks throughout the world into an informal network, and there can be no doubt that international liquidity has been enhanced in the process. However, it is clear that there are dangers in moving around vast sums of money without there being any institution in overall control of proceedings. This can arise first of all with respect to individual banks. Eurocurrencies tend to travel through a succession of banks on their route between ultimate lender and ultimate borrower. An individual bank cannot, therefore, know to what extent its lending may end up with any particular borrower, and thus how vulnerable it is to that borrower's financial health.

Second, from the point of view of sovereign states, it is clear that domestic monetary policy may be rendered ineffectual by the Eurocurrency markets. The movement of 'hot money' has, for example, recently been of considerable concern to the UK government. It should be noted, in particular, that interest rate differentials between countries are critical in determining the direction of flow of hot money, and hence that no individual country can set its interest rate structure in isolation. The loss of control implied by these developments is inevitably a considerable irritant to banks and governments alike, but attempts to regulate Eurocurrency markets would simply result in their replacement by other markets not subject to the new regulations.

Growth in the largest market, for Eurocommercial paper, has gone into reverse over the past year, reflecting the maturity of the market, slower economic growth, a reduction in longer-term interest rates and a fall-off in the credit quality of issuers. Overcapacity has led to the withdrawal of several banks, leaving roughly ten active dealers. Euromedium-term notes (EMTNs), on the other hand, have become increasingly popular, as shown in **Figure 4.6**. Over the past two years outstanding issues have risen threefold to $61 billion, and the large building societies have become prominent issuers of EMTNs.

ECU Securities

In 1981 a market was developed for Eurobonds denominated in ECUs. As shown in **Figure 4.7**, the market built up rapidly in 1985, then subsided. An initial problem was the absence of any parallel market in short-term (up to six-month) ECU bills. The market picked up again in 1988, as the SEM

Figure 4.6   *Stock of Outstanding Euronotes*

Source: Bank of England Quarterly Bulletin.

Figure 4.7   *ECU Bond Market: Volume Outstanding[1]*

Note:
[1] Fixed-rate Euro plus domestic; excludes Italian and Greek domestic issuance amounting to 30 billion and 4 billion respectively at 13 March 1992.

Source: Bank of England Quarterly Bulletin.

began to exert an influence. In August 1988, the UK Government launched a series of ECU Treasury bill tenders, partly as a pre-emptive measure to concentrate the ECU markets in London.

These and other issues were hugely successful. By the end of 1990 there were $60 billion of fixed-rate ECU bonds outstanding in the international bond market, making it the fifth-ranking currency by value of outstanding bonds. At the end of the 1980s a number of central banks, including the Bank of England, began to use the ECU markets for their own reserves management operations. As a result issuance surged to ECU 27.5 billion in 1991. The Bank of England also began issuing ECU Treasury notes (for details of the development of the ECU markets, see Bank of England, 1992). ECU denominated securities were particularly attractive to the Japanese, who preferred them to bonds issued in individual currencies on the grounds that they combined relatively high yields with relatively low risk. A futures contract in ECU bonds was also been launched by LIFFE/LTOM and in France.

With the single European currency increasingly on the minds of investors, it seemed that the ECU would be playing an ever-greater role in the international securities markets. However, the rejection of the Maastricht Treaty by Denmark in 1992 caused a crisis in the ECU bond market, with dealing suspended temporarily in July. The market may never recover fully from this shock, and it is increasingly the case that activity has recently become concentrated in larger, more liquid, issues.

■ 4.7 Capital Markets

When companies need more medium- and long-term capital than is available from retained profits, and when the government cannot cover its expenditure from its tax revenue, they make up the shortfall by recourse to the capital markets. These thus encompass both the **institutions** which provide medium- and long-term finance, illustrated in **Figure 4.8**, and the **forms of financial instrument** which are traded there.

Figure 4.8 *The Capital Markets*

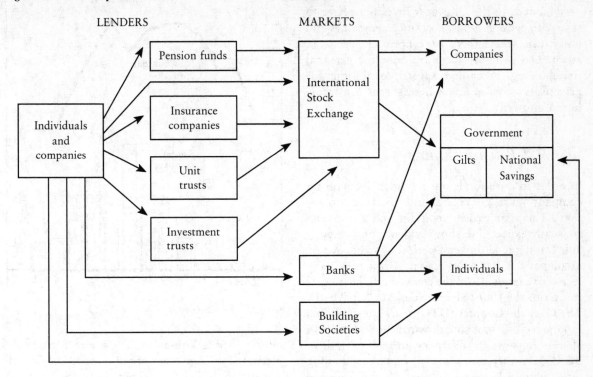

4.7.1 New-Issue and Secondary Markets

There are two markets. The first, called the **new-issue** or **primary market**, is where new securities are offered to investors. The second, called the **secondary market**, is where existing securities are traded. The securities traded fall into two basic categories. Equities, or shares, are issued by companies and pay dividends, usually half-yearly, which are variable and linked to profitability. Most shares carry voting rights at the annual general meeting, although these are rarely exercised in practice. The value of a share is also variable, being determined by the forces of supply and demand, and a shareholder may, therefore, make either a capital gain or loss over time. Interest-bearing securities (stocks) come in a variety of forms. They are mostly issued by the government in the form of **gilts**. Those issued by companies are called **debentures**. There is also an active market in **Eurobonds**, as outlined earlier. Stocks almost universally become redeemable at a specific future date, and yield a fixed rate of return. However, some are convertible into equity, and others are in the form of FRNs, or are index-linked to guarantee their return in real rather than money terms. Stocks may also be subject to capital gains and losses as interest rates vary if sold before maturity.

The secondary market is essential if the primary market is to operate successfully. In other words, stocks and shares are regarded as liquid assets by investors even though they are frequently held for long periods of time by the original purchaser, and it is essential that there is a mechanism for rapid trading. The London Stock Exchange (LSE) lies at the centre of the capital markets, but it is by no means necessary to use its services in order to raise longer-term capital. This is related to the role of financial intermediaries which hold the bulk of all stocks and shares in the UK. Whereas it is quite easy for individuals to deal in shares, personal portfolios are still, despite privatisation, very modest. In the UK, most investors prefer to save with pension funds, insurance companies and unit trusts where there have normally been tax advantages, whereas there are none for personal shareholdings other than special concessions for privatisation issues and where shares are transferred into PEPs.

☐ 4.7.2 Raising Funds

In order to raise funds on the Stock Exchange a company must 'go public' and obtain a 'quotation'. This is an expensive affair, and a company is usually expected to show evidence of a respectable trading record over a period of years. Where a company is too new, operates in a very risky sector or cannot afford the costs of a full listing, it can go to the **Unlisted Securities Market** (USM). The **Over the Counter** (OTC) market established in January 1987 was shut down at the end of 1990. Shares are, however, relatively difficult to trade in the USM as there are few market-makers and big differences in buy and sell prices, and there has been a significant decline in the amount of money raised in the last four years, as shown in **Figure 4.9**.

When the USM was established, a five-year trading record was required before companies could obtain a full listing, as against three years for the USM. In 1991 these became three and two years respectively, and many companies responded by waiting until they could go directly to a full listing. As a result, the Stock Exchange decided at the end of 1992 to scrap the USM by 1995, with new members permitted to join only until June 1993. The 308 members would be allowed to transfer cheaply to the full market. However, this decision did nothing to resolve the fundamental problem of lack of liquidity in the market for small companies' shares, and it has recently become unclear whether the recommended timetable for closure will need to be extended.

Where a full listing on the Stock Exchange is required, but the value of the new issue is modest, it is customary to opt for a 'public placing' where-

Figure 4.9   *The USM*

Source: The Economist, 6 March 1993.

by the issuing house (usually a merchant bank) places up to 75 per cent of the shares directly with institutional clients, the remainder being made available on the Exchange. Not surprisingly, shares issued in this way tend to end up concentrated in a very few hands. For issues raising more than £30 million an Issue by Prospectus or an Offer for Sale is normally required, with up to half the shares being sold to institutions, the difference being that in the latter case the issuing house first acquires the shares and then sells them to the public (favoured where the company is obscure but the issuing house is well known).

These methods are expensive because a prospectus has to be drawn up, containing a full financial history of the company. The issue must be advertised nationally, and the issuing house and other advisers paid a commission. If oversubscribed, a system of allocation will have to be chosen and implemented. In the great majority of cases, the issue will be underwritten for a further fee as a precaution against an undersubscription, the underwriter then being obliged to purchase the outstanding shares. An Offer for Sale may be either at a fixed price or, less commonly, by tender at (or above) a predetermined minimum price. The latter prevents the shares being seriously underpriced with attendant capital gains for 'stags' who immediately resell, but will almost certainly leave virtually all of the shares with the institutions.

Occasionally there are 'scrip' issues whereby, perhaps to make each share cheaper and hence more marketable, the number of shares may, for example, be doubled and their price halved. This does not raise any new capital as such, unlike a **rights** issue which is where existing shareholders are offered the right to buy additional newly-issued shares. If they do not wish to acquire the extra shares then the rights can be sold on the Stock Exchange. Strictly speaking, the price of the old shares should fall to bring into line the higher total number of shares and the higher total capitalisation of the company. Rights issues are popular with companies themselves because all the company has to do is send a circular to existing shareholders, who also benefit because there are no brokerage charges to pay but who may find their shareholdings diluted if they cannot afford to take up their rights.

The LSE is the world's third largest, although it is dwarfed by total turnover in New York and Tokyo. More importantly, however, the LSE is the world's biggest foreign equity market, where two-thirds of reported trading of equities outside their country of origin takes place. The advantage of the LSE lies in its low trading costs and in its structure, with market-makers taking positions between buyers and sellers, and thereby providing superior liquidity for large wholesale trades.

The existence of **SEAQ International** has been important in this respect. This is a lightly regulated, computerised arena in which more than 50 large securities firms, mostly British, American and Japanese, trade huge blocks of shares among themselves and with institutions. SEAQ (Stock Exchange Automated Quotation System) was founded in June 1985, and currently accounts for anything between 10 and 60 per cent of the turnover in the stocks of other European countries. It is due for replacement, and in June 1993 the LSE opted for a system it had developed with Anderson Consulting which will replace SEAQ and roll in SEATS, the order-driven system for illiquid shares. The target date for the new system to be operational is 1996.

☐ 4.7.3 Gilt-edged Securities

The issue of **gilts** is the responsibility of the Bank of England, and the total value outstanding grew rapidly as a result of new borrowing by the government in the majority of postwar years. However, in the Autumn Statement of November 1988 the Chancellor declared that he would 'fully fund' the Public Sector Debt Repayment (PSDR, see **p. 178**), the effect of which was to withdraw £9 billion of gilts from the market during the financial year 1988–89. This did not merely have the effect of altering considerably the shape of the yield curve which relates short-term to long-term yields, but caused problems for institutions such as pension funds which like to hold long-dated assets that match their long-dated liabilities. Indeed, given a shortage of alternative long-dated securities denominated in sterling offering an attractive rate of return, institutions turned increasingly to investment in foreign bonds. The Chancellor followed this up in December by announcing that, commencing in January 1989, the Bank of England would conduct reverse gilts auctions, concentrating on short-dated gilts.

There were no new issues of gilts during 1990. In the light of the shrinking market, a reduction in the number of actively traded stocks was brought about in 1990 by inviting investors in small, less-liquid issues to convert into larger, more liquid issues. Somewhat surprisingly, the number of gilt-edged market-makers (GEMMs) remained constant at 19 throughout 1990, the first full year post-Big Bang not to have seen any withdrawals (there are 19 in 1993).

In January 1991, faced with the certainty of the reappearance of the PSBR in 1991–92, the Treasury began issuing new gilts. Subsequently, the rapid growth of the PSBR caused new issues to escalate to such a degree that fears were expressed about the Bank of England's ability to dispose of all that were on offer. So far it has been successful in that regard, but there has been very little excess demand for several of the issues in 1993.

■ 4.8 'Big Bang' and its Aftermath

The term 'Big Bang' is the colloquial name for the **deregulation of the Stock Exchange** in October 1986. A variety of circumstances conspired to bring it about at that particular point in time. Historically, there were two major groups of participants in the Exchange. The first, the **stock-brokers**, acted on behalf of clients, both personal and institutional, who paid a commission for stockbroking services. Brokers primarily traded equity, but also gave advice on portfolios. In order to obtain shares the brokers had to go to a **jobber** who acted as a **market-maker**: that is, he held a portfolio of shares which he bought and sold on his own account. Since jobbers could not deal directly with the general public, they were independent of the brokers in a so-called 'single capacity' system. The Stock Exchange's own rules enforced the system, the main attractions of which were superficially that there were always jobbers willing to trade and that, since the brokers had nothing personally to gain by using one jobber rather than another, they would get the best deal they could for their clients.

However, the system had two particularly serious defects. In the first place, the scale of commissions paid to brokers was fixed by the Exchange. An institution buying shares worth £10 million thus had to pay virtually the same rate as a personal investor buying shares worth £1000. Second, the Stock Exchange would not allow individual member firms to grow at the expense of others.

In 1983, under pressure from the government, the Stock Exchange agreed to **forgo fixed commissions and single capacity trading** as from 27 October 1986. Commencing in March 1986, any Stock Exchange firm could be **wholly taken over by outsiders**. This also held true in the gilt-edged market, which had previously been dominated by only two firms of jobbers.

As Big Bang approached there was a mad rush to organise the new 'dual-capacity' market-making firms which stood ready to deal directly with investors, to trade on their own account and to make markets in as many shares as they wished. Brokers and jobbers were taken over by UK and foreign banks, **thereby destroying the historic distinction between banking and security trading** in the UK. The number of trained personnel was understandably totally inadequate, and vast sums of money were offered to attract qualified staff.

One significant problem related to **technology**. Very few old-style jobbers had modern electronic dealing rooms, so there was also a mad scramble to obtain new premises and to get them wired up. The system for transmitting data throughout the Exchange, known as SEAQ, was only just about up and running in time for Big Bang. Once the electronics were in place, the Stock Exchange floor suffered a virtual mass desertion.

For a year, all went very well. The stock market boomed and the volume of business rose to new heights. However, in October 1987 there was a market collapse which made even the Wall Street Crash of 1929 look insignificant. The authorities in the UK and elsewhere reacted positively on this occasion, making large amounts of liquidity available to prevent market-makers going to the wall, and in the event remarkably little damage was done. The real economy carried on working pretty much as before. The enormous cuts in the capitalisation of firms did not make any real difference because, at the end of the day, share prices simply reflect the use of capital which has already been invested. One thing that understandably was affected was the amount of new equity capital which could be raised, because that is not normally allowed to exceed a given proportion of the value of existing capital. The issue of 'rights' came to a grinding halt, and has yet fully to recover although there have been a significant number in Spring 1993 taking advantage of the relative buoyancy of the market.

Equally, on paper, investors became less wealthy, which might have caused them to cut consumption and save more with consequent effects upon GDP. However, this did not take place. What happened is that many personal and institutional investors stayed out of the equity market until early 1991, and the daily volume of shares traded fell well below 1987 levels. As a result, many market-makers and brokers struggled to break even, and there were eventually extensive redundancies in the City. Personal investors switched back to the building societies, which regained much of the mortgage market share previously lost to the banks.

As can be seen in **Table 4.8**, twice as many foreign securities houses set up shop in London in 1986 compared to 1984 and 1985, and even more in 1987. This increase in capacity neatly coincided with the cyclical downturn after the October 1987 crash, and caused the members of the Stock Exchange to lose £27 million in 1987 and £265 million in 1988. Subsequently, market activity peaked and the LSE returned to profit in 1989, but the volume of trading in UK and foreign equities, government securities and other fixed-income stocks struggled to rise above levels prevailing before the crash.

What is surprising is not the reduction in the number of new entrants in 1988 and 1989, but rather that there were as many as there were and that they exceeded the negligible number of departures. Such departures, either of UK or overseas houses, as did occur received much publicity, but they were in fact atypical. This was not, however, merely the triumph of hope over experience, since the LSE managed to replace much of its sagging domestic business with trading in international securities. In 1991, there were twice as many entrants as departures, creating a record number of participants, but even though there were as many entrants again in 1992 the number of departures was extraordinarily high, with Japanese houses departing for the first time. Whether this is the beginning of a new trend remains to be seen.

There has been an ongoing debate about the LSE's trading rules. These require immediate publication of most trades and a delay of only 90 minutes in the publication of the very biggest, which market-makers claim leaves them insufficient time to make a profit. It is also argued that the quote-driven system is a boon for those (mainly institutions) who trade large blocks of shares, but is expensive and cumbersome for small investors.

■ 4.9 Investor Protection

In the run up to Big Bang it became clear that deregulation on the intended scale could have

Table 4.8   *Foreign Securities' Houses in London*

	US			Japan			Europe			Other			Summary		
	Total	*In*	*Out*	*Total*	*In*	*Out*	*Total*	*In*	*Out*	*Total*	*In*	*Out*	*Total*	*In*	*Out*
1980	43	4	1	21	1	0	13	3	0	27	1	0	104	9	1
1981	45	2	0	23	2	0	13	0	0	30	3	0	111	7	0
1982	47	2	0	25	2	0	15	2	0	31	1	0	118	7	0
1983	52	5	0	25	0	0	17	2	0	33	2	0	127	9	0
1984	51	0	1	27	2	0	17	1	1	35	3	1	130	6	3
1985	51	0	0	29	2	0	17	1	1	37	3	1	134	6	2
1986	52	1	0	34	5	0	18	1	0	39	5	3	143	12	3
1987	54	2	0	41	7	0	21	3	0	39	1	1	155	13	1
1988	54	0	0	41	0	0	24	3	0	37	2	4	156	5	4
1989	55	1	0	42	1	0	23	1	2	38	1	0	158	4	2
1990	54	2	3	44	2	0	28	5	0	34	1	5	160	10	8
1991	55	2	1	47	3	0	27	5	6	40	8	2	169	18	9
1992	53	5	7	45	1	3	24	5	8	43	7	4	165	18	22
Total		26	13		28	3		32	18		38	21		124	55

Source: Noel Alexander Associates.

highly adverse effects upon investors. The government therefore appointed Professor Gower to look into the issue of investor protection, and his Report was published in 1984. Gower raised a good many objections to existing practices, which were generally based upon the principle of letting the professionals look after their own because only they were competent to do so. With more and more cases of practices such as insider dealing coming to light, and wholly inconsequential punishments being meted out by the professionals, the government decided to build many of Gower's criticisms into a Financial Services Act which became law in 1986.

☐ 4.9.1 Financial Services Act 1986

The Financial Services Act is intended as a **system of regulation covering the entire investment sector,** from the largest bank to the smallest investment adviser. It is intended to ensure that financial services are provided only by those who are fit and proper to do so, that legitimate complaints can be laid before the relevant authorities and that compensation is available where appropriate. For the past six years the regulatory framework has been painfully pieced together. At its centre lies the Securities and Investments Board (SIB) whose powers are delegated to it by the Secretary of State for Trade and Industry. The SIB is a private company, financed by levies on its members. The main responsibility of the SIB is to oversee the Self Regulatory Organisations (SROs) of which there were originally five (now four).

AFBD	Association of Futures Brokers and Dealers
FIMBRA	Financial Intermediaries, Managers and Brokers Regulatory Association
IMRO	Investment Management Regulatory Organisation
LAUTRO	Life Assurance and Unit Trust Regulatory Organisation
TSA	The Securities Association

The TSA and AFBD have now merged to form the

SFA	The Securities and Futures Authority

The SIB's first task was to draw up its rulebook. Each SRO then had to draw up its own rulebook which had to be at least as rigorous as that of the SIB. All investment businesses have to register with an SRO of their choosing, or may opt to be regulated directly by the SIB. Failure to register is a criminal offence. The SIB can investigate any alleged malpractice, and apply sanctions as appropriate, and in certain circumstances bring legal proceedings.

The key elements of all rulebooks are that:

a   clients' money must be kept separate from that of investment businesses;
b   written contracts must be provided to clients specifying agreed services;
c   there must be 'polarisation' (see below);
d   investigations of clients' needs must be undertaken and best possible advice given in the light of their findings;
e   clients should be advised to go elsewhere if expertise is lacking;
f   an established complaints procedure must be followed.

Polarisation requires all registered bodies to state clearly whether they are acting as a seller or agent for the services of only one intermediary, or as independent advisers choosing the best services on offer: there is no middle ground. If a bank elects to be an independent adviser then it cannot recommend its own services although a client can expressly ask for them. Polarisation has caused particular controversy because of differences between the amount of information on commissions which has to be disclosed to clients by salespeople in each category.

The compensation scheme has operated since August 1988. It pays out a maximum of £48 000 to any investor who loses money when a registered firm goes into liquidation. Complaints must be taken up with the appropriate SRO, as plans for an ombudsman have fallen through.

The extent of regulation is a critical issue. On the one hand, too much regulation drives business away to less regulated markets elsewhere in the EU. On the other hand, too little regulation fosters abuse and fraud. The SIB has come up with the 'new deal', comprising 10 principles (**tier 1**, introduced in July 1990) and 40 'core rules' (**tier 2**, introduced in January 1991), all written in clear, straightforward English. The principles are along the lines of 'A firm should observe high standards of integrity and fair dealing.' The core rules are designed to draw a clear distinction between business carried out between professionals and the sale of investment products to the general public.

Unfortunately, the key to the regulatory edifice lies in the SRO's 'third-tier' rules which are by no means simple and easy to comprehend. In any event, interpreting simple rules is much harder than writing them, and the notes and appendices tend to be longer than the rulebook itself. Life has been made slightly easier by the fact that on 1 April 1991 the TSA and AFBD merged to form the SFA, so there are now only four SRO rulebooks.

4.9.2 Disclosure of Life Assurance Commissions

Polarisation created independent financial advisers (IFAs) and tied agents (or as they prefer to be known, appointed representatives) selling the products of one company. IFAs were to rely upon commissions for their income. As some life companies could be tempted to bias proceedings by offering excessive commissions, a maximum commissions agreement was introduced by LAUTRO. The Office of Fair Trading (OFT) promptly struck this down as anti-competitive, causing commissions to rise by 20–30 per cent. This did at least keep some agents as IFAs, given that direct-selling life assurance companies had previously managed to induce large numbers of IFAs to become their tied agents by offering commissions well in excess of the maximum commissions agreement.

The trouble was that the remaining IFAs were told to disclose more about their commissions to clients, which they could fudge as IFAs but which

they did not need to do at all as tied agents, so virtually every bank and building society ceased to be an IFA. This caused FIMBRA's income to fall drastically and it got into financial difficulties. The IFA share of the life and pensions market is under 40 per cent at the present time, yet the SIB had originally set out to ensure that there would be a strong independent sector. However, the trend is moving back towards IFAs as problems of monitoring tied agents have increasingly surfaced.

Disclosure has become a critical issue. A personal pension plan can carry as many as seven different layers of charges and first-year payments in endowments mostly go as commission. IFAs are subject under SIB rules to 'soft' disclosure of commissions. This means that, at the time of sale, the client must be told the method by which the IFA is paid for his or her services. The insurance company provides details of the commission after the sale takes place, hidden among the small print. Tied agents need not disclose commissions. The playing field is not level, and the client rarely gets to know the truth.

In March 1991, the SIB announced a new review of the regulatory system, with especial emphasis upon disclosure. The Financial Services Act was supposed to usher in a new era of clearly defined relationships. It would appear that this was optimistic because in March 1992 the SIB

Table 4.9 *Disclosure Regimes*

Information disclosed	At Present	SIB proposal	OFT proposal
Reduction in yield	✓	✓	✓
Wealth warnings	✗	✓	✓
Adviser's status	✗	✓	✓
Five-year surrender values	✗	✓	✓
Later surrender values	✗	✗	✓
Independent adviser's commission	✗	✗	✓
Companies' total charges	✗	✗	✓
Tied agents' commission	✗	✗	✗

Source: Financial Times, 19 March 1993.

rejected calls for the full disclosure of commission at point of sale, and opted instead for investors to be told the surrender values of their policies during their first five years. The pay-out figures used for these calculations are standard industry-wide projections provided by LAUTRO rather than individual company performance figures, and do not enlighten the investor. As a consequence, the OFT issued a report in March 1993 which recommended more extensive changes, as shown in **Table 4.9** on the previous page.

4.9.3 The Proposed Personal Investment Authority

Early in 1992 Sir Kenneth Clucas proposed in a report to the SIB that a single body incorporating FIMBRA, LAUTRO and parts of IMRO be created, to be known as the **Personal Investment Authority** (PIA). Unfortunately, however, the banks and building societies have so far refused outright to join, primarily because they fear that they will be forced to increase substantially their contributions to the Investors Compensation Scheme to cover defaults among small independent intermediaries (which might anyway vote not to liquidate FIMBRA). The life insurance companies have responded that they will not join unless the banks also join.

The SIB wants the proposed PIA to introduce improved practices, but intermediaries reject tougher enforcement on the grounds that it will mean higher costs. The SIB could withdraw recognition from existing SROs but is unlikely to do so, although it is determined that a solution to the problem must be found soon.

4.10 Financial Intermediation in the Future

Let us turn, by way of summary, to pick out from the above discussion the most important themes which will determine how the financial system will evolve during the remainder of this century.

4.10.1 Deregulation and Regulation

A particularly interesting issue is the balance between **deregulation** and **regulation**. Historically, the financial system in the UK was heavily regulated by the government, acting through the Bank of England. In addition, specific kinds of financial assets and liabilities were favoured by tax concessions to lenders and/or borrowers. As a result, certain parts stagnated. This imbalance was recognised in the UK when the present government came to power and, starting with the abolition of exchange controls in 1979, it set in train a process of freeing up the system. Most of the monetary controls were subsequently terminated or put into abeyance; public corporations were sold, partly to small shareholders; the Financial Services Act 1986 and Building Societies Act 1986 became law; the Stock Exchange was reformed via Big Bang; portable pensions were introduced as were PEPs, and so on.

However, these processes have been incomplete and the government has been forced to recognise that free-for-alls in financial markets are a recipe for widespread abuse, and hence **deregulation has dragged regulation in its wake**. Whereas the Financial Services Act and Building Societies Act, for example, have allowed NBFI to provide services previously forbidden to them, they have also made it necessary to set up regulatory bodies to ensure that the new services are provided by fit-and-proper intermediaries, and that the new rules are obeyed to the letter. This in turn has caused many disputes about what kinds of regulatory body are needed, and how they should be financed. It must be recognised that financial markets always have been regulated in the sense that, for example, the Stock Exchange imposed a rulebook upon its members, but this kind of self-regulation is bound to be treated with considerable scepticism by outside parties who read about scandals and their resolution behind closed doors. However, it is clear that other existing bodies, such as the Bank of England and the Monopolies and Mergers Commission (MMC) do not have the resources to cope with the huge increase in regula-

Figure 4.10   *The Framework for Financial Regulation in the UK*

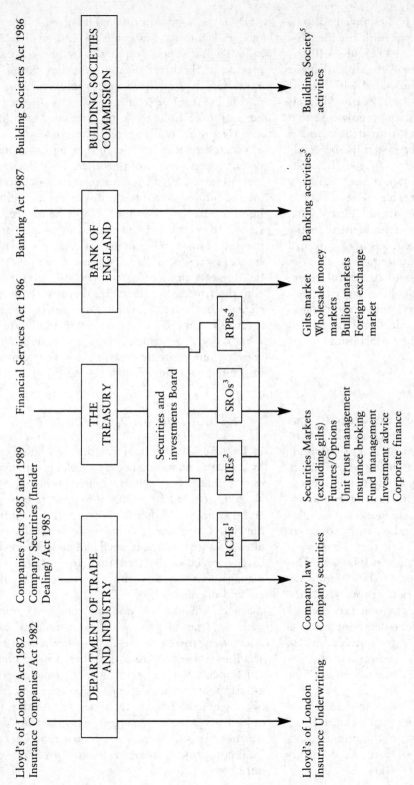

Notes:
1 RCHs = Recognised clearing houses.
2 RIEs = Recognised investment exchanges.
3 SROs = Self regulatory organisations.
4 RPBs = Recognised professional bodies.
5 The investment business of banks and building societies is supervised within the Securities and Investments Board regime.

Source: D. Goacher (mimeo).

tory work, and hence other bodies have had to be created. The full current framework for financial regulation in the UK is set out in **Figure 4.10**.

Matters have recently come to a head in the aftermath of the scandals associated with Barlow Clowes and especially Robert Maxwell. It is alleged that there are too many regulators; that the regulatory system does too little to deter illegal activities; and that the system is too costly to operate. In particular, it is alleged that self-regulation has been such a failure that statutory regulation would be preferable. The reality is that, while these criticisms are all partly true, they represent much less of a problem than the fact that the regulatory system has a poor record in detecting improper behaviour, and an even worse record in bringing about successful prosecutions. The government has shown little inclination to act on these failings, and it is anyone's guess how many more scandals will be needed before decisive action will be forthcoming.

☐ 4.10.2 Innovation

At the present time these new regulatory systems are beginning to settle down, but it is too early to form a judgement about their success or failure. It is reasonable to expect that many amendments will be forthcoming in the years to come. Indeed, this is almost inevitable in the face of ever more rapid **innovation** in financial markets. Regulations can ultimately be applied only to cover existing practices, and it is clear that a rulebook set up to cover existing practices in 1980 would by now be looking totally out of date. Financial innovation is driven by a variety of forces, including (most obviously) changes in monetary control systems; the desire to avoid regulation; vast increases in the total sums being transacted; a wider variety of both lenders and borrowers; and increasing sophistication on the part of both in specifying their needs.

We have already referred to the rapid growth of Eurobonds. It is worth noting that, hand in hand with these, it is increasingly common to find transactions in the **swaps** market. According to the International Swap Dealers Association

(ISDA), the nominal principal involved in interest rate and currency swaps is in excess of $2000 billion in mid-1993. Despite their superficial complexity, at the heart of any swap lies simply an agreement between two institutions receiving or paying interest to exchange payments or receipts. For example, if one bank has borrowed in dollars at a fixed rate, and a second bank has borrowed in yen at a floating rate, each then agrees to meet the interest payments of the other. Their decisions are influenced by different expectations concerning the future path of both the currencies and the interest rates in question. Whole sequences of swaps can be placed end-on-end in a single programme. However, most swaps currently involve simple swaps in dollars between fixed-rate and floating-rate notes. Currency swaps carry more risk than interest rate swaps because both exchange rates and interest rates may move adversely at the same time. Banks accordingly run a 'swaps book' in which swaps are matched up, thereby limiting their exposure to exchange rate or interest rate movements.

☐ 4.10.3 The Swaps Débâcle

In 1989 a case was bought before the High Court by a district auditor who, on checking the books of a London borough (Hammersmith and Fulham), uncovered £6 billion of interest rate swaps and was unsure of their legality. On 1 November, the High Court ruled that not only were the swaps **ultra vires** (that is, the council had no legal powers to engage in swaps) but that any interest rate management contacts with any council were illegal and unenforceable.

Some 78 banks had traded swaps and options with local authorities. All the outstanding contracts were frozen at the time of the judgement, and the banks stood to lose at least £500 million. On appeal, the Court of Appeal ruled unanimously that legality depended upon the objective of the council official at the time of the deal. If the objective was money management, then the deal was in order since this was a proper function of a local authority. If it was to make a profit, it was **ultra vires**.

On further appeal, the House of Lords ruled on 14 January 1991, again unanimously, that the Court of Appeal was wrong and annulled not merely Hammersmith's swaps but over 1000 other local authority swaps dating back to 1982. The banks were appalled. After all, both the Bank of England and the Audit Commission had sanctioned swaps as tools for managing interest rate risk. The banks and the Bank of England appealed to the government to introduce retrospective legislation to validate the illegal transactions but the government refused. The banks were recommended to issue writs for repayment. These were expected to recover about £125 million and, with the Treasury meeting 35 per cent of the residual losses through tax repayments, the banks were expected to suffer a net loss of £275 million.

A series of out-of-court settlements commenced in February 1992, with six test cases settled for undisclosed sums by June. However, the first case to be argued in the High Court resulted in a ruling in February 1993 that Islington Council should repay £1 million to Westdeutsche Landesbank. The High Court also ruled that restitution could be applied to swap agreements that had already been closed. In March Islington decided to appeal, but Kleinwort Benson won a second case against South Tyneside Council.

☐ 4.10.4 Disintermediation

It is important to note that much innovative activity, such as swaps, is **off-balance sheet**. In other words, the bank concerned in a transaction does not lend to the borrower funds which the bank has itself previously borrowed, which would cause both transactions to appear on its balance sheet, but rather acts as the agent organising a loan directly between ultimate lender and ultimate borrower. The process in which funds flow from lender to borrower other than via the banks is known as **disintermediation**, and has obvious consequences for monetary controls which are intended to operate via regulations imposed upon specified intermediaries (traditionally banks).

It also involves the process known as **securitisation**, whereby conventional bank or building so-ciety lending is replaced by other forms of financial instruments. A Eurobond, for example, is a 'securitised' debt, which means that it is sold by a borrowing institution to a lender without the money being either lent to, or by, a bank. The purchaser may subsequently resell the debt in the secondary Eurobond market, and the debt may be resold any number of times before maturity. The obvious consequence of securitisation is that the issuer of the security has no real idea who actually holds it as an asset at any given time. However, securitised debt is set to become increasingly popular as top quality borrowers such as blue-chip companies take advantage of the fact that they can actually borrow more cheaply in their own names than through the intermediation of a bank, the credit rating of which may have suffered as a result of bad debts.

On the face of it, financial innovation should permit independent groups of intermediaries to carve out their own market niches, and indeed specialist intermediaries are often successful as niche operators. However, a successful niche operator with a limited capital base is sooner or later going to attract the attention of an intermediary in another part of the system which has spare capital and limited capacity to expand in its major lines of business. Historically, the process of merger and takeover between different kinds of intermediary was heavily restricted, but in a de-regulated environment the key issue is simply whether the merged company will be a fit-and-proper operator in every market in which it wishes to operate. The process of merger and takeover may allow an intermediary to reduce the risk inherent in its exposure to a single or to a very small number of markets. It may provide a short cut, via merger with another intermediary overseas, to becoming an international, as against a national, operator. There are also going to be circumstances in which a company outside the financial system will want to merge with a financial intermediary, especially if it wants, for example, to provide credit facilities to its customers.

It is unclear where the adjusments implied by the above will end. It is certain that for many companies the process of merger will prove to be an unhappy and costly business, and parts of the merged organisations may subsequently need to be shut down or resold. It was clear at the time of Big Bang, for example, that there were too many players and too little talent in almost every part of the equity and bond markets. The crash of October 1987 caused the process of readjustment to be speeded up, but it is by no means complete as yet. The link between economic efficiency and concentration in the financial markets cannot be determined by historical precedent. There is much evidence of a 'clash of cultures' when different kinds of intermediary are brought together. At the end of the day, the authorities must also form a judgement both about their ability to oversee the system and also the compatibility of different kinds of financial system with the pursuit of their major objectives.

☐ *4.10.5 Internationalisation*

One of the trickier issues is raised by the **internationalisation** of the financial system. Predominantly national intermediaries still dominate the UK retail markets, particularly the building societies, but the process of merger and takeover is gradually becoming more international in scope. Big Bang specifically encouraged the inflow of foreign capital, but it would be wrong to suppose that this can be interpreted as a completely **laissez-faire** attitude on the part of the authorities. They have indicated that there are distinct limits beyond which internationalisation will not be permitted to go, although they are evidently prepared to accept the takeover of a clearing bank, such as the Midland provided the acquirer is a well-established denizen of the City.

☐ *4.10.6 New Technology*

To be a major international intermediary it must be possible for the head office to know what is going on in the farthest-flung outposts of the company. This has increasingly been made possible by the introduction of **new technology**, and especially of computers, which can communicate information instantaneously over vast distances.

However, the introduction of computers has had much more widespread effects, because it has permitted an individual intermediary to handle an enormously increased range of data and has therefore made it possible for it to compete in many more markets than in previous periods when a lack of skilled manpower could not produce enough detailed information for rational decisions to be made. Dealing with a multiplicity of currencies is no longer more than a technicality, and the full spread of interest rates can be arranged on a screen at the touch of a button. Much of the software is marketed commercially, so it is not even necessary for organisations to develop their own software before joining in a new market. It should, however, be borne in mind that computers cannot think for themselves so that, if information is mistakenly or fraudently inserted, serious consequences can easily arise involving losses on a scale which would have been spotted much more quickly in less sophisticated systems.

Dealing in equities and gilts is almost totally dependent upon modern technology, but this technology barely touches upon the everyday lives of individuals. However, ATMs are now in widespread usage, and the National Westminster Bank, for example, has spent £1 billion in order to create a computerised system which will allow it to deal with deposits, cash dispensing and account information at branches entirely through machines.

EFTPOS (electronic funds transfer at point of sale) has become popular very quickly. EFTPOS is a system whereby, for example, a supermarket uses an individual's debit card to debit his or her purchases direct to a bank account, thereby rendering unnecessary the use both of cash and cheques. By the end of 1990, 45 per cent of adults in Britain owned a debit card, and the number of debit card transactions grew by 400 per cent in 1989 alone. In 1992 the number of debit card transactions grew by 45 per cent to 522 000 000. It was predicted that Switch and Visa cards would be used ten times as often as credit cards by the year 2000, but the amount spent on credit cards remains above that for debit cards, which are seen as a replacement for cheques and cash cards and as complementary to credit cards. It is currently anticipated that electronic payments will largely have replaced cheques by the year 2000, but the banks have struggled to make a profit from issuing debit cards which are far more costly for retailers than cheques.

In January 1991, the big five clearing banks announced that they had agreed upon a scheme that would eliminate paper for corporate customers and replace it with electronic messages. Inter-bank electronic data interchange (EDI) enables companies to make payments by sending messages directly from their computers to their banks. The banks then transfer the funds and notify the recipient electronically.

In March 1993, the much-delayed LSE system called TAURUS, which was designed to replace share certificates with electronic records, was finally cancelled despite an investment of £400 million. This was a major set-back since it left London as the only big international centre which did not meet the 1990 recommendations of the Group of 30 for faster electronic share settlement.

A Bank of England taskforce produced a report on how to replace TAURUS in July. This recommended that the LSE's Talisman settlement system should be adapted to accommodate 10-day 'rolling' settlement by July 1994 and 5-day settlement by January 1995 (compared to the current two weeks). This is likely to force private investors to place their stock in the nominee name of their broker which many are likely to resist. Because Talisman is old, paper-based technology, it is to be replaced by an electronic system called CREST, which it is hoped will be operational in 1996. CREST will not make it compulsory to get rid of share certificates. The failure of TAURUS has, incidentally, benefited the Treasury since the government has promised to abolish the 0.5 per cent stamp duty on share transactions once a fully electronic system is operational.

Other recent innovations are electronic gadgets which allow individuals sitting at home to access their bank accounts or a share-dealing service via a telephone link, with the information shown on a home computer screen. In the 1980s most experiments with 'home banking' failed because they were too sophisticated. The Midland Bank set up

Firstdirect in 1989 as a retail bank without branches. All transactions are done over the telephone on a 24-hour a day basis, and no computer is required by the customer. Cash is withdrawn from ATMs.

Firstdirect is forecast to have 500 000 account holders by the end of 1993. Most have been opened by defectors from other banks. So far it has yet to make a profit due to high start-up costs, but an eventual cost-to-income ratio of well under 40 per cent is predicted. Other banks have belatedly responded not by setting up a service to replace branches but by adding a more limited telephone facility to their existing branch structure. This is likely to add to costs unless some branches are simultaneously shut down or automated, but there is a general reluctance to follow the example of Firstdirect in case it also gets overtaken by new technology.

These developments represent progress towards a cashless society but, as noted above there remains, and will remain for the foreseeable future, very large numbers of the 'unbanked'. In 1992, two-thirds of payments of more than £1 in value were still being made by notes and coins. Furthermore, the use of ATMs requires relatively large amounts of cash to be held, so what is being replaced is not so much cash as cheques which, as noted above, makes the banks happy as cheques are expensive to process.

■ *4.11* Conclusion

It is clear from this discussion that the circumstances of the financial markets post-Big Bang are somewhat different from those anticipated in 1986. There was an almost universal belief that the markets would be transformed by the quest for globalisation, and that in order to compete a financial supermarket would have to be created.

This would require the elimination of the weakest players from the markets, leaving the survivors with profitable businesses with significant shares of each market. The reality has been a fascinating illustration of the forces of competition, which in this case are dependent upon information flows. The quest for globalisation was based upon the assumption that the market players with the most sophisticated, and by implication the most expensive, communications would have an advantage over the less-well capitalised players. To the discomfiture of those companies that spent vast sums of money following the path mapped out by this line of reasoning, it proved possible for all the players, even those operating on a small scale and with relatively little capital, to access the necessary information on equal terms. Furthermore, it has become possible for customers to shop around at the touch of a button on a computer screen. They are largely indifferent from whom they buy, so they may simply opt continuously for the cheapest (and probably not very profitable) bargain such as is offered by a basic share-dealing only service. Alternatively, they may be willing to pay a premium for high quality advice, but if this fails to meet expectations they can readily transfer his allegiance elsewhere.

Building up allegiance is largely a matter of personal relationships and trust. This is why, following American precedents, department stores began to offer a limited range of financial services. Marks & Spencer obtained a banking licence and started to market investment products, most recently unit trusts in October 1988. Most department stores offer credit cards and personal finance. Given the rather poor image of banks, there is every reason to suppose that many people will be at least as happy to deal with Marks & Spencer. In any event, it is evident that most functions performed by clearing banks can be done satisfactorily by a different type of financial intermediary, such as a building society.

It is also probable that many of the new ventures in financial services by non-financial companies will be at least as successful as diversification by existing financial intermediaries. As has been recounted at various stages in the preceeding analysis, there is a good deal of licking of wounds going on, and the financial sector is still some way from reaching a post-Big Bang equilibrium. The winners have undoubtedly been the stockholders and estate agents who were bought out by financial intermediaries for highly inflated prices in the belief that there would be lots of synergy to tap. Some of these fortunate sellers have recently been able to buy back their old companies for a fraction of their selling price. If there is one lesson to be learned above all others, it is that there is no substitute for local knowledge of the customer.

Bibliography

Alesina, A. (1989) 'Politics and Business Cycles in Industrial Democracies', *Economic Policy* (April).

Bank of England (1992) 'Ecu Securities Markets', *Bank of England Quarterly Bulletin* (May).

Bank of England (1993) 'Cross-border Alliances in Banking and Financial Services in the Single Market', *Bank of England Quarterly Bulletin* (August).

Blake, A. and P. Westaway (1993) 'Should the Bank of England be Independent?', *National Institute Economic Review* (February).

Callen, T. and J. Lomax (1990) 'The Development of the Building Societies' Sector in the 1980s', *Bank of England Quarterly Bulletin* (November).

Colwell, R. (1991) 'The Performance of Major British Banks, 1970-90', *Bank of England Quarterly Bulletin* (November).

Davis, E. (1991) 'The Development of Pension Funds – An International Comparison', *Bank of England Quarterly Bulletin* (August).

Fraser, I. and P. Mortimer-Lee (1993) 'The EC Single Market in Financial Services', *Bank of England Quarterly Bulletin* (February).

Healey, N. and P. Levine (1992) 'Unpleasant Monetarist Arithmetic Revisited: Central Bank Independence, Fiscal Policy and European Monetary Union', *National Westminster Quarterly Bank Review* (August).

Ingham, H. and S. Thompson (1993) 'Structural Deregulation and Market Entry: The Case of Financial Services', *Fiscal Studies*, 14(1).

Peet, J. (1992) 'Financial Centres: Rise and Fall', *The Economist*, 27 June.

Unger, B. (1992) 'World Banking', *The Economist*, 2 May.

Wood, G., T. Mills, and F. Capie (1993) *Central Bank Independence: What Is It and What Will It Do For Us?* (London: Institute of Economic Affairs).

■ *Chapter 5* ■

Spending, Taxing and Borrowing

Peter Curwen

■ 5.1 Introduction

Our purpose in Chapter 5 is to describe the components of the UK fiscal system and to provide an up-to-date statistical analysis of government expenditure, taxes and borrowing. We do not seek to discuss the operation of fiscal policy instruments as such, which is left to the concluding chapter because it is unhelpful to discuss fiscal policy independently of monetary policy. Furthermore, it is impractical to discuss the use of policy instruments until all of the relevant policy objectives have been thoroughly reviewed, and their inter-relationships assessed.

Our first task is to examine the available data on public spending. Whereas the government has shown some ambivalence about the presentation of its policy objectives since 1979, its public spending plans have always been an important element of its strategy. The government's stated objective has long been to hold the rate of growth of public spending (excluding privatisation proceeds) below the growth rate of the economy as a whole, and thus to reduce public spending as a proportion of NI. This should then make it possible to ease the burden of taxation without any accompanying increase in the overall burden of the national debt, and from this should flow the enterprise and efficiency which leads to growing output and employment. Once our discussion of public spending is complete we will move on to examine, first, the burden of taxation, and subsequently the government's borrowing requirements and their impact upon the national debt.

■ 5.2 Public Expenditure

5.2.1 *The Growth of Public Expenditure*

As will be shown in **Figure 5.3**, public expenditure has grown enormously during the twentieth century, a phenomenon common to all advanced industrial economies, albeit to varying degrees. The lesson of history is that it is very difficult to reduce public expenditure once it has taken root, so it is of considerable interest briefly to review the origins of the growth of public expenditure in the UK.

At the microeconomic level, it is possible to argue that governments are constantly intervening in order to offset the undesirable side-effects of free markets. In the case of what are known as **public goods**, such as national defence and street lighting, there is unlikely to be adequate provision in a private market since the provider will be

143

unable to obtain payment from the beneficiaries of his provision. Equally, in the case of **merit goods**, such provision in a private market of such things as health and education will be limited to those with the ability to pay.

At the macroeconomic level the basic premise is that goods and services provided by the public sector have **high income elasticities**: that is, demand for them grows faster than the rate of growth of incomes. This sharp rise in demand manifests itself not only in the case of merit goods, including public housing, but also in the case of income support, including pensions, sickness pay and unemployment benefits. The 'displacement theory' suggested that the growth in public spending was not a broadly smooth and continuous process as previously thought, but rather was periodically ratcheted upwards on to a permanently higher level by events such as wars, which caused a radical reappraisal of the status quo.

It is difficult, however, to decide whether such upwards displacements in public expediture are permanent or transitory, especially since they are divorced from the more general political influences that were referred to in Chapter 1. What is evident is that if public expenditure is maintained in a recession – which is both standard Keynesian practice and a necessary consequence of needing to pay out much larger sums to the unemployed – the proportion of public spending in total NI is bound to rise, albeit temporarily. Logically, of course, as discussed later, the opposite argument holds during periods of rapid growth.

5.2.2 A Breakdown of Public Expenditure

Figure 5.1 shows, for the financial/fiscal year (commencing 5 April) 1992–93, the departments responsible for planning the largest parts of the recently introduced **new control total** (previously the planning total: see below), and gives details of the areas in which the majority of general government expenditure (GGE) is incurred. It also shows who spends the money and what it is spent on.

There are different ways of defining 'public spending', and different aggregates are relevant for different purposes. The measure which is used for the formulation of macroeconomic policy and the Medium Term Financial Strategy (MTFS) is **general government expenditure** (GGE), consisting of the combined capital and current spending of central and local government including debt interest. This represents the amount which needs to be raised by taxation and borrowing. However, for the purposes of planning and control of programmes, the public expenditure new control total (NCT) is the relevant figure, since it is built up from the control totals for departmental programmes including public corporations.

Table 5.1 illustrates GGE and the NCT over a five-year period. The period 1991–92 is retrospective and the figures given are known as an outturn. The period 1992–93 is an estimated outturn, and the other years represent plans and projections. The figures are published in the Financial Statement and Budget Report (FSBR), known as the 'Red Book' and published in the Spring at the end of each financial year, and are subsequently revised in November. The Red Book and Autumn Statement also contain estimates for the ongoing financial year and forecasts for the three subsequent years. These latter figures will be subject to extensive revision over time, and should be treated as indicative rather than as gospel.

As can be seen, the major difference between the NCT and GGE is interest on debt instruments issued by the central government. This amount depends both upon the total debt outstanding and upon interest rates, so it is very difficult to forecast accurately. Its size is related to the historic and current borrowing needs of government which are discussed towards the end of this chapter. In practice, it was stable in nominal terms during the late 1980s, implying that it was falling in both inflation-adjusted terms and as a percentage of GDP, but this is no longer the case as can be seen in the table. The other major difference between the two parts of **Table 5.1** relates to cyclical social security, and represents an innovatory element in the presentation of public expenditure. It should also be observed

Figure 5.1 *The NCT and GCE: How it is Planned and Spent, 1992–93 (£ bn)*

By department etc.

Value	Label
61.5	Department of Social Security
41.1	Department of the Environment[1]
28.2	Department of Health
25.3	Scotland, Wales Northern Ireland
23.8	Ministry of Defence
41.4	Other departments
10.4	LASFE[5]
13.2	Cyclical Social Security
17.7	Central government debt interest
9.0	Other[4]

New control total

By sector

Value	Label
193.6	Central government[2]
69.8	Local authorities[3]
5.3	Other[4]

By function[1]

Value	Label
79.2	Social security
41.0	Health and personal social services
32.3	Education
23.8	Defence
14.3	Law, order and protective services
10.8	Transport
8.6	Environmental services
30.4	Other functions
18.4	Central government debt interest
9.9	Other[4]

By economic category

Value	Label
123.0	Pay and other current expenditure on goods and services
98.6	Current grants to persons
12.3	Net capital expenditure on assets
15.4	Subsidies, capital grants and lending
18.4	Central government debt interest
9.9	Other[4]

GGE (excluding privatisation proceeds) £268.7 billion

Notes:

1   Includes revenue support grant and non-domestic rate payments and certain transitional grants to local authorities in England. Comparable items are included in the figures for Scotland and Wales.

2   Includes grants, subsidies and net lending to public corporations, including nationalised industries. It also includes central government debt interest (£17.7 billion).

3   The total is made up of £59.4 billion financed by support from central government and £10.4 billion financed from local authorities' own resources. It includes local authority debt interest (£5.3 billion).

4   Includes the national accounts adjustments. The differences in these figures reflect the different treatment of LA debt interest and market and overseas borrowing of public corporations in the analysis of GCE by function and economic category.

5   Self-financed expenditure.

Source: Statistical Supplement to the 1992 Autumn Statement, Chart 1.2.

Table 5.1 *Public Expenditure Totals (£ bn)*

	1991–92 Outturn	1992–93 Estimated Outturn	1993–94 Plans and Projections	1994–5 Plans and Projections	1995–96 Plans and Projections
Central government[1,2]	144.6	158.7	166.4	172.1	177.0
Central government support for local authorities	53.3	59.4	58.4	61.6	63.8
LA self-financed expenditure	11.0	10.4	11.1	11.0	10.8
Nationalised industries' financial requirements	2.5	3.4	3.9	1.9	1.7
Reserve	–	–	4.0	7.0	10.0
Adjustment	–	–0.2	–	–	–
NCT	211.4	231.7	243.8	253.6	263.3
Cyclical social security[3]	10.9	13.2	15.5	16.5	17.0
Central government debt interest	16.3	17.7	20.0	24.5	27.5
Accounting adjustments	5.4	6.0	7.5	8.5	9.0
GGE EXCLUDING PRIVATISATION PROCEEDS	244.0	268.7	286.6	302.5	316.4

Notes:
[1] Excluding cyclical social security.
[2] Comparisons between 1992–93 and 1993–94 are distorted by the effects of transfers between departments and spending sectors.
[3] UK.
Source: Statistical Supplement to the 1992 Autumn Statement, Table 1.1.

that it is customary to insert a rolling reserve in what is now the NCT. It is not unusual for this to be consumed by unforeseen demands upon the public purse almost as soon as the financial year begins, especially at a time of recession.

☐ 5.2.3 Local Government Financing

The approach to the calculation of public spending contained in this discussion dates back to the original surveys of public spending which were set up in accordance with the recommendations of the Plowden Committee (Cmnd 1432, 1961).

However, in a White Paper entitled **A New Public Expenditure Planning Total** (Cmnd 441, 1988), the government proposed a change in the coverage of the planning total, to take place when the new arrangements for local government financing came into operation in England and Wales in 1990. Under this proposal the planning total included (a) spending on the government's own programmes; (b) grants, current and capital, paid to local authorities; (c) credit approvals issued by government for LA borrowing for capital expenditure; (d) payments to the LAs from the proceeds of the national non-domestic rate; (e) the external financing limits of public corporations; (f) privatisation proceeds; (g) a Reserve. Data collection in the appropriate form could not be integrated into the 1988 Public Expenditure Survey because it was already in progress, but commenced wuth the 1989 Survey.

The underlying purpose of this change was to distinguish that part of LA spending which was the responsibility of central government from that part which LAs determined and financed for themselves. Public spending control was thereby enhanced in a number of ways: for example, by the inclusion of grants in the planning total for the first time. Furthermore, since this required the grants to be planned for three years ahead, it helped the LAs to plan their own expenditure more effectively.

It should be noted that this change had no effect upon the total for GGE. The effect, in accounting terms, was to remove LA self-financed expenditure from the planning total and to place it, in terms of **Table 5.1**, together with interest and other adjustments.

The NCT was introduced in the 1992 Public Expenditure Survey. It differs from the planning total in three ways:

a   Cyclical social security does not score in the NCT but did score in the planning total.
b   LA self-financed expenditure (LASFE) scores in the NCT but did not score in the planning total.
c   Privatisation proceeds are excluded from the NCT but they did score in the planning total.

The justification for these changes is that the government wishes to include as much public spending as possible in the NCT, given the fundamental objective of controlling GGE over time, but nevertheless wishes to insulate programme spending so far as is possible from the effects of the cycle. For this reason LASFE has been included in the NCT, given that it is a significant component of GGE and is not primarily cyclical. Equally, the main unemployment-related elements of social security (unemployment benefit and income support for non-pensioners) have been excluded from the NCT, whereas non-cyclical elements have been included.

It is important to note that the NCT implies a change in the approach to bargaining between spending ministers and the Treasury. Previously, spending ministers would submit bids, and after they had been totted up the Treasury would decide how many of them it was willing to sanction, so spending was partly driven by the size of bids. By comparison, the new 'top-down' system begins with the Chancellor and Prime Minister fixing the total in advance. As a result (at least in theory), any additional resources for one department can only be generated by reducing those available to other departments by an equivalent amount. In the event of dispute, a Cabinet committee chaired by the Chancellor will adjudicate.

5.2.4 *Trends in Public Expenditure*

The relationship between the planning total and the NCT is shown, in inflation-adjusted terms, in **Figure 5.2**. As can be seen, the NCT began to grow rapidly with the onset of recession in 1989–90, but is projected to grow very slowly with recovery beyond 1993–94. Taking the six-year period from 1989–90 to 1995–96, the overall growth in real terms is 15 per cent, which can be compared to the 18 per cent growth projected for GGE which includes cyclical elements. **Table 5.2** provides the wider overview of public expenditure spanning the period 1971–72 to 1995–96. Various aspects of the overall picture are picked up in the subsquent discussion. For the moment it is necessary merely to remark upon the missing data for the planning total/NCT. This arises because it has not proved to be possible to recalculate the local authority element in the planning total/NCT on the current definition for the years preceeding 1984–85.

Table 5.2 indicates the path of GGE (excluding privatisation proceeds) in real terms and as a percentage of GDP. The growth of real GGE was exceptionally rapid from 1963–64 to 1967–68, and then again from 1969–70 to 1974–75. After a set-back during the first OPEC crisis, it moved upwards again until 1984–85, albeit not quite as fast as during the previous two upturns. Subsequently, it barely grew at all until the end of

Figure 5.2   *Planning Total and NCT in Real Terms*[1]

Note:
[1] Cash figures adjusted to levels of 1991–92.
Source: Autumn Statement, 1992, Chart 2.2.

the decade, but is now once again growing quite strongly.

The early 1960s surge in real spending was much faster than GDP growth. The second surge, commencing in 1968–69, resulted in a 8 per cent rise in the real GGE/GDP ratio, with an overall effect, allowing for a brief fall at the end of the 1960s, of 12.5 per cent. There were a few countries (such as Sweden) where this figure was easily exceeded, but the OPEC crisis subsequently forced real spending down at a time when GDP continued to rise, thereby hauling back the ratio by 6 points within only two years.

Although much of this improvement proved to be transitory once the crisis was over, no government post-1976 has ever showed as much enthusiasm for public spending as was manifested in the mid-1970s. Nevertheless, it is notable that the 1980–81 recession prevented the first Thatcher Government from getting to grips with spending. Only after 1985–86 did the ratio of real spending to GDP start to fall rapidly, yet even at its lowest level in 1988–89 the ratio was back

only to the level of 1966–67, and it is currently back to the levels customary in the late 1970s.

As shown in **Figure 5.3**, which reflects the discussion at the beginning of the chapter, this is less of an achievement when viewed over the long term. Furthermore, for reasons discussed below, there is no foreseeable likelihood that the ratio of GGE to GDP will unwind to levels customary pre-1970. It is interesting to note, however, the difference between the two lines shown in **Figure 5.3**. GGE includes transfers, and shows the extent to which the government has to raise taxation and to borrow on the financial markets in order to finance its activites. The narrower measure, which covers goods and services only, shows the extent to which the nation's resources are being directly absorbed by the government. It is very evident that the latter has changed remarkably little over the past four decades. In other words, it is transfer payments of all kinds which have largely accounted for the much enlarged role of central government in people's lives.

Table 5.2 *Public Expenditure, 1971–72 to 1995–96*

	NCT[1]		Planning Total[1]		GGE		Privatisation Proceeds	GGE (excluding privatisation proceeds)		
	£ bn	Real terms[2] £ bn	£ bn	Real terms[2] £ bn	Spending on goods and services £ bn	Total £ bn	£ bn	£ bn	Real terms[2] £ bn	% of GDP[3]
1971–72					13.4	24.4		24.4	163.7	41¾
1972–73					15.2	27.6		27.6	171.7	41¾
1973–74					17.9	32.0		32.0	185.8	43¼
1974–75					22.9	42.9		42.9	208.1	48¾
1975–76					29.4	53.8		53.8	208.2	49¼
1976–77					32.9	59.6	−0.5	59.6	203.0	46¼
1977–78					35.2	63.9		64.4	193.0	43¼
1978–79					39.1	75.0		75.0	202.7	44
1979–80					46.6	90.0	−0.4	90.4	209.3	44
1980–81					56.8	108.6	−0.2	108.8	213.1	46½
1981–82					61.1	120.5	−0.5	121.0	216.0	47¼
1982–83					67.5	132.7	−0.5	133.1	221.8	47½
1983–84					73.0	140.3	−1.1	141.4	225.3	46½
1984–85	126.0	191.0	127.0	192.5	78.6	150.9	−2.0	152.9	231.8	47
1985–86	129.5	186.2	130.7	187.7	82.6	158.6	−2.7	161.3	231.8	45
1986–87	136.0	189.4	135.8	189.1	87.4	164.8	−4.5	169.2	235.7	44
1987–88	148.6	196.2	142.4	187.9	94.5	173.2	−5.1	178.4	235.4	41¾
1988–89	156.1	192.1	145.4	178.9	99.7	179.7	−7.1	186.8	229.8	39¼
1989–90	175.1	202.2	162.0	187.1	112.6	200.8	−4.2	205.0	236.7	39¾
1990–91	192.1	205.4	179.5	191.9	124.4	217.4	−5.3	222.7	238.1	40¼
1991–92	211.2	211.2	203.5	203.5	137.4	235.9	−7.9	243.8	243.8	42
1992–93	232.0	222.5	226.1	216.9	4	260.8	−8.0	268.8	257.8	44¾
1993–94	243.8	227.6	242.5	226.4	4	281.1	−5.5	286.6	267.6	45½
1994–95	253.6	229.3			4	297.0	−5.5	302.5	273.5	45
1995–96	263.3	231.7			4	315.4	−1.0	316.4	278.4	44¼

Notes:
[1] Figures for the control total and planning total are available on a consistent basis only for the years shown. Figures are estimated outturn for 1992–93 and plans for 1993–94 onwards.
[2] Cash figures adjusted to 1991–92 price levels by excluding the effect of general inflation. The deflator series used is that for GDP at market prices adjusted to remove the distortion caused by the abolition of domestic rates.
[3] Based on money GDP figures adjusted to remove the distortion caused by the abolition of domestic rates.
[4] Figures are available on a consistent basis for outturn years only.
Source: Statistical Supplement to the 1992 Autumn Statement.

Figure 5.3 *GGE as % of GDP, 1890–1996*[1]

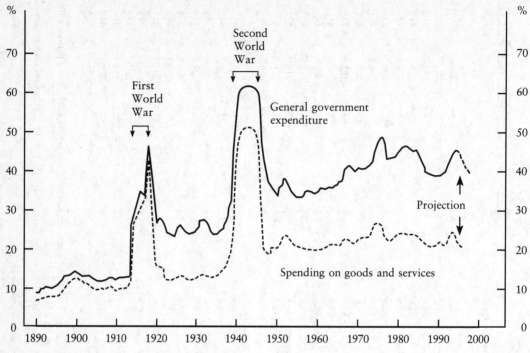

Note:
[1] Excluding privatisation proceeds and adjustments to remove the distortion caused by the abolition of domestic rates.

Source: Economic Trends (October 1987); *Statistical Supplement to the 1992 Autumn Statement*; *FSBR 1993–94*.

Given that the government does not itself consume transfer payments, there are those who prefer to discuss the role of government in terms of the lower rather than the upper line. On the other hand, taxes and social security levies must be raised to cover the entire sum spent by government, and the upper line is accordingly more appropriate in terms of the coverage of this chapter.

☐ 5.2.5 Public Expenditure Targets

In the course of the Autumn Statement for 1990 the government restated its position in relation to both expenditure and taxation as follows:

The Government's medium term objective for public spending is that, over time, it should take a declining share of national income,

while value for money is constantly improved. This is consistent with the policy of maintaining a balanced budget over the medium term and reducing taxation when it is prudent to do so. The public spending objective is expressed in terms of the ratio of general government expenditure (GGE), excluding privatisation proceeds, to gross domestic product (GDP). GGE is the main spending aggregate used in the Medium Term Financial Strategy (MTFS).

Throughout the 1980s it was the custom for the government to produce figures for its expenditure which showed a clear downward trend over time as a percentage of GDP. Initially, the planned percentages were consistently overoptimistic by a wide margin. By the mid-1980s the outturns were proving to be only modestly worse than the plans, and by the end of the decade the outturns were an improvement on the plans.

During the recent recession public spending inevitably rose as a percentage of GDP, but the government remains proud of its record, claiming that unlike its predecessors it has got to grips with public spending. But has it? In the first place, it must be remembered that we are dealing here with a **ratio**, which can fall in value for a variety of different combinations of changes in numerator and denominator. Originally, in the 1980 White Paper, the government expressed its spending objective as a progressive reduction of its expenditure in real terms over the subsequent four years. When this failed to transpire in practice, its objective became to hold expenditure constant in real terms, but this was not achieved either, despite the best efforts of the 'Star Chamber', a small committee of senior politicians set up specifically to bring into conformity the desire on the part of ministers to spend and the desire on the part of the Treasury not to spend.

Clearly, therefore, the government expressly never wanted its spending to rise in real terms, yet that, as we have seen in **Table 5.2**, is precisely what did happen if we take the 1980s as a whole (although the second half was better than the first and there was a modest reduction in 1987–89). Not surprisingly, the government also failed to bring spending down as a percentage of GDP on an ongoing basis until 1985–86, after which point it fell rapidly for three successive years despite the fact that real spending remained almost constant. In other words, real spending as a percentage of GDP essentially fell **not because real spending was itself falling but because GDP was rising rapidly**, as shown in **Table 5.2**.

Our conclusions from the above discussion are that (**a**) in terms of its original public spending targets the government has been a failure; (**b**) by moving the goalposts the government did manage, during the late 1980s, to hit its targets; but (**c**) this could be ascribed much less to successful curbs on real spending than to the effects of rapid economic growth; and hence (**d**) the government will be unable to hit its targets again until the recession is well and truly over, and probably not for some time after that.

It is evident that the government puts a favourable gloss on its spending performance. It is particularly interesting that when reference is made to public expenditure **cuts** this actually means a **reduction in the forecast rate of growth of spending**. It is also evident that the government has missed its spending targets more often than not. But **just how much of a failure has it been?** It must be recognised, first of all, that the government took office at the end of the era of profligate public spending which not merely rose sharply in real terms but as a percentage of GDP – up from 36 per cent in 1964–65 to 49 per cent in 1975–76, although the Labour government stemmed the tide in the late 1970s. Some of the blame for that rise could be laid at the door of the Plowden Committee. In the first place, planning subsequently came to be done on a volume basis which meant that spending Departments could expect their real spending to be maintained. Second, the volumes were adjusted upwards on the basis of forecast economic growth which never fully transpired in practice, with the result that real spending rose faster than real GDP.

In setting out to cut real spending the first Thatcher government was, therefore, trying like King Canute to turn back the tide, and although it failed **so did almost everyone else**. On average, public spending as a percentage of GDP rose sharply in OECD countries during the 1970s (and in absolute terms also). Table 5.3, which covers the EU over the period 1974–94, reveals that the position in 1985 was generally much worse than the average for the previous decade, with the ratios typically falling back after 1985 as public spending became, temporarily, less fashionable. During the 1980s only Britain and West Germany among the larger economies managed to rein back their ratios at all significantly. Elsewhere in Europe high spenders, such as Sweden and Holland, made negligible progress overall, although in many cases quite sharp reductions towards the end of the decade more than offset rising ratios at the beginning. Compared to the long-term trend the position in Spain, Italy and Greece had deteriorated seriously by 1990, and even the USA moved up towards European levels of spending, Reagan notwithstanding.

It was fortunate for Britain that its difficulties in the mid-1970s brought the desirablity of spiral-

Table 5.3 *Total Public Expenditure (as % of GDP) 1974–94.*

Country	1974–84	1985	1986	1987	1988	1989	1990	1991	1992	1993	1994
B	51.8	56.3	55.6	54.1	52.0	50.8	50.2	51.2	50.4	50.2	49.4
DK	52.6	58.9	54.3	55.7	58.0	58.1	57.2	57.1	58.1	58.5	57.9
D	48.2	48.1	47.1	47.4	47.0	45.5	45.9	49.2	49.7	50.5	50.4
D+	–	–	–	–	–	–	–	49.8	50.5	50.9	50.7
GR	–	44.1	47.2	47.7	47.9	49.4	53.1	52.0	51.3	49.6	48.0
E	31.5	39.6	41.9	40.8	41.0	42.2	43.3	45.0	46.0	46.5	46.5
F	46.7	52.5	52.2	51.7	50.8	49.8	50.3	50.6	51.5	52.4	52.9
IRL	49.0	53.1	53.7	51.5	48.1	41.3	42.0	42.2	43.2	43.8	44.1
I	42.0	49.4	50.7	50.2	50.3	51.4	53.2	53.5	55.4	55.8	55.1
L	52.2	53.6	51.3	55.2	52.9	48.6	48.9	49.3	50.2	50.8	50.9
NL	54.5	59.0	57.9	59.4	57.6	54.8	55.0	55.2	55.1	55.2	55.0
P	–	46.6	44.6	43.0	43.0	42.9	44.3	46.4	46.9	45.9	44.7
UK	43.5	45.3	42.6	40.8	38.1	37.8	40.0	40.8	42.7	44.3	44.7
EUR	45.0[1]	48.9	48.4	47.9	47.0	46.5	47.6	48.9	49.9	50.6	50.5
EUR+	–	–	–	–	–	–	–	49.0	50.1	50.7	50.6

Note:
[1] EUR without Greece and Portugal.
Source: European Economy, Supplement A.

ling public spending into question at a relatively early point in history. Gradually, expenditure was transformed on to a cash basis, a process completed in 1981, and this was accompanied by a more determined pursuit of value for money in public spending during the Thatcher years. The government's **efforts** could not be denied, but such progress as was made has to be set against a decade of Thatcherite determination. A recession combined with a 'wetter' government has already served to unwind most of the gains made in the late 1980s.

This does not bode particularly well for the future, yet there is one saving grace of a kind. In Britain, almost uniquely, the old-age dependency ratio (the number of people aged over 65 as a percentage of the working population) is set to fall up to the year 2010. As the dependency ratio rises so does the bill for health care and pensions, so whereas the Japanese Government, for example, currently spends a much lower proportion of GDP than the British (yet provides excellent services), its dependency ratio is set to rise from 17 per cent in 1990 to 28 per cent in 2010.

Looking further ahead to 2030, Britain's dependency ratio is set to rise, and the effect of health and pensions expenditure alone will possibly be to raise the spending/GDP ratio by 3 per cent. However, this is less than half the projected rise in other major economies, so in the longer term Britain will be well down the league table of big spenders even if the ratio of public spending to GDP is higher than currently.

5.2.6 *Functional Analysis of Expenditure*

In seeking to analyse why even a decade of Thatcherism failed to make any inroads into the absolute level of real public spending we need to disaggregate public spending into its main functions, as in **Figure 5.4**. The key lesson of **Figure 5.4** is that roughly 70 per cent of public spending is accounted for by only four functions, namely health, social security, education and science and defence. Over the period 1980–81 to 1992–

93 these four functions absorbed an increasing share of total spending, as shown by the dotted line.

It is important to remember that real spending rose during this period by £45 billion, so this was an **increasing share of an increasing real total**. In other words, any increase in the share necessarily means that additional **real** (not simply nominal, but inflation-adjusted) resources are being pumped into the function in question, and this may still be true even if the share declines slightly. Given the current controversy over health care, it has been put at the foot of each column in order to bring out the essential reality that the government has **pumped significant additional real resources into health care over the past decade**. The biggest share has long been taken by social security, reflecting in particular long-term growth in

pension liabilities and, up until the late 1980s and also recently, substantially higher unemployment benefits. As unemployment eased after 1986, so social security began to absorb a smaller share of the total, and that should continue in 1994–95.

Education and science has had a patchier time, partly because of the adjustment necessitated first by falling then by rising school rolls, but currently has the same share as a decade ago. Defence, on the other hand, after peaking in the middle of the 1980s, is on a downward trend in terms of its share of total spending, and this is set to continue, the Gulf War notwithstanding. Housing is also included in **Figure 5.4** because it took a significant share of total spending in 1980–81, but the sale of council houses and the upgrading of rents towards market levels halved housing's share of total spending by 1985–86. By way of

Figure 5.4 *GGE on Services by Function, % Share of Total, 1980/81 to 1992/93*

Note:
[1] Estimated outturn.
Source: Statistical Supplement to the 1992 Autumn Statement, Table 2.2.

contrast, law and order started off in 1980–81 with a much smaller share than housing and ended the decade with more than twice the share. It would therefore appear to be the case that the present governement is indeed the party of law and order.

These changes are brought out more clearly in **Table 5.4** which shows the percentage change in real spending between 1979–80 and 1992–93 and also between 1980–81 and 1992–93 (in order to avoid disputes about whether the government should be held responsible for spending during its election year). In either case the biggest increase was in spending on law and order, with both health and social security showing very substantial increases. With real spending on health up by over 40 per cent, it is, frankly, rather **unrealistic to accuse the government of undermining the NHS.**

On the other hand, education and science did only half as well, and real spending on defence was only slightly larger overall. The really significant reduction, as can be seen, was in real spending on housing, down by roughly one-half.

These developments can also usefully be reexpressed in terms of capital (investment) versus current spending. In 1973, investment constituted 12 per cent of GGE whereas by 1986 it constituted only 4.5 per cent. The reduction in the real level of fixed investment by roughly one-half during the

Table 5.4 *Increase in Real Expenditure by Function (%)*

	1992–93 / 1979–80	1992–93 / 1980–81
Law and order	80.3	75.6
Health	53.7	41.9
Social security	62.9	59.8
Education and science	27.0	23.5
Defence	4.6	1.8
Transport	22.4	23.8
Agriculture and fisheries	6.7	0.0
Housing	−54.7	−47.3

Source: Statistical Supplement to the 1992 Autumn Statement, Table 2.3.

decade beginning in 1975 was particularly pronounced in housing. Public corporations were also squeezed, as were investment grants to private sector organisations. It was also noticeable that subsidies were cut sharply, but although this tendency to make investment obey the rules of the market place sits comfortably within the philosophy of the present government, the reduction in investment was ironically much sharper under the Labour government in the late 1970s than under its Tory successor. By the late 1980s the government was obliged to increase real investment in, for example, roads and prisons (because it was increasing the prison population), but it is trying to involve private capital in these and other areas in order to keep its own capital investment under control.

One reason for the erratic approach to capital spending arises from the accounting system which writes off investment in the year the money is spent, exactly as though it was current spending, thereby ignoring the stream of future benefits that it generates. This is at odds with private sector practice, and makes it only too easy to cut spending on replacing sewers, for example.

One obvious conclusion to be drawn from the above discussion is that the government's efforts to control real spending during the 1980s were successful only in areas which did not absorb a big share of its spending: trade and industry was another in this category. Now these functions have been cut back to the bone there is no more fat to trim. Hence further reductions can occur only in major heads of spending yet, as we have seen, those are precisely the areas where even the current government has had little or no success. The number of pensioners cannot be reduced; unemployment will remain high by 1970s standards; the number of school children and college students is set to rise; and the health service is impervious to cuts.

☐ 5.2.7 The Spending Conundrum

It is surely one of the greatest ironies of Mrs Thatcher's decade in power that, having claimed for many years that a major objective was to **cut** public spending (but having failed in real terms to do so), it eventually became politically expedient to claim to the **contrary** (for example, in the case of the health service). But by that time the propaganda machine had been so successful that no-one would believe the government, even though what it claimed was true!

We already know that real spending on the health service rose significantly during the 1980s, yet the medical establishment has complained endlessly that the health service is underresourced, and (prospective) patients certainly believe that the service they receive (or cannot obtain) is deteriorating. How can this be?

Many categories of public expenditure, such as health and education, are currently labour-intensive. This means that the public expenditure debate has been dircted primarily towards **inputs** rather than **outputs**. The GDP deflator, which is used to express spending in real terms is, however, output-based and is therefore inappropriate for evaluating the **volume** of provision of **labour-intensive services**. This suggests that an own-cost deflator should be used in such circumstances, namely one based upon the **costs of inputs** used in each category. A study by Levitt and Joyce (1987) has demonstrated what a difference this can make. In the case of health, real GDP-deflated spending rose by 25 per cent between 1979 and 1986, whilst own-cost deflated spending rose by only 9 per cent. Since population growth absorbed over half of this latter increase, and technological advances absorbed the rest, the actual volume of health care delivered **per capitum** was **effectively identical** throughout the entire period. Thus, when the government claims to have increased real spending on the NHS, and the medical profession categorically denies that the resource base has improved, they are **both in their respective ways telling the truth!**

The obvious difficulty this creates is that, if real spending has to be constantly increased simply in order to deliver an unchanged volume of provision in crucial labour-intensive areas such as health, the only painless way to cut public spending as a percentage of GDP is to make GDP grow rapidly. One could alternatively, of course, move public spending into the private sector, so it is hardly surprising that educational loans rather than grants, and the tendering-out of NHS services, are being actively promoted. However, these changes are very difficult to deliver politically even for a government with a clear majority.

The demand for more resources in, for example, the NHS is inevitably couched in terms of inputs: too few nurses, hospital beds and so on. However, this tells us nothing about how **efficiently** these resources are going to be used, so the government has understandably tried to switch the emphasis of the public expenditure debate on to **outputs and productivity**. It introduced the Financial Management Initiative (FMI) in 1982; the programme of scrutinies of efficiency by the Cabinet Office under Lord Rayner in 1979; and the publication of performance indicators in the Autumn Statement. The drawback here is that one can, for example, show an increase in the number of in-patients treated per available bed by discharging patients more quickly than before! If, as a consequence, this means that many of them need to be readmitted, then they count as new patients and productivity remains high. There is also an inevitable tendency to use readily accessible measures of performance such as the size of GPs' lists, the pupil:teacher ratio in schools or the crime clear-up rate per police officer. However, there is no guarantee that reducing either of the first two will improve the quality of output, which would need to be measured by the ratio of cured patients per doctor or examination passes per teacher.

■ 5.3 The Overall Tax Burden

Between 1948 and 1985, in money terms, the gross receipts from taxation rose by 3200 per cent. Starting from 1948 it took 14 years to double tax revenue. It doubled again in eight years, and again in five. This acceleration was clearly associated with a sharp rise in the rate of inflation, and since 1975 the rate of increase has slowed down. However, prices rose by a total of only 1200 per cent during the equivalent period, which means that gross tax receipts more than doubled in real terms. As the population has remained fairly constant, the gross real burden of taxes **per capitum** has also clearly more than doubled.

However, individuals are not simply interested in their total tax bill but also in the **proportion of their total earnings which is taxed away**. This makes it sensible to express the tax burden in the form of total taxation as a percentage of GDP. Interestingly, this has shown no long-term continuous tendency to rise. Taxation as a percentage of GDP fell from 1948 to 1960, admittedly from the high percentage required for postwar reconstruction. However, it was back to the 1948 level by 1970. Having fluctuated somewhat during the 1970s, it rose sharply after the election of the present government in 1979, as shown in **Figure 5.5**.

As in the case of public expenditure, there are various methods which can be used to calculate the tax burden, but the trends have been almost identical so it is sensible to stick to the definitions which match up with the government's expenditure data. It is very interesting to note that on that basis the tax burden levelled out somewhat at the

end of the 1980–81 recession, and particularly during the period 1985–86 to 1990–91 when the two measures used in **Figure 5.5** became effectively one and the same. Thus, **it took from 1979–80 to 1992–93 for the tax burden to fall back below that prevailing at the time the first Thatcher Government was elected,** and it has yet to fall below that prevailing when the last Labour government was in power. Furthermore, with delayed tax increases already pencilled in as part of the Spring 1993 Budget, the trend line can be expected to turn up again shortly.

Fiscal drag, discussed below, is clearly a more powerful phenomenon than is commonly understood. In fact, the most markedly cyclical effect is shown by corporation tax receipts which soared with rising profitablity during much of the 1980s. In 1989–90 corporation tax accounted for 10.9 per cent of total tax revenue, but this has fallen to a forecast of only 6.4 per cent in 1993–94 as profitability has collapsed back much faster than GDP. This accounts in good part for the recent fall in the tax burden, but as it is a cyclical

Figure 5.5   *Taxes and Social Security Contributions*

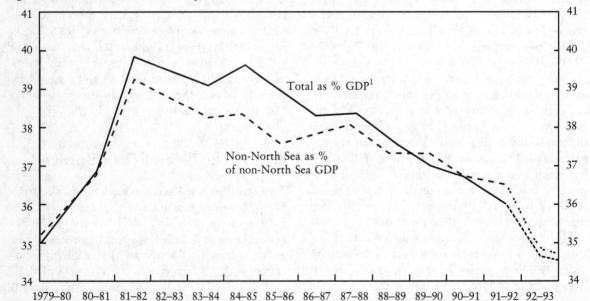

Note:
[1] Includes the Community Charge with taxes from 1989–90.
Source: FSBR 1993–94, Chart 6.2.

phenomenon it is another likely reason why there could well be a rise in the tax burden once the recession is fully over.

☐ 5.3.1 *The Marginal Rate of Tax*

The tax burden represents the **average** rate of **direct tax**: that is, total direct tax divided by total GDP. Given the existence of tax allowances, it is evident that the rate levied on an **extra** £1 of income, the **marginal** rate of direct tax, will be **higher**. Suppose, for example, an employer wishes to pay an extra £1 to a worker. In every case he or she must him- or herself pay 10.2p in NICs. The employee may, or may not, pay 10p in NICs (because they are levied only up to a maximum income: see **p. 163**) and will pay either 20p, 25p or 40p in income tax. Out of what is left, the employee will subsequently incur VAT, excise duties and other indirect taxes.

Thus, out of every additional £1 earned, a higher rate income tax payer will initially pay 40p (income tax) but the employer will also pay NICs of 10.2p: a total tax bill of 50.2p. For a standard rate payer it will be either 25p+10.2p +10p= 45.2p or, without employee NICs, 35.2p. The Labour Party promise to uncap NICs: that is, to make the 10p apply in all cases. Under such circumstances we get 60.2p for the higher rate payer and 45.2p for the standard rate payer. They also propose to raise the higher rate of income tax. And this, remember, only relates to **direct** tax. When what remains is spent, all kinds of additional **indirect** taxes are incurred.

The Labour Party argues that this will yield sufficient extra revenue to finance improved child benefits and State pensions, but this is most unlikely to occur. In 1978–79, the last Labour government's final financial year in power, with higher rates of income tax **alone** rising to 83 per cent, the highest-paid 10 per cent of the working population contributed 34 per cent of all income tax collected. In 1989–90, with the higher rate set at 40 per cent, the highest-paid 10 per cent contributed 42 per cent of all income tax. On the other hand, the share contributed by the bottom 70 per cent of income tax payers (including almost all Labour voters) fell from 38 per cent to 32 per cent. It is widely recognised that when higher rates of income tax go up almost everyone in a position to do so **looks for ways to avoid them,** so the tax burden will simply be redistributed back from the highest paid to the lowest paid; **little or no extra spending will be financed**.

Opinion polls consistently reveal that UK residents **prefer** more public spending to tax cuts, but since 1979 they have just as consistently failed to elect governments who have promised tax increases to pay for higher spending. Readers may draw their own conclusions.

■ 5.4 Fiscal Drag

It may come as something of a surprise, in view of the sharp reduction in the marginal rates of income tax in recent years, that the burden of taxation has fallen so little in response. This can primarily be explained by the phenomenon of **fiscal drag** which arises because, whereas the Rooker-Wise-Lawson amendments to the 1977 Finance Bill provided that tax allowances be raised in line with inflation unless the Budget specifically provided otherwise, the index used to adjust for inflation is for **prices** rather than **incomes**.

When the economy is growing strongly incomes tend, on average, to grow noticeably faster than prices. Hence, even if tax allowances are adjusted to compensate for rising prices, an increasingly larger proportion of total income is subjected to tax. In 1987–88 this caused tax revenue to be some £2 billion higher than forecast, and this was comfortably exceeded in 1988–89. As a rule of thumb, each 1 per cent rise in real income increases the average personal tax rate by between 1.5 and 1.75 per cent.

Though not technically fiscal drag, precisely the same effect will occur for corporate taxation when profits are rising much faster than GDP, as can clearly be seen in **Figure 5.6**. Equally, spending tends to rise with real incomes, with the result that indirect tax receipts rise sharply.

During the recession commencing in 1990 fiscal drag operated in reverse, with incomes rising

Figure 5.6 **Corporation Tax Receipts**

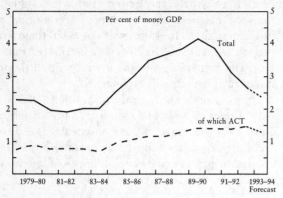

Source: FSBR 1993–94, Chart 6.1.

more slowly for the employed, large numbers losing their jobs, falling profits and a collapse in household spending. The consequent rapid erosion of the tax base made it difficult for the government to maintain tax revenue (which is projected to be lower in real terms in 1993–94 than in 1991–92). The only way to compensate for this is to reduce tax thresholds (allowances), but this is politically unacceptable (although freezing them in money terms, and hence reducing their real value, has become an increasingly popular option for the government).

■ 5.5 International Comparisons

The CSO calculates the tax burden for OECD member countries on a standardised international definition used by the OECD, as shown in **Figure 5.7**. This reveals, firstly, that in 1990 the overall tax burden in the UK as a percentage of **GNP at factor cost** was in the lower half of the list of countries illustrated, well below the Nordic countries and France and similar to West Germany, albeit appreciably above Japan.

For studies of the UK alone, **GDP at market prices** is often used as a denominator, as in **Figure 5.5**. This has the effect of reducing the size of all the ratios in **Figure 5.7**, but does not affect the UK's ranking as shown in **Table 5.5**.

Clearly, therefore, the UK is **not overburdened by taxation relative to most other industrialised**

Figure 5.7 **Taxes and Social Security Contributions as a % of GNP at Factor Cost, 1990**

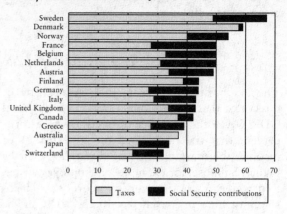

Source: Economic Trends (December 1992), p. 104.

countries. As shown in **Figure 5.7**, many of the misconceptions about the burden of taxation arise because of the very different balance between

Table 5.5 **Taxes and Social Security Contributions as a % of GDP at Market Prices by Rank**

	1980		1985		1990	
	Percentage and Rank		*Percentage and Rank*		*Percentage and Rank*	
Sweden	49	2	50	1	56	1
Denmark	45	4	49	3	49	2
Norway	51	1	50	2	47	3
Netherlands	46	3	46	5	45	4
Belgium	45	5	48	4	45	5
France	42	7	44	6	44	6
Austria	42	6	44	7	42	7
FR Germany	42	8	42	8	40	8
Italy	30	11	35	11	39	9
Finland	33	10	36	10	38	10
UK[1]	36	9	38	9	37	11
Canada	30	13	32	13	36	12
Greece[2]	28	15	33	12	34	13
Switzerland[2]	30	12	32	14	32	14
Japan	26	16	28	16	32	15
Australia	28	14	30	15	31	16

Notes:
[1] Includes the Community Charge.
[2] Calculations based upon current system for National Accounts except for Greece and Switzerland, which are based up on the pre-1968 System of National Accounts.
Source: Economic Trends (December 1992), p. 104.

Table 5.6 *The Structure of the UK Tax System since 1948*

Ongoing Taxes	New Taxes	Repealed Taxes
Beer duty	Selective employment tax (1967)	Profits tax (1965)
Customs and protective duties	Capital gains tax (1967)	Selective employment tax (1972)
Hydrocarbon oil duty	Corporation tax (1967)	Purchase tax (1973)
Income tax	Car tax (1973)	Estate duty (1974)
Local authority rates	Value added tax (1973)	Capital transfer tax (1976)
National Insurance	Capital transfer tax (1974)	Community Charge (1993)
Stamp duty	Petroleum revenue tax (1978)	Car tax (1993)
Tobacco duty	Inheritance tax (1986)	
Vehicle licences	Community Charge (1989)	
Wine and spirits duties	Council tax (1993)	
	Air passenger duty (1994)	
	Insurance premium tax (1994)	

what are officially called 'taxes' as against 'social security contributions' in different countries. The 'tax' burden in the UK is relatively high but the **overall deductions** in relation to GDP are nothing exceptional.

Unfortunately, what this means in policy terms is that there is equal ammunition (a) for those who believe that taxation should be set at a Japanese level in a free society and (b) for those who believe that the UK can afford to increase public expenditure, financed out of taxation, without raising the tax burden above that commonly ruling elsewhere in the EU, or indeed in Europe generally.

■ 5.6 The Tax System

☐ 5.6.1 Introduction

The tax system in the UK is somewhat out of line with that typically found elsewhere in the OECD. Only in the UK, between 1955 and 1985, did the importance of income tax, measured as a percentage of GDP, fall rather than rise. However, the UK has been typical in its increased emphasis upon NICs (or its equivalent) which, though not technically a tax, has precisely the same effect as income tax upon disposable income.

The UK tax system has been developed in an **evolutionary** rather than a **revolutionary** manner

since 1948. Although no chancellor has chosen to institute a major programme of tax reform (unless, as some believe, Nigel Lawson is to be regarded as the exception in this respect), the long-term consequence of continuous small adjustments has been to alter the relative importance of different taxes quite dramatically (Keen, 1991). The preference for evolution is unsurprising from a political perspective since it has been calculated that, as a rule of thumb, tax reform is politically acceptable only if the beneficiaries outnumber the losers by a ratio of four to one. Furthermore, it is much easier to sweeten a reform that hurts the pockets of a large number of voters by giving them back bigger sums via tax cuts elsewhere in the system, and this can be done only if tax revenue is buoyant. In any event, the Inland Revenue is never keen on major administrative changes. The structure of the tax system since 1948 is set out in **Table 5.6**.

☐ 5.6.2 Taxes on Income

Income Tax

Income tax remains the most important element of the tax system, but its importance has declined since 1979. In general, income tax is charged **on all income that originates in the UK** (including, since 1987, the earnings of overseas entertainers and sportsmen), and on **all income arising abroad of people resident in the UK.**

However, every taxpayer is entitled to a **personal allowance** to set against his or her gross taxable income (which is itself taken net of any pension fund contributions). There is currently a separate allowance for the single and for the married (but see discussion of personal allowances reform below). This is generally referred to as the **standard rate tax threshold.** It may also be supplemented by a whole variety of other allowances, of which the most common is tax relief on interest paid on mortgages. Currently this is almost always paid direct (at source) to the building society or bank acting as mortgagor by the Inland Revenue, with the mortgagee paying a net-of-tax relief monthly figure (the MIRAS system), so it does not normally affect an individual's tax code. Tax relief may also be given for such things as covenants, or for payments under the Business Expansion Scheme (BES). Once all allowances have been deducted the residual sum becomes the **taxable income.**

Historically, income tax was designed to be **progressive**: that is, to take a higher proportion of income in tax as income rises. This was based upon the principle of **ability to pay**, and provided the main mechanism whereby the redistribution of spending power between households could be effected. Progressivity was thought to require a significant number of different tax rates, although in practice there is progressivity if there is a single tax threshold below which the tax rate is 0 per cent and above which it is positive. During the early postwar period the standard rate rose sharply, and was held at over 40 per cent throughout the period from 1948 to 1968, although until 1971 two ninths of earned income was exempt from tax so that the effective rate was lower than the nominal rate.

The higher rates were ultimately raised to punitive levels, and predictable consequences followed. During the 1970s everyone in a position to do so earned 'income' in the form of legitimate tax-relieved 'perks', and taxable income fell to half the total income declared to the Inland Revenue. Furthermore, a good deal of income was undeclared (the black economy). But with the tax base shrinking in leaps and bounds, the only way to maintain total tax revenue was assumed at the time to be to raise tax rates even higher, setting off the vicious circle yet again.

The disincentive effects of high tax rates on hard work understandably did nothing for economic growth, and in recognition of this the standard rate had been brought down to 33 per cent by the beginning of the present government's term of office. The government declared its intention of bringing down the basic rate as part of the MTFS, and managed to reduce it steadily to 25 per cent by 1988–89. In so doing, it reduced both the rewards of non-declaration relative to the drawback of a possible prison sentence, and the benefits of perks compared to cash. At the same time, many perks were either abolished (for example, tax relief on life insurance premiums) or were held roughly constant in money terms, thereby reducing their real value (for example, mortgage interest relief). As a result, taxable income rose to two thirds of total income by 1987–88.

The possibility of moving to a 25 per cent standard rate, which the government had declared to be its ultimate goal but which was widely regarded at the time as little more than a pipe-dream, arose as a result of the immense fiscal drag in 1987–88. Chancellor Lawson was very keen to emulate the USA which had already moved to a two-rate system of 15 per cent and 34.7 per cent (adjusted for local income tax), in the process abolishing a whole host of tax reliefs as a quid pro quo. The Chancellor had always been ambivalent about perks, inventing new ones (such as the Business Expansion Scheme) whilst abolishing existing ones. However, he found himself able in the Budget of 1988 not merely to fund higher levels of spending and to reduce the PSBR, but also to produce his own two-rate structure with the standard rate set at 25 per cent and the higher rate set at 40 per cent (compared to the five higher rates ranging from 40 per cent to 60 per cent only the previous year). Furthermore, he did not need to eat heavily into perks.

Compared to other major industrialised countries the standard rate tax threshold in the UK still remains low (at £3445 for a single person in 1994–95), and the standard rate itself is almost the highest. However, the top rate is lower than all except that of the USA (although it bites at the very low threshold of £23 700 of taxable income), and there is a 20 per cent rate on a modest amount of taxable income. This was introduced in the 1992 Budget encompassing the first £2000 of taxable income, extended to £2500 in the Spring 1993 Budget and is set to rise to £3000 in 1994–95. There is, therefore, still considerable scope for further rate reductions, but fiscal drag will be needed to provide the means to achieve them. Indeed, in his 1988 Budget speech Nigel Lawson stated that the objective was to be a standard rate of 20p, and that rate has been introduced as indicated as a token of the government's desire to meet that objective at some time in the future.

Three issues also need to be carefully noted. In the first place, the sharp reduction in the top rate of tax inevitably transferred huge sums of money to the highest income earners without offsetting reductions in perks, whereas the minor reduction in the standard rate made little difference to the bulk of the working population. This inevitably made the distribution of post-tax income less equal. Against this can be set the benefits of a simplified tax structure and the hoped-for incentive effect on work effort and entrepreneurial activity, but it is doubtful whether the balance between equity and efficiency can be pushed even further towards the latter by repeating the exercise. Second, the very high levels of consumer spending during 1988, and their consequences for overheating and inflation, made Lawson wary of anything that smacked of fiscal giveaways in his 1989 Budget, and his successors, Major and Lamont, have chosen to proceed very cautiously even in the face of a deepening recession. Third, the creation of a 20 per cent band has been accompanied by a reduction, first to 20 per cent in the Spring 1993 Budget and then to 15 per cent in the Autumn 1993 Budget, in the tax relief available on mortgage interest payments, tax credits and tax relief for married couples, operative from April 1995, so the Chancellor is certainly not treating the objective of a 20 per cent standard rate as an exercise in transferring large sums into people's pockets.

Nevertheless, the 1991 Budget undoubtedly represented a move back towards more progressivity in the income tax structure. In particular, the abolition of tax relief on MIPs at the higher rate of tax imposed additional burdens only upon high-income households. The more recent introduction of a lower tax rate has benefited primarily low earners, and the freezing of the higher rate threshold in 1993–94 and 1994–95 has also had a rebalancing effect.

5.6.3 Independent Taxation for Married Couples

Recent changes in the structure of income tax have altered it to a greater degree and at a faster rate than at any other time since 1945. Nevertheless, these changes still represent tinkering rather than true reform. There is little sign of the latter on the horizon, but one issue is worthy of mention: namely, that of independent taxation for married couples. The pre-1990 system of taxing husbands and wives treated a married woman's income in law as if it belonged to her husband, a procedure dating back to the time when it was uncommon for wives to earn outside the home. This gave rise to dissatisfaction because such a high proportion of married women were in employment outside the home. Furthermore, the married man's allowance, originally intended to compensate for the added burden of supporting non-earning members of a household, had become something of an anomaly in a world of two-income households where the working wife was given an additional single person's allowance in her own right. As a consequence, a household containing a married couple where both were working was in receipt of 2.5 times as much in allowances as a single-person household. Even more anomalous was the fact that if the wife alone was at work she was entitled to the full set of allowances, whereas if the husband alone was at work he was entitled only to the married man's allowance.

Green Papers, published in 1980 and 1981, considered how to eradicate these anomalies, and in his Budget speech in 1988 the Chancellor announced that, from 6 April 1990, husbands and wives would be taxed independently on their income and chargeable capital gains. This has meant that (a) husband and wife become independent taxpayers, each with his or her own allowances to set against income from whatever source, and each responsible for dealings with the Inland Revenue; (b) every taxpayer receives the single person's allowance; (c) in addition, a married couple receives the difference between the current single allowance and the married allowance, which from 1993–94 can be set either against the income of husband or wife or shared equally between them (although this attracts only a 15 per cent rate of relief from April 1995); (d) special arrangements apply for those aged over 65; (e) a husband and wife's capital gains are taxed independently, with each entitled to a single person's exempt allowance; (f) the existing exemptions from CGT and inheritance tax on transfers of capital between husband and wife continue as before.

5.6.4 National Insurance Contributions (NICs)

NICs were introduced as a universal tax in 1948. Unusually for the UK tax system they are a hypothecated tax, which means that they exist to finance specific items of expenditure, in particular retirement pensions and unemployment and sickness benefit. Originally NICs were levied at a flat rate which was regressive in its impact. Benefits were related to contributions, but this became impractical as benefits grew rapidly because flat-rate NICs would have had to be levied at a level which would have borne down too heavily on the poor. Earnings-related NICs were therefore introduced in 1961 on a partial basis, and this became the only form of NICs after 1975.

An annual review of NICs is required by the provisions of the Social Security Act 1975. It is necessary to comment briefly on this because,

from the taxpayer's point of view both income tax and NICs have the same effect since they are deducted at source on Pay As You Earn (PAYE), which applies to all except the self-employed in the UK. Although the income tax structure was simplified in the 1988 Budget, the structure of NICs retained the perverse principle that once a threshold was triggered the relevant rate was applied not only to income between the thresholds but to all income, thereby generating very high marginal rates at the threshold points.

The reform of NICs introduced in the 1989 Budget took effect in October 1989. This simplified the system in that those with earnings below £57 per week in financial year 1994–95 continue to pay nothing, while those with earnings at or above £57 pay 2 per cent on the first £57 (112p) and 10 per cent on the rest up to the upper earnings limit of £430 per week.

Removal of all except a very modest NICs' liability on the first £57 of weekly earnings undoubtedly benefits the low paid (and helps to offset fiscal drag), but it remains the case that the lower earnings limit is indeed very low (below that for income tax) and also that, once earnings in 1994–95 rise above £430 per week, the combined rate of income tax plus NICs falls back at the margin from 35 per cent to 25 per cent, (the 1993–94 position is shown in **Figure 5.8**). This can hardly be called a progressive structure, and it must also be borne in mind that it is only those whose incomes are high enough to provide spare cash who can afford to spend money in tax-deductible ways (by taking out a £30 000 mortgage, for example). Furthermore, employee benefits do not attract NICs. Despite the 1989 reform, the employer continues to pay NICs on all employee earnings at the rates shown in **Table 5.7**.

The government has come under pressure to make employee NICs open-ended in terms of income, which would have the effect of a permanent marginal rate of deduction of either 35 per cent or 50 per cent on taxable income alone. This is Labour policy, but has so far been ignored by Conservative chancellors. Instead, in the 1991 Budget, Chancellor Lamont made employers pay NICs on the benefit of cars provided for the

Figure 5.8 *Marginal Tax Rates, 1993–94[1]*

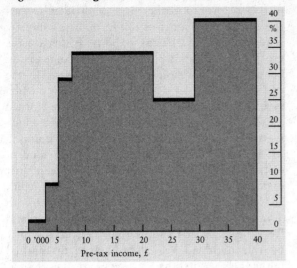

Note:
[1] Income tax and NICs for married man.

Table 5.7 *NICs, 1994–95*

Weekly Earnings	Percentage NIC Rate	
	Employees	*Employers[1]*
Below £57	0	0
£57 to £100	2% of £57	3.6
£100 to £145	plus	5.6
£145 to £200	10% of earnings	7.6
£200 to £430	between £57	10.2
Above £430	and £430	10.2

Notes:
[1] Rates apply to all earnings.
Source: Autumn Statement 1992, p. 85 as amended by Budget statement (November 1993).

private use of employees, based on the scale charges set for income tax. Employees are, however, exempted.

☐ 5.6.5 *Corporation Tax*

During the 1970s, corporation tax, which is levied on company profits, had much in common with income tax. On the face of it the marginal rate was high, but deductible allowances were so extensive, particularly those concerned with capital investment, that large companies were able to adjust their balance sheets so as to incur little or no tax liability.

As a result, Nigel Lawson reformed the tax in 1984 by phasing out many of the allowances and by simultaneously cutting the tax rate progressively from 52 per cent to 35 per cent. The matching rate for small companies earning profits below £100 000 per annum was initially set at 29 per cent (to match the existing income tax basic rate), and was reduced to 25 per cent for the financial year 1988–89. By international standards, company taxation in the UK thereby became modest.

However, care must be taken to **adjust for the phasing out of capital allowances**, and for the **failure to inflation-adjust** those that remained. Furthermore, the abolition of tax relief on the increase in the value of stocks due to inflation, which seemed uncontroversial at the time because inflation had fallen rapidly, temporarily became a problem once again when inflation rose towards the end of the decade. Hence, as we have seen in **Figure 5.6**, many companies actually found themselves paying more tax than before even though the rate was much lower.

With the onset of recession in 1990, the need for a Budget to assist businesses resulted in the retrospective reduction in the rate of corporation tax in the 1991 Budget to 34 per cent for the 1990–91 financial year and to 33 per cent for 1991–92, at which rate it has subsequently remained. In addition, companies were to be allowed to carry back trading losses for three years instead of one year, and the profits limit for the small companies' corporation tax rate of 25 per cent was raised from £200 000 to £250 000 for 1991–92. It has been set at £300 000 for 1993–94.

The remaining allowances of any consequence are concerned with **depreciation provisions**. These exist in order to permit companies to build up a stock of money (often itself confusingly called 'capital') which can be used to replace their worn-out or obsolete physical capital stock. Since money set aside for this purpose is needed merely to keep the company in business as a going concern, it is clearly not 'profit' and should not be taxed as such. There are basically two ways of calculating how much money can be set aside each year without incurring a tax liability on the equivalent amount of gross profit. The first is the straight-line method whereby a given proportion of the original capital cost is set aside each year: for example, 15 per cent each year for four years. Alternatively, the declining-balance method is used whereby a specified proportion of the original outlay is set against tax liability in Year 1, and the same proportion of the residual amount is written down in Year 2, and so on. This has the effect of setting aside the largest absolute amount of tax liability in Year 1, and successively smaller absolute amounts in successive years. It is up to the tax authorities to determine which depreciation method is to be applied. Historically, when inflation was unusually high, adjustments also needed to be made for the fact that the replacement cost of a unit of capital was much higher than the original cost, but this is no longer considered to be necessary.

Prior to 1984 it was customary to allow a very high proportion of all capital expenditure to be set against corporation tax liability in the year of purchase, but since 1986 these provisions have been made much less generous in view of the much lower rates of tax. Each year 25 per cent of the cost of plant and machinery can in principle be set against corporation tax liability on a declining-balance basis (although a special first-year rate of 40 per cent applied between November 1992 and October 1993), while only 4 per cent of the cost of industrial or agricultural buildings and hotels can be written down on a straight-line basis each year since buildings last much longer than machines (although a special initial allowance of 20 per cent applied between November 1992 and October 1993). Short-life machinery and plant may be wholly written down over its lifetime. These provisions are universal because it would be far too difficult and expensive to deal with companies on an individual basis. However, it remains possible for the government to make exceptions, usually in the context of **regional policy**.

Corporation tax is levied on all profits, whether retained within the company or distributed to shareholders. However, if a company wishes to distribute profits in the form of dividends, then these are paid in a net-of-tax form. The company is obliged to pay the tax liability arising on the gross dividends at an agreed rate of **income tax** on behalf of the shareholders. This is collected by the tax authorities in advance of the time when dividends are paid out and is therefore known as advance corporation tax (ACT). ACT, which is strictly not a corporation but an income tax, in 1993–94 represents 29 per cent of the value of distributed profit (tax rate of 22.5 per cent: net dividend equals 77.5 per cent of gross dividend). Shareholders receive their dividend together with a 'tax credit' which they can pass on to the Inland Revenue in order to show that their tax liability on this dividend has already been discharged (although they will have to pay extra tax if their marginal rate is 40 per cent). Any shareholders exempt from income tax can claim a refund.

It is intended that the tax credit will be reduced to 20 per cent in 1994–95. However, since the rate of tax on dividends will simultaneously be reduced to 20 per cent, the net dividend will remain exactly as before. Non-taxpayers and investing institutions will suffer because they will only be able to reclaim the reduced tax credit, but companies will be better off.

At present a company subtracts the ACT payment from the total corporation tax liability on its profits, and the outstanding sum is paid over at the end of the relevant financial year in the form of **mainstream** corporation tax. It will now have to hand over less tax in advance, thereby improving cash flow, although the total tax bill will remain the same. However, not all companies pay sufficient mainstream tax to offset the ACT fully, and this was tempting foreign-owned multinationals to move their headquarters out of the UK. A special tax regime for such companies has accordingly been promised for 1994–95.

☐ 5.6.6 North Sea Taxes

North Sea taxation consists of royalties, petroleum revenue tax (including advance payments) and corporation tax from North Sea oil and gas

Table 5.8 *North Sea Revenues (£ bn)*

	1991–92	1992–93		1993–94
	Outturn	1992 Budget	Latest Estimate	Forecast
North Sea corporation tax[1]	0.6	0.6	0.7	0.8
Petroleum revenue tax	−0.2	0.1	–	0.6
Oil royalties	0.6	0.5	0.5	0.7
Total North Sea revenues	1.0	1.2	1.3	2.2
Note:	0.4	0.3	0.5	0.6

[1] Before ACT set-off of:
Source: FSBR 1993–94, Table 6.3.

production (before ACT set-off). In 1984–85 these amounted to £12 billion, but in 1986–87 there was a very sharp fall to £4.8 billion, a figure which was halved again by 1989–90. **Table 5.8** indicates how unimportant this element of the tax system has become.

Royalties are levied on the production of oil and gas fields on an individual basis. However, in order to induce oil companies to explore for oil and gas in less accessible – and hence more costly – tracts of the North Sea, the government first abolished royalties on newly-developed fields in the central and northern sectors in 1982, and in the 1988 Budget subsequently abolished royalties on post-1982 oil and gas fields in the Southern Basin and onshore areas. The latter development was primarily intended to stimulate gas production.

As a consequence, North Sea taxation became almost entirely dependent upon profit-related taxes. Prior to the March 1993 Budget, petroleum revenue tax (PRT) was charged at a rate of 75 per cent on profits (net of royalties) from the production, as opposed to the refining, of oil and gas under licence in Britain and on its continental shelf. Various allowances could be set against PRT, in particular certain costs incurred in oil exploration. Corporation tax was payable on profits in the usual way, but was levied on profits net of royalties and PRT.

The PRT rate on existing oilfields has been reduced to 50 per cent, and it has been abolished

altogether for new fields as part of the Spring 1993 Budget, but by simultaneously disallowing offsetting exploration costs the Treasury expects PRT to start contributing once again to receipts, as shown in **Table 5.8**.

Events in the North Sea, such as the Piper Alpha fire, and the instability of oil prices due to the Gulf War have had an erratic effect upon recent North Sea production. Also, the effect of much increased investment in the North Sea caused profitability to fall, and as a consequence PRT needed to be repaid in 1991–92. North Sea revenues currently represent less than 1 per cent of total tax revenue: a far cry from the 9 per cent which they represented at their peak in 1984–85.

☐ *5.6.7 Customs and Excise Duties*

Customs duties are charged on imported goods in accordance with the Common Customs Tariff of the EU. This exempts community goods imported from other EU member states, and provides a uniform EU-wide tariff barrier against goods from elsewhere in the world. Special arrangements apply for agricultural products in accordance with the CAP. As these duties are an EU rather than a purely national policy, their proceeds are transferred to Brussels to help finance the EU.

Excise duties, on the other hand, are not concerned with controlling trade flows but purely with raising revenue from goods and services which are either in inelastic demand (their consumption varies less than in proportion to price) or anti-social, or both. They apply to oils used for road fuel (and for other uses at a reduced rate); to alcoholic drinks (taxed largely in accordance with alcoholic strength); to tobacco products (in accordance with number, price or weight); to betting; to gambling machine and casino licences; and from 1 April 1994 to air travel from the UK. Road usage is additionally taxed through vehicle licences.

These duties are very unpopular, but have the virtue (from the Chancellor's viewpoint) that consumers are really aware only of how much they are going up and not of how much has cumulatively been levied in the past. Each increase therefore causes great aggravation at the time, but very rapidly gets forgotten as consumers get used to the new levels of prices, which are anyway constantly being adjusted for other reasons. Furthermore, as they are levied in incremental amounts expressed in pence, their incidence is very erratic. VAT receipts automatically rise in money terms when product prices rise, but excise duties do not and therefore can – and often do – fail to keep pace with inflation. Surprisingly, some products, such as whisky, are currently very cheap by historical standards once inflation is taken into account, partly as a result of a move to uniform taxation of alcohol content.

Alcohol and tobacco products bear VAT on the total cost after levying excise duties: that is, the tax is taxed! In the case of cigarettes EU harmonisation proposals (see below) resulted in a specific tax of 3.2p per cigarette and a special ad valorem tax of 21 per cent of retail price. As a result roughly 75 per cent of the retail price of a packet of cigarettes consists of tax of one kind or another, whereas it is only roughly one third for a pint of beer.

In recent years increasing attention has been paid to the wider social costs associated with the misuse of alcohol, tobacco and vehicles by individuals, but there has been no clear attempt to force a reduction in consumption via the price mechanism. This may partly reflect the desire to maintain revenue, since sharp increases in prices may, at least temporarily, cause demand (and hence revenue) to fall disproportionately. Perhaps more importantly, excise duties feed straight through to the rate of inflation, control of which is the primary macroeconomic objective.

One innovation, in the 1988 Budget, was the introduction of a reduced rate of duty on unleaded petrol which causes less pollution than its leaded equivalent.

☐ 5.6.8 Taxes on Wealth

For the most part, income has to be **earned**. By saving part of this income a pool of wealth can be accumulated. However, a very large proportion of the total pool of wealth currently results from capital gains (especially rising house values) and from inheritance, neither of which requires much effort to acquire. Thus, in principle, one would expect wealth to be taxed much more harshly than income on grounds of equity.

There are, however, a number of practical difficulties. Much wealth is, for example, tied up in physical assets (houses, businesses, farms, etc.) and to pay a wealth tax in cash could require a part of these assets to be sold. This could be very damaging to efficiency (for example, farms could become progressively smaller). Equally, the incentive for an entrepreneur to build up a business would be much reduced were it to be necessary for the business to be sold off by his or her heirs in order to pay wealth taxes, since it is reasonable to suppose that the entrepreneur is often driven by a desire to build up a business dynasty. Furthermore, it is inequitable and impractical to force surviving spouses to sell up the family home upon the death of their husbands or wives. As a result, wealth taxes have never accounted for more than a very small proportion of total tax revenue.

Inheritance Tax

It is possible to value assets on an annual basis and to tax their value on an ongoing basis. Annual wealth taxes are levied elsewhere in Europe, but have never been implemented in the UK. Instead, wealth is liable to tax only upon its **transfer from one individual to another**, whether in the form of a gift during the donor's lifetime, or upon the donor's death. This is administratively convenient since estates must be valued for probate purposes when a person dies.

Inheritance taxes have been levied in the UK since 1894. Until 1974 they were known as Estate Duty (or death duty) and applied only to transfers at death. The Labour government introduced Capital Transfer Tax (CTT) in 1974 in order to incorporate certain lifetime gifts. These were accumulated over time, with the tax rate applied to each gift being determined by the cumulative total. However, transfers of property between husbands and wives, both during life and at death, were tax-exempt, together with gifts and bequests to charity. Tax-exempt thresholds also applied to transfers upon death, and to gifts both to individuals and in total during any one year.

In practice, CTT proved to be scarcely more punitive than its predecessor because of the widespread exemptions and the low rates levied on lifetime gifts. When elected in 1979, the Conservatives nevertheless set about 'drawing the teeth' of CTT by raising thresholds, lowering rates and reducing aggregation periods during which lifetime gifts were accumulated (those made pre-1979 being exempt). In 1986 CTT was renamed inheritance tax. The period of accumulation was reduced from 10 to seven years and the rate of tax was lowered. Anyone making a 'potentially exempt transfer', and living for a further seven years, could subsequently expunge that transfer from their cumulative lifetime total of taxable gifts. If that person lived on for between four and seven years, a proportion of the tax would become payable, ranging from 100 per cent for deaths occurring within three years of making a gift to 20 per cent in the seventh year.

Between 1979 and 1988 prices in general less than doubled. However, the tax threshold for inheritance tax (CTT) rose from £25 000 in 1979 to £110 000 in the Budget of 1988, representing a more than doubling in real terms. Furthermore, the multiple rate structure of previous years was abolished, and a single rate of 40 per cent introduced. The threshold and rate changes in 1988 had little effect upon modest estates, but reduced the tax bill on an estate of £1 million by £145 000

(and by even more where legitimate tax shelters had been used). The 1994–95 threshold stands at £150 000. Owner-occupied farmlands and interests in unincorporated businesses are also tax-exempt.

In 1965 annual wealth taxes and capital transfer taxes accounted for 1.6 per cent of the total tax revenue of OECD countries, with the UK well above that figure. In 1985 the OECD average was down to 0.7 per cent with the UK below average at 0.5 per cent. It is therefore fair to conclude that, whilst becoming wealthy is problematic (although becoming progressively easier as houses are inherited), staying wealthy is no problem at all.

Capital Gains Tax (CGT)

This tax is levied on the difference between the purchase and sale price of any asset. This price difference might occur entirely because of inflation, and CGT has accordingly been index-linked since 1982 so that only **real gains** are currently taxed. Were there no CGT it would pay those with spare income to invest it almost entirely in assets with potential for capital gains rather than in those which accrue interest or other forms of unearned income.

It has to be said that this tends to occur anyway because a large variety of assets are exempt from CGT, including principal private residences (but not second houses), agricultural property, winnings from the football pools and other forms of gambling, motor cars, National Savings instruments and so forth. Furthermore, there is a threshold below which gains are tax-exempt, and a provision to set losses against gains before tax liability is assessed.

Before April 1988 the tax threshold stood at £6600, and the tax at 30 per cent. However, the tax was based on any assets acquired since 1965, and the high threshold existed partly to adjust for the fact that gains between 1965 and 1982 were not index-linked. In April 1988, the threshold was reduced to £5000, and is £5800 in 1994–95. Gains are currently taxed at the individual's highest income tax rate. However, any gains accruing prior to April 1982 are wholly tax-exempt.

The similar tax treatment of earned income and capital gains is at variance with the traditional view that earned income is morally superior to unearned income, and should accordingly be less heavily taxed. However, the widespread exemptions allowed under CGT have made rather a mockery of this principle, and the government effectively wish it to be known that for tax purposes 'income' is simply income irrespective of source (it was in any case never exactly clear whether a capital gain was wealth or unearned income, although CGT has been listed here as a tax on wealth for convenience). This view is also consistent with the change made in March 1987 for companies, since which time their gains have been taxed at normal corporation tax rates.

Stamp Duty

Transfers or sales of property (other than of stocks and shares) above a value of £60 000 are subject to stamp duty of 1 per cent on the entire purchase price. Transfers of stocks and shares are subject to stamp duty of 0.5 per cent, regardless of the amount. There is no stamp duty on transfers of property other than land and buildings.

☐ 5.6.9 *Taxes on Expenditure*

Value Added Tax (VAT)

VAT is the most wide-ranging tax on expenditure, and has been in force since the UK joined the Community in 1973. It is levied in one instalment directly by the retailer upon the customer. The standard rate of VAT was raised sharply to 15 per cent in 1979 as part of the switch by the first Thatcher Government from direct to indirect taxation (initially with predictably inflationary consequences). It was raised to 17.5 per cent in April 1991 as a quid pro quo for the £140 per head reduction in the Community Charge. There is also a zero rate. These rates are not uniform throughout the EU, and this is therefore one of the areas where harmonisation has yet to be achieved. However, this represents a highly elusive goal in

practice because of the enormous problems which would need to be overcome if it became necessary to switch some of the burden of taxation back onto income taxes.

VAT is collected at each stage in the production and distribution of goods and services by taxable persons (running a business with a turnover in excess of £45 600 per annum in fiscal year 1994–95). The burden of the tax is ultimately borne by the consumer as part of the final purchase price, but the tax is built up in stages. When a taxable person purchases taxable goods or services (say at £10), the supplier adds VAT to the supply price. This is called the taxable person's input tax (£1.75). When the taxable person subsequently adds value to the good or service, and sells it on to another taxable person, he or she adds VAT to the price charged (say at £20 which includes the input tax). This is known as the output tax (£3.50). Since the input tax has already been paid by the original supplier, it is necessary only for the taxable persons to pay over to the Customs and Excise the difference between the output tax and the input tax, or in other words the tax on the **value which has been added to the good or service**. As the final price in our example is £23.50 of which £3.50 is tax, the taxable person has added £10 to the supply price of £10 and paid a second instalment of £1.75 in tax.

There will normally be several such instalments before the final customer is reached, once account is taken of both wholesalers and retailers. VAT is further complicated by the fact that not all goods and services are taxable. This arises primarily because everyone pays 35p in tax on a taxable item costing £2.35 irrespective of income, so the tax bears down more severely on the low-paid than on the high-paid. In order to offset this there are two methods by which goods and services, especially those heavily consumed by the relatively poor, can be tax-relieved. The first method is where a taxable person does not charge any VAT to a customer and also reclaims any VAT paid to suppliers. In this case total VAT is zero. **Zero rating** applies, **inter alia**, to most food, reading matter, construction of new buildings, exports, public transport fares, young children's clothing and footwear, prescription medicines and caravans, encompassing in aggregate nearly one-quarter of total consumer spending.

The second method is where a taxable person does not charge any output tax to a customer, but is not entitled to deduct or to reclaim the input tax. In this case total VAT is not zero and the final good or service is said to be **VAT-exempt**. Exemption applies, **inter alia**, to land (including rents), insurance, postal services, betting, finance, education, health, and burial and cremation, encompassing in aggregate roughly 4 per cent of total consumer spending.

In the Spring 1993 Budget Norman Lamont moved to boost tax receipts by introducing VAT for the first time on domestic fuel and power, at 8 per cent in fiscal 1994–95 and at 17.5 per cent in 1995–96. There is compensation for pensioners.

☐ 5.6.10 Taxing Savings

In the UK savings have not generally been encouraged by the tax system. First income is taxed, and then the savings set aside out of net-of-tax income are frequently taxed as well. This is not universally the case because, for example, pension contributions are deducted from gross income without incurring a tax liability, but it is sufficiently common to be a matter of considerable contention in tax-reforming circles.

It has often been argued that only **spending** should be taxed, which would provide an incentive to save more. However, most of the recent discussion has been concerned with tax **neutrality**: that is, the desire to treat all savings in the same way by taxing **all of them** either once or twice (see Robinson, 1990). In the 1990 Budget the then Chancellor, John Major, moved several steps towards single taxation by extending tax exemptions on savings. This was in the form of TESSAs which could be added to the PEPs (Personal Equity Plans) introduced by Nigel Lawson. It is important to bear in mind, however, that Lawson was concerned primarily with the abolition of tax breaks for savers such as tax relief on insurance premiums, and that both PEPs and TESSAs were expected to divert sav-

ings out of one channel and into another, more tax efficient one rather than to increase substantially the total level of saving.

Personal Equity Plans (PEPs)

PEPs were first announced in the 1986 Budget and brought into operation in January 1987 as a simple way to invest in shares, especially for small savers and first-time investors unfamiliar with the stock market. The amount which could be invested in a single plan in any one year was originally £2400. In 1987, 270 000 PEPs were taken out and £480 million invested. The year 1988 was a poor one for PEPs, but in 1989, 300 000 were taken out and so PEPs became firmly established as a savings vehicle, with over £8 billion invested to date.

In the 1990 Budget the requirement that investors had to keep their investments in their PEPs for at least a complete calendar year to qualify for tax benefits was abolished. Currently, up to £9000 in total can be invested in any one year in two separate PEPs with returns free from income and CGT, of which £6000 can be placed in a general plan and £3000 in a single company plan. Up to £6000 of this total can be invested in investment and unit trusts.

Tax Exempt Special Savings Accounts (TESSAs)

TESSAs were introduced in the 1990 Budget to become operational as from 1 January 1991. A taxpayer is permitted one TESSA which confers the right to receive interest on building society and bank deposits tax-free. A maximum of £9000 can be deposited over a five-year period, either in lump sums or in irregular amounts, up to £3000 in the first year and then up to £1800 a year for the subsequent years subject to the overall limit. If capital is withdrawn early all tax relief is lost, but interest earned can be withdrawn at any time at the net-of-tax rate. At the end of five years the TESSA is wound up, although a new TESSA can be started with up to £3000 transferred into it from the previous one.

5.6.11 Hybrid Taxes: The Council Tax

The UK tax system has long been dependent upon taxes raised within the confines of an LA rather than of the UK as a whole. These taxes were traditionally based upon property, whether domestic and commercial (but excluding farms). The calculation of tax liability required that each property be given an imputed rental value, called a **rateable value**, in accordance with a complex formula devised by the responsible local authority to take into account location, size, amenites, provision of public services and so on. The LA then levied a uniform rate per pound of rateable value, with a small rebate for domestic as against commercial property. A supplementaty rate was then added to cover water, sewerage and environmental services.

The **rates**, as they were known, were a hybrid tax in the sense that whilst they were wholly divorced from a property occupier's income and clearly therefore not an income tax, they were not based directly upon the market value of a property and hence not exactly a wealth tax either. Obviously, house prices varied considerably over time, thereby making it necessary to revalue periodically in order to preserve equity between different properties. The sheer cost of the exercise militated against intervals of less than 10 years, but this in turn meant that some people would find their rateable values sharply increased, to their immense annoyance, whereas those who had seen their bills reduced thought this no more than their just desserts. The political ill-will engendered by the revaluation of 1973, coming as it did at the end of a period of sharply rising house prices, discouraged a repeat of the exercise in both 1978 and 1984. The Scottish revaluation of 1985 was blamed for the severe loss of Conservative electoral support in the subsequent General Election.

The failure to alter rateable values did not imply an inability to raise the yield from the rates. The ruling political party in a local authoriy could impose any rate poundage that it thought fit, although it would have to be subject itself to periodic re-election. However, a number of local councils, especially in the larger towns and cities, had such large majorities that they could do virtually anything they liked and make their ratepayers, including local businesses (with no right to vote independent of the rights of their employees to vote as individual ratepayers if eligible), and also the government (which supplied over one-half of all local authority revenue via a **rate support grant**), foot the bill. The ability to charge high taxes, yet remain politically popular, reflected the high proportion of the total bill laid at the door of government and businesses (over 75 per cent by 1970 and higher still by 1980), and also the fact that domestic rates took no account of the number of individuals living in a property. Large, underoccupied properties in expensive areas could be made to pay very high rates, whereas small, overoccupied properties were frequently exempted from rates altogether because their main occupier was entitled to a rate rebate by virtue of his or her income.

Not surprisingly, those who paid heavy rates wanted services to be cut and rates to be reduced, whereas those who paid little or no rates demanded more and more services regardless of expense. In the bigger towns the latter were often in a clear majority, and elected councils committed to ever-higher expenditure. When the Conservatives were elected in 1979 on a platform of reductions in public spending, their attention was inevitably drawn to the alleged profligacy of the local authorities. Since the highest-spending local councils were all Labour-controlled the issue inevitably became political as well as economic. The power of such councils, democratically elected though they were, had, in the government's view, to be subjugated to the constitutionally superior power of the democratically elected central government.

How was this to be achieved? For several years the government sought desperately for a foolproof method of keeping LA spending in check. However, the fatal flaws in most schemes were either that the local authorites could raise the rate poundage to substitute for reductions in revenue supplied by central government, or that, if prevented from so doing by **rate capping**, they could introduce increasingly innovative methods of raising finance such as swaps and sale-and-lease-back deals on LA-owned assets. The government's position was that all local voters had to be made to pay personally for increases in spending if that was what they wanted and voted for. The chosen solution was, first, to take the **non-domestic (business) rate** away from the local authorities and transfer it to central government which set it nationally at a uniform level (to be known as the **Uniform Business Rate**). The revenue was then distributed to local authorities as a **per capitum** grant. Second, the **Community Charge** (often referred to as the **poll tax** because it required everyone above the minimum voting age of 18 to register with their local authority), to be paid by all voters either in full or in part (if eligible for a rebate) at a **flat rate**. The changes were introduced in Scotland in April 1989 and in England and Wales in April 1990.

This solution was not without its drawbacks. It clearly implied a major redistribution of the burden of taxation, both from the single-adult household to the multiple-adult household, and from the well-off to those previously considered too poor to pay any rates at all. It was also costly to administer because it was problematic to get all those who should be paying the Charge to register for that purpose, and to track them down if they refused to do so. This did not necessarily imply that spending on the rump of services left in the hands of local authorities would fall, because voters could opt for as many such services as they were willing to pay for, but the underlying assumption was that spending would indeed fall in order to keep the Charge as low as possible. However, it would still be the case that most spending by local authorities would be covered by central government grants and the apportioned non-domestic rates, as shown in **Table 5.9**.

The local authorities raised only 27 per cent of their total spending via the rates (domestic+business) in 1971. From a low point of 24 per cent in fiscal 1975–76, the proportion rose to 37 per cent by 1989, but throughout the 1980s well over 40 per cent of their spending was financed by central government grants.

Table 5.9 *LA Revenues, 1991–94 (£ bn)*

	1991–92 Outturn	1992–93 Estimate	1993–94 Forecast
Community Charge and council tax[1]	7.2	8.3	8.2
Capital grants from central government	2.7	8.0[2]	3.3
Current grants from central government[3]	50.4	55.5	54.6
Other sources[4]	7.8	8.9	9.0
Total	68.0	80.7	75.0

Notes:
[1] Net of rebates, community charge benefit, transitional relief and community charge reduction scheme.
[2] Includes commutation grant of £5.1 billion used to repay debt.
[3] Includes domestic rate income.
[4] Includes interest receipts, rent, etc.

Source: FSBR 1993–94, Table 6.7.

The way the poll tax system worked was (a) for each LA to be given a spending target according to its needs; (b) the central government then set a 'community charge for standard spending' or 'headline' charge; (c) non-domestic rate income was distributed; and (d) the difference between (a) and (b + c) was supplied as a grant. Although any local authority could exceed its standard spending, the extra spending fell **entirely** on local charge-payers. This could raise the local tax sharply, but so could a miscalculation by civil servants of local needs.

As part of the 1991 Budget the government sought to reduce the political fallout of the poll tax by reducing the headline Community Charge by £140 per charge-payer in Britain (down from £385 to £245), to be financed by a 2.5 per cent increase in VAT from 15 to 17.5 per cent. Net of rebates and reliefs, the average charge was expected to be roughly £175. This left only 11 per cent of LA spending to be raised locally, inducing many commentators to wonder why central government did not simple scrap local taxes and be done with it. But on 23 April 1991 the Environment Secretary, Michael Heseltine, came up instead with a new **Council Tax**, introduced in April 1993, the main features of which are as follows:

a   It reflects the capital value of a property occupied by two adults and gives a 25 per cent discount to a single person;

b   Properties are assigned to eight bands based upon value;

c   Payment in the top band is limited to three times that levied in the bottom band;

d   There is a single bill for each household;

e   The poor are protected by discounts;

f   There is no minimum contribution;

g   Second homes receive a 50 per cent discount;

h   Transitional relief in the form of a £340 million Transitional Reduction Scheme (TRS) exists to prevent an individual from incurring too large an increase in his or her tax bill.

As indicated above, the poll tax proved to be a costly blunder, both politically and economically. As early as April 1989 the government was obliged to produce a £500 million package of adjustments to income-related social security benefits. To this must be added the £1.7 billion poll tax reduction package of January 1991, transitional relief, extra collection costs and at least £1 billion of extra non-payment each year. If the shift to the higher rate of VAT is added on, the extra annual cost compared to the rates for the final two years of the Community Charge amounted to roughly £7 billion.

In the end, the poll tax had to go because at realistic levels in relation to LA spending it would impose a crippling burden on millions of households, whereas at realistic levels in relation to household incomes it would contribute an unacceptably small proportion of LA finance. The Community Charge is an improvement in that, although it remains somewhat regressive because properties of below average value pay proportionately more tax, the tax does rise with property values. It should also be relatively cheap to administer because it is based upon the household rather than the individual. This is important because at the end of 1992, court summonses were issued to 2.3 million people for non-payment of poll tax, but 1.9 million of these still did not pay up and were issued with a liability order. However, the fall in property values in

1991 and 1992 has inevitably caused a large number of appeals against property valuations in order to move to a lower tax band, albeit fewer than were anticipated.

5.6.12 *The EU and Tax Harmonisation*

The UK is obliged, as a member of the EU, to contribute tax revenue to cover EU expenditure in the areas of agriculture, social policy and regional policy. The EU Budget is financed by its 'own resources', comprising the proceeds of the common external tariff (less 10 per cent); a share in national VAT proceeds and a share of GNP (see **p. 240**). EU members have compiled a collection of goods and services known as the **common assessment base**. The UK calculates the total value of sales of the base every year, applies VAT, and remits the EU's share to Brussels. This share is currently 1.4 per cent. In practice, the UK has always argued that its contribution is excessive compared with that made by other member states, and has had part of it returned each year. It is also obviously the case that some of the money is returned in the form of EU expenditure in the areas set out above.

Under the terms of the Single European Act 1985 (see **pp. 234**) there is supposed to be **fiscal harmonisation** in the EU. Initially, progress towards this objective achieved very little since, whereas VAT is levied in every country, each member state wished to impose its own preferred rates upon the others. The only progress of any note arose in that, since taxes within the EU are not supposed to favour domestic as against imported goods, the European Court of Justice felt obliged periodically to implement this principle in a piecemeal way by, for example, obliging the UK to reduce excise duties on wine (largely imported) relative to beer (largely domestic).

However, the debate about tax harmonisation became considerably more heated with the onset of the SEM. The original blueprint was proposed by the then European Commissioner, Lord Cockfield, on behalf of the EU in late 1987. In the

Single European Act 1985 the internal market is defined as 'an area without internal frontiers'. What the Cockfield plan proposed was that all border controls within the EU should be abolished by 1992, and it concluded that this could not be achieved without first harmonising rates of VAT and excise duties within the EU. It thus proposed that the wide array of VAT rates should be grouped into two 'bands', comprising a **standard rate band** at 14–20 per cent and a **reduced rate band** at 4–9 per cent covering goods which member states wished to keep cheap for social reasons.

The Cockfield plan also recommended a single EU-wide excise duty for alcohol, petrol and tobacco. This arose because VAT is levied on the price of goods **inclusive of** excise duty, and were excise duties to vary the proposed VAT bands would be distorted. This is an important consideration because, like VAT, excise duties historically varied enormously within the EU, being very low in the South – where, for example, most wine is produced – and high in the North for health and environmental reasons.

It is hardly surprising that the Cockfield proposals were contentious. On the one hand, if existing VAT rates were retained but frontier controls abolished, the citizens of high-VAT-rate countries would be expected to pour across their frontiers with countries where VAT rates were lower in order to shop there, which would be unacceptable to the former countries. On the other hand, harmonising tax rates would force prices up in those countries where rates were below the designated minima while at the same time causing tax revenue to fall in those countries where rates were above the designated maxima.

EU member states, with the exception of the UK, always favoured a minimum rate of VAT in order to protect their tax revenue (and hence their ability to spend). Reflecting this majority view, the European Commission came up with a proposal to set a legally binding 15 per cent minimum standard rate of VAT, together with a number of special lower rates where their abolition would be politically damaging. Ironically, given that the UK would be less affected by these rates than almost any other country, the UK used its veto on tax matters (which require unanimity) to stop the proposal, which was somewhat difficult to justify given that the UK had accepted the principle of a minimum for excise duties on alcohol and tobacco. Clearly, an (unspoken) consideration was that a minimum rate of VAT would make it impossible to rebalance the tax system from indirect to direct tax on a future occasion should it be politically expedient.

In June 1991 the Council of Ministers declared that they would all apply a minimum standard rate of VAT of 15 per cent from 1 January 1993, and a directive to that effect was finally sanctioned in October 1992. The Council also agreed that there should be one or two optional reduced VAT rates of not less than 5 per cent. For member states with existing VAT rates below the reduced rate minimum, a super-reduced rate (as well as a zero rate) may be retained during a transitional period which is expected to last until 1 January 1997, at which point changes may be introduced by unanimous agreement in the Council. Until that date VAT is to be levied in the country of destination, but after that date VAT is to be levied in the country of origin with goods despatched on a tax-paid basis.

The VAT regime ruling in 1993 is set out in **Table 5.10.** Attempts to harmonise VAT are only a relatively modest step along the path towards tax harmonisation because, by virtue of the fact that VAT is payable only in the country of sale, there can be no biasing effect on the location of firms. This is not, however, the case if one considers taxes on companies, for example. The UK currently has the lowest EU rate of mainstream corporation tax at 33 per cent, and other countries have been obliged to bring their rates into rough conformity (the highest is currently 40 per cent in Ireland) in order to avoid excessive tax competition. For the foreseeable future, 'approximation' rather than 'harmonisation' is likely to remain the order of the day in this respect. The issue of harmonisation is, ultimately, bedevilled by the fact that firms in countries with special concessions are most reluctant to give them up in the cause of greater European harmony (see Kay and King, 1990, **p. 218**). As for harmonisation of income tax, that is too far off even to worry about.

Table 5.10 *VAT Rates Applied in the Community Member States (%)*

	Zero rate	Reduced rate(s)	Standard rate	Increased rate
Luxembourg	No	3/6	15	–
Spain	1	6	15	28
Germany	No	7	15	–
Portugal	No	5	16	30
UK	Yes	–	17.5	–
Greece	No	4/8	18	–
Netherlands	No	6	18.5	–
France	No	2.1/5.5	18.6	–
Italy	1	4/9/12	19	38
Belgium	1	1/6/12	19.5	–
Ireland	Yes	2.7/12.5	25	–
Denmark	1	–	25	–

Note:
1 Minimal coverage.

■ 5.7 The Budget

□ 5.7.1 Budgetary Changes

The Budget is an annual event, held up to and including 1993 in either March or April, but switching to November in 1993 (requiring a second Budget in that year) for reasons discussed below (Dilnot and Robson, 1993). It exists both to set out the government's proposals for changes in taxation and to provide an occasion for the annual review of economic policy. Normal procedure was for the proposals to be announced to the House of Commons by the Chancellor of the Exchequer in the Budget Statement, and to be published in the **Financial Statement and Budget Report** (FSBR).

The Budget statement is followed by the moving of a set of Ways and Means resolutions embodying the Budget proposals, and these form the foundations for the **Finance Bill** which goes forward for debate in Parliament. The Ways and Means resolutions exist so that taxes can be levied at the new levels set out in the Finance Bill pending its enactment. The Finance Bill, subject to any amendments volunteered by, or forced

upon, the Chancellor during debate, is then passed as the **Finance Act**.

Tax proposals are concerned primarily with changes in the rate or coverage of taxes, the introduction of new taxes and the abolition of existing ones, or changes in methods of administration. Most taxes are permanent, but in the case of income tax and corporation tax the Finance Act is needed every year to keep them in existence. It is, however, perfectly proper either to have a mini-Budget at any time of year, which necessitates amendments to the Finance Act, or simply to operate the Regulator which permits VAT to be varied by up to 25 per cent and the main excise duties by up to 10 per cent between Budgets.

Figure 5.9 represents the breakdown of total government revenue forecast for 1993–94. As can be seen, 33.5 per cent of all revenue comes under the control of the Inland Revenue (down from 37 per cent in 1991–92), while a further 29.5 per cent is handled by Customs and Excise (up from 27.5 per cent in 1991–92). It is not generally appreciated how dependent tax revenue is upon a narrow range of taxes. NICs account for slightly less than VAT, which is itself exceeded only by income tax. Not so long ago, in 1985, duty on petrol/derv plus PRT were the next most important, followed by corporation tax, but the effects of the fall in the price of oil and of fiscal drag resulted in corporation tax yielding almost twice as much (8.6 per cent) as the other two combined in 1991–92. However, corporation tax is only expected to produce 6.4 per cent of total tax receipts in 1993–94, much the same as petrol/derv plus PRT, although this remains a much higher proportion than for any other individual tax levied at a national level.

The Budget contains an array of changes to the tax system. It is clear, however, from the above discussion, that very few of these have other than marginal effects upon total revenue, whereas changes in income tax of an apparently modest kind (for example, a 1p reduction in the marginal rate) have quite dramatic effects (altering revenue by more that £1 billion). **Table 5.11** gives an indication of the sorts of change that have a reasonably significant effect upon tax receipts, in the context of the Budget in Spring 1993 which

Figure 5.9 *Sources of Revenue, 1993–94*

Source: FSBR 1993–94, Table 1.2.

was notable for the fact that many of the changes were introduced with a delayed effect.

The purpose of raising revenue is primarily to fund expenditure, so it was a little curious that the Budget was traditionally divorced from the two main discussions of public expenditure set out in the Autumn Statement and Public Expenditure White Paper. The Treasury did not like making statements about revenue in the Autumn because tax receipts could alter sharply between November and April (perhaps due to fiscal drag). On the other hand, public expenditure needed to be planned well in advance and did not have to be financed solely through tax receipts. The drawback to the separation in time was that any increases in spending in the Autumn had been largely forgotten by April, so any buoyancy in tax receipts immediately led to demands for yet further spending.

In 1993 the Chancellor finally decided to bite the bullet and announced that henceforth there would be a unified tax and spending Budget, of which the first would take place in November 1993. This necessitated a second Budget in 1993, although the first was set up so as to eliminate the need to take much action in the Autumn. The Finance Bill is thereby set back to January, which has the advantage of giving taxpayers a clear idea of most tax changes well before the date that they take effect, as compared to the previous situation where legislation was not enacted until well after the start of the tax year. Nevertheless, excise duties will still need to be raised on the day of the Budget. The FSBR will be published at the time of the Budget and will contain spending plans covering the three years commencing the following April.

Table 5.11   *Direct Effects of Budget Measures, Spring 1993*

	£ million	yield (+)/cost (−) of measure		
	Changes from a non-indexed base 1993–94	Changes from an indexed base 1993–94	1994–95	1995–96
INLAND REVENUE (28 changes) of which:[1]	−475	265	2925	4055
Lower rate band – increased to £2500	−370	−300	−390	−400
Married couple's allowance – restricted to 20 per cent, etc.	–	–	910	1170
Lower rate band – increased to £3000	–	–	−320	−450
Mortgage interest relief – restricted to 20 per cent	–	–	820	870
Taxation of dividends	−100	−100	100	900
PRT – reformed	–	–	300	400
Land and property – stamp duty threshold increased	−220	−220	−270	−265
CUSTOMS AND EXCISE (19 changes) of which:[1]	825	295	1900	3655
VAT on domestic fuel and power	–	–	950	2300
petrol and derv up 10% (net of car tax recoupment)	380	90	120	70
petrol and derv up 3 per cent in real terms in future Budgets	105	105	520	950
cigarettes – specific duty up to 10% **ad valorem** duty down 1%	360	230	280	290
VEHICLE EXCISE DUTY (2 changes) of which:[1]	385	300	310	320
Duty on cars, etc. up to £125	380	310	320	330
BUSINESS RATES (1 change) No real increase under transitional arrangements	−370 −370	−370 −370	−260 −260	... ...
NATIONAL INSURANCE CONTRIBUTIONS (3 changes) of which:[1]	0	0	1850	2275
1% increase in employees' main rate	–	–	1750	2100
TOTAL RECEIPTS	365	490	6725	10305

Note:
[1] Separate listing where effect is at least ± £270 million in the financial year.
Source: FSBR 1993–94.

5.8 The Public Sector Borrowing Requirement (PSBR) and Public Sector Debt Repayment (PSDR)

The difference between the total receipts and total expenditure of the public sector is known as the PSBR. The public sector consists of central government, local government and the public corporations. The global figure for the PSBR does not, therefore, show flows between the three sectors, normally from central government to the other two and on a very large scale, but does include public corporations' borrowing from the money markets and overseas. The figures for the past two years, and projections for the next four are to be found in **Table 5.12**. These are in cash terms, and the PSBR is also expressed as a percentage of GDP.

The longer-term trend of the PSBR can be seen in **Figure 5.10**, again expressed as a percentage of GDP. During the oil crisis in the mid-1970s the

percentage came close to reaching double figures and, despite some subsequent improvement, rose back to 5 per cent when the present government was first elected.

It is important to note at this point the accounting convention used for privatisation proceeds. As shown earlier, on **p. 149**, these are recorded as **negative spending**. The government argues that, since the purchase price appears as public expenditure when assets are taken into public ownership, it is only logical to treat any monies arising when they are sold back to the private sector as negative spending. A more cynical view might be that the purpose of this exercise is to reduce the declared amount of public spending in order to reduce the PSBR. Certainly, it is undeniable that the government actually does spend the amount indicated before privatisation proceeds are subtracted, and it therefore seems to be more sensible to treat the PSBR as the excess of gross public expenditure over total tax revenue, and to treat privatisation proceeds as a **means of financing the**

Table 5.12 *Borrowing Requirements of Central Government (CGBR) and Public Sector (PSBR) (£ bn, cash)[1]*

	1991–92	1992–93	1993–94	1994–95	1995–96	1996–97
GGE	236.1	260	280	296	314	329
General government receipts	222.2	224	229	257	275	293
CGBR	14.0	36	51	45	40	36
Public corporations' market and overseas debt repayment	−0.2	−1	−1	−1	−1	−1
PSBR	13.8	35[2]	50	44	39	35
Money GDP at market prices[2]	580.4	599	628	671	716	756
PSBR as % of GDP	2.4	$5\frac{3}{4}$	8	$6\frac{1}{2}$	$5\frac{1}{2}$	$4\frac{1}{2}$

Notes:
[1] Rounded to the nearest £1 billion from 1992–93 onwards.
[2] The outturn proved to be higher at £36.5 billion as a result of a £9.5 billion PSBR in March 1993, the highest monthly figure ever.
[3] Figures adjusted for the distortion caused by the abolition of domestic rates.

Source: FSBR 1993–94.

Figure 5.10 *PSBR as a % of GDP*

Note:
[1] Forecast.
Source: FSBR 1988–89; 1993–94.

shortfall. Were this alternative convention to be adopted then the PSBR data in **Figure 5.10** would obviously look markedly worse.

During the major part of the present government's period in office the PSBR remained stubbornly higher than forecast, for reasons familiar from our previous discussion. In five of the seven years after 1981–82 public expenditure exceeded its forecast value on four occasions, falling short only in 1986–87 because of a sharp drop in North Sea taxes. However, these overshoots were generally more modest than those for spending, and the PSBR consequently did no better than hit its target value for the six consecutive years beginning in 1981–82.

5.8.1 Public Sector Debt Repayment (PSDR)

The dramatic turnaround came in 1987–88 when tax revenue overshot the forecast by an astonishing £7.5 billion, with the result that, despite a serious £4 billion overshoot in spending, the PSBR became negative for the first time since 1971. It became the custom to refer to the PSDR instead. Strictly speaking, a PSDR did not arise excluding privatisation proceeds until 1988–89. The then Chancellor, Nigel Lawson, never did advocate the desirability of a PSDR as such, however. Indeed, he formally advocated the desirability of a **balanced budget** only in the FSBR of 1988, and did so then on the grounds that 'it provides a clear and simple rule, with a good historical pedigree'. In the event, his avowed strategy could not cope with the buoyancy of tax revenue, and on either definition there was a PSDR in 1988–89 and 1989–90: quite substantial ones if privatisation proceeds are included. As the economy sank into recession during 1990, the original forecast of a further substantial PSDR gradually gave way to less-optimistic views about the eventual outturn.

There can be no doubt that the turnaround from massive and apparently uncontrollable PSBRs in the 1970s to PSDRs in the late 1980s was an extraordinary achievement. Indeed, merely in achieving a PSDR the UK could be compared only with Japan among the major industrialised nations, as shown in **Table 5.13**. Unfortunately, the PSDR has proved to be a

transitory phenomenon in the UK, and indeed for those smaller EU economies such as Denmark which also achieved a PSDR in the mid-1980s. In 1990–91 the fiscal books were in balance, but only if privatisation proceeds were included. However, with the onset of recession the situation deteriorated alarmingly, with a PSBR of almost 6 per cent of GDP, including privatisation proceeds, in 1992–93, and a forecast of a 8 per cent PSBR on the same basis for 1993–94. Precisely what will happen beyond that point no-one really knows, apart from a general belief that as growth picks up again the situation should improve somewhat.

The official estimates are contained in **Table 5.12**, which indicates a modest reduction to 4.5 per cent of GDP by 1996–97. This is a rather unpleasant prognosis, but it has to be borne in mind both that official estimates have tended to be overoptimistic in recent years, and also that privatisation proceeds are well past their peak.

Table 5.13 *General Government Lending (+) or Borrowing (−) as a % of GDP, 1974–9[3]*

	1974–84	*1985*	*1986*	*1987*	*1988*	*1989*	*1990*	*1991*	*1992*	*1992[1]*	*1993[1]*
B	−8.3	−9.5	−9.4	−7.5	−6.7	−6.7	−5.7	−6.6	−6.7	−6.0	−6.3
DK	−2.9	−4.1	3.4	2.4	0.6	−0.5	−1.4	−2.0	−2.3	−2.7	−1.9
D	−2.9	−1.9	−1.3	−1.9	−2.2	0.1	−2.0	−3.6	−3.4	−3.9	−3.8
D + [2]	–	–	–	–	–	–	–	−3.2	−3.2	−3.6	−3.7
GR	–	−9.8	−12.0	−11.6	−13.8	−17.7	−18.8	−15.4	−13.4	−9.8	−7.7
E	−2.4	−5.4	−6.0	−3.1	−3.3	−2.8	−4.0	−4.9	−4.6	−4.2	−3.8
F	−1.6	−2.8	−2.7	−1.9	−1.7	−1.1	−1.4	−1.9	−2.8	−3.2	−3.6
IRL	−10.9	−9.8	−11.1	−8.9	−4.8	−1.8	−2.5	−2.1	−2.7	−3.0	−3.7
I	−9.3	−11.6	−11.6	−11.0	−10.7	−9.9	−10.9	−10.2	−10.5	−10.2	−9.1
L	1.4	2.8	4.3	2.4	3.1	5.3	5.0	−0.8	−0.4	−1.0	−0.7
NL	−3.9	−6.3	−6.0	−5.9	−4.6	−4.7	−4.9	−2.5	−3.5	−3.5	−3.3
P	–	−12.0	−7.2	−6.8	−5.4	−3.4	−5.5	−6.4	−5.6	−4.8	−3.8
UK	−3.6	−3.9	−2.4	−1.3	1.0	0.9	−1.3	−2.8	−6.1	−8.2	−8.1
EUR[3]	−4.2[3]	−5.3	−4.8	−4.1	−3.6	−2.8	−4.1	−4.7	−5.4	−5.8	−5.5
EUR +	–	–	–	–	–	–	–	−4.6	−5.3	−5.7	−5.4
USA	−1.7	−2.9	−3.5	−2.5	−2.0	−1.5	−2.5	−3.4	−4.8	−4.8	−4.5
JAP	−3.6	−2.1	−0.9	0.5	1.5	2.5	3.0	2.4	2.2	0.4	0.4

Notes:
[1] Forecasts based upon individual countries' national accounts.
[2] Including East Germany.
[3] EUR without Greece and Portugal up to 1983.

Source: European Economy, Supplement A (January 1993).

The deterioration in the fiscal outlook between 1988–89 and 1993–94 is equivalent to the better part of 10 per cent of GDP, and as such is the worst by far of any EU member state. However, the situation has also deteriorated badly in Luxembourg, and the PSBR also remains higher in Italy and, outside the EC, most notably in Sweden. Although the USA has been heavily criticised for the size of its PSBR, it has to be said that the EU is by comparison hardly a paragon of fiscal virtue.

■ 5.9 The National Debt

It is of some importance to remember that the first claim on tax revenue is **interest on the national debt**. Were there to be no such debt, public spending on real goods and services could be increased by £20 billion in 1993–94 without any need to raise further taxes. While this may currently appear to be a pipe-dream, there was much discussion of such an outcome as a result of the succession of debt repayments at the end of the 1980s.

The ability to repay debt exists provided there is an excess of taxation over expenditure adjusted for privatisation proceeds. This, as we have seen, occurred during the financial years 1987–88 to 1990–91 inclusive, and although the government was not obliged to use the surplus to repay the debt, it chose to do so, thereby expunging well over £20 billion of debt in 1988–89 and 1989–90 alone. At the beginning of the fiscal year 1991–92, the outstanding **net** debt was accordingly worth a 'mere' £150 billion. It is also possible to treat total debt in its **gross** form, in which case the equivalent figure was £190 billion. The transformation from gross to net debt requires the deduction of liquid assets held by the public sector, of which well over half is currently in the form of gold and foreign exchange reserves.

It has been claimed that the national debt is in reality nearly twice as large as is officially admitted. This arises because certain public sector pension schemes are notionally rather than actually funded. The government borrows the excess of pension contributions over expenditure and

dummy gilt-edged securities are created (but not actually issued). This, it is alleged, is the national accounts equivalent of off-balance-sheet borrowing by corporations.

With this proviso in mind, we will continue the analysis using the official figures. The gross and net debt, expressed as a percentage of GDP, are set out in **Figure 5.11** over the period from 1970 to 1993. In 1985–86, prior to the first PSDR, the ratio for the gross debt was 54.5 per cent and it was 46 per cent for the net debt, roughly the same level each had been at the turn of the 1980s. By the beginning of the 1990s the situation had changed dramatically such that both ratios had fallen by almost 20 per cent. It is enlightening to compare the UK's experience during this period with that of other EU countries on the basis of the figures for gross public debt as a percentage of GDP. Over the 20-year period beginning in 1970, only two EU countries managed to reduce this ratio, namely the UK and Luxembourg. In the latter case it started out relatively low, whereas the ratio for the UK was the highest in the EU in 1970. By 1990 the UK ratio had halved, whereas the EU average had risen by 50 per cent and that for West Germany had more than doubled. At this point only Luxembourg had a lower ratio than the UK, while the ratios for Belgium, Italy

Figure 5.11   *Measures of Public Sector Debt in Relation to GDP*

Source: Bank of England Quarterly Bulletin.

and Greece had all risen above 100 per cent as a consequence of the string of massive borrowing requirements shown in **Table 5.13**.

The debt/GDP ratio in the UK has turned up sharply over the past two years, and is expected to continue to climb for some time to come, even assuming some growth in GDP. The gross debt/GDP ratio is currently approaching 50 per cent, but despite this the ratio remains one of the lowest in the EU, and the situation should not be viewed as excessively alarming.

The precise implications of the trend in the absolute size of the debt for **debt interest payments** is complicated by such matters as interest rate volatility and the effects of inflation on index-linked debt. The situation for the UK over the past decade, again expressed as a percentage of GDP, is shown in **Figure 5.12**. Here again the enormous improvement over the 1980s, high interest rates notwithstanding, is especially notable, but the upturn in the ratio is also clearly visible over the past two years.

It is fortunate that interest rates are somewhat lower than they were, since the problem can rapidly spiral out of control. This is due to the fact that the gross debt and its associated interest charge need to be rolled over from year to year. Each year's interest charge gets added to the gross debt of that year, and in the following year interest would have to be paid on the previous year's interest unless the gross debt has itself been reduced in the meantime by running a budget surplus. In the case of Belgium, Italy and Greece, where a string of deficits has added greatly to the gross debt for many years past, this has caused annual debt interest payments to escalate

Figure 5.12   *General Government Debt Interest Payments*

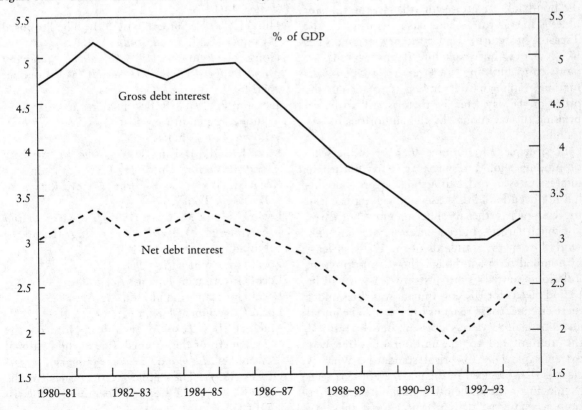

Source: Autumn Statement 1992, Table 2A.12 for latest figures.

to roughly 10 per cent of GDP, beyond which point little short of draconian measures can forestall a fiscal disaster.

A fundamental concern, already apparent in the case of the UK, is how to finance large-scale deficits, particularly if the financial markets have lost faith in the government's determination to seek a solution. The total additional amount to be financed in 1993–94 is expected to be £50 billion, on top of which must be added the need to refinance all debt that matures during the year as well as any underlying increase in the foreign exchange reserves. As a consequence, the government was obliged to announce a change in its policy of **fully funding** this aggregate (that is, the sale of debt instruments equal in value to this) as part of the 1992 Autumn Statement.

The rationale for fully funding government borrowing is to ensure that it is financed in a non-inflationary way, and this was long interpreted to require sales of securities exclusively to the non-bank private sector (that is, the transfer of existing privately-held cash deposits to the Treasury in return). Under the new regime sales of securities (but excluding Treasury bills) to banks and building societies are to count as funding, although full funding is to remain the order of the day (that is, there is still to be no printing of new money by the authorities to pay its bills).

In principle, an enormous increase in the scale of funding should result in a sharp upturn in interest rates in order to attract buyers, but this has not occurred in this case (and neither has it in the USA where the absolute amounts borrowed are much larger). Indeed, interest rates are currently low by the standards of the 1980s, at least in nominal terms, although they are positive in inflation-adjusted terms. Just how easy it will be to find buyers for UK government securities under these circumstances remains to be seen. The initial auctions in 1993 were successful, but the ratio of the amount bid to the amount on offer was extremely low by historical standards. What is clear is that the need to finance the PSBR is seen as placing a floor below which interest rates cannot readily be driven, especially if they are rising in other EC member states.

Bibliography

Cmnd 1432 (1961) *Control of Public Spending* (London: HMSO).

Cmnd 9714 (1986) *Paying for Local Government* (London: HMSO).

Cmnd 441 (1988) *A New Public Expenditure Planning Total* (London: HMSO).

Cmnd 1867 (1992) *Budgetary Reform* (London: HMSO).

Cmnd 2096 (1992) *Autumn Statement 1992* (London: HMSO).

Cmnd 2219 (1993) *Public Expenditure Analyses to 1995–96. Statistical Supplement to the 1992 Autumn Statement* (London: HMSO).

CSO (1992) 'International Comparisons of Taxes and Social Security Contributions in 20 OECD Countries 1980–1990', *Economic Trends* (December 1992).

Dilnot, A. and M. Robson (1993) 'The UK Moves from March to December Budgets', *Fiscal Studies*, 14(1).

Hills, J. and H. Sutherland (1991) 'The Proposed Council Tax', *Fiscal Studies*, 12(4).

House of Commons (1993) *Financial Statement and Budget Report 1993–94. HC 547* (London: HMSO).

Jackson, P. (1990) 'Reflections on the Growth of Public Expenditure', *British Review of Economic Issues* (June).

Kay, J. and M. King (1990) *The British Tax System* (Oxford University Press), 5th edn.

Keen, M. (1991) 'Tax Reform', *Oxford Review of Economic Policy*, 7(3).

Levitt, M. and M. Joyce (1987) *The Growth and Efficiency of Public Spending* (London: NIESR).

Local Government Act 1988.

Local Government Finance Act 1988.

Local Government and Housing Act 1989.

Local Government Finance Act 1992.

Macleay, I. (1993) 'A Technical Note on the Treatment of the Council Tax in the National Accounts', *Economic Trends* (January).

OECD (1991) 'The Public Sector: Issues for the 1990s', *OECD Working Paper No. 90* (Paris: OECD).

Robinson, W. (1990) 'How Should Savings Be Taxed?', *National Westminster Bank Quarterly Review* (November).

Skinner, D. and M. Robson (1992) 'National Insurance Contributions: Anomalies and Reforms', *Fiscal Studies*, 13(3).

The Economist (1992) 'Taking the State to Task', 2 May.

Chapter 6

External Tranactions

Peter Curwen

6.1 Introduction

There are enormous differences in the extent to which individual nations are dependent upon transactions with the outside world. The UK has always been an 'open' economy, both importing and exporting on a massive scale. Superficially, this may simply be seen to reflect the difficulties which any nation the size of the UK must inevitably face in trying to be self-sufficient across the whole range of goods and services. However, it is important to note both that the UK's degree of openness has been increasing steadily over the past several decades (as has also been true elsewhere in the EU), and that external transactions increasingly involve one-way flows of capital which are unrelated to the immediate consumption requirements of UK residents.

In recent years the value of both imports and exports has grown to exceed 30 per cent of the UK's GDP, and it is obvious that these trade flows have a significant impact upon the UK's industrial structure, the level of employment, the standard of living of UK nationals and so on. In other words, the **internal and external sectors are inex-** tricably linked, and it is impossible to control internal macroeconomic objectives (such as the level of employment and the rate of inflation) without taking into account their links with the external sector. Indeed, as we shall see, much of the postwar history of UK macroeconomic policy can be viewed in terms of a struggle **to find acceptable trade-offs between the internal and external objectives of policy.**

Economic policy is frequently focused upon the **balance of payments**, and our first task is, therefore, to set out the accounting system used to measure it, and to explain how policy objectives are expressed in relation to these accounts. The other central task is to examine the primary instrument used to achieve this objective, namely the **exchange rate**. However, as we will discover, these apparently straightforward tasks are in practice greatly complicated by the need to take account of other related policy objectives and instruments, of the behaviour of other countries insofar as it impinges upon the UK, of international institutions and of the whole plethora of arrangements which govern the conduct of the world economy.

6.2 The System of Balance of Payments Accounts

☐ 6.2.1 Recording Transactions

The BoP may be defined as a **systematic record, over a given period of time, of all transactions between residents and non-residents of the UK.** The term 'resident' covers both individuals living permanently in the UK and corporate bodies located therein, but not their overseas branches and subsidiaries. It also includes government agencies and military forces located abroad. 'Permanent' residence is determined by the intention to remain in the UK for at least one full year.

The object of the accounting system is to record these transactions in a format that is suitable for analysing the economic relations between the UK economy and the rest of the world. The transactions may represent **resources** provided by or to UK residents (imports and exports of goods and services, and the use of investments); changes in the UK's **foreign assets or liabilities**; or **transfer payments.**

In principle, transactions are recorded when the ownership of goods or assets changes and when services are rendered. In practice, however, trade flows are recorded on a **shipments basis**, and the payments which match these shipments are not only almost invariably delayed, but the length of this delay is quite erratic from one period to another. In the longer term all the shipments and monetary flows can be matched up, but the short-term picture is almost inevitably quite heavily distorted. This is important because, first, both foreign exchange markets – and indeed sometimes the government – respond in a volatile way to monthly or quarterly BoP statistics and, second, because the annual accounts are constantly being adjusted retrospectively to a degree that can turn surpluses into deficits or vice versa. In other words, the short-term picture can conflict with the longer-term perspective, yet by the time the latter is visible it is too late to take appropriate action.

A further element of ambiguity is introduced by the need to **convert currencies**. The general rule in international trade is that the exporter dictates the form in which payment is made which, in the case of a developed nation like the UK, is mostly in its own currency. A much smaller proportion of UK imports will also be paid for in sterling. All non-sterling payments must then be converted into sterling at the ruling exchange rates, but these may fluctuate enormously during the course of a financial year, with the result that the valuation of imports and exports can be influenced by the **precise timing of currency conversion**.

☐ 6.2.2 Double-entry Accounting

The BoP accounts are, like any accounting system, constructed according to the **double-entry principle**. Every transaction involves equal credit and debit entries but, instead of arranging these in separate columns, all BoP entries are arranged in a single column, and given different signs so that they sum to zero. It is therefore the case that the BoP accounts **must balance by definition**. This should not, however, be confused with the concept of **equilibrium**, which is discussed below. This method accommodates account items which are generally recorded only on a **net** basis.

Under the conventions of the accounts all credit items are entered with a **plus** (+) **sign**. The credit relates to the **flow of currency** and not to the flow of resources. If resources are provided in the form of exports of goods or services, then the corresponding payment in currency **flows into the UK** and is recorded with a plus sign in the accounts. Where resources are provided to UK residents – for example, as imports of goods or services – payment **flows out of the UK** and is recorded with a **minus** (−) **sign** in the accounts.

Every positive entry must, as indicated, have its matching negative entry, but this may appear in a variety of forms. For example, an export of goods can be matched by either (**a**) an increase in the foreign assets owned by UK residents (where the export receipts are, for example, deposited in a bank outside the UK); (**b**) a reduction in non-residents' holdings of sterling in the UK (which are transferred to the exporter's bank account); or (**c**) a direct exchange for imports of equal value (barter trade). It is undoubtedly rather confusing, at first, to regard an **increase in foreign assets** as a **negative** item in the accounts, but it makes sense in terms of identifying **where the currency goes**. The above example works exactly in reverse where one starts with a negative entry for an import of goods.

In order to make things somewhat easier to follow, the BoP accounts are currently divided into two. This division is relatively recent, and while the accounts have been recalculated in this format going back as far as is necessary for the purpose of this book, it should be recognised that variants of the accounts published before 1987 are in the original format which is difficult to match up with the new and should, therefore, no longer be used. The upper half of the accounts is called the **current account**. In this are to be found transactions covering exports and imports of goods and services, investment income, and transfers. The lower half of the accounts is called **transactions in UK external assets and liabilities**. In this are to be found inward and outward investment; external transactions by banks in the UK; borrowing and lending overseas by other UK residents; drawings on and additions to the official reserves; and other capital transactions. For simplicity this will be referred to as the **capital account**.

Where there is a positive entry in the current account – arising, for example from the export of goods – the corresponding negative entry is, as indicated above, normally to be found in the capital account as in (a) or (b) above. However, it must also be noted that corresponding plus and minus entries may both appear in the capital account, as would be the case if a UK resident borrowed from a bank in France in order to buy shares in a French company. An interesting illustration of this phenomenon is Japan in the 1980s, where despite a substantial current account surplus, large sums were borrowed from abroad in order to finance overseas investment.

It is also necessary to remind ourselves about the difficulties of estimation with respect to items in the BoP accounts because, as previously noted, the accounts must balance as a matter of definition. The two entries made in respect of each transaction are generally derived from separate sources, and the methods of estimation are neither complete nor precisely accurate. As a consequence the two entries either may not match precisely, and/or may fall within different recording periods. It is also possible that two entries, both in the same foreign currency, have been converted at different exchange rates. Hence, when all the entries in the accounts are added together, they never actually do sum to zero, and in order to make them do so the **balancing item** has to be added at the foot of the accounts.

6.3 The Structure of the Accounts

6.3.1 *The Current Account*

The full set of accounts is set out for the period of 1987 to 1992 in **Table 6.1**. The first part of the accounts covers exports and imports of goods, and the **net** figure is called the **visible balance**. It is more commonly referred to as the **balance of trade**. Note that both exports and imports are entered as positive amounts, but the net figure is plus or minus as appropriate. The next entry relates to credits and debits generated by trade in services, which are again entered as positive amounts with the net figure, called the **invisibles balance**, signed as appropriate. This net balance is then broken down into its three component parts: services (primarily sea transport, civil aviation, tourism and financial); interest, profits and dividends; and transfers (primarily central government grants to overseas countries and contributions to the EU Budget and to international organisations, and private transfers of assets by migrants). It should be noted that only the services part of the invisibles balance arises from trading, while the larger part arises as a result of movements of money.

The sum of the visible and invisibles balances, signed as appropriate, is called the **current balance**. Adjustments to the current balance usually occur as a result of changes in national income

Table 6.1   *UK BoP Accounts, 1987–92 (£ m)*

	1987	1988	1989	1990	1991	1992
CURRENT ACCOUNT						
Visible trade						
Exports (fob)	79 153	80 346	92 154	101 718	103 413	107 047
Imports (fob)	90 735	101 826	116 837	120 527	113 697	120 453
Visible balance	−11 582	−21 480	−24 683	−18 809	−10 284	−13 406
Invisibles						
Credits	79 194	87 307	107 203	114 624	114 373	108 438
Debits	72 595	82 444	105 032	114 083	111 741	103 652
Invisibles balance	6 599	4 863	2 171	541	2 632	4 786
of which:						
Services balance	6 242	3 957	3 361	3 808	3 657	4 069
Interest, profits and dividends balance	3 757	4 424	3 388	1 630	320	5 777
Transfers balance	−3 400	−3 518	−4 578	−4 897	−1 345	−5 060
Current balance	−4 983	−16 617	−22 512	−18 268	−7 652	−8 620
TRANSACTIONS IN EXTERNAL ASSETS AND LIABILITIES						
Investment overseas by UK residents						
Direct	−19 147	−20 863	−21 503	−10 544	−8 841	−9 424
Portfolio	5 418	−11 225	−36 341	−16 470	−29 240	−32 818
Total UK investment overseas	−13 729	−32 088	−57 844	−27 014	−38 081	−42 242
Investment in the UK by overseas residents						
Direct	9 449	12 006	18 567	18 520	9 032	10 343
Portfolio	22 233	16 533	16 079	7 724	19 230	21 390
Total overseas investment in the UK	31 682	28 539	34 646	26 244	28 262	31 733
Foreign currency lending abroad by UK banks	−45 757	−15 065	−25 688	−37 430	27 401	−14 995
Foreign currency borrowing abroad by UK banks	43 518	20 447	32 384	34 930	−14 805	21 460
Net foreign currency transactions of UK banks	−2 239	5 382	6 696	−2 500	12 596	6 465
Sterling lending abroad by UK banks	−4 636	−4 626	−2 923	−3 800	4 828	−10 842
Sterling borrowing and deposit liabilities abroad of UK banks	8 633	13 641	12 470	12 638	−9 395	2 840
Net sterling transactions of UK banks	3 997	9 015	9 547	8 838	−4 567	−8 002
Deposits with and lending to banks abroad by UK non-bank private sector	−5 291	−4 026	−9 553	−9 023	−4 642	−7 871
Borrowing from banks abroad by:						
UK non-bank private sector	2 612	3 973	9 964	7 934	13 576	8 018
Public corporations	−166	−253	−1 726	−124	−49	−506
General government	105	−10	529	−498	−65	993
Official reserves (additions to −, drawings on +)	−12 012	−2 761	5 440	−76	−2 679	1 406
Other external assets of:						
UK non-bank private sector and public corporations	−278	993	1 352	−3 821	−4 856	−9 749
General government	−796	−887	−873	−1 025	−894	−682
Other external liabilities of:						
UK non-bank private sector and public corporations	1 414	1 635	20 975	8 799	10 392	31 319
General government	1 725	842	2 293	1 197	−2 264	−2 562
Net transactions in assets and liabilities	7 026	10 352	19 415	10 960	6 728	8 319
Balancing item	−2 043	6 265	3 097	7 308	924	301

Source: UK National Accounts Pink Book (CSO, 1993), Tables 1.3 and 1.4; *UK Economic Accounts*, No. 1.

both at home and abroad, the proportion of it which is spent, and the proportion of that spending which goes on domestic as against overseas goods and services. A sharp deterioration in the current balance is usually taken to indicate an upturn in consumption (either private or public) which has spilled over into imports, but an alternative, and more beneficial, interpretation is that it indicates the importation of capital goods for investment by UK companies to improve their productive capacity. Unfortunately, it is very difficult for analytical purposes to distinguish in the short term between these interpretations.

☐ 6.3.2 *The Capital Account*

The rest of the accounts can be distinguished by virtue of the fact that no goods and services flow in the opposite direction to the flows of currency. What are being acquired are foreign assets such as shares and securities. When such flows of currency are recorded they can be attributed to a number of basic influences. The first – of critical importance in recent years – is the **structure of interest rates** in the UK compared to that overseas. If interest rates are higher in the UK than elsewhere, after adjusting for any risk of default, currency will tend to flow into the UK in very large amounts. For the most part, such currency flows will be **short-term** (colloquially called **hot money**). The second influence is the **rate of return on investment**. If a UK company takes over a foreign company, it does so in the belief that the investment will yield a higher rate of return than would result from the takeover of another UK company. Equally, private investors in the UK will buy shares in foreign companies if they believe that the dividend yield and/or the prospect of capital gains is better than that to be achieved in the UK. These currency flows are mostly **long-term**. If interest rates are relatively low in the UK, or rates of return in the UK are relatively low, the flows will operate in the reverse direction.

It should be noted that the distinction between short-term and long-term capital flows is much easier to establish in principle than it is in practice. The capital account is not divided up specifically to illustrate this distinction, and we will accordingly be using the term 'hot money' to refer to highly mobile international capital.

The third influence is the **exchange rate**. All capital flows must take place in a particular currency, the value of which can vary quite considerably over time. While long-term investment is not much affected by this influence, given that exchange rate movements in the longer term are impossible to predict and that the investor can anyway hedge against changes in currency value, hot money flows are a different matter. Even where the interest rate on offer is higher than in other financial centres, a financial asset, denominated in a currency whose value is expected to rise sharply, will prove popular even if its yield is very poor, as this will be more than compensated by the prospect of a capital gain in the asset. This proposition is developed in more detail on **p. 219**.

Direct investment primarily comprises net investment by overseas companies in their UK affiliates including the reinvestment of retained profits, and by UK companies in their overseas branches, subsidiaries and associates.

Portfolio investment by UK residents comprises net purchases and sales of overseas government, municipal and company securities, while portfolio investment in the UK primarily comprises net purchases and sales of UK company securities and government stocks. These flows clearly affect the **net asset/liability position** of the UK relative to the rest of the world. In principle, one simply adds or subtracts the net annual change to the existing cumulative net value of assets, but in addition there may be capital gains and losses arising from, for example, changes in share prices which cannot show up in the BoP accounts until such time as an asset is sold. The scale of financial asset acquisition by UK residents resulted in the UK becoming temporarily one of the world's three largest net creditor nations in 1989. This was obviously balanced by growing net indebtedness elsewhere and, although it was hard to accept, the USA appeared to have become a net debtor, indeed the world's largest net debtor. This is a highly contentious issue and it is discussed in some detail on **pp. 205–7**.

Net foreign currency transactions of UK banks consist of changes in deposits of foreign currencies made with UK resident banks by non-residents, and loans by the banks in those currencies to non-residents. **Net sterling transactions** of UK banks consist of sterling advances and overdrafts (net of repayments) provided to overseas residents (including banks abroad) by UK banks, sterling commercial bills discounted, acceptances, and sterling borrowing and deposit liabilities abroad.

Deposits with, and lending to, banks abroad by the UK non-bank private sector consist of UK residents' deposits with banks in the Bank for International Settlements (BIS) reporting area, together with assets held in the custody of banks in the USA. **Borrowing from banks abroad** predominantly covers borrowing from commercial banks in the BIS reporting area, the European Investment Bank and the United States Export–Import Bank.

We come next to changes in the **official reserves**, which are also analysed in more detail below. Other external assets include identified trade credit between unrelated companies, inter-government loans by the UK and subscriptions to international lending bodies, while other external liabilities include broadly the same items. The balancing item has already been discussed above.

■ 6.4 The Accounts in Retrospect

In taking a retrospective view of the BoP accounts it is clearly not practicable to operate at the detailed disaggregated level presented in **Table 6.1**, except insofar as it is needed to shed light on the peculiarities of recent policy in relation to the external sector. **Table 6.4** (see below), which covers the period commencing with the present government's election and its full period in office, accordingly treats transactions on external assets and liabilities only in the aggregate. This accords with the customary presentation of the accounts in the media.

6.4.1 The Meaning of Equilibrium

Before proceeding we need first to consider the meaning of the term 'equilibrium' in the context of the accounts. As we have explained, the accounts as a whole must balance by definition, but to achieve that it is not necessary for any individual component of the accounts, (for example, the current balance) to have a zero value. The main issue accordingly is how best to express the objective of policy concerning the BoP. The messages sent out about the state of the economy by the current and capital accounts are rather different, and the focus of concern about the accounts has always been upon the **current balance**. It is, therefore, often argued that this should be in equilibrium in the sense that it should have a value of zero.

However, given that the UK has historically been predominantly a manufacturing nation, it is sometimes argued that attention should be focused more narrowly upon the **visible balance**, more commonly referred to as the **balance of trade**, and that this should be kept in equilibrium with the value of zero.

Occasionally, reference is made to the **basic balance**, which is the sum of the current balance plus the balance of long-term capital flows (that is, it excludes hot money). It can be argued that hot money merely 'accommodates' the basic balance, which thus gives a true insight into the current and longer-term prosperity of the trading sector. However, as we have noted, the basic balance cannot be estimated accurately because of the difficulty of separating out the short-term from the long-term capital flows.

The first important lesson from the above is that when the word 'equilibrium' is encountered, one must look carefully to see to which part of the accounts it is being applied. In the second place, there is clearly a time dimension to the issue. The current balance might sum to zero over a period of years, and hence yield an equilibrium, albeit possibly more by chance than by design. This may be preferable to the requirement that it be in equilibrium over a period of months, or in any given year, since it will allow for cyclical adjustments and the problems of data collection discussed above. But unless a government is prepared to state in advance that it is pursuing a set of policies intended to achieve equilibrium within a specified period, the fact that it can retrospectively identify such an equilibrium cannot be said to prove anything one way or another about its policies.

In any event, the whole issue is clouded by the choice of a particular exchange rate regime. Without discussing this in detail here as it is covered below, the essential point is that it is possible to choose a regime which will, other than in the very short term, keep the visible balance in equilibrium. However, it will not keep the other components of the accounts in equilibrium, and there are also likely to be conflicts with other objectives of policy which rule out this approach to the achievement of equilibrium. It is finally worth reminding ourselves that it is current practice to isolate the balancing item from both the current and capital account balances. But if, as generally been the case, the balancing item is initially (and in some cases will always be) large, and if it is unclear how it should be divided between current and capital accounts, it becomes almost impossible to surmise whether either account is anywhere near, let alone specifically at, its equilibrium value, be it in the short or the longer term.

☐ 6.4.2 The Balancing Item

The balancing item is a very volatile item in the accounts. Some part of it will be permanent insofar as, for example, the data collection system consistently fails to record certain transactions. Other parts will be erratic and arise because, for example, the data collection system either becomes able to record transactions in the capital account which could not previously be attributed to any of its headings, and therefore had to be lumped into the balancing item, or cease to be able to do so, with the reverse effect. Large balancing items (whether plus or minus) have been a feature of the 1980s in the accounts. This is partly because, since 1982, a substantial proportion of trade credit between unrelated companies, required to bridge the gap between the time goods are shipped and the settlement of the invoice, has been switched from the capital account to the balancing item. Furthermore, in 1986, the high level of capital flows during the period leading up to and following 'Big Bang' created difficulties of attribution to appropriate headings in the capital account.

Hopes that the balancing item would settle down, as it did in 1987, have in most years been confounded. This is more important that it seems because, if the balancing item is large, and if it is not known whether it is created by under- or overrecording in the current account, it is difficult to know how seriously to take the recorded data. Recently, the situation has improved.

Since 1975 the balancing item has been positive in every year except 1982 and, possibly, 1987 where the most recent revision sets it (temporarily, no doubt) at −£2,043 million. A positive balancing item implies either unrecorded net credits in the current account or unrecorded net inflows in the capital account, or both. In practice, the balancing item is highly volatile on a quarterly basis, and individual quarters have been as large as +£10 billion and −£5 billion in recent years. Nevertheless, the Bank of England considers that of late the underrecording of inflows has become a structural problem. Transfers from the balancing item to portfolio inflows in the accounts have ameliorated the situation somewhat (the cumulative balancing item was, at the time, shown as £35 billion for 1986–88), but it remains unclear exactly where the problem lies.

The Bank believes that the recording of visible trade should be highly accurate, although anyone who has cause to examine trade data at a disaggregated level is fairly sure to believe to the contrary. It believes that there are problems with data on services, but does not see how these errors could account for more than a small part of the overall balancing item. Hence, 'it seems likely that the explanation for the majority of the balancing item lies in the capital account' (Bank of England, 1990, **p. 498**). In particular, the Bank considers that 'the bulk of omission may be in portfolio inflows'.

There is an additional factor to consider. Taking the world as a whole, while as a matter of simple definition total world exports must equal total world imports, they fall short in practice by a wide margin. It therefore follows that in many parts of the world exports are significantly underrecorded. The situation is fluid because the discrepancy for a given year tends to decline over time as the data are improved, but imbalances remain large.

The IMF indicate where they believe the problem arises, and in recent years their preference has been to attribute it to underrecorded investment flows in industrial countries. The official version of events thus has it that the balancing item consists of underrecorded capital account **inflows** and, taking the IMF line, that missing world exports are predominantly not of goods but of services, and anyway do not originate from the UK at all. If they are right then this has serious implications for the value of the UK's net overseas assets. The sceptics' view, on the other hand, is that a significant part of the balancing item is unrecorded exports of goods and services, and that these also exist for the UK as part of the black hole in the world's trading accounts. If the sceptics are right then the trading account is healthier than it appears to be.

In many ways the most surprising aspect of the above debate is that both politicians and currency dealers set so much store by the monthly data on the BoP which should clearly carry a government warning concerning their use (and abuse). This does not arise solely because of the constant process of re-attribution from the balancing item to other items in the accounts, but also because of the acknowledged misrecording of both current account and capital account flows.

6.4.3 Index Numbers of UK Visible Trade

It must be recognised that when one has become used to regarding a current account deficit of £10 billion as giving cause for concern, there is a tendency to be dismissive of historic deficits of a 'mere' £1 billion, let alone those of £100 million. Yet these figures, in their historic context, were regarded with equal dismay because of their size in relation to the then value of GDP. The escalation in the numbers partly reflects the effects of economic growth, but primarily those of continuous – and in many individual years very rapid – inflation. It is possible to give a general impression of the relative effects of growth and inflation by the use of index numbers, as in **Table 6.2**.

The **volume** index for visible exports rose by roughly 60 per cent between 1970 and 1980, a markedly better performance than for the volume of imports. However, from 1982 to 1989, as shown in **Table 6.2**, growth in the volume of imports was twice that of exports (although 1985 was the one year which went against the trend). Nevertheless, the growth differential was shrinking from 1987 onwards and became positive in 1990. In 1991 the volume of imports actually fell for the first time since 1981 whereas, unlike in 1981, the volume of exports continued to rise.

Over the period 1970 to 1980 the **value** of both visible exports and imports roughly quadrupled, so prices of both exports and imports were clearly rising rapidly, albeit faster for imports than for exports. The unit value indices continued to outrun the volume indices until 1985, although prices of imports and exports were rising in unison during this period. However, from 1986 to 1992 the situation reversed itself, with volumes outrunning unit values by a substantial margin. During this period the unit value indices moved more or less in unison, but with that for imports always remaining slightly above that for exports.

If the unit value of visible exports is divided by the unit value of visible imports we get a measure of the **terms of trade**. As can be seen, these worsened sharply between 1972 and 1974, but subsequently improved more steadily until 1981. They worsened sharply again in 1986, but after climbing back steadily they have almost regained the level of 1985.

The terms of trade must be treated with care. On the face of it, an improvement, resulting perhaps from relatively high inflation in the UK, enables the same volume of imports to be bought in exchange for a lesser volume of exports than

Table 6.2   *Index Numbers, UK Visible Trade (1985 = 100)*

	Volume indices[1]						Unit value index[2]		Terms of trade ((a)/(b))
	Exports			Total	Imports		(a) Exports	(b) Imports	
	Manufactures		Share of world exports of manufactures		Total	Manufactures as % Total Final Expenditure			
	Semi	Finished							
1972				55.9	64.1		20.3	18.6	109.2
1973				63.4	73.0		22.8	23.7	96.3
1974				68.0	73.3		29.0	34.6	83.7
1975				65.2	66.9		35.6	39.5	90.2
1976				71.7	71.3		42.6	48.4	88.1
1977				77.6	72.8		50.5	55.9	90.3
1978	97	91	117	79.6	76.1	11.4	55.5	58.0	95.5
1979	99	98	110	83.1	83.5	11.8	61.4	61.8	99.4
1980	93	89	105	84.1	79.0	10.8	69.9	67.8	103.1
1981	85	86	96	82.6	75.8	10.1	76.2	73.7	103.4
1982	86	87	102	85.3	80.3	10.7	81.4	79.9	101.9
1983	91	84	99	87.2	87.2	11.7	88.0	87.6	100.5
1984	97	93	98	94.5	96.5	12.7	95.0	95.3	99.6
1985	100	100	100	100.0	100.0	12.8	100.0	100.0	100.0
1986	106	102	102	104.0	107.2	12.9	90.1	95.4	94.4
1987	113	112	105	109.8	114.8	13.3	93.5	98.0	95.4
1988	120	120	103	112.5	130.5	14.0	93.4	96.9	96.4
1989	123	136	105	117.3	140.8	14.6	100.8	104.1	96.8
1990	131	147	107	125.1	142.7	14.0	106.2	108.0	98.3
1991	135	151	107	126.9	138.6	12.9	106.4	108.4	98.2
1992	142	152	107	130.7	147.4	13.2	108.9	109.3	99.6

Notes:
[1] Seasonally adjusted.
[2] Unadjusted.
Source: UK National Accounts Pink Book (CSO, 1993); *National Institute Review; Economic Trends; Monthly Digest of Statistics*, Table 15.8.

before. However, much depends upon the price elasticity of demand for exports and imports. If demand for UK visible exports is elastic, as is generally the case, an increase in price results in a reduction in revenue. Equally, if demand for visible imports its inelastic, as is generally the case, a reduction in price results in an increase in payments. Thus, overall, the balance of trade (visible exports **less** visible imports) will worsen rather that the reverse. In other words, a dose of domestic inflation in the UK is likely to cause serious damage to the visible trade balance, and

is also likely to damage invisibles trade in an increasingly competitive world. The (albeit modest) improvement in recent years has not, therefore, been beneficial to the UK.

It is of particular interest to examine the other columns in **Table 6.2** in the light of the alleged collapse of manufacturing capability in the UK. What the first two columns show is that at the end of the 1970s, and through the 1980–81 recession, the volume of exports of semi-manufactures and finished manufactures suffered a set-back, particularly as the exchange rate was driven up by

North Sea oil coming on stream. There was a sharp recovery in 1982 and 1983 respectively, with both categories back to their 1978 volumes in 1984. From that point on to the end of the decade export volumes rose rapidly, demonstrating that the manufacturing capability which survived the 1980–81 recession was fully capable of selling competitively in international markets.

This has continued to be the case, albeit to a lesser degree, during the 1990s. As a result, the volume of finished manufactures is more than half as great again as in 1985, and may soon reach twice the level of 1983. The consequences for the UK's share of world exports of manufactures are important because so many attacks on government policy include a claim that it is continuously falling, but **this is untrue**. It did indeed fall rapidly at the end of the 1970s, but once the 1980–81 recession was over it stabilised around its 1983 level. This can be seen more clearly in terms of both volume and value (up to 1986) in **Figure 6.1**, which covers the period 1972–93. Bearing in mind

the export success of, for example, Japan and Taiwan, this was a creditable performance, and it would be unreasonable to expect a mature economy like the UK to gain much market share in the intensely competitive environment of international trade in manufactures (but see the discussion of the car market below).

On the imports side the picture is less rosy, with manufactured imports rising as a proportion of TFE from 1981 to 1989, at which point UK domestic demand fell away, taking the demand for exports with it. The fact that import and export volumes of manufactures rise together is a commonplace of advanced countries which, for example, trade different makes of car and electronic goods. The purchase of cheap, high quality, imports is not to be deplored as such, provided, of course, one believes more or less in free trade. The key issue is whether or not a country can compensate by maintaining exports of goods and services in order to keep the current account balance in rough equilibrium.

Figure 6.1   *UK Share of World Trade in Manufactures (%)*

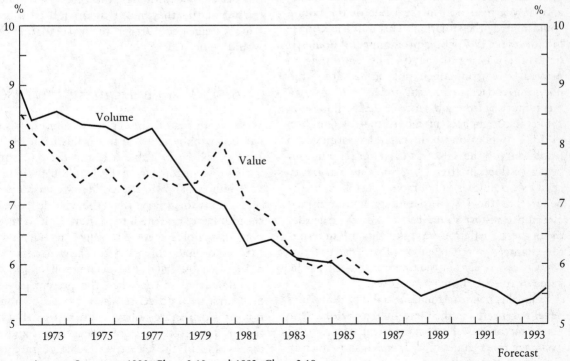

Source: Autumn Statement 1990, Chart 2.10, and 1992, Chart 3.18.

□ 6.4.4 *Visible Trade in Retrospect*

Prior to 1967 the UK managed to keep the current balance in surplus but, with the exception of 1956 and 1958 when the visible balance was positive, the pattern of a negative visible balance more than compensated by a positive invisibles balance was already well-established. There was considerable volatility with respect to short-term capital flows, but long-term capital flows were mostly outflows, and hence negative in the accounts. In looking at the current situation one might be tempted to believe that nothing much has changed since the 1960s. However, as we shall see, this is not the case because of differences in the exchange rate regime in operation, in the UK's reserve position, and in the contribution of North Sea oil.

The steady deterioration in the UK's share of world trade in manufactures, exacerbated by an uncompetitive fixed exchange rate and combined with a tendency for hot money to pour out of the UK whenever a crisis loomed, thereby draining the inadequate reserves, was an unsustainable situation. The BoP accounts gave every appearance of being in 'fundamental disequilibrium', and only a reduction in the value of the pound could remedy the situation. This duly took place in November 1967, and a programme of domestic deflation was set in hand. The combination proved successful, albeit not immediately and not soon enough to prevent a change of government. Starting from a balance of −£286 million in 1968, the current account moved to +£460 million in 1971. While long-term capital continued to flood out of the UK, an even larger amount began to flood in after 1969, and this was paralleled by net inflows of hot money sustained by the belief that the UK was making a determined attempt to restore sound finance. It was true that the domestic deflation was taking its toll in terms, for example, of rising unemployment, but this was of less concern at the time than the symbolic value of the deflationary measures.

From this point on fundamental disequilibrium never reappeared in the same guise as before. One major factor was the abandonment of the fixed exchange rate regime in 1972, which subsequently permitted the exchange rate to be used more

positively to regulate the current balance. A second factor, which was initially of much less help, was the sharp increase in the price of North Sea oil. From 1975 to 1979 the visible balance remained heavily in deficit. The invisibles largely offset the damage, although the negative transfer component (including contributions to the EU) grew too rapidly to allow for a substantial current account surplus other than in 1978, at the end of a long period of oil price stability. The exceptionally high rate of inflation, partly triggered by the first oil price rise, was ultimately the key problem, because although long-term capital was flowing in to finance the development of the North Sea oilfields, international confidence in the UK's ability to deal with its domestic problems caused a massive outflow of hot money. This forced the then Labour government both to deplete the reserves and to borrow from the IMF (agreeing in return to deflate the economy along 'monetarist' lines), as shown in **Table 6.3**.

With confidence restored by the IMF intervention, the reserve position took a dramatic turn for the better, and although the reserves remained fairly volatile they never again fell to a level which suggested further recourse to the IMF would be needed.

□ 6.4.5 *Visible Trade in the 1980s*

With North Sea oil coming on stream, the visible balance actually returned to surplus from 1980 to 1982 as shown in **Table 6.4**, and the oil surplus itself grew steadily from £0.3 billion in 1980 to £8.1 billion in 1985. Under the circumstances it seems extraordinary that the visible balance should have returned to deficit, but whereas non-oil visibles were £1 billion in surplus in 1980, they had collapsed to show a deficit of £11 billion by 1984. The decimation of the UK manufacturing sector when the present government first took office, resulting from a combination of a deliberate policy of domestic deflation, the UK's relatively high rate of inflation and the high value of the effective exchange rate (see **pp. 461, 82** and **223** respectively) was largely to

Table 6.3   *UK Official Reserves, 1975–92, End-Year Values*[1] *($ m)*

	Gold	SDRs	Reserve position at IMF	Convertible currencies	TOTAL
1975	888	840	366	3 335	5 429
1976	888	728	–	2 513	4 129
1977	938	604	–	19 015	20 557
1978	938	500	–	14 230	15 694
1979	3 259	1 245	–	18 034	22 538
1980	6 987	560	1 308	18 621	27 476
1981	7 334	1 048	1 513	13 457	23 352
1982	4 562	1 233	1 568	9 634	16 997
1983	5 914	695	2 168	9 040	17 817
1984	5 476	531	2 110	7 577	15 694
1985	4 310	996	1 751	8 486	15 543
1986	4 897	1 425	1 820	13 781	21 923
1987	5 792	1 229	1 579	35 726	44 326
1988	6 466	1 341	1 694	42 184	51 685
1989	5 457	1 125	1 610	20 453	38 645
1990	5 235	1 142	1 534	30 553	38 464
1991	5 039	1 232	1 733	36 122	44 126
1992	4 770	539	2 007	34 338	41 654

Notes:
[1] The level of the reserves is affected by changes in the dollar valuation of gold, Special Drawing Rights (SDRs) and convertible currencies as well as by transactions.
Source: Bank of England Quarterly Bulletin.

blame, since the damage done at the time has never been fully rectified. Whereas the effective exchange rate fell to an historic low by 1986, and the rump of the manufacturing sector performed very creditably in export markets, the growth in the UK economy sucked in vast amounts of foreign manufactures, many of which could no longer be produced at all in the UK. Individual events (such as the coal-miners' strike in 1984–85) added to the difficulties, and it is possible to argue that, although many UK products were highly competitive on price alone, they fell down with respect to non-price factors such as quality and speed of delivery.

It is also necessary, in looking at the visible balance, to appreciate a peculiarity of the way in which exchange rates work. In practice many products, and especially raw materials including oil, are priced in dollars. Thus if the pound rises in value against the dollar these become cheaper in sterling and vice versa. However, exports to the EU are affected by the rate at which the pound is exchanged for EU currencies. If the pound rises against these currencies then UK exports become expensive and vice versa. The worst combination for the UK is, therefore, for the pound to fall against the dollar, making raw material imports expensive, and to rise simultaneously against EU currencies, making exports expensive. From 1979 to 1985 this combination broadly held true and the visible balance was only salvaged by North Sea oil coming on stream.

From 1980 to 1987 the invisibles balance remained very healthy. The balance on private services was the major contributory factor. Equally, while interest payments needed to be made on outstanding government borrowings from abroad, the long-term capital outflows in the 1970s mentioned above resulted in a sharp upturn in private sector interest, profits and dividends (appearing, note, in the **current** rather than the capital account).

Table 6.4 *BoP of the UK, 1979–92, (£ m)*

	1979	1980	1981	1982	1983	1984	1985	1986	1987	1988	1989	1990	1991	1992
CURRENT ACCOUNT[1]														
Visible Balance	−3342	1357	3251	1911	−1537	−5336	−3345	−9559	−11582	−21480	−24683	−18809	−10284	−13406
Invisibles:														
Services	3895	3653	3792	3022	3829	4205	6398	6223	6242	3957	3361	3808	3657	4069
Interest, profits and dividends	1205	−182	1251	1460	2830	4344	2296	4622	3757	4424	3388	1630	320	5777
Transfers	−2210	−1984	−1547	−1741	−1593	−1732	−3111	−2157	−3400	−3518	−4578	−4897	−1347	−5060
Invisibles Balance	2890	1487	3496	2741	5066	6817	5583	8688	6599	4863	2171	541	2632	4786
CURRENT BALANCE	−453	2843	6748	4649	3529	1482	2238	−871	−4983	−16617	−22512	−18268	−7652	−8620
TRANSACTIONS IN EXTERNAL ASSETS AND LIABILITIES[2]														
Net Transactions[3]	−742	−3940	−7436	−2519	−4562	−8688	−3797	−3173	7026	10352	19415	10960	6728	8319
Allocation of SDRs	195	180	158	0	0	0	0	0	0	0	0	0	0	0
Balancing Item	1000	917	530	−2130	1033	7206	1559	4044	−2043	6265	3097	7308	924	301

Notes:
[1] Seasonally adjusted.
[2] Assets: increase −/decrease +. Liabilities: increase +/decrease −. Not seasonally adjusted.
[3] *Financial Statistics*, Table 10.2; UK National Accounts Pink Book (CSO, 1993), Table 1.1; *UK Economic Accounts*, No. 1.

Source: Financial Statistics, Table 10.2; UK National Accounts Pink Book (CSO, 1993), Table 1.1; *UK Economic Accounts*, No. 1.

As a consequence of its diversity, the capital account is much more difficult to interpret. Account must be taken of the lifting of exchange controls in October 1979, which resulted in a sharp upturn in investment overseas by UK residents (rising from £12.6 billion in 1983 to £34.4 billion in 1986). These were offset by large amounts of foreign currency borrowing by UK banks and, as already mentioned, short-term inflows were heavily influenced by sterling's new status as a petro-currency and by the government's determined attack upon inflation, initially via its 'monetarist' policies and subsequently via high interest rates. UK companies continued to perform creditably in export markets, but **Table 6.4** indicates the scale of the problem. From 1985 to 1987 the volume of visible exports rose by roughly 10 per cent, but the volume of imports rose by 15 per cent, and the gap continued to widen during 1988. If the comparison is linked only to manufactured goods, then the margin of difference was considerably wider. The consequences, taken in conjunction with the collapse in the price of North Sea oil, show up clearly in the visible balance which worsened sharply in 1986 to record a deficit of £9.6 billion. This would have been worse had sterling not risen against the dollar, thereby cheapening raw material imports, and fallen against EU currencies, thereby cheapening UK exports. The invisibles balance, on the other hand, improved sharply in 1986, and almost matched the visible deficit.

□ 6.4.6 Recent History

In 1987 the visible balance deteriorated further to show a deficit of £11.6 billion. The invisibles balance registered a surplus of £6.6 billion resulting in a current account deficit of £5 billion for the year, the first major deficit of the 1980s. At first 1987 seemed to be exceptional in relation to earlier years in the decade in that net transactions were recorded in the 1988 Pink Book as being only marginally negative, a turnaround of £13 billion in one year. This was widely thought to be due to the appreciation of sterling which lowered the sterling value of assets priced in other curren-

cies, and also because UK residents ran down their overseas investments, mainly after the stock market crash in October. The attraction of the UK as a haven for hot money grew even stronger because of the combination of fiscal rectitude and high nominal interest rates. The year was also unusual in that the balancing item appeared to fall sharply. However, the revisions published in subsequent Pink Books swung from a £7 billion outflow on net transactions to the latest £7 billion inflow, and from a +£11 billion balancing item to the latest estimate of a negative balancing item of £2 billion. No wonder the government set in hand a major overhaul of the statistical service!

In 1988 the current account deteriorated rapidly, as shown in **Figure 6.2** where the data are presented as percentages of GDP. The visible balance recorded an unprecedented deficit of £21.5 billion, which was only partially compensated for by an invisibles surplus that was itself falling sharply from its 1986 peak. Hence the current account deficit was an alarming £16.6 billion which even the large positive balancing item could not explain.

One factor, apart from the general surge in imports of all kinds, was a sharp decline in the oil surplus as domestic industry increased its oil consumption and the Piper Alpha platform disaster affected supplies. This appeared to herald the end of an era for North Sea oil and gas insofar as it affects the BoP, an issue addressed in the next section.

The visible trade deficit worsened in 1989, as shown in **Figure 6.3**, and with the invisibles surplus shrinking further, so did the current account deficit. It goes without saying that in many quarters these figures were taken as evidence that the obsolete ship SS Great Britain was sinking without trace. As a result the government was forced to scratch around with increasing desperation to explain why they were merely a 'blip' rather than a trend.

The situation began to improve noticeably in 1990 as the recession began to take hold, as shown in **Figures 6.2** and **6.3**, and in the second quarter of 1991 the current account appeared to be once again in balance. Unfortunately, this proved to be a false dawn, with the deficit on visibles promptly

Figure 6.2   *Current Balance as % of GDP*

Source: CSO.

building up again at the same time as the surplus on invisibles began to erode. The current account deficit for the year, at £7.7 billion was indeed a big improvement on 1990, but there was a further modest deterioration, allowing for inflation, in 1992.

Given the role played by manufactures in explaining the size of the current account deficit, at this stage it is worth examining a number of sub-sectors of the accounts in order to gain some insight into the UK's future prospects.

Trade in Cars

The general tone of commentators is so pessimistic that it seems almost sacrilegious to suggest that there are rays of sunshine amid the gloom, yet that is truly the case where trade in cars is concerned. It is not so long ago that the traditional British car industry more or less disappeared without trace. Although the American/British car industry in part replaced it, this was not on a scale such that a massive trade deficit in cars could be prevented, especially since many Fords and Vauxhalls were actually imports.

Nevertheless, the most notable improvement in the balance of trade during 1990 resulted from an end-year surge in exports of cars and commercial vehicles (motors). In the whole of 1990, 414 000 cars were exported, with the final quarter figures up 60 per cent on 1989. Overall, the motor trade account remained in deficit to the tune of £4.6 billion, but this was much better than the 1989

Figure 6.3   *Visible Trade Deficit (£ bn)*

Source: UK *Economic Accounts*, No. 3, Chart 8.

deficit of £6.6 billion. Ford and Vauxhall resumed large-scale exports to the Continent for the first time in over a decade, and the Nissan factory in Sunderland became the first Japanese plant to produce 'UK' exports of cars.

In the final quarter of 1991 the motor industry achieved its first trade surplus for almost a decade, and the deficit for the year fell to £1 billion. The situation deteriorated in 1992 with a deficit of £2.4 billion, but the longer-term perspective is much rosier than is generally admitted. By 1995, Japanese car-makers will be building 500 000 cars a year in Britain. Nissan is expected to increase its exports from Britain to at least three times their current level by the end of the decade. Both Toyota and Honda will also have the capacity to export at this time, and as many as 1.5 million vehicles may be exported in total. Furthermore, these companies' cars will displace existing imports to a considerable extent. The ultimate impact of these developments is dependent upon the UK home market and the proportion of UK content in both exports and imports of cars (Rhys, 1990). In principle, all EU member states are obliged to remove barriers against the importation of Japanese/UK cars by the end of the decade, although the current recession in mainland Europe is causing some rebellion about concessions in the short term. It is not altogether clear either if or when the motor trade deficit will ever completely disappear, although the indications are that it will eventually, and the 1992 fall in the value of the pound has led some to argue that it will be sooner rather than later (for example, Rhys now opts for 1996). Either way, as the motor trade constituted roughly one-quarter of the total visible trade deficit in 1990 (and slightly more in 1989), this does offer some support for the expectation that the visible trade deficit will shrink to a more manageable size.

Trade in Electronics

The process described above is by no means confined to cars. Even though, for example, there are no longer any UK-owned television manufacturers, colour television exports began to exceed imports in 1989. Ferguson, the last substantially UK-owned manufacturer of television sets, was bought by Thomson of France in 1987, but once again it is primarily the Japanese who have spearheaded the attack on overseas markets. Sony, the largest UK-based manufacturer, has won three Queen's Awards for Export Achievement since it established its factory in South Wales in 1974. The UK is currently the possessor of the fourth largest electronics industry in the world after the USA, Japan and Germany. In 1992 electronics exports were 15 per cent smaller than imports, but a decade ago the gap was twice as large. In June 1993 it was announced that a new £42 million electronics plant was being set up in South Wales by a subsidiary of QPL of Hong Kong, creating 1000 jobs.

Needless to say, the invasion by foreign companies has generated an intense debate about whether ownership as such is important, but in simple BoP terms the consequences for the visible balance are undoubtedly positive. We will return to this issue in our subsequent analysis of the commodity composition of visible trade.

In examining the reasons for the UK's poor performance in manufacturing trade such as poor education and training, bad design and quality and too little research and development (R&D), it is salutary to remember that the sectors in which the UK trades successfully – such as chemicals, pharmaceuticals and aerospace – operate in exactly the same domestic environment as the sectors in which the UK trades unsuccessfully. It is possible to hypothesise that sectors which are currently successful are successful precisely because they always had to operate in international markets, whereas those (such as white goods and motor cycles) which relied almost entirely upon the home market proved easy pickings for internationally competitive overseas producers.

The situation may, therefore, become more stable than in the recent past, especially if continued inward investment serves to replace uncompetitive UK-owned business with Japanese-owned subsidiaries, as in the case of cars. It is not the case that the UK's problems are particularly in high-technology sectors since the aerospace industry trades successfully. Indeed, it is in areas such as white goods, which are essentially low-tech, that the worst problems have typically arisen.

However, the pessimists can still make out a fairly convincing case in the short term, as shown in **Figure 6.4**, since it was widely expected that import penetration would fall back in the recent recession, much as it did in the early 1980s, and this did not happen. Simple extrapolation of the trend in **Figure 6.4** certainly gives cause for concern, although it should be noted that virtually all advanced countries have suffered increased import penetration over the past decade. It is slightly ironic that part of the 'problem' lies in the exceptionally efficient UK retail sector. The inefficient system of retail distribution in Japan is undoubtedly one of the subtle protectionist devices used to keep out imported manufactures, whereas the ease with which such products find their way into British stores, and the simplicity of 'comparison shopping' in such outlets, has ruthlessly exposed price and quality shortfalls in domestic products.

Figure 6.4 *Import Penetration*[1]

Notes:
[1] Imports as a proportion of domestic demand.
[2] The first observation is 1988 Q3.
Source: Bank of England Quarterly Bulletin.

☐ 6.4.7 *Balance of Payments Effects of North Sea Oil*

The BoP effects of the North Sea show up in four ways. The first two are current account items, appearing mainly in the visible balance. First, there is the balance of trade in oil and gas. This, as discussed above, was heavily in deficit during the 1970s, but showed a healthy surplus during the 1980s until the more than halving of the price of oil in early 1986. This surplus is no longer of sufficient size to warrant the level of attention accorded to the oil balance over the period to 1987. The second item relates to the net purchase of goods and services required to discover and extract the oil and gas. This was a significant deficit item in the early 1970s, but is no longer of any consequence. One of the other two effects appears in the capital account, namely capital inflows to finance the discovery and extraction activities. These basically can be set against the cost of purchasing goods and services and, like them, have been inconsequential for a good many years. However, in the usual way, these inflows of capital generate the final effect, namely a requirement to pay interest, profits and dividends at a later date, which have accordingly been a negative item in the invisibles during the 1980s.

If this is set against the worsening in the balance of trade in oil and gas, it is clear that net revenue from the North Sea is unlikely to be able to offset any further deterioration which may occur in trade in manufactures. It is possible to speculate that this offset will continue because the price of oil will rise over time, but this is less than probable. It is equally possible to argue that the output of oil and gas will rise rapidly, subject to a supportive tax regime, since there is no shortage of reserves, but there are no immediate signs of this and it is in any case dependent upon trends in prices.

If the BoP benefits of North Sea oil and gas have now largely come to an end, but the non-oil variables remain in deficit, it is certainly possible to argue that the existence of North Sea resources has simply been used as an excuse for not tackling some of the most deep-rooted problems of the economy. On the other hand, it has to be asked whether the huge increase in the net overseas assets of the UK in the 1980s had anything to do with the use of the money generated by the production of North Sea oil. If so, then it is unreasonable to regard the money as 'wasted' even if it has not been put to the purpose preferred by all parties.

It is also possible to argue that the UK's net trading postion with respect to manufactures has been permanently damaged by the effects of North Sea oil on the exchange rate. As noted elsewhere, the willingness of the government to let the exchange rate appreciate rapidly at the beginning of the 1980s, in response both to the current account benefits of oil and to the boost to foreign confidence in the UK which accompanied it, made it very difficult for many firms to sell in export markets. The subsequent decline in the oil balance was not, however, accompanied by a parallel resurgence in manufactured exports.

□ *6.4.8 The Invisibles Balance*

In aggregate, as shown in **Table 6.1**, UK exports of invisibles are normally worth more than visible exports. The UK is second only to the USA as an exporter of invisibles, with roughly 16 per cent of the world total. However, this represents a greater dependency on invisibles than for any other industrial country. Tradable services account for 20 per cent of GDP, whereas the comparable figure is nearer 5 per cent for both the USA and Japan.

Despite this, the invisibles balance has for some time been a cause for concern. In money terms it has been on a declining trend since 1986, and hence its real value has been falling even faster. Traditionally, an invisibles surplus offset a balance of trade deficit, but on a monthly and quarterly basis invisibles deficits are no longer exceptional, as shown in **Figure 6.5**. It is useful, as ever, to express the balance as a percentage of GDP, as in **Figure 6.6**, to bring the trend out more clearly.

Figure 6.5   *Invisibles Trade Balance (£ bn)*

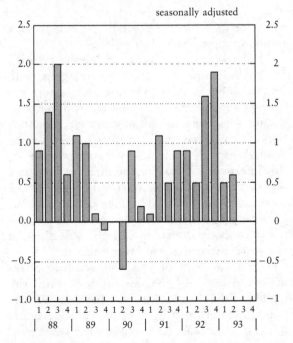

Source: *Economic Accounts*, No. 3, Chart 9.

The UK remains the world's largest exporter of financial services (the Cayman Islands, interestingly, is the UK's main rival), so it is tempting to see the problem as an excess of foreign transfers, primarily to EU institutions. Given the political unanimity concerning the UK's membership of the EU, and given the fact that the UK has wrung whatever concessions it is likely to get from other EU members, the long-term negative impact of such transfers upon the invisibles balance is best treated as a simple fact of life. The issue is thus whether the other elements in the balance can rise to compensate for this difficulty.

It is hard to be optimistic on this matter. The raising of virtually all barriers to the free flow of international capital cannot help but put the City of London under increasingly competitive pressure and, although it looks certain to hold its own, it cannot be expected to make much headway. This is especially true in the short term as a series of natural disasters has inflicted considerable punishment upon the insurance sector. Equally, the British have become rather fond of their holidays abroad, and there seems little prospect of them staying at home for the sake of the invisibles balance.

The key issue probably relates to interest, profits and dividends (IPD). The holdings of overseas assets should be generating a substantial inflow of capital, but there is no need for such capital to be repatriated. If, for example, it is reinvested abroad then the short-term effect is a deterioration in IPD, although the longer-term outlook is clearly improved. It is also significant that the large deficits of 1988 and 1989 necessitated an inflow of hot money which caused UK banks to become net borrowers from overseas, rather than the reverse. Furthermore, interest rates were considerably higher in the UK than in most other advanced economies, so these borrowings were expensive to service.

IPD has improved since 1991, partly as a reflection of lower absolute and relative interest rates in the UK, but the best thing that could happen would undoubtedly be an agreement under GATT auspices to lift barriers to trade in services in which the UK has a comparative advantage. Failing that, fewer natural disasters would be a

Figure 6.6 *Invisibles Balance, 1972–92, % of Money GDP at Factor Cost*

Source: CSO.

boon to the insurance sector, which has taken a hammering at a time of softening premiums.

☐ 6.4.9 Prognosis for the 1990s

There is increasing evidence that the trough of the recession has passed, with predictable short-term adverse effects upon the balance of trade. At the end of 1990 the growth of import volumes was negative after a period of two years during which it had once again shot ahead of export growth. Meanwhile the buoyancy of exports, resulting from continued growth overseas, especially elsewhere in the EU (which lagged the UK in the economic cycle), opened up a large positive gap between export and import volume growth. Commencing in mid-1991, the import volume growth line rose sharply once again and caught up with the more slowly rising export growth line. The fact that most of the EU collapsed into recession was a negative factor in relation to exports, while

the tendency for rising domestic demand to suck in imports remained a fact of life.

The latest figures reflecting the period since the 1992 devaluation are mildly encouraging, with import volumes down sharply and export volumes flat since the beginning of 1993. This indicates some substitution of domestic goods for imports, combined with imports limited by the sluggish growth of domestic demand. However, this improvement has been confined to countries outside the EU, which account for the minority of total trade, and the visible trade deficit with the EU doubled in the second quarter of 1993 compared to the first quarter of 1993, reflecting the recession throughout the EU mainland.

Current account deficits will accordingly remain the order of the day, at least until the middle of the decade. Just how big these deficits will ultimately prove to be in value terms is difficult to forecast (especially in the short term because of data collection problems). We have already commented on the improvement in certain parts of the trading accounts, but much will ultimately depend upon the growth path of other EU member states, and (to a lesser degree) of the USA. The trade deficit is unlikely to return to pre-1990 levels other than very temporarily, and it is possible to anticipate a much improved situation towards the end of the decade. Meanwhile, the government should set about trying to attract inward investment, since manufacturing salvation is most unlikely to arrive on the back of purely domestic companies.

The significant depreciation in the value of the pound since the UK left the ERM in October 1992 (see **pp. 223**) cannot help but improve the current account, although the government appears to be intent upon boosting the exchange rate in order to restore its tarnished image; never the best of reasons, and certainly not at this juncture. Much therefore depends upon the eventual equilibrium value for the pound, and upon the demand elasticity for British exports.

A final caveat relates back to the exercise in NI accounting, as discussed on **p. 25** There we concluded that investment in the UK economy must be financed either by domestic savings, a budget surplus or by running a current account deficit. Domestic savings have indeed risen in recent years, as noted earlier, but the budget deficit has escalated rapidly, thereby effectively neutralising domestic savings as a source of investment funds. It therefore follows that as the recovery gets under way, and investment surges, it will have to be financed by drawing in overseas capital. As we have shown, a surplus on the BoP capital account has its mirror image in a deficit on the current account, and this kind of deficit is not amenable to improvement via devaluation. It follows, therefore, that the current account will not return to surplus until the budget deficit is itself brought under control.

■ 6.5 International Perspectives

□ 6.5.1 *The Current Deficit*

The deterioration in the domestic current account balance needs to be seen in a wider context, as in

Figure 6.7 *Current Account Balances as % of GNP/ GDP*

Note:
[1] West Germany
Source: The Economist.

Figure 6.7. This indicates (**a**) that the current account deficit is not excessively large as a percentage of GDP; (**b**) that the recent deterioration is nothing unusual and far less severe than that of Germany, Spain and Portugal; (**c**) that it **is** possible to produce an equivalent swing in the opposite direction, as in the case of Ireland and Denmark (in surplus in the 1990s unlike the previous three decades).

□ 6.5.2 *Trade with Japan*

From the beginning of 1987, until the third quarter of 1990, Japan's plans to reduce its trade surplus were widely acknowledged to be succeeding. Imports grew, on average, by 17.7 per cent whilst export growth slowed down to average 2.9 per cent. Furthermore, Japan exported capital on a much increased scale, thereby easing the adjustment problems of countries with which it was running big current account supluses.

The overall current account surplus for 1990 was the lowest for five years at £18.3 billion, in particular because of a big rise in the deficit on invisibles. As a proportion of GNP this represented 12 per cent compared to 4.4 per cent in 1986, and Japan was loudly proclaimed to be behaving like a model world citizen.

However, throughout the latter half of the 1980s Japan's trading relationship with the USA continued to deteriorate, and the USA made it increasingly clear that it would use the provisions of the 1988 Omnibus Trading Act to resist further Japanese incursions into the US market. As a consequence, Japan began to search for alternative markets, and found them in Asia and Europe. Had the Japanese current account deficit continued to shrink this would not have mattered, but in the fourth quarter of 1990, despite the recession in the USA and Canada, Japan exported $81 billion of goods, the largest ever quarterly amount by value. Importantly, the surplus with the EU exceeded that with the USA, beginning in the Spring of 1991.

In 1992 Japan's trade surplus rose by 37.6 per cent to a record $107 billion on a customs basis, and included a 14 per cent rise in relation to the EU. The equivalent surplus on a BoP basis was $135 billion. Hence there is once again the distinct probability of a massive Japanese current account surplus for the entire decade. Furthermore, this surplus will increase with the EU. In practice, the EU member with the worst trading imbalance with Japan is currently the UK, which ran a trade deficit of $7.5 billion in 1992, whereas not all members are even in deficit. Understandably, therefore, that the UK Government has voiced its concern about its trade with Japan, but it would be surprising if this were to produce any concrete response. The current account surplus in Japan is the inverse of the capital outflow which is the result of domestic savings exceeding domestic investment. Until the UK ceases to need to attract Japanese capital the imbalance in trade is set to continue.

■ 6.6 Direct Investment

For centuries past an unfailing characteristic of the UK has been the willingness of its inhabitants to engage in foreign direct investment. That this enthusiasm has continued in recent years is not, therefore, altogether surprising; what is surprising is that it reached unprecedented levels during the latter half of the 1980s, as shown in **Table 6.1**. As a consequence, the gross stock of UK-owned foreign assets grew very rapidly.

The second surprise is that, after dipping below zero in 1984, **inward** investment first rose sharply to £9.4 billion in 1987 and then shot up to £18.5 billion in 1989 and 1990, to such an extent that it not merely constituted a much higher proportion of GDP (over 4 per cent) than for any other equivalent economy, but also exceeded outward investment in 1990 by a significant margin for the first time in several hundred years (a feat repeated in both 1991 and 1992).

The Japanese have located more than one-third of their investment in the EU in the UK. They are encouraged by relatively cheap but acceptably skilled labour, good telecommunications and golf. They are, interestingly, also able to generate much higher levels of productivity than British managers. The past two years have, however, seen a considerable reduction in the value of such investment, partly because of the apparent lack of enthusiasm in the UK for the Maastricht Treaty, although the gross number of investments in 1992 (197) was much higher than in 1991 (22). Until this issue is resolved there must remain some uncertainty over the scale of future investment although, as noted elsewhere, it is important for the revitalisation of the UK's manufacturing sector that Japanese companies are induced to set up in the UK.

▌ 6.6.1 Foreign-owned Multinationals

The existence of foreign-owned multinationals in the UK is not a new phenomenon. Indeed, many

US companies such as (Ford and General Motors) have been around for so long that their cars are widely regarded as British rather than foreign.

The more recent influx of investment has been particularly associated with Japan: for example, the takeover of ICL by Fujitsu and the car plants set up by Nissan, Honda and Toyota. During 1988–90 some 80 Japanese manufacturers set up in the UK, but their role should not be exaggerated since the USA accounts for roughly 40 per cent of all foreign-owned assets in Britain (worth around £30 billion), Holland for another 18 per cent and Japan for only 5 per cent.

It is unsurprising that the arrival of the SEM has triggered an influx of foreign direct investment into the EU. Nevertheless, the fact that 60 per cent of US investment in the EU is in the UK, as well as over 30 per cent of Japanese EU investment, indicates that the net inflow of direct investment is set to be an ongoing rather than a temporary characteristic of the UK BoP accounts. Indeed, if the Uruguay Round ultimately breaks down (see **p. 285**) and the USA becomes more inhospitable to inward Japanese investment, the Japanese may turn increasingly to the UK as their preferred investment location. On the other hand, there are signs in the data for recent years that the UK's share of inward investment into the EU is on the wane, so it will probably be necessary to wait until the recession is fully over before a clearer longer-term trend is perceptible.

The importance of inward investment cannot be exaggerated. The Invest in Britain Bureau, part of the Department of Trade and Industry (DTI), recently calculated that although overseas companies investing in the UK represent only 1 per cent of businesses, they account for 16 per cent of UK manufacturing jobs, 22 per cent of net output and 27 per cent of net capital expenditure. Curiously, the continuation of this development is not welcomed in all quarters. It is often argued that the BoP will deteriorate as a consequence, since the Japanese will use the UK as a glorified assembly plant while manufacturing high value-added products in Japan and exporting them to the UK. Furthermore, profits made in the UK will subsequently be repatriated. However, this argument is less than convincing for several reasons. In the first place, it is evident that if the Japanese do not, for example, set up car plants in the UK and use them as a base for exporting to other EU countries, then there will be no substitute exports for UK-originated products that no longer sell well overseas. The same applies for any products no longer manufactured at all by UK firms. Second, as a result of infighting between the EU and Japan, the Japanese have conceded the need to create much more value-added in the EU then they had originally intended. Finally, their imposition of much higher quality standards compared to UK manufacturers has caused some UK suppliers to improve their products to the point at which they are attractive in export markets.

6.6.2 *The External Balance Sheet of the UK*

We have previously referred to the external balance sheet of the UK which has been analysed in great detail in the **Bank of England Quarterly Bulletin** of November 1990, 1992 and 1993. The first point to note is that, because it is denominated in dollars, the equivalent sterling value can be highly variable. This can be seen in **Figure 6.8** where the net capital flows (above the line is an outflow and below the line is an inflow) are rather small (mostly below £10 billion), whereas the effects of revaluation due to exchange rates changes and the movement of security prices are very large.

In 1987, 1989 and the first half of 1990 the revaluation was primarily due to the exchange rate effect – when the pound rises against the dollar the value of external assets falls in dollar terms and vice versa – whereas in 1988 it was almost entirely due to revaluations of share and bond prices. The collapse of the dollar in the second half of 1989, followed by its equal and opposite rise during the first half of 1991, caused the external balance sheet to fluctuate widely in value even though net capital flows remained quite small.

Figure 6.8   *Contributions to the Change in UK Net External Assets (£b)*

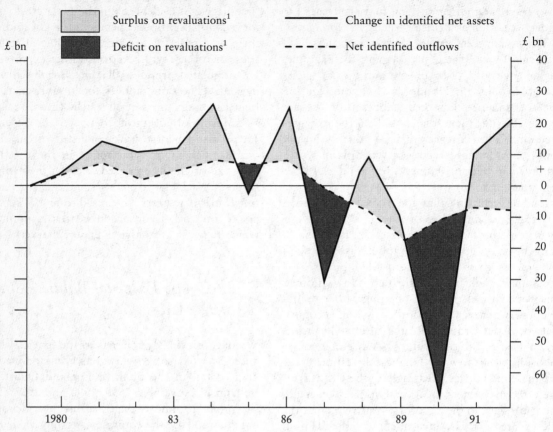

Note:
[1] Residual component = difference between change in recorded net stock and net identified outflows.
Source: Bank of England Quarterly Bulletin (November 1990), p. 488 and (November 1993), p. 509.

As we have seen in **Table 6.1**, the biggest shifts between 1988 and 1989 took place firstly in inflows of direct investment (up from £12 billion to £18.6 billion), and second in UK residents' purchases of overseas portfolio investments (up from £11.2 billion to £36.3 billion). Direct investment overseas remained at its previously high level. This latter item collapsed back by more than half in 1990, as did portfolio investment overseas, while portfolio investment into the UK fell back by 65 per cent although the absolute difference was much smaller. Direct investment overseas has yet to recover from its 1990 level, but portfolio investment has risen most of the way back to its 1989 level. Meanwhile, direct investment into the UK is well below what it was in 1990, although

portfolio investment is running at three times the level of that year.

The acquisition of £197 billion of overseas assets in the course of the last five years is really rather extraordinary for a country running large current account deficits and – in the mistaken view of many critics – allegedly brought to its knees by a decade of Thatcherism. One obvious consequence of this capital outlow at a time of current account deficits (which, added together, constitute the **basic balance**) was the need to borrow to cover the gap at high interest rates (see Davies, 1990 **pp. 34–9**). This, in turn, had a detrimental impact upon the interest, profits and dividends item in the invisibles account, causing the current balance to worsen further in subsequent years. Given that the dividend yield on overseas investments was lower than the interest costs of financing those investments, this appeared to be irrational behaviour on the part of UK investors.

It has to be borne in mind, however, as argued by Cliff Pratten (*Financial Times*, 18 July 1990, p. 15 and Pratten, 1992) that no account was taken of capital gains in this respect. It was the case in almost every year during the 1980s that part of the return on investments took the form of capital gains which **did not appear in the current account** of the BoP. In 1990 Pratten estimated the total capital gains during the 1980s as £95 billion and during 1990 as £12 billion (adjusted for inflation). In Pratten (1992) a figure of £82.3 billion is estimated for the 1980s. The methodology is complicated, and the estimates are precisely that, but there is considerable justification for his conclusion that 'During the 1980s capital gains more than offset deficits on the current account of the balance of payments.' This would suggest that concern over the state of the current account is overdone, although it should be noted that since the gains were mostly unrealised, there was, and there remains, a **liquidity** problem resulting from short-term borrowings to cover the capital outflows.

This view is not universally shared. Coutts and Godley (1990), for example, conducted their own analysis of the accounts and concluded that, first, only £3 billion of the (then) £20 billion current account deficit in 1989 could be compensated by adjustments for capital gains and inflation and, second, that if the balancing item represented underrecorded net exports, then the net stock of overseas assets was much smaller than official estimates suggested and hence that Britain would become a debtor nation if the balance of trade was not rapidly restored to a surplus. According to a calculation by Keith Skeoch, the chief economist at James Capel, adjusting for capital gains of foreign assets in Britain which he assumed to have accumulated as a result of, first, officially identified investments and, second, underrecorded capital inflows, meant that Britain already was a net debtor.

All of this may, understandably, leave the reader wondering just what is the real truth of the matter. If so, he or she is not alone, since by the same reasoning it has been alleged that the USA is not really a net debtor at all but a net creditor. The US Government actually refuses to publish the official (horrendously large) figure for the net debt, claiming that it is erroneous and misleading. Nevertheless, respected US analysts claim that a proper revaluation of both assets and liabilities leaves the official net position almost unchanged.

□ 6.6.3 Rejigging the Accounts

Measured in constant 1980 dollars, the value of world-wide direct foreign investment was roughly ten times as large at the end of the 1980s as it had been at the beginning of the 1970s. The effect of these enormous overseas investments has been to change the ownership structure of business in many countries, and at the same time to cast doubt upon the conventional way of calculating trade balances.

For example, an increasing amount of trade takes the form of transfers between the domestic operations of a multinational business and its overseas subsidiaries. On an 'ownership-based' accounting system these would not be counted as international trade. In addition, some sales in a domestic market are to the subsidiaries of foreign businesses which it may be argued are analogous to exports, as are the sales of overseas subsidiaries in overseas markets. On the other hand, it may be argued that domestic purchases from the subsidiaries of foreign-owned businesses are analogous to imports, as are purchases by overseas subsidiaries in overseas markets.

Until the 1980s rejigging trade flows on to an ownership basis would not have made much overall difference, and it currently makes relatively little difference in the case of, for example, Japan. In the case of the USA, however, it totally transforms the trade balance, converting a very large deficit into a modest surplus. The effects upon the UK accounts are not known, but given the surge in outward investment during the 1980s, an ownership-based system of trade accounts would presumably look much more favourable today than it did a decade ago, and thus help to allay fears about the overall trading position.

6.6.4 Is There a Current Account Crisis?

It is now possible to draw some tentative conclusions about the alleged crisis in the current account. At the end of the 1980s the so-called 'Burn's Doctrine' held that such a crisis was an illusion because (a) it was temporary, (b) invisibles were replacing visibles, (c) the external asset base was growing, and (d) the deficit could be financed without difficulty. It is our considered view that (a) the imbalance is clearly not temporary in that it will be with us for several years to come, but that it should not be seen as permanent either, at least not on a scale such as to cause concern; and (b) as regards invisibles and visibles, this is no longer taking place and is not likely to take place in the near future. However, (c) does appear to be true and is likely to remain so, and as for (d) this has been true so far and should also remain so. Overall, therefore, we are inclined to see a 'problem' where others see a 'crisis', but it nevertheless requires the constant attention of the government to prevent it from slipping into the other category.

■ 6.7 Competitiveness

6.7.1 Measuring Competitiveness

It is appropriate to refer, at this point in our discussion of trade performance, to the **competitiveness** of the UK. Competitiveness is impossible to measure in any absolute sense, so it must be judged by compiling indices of **relative performance** compared to other relevant countries. Even this is fraught with data collection difficulties, because we need to take some relevant characteristic of the UK economy, measure it over time as an index, and compare that index with the corresponding indices for other countries.

Since no single index can be expected to tell the whole story, we need to provide as wide a variety as possible. However, while some of these should incorporate non-price characteristics, they cannot realistically be measured, so indices must concentrate upon **cost and price competitiveness**, on the assumption that price and non-price factors are interdependent.

Many goods are in practice sold almost entirely on the home market, so the indices need to incorporate only those goods that are internationally traded on a major scale. As manufactured goods comprise the largest element in both UK imports and exports, they are used exclusively for the indices. Additionally, because competitiveness is affected by the exchange rate, all the costs and prices need to be converted into a common currency (in this case, dollars) at the ruling spot rate. With every country's index valued in a common currency, the ratio expressing one relative to another can then be measured as an absolute number.

Figure 6.9 illustrates the most important measures of competitiveness on a quarterly basis for 1982–92. These measures represent changes in the degree of competitiveness over time. The ratios are compiled as follows:

Import price competitiveness: UK wholesale price index for home market sales of manufactures (other than food, drink and tobacco) divided by the unit value index of imports of finished manufactures (SITC sections 7–8, Revision 2).

Relative normal unit labour costs: index of normal labour costs per unit of output in the UK divided by a weighted geometric average of competitors' normal unit labour costs adjusted for exchange rate changes.

Relative producer prices: UK wholesale price index for home sales of manufactures (including food, drink and tobacco) divided by weighted average of the indices of competitors' wholesale prices.

Relative profitability of exports: ratio of the UK export unit value index for manufactured goods (SITC sections 5–8, Revision 2) to the UK whole-

Figure 6.9   *Measures of UK Trade Competitiveness (1985 = 100)*

Source: Economic Trends, Table 20.28.

sale price index for home market sales of the products of manufacturing industries (other than food, drink and tobacco).

Relative export prices: unit value index of UK exports of manufactured goods divided by a weighted average of competitors' export price indices for manufactures.

All of these indices are subject to data measurement problems (see *Economic Trends* No. 304, February 1979, and No. 319, May 1980, for details). However, the various measures of competitiveness do appear to follow the same pattern, so the overall picture can be taken as acceptably accurate.

☐ 6.7.2 The Historical Pattern

During the 1970s, as shown in **Figure 6.13** below, sterling's effective exchange rate (EER) fell stea-

dily, thereby cheapening exports and making imports more expensive. Unfortunately, this did not, as we have seen, prevent the trade balance from remaining firmly in deficit. The reason can partly be seen in the data for relative normal unit labour costs, where the index, standing at 80.9 in 1978, rose sharply to 100.0 in 1980, and actually peaked at over 120.0 in the first quarter of 1981. Irrespective of non-price factors, which in any event were unfavourable for the UK, it is understandable that the UK's relatively high costs caused relative export prices to move unfavourably despite the advantage of a falling exchange rate. Equally, even though this caused import prices to rise, domestic prices also rose steadily, albeit less dramatically relative to import prices. The only positive feature was that the steady rise in relative export prices maintained the relative profitabilty of exports on an even keel, although it was showing clear signs of sagging at the end of the decade.

A generally similar picture is shown in **Table 6.2.** The UK's share of world exports of manufactures had been falling throughout the postwar period. This, of itself, was only to be expected since the initially very high share held by the UK reflected the early date of industrialisation, and progressive entry into her markets by newly industrialising countries, using more modern technology, was bound to have a profound impact. The disturbing aspect was, however, that the total volume of world trade in manufactures was itself rising very rapidly, commonly at over 10 per cent per annum, so there was plenty of room for new entrants without the need to eat heavily into the market share of existing producers; indeed the UK was unique amongst the established industrial nations in suffering more than a marginal loss in market share.

The increased share of imports in TFE was also to be expected as industrialised nations increasingly traded manufactured goods with one another, and in fact this was characteristic of all such nations. Again, however, the disturbing aspect was the relatively rapid pace at which this occurred in the UK, reflecting in part the UK's relatively high income elasticity of demand for imports.

However, the overall picture during the period from 1981 to 1984 was a generally much happier one. As shown in **Table 6.2,** the UK's share of world exports of manufactures appeared to have reached an equilibrium situation. **Figure 6.9** shows that relative normal unit labour costs declined steadily, and with the EER moving sharply downwards, relative export prices became significantly more competitive, and the relative profitability of exports rose slowly but steadily. Despite the rise in import prices, the competitiveness of imports also improved, albeit understandably more slowly, and the visible balance showed several years of surplus. The major problem was, however, the fact that imports as a share of TFE had bottomed out in 1981, and by 1984 was up 2.6 percentage points. The visible balance in 1984 was accordingly back in substantial deficit.

During 1985 competitiveness suddenly deteriorated, in particular because of a sharp rise in relative normal unit labour costs and in the EER; and, although the following year witnessed a recovery, it was clear that the first quarter of 1985 was going to prove difficult to emulate, let alone outperform. The situation from 1985 to the end of 1988 was very gloomy. Relative normal unit labour costs resumed their upward climb, and both relative export prices and import competitiveness followed suit. Imports as a percentage of TFE rose yet further, but the one modest saving grace was an increase in the UK's share of world exports of manufactures and the resilience of relative export profitability. With the EER being prevented from falling much as a matter of policy, and wage demands showing signs of escalating, it was reasonable to suppose that competitiveness would continue to deteriorate for the foreseeable future.

In practice, relative normal unit labour costs did dip again in 1989 only to concede all the ground gained, and more, during 1990. Relative export prices followed suit and relative export profitability dipped significantly below the 100 index at the end of 1990 for the first time since 1984. With inflation rising relative to its trading partners, the UK inevitably suffered a loss of competitiveness in 1990 and 1991.

As ever, it is important not to get too fixated with domestic problems taken in isolation. Compared to most OECD advanced countries, Britain managed to remain relatively competitive during the latter part of the 1980s, as shown in **Figure 6.10** which measures the growth of manufacturing exports relative to the growth of their export markets (measured as a weighted average of the import growth in each exporting country's markets). The likes of Taiwan and Hong Kong were the real exporting successes of the decade, but Britain held on to its markets better than Japan and most of the EU.

6.8 Area Composition of UK Visible Trade

During the nineteenth century circumstances conspired to create a pattern of trade in the UK, consisting essentially of the importation of raw

Figure 6.10 *Relative Export Performance*[1]

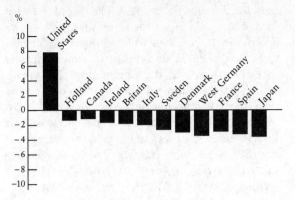

Note:

1 Manufacturing export growth (volume) *minus* export market growth, 1985–88 average.

Source: OECD.

materials and the exportation of finished goods. This arose in the first place because the UK was the earliest country to industrialise, and second because most of the trade was conducted with former or existing colonies. The latter was to a considerable extent a consequence of the former,

since other newly-industrialising countries erected barriers against imports from the UK in order to protect their infant industries; but, in any event, the existence of a common language facilitated trade even with ex-colonies such as the USA.

Trading links with Europe developed gradually during the twentieth century but, as **Tables 6.5** and **6.6** indicate, Europe accounted for only one quarter of UK imports and a slightly higher proportion of exports even in 1955. At that time the LDCs accounted for roughly 40 per cent of both UK imports and exports, of which very little was contributed by the Eastern bloc countries. Over the past three decades the UK has come to trade increasingly with other developed countries. In the case of exports the share has risen to over 80 per cent, although there was a marked temporary dip in the mid-1970s due to the oil-price effect discussed below. In the case of imports the growth in the share taken by the developed countries has been much steadier, with no comparable mid-1970s effect, and the current figure is, as a consequence, even higher than that for exports. It is clear that this growth cannot continue if the UK is to maintain any meaningful trade links with the

Table 6.5 *Area Composition of UK Exports, f.o.b., 1955–92, % Total Value*

	1955	1965	1970	1975	1980	1985[1]	1989[2]	1990	1991	1992
EC	15.0	26.3	28.9	32.2	45.4	48.6	50.7	53.1	56.7	55.9
Rest of Western Europe	13.9	15.5	17.1	15.9	12.1	9.7	8.5	8.7	8.2	7.8
North America	12.0	14.8	15.0	11.8	11.2	17.0	15.4	14.4	12.5	12.9
Other OECD[3]	20.5	14.8	12.0	9.5	5.6	4.9	4.8	4.7	3.8	3.7
Oil exporting	5.1	5.6	5.8	11.6	10.2	7.6	6.2	5.4	5.5	5.5
Other[4]	31.8	20.1	17.5	15.7	12.5	9.8	11.8	11.7	11.5	11.6
E. Europe and former USSR[5]	1.7	2.9	3.7	3.3	3.0	2.4	1.6	1.4	1.2	1.6

Notes:
[1] Old definitions up to 1985. For new definitions post-1985 see notes 3, 4 and 5.
[2] From 1989 onwards columns exclude low value trade and hence do not sum to 100%.
[3] Japan, Australia, New Zealand. Previously included South Africa. 1985 equivalent on new definition =3.6%.
[4] Previously 'other developing'. Becomes larger on new definition.
[5] Previously 'centrally planned'. Becomes larger on new definition.
Source: Annual Abstract of Statistics; Monthly Digest of Statistics, Table 15.4.

LDCs, and **Tables 6.5** and **6.6** give some reason to believe that the ultimate equilibrium between developed and less-developed countries has just about been reached of late.

The increased share of both imports and exports taken by developed countries has not, however, been evenly distributed. The UK joined the Community in 1972 at a time when trade links with Western Europe were already significantly outweighing those with developed countries outside Europe. Exports to America were still fairly buoyant, whereas imports had only very recently begun to decline, but a marked reduction in trade with other English-speaking ex-colonies had by then become evident.

Prior to 1972 the switch from non-Community to Community countries was already quite marked, but the sharp increase in the share of UK imports from the Community between 1970 to 1975, and the even bigger increase in the share of UK exports taken by Community countries between 1975 and 1980, can reasonably be attributed to UK membership. The share of UK exports taken by EU countries continued to rise in the early 1990s, but this in part reflected the exchange rate effects which favoured the Community as a market compared to the USA. The rest of Western Europe provides much the same share of imports as it did in 1955 (albeit well below its 1975 peak) but it has been in decline as an export market since the UK joined the Community. The quadrupling of the share of UK imports originating from the EU has undoubtedly been the most dramatic adjustment of UK trade patterns over the past three decades, and it is hardly surprising that the UK economy has been reoriented geographically, swinging around from North-west (feeding trade with America) to South-east (feeding trade with Europe).

As previously mentioned, the oil price has affected the pattern of UK trade with the LDCs. The effect of the sharp increase in the oil price in 1974 was to transfer huge sums to OPEC countries, and as **Table 6.5** shows this resulted in a doubling of the share of UK exports to oil exporting countries in 1975. Imports did not follow suit on the same scale because only one product was involved, but in the short term the low price elasticity of UK demand for oil did result in a marked increase in the value of oil imports. The

Table 6.6   *Area Composition of UK Imports, c.i.f., 1955–92. % Total Value*

	1955	1965	1970	1975	1980	1985[1]	1989[2]	1990	1991	1992
EC	12.6	23.6	28.3	36.5	45.1	50.0	53.1	52.3	51.6	52.1
Rest of Western Europe	13.1	12.2	14.9	14.9	13.0	14.3	12.4	12.5	12.0	11.5
North America	19.5	19.6	20.9	13.3	14.9	13.5	13.1	13.3	13.2	12.5
Other OECD[3]	14.2	11.9	10.1	7.7	6.2	7.3	7.0	6.7	6.8	7.1
Oil exporting	9.2	9.8	7.2	13.5	8.4	3.2	1.9	2.4	2.3	2.4
Other[4]	28.7	18.4	14.7	11.4	10.0	9.5	11.2	10.9	11.9	12.3
E. Europe and former USSR[5]	2.7	4.5	3.9	2.7	2.4	2.2	1.5	1.4	1.4	1.3

Notes:
[1] Old definitions up to 1985. For new definitions post-1985 see notes 3,4 and 5.
[2] From 1989 onwards columns exclude low value trade and hence do not sum to 100%.
[3] Japan, Australia, New Zealand. Previously included South Africa. 1985 equivalent on new definition = 3.6%.
[4] Previously 'other developing'. Becomes larger on new definition.
[5] Previously 'centrally planned'. Becomes larger on new definition.
Source: Monthly Digest of Statistics, Table 15.4.

oil price rose sharply again in 1980, but by then the UK was becoming self-sufficient. Subsequently, imports from OPEC have virtually disappeared, although exports remain high compared to the 1960s because the OPEC countries have much greater spending power.

The reasons behind some of the changes described above are fairly obvious, but the heavy dependence upon imports from other developed countries is less so, given that they must consist primarily of finished manufactures which traditionally formed the bulk of UK exports. However, it is increasingly a phenomenon of advanced industrial countries that they simultaneously import and export the same types of product, such as cars and electronic apparatus, and there has also been a marked reduction in the dependence of the UK economy upon the exportation of finished manufactures.

6.9 Commodity Composition of UK Visible Trade

As indicated above, the UK was traditionally an importer of raw materials and an exporter of manufactured goods. Even in 1955, as shown in Tables 6.7 and 6.8, raw materials constituted some 75 per cent of UK imports, whereas over 80 per cent of UK exports consisted of semi-manufactured or finished manufactured goods. However, the switch towards European markets documented above went hand-in-hand with a sharp change in the nature of imports during the 1970s, such that raw materials currently constitute only one fifth of the total value of imports.

As can be seen in Table 6.8, the steady decline in this share disguised some volatile behaviour among the sub-aggregates. In particular, fuel imports show up as a result of OPEC during the mid-1970s, only to decline sharply thereafter as the UK became self-sufficient in oil.

The share of semi-manufactured imports has also been rather volatile, while that of finished manufactured imports rose steadily to 1990 before falling back slightly with the onset of recession. As a result, the two parts of Table 6.8 currently stand in approximately the inverse ratio to that of 1955. The shares are of a total value which has grown steadily in monetary terms throughout the period examined, but it is difficult to assess whether the current position is near to its ultimate equilibrium because sharp changes in sub-aggregates – such as the virtual halving of fuel imports in money terms during 1986 – have

Table 6.7 *Commodity Analysis of Exports, % Total Value*

	1955	1965	1970	1975	1980	1985	1990	1991	1992
Food, beverages and tobacco	6.0	6.6	6.2	7.1	6.8	6.3	6.8	7.4	8.0
Basic materials	3.9	4.0	3.2	2.7	3.1	2.7	2.2	1.9	1.8
Fuels[1]	4.9	2.7	2.2	4.2	13.6	21.5	7.5	6.8	6.4
Total	14.8	13.3	11.6	14.0	23.5	30.5	16.5	16.1	16.2
Semi-manufactured	36.9	34.6	34.4	31.2	29.6	25.6	27.5	29.4	28.5
Finished manufactured	43.5	49.0	50.2	51.0	44.0	41.2	53.8	52.7	53.4
Total	80.4	83.6	84.6	82.2	73.6	66.8	81.3	82.1	81.9
Unclassified	4.8	3.1	3.8	3.8	2.9	2.7	2.2	1.8	1.9

Note:
[1] Roughly 95% oil.
Source: Annual Abstract of Statistics; Monthly Digest of Statistics, Table 15.1.

Table 6.8 *Commodity Analysis of Imports, % Total Value*

	1955	1965	1970	1975	1980	1985	1990	1991	1992
Food, beverages and tobacco	36.9	29.7	22.6	18.0	12.2	10.6	9.8	10.4	10.6
Basic materials	29.0	19.3	13.7	8.4	7.4	6.0	4.8	4.3	4.1
Fuels	10.6	10.6	8.3	17.5	14.2	12.8	6.2	6.4	5.6
Total	76.5	59.6	44.6	43.9	33.8	29.4	20.8	21.1	20.3
Semi-manufactured	17.9	23.8	29.2	23.9	27.3	24.8	26.2	26.6	26.9
Finished manufactured	5.3	15.4	24.6	29.9	36.6	44.0	51.7	50.9	51.5
Total	23.2	39.2	53.8	53.8	63.9	68.8	77.9	77.5	78.4
Unclassified	0.3	1.2	1.6	2.3	2.3	1.8	1.3	1.4	1.3

Source: Annual Abstract of Statisticsof Monthly Digest of Statistics, Table 15.1.

introduced an element of instability which may prove either to be an aberration or the beginning of a new long-term trend. It may be argued that the UK is no longer much dependent upon imports of food, beverages and tobacco. Nevertheless, this sector currently presents major trading problems, as noted below, once exports are taken into account.

The situation with respect to exports has generally been much more stable until relatively recently. However, from 1980 to 1985 the share of exports taken by manufactured goods of all kinds declined quite sharply. This was not altogether surprising given the effects of the recession brought on by the MTFS combined with an overvalued exchange rate, and it reflected in part the sharp increase in the share taken by fuels.

Fuel exports collapsed after 1985, and their share of total exports was entirely taken up by manufactures on the back of rising productivity and a sustainable exchange rate in relation to other EU countries. Overall, the situation bears a remarkable resemblance to the position between 1975 and 1980.

The aggregates disguise some significant switches between industrial sectors. Amongst the semi-manufactured exports the share taken by chemicals rose steadily throughout the period from 1955, whereas that of metals fell by almost one half and that of textiles by three quarters. The

chemicals industry has been a major success story for UK exports, although its 13 per cent share of total exports has risen only slightly since 1985.

Engineering products constituted roughly one third of all exports in both 1955 and 1985. However, their share peaked some 10 per cent higher in 1970, and there has been a steady decline since that time. A good part of this was in the road motor vehicles classification. This accounted for only 1.5 per cent of total exports in 1984, but its share has subsequently more than doubled.

It is also of interest to look at the visible balance for each of the aggregates as depicted in **Figure 6.11**, although it should be borne in mind that this is based upon a different accounting system from that used in **Table 6.1**, and sums to a total trade deficit of £17.6 billion in 1992 compared to the £13.8 billion in **Table 6.1**. Throughout the period 1970–92 imports of food, beverages and tobacco consistently exceeded exports, and this has also been the case for basic materials. The oil aggregate fell to a record deficit of £4 billion in 1976, but moved into surplus by 1980. The record surplus of £8 billion in 1985 therefore represented a turnaround of £12 billion over a 10–year period (although less marked after adjusting for inflation), but the surplus remained at half that value for the next two years and fell sharply again in 1988 and 1989, after which it stabilised. Semi-manufactured goods remained in

Figure 6.11 *Visible Trade Balance, Current Prices*

Source: Pink Book (CSO, 1993), Table 2.3; *Monthly Digest of Statistics*, Table 15.1.

surplus until 1983, but recorded deficits there-after, and the problem deteriorated rapidly from 1985 to 1989, since when it has improved some-what.

However, even this is insignificant compared to the situation with respect to finished manufac-tured goods, which also remained in surplus until 1983 before moving sharply into deficit thereafter. The surplus of £4 billion in 1980 was transformed

into a £6 billion deficit in 1987, a somewhat smaller turnaround than for oil but accomplished in half the time. In 1988 the deficit soared to nearly £12 billion followed by £13.5 billion in 1989. Not surprisingly, much of the policy debate over the past few years has focused on this phe-nomenon even though the situation did improve dramatically in 1990 and 1991 with the onset of recession.

During the greater part of the 1980s, the sector which contributed most to the deficit in manufactures was motor vehicles. As we have noted, this sector is on the mend, and is unlikely ever to play that undesirable role again. What is rather alarming is that the food, beverages and tobacco sector has been performing so badly even though it is non-manufacturing and even though one-half of the deficit is accounted for by products that can be grown in the UK. It would appear that British farmers' ability to market their products is put into the shade by their continental rivals.

Davies (1990) has calculated that well over two-thirds of the worsening in the trade balance between 1986 and 1989 was derived from those items which relate to goods that are used in the process of production: raw materials, semi-manufactures and intermediate finished manufactures. As a consequence, it would appear that the government was correct in claiming that it was a deterioration in these inputs rather than any direct increase in the deficit on consumer goods which 'explained' most of the deterioration in the trade deficit, but also that the Opposition was correct in claiming that it had not been caused by an inflow of capital machinery which would have enhanced the UK's capacity to produce in the future. As Davies notes, a key issue is whether the industrial inputs have been used, after being subjected to further processing, for investment or consumption. His conclusion is that these were almost equally responsible for the deterioration in the current account during 1986–89. However, taking the period 1979–89 as a whole, private consumption appeared to be the villain of the piece.

■ 6.10 Exchange Rates

□ 6.10.1 Introduction

An 'exchange rate' is the **price of one currency**, for our purposes the £ sterling, **in terms of another currency or set of currencies**. As such it is in principle determined in the market place for currencies, and moves up or down in accordance with the relative forces of demand and supply. In this case the market place is no longer physical, since currency transactions are these days conducted on electronic screens, and this in turn means that anyone can deal in currencies at any time of the day or night anywhere in the world. Not surprisingly, exchange rates are as a consequence constantly on the move as dealers try to make money by taking advantage of very small movements in rates. Most transactions are for immediate delivery at the current price on the **spot** market, but it is possible to transact in the **forward** market where a price is agreed today for delivery **at some future date**. Buying or selling forward is valuable for firms engaging in trade, since it guarantees for them the amount of pounds sterling which they will have to pay for imports or receive for exports.

However, although currency transactions are open to all, there are huge discrepancies between the market power of different participants. In particular, governments, especially of industrial nations, have powers derived from being the ultimate suppliers of currencies which are widely traded, and they are therefore in a position to influence strongly the way the currency markets behave. At the one extreme they may be happy to allow the markets to trade freely, neither deliberately adding to, nor subtracting from, the amount of their own currencies in circulation that arise from imbalances in their BoP accounts. At the other extreme, they may set out to prevent the exchange rate from varying at all, by buying and selling their own currencies on whatever scale is necessary to neutralise exactly any buying or selling in the market place. Between these extremes there are a host of variants which reflect gradations in the extent to which governments seek to prevent the market working freely. Nevertheless, it must be borne in mind that non-governmental traders are **in aggregate** also very powerful, and it is not altogether clear in priniple whether they, or governments, will be the dominant influence on exchange rates. The average **daily** turnover in the London foreign exchange market is $300 billion, and in total world forex markets turn over roughly $900 billion a day, as shown in **Figure 6.12**. A reasonable view might accordingly be that whereas traders in

Figure 6.12 *Major Centres: Average Net Daily Turnover*

Source: Economic Trends.

currency and/or suffering too great a trading loss, whereupon the currency will drop sharply in value and produce huge speculative gains for sellers.

It follows that half-hearted inventions by the authorities are largely counterproductive. Intervention is only successful **insofar as it imposes losses on speculators**. If the authorities in several major economies, acting in concert, suddenly enter the markets with large-scale buy orders for a particular currency which speculators are selling on a modest scale, or vice versa, speculators will get their fingers burned and act more circumspectly on future occasions. However, it may strictly be necessary only to **threaten** such behaviour to discourage a good deal of speculation, since if one group of speculators is selling heavily another group may move to buy in anticipation of similar behaviour by the authorities should the rate fall too far (which naturally, does not then happen).

When the forces of the market are dominant, and the exchange rate is constantly on the move in response either to excess demand or supply, an upwards movement is called an **appreciation** and a downwards movement is called a **depreciation**. Where, however, the government engineers a **unilateral change** in the rate from one value to another, an upwards adjustment is called a revaluation and a downwards adjustment is called a **devaluation**. The action of the government may not be intended to alter the rate, but rather to halt its upward or downward movement. When it intervenes in the foreign exchange markets in order to prevent sterling from rising, it is obliged, via the Bank of England, to sell sterling and to buy foreign currency in exchange. This is then mostly deposited in the official reserves. When, however, the government wishes to prevent sterling from falling, though, it is obliged to buy sterling and in exchange to sell foreign currency which is withdrawn from the official reserves.

As suggested above, the government may, or may not, be successful in its endeavours. To some extent this is conditioned by whether or not the government has openly declared the value of the pound at which it wishes it to be stabilised, since

aggregate can dominate **individual** governments, they cannot dominate the major industrial nations **acting in concert** over extended periods of time. Since in practice, as we will see below, this latter eventuality is very uncommon, it is fair to say that in the long term exchange rates are broadly determined by market forces irrespective of which exchange rate system is nominally in operation.

The very appearance of the authorities in the foreign exchange markets is potentially an encouragement to speculation. In the absence of intervention, a speculator can make gains only at the expense of other speculators, and hence tends to tread a little carefully for fear of being outwitted. However, once the authorities enter the markets to buy a particular currency it becomes obvious to all speculators that this currency cannot otherwise be held at its desired level, and they realise that they can all become sellers and impose losses upon the authorities rather than upon others of their kind. Furthermore, if they can create sufficient selling pressure then the authorities may have to withdraw from the markets in order to avoid using up scarce foreign this is bound to affect market expectations. Even if there is no official upper or lower limit to the value of the pound, the currency markets can work out the unofficial policy by retrospective inspection of changes in the reserves. Clearly, if there has been, for example, a rise of $1 billion in the monthly reserves figure, it follows that the Bank of England must have been intervening heavily in order to prevent the value of the pound from rising against the dollar (by selling pounds and buying dollars).

It is reasonable to suppose that, officially or unofficially, the government will usually have a clear view about the appropriate level for the exchange rate because of its effects upon the BoP. However, it must be recognised that the currency markets are not interested in the official position other than as a pointer as to whether to buy or sell a currency at a particular point in time. They do not necessarily agree with the government about the consequences of its economic policy and, having formulated their own view about the probable direction of change of the pound, will be looking for signals from the Bank of England in order to determine whether they will be allowed to push the rate to what they believe it should be, or whether – and to what extent – they are likely to be thwarted by intervention.

The view about the exchange rate, whether governmental or market, will be influenced by a whole host of factors, of which the following are the most important: the rate of inflation compared with that of major competitors, the structure of interest rates compared with that of major competitors and the BoP on current account. In addition the market view will, as indicated, be influenced by its forecast of how the government will respond to these factors. Clearly, in order to form an opinion about these matters their underlying causes will themselves have to be studied with care (including, for example, the rate of growth in the economy, capacity constraints, unit labour costs, the fiscal and monetary aggregates and so on). Under the circumstances, it is hardly surprising that there should be disagreement about the 'proper' value for the exchange rate.

6.10.2 The Theory of Purchasing Power Parity (PPP)

This theory, which dates back to the 1920s, has traditionally been used to explain long-term trends in the exchange rate. PPP states that the exchange rate between two currencies depends upon the **purchasing power of each currency in its country of origin**. If both the UK and USA can produce a set of identical products, in the former case for £100 and in the latter for $100, PPP dictates an exchange rate of £1=$1.

The change in the exchange rate comes about through adjustments to trade flows. In the above example, at the original exchange rate, it would pay UK residents to buy US exports for £100 in preference to identical domestic products at any higher price, and that would continue to be the case until the £/$ exchange rate had fallen in value (by one half if UK prices had doubled). Unfortunately, this is an oversimplified view of the real world in which sets of identical products are difficult to identify, and are certainly less than comprehensive. In addition, allowance must be made for **trading costs**, including transportation costs, when comparing prices in domestic and foreign markets. In any event, these matters relate only to **visible trade flows**, and the exchange rate is likely to be affected by capital flows which fall outside the confines of the theory.

A looser – and hence by implication a more accurate but, at the same time less analytically helpful – definition of PPP is that the currency of a country which has a **higher inflation rate** than its main trading partners will **depreciate**, and vice versa. Such testing of the theory as has been undertaken (and even that has to be treated with care because of problems with respect both to the measurement of the price level and of the exchange rate and to the choice of countries) indicates that, starting at any particular year, the exchange rate eventually reaches an equilibrium level compatible with PPP, but that in the intervening period it may deviate significantly from it in either direction, and probably both. Hence it follows that PPP is of little value of itself, but it does have the virtue of focusing attention on the reasons why deviations of the exchange rate from PPP actually occurred.

☐ 6.10.3 Interest Rates

We have already remarked upon the fact that hot money is attracted to countries which, after allowing for risk, offer the highest short-term rates of interest. This is also true, but on a much lesser scale, where non-residents wish to hold longer-term interest-bearing securities. If UK interest rates exceed those in the USA, West Germany and Japan there is going to be great demand for pounds to invest in the UK, and hence upwards pressure upon the exchange rate. The sums involved can best be thought of in terms of billions rather than millions, but there is fortunately a limiting device in operation.

This arises because, when a non-resident buys sterling at the current or 'spot' exchange rate in order to acquire an interest-bearing asset, he or she may wish to protect against a capital loss, should interest rates rise further, by arranging to sell the asset 'forward' at an agreed price. Buying in the present pushes the spot rate up, while selling in the future pushes the forward rate down. The greater the volume of sterling being bought and sold, the greater the difference between purchase and sale prices. Hence, beyond a certain point, the extra interest earned by investing in the UK is in principle entirely offset by the loss resulting from the need to sell at an exchange rate lower than at the time of purchase. The **interest rate parity theory** argues that the difference between spot and forward rates will automatically adjust to neutralise differences in short-term interest rates between countries, thereby greatly limiting flows of hot money. However, this argument may be defeated by the sheer volume of hot money, since it follows that a flood of hot money will drive up the exchange rate even higher, and so even though forward rates are below the matching spot rates at any point in time, they will be rising above the spot rates which ruled in the preceding period. If sterling becomes a 'one-way bet' to continue rising, there is thus no necessity to accept a forward rate until

it has risen above the spot rate at the time of purchase, or even perhaps to trade forward at all, since the spot rate at the time of sale will almost certainly be higher than any forward rate contracted previously.

In practice, the above effect is frequently stronger than any influence which the current account surplus or deficit may have upon the exchange rate. This is not to argue that the latter cannot be significant, but it follows logically that if the exchange rate is driven by the current account, then the current balance should be perpetually close to, or at, equilibrium. Since this has rarely been the case for the UK it follows that, particularly in the short term, **the exchange rate is more responsive to capital flows**. The obvious exception is where the current account deficit becomes so large that, even after adjusting for offsetting capital inflows, the reserves will run out unless the exchange rate is devalued. Where this is not an issue, it is quite possible that even a massive current account deficit will have less influence upon the exchange rate than hot money responding to rising interest rates, and hence that the **exchange rate will itself continue to rise**.

☐ 6.10.4 Interest Rates and Exchange Rate Risk

Let us assume that:

A US investor has $100 to invest.
The interest rate is 5 per cent in the USA and 10 per cent in the UK.
The exchange rate is initially $1=£1 and does not vary.

Hence:

If $100 is converted into sterling it becomes £100 (ignoring transaction costs).
After earning interest in the UK at 10 per cent it becomes £110.
When converted back into dollars it becomes $110.

This then compares **favourably** with the $105 which would have arisen in the USA.

However:

Suppose the value of sterling can vary, and it **falls** by 10 per cent (i.e. £110=$100).
Then the £110 earned in the UK will convert back to $100.

This then compares **unfavourably** with the $105 which would have arisen in the USA.

On the other hand:

Suppose the value of sterling can vary, and it **rises** by 10% (that is, £100=$110).
Then the £110 earned in the UK will convert back to $121.

This represents a return of 21 per cent compared to only 5 per cent if the money is left in the USA.

It follows, therefore, that whether a higher nominal interest rate in one country compared to another is sufficient to attract an inflow of capital depends upon **expectations** of changes in exchange rates. If a country is expected to have a strengthening exchange rate then it will not need to have a high nominal interest rate. This was traditionally the situation for Japan and Germany, but circumstances have changed considerably since 1990.

For example, at the end of 1990 the US Government was determined to reduce interest rates in order to offset the recession. The Germans, on the other hand, were anxious to raise interest rates in order to offset the inflationary impact of reunification. Ordinarily this would have caused the Deutsche Mark (DM) to surge against the dollar, whereas precisely the opposite happened because the post-Gulf War euphoria and hopes of recovery made investors buy the dollar, and fears about the cost of reunification made investors sell the DM. Once it was clear that this was going to continue well into 1991 it became possible for the US Government to cut interest rates even further without triggering a run on the dollar. Meanwhile, in the UK the government refused to follow suit, only reducing interest rates slowly and by small increments, for which it was quite properly much criticised.

Where a country's exchange rate is expected to weaken, it will normally need to have a much higher nominal interest rate than elsewhere. The only way to eliminate exchange rate risk is to lock exchange rates together, a factor which underlay the decision to enter the ERM, but even the wide band was clearly sufficient to create expectations of exchange rate variability in the UK, and to create worries in the minds of the government that interest rate reductions would trigger a sharp fall in the value of the pound.

Once the above is understood, it is possible to unravel the mystery posed on **p. 62** as to why the correlation between saving and investment in any given country is stronger than one would expect in a world of freely mobile capital. At the end of the day, no matter how high the nominal interest rate on offer in, say, the UK, the fear of capital losses on the exchange rate will be enough to deter the more timid investor who will keep his or her money firmly at home. This is borne out by the astonishing size of capital flows during the era of the gold standard when exchange rate risk did not exist. When the topic of capital flows is under discussion, few remember that prior to 1915 the UK ran an average current account surplus of 5 per cent of GDP over a period of three decades, and that the money was exported all over the world to finance development in, for example, North and South America. It would appear, therefore, that talk of a global capital market is a touch premature, and this is anyway not a new concept.

6.10.5 *Measuring the Exchange Rate*

It is such a commonplace to read about movements in 'the' exchange rate that few non-economists ever bother to question whether it is always the **same exchange rate** which is moving. In fact it is not, so we must consider below the appropriate ways to measure exchange rate movements.

It is clear, to begin with, that there is an exchange rate linking sterling to every other currency belonging to a country with which the UK conducts trade. Naturally, some of these are much more important than others, either in terms of the pattern of UK trade or because of their significance for world affairs. For both these reasons it is customary to place most attention, in terms of individual exchange rates, upon the dollar, and it is indeed the £/$ rate which is most often quoted in the media. However, as shown in the section on the area composition of trade, the UK now trades increasingly with the EU, and within the EU the German currency, the DM, plays a central role, so there are often good reasons to concentrate upon the £/DM rate. While Japan is also very important from the point of view of its share of total world trade, the yen has less significance that the dollar or DM specifically in terms of UK trade patterns. Nevertheless, it must be recognised that if the $/yen rate alters sharply, then this is bound to have some repercussions for the £/$ rate as well.

Measuring exchange rates in terms of individual currencies does, however, have drawbacks. In the first place, such rates can be very volatile, as the discussion of recent history below will demonstrate. Moreover, this volatility is much greater in certain cases, such as the dollar, compared to others such as the DM, and individual rates may not simply move in the same direction but at **different speeds** and in **opposite directions**. Clearly, to concentrate exclusively on the dollar when it is rising against the pound, at a time when the DM is simultaneously falling against the pound, may prove highly misleading in terms of consequences for the UK economy.

In order to adjust for this, the sensible procedure is to measure the exchange rate in terms of a **basket of currencies** which includes all those of any significance in terms of the UK, and, by implication, of world trade. One could simply take the arithmetic average of all the rates included in such a basket, but it also seems sensible to make adjustments for the **relative importance of different countries in terms of UK trade** through a system of **weights**. Such a weighted average is in use, and is called the **effective** exchange rate, where the weights used represent the share of total UK world trade conducted with each country whose currency is included in the basket. It follows that, if a volatile currency is highly weighted, as is true of the dollar, then the EER will itself show a tendency to be volatile, albeit on a much reduced scale. However, a low-weighted currency will have little effect upon the EER, no matter how volatile it is.

Unfortunately, because the EER measures the pound in relation to other **currencies**, it may be a poor guide to changes in the **competitiveness** of UK goods and services. For this reason, it is preferable for certain purposes to use a **real** exchange rate (RER), which measures the price of UK goods (and hence of UK exports) relative to the average price of foreign goods (and hence of UK imports). Since the latter need to be converted into sterling, the average price of foreign goods is multiplied by the EER for this purpose, and the RER is given by: UK price index divided by overseas average price index multiplied by EER. If the RER **falls** then UK competitiveness **improves** because, converted to sterling, imports have become more expensive relative to exports. One obvious drawback to the RER is that not all UK and foreign goods are traded, so the formula is something of an approximation as a measure of competitiveness in the traded goods sector, but it provides a useful supplement to other exchange rate measures.

Table 6.9 sets out the data for the three most important bilateral exchange rates, for the EER and the ECU. During the period 1975–88 the DM and the yen were the world's strongest currencies, and as can clearly be seen, the pound depreciated steadily against both currencies other than during 1980 and 1981 and, more recently, against the DM in 1988 and 1991 and the yen in 1990. However, the £/$ rate was much more volatile, with peaks in 1972, 1980, 1988 and 1990, and troughs in 1977, 1985 and 1989. As these are annual averages they obviously understate the daily high and low values for each year, some of which are also referred to in the following sections. Again, it is important to remember in the wider context that, even if the pound is falling against the DM while simultaneously rising against the dollar, the DM is not necessarily also rising against the dollar, and so forth.

Table 6.9   *Selected Sterling Exchange Rates and Effective Rate Index (ERI), 1975–92, Annual Averages*

| | Exchange value of sterling in | | | | Sterling effective ERI[1], (1985 = 100) |
	US$	DM	Yen	ECU	
1975	2.220	5.447	658.1		124.8
1976	1.805	4.552	535.4		107.0
1977	1.746	4.050	467.7		101.2
1978	1.920	3.851	402.6		101.0
1979	2.123	3.888	465.6		107.0
1980	2.328	4.227	525.6	1.674	117.7
1981	2.025	4.556	444.6	1.811	119.0
1982	1.749	4.243	435.2	1.785	113.7
1983	1.516	3.870	359.9	1.704	105.3
1984	1.336	3.791	316.8	1.694	100.6
1985	1.298	3.784	307.1	1.700	100.0
1986	1.467	3.183	246.8	1.495	91.5
1987	1.639	2.941	236.5	1.420	90.1
1988	1.780	3.124	228.0	1.506	95.5
1989	1.638	3.080	225.7	1.489	92.6
1990	1.786	2.876	257.4	1.400	91.3
1991	1.768	2.925	237.6	1.428	91.7
1992	1.767	2.751	223.7	1.362	88.4

Note:
[1] The weights used for the ERI used to be calculated by the IMF using its Multilateral Exchange Rate Model. However, as from January 1989, the index is that published in the IMF's *International Financial Statistics*, where the weights reflect the relative importance of other countries as competitors to the UK in both domestic and overseas markets. The base year is 1985. The weight of the $US in the new ERI has fallen compared to the old ERI, whilst that of the DM has risen.

Source: Bank of England Quarterly Bulletin; Economic Trends.

The EER is also plotted graphically, on a quarterly basis, in **Figure 6.13** since the annual averages are a little misleading. As can be seen, the EER stood at 120 in mid-1975 in the midst of a massive depreciation lasting from early 1972 to the end of 1976, with only one temporary abatement in 1974–75. From early 1977 to early 1981 it subsequently appreciated steadily to stand once again at a value of 120, only to collapse back to a value of 95 at the end of 1984. On an annualised basis the EER continued to fall until the end of 1987 but, as **Figure 6.13** shows, the quarterly pattern was actually quite volatile, and showed a rising tendency from 1986 to 1988 before falling sharply again in 1989. During the latter half of

1990 the EER rose sharply (gaining 15 per cent against the dollar alone), but the sudden recovery of the dollar against the pound at the beginning of 1991 promptly reversed the sequence. The collapse of the EER in October 1992 is set aside for discussion in the chapter which follows.

It is worth noting that the UK's EER has **in general** shown considerably less volatility that that of other major countries, especially Japan and the USA, as can be seen in **Figure 6.14** which includes events post-October 1992. Hence a quite different perspective is gained in the longer term when comparing volatility in the EER with volatility in, say the £/$ rate. In the short term the EER normally shows little volatility, even though

Figure 6.13   *Sterling ERI, 1974–93, Quarterly Averages (1985 = 100)*

Source: Compiled from the *Bank of England Quarterly Bulletin.*

bilateral rates may be highly volatile, which might be taken as a lesson for financial markets that what you see depends upon where you look.

The RER is rarely mentioned in the media, so detailed figures are not given here. By and large the RER is affected mostly by the EER in the short term, and mostly by relative inflation rates in the longer term, much as one would expect. Since the UK has almost continuously suffered more inflation than her main competitors since 1975, this has exerted constant upward pressure upon the RER and led to a corresponding loss of competitiveness. During those periods in which the EER has risen sharply, for example in 1979–80, this has combined with the relative price effect to produce a disastrous loss of competitiveness. The same combination, albeit on a lesser scale, was evident in 1988 and 1990. At other times, however, the decline in the EER has more than outweighed the relative price effect, and the RER has fallen (as in 1986–87). It is finally worth noting that a country which is undergoing a strong currency appreciation need not necessarily become uncompetitive. As the Japanese have shown in recent times, the

Figure 6.14   *EERs (1985 = 100)*

Source: Bank of England Quarterly Bulletin.

RER can still be induced to fall provided domestic prices can be kept down relative to world prices.

☐ 6.10.6 *Exchange Rate Regimes*

Gold Standard

Although there is no realistic prospect of an equivalent exchange rate regime being restored, it is of some importance to explain briefly the workings of the old **gold standard** which involved strict rules, but which did not require any international cooperation since each country could apply the rules independently of the others. The gold standard operated in the UK from 1821 to 1914, and from 1925 to 1931. During these periods the UK money supply was determined by the gold reserves, and gold was the medium used to settle international indebtedness. Each country's currency was absolutely fixed in value in terms of gold, which in turn meant that the value of each currency was absolutely fixed in terms of all other currencies. If a country ran a BoP deficit, it would have to transfer gold to the country in surplus. This in turn would lower the money supply in the former and raise it in the latter, with prices subsequently following suit. This movement in relative prices would then boost the exports of the deficit country, and reduce those of the surplus country, until equilibrium was restored.

At the time, the fact that the gold standard left no leeway for discretionary behaviour on the part of individual governments, while restoring BoP equilibrium and bringing prices into line, was seen as a great virtue. In practice, the adjustment mechanism was far from smooth since, for example, prices tended to be insufficiently flexible. The attempt to go back to the gold standard in the UK in 1925 was fairly disastrous because the conversion rate of sterling into gold was set at too high a level, and after the 1929 Crash the world-wide rush to convert currencies into gold forced the UK, whose gold reserves were limited, to suspend convertibility and to float the pound in 1931.

From a more modern perspective, a gold standard type of mechanism is sometimes advocated because it provides a strong brake upon inflation. However, against this has to be set the fact that an individual country cannot **choose** its rate of inflation, it cannot use money supply control as an instrument of demand management, and it cannot vary the exchange rate to deal with BoP problems arising either because of differences in national inflation rates or because of unforeseen external shocks. The fact that it might no longer be possible to use gold to underpin the mechanism because it is unavailable in sufficient quantities does not rule out the use of the mechanism as such. Something else which is available can quite easily be used instead. This could either be an existing currency such as the dollar, or an artificial currency linked to a basket of existing currencies.

Bretton Woods 1944–71

At the end of the Second World War a new set of rules was introduced for controlling the world's monetary system. These included a fixed exchange rate mechanism harking back in many respects, but in a less rigid manner, to the gold standard. All members of the IMF had to peg their currencies to the dollar, which was in turn pegged to gold at a rate of $35 per ounce. However, this peg was not immovable, but 'adjustable'. Any individual currency could freely move up or down by up to 1 per cent in relation to its $ par value, but beyond that point the relevant central bank would have to intervene and use its reserves in order to keep within the permitted variance about the par value. In addition, any country could, without seeking the permission of the IMF, unilaterally lower (devalue) or raise (revalue) its currency by up to 10 per cent. If a larger alteration was thought to be necessary, then the permission of the IMF had to be sought, but this was certain to be forthcoming provided the country could demonstrate that its BoP was in 'fundamental disequilibrium'. Since no specific definition of this term existed, it was hard to see how the IMF could refuse a country which claimed that such a condition was indeed in force.

For the most part the adjustable peg worked quite well until the later 1960s. It was a period of generally sustained growth, and the gold reserves of the USA were sufficient to settle trade imbalances in the few cases where dollars, effectively as good as gold, were unacceptable. Compared to the gold standard, inflation control was weakened because currencies could be realigned, but the widespread adoption of fiscal policy as an instrument of demand management overcame a serious deficiency of the gold standard in that it had no instruments for demand management.

However, the Bretton Woods system came under increasing pressure, primarily because (1) countries arguably in fundamental disequilibrium, such as the UK in the 1960s, were afraid to admit it and to devalue, since their governments feared the political consequences of being seen as unable to manage their economies. While devaluations did occur, as in the UK in 1967, these were always by too little and too late. (2) Since such countries preferred instead to deflate their economies by fiscal means, their growth was held back. (3) Countries in surplus generally refused to revalue, arguing that this would stimulate spending on cheap imports and impart an inflationary bias to their economies. (4) Consequently this meant that speculators could be fairly certain that a fundamental disequilibrium would be resolved by a devaluation, effectively yielding a one-way bet which in turn put further pressure on deficit countries' reserves. (5) The dollars needed to maintain international liquidity, and to allow for BoP deficits to be paid for, had to come as a result of the USA running a BoP deficit and paying its debts in its own currency (which no other country could do). Eventually these dollar holdings outside the USA grew larger than the value of the gold reserves held in the USA to which they were fixed, and the whole system became over-dependent upon US macroeconomic policy. Confidence in this policy could not be restored and, as a result, attempts were made to convert dollars into gold at the fixed parity, and the USA was forced to suspend convertibility in August 1971. This signalled the end of the era during which gold played an important role in international trade.

In an attempt to salvage the adjustable peg, agreement was reached at the Smithsonian Conference in December 1971 to increase the permitted fluctuation around par values from +/− 1 per cent to +/− 2.25 per cent, to revalue certain strong currencies, and to raise the dollar price of gold (which was worth far more in the free market than when held in reserves). However, the situation could not be salvaged, and in the particular case of the UK the BoP problems of the early 1970s forced the government to float the pound in June 1972. One year later, floating exchange rates were the norm rather than the exception.

Managed Floating

The floating exchange rate system adopted after 1973 was 'dirty' (managed) rather than 'clean'. Even so, it was considered that a number of advantages would follow compared with the adjustable peg, many of which were compatible with the newly popular monetarist doctrines. In this latter respect it was argued that the adjustable peg had necessitated the use of monetary instruments to manage demand, with a view to keeping the BoP in equilibrium. Once the exchange rate was floating, equilibrium would automatically be restored by appreciation or depreciation of the currency, and as a result monetary instruments could be transferred to their proper use, namely control of inflation. Strictly speaking, this required the float to be clean if it was to work properly, but even a dirty float would free up the hands of the authorities to some extent.

In principle, any country experiencing relatively rapid inflation should not suffer a permanent competitve disadvantage. As prices rise faster than in competing countries, so the exchange rate should depreciate to offset this. The nominal exchange rate thus adjusts to keep the real exchange rate constant. However, this should not create unemployment in uncompetitive countries. As their currencies depreciate, the price of imports – and hence retail prices in general – will begin to rise. Provided nominal wages stay more or less unchanged, real wages will accordingly fall and bear the brunt of the adjustment rather than the number of jobs on offer. Furthermore, there should be much reduced scope for destabilising speculation compared with the adjustable peg. By buying cheap and selling dear, speculators actually move the currency towards its equilibrium value, and hence reduce the opportunities for further speculation.

Unhappily, the era of managed floating was not an unqualified success, and a number of serious drawbacks manifested themselves in practice. Most importantly, (1) certain currencies remained overvalued in relation to the current account, which accordingly remained heavily in deficit with the deficit financed by capital inflows. (2) Monetary policy often did not succeed in controlling domestic inflation because, for example, of the problems of defining the monetary aggregates for this purpose, and so the exchange rate needed to be depreciated further, once again driving up import prices. Where domestic wage rises were demanded by way of compensation, further damaging effects upon inflation and employment ensued. (3) Exchange rates were much more volatile than could be accounted for by differences in inflation rates, leading to large fluctuations in RERs which had damaging effects upon world trade flows. (4) Speculation at times was very heavy. Whereas it is clear that if one party gains £1 another party must have lost £1, it does not necessarily follow that winners and losers come from the same group. Professional speculators may gain continuously at the expense of the ill-informed.

In essence, acknowledgement of these difficulties led to two distinct developments. First, the Community States introduced the EMS (discussed in detail in Chapter 7), which harks back to the adjustable peg in that it requires much the same degree of cooperation between participants, but in the context of a somewhat less rigid set of rules. Second, the USA under President Reagan attempted to move away from unco-ordinated floating towards a system centred essentially on the dollar, the yen and the DM (and hence linking in to the EMS), requiring progressively more cooperation and the adherence to progressively more specific rules. Before discussing this, it is worth noting that the UK was party to both these developments, either as a member of the EU or as a member of the Group of 5 (G5) or 7 (G7) major

industrial countries, but until 1990 remained on the side-lines pursuing a policy of an essentially **ad hoc** nature.

There have been a large number of minor milestones along the road which may, perhaps, best be labelled 'informal' management of the world's major three currencies. Among them the more notable ones were the **Plaza Agreement** of September 1985, the **Louvre Accord** of February 1987 and the G7 Statement of December 1987 (issued in the absence of a formal meeting).

In March 1985 the dollar stood at Y260 and DM3.4, a rise of roughly one-half in its RER since 1980. This was viewed in the USA as a virtue insofar as it reflected the strength of the US economy, and simultaneously as a vice insofar as it produced huge BoP deficits and stirred up strong protectionist sentiments. The dollar then began to fall of its own accord, but only temporarily. The Plaza Agreement (between the members of G5 including the UK) was designed to talk it down a further 10 per cent or so, essentially by stating that it was too high. The sum of $18 billion was made available for supportive intervention. By October the dollar had fallen to its desired level, but it continued to fall sharply, thereby raising fears in Japan and Germany that it was not going to achieve a 'soft landing'. Eventually this led to the Louvre Accord which agreed 'reference rates' for the dollar of Y153.50 and DM1.825.

Intervention to maintain these reference rates was initially successful, but the G7 summit in Venice in June 1987 failed to instil confidence in the financial markets that the USA was determined to deal with its twin budget and BoP deficits, and this provided the trigger for the stock market crash of October 1987, subsequent to which the dollar fell sharply. Initially this did not please the Japanese, but they soon came to realise that their exporters could learn to live with a highly valued yen, and thereafter they lost interest in active intervention. The West Germans saw little reason to support the dollar until the USA got to grips with their domestic problems. Meanwhile the UK allowed the pound to float around for a while, before adopting a policy of shadowing the DM prior to officially joining the ERM.

■ *6.11* Exchange Rate Issues

It is helpful at this stage to summarise some of the threads which run through the preceding discussion. We may note, for example, that each exchange rate system can be designated according, first, to the rigidity of its rules, and second to the degree of cooperation required of participants.

The postwar years have witnessed a considerable diversity of systems, all quite distinct from the pre-war gold standard. This, as explained above, required currencies to be fixed in terms of gold, with no discretion to alter the rate and with each country able to fix its rate wholly independently of other countries. Subsequently, countries have periodically reimposed either fairly rigid rules or adopted an independent stance, but never both together. The Bretton Woods 'adjustable peg' allowed for some variation around par values, and also for periodic realignment of currencies, so it was less rigid than the gold standard, but it differed from the latter primarily insofar as it could only operate successfully through cooperative behaviour. However, the willingness to set supranational interests above national interests was distinctly limited, and indeed the system ultimately faltered because of a general unwillingness to adopt cooperative solutions.

The EMS is essentially a more flexible version of the adjustable peg, but like that system it allows participants to behave in somewhat different ways. The country at the centre of the system, Germany, has more room for manoeuvre than any of the others. Those participants which peg themselves to the DM, such as Holland, are relatively rule-bound compared with those that are willing to realign their currencies.

The UK, from 1979 to 1990, largely did its own thing. It avoided becoming rule-bound by not pegging sterling to any other currency, although it latterly shadowed the DM prior to entry into the ERM. This once again holds true now that the UK has once again left the ERM. For most of the earlier period the dollar was also managed very independently, although it subsequently showed a clear preference for international cooperation, albeit of a flexible kind.

Countries which are eager to grow at above-average rates tend to prefer an undervalued exchange rate, since this keeps down export prices. Equally, if control of inflation is the primary concern, an overvalued exchange rate becomes more desirable because it keeps down import prices. It is difficult to prove that exchange rates are deliberately managed in order to pursue national interests (at the expense of other countries) since governments are overtly dedicated to better cooperation. But insofar as it does occur, it prevents rather than enhances the move towards equilibrium in international trade.

■ *6.12* The International Monetary System

□ *6.12.1 International Liquidity*

As has become clear from our previous discussion, it is impossible to isolate an individual country such as the UK from the economic forces which affect the rest of the world. The UK is not merely linked to these forces via the institutions which try to control them, but also through the flows of international liquidity that are the physical manifestation of these forces.

International liquidity is the stock of assets that is held by the appropriate body in each country on behalf of its government, in order to settle BoP deficits and to defend the exchange rate. The assets in question must obviously be acceptable throughout the non-Eastern bloc world, and at any point in time the great bulk of them are to be found in the official reserves of the major industrialised countries. However, since few individual countries are either able – or indeed wish – to hold sufficient reserves to cover every eventuality, existing reserves need to be supplemented by a variety of sources, whether money markets or international institutions, from which additional liquidity can be obtained as required.

International liquidity is no different from domestic money in terms of its functions, such as acting as a medium of exchange or a unit of account, but it is much more restrictive in its physical forms. A greatly expanded volume of world trade has caused a dramatic escalation in the need for such liquidity since the 1970s. This was to be expected, since it is obviously a precondition for international liquidity that it is acceptable not merely within an individual country, but well beyond its borders.

International liquidity takes three basic forms: namely, gold, the domestic currencies of individual countries which are acceptable as 'reserve' currencies, and non-domestic currencies artificially created by international bodies such as the IMF. The holdings of gold and reserve currencies are largely to be found in the reserves of individual countries, but substantial quantities are also held by the IMF independently of its own 'artificial' currency.

Until fairly recently, gold was the most favoured form of international liquidity, since it has always been universally desired for its intrinsic qualities. Given that its value has always greatly exceeded its production costs, those countries which mine it – mainly the ex-USSR and South Africa – have profited enormously from its supply, but the main economic issue is that this supply is inflexible even in the face of a rapid increase in its price; hence the enormous increase in the demand for international liquidity after 1945 could not be met via an increase in the supply of gold at its existing price. Whereas it would have been possible to raise the value of the existing stocks to the required level, this would have seriously affected the world economy because of the very unequal distribution of gold stocks between countries. Thus, so long as gold was fixed in terms of dollars (as was the case until 1972), the increasing demand for international liquidity had to be met in other ways, although gold still constitutes a significant proportion of the value of reserves held by industrialised nations.

The use of domestic currencies as reserve currencies has many advantages. Paper money is cheap to produce and to store, it can be supplied on any scale that can conceivably be required; and there is widespread familiarity with its use. It is also worth noting that reserves do not have to be held in the form of currency as such. Rather, the currency can be placed on deposit and hence earn interest, or be converted into financial instruments denominated in the relevant currency.

Most international liquidity has been held in the form of reserve currencies since 1945. The obvious drawback is that no-one wishes to hold reserves in the form of a currency that is subject to capital losses. Until 1972 the dollar was pegged to gold, and hence was a universally popular reserve currency, unlike the pound which devalued in 1949 and 1967. Since 1972 the volatile behaviour of the dollar has considerably undermined its desirability, and the yen and the DM have tended to replace the dollar. However, the vast dollar reserves built up over the years (issued in settlement of US BoP deficits) mean that international liquidity will remain dominated by the dollar for the rest of the decade and well beyond.

There are clear advantages accruing to a country whose currency is used for reserve purposes, not least of which is its ability to settle its debts in its own currency which it can print endlessly at very little cost to itself. The main drawback is that if there is a severe loss of confidence in the currency, attempts by outsiders to convert into other, stronger, currencies may have severe implications for the domestic economy. When there is a run on a currency, it is unlikely that the country whose currency it is will by itself have the reserves in other currencies to stem the tide. Hence international cooperation is a prerequisite for stability in the international monetary system.

6.12.2 *Special Drawing Rights (SDRs)*

The shortage of gold, and the increasing overdependence upon the dollar, stimulated moves towards the creation of an 'artificial' form of currency (that is, one controlled not by the monetary authorities of an individual country but by an international body). As part of the Bretton Woods agreement discussed above, the IMF had been set up to oversee the adjustable peg mechanism and to help countries in BoP difficulties to set their houses in order. To facilitate this it received funds from member countries, varying according to their ability to pay. Originally, these funds were paid as a quota, of which 75 per cent constituted the domestic currency of the contributor and 25 per cent constituted gold. The funds were then lent in the same form by way of temporary loans to countries in difficulties, in the expectation that they would be repaid within three to five years once the difficulties had been resolved (in accordance with guidelines laid down by the IMF).

In 1969 the IMF managed to obtain international agreement for the introduction of an international currency called SDRs, and these first began to circulate in 1970 following an amendment to the IMF's Articles of Agreement. The SDRs are not put into circulation in the form of banknotes, but rather exist as **credits in ledgers to be drawn on as required in relation to member's quotas**, as explained below.

The creation of SDRs was certainly a major improvement on preceding arrangements because it offered a permanent solution to the shortage of international liquidity that existed at the time, rather than the kind of **ad hoc** arrangement adopted previously. In particular, the General Agreements to Borrow (GAB) had been brought into being in 1962 whereby members of the Group of Ten (major industrial countries) agreed to increase allocations of their domestic currencies to the IMF if other members of the group needed to withdraw larger amounts than the IMF had in stock. The UK was itself able to utilise GAB during its periodic BoP crises in the 1970s, and especially in 1976. Over the years, the sums allocated to GAB have occasionally been periodically revised, with Switzerland joining the other ten members in 1984, and the possibility of access to GAB being extended beyond its immediate membership.

Like GAB, SDRs are available only temporarily (the World Bank being the appropriate body to approach for more permanent financing). Each country paying over its quota to the IMF is guaranteed a borrowing facility related to the size of the quota, which is measured in terms of SDRs. Furthermore, this facility rises in value over time as the size of the quotas is periodically raised.

A country seeking to borrow from the IMF obviously desires reserve currencies and/or gold. It purchases these with its SDRs, acquired either in return for its quota payments or as a loan from the IMF, thereby transferring the SDRs to the country supplying the currency which is being borrowed.

The IMF expects to influence a borrowing country's macroeconomic policy in order to ensure that the borrower creates the capacity to repay. However, no conditions are imposed where the borrower seeks a loan no greater than 25 per cent of its quota. This is called its **reserve tranche**, and is contained in the figure for the borrower's official reserves (denoted 'reserve position at IMF' in the BoP accounts). Conditions begin to be imposed when a loan exceeds this figure, and are made increasingly stringent as the size of the loan increases. Loans in excess of the reserve tranche are available in four equal instalments, each amounting to 25 per cent of a country's quota. These **credit tranches** can thus bring total borrowings up to a maximum of 125 per cent of a country's quota but, unlike the reserve tranche they are recorded (where relevant) in the BoP accounts as 'allocation of Special Drawing Rights'.

The conditions placed upon credit tranches are understandably somewhat unpopular in the borrowing country. When the UK was forced to borrow in 1976, the IMF demanded that public spending be sharply reduced and that the growth of the money supply be curtailed, neither policy being likely to appeal to the Labour Government of that time. Inevitably, borrowers are wont to place the blame for austerity measures at the IMF's door, since this avoids explaining why the problems arose in the first place, so the IMF has something of an image problem. It also has something of a credibility problem because it is dealing in an artificial currency on a scale which is deliberately restricted by the major industrial countries which can wield large blocks of votes on its governing board.

The size of quotas is subject to five-yearly reviews, but the initial intention steadily to replace reserves held in other forms by SDRs has never found favour with the major industrial countries, which are understandably wary of handing over control regarding monetary matters to a supranational body. Certainly, some attempts were made over the years to bring the SDR into increasing prominence, including the partial or full payment of increases in quotas in the form of SDRs rather than gold, and the payment of attractive rates of interest to countries receiving SDRs in exchange for their currencies, but a major consideration has been the ready availability of dollars, as noted previously.

6.13 The International Debt Crisis

☐ 6.13.1 Origins of the Crisis

During the period prior to the early 1970s, the volume of world trade was growing rapidly, to the mutual benefit of developed and less-develoed countries. Lending to the LDCs, whether via the banks or bodies such as the IMF, was not considered to be at widespread risk of default since these countries were, with occasional exceptions, generating sufficient NI to service the interest payments on their debts. However, the sudden sharp rise in the price of oil engineered by OPEC in 1974–75 severely affected not merely the non-oil LDCs but some of the more developed countries as well, and so reduced their national income as to prevent full payment of outstanding debt interest. The second oil price rise in 1979 worsened their situation still further, partly via increased costs of production, and partly via the resultant recession amongst their industrialised customers.

During the 1970s the IMF provided very limited assistance. The largest sum lent in any one year was $3 billion, and that included loans to developed countries in difficulties. The burden of lending accordingly fell upon the commercial banks in industrialised countries which, rather foolishly in retrospect, were happy to offer short-term loans tied to floating interest rates. At the time, such behaviour did not appear to be quite so foolish. In the first place, the bor-

rowers were sovereign states which, unlike industrial concerns, were not thought to be in any danger of bankruptcy. Second, the OPEC surpluses were swilling around the banking system looking for a profitable home, and with industrial profitability falling sharply in domestic markets, the number of clients wishing to borrow expensive money was on the decline.

With interest rates floating upwards rather than down, it gradually became clear that sooner or later a major default on interest payments was going to occur, and that this could have a disastrous impact if such a default threatened to bankrupt commercial banks, which would then call in other loans to LDCs, and so on. In 1982, the three largest debtors, Mexico, Brazil and Argentina, between them owed $220 billion of debt, with an annual interest bill of $13 billion. Since it was clear that countries such as these literally – at least, for the time being – lacked the capacity to repay, some kind of debt rescheduling operation was clearly required.

Between them, the IMF and the banks devised a way to proceed. The IMF stood ready to make further loans available, albeit on a relatively modest scale, through a variety of programmes such as the extended fund facility (EFF), the supplementary financing facility (SFF), the compensatory financing facility and the enlarged access policy (EAP). Most of the loans were not merely made 'conditional' upon changes in the macroeconomic policies of the debtor nations, but also conditional upon the creditor banks accepting a restructuring of those debts and, if necessary, further increases in their lending. In other words, the banks needed the reasssurance of an IMF-imposed austerity programme, while the IMF needed the banks' cooperation in order to induce the debtor countries to accept such a programme.

During 1983 and 1984 the IMF lent some $20 billion to 70 countries, although the effect was multiplied many times by the debt rescheduling which accompanied this lending, and the feared collapse among the banks, whose balance sheets contained what, on any definition, were bad debts in excess of their issued capital, was headed off. However, the problem did not go away. The drop in the oil price did provide some relief for the non-oil LDCs, but it simultaneously created problems for oil-producers such as Mexico and Nigeria.

Between 1982 and mid-1987 the 'Paris Club' creditor governments rescheduled $48 billion of debt for 39 countries, as shown in **Figure 6.15**. Meanwhile the banks set out to strengthen their balance sheets and began to make provisions for the probability that some debts would never be repaid, a reasonable assumption given that the ratio of debt to export earnings was continuing to rise in most debtor countries. In spite of this, the IMF was obliged to acknowledge at the end of 1988 that, instead of it financing debtor nations, the debtor nations were financing the IMF as a result of loan repayments.

□ 6.13.2 Recent Developments

In early 1989 the debt problem was suddenly pushed back into prominence by rioting in Venezuela, triggered by price rises introduced to qualify for new IMF loans. The US Treasury Secretary, Nicholas Brady, hastily cobbled together a plan which proposed that commercial banks voluntarily exchange loans for bonds with either lower face values or lower interest rates, thereby reducing the cash burden on debtors. The problem was to get something concrete in return. Debtor nations wanted the resolution of their problems to be divorced from internal reform, but this provoked a protest which centred around the argument that debtor countries should privatise their inefficient State enterprises, crack down on corruption and introduce market forces.

The refusal by debtor nations to implement structural reforms had previously caused the demise of the Baker Plan of 1985, but the softer line contained in the **Brady Plan** induced a more positive reaction by debtor nations. By the end of 1990 three 'Brady-style' deals were accordingly completed with Mexico, the Philippines and Costa Rica, and countries such as Venezuela and Uruguay were negotiating further deals. However, the overall problem was not improving because arrears of interest payments had built up

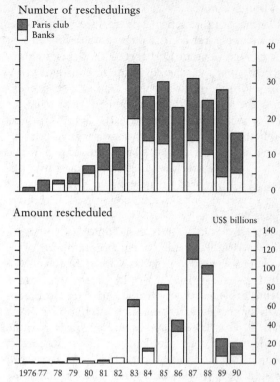

Figure 6.15 *LDC Debt Rescheduling*

Source: Bank of England Quarterly Bulletin (November 1991).

rapidly after 1988, and the banks were losing their patience, especially as they had come to believe that the IMF was giving the impression to debtor countries that failure to pay off arrears would not disqualify them from further official assistance.

Faced with insufficient progress under the Baker Plan, attempts had been made to enhance the existing secondary market in LDC debt with additional financial innovations. By selling all of its outstanding debt, a bank could clean up its balance sheet but only by taking an actual rather than a theoretical loss. For the most part the debt was bought by other banks which raised loans to pay for it. Brazil and Argentina introduced 'exit bonds' which, if taken up, relieved a bank of the obligation to supply new money. Some debtors (such as Chile) permitted debt to be converted into equity, whereas others ran auctions at which banks bid to swap their customers' foreign debt for local currency which they needed for projects in those countries.

Some of these schemes were successful. Chile, for example, raised its debt's value to 80 per cent of its face value in 1991 through a debt-to-equity scheme, but the schemes made few inroads given the enormity of the problem, and in almost every case the secondary market value of debt fell after 1986, as shown in **Figure 6.16**. Since this was something of a deterrent to prospective purchasers, action on the official debt seemed to be essential, and in June 1990 President Bush followed up the Brady Plan with an 'Enterprise for the Americas' initiative involving partial forgiveness, on a case-by-case basis, of official bilateral debts for South American countries pursuing IMF/World Bank adjustment programmes.

There were also proposals for **debt-for-nature** deals whereby LDCs would be forgiven their debts provided they refrained from environmentally damaging activities, such as chopping down rain forests. However, it simultaneously became evident that debt problems in Eastern Europe, which had previously attracted little attention, would also need to be addressed as a matter of some urgency, particularly in view of the overthrow of communist regimes in 1990. Eastern European debt rose from $70 billion in 1985 to $99 billion in 1987, and by 1989 Poland's debts alone amounted to $40 billion.

A major difference in the Polish case was that most of the debt was official, and it instigated economic reforms subsequent to the overthrow of communism. These considerations made it much easier to forgive the debt than in the case of other LDCs, and early in 1991 it was accordingly agreed by the Paris Club that half of the official debt would immediately be forgiven, which did not go down well in South America. The same facility was extended to Egypt in gratitude for its role in the Gulf War.

Over the past two years a dramatic turnaround has been evident in respect of many South American debtors, as shown by the rise in debt prices in **Figure 6.16**. Where governments have welcomed international capital, opened their economies to outside influence through a lowering of trade barriers, set their fiscal books in order and

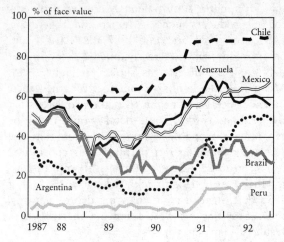

Figure 6.16   *Secondary Market Bank Debt Prices*

Source: Salomon Brothers.

shrunk their public sectors, their own citizens have repatriated their capital with foreign investors following hard on their heels. With lower interest rates and inflation, and a more benign attitude towards debt rescheduling, the short-term position has improved immeasurably.

However, the capital inflows include a good deal of 'hot money', and may flow out again if interest rates rise again in the USA and EU. Equally, countries beset by corruption and political instability such as Brazil have fared less well, and some commentators (for example, Bird, 1992) are less than sanguine about the longer-term prognosis. The adjustment process is certainly painful, and social unrest remains a worry. This is even truer of the former members of the Soviet bloc. Estimates of Russia's total foreign debt range from $80 billion to $87 billion, of which $38 billion is owed to official creditors and another $20 billion to commercial banks. In April 1993 Western creditor nations came to the rescue of Boris Yeltsin by agreeing to reschedule the bulk of the estimated $20 billion of debt service obligations for the year, but this provides a breathing space rather than a solution.

The situation also remains dire in Africa, where formerly oil-rich Nigeria has a foreign debt of $28 billion. Sub-Saharan nations have received official support via concessional lending, debt restructuring and forgiveness, but their **per capitum** incomes have shrunk by 20 per cent over the past decade, and little short of a total debt write-off can resolve the problem. At the end of the day, the only long-term solution is to speed up the rate of growth in debtor nations so that they acquire the capacity to repay debts without eroding the standard of living of their inhabitants. There is clearly a strong case to be made for requesting the industrialised nations to open up their markets, especially to agricultural products, and for the debtor countries to become more export-oriented. Unfortunately, as the subsequent section on the GATT demonstrates, that is not seen as a priority at this time.

Bibliogrpahy

Ayres, R. (1992) 'Britain's Trade in Invisibles', *British Review of Economic Issues* (February).

Bank of England (1990) 'The External Balance Sheet of the United Kingdom: Recent Developments and Measurement Problems', *Bank of England Quarterly Bulletin* (November).

Bank of England (1991) 'The LDC Debt Crisis', *Bank of England Quarterly Bulletin* (November).

Bank of England (1992a) 'The External Balance Sheet of the United Kingdom: Recent Developments', *Bank of England Quarterly Bulletin* (November).

Bank of England (1992b) 'The Foreign Exchange Market in London', *Bank of England Quarterly Bulletin* (November).

Bird, G. (1992) 'Ten Years Older and Deeper in Debt? The Developing Country Debt Problem in Retrospect and Prospect', *Economics* (Spring).

Bordo, M. (1993) 'The Gold Standard, Bretton Woods and Other Monetary Regimes: A Historical Appraisal', *Federal Reserve Bank of St Louis Quarterly Review* (March/April).

Coutts, K. and W. Godley (1990) 'Prosperity and Foreign Trade in the 1990s: Britain's Strategic Problems', *Oxford Review of Economic Policy*, 6(3).

Davies, G. (1990) 'The Capital Account and the Sustainability of the UK Trade Deficit', *Oxford Review of Economic Policy*, 6(3).

Holtham, G. (1990) 'World Current Account Balances', *Oxford Review of Economic Policy*, 6(3).

Muellbauer, J. and A. Murphy (1990) 'Is the UK Balance of Payments Sustainable?', *Economic Policy* (October).

Pain, N. and P. Westaway (1990) 'Why the Capital Account Matters', *National Institute Economic Review* (February).

Pratten, C. (1992) 'Overseas Investments, Capital Gains and the Balance of Payments', *Research Monograph 48*, Institute of Economic Affairs.

Rhys, D. (1990) 'The Motor Industry and the Balance of Payments', *Bank of Scotland Review* (December).

Thirlwall, T. (1992) 'The Balance of Payments and Economic Performance', *National Westminster Quarterly Bank Review* (May).

■ *Chapter 7* ■

External Relations

Peter Curwen

■ 7.1 Introduction

The distinction between external transactions and external relations is necessarily a rather fine one, and there are clearly other ways to manage the division of material. Essentially, there seemed to be advantages in assembling together most of the material that impinges upon the role of the UK as a member of the EU (see box below) and Chapter 7 is broadly given over to this topic. This means that the issues pertaining to exchange rate relationships within the EU are also contained within Chapter 7, even though the more general discussion of exchange rates appears in Chapter 6.

Readers may understandably find it difficult to distinguish between the ERM, EMS, Economic and Monetary Union (EMU) and the SEM and

these are accordingly dealt with at the beginning of the chapter. We then go on to examine relationships between the EU and the rest of the world, treating the UK in its capacity of EU member state, and conclude with a detailed examination of the CAP, which is simultaneously an issue in terms of the UK's relationship with the EU and also in terms of the EU's relationship with other agricultural trading blocs.

■ 7.2 The Single European Market

☐ 7.2.1 *The Single European Act 1985*

The SEM which came into being on 1 January 1993 has its origins in the Single European Act (SEA) of 1985. This was one in a line of Acts that had the underlying purpose of amending the original Treaty of Rome which brought the Community into being in 1958 (see box). The institutions that existed in 1985, and still do, are set out below, and there is also a list of the Commissioners who are currently in post.

When he was first appointed in 1984, Jacques Delors considered carefully the areas in which to

---

1958 (6)	:	Belgium, France, Italy, Luxembourg, Netherlands, West Germany (now reunified with its eastern counterpart and referred to as 'Germany')
1973 (9)	:	Denmark, Ireland (Eire), United Kingdom
1981 (10)	:	Greece
1986 (12)	:	Spain, Portugal

1	European Commission	17 members of whom 1 (Jacques Delors) is president. Commissioners are allocated by country. The UK has 2: Sir Leon Brittan and Bruce Millan. The Commission is the EU's civil service and has no direct political power. Its main role is to instigate proposals such as directives and see them through to acceptance or rejection (see **Figure 7.1**).
2	The Council of the European Union	Consists of 12 representatives, one from each member country. The make up of the Council varies according to the subject under discussion (12 agricultural ministers if the subject is agriculture, and so forth). Voting is either **unanimous** or by **qualified majority**. Only the Council has the power to ratify a proposal. Grand strategy is left to the meeting of the 12 heads of state: the **European Council**.
3	European Parliament	536 Euro MEPs who sit according to their position on the political spectrum rather than by country. Main groups are socialists and Christian Democrats. The Parliament's powers have been enhanced under the new *cooperation procedure* (see **Figure 7.1**), but are not comparable to those of the Council.
4	The European Court of Justice	Consists of 13 judges and 5 advocates-general. The rulings of the Court are supranational and take precedence over legal rulings in member countries.

concentrate his attention. His first priority was to create an EMU within the Community, but neither the UK nor West Germany showed sufficient enthusiasm for that idea. He accordingly turned next to matters of foreign policy, but again found no takers for a policy of increased coordination. His third choice proved more inspired. Noting the movement towards deregulation and liberalisation in economic affairs, he advocated **freedom of movement for goods and services, people and financial flows** throughout the EU, now enshrined in Article 8A of the SEA.

At the present time, there are still a number of developments working their way through the

President:	Jacques Delors (France)
Economic and financial affairs:	Henning Christophersen (Denmark)
Development:	Manuel Marin (Spain)
Industry:	Martin Bangemann (Germany)
External economic affairs:	Sir Leon Brittan (UK)
Energy, transport:	Abel Matutes (Spain)
Budget:	Peter Schmidhuber (Germany)
Customs, taxation:	Christiane Scrivener (France)
Regional Policy:	Bruce Millan (UK)
Competition:	Karel Van Miert (Belgium)
External political relations:	Hans van den Broek (Netherlands)
Internal political relations:	Joao de Deus Pinheiro (Portugal)
Social affairs and employment:	Padraig Flynn (Ireland)
Science, research and development:	Antonio Ruberti (Italy)
Agriculture:	René Steichen (Luxembourg)
Environment:	Ionnis Paleokrassas (Greece)
Single market:	Raniero Vanni d'Archirafi

Figure 7.1 *Community Legislative Process: New Cooperation Procedure*[1]

```
                    ┌─────────────────────┐
                    │      COMMISSION      │
                    │       Proposal       │
                    └─────────────────────┘

        ┌─────────────────────┐   ┌─────────────────────┐
        │       COUNCIL        │   │     PARLIAMENT       │
        │  begins deliberating │   │       Opinion        │
        └─────────────────────┘   └─────────────────────┘

                    ┌─────────────────────┐
                    │      COMMISSION      │
                    │  takes a view on the │
                    │  Parliament's opinion│
                    └─────────────────────┘
```

(Traditional Procedure)   (New Cooperation Procedure)

```
    ┌─────────────────────┐        ┌──────────────────────────┐
    │       COUNCIL        │        │         COUNCIL          │
    │ takes final decision │        │ adopts a common position │
    └─────────────────────┘        │   by qualified majority  │
                                    └──────────────────────────┘
```

within 3 months the		PARLIAMENT		
approves Council position	or *takes no position*	or	*amends* Council common position by absolute majority of members	or	*rejects* Council common position by an absolute majority

COUNCIL	within one month COMMISSION	COUNCIL
adopts act	reviews EP amendments and may revise its proposal	may act only by authority

within 3 months the		COUNCIL		
may adopt the Commission proposal on the table by qualified majority	or	may adopt EP amendments not approved by the Commission by unanimity	or	otherwise amend the Commission proposal by unanimity	or may fail to act

Possible one-month extension if agreed by the Parliament

Commission proposal lapses if Council does not act

Note:
EP=European Parliament.
Source: The Single Market – the Facts (London: DTI, 1990).

complicated and time-consuming process of ratification by all EU members, as shown in **Figure 7.1** (though subject to certain amendments once the Maastricht Treaty is finally ratified by all members), even though the SEM is officially already in existence.

Most decisions under the SEA are subject to **qualified** (weighted by size of member states' economies) **majority voting**, although some important and sensitive issues, such as those concerned with **taxation**, require **unanimous** approval. The qualified majority is **54** votes out of a total of **76** (see below), of which the UK has **10**. Should other countries be permitted to join the EU these proportions will obviously have to be altered, as shown in **Table 7.1**. It can be seen that the idea behind majority voting is to prevent, say, two large countries from vetoing legislation in the face of agreement by the other ten, although this necessitates allocating them rather less voting power than is strictly warranted in relation to their economic strength. Whereas the big four members represent roughly 75 per cent of EU GDP, they control only 53 per cent of the votes.

10 votes	Germany, France, Italy, UK
8 votes	Spain
5 votes	Belgium, Greece, Netherlands, Portugal
3 votes	Denmark, Ireland
2 votes	Luxembourg

76 votes in total: qualified majority = 54 votes

The SEM consists essentially of a set of measures, primarily in the form of **directives**,[1] which are initially tabled by the European Commission. There are **282** such measures and, when they have passed through the procedure illustrated in **Figure 7.1**, and have thereby become Community law, the majority must subsequently be placed upon the statute book of individual member states by a specified date unless there is a derogation exempting a member from the measure for a stated period.

At the beginning of February 1993, 261 of the measures had been adopted by the Council of the European Union, in three cases common positions had been agreed and the remaining 18 were under

Table 7.1 *Enlarging the Community*

In the club	People, (m)	Council votes[1]
Germany	79.8	10
Britain	57.6	10
Italy	57.1	10
France	57.1	10
Spain	39.0	8
Holland	15.1	5
Greece	10.3	5
Belgium	10.0	5
Portugal	9.8	5
Denmark	5.2	3
Ireland	3.5	3
Luxembourg	0.4	2

In the queue[2]		Potential votes[3]
Austria	7.8	5
Finland	5.0	5
Norway	4.3	3
Sweden	8.6	5
Switzerland	6.8	5
Cyprus	0.7	2
Malta	0.4	2
Turkey	57.7	10

In the distance		
Albania	3.1	3
Bulgaria[4]	8.6	5
Czech Rep.[4]	10.4	5
Estonia	1.6	3
Hungary	10.3	5
Latvia	2.7	3
Lithuania	3.7	3
Poland[1]	38.3	8
Romania[4]	23.2	6
Slovakia[4]	5.2	3
Slovenia	2.0	3

Notes:
[1] It currently takes 54 votes out of 76 to pass a law by 'qualified majority'.
[2] Applied to join the Community.
[3] Estimated, under extension of existing rules.
[4] Countries with 'Europe agreements' with the EU.
Source: Financial Times.

consideration. In principle, the SEM is accordingly close to completion. However, member states have varying difficulties in passing the necessary national laws, sometimes intentionally, so that in practice it will be some time before the SEM is completed at a national level. In mid-1993, for example, less than half of the directives had become law in all 12 member states. The UK, somewhat surprisingly given its reputation as an unenthusiastic member, has a generally good record in implementation, as shown in **Figure** 7.2, although the Danes are the clear leaders. The Belgians, and especially the Italians, have less to be proud of, and this shows up in the number of times they have been dragged before the European Court of Justice to be reprimanded for their dilatory behaviour. Whereas Denmark had only been rebuked once by the end of 1991, and the UK three times, the Belgian score was 17 and the Italian was 35.

The directives cover such an enormous range of issues that it is impossible to engage in a detailed discussion in a book of this kind. However, certain sensitive matters were excluded from the SEM – for example energy policy – and notably little has been achieved in respect of a common policy towards the liberalisation of telecommunications and postal services.

Figure 7.2   *Percentage Share of EU Directives Incorporated Into National Legislation as of 8 December 1992*

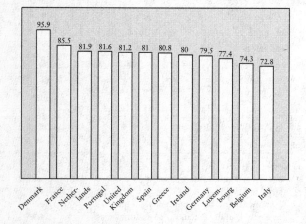

Source: EC Commission.

7.2.2 Supranationality

At this juncture we do need, however, to take a general look at the SEM, concentrating in particular upon those aspects which affect trade flows between member states.

It has to be borne in mind that every step towards a single market implies a loss of national sovereignty on the part of member states. The original impetus towards a Europe of independent nation states came from de Gaulle in France. However, when the French attempted to expand their way into prosperity in the early 1980s, their failure caused them to reverse direction and become the arch advocates of the single market. The fact that M. Delors has maintained close links with the French Socialist Party has created a suspicion in other countries that he is pressing for a predominantly French version of the single market. This has never gone down well in the UK. When M. Delors was ill-advised enough to boast that 80 per cent of economic legislation, and perhaps tax and social legislation, would be decided in Brussels by the end of the millenium, he was abruptly brought back to earth by Mrs Thatcher, who pointed out that she did not expect the loss of national sovereignty on such a scale to take place during her lifetime.[2] The UK's attitude has mellowed somewhat since her replacement as Prime Minister, but the backbench rebellion over the Maastricht Treaty has demonstrated more recently that a referendum would almost certainly result in a vote against the Treaty.

7.2.3 Harmonisation and Mutual Recognition

One of the primary reasons underlying the failure of the Community to develop much beyond the running of the Common Agricultural Policy prior to the 1980s was the issue of **harmonisation**. By insisting, for example, that imports of beer would have to match the purity of the domestic product, the West Germans were able to create an effective non-tariff barrier against imports. Attempts by the European Commission to introduce rules which, if adhered to, would make products universally accepted throughout the EU, foundered constantly because member states with the highest standards tried to harmonise the proposed EU-wide standards with their own.

The pointer to a way out of this dilemma came in the form of the **Cassis de Dijon Judgement** of the European Court of Justice. This ruled that if a product satisfied the laws governing its production and sale in one member state, then it could also be sold in an identical form in any other member state even if the laws of those states prohibited its domestic production in that form. Importation of the product would not affect domestic laws, so it would remain illegal to make the product domestically. In this respect 'domestic' was taken to mean production by a national company, its subsidiaries and branches and subsidiaries of foreign companies operating within the boundaries of that nation.

Up to that time, products which were exported had to be compatible with the laws of the **importing** country. It was now proposed by the Commission that they had to be compatible only with the laws of the **exporting** country. This is known as **mutual recognition**, and it obviously simplified enormously the problems facing a company wishing to engage in intra-EU trade. If exporters were already making products in conformity with the laws of the importing country, they could either continue to do so or they could opt to produce in conformity with their domestic laws. One situation where exporters would wish to continue to adhere to the laws of the importing country would be where the product exported was illegal on the home market. Although it appeared to be reasonable, this ruling was not without its own problems. In the first place, once frontier controls are dismantled it becomes relatively easy to move a product from a country where it is legal to one where it is not. Second, the ruling favours imports from outside the EU altogether. Once imported legally into any one EU country these can, in accordance with Article 9 of the Treaty of Rome, be sold in every EU country without restriction. Hence, importers have only to get their product accepted in an EU country of

their choosing to gain access to countries where the product cannot legally be produced for domestic consumption.

Under certain circumstances set out either in the Treaty of Rome or in judgements of the European Court of Justice (for example, concerning health and safety), a member state can prohibit imports from any source. However, these circumstances are much less pervasive than might be imagined. In the example cited above, the West Germans were unable to prohibit imports of beer on the grounds that they were adulterated and hence harmful to health, and the same principle was applied when the Italians tried to prohibit imports of pasta. In both cases the Court of Justice ruled that the health of consumers was not seriously threatened and that their interests could be adequately protected by labelling clearly the contents of the products.

It is interesting to speculate whether mutual recognition will bring about a condition akin to total harmonisation. It is evident that a country which prohibits the domestic manufacture of a product cannot exclude the importation of that product in a form which is compatible with the laws of any other member state. Hence it follows that the domestic prohibition serves only to deny opportunities to domestic producers. Equally, if higher standards are required of a domestic producer than of producers who export from other states, the domestic producer must suffer some competitive disadvantages. It may accordingly make sense for prohibitions to be lifted and for exceptionally onerous domestic rules to be eased, not merely in order to permit domestic producers to reclaim the domestic market, but also to permit them to export successfully. Market forces may in this manner harmonise national standards, albeit not in accordance with the pre-existing highest standards of any individual country but in accordance with those set at a less onerous level.

Unsurprisingly, this scenario holds little appeal for countries such as Germany, which can foresee their high-quality domestic products driven out of both domestic and export markets by lower-quality foreign products. Furthermore, in order to discover whether the foreign products should be sold in the domestic market, they must be checked not against the domestic standards, which are well known, but against the standards set in each country of origin, which are unfamiliar. In order to avoid excessive bureaucracy an importer will generally have to trust the exporting country's own inspectorate, but it is understandable that, for example, Germans are suspicious of quality controls in Greece.

7.3 The Community Budget and the UK

☐ 7.3.1 The Community Budget

The Community Budget is agreed annually between the Council of Ministers and the European Parliament on the basis of a draft by the European Commission. It is formally adopted by the Parliament which has the final say on 'non-compulsory expenditure', whereas the Council has the final say on 'compulsory' expenditure. Spending which is **compulsory** is that which arises directly from the provisions of the Treaty of Rome or from other Acts adopted in accordance with the Treaty. In practice, it is almost all related to agricultural support and overseas aid. Spending which is **non-compulsory** includes that on regional development and social policies. Agricultural spending, together with the Regional Development Fund, the Social Fund and grants to farmers for modernisation or environmentally beneficial projects, are known as the **structural Funds**. These Funds require **additionality**: that is, they must supplement, and not replace, existing local and central government commitments to the projects selected.

The Community Budget relies, apart from periodic inter-governmental agreements (IGAs), upon its **own resources**. These comprise:

(a)   the Common Customs Tariff, which relates to duties and levies on goods imported from non-EU countries (net of a 10 per cent contribution to cover collection and administration costs);

(b)   agricultural levies on imported produce;

(c)   the amount which would be raised if VAT up to a specified rate were levied on the same basket of spending on goods and services in each member state (itself worth a maximum of 55 per cent of GNP at market prices);

(d)   payments related to each member state's GNP at market prices, set at a level sufficient to bridge the gap between total expenditure and the yield of the other three own resources.

There is a legally-binding ceiling, called a **guideline**, on the total own resources available to finance the Budget, which is expressed as a proportion of EU GNP. The Budget is set initially to provide some leeway below the guideline, but if there are problems with, for example, agricultural spending, that leeway can be rapidly eroded. The various contributions made by the UK are itemised as UK debits in **Table 7.2**. In return for these the UK receives credits, primarily from the European Agricultural Guarantee and Guidance Fund (EAGGF), the European Social Fund and the European Regional Development Fund. The difference between debits and credits represents the UK's net contribution to the Community Budget.

Gross of any abatements, the UK's share of total Community own resources is roughly 20 per cent. This can be compared with the fact that the UK accounts for roughly 16 per cent of Community GNP. More importantly, the UK receives back only 7–8 per cent of total Community expenditure. It is hardly surprising, therefore, that the UK is a major net contributor to the Community Budget, as shown in **Table 7.2**. This arises because agricultural and other levies and duties are boosted by the UK's relatively heavy dependence on non-EU imports, because UK citizens' high propensity to consume generates large amounts of VAT and because the UK's relatively efficient agricultural sector attracts only modest levels of support.

In 1979 debits were 2.5 times as large as credits, and the net contribution amounted to almost £1 billion. As a consequence the UK government sought, and obtained, agreement for a series of annual **refunds** based upon the UK's excess net

Table 7.2   General Government Transactions with the Institutions of the EU (£ m)

	1981	1982	1983	1984	1985	1986	1987	1988	1989	1990	1991	1992
EU BUDGET												
UK CREDITS												
Services	122	150	148	186	157	157	126	85	5	5	8	5
Transfers												
EAGGF	683	791	1082	1353	1151	1385	1345	1379	1315	1496	1761	1813
Social Fund	107	152	128	283	256	335	428	277	406	225	618	437
Regional Development Fund	145	111	139	184	274	298	404	370	347	441	370	551
Negotiated refunds[2]	693	1019	807	528	61	–	–	–	–	–	–	–
Other	27	36	24	11	15	41	42	72	43	16	9	17
TOTAL	1777	2259	2328	2545	1914	2216	2345	2183	2116	2183	2766	2823
UK DEBITS												
Transfers												
Agriculture and sugar levies	218	307	232	260	189	244	354	226	192	135	205	206
Customs protective duties	861	1001	1075	1276	1291	1244	1417	1521	1638	1555	1029	1558
GNP financial contribution	–	–	–	–	–	–	–	–	–	–	–	–
Budget adjustments[3]	–	–	–	–	–	–	–	–	–	–	–	–
VAT (gross before abatement adjustments)	960	1497	1712	1720	1930	2742	3347	2886	3444	4149	4610	5291
Abatement[3]	–	–	–43	–55	–166	–1701	–1153	–1595	–1156	–1697	–2497	–1881
Adjustments[3]	135	57	–	–	145	263	84	–127	311	516	–538	–317
IGAs	–	–	–	–	370	–	–	613	–	–	–	–
TOTAL	2174	2862	2976	3201	3759	2792	4049	3524	4429	4658	3309	4857
BALANCE	–397	–603	–648	–656	–1845	–576	–1704	–1341	–2313	–2475	–543	–2034

Notes:
[1] For all years sterling figures reflect actual payments made during the year, not payments in respect of particular Budgets.
[2] Refunds and abatements received in respect of the UK's excess net contributions to EU Budgets in earlier years.
[3] Adjustments reflecting reassessments of the gross contributions required for the EU Budgets for the previous years.
Source: UK National Accounts Pink Book (CSO, 1993), Table 9.2.

contributions to Community Budgets in earlier years. In addition, certain modest **adjustments** were made with respect to previous years' gross contributions. In 1984, at the Fontainebleau Summit, an **abatement** mechanism was negotiated which is now formally part of Community law. Under this agreement the UK's **gross** contribution to the Budget in any given year is currently abated by an amount which is broadly equivalent to two thirds of the UK's **net** contribution in the previous year.

As can be seen in **Table 7.2**, the UK's net contribution is rather erratic. This arises because of the need to make adjustments for inaccurate forecasts in previous years. It should be noted that between 1979 and 1991 the Community Budget rose on average by 4.3 per cent annually whereas the UK's contribution rose on average by 0.5 per cent. If nothing else, Mrs Thatcher knew how to tough it out at the bargaining table. The position for the UK relative to other member states in 1992 is set out in **Figure 7.3**. As can be seen, Germany bears the brunt of making contributions, but it has understandably lost some enthusiasm for that role now that it carries the burden of paying for the integration of former Eastern Germany.

In order to understand recent events, it is helpful to begin by looking back to the key Budget negotiations which took place in 1988. These negotiations were, as usual, conducted in an atmosphere of impending crisis. On this occasion, however, there was clear evidence that previous measures to reduce both the degree of price support and also surplus production had failed to rein back expenditure on the CAP. In 1975 the EU Budget amounted to ECU 6.5 billion, of which ECU 4.5 billion went to the EAGGF. By 1980 the respective figures were ECU 16.2 billion and ECU 11.5 billion, subsequently rising to ECU 28.4 billion and ECU 20.0 billion respectively in 1985. In each year the percentage allocated to the EAGGF was 70 per cent. However, although in 1987 the EAGGF allocation had risen to ECU 22.8 billion, this represented only 63.5 per cent of the total Budget of ECU 36 billion, with a much enlarged share allocated to the Regional Fund and the Social Fund.

Figure 7.3   *Community Budget, 1992*

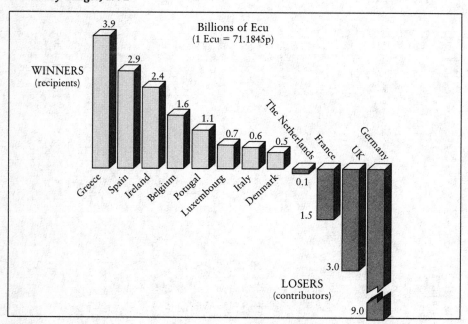

Source: European Commission.

It was widely accepted that the Budget should continue to be readjusted towards regional and social spending, and within the EAGGF towards structural support. However, there were problems of implementation given that allocations to the CAP were the only obligatory element in the Community Budget, and that the Council of Agricultural Ministers, backed by the business interests dependent upon agriculture, had a strong vested interest in maintaining the status quo. Nevertheless, the package put forward by M. Delors, known as **Delors I**, included a proposal to double the Regional Fund and Social Fund by 1992.

A Summit was called in February 1988 to discuss the proposed package, and for once Mrs Thatcher was obliged to make significant concessions. It was agreed, with retrospective effect as from 1 January 1988, that the EAGGF growth rate would be limited to 74 per cent of the annual growth of EU GNP in volume terms; that the Budgets should absorb no more than 1.2 per cent of EU GNP; that the VAT base of each member state would be capped at 55 per cent of its GNP, with the continuation of the ceiling of 1.4 per cent of VAT proceeds to be given over; that a fourth source of revenue should be introduced based on shares in GNP, the rate levied to be that which is required, given all other revenue, to balance the Budget; that a production levy of 3 per cent would be placed on cereal production, at the beginning of each year up to 1992, which would be reimbursed only if total output fell below a ceiling of 160 million tonnes (with small farmers exempted), and that if this figure was exceeded the price in the following year would be reduced by 3 per cent (a policy known as a budget **stabiliser**); that a similar scheme would be applied to oilseeds; and that farmers agreeing to take land out of production for five years would receive **set-aside payments** of between ECU 100 and 600 per hectare by way of compensation, provided at least 20 per cent of arable land was set aside and also not reutilised as grazing.

ECU 600 million was allocated for set-aside payments up to 1992, enough to fund 2 million hectares. The EAGGF was also to be rebalanced, with 50 per cent of the funds being used for structural purposes by 1992, and with a greater proportion directed towards the less edveloped member states. These various changes served to raise the Budget ceiling by roughly 40 per cent compared to what it would have been had the financial system which prevailed until 1985 not been changed. Whereas part of the intention was to provide funds other than for the CAP, it was ultimately the ongoing costs of the CAP which largely accounted for this substantial increase in budgetary resources.

The 1989 and 1990 negotiations were as usual acrimonious, but for the reasons discussed on **pp. 282–3**. CAP spending was reasonably under control. However, with mountains and lakes reappearing in 1991, and an adjustment needed to allow for the incorporation of former East Germany into the CAP, it looked like the guideline would sooner or later be breached unless remedial action was taken. The Budget for 1992 is set out in **Figure 7.4**, which shows that the share of spending taken by the CAP had fallen by this time to just over 50 per cent of the total, with the structural Funds absorbing half as much again.

The structural Funds were an increasingly thorny issue. When the Commission drew up its first five-year spending plan in 1988, covering the period 1988–92 inclusive, the key to harmony lay in the doubling of structural Funds and the associated ceiling on CAP costs. However, in return for their signatures on the Maastricht Treaty, the poorest four EU members demanded an additional transfer of resources from richer northern members on the grounds that the latter would be the main beneficiaries of the treaty. This transfer, in the form of a **Cohesion Fund**, was to be incorporated in the new five-year plan commencing in 1993, known as **Delors II**.

The scope of Delors II can be seen in **Table 7.3**. It was proposed that the structural Funds would be increased by roughly 60 per cent. In addition, the funds allocated to external action were to be doubled. Unfortunately, these proposals would cause the Budget, in real terms at 1992 prices, to rise to ECU 87.5 billion, an annual growth rate of 5 per cent. It was accordingly proposed that the own resources ceiling be raised from 1.20 to 1.37

Figure 7.4 *1992 Budget Commitments and Resources*[1]

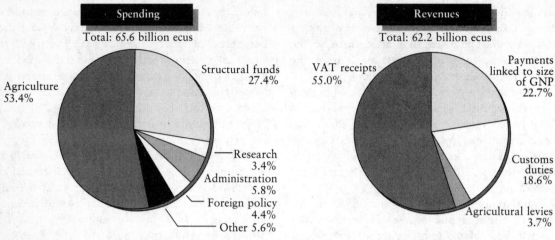

[1]The EU cannot run a budget deficit. Spending does not match revenues as some money authorised now may be spent later.
Source: The European Commission.

per cent of EU GNP. This in turn meant that a fifth own resource might need to be tapped.

In June 1992 the Council of the EU agreed to set up the Cohesion Fund, which was to benefit any member state with a GNP **per capitum** of less than 90 per cent of the Community average and which

Table 7.3 *Community Budget plans (spending commitments in billion ecus, 1992 prices)*

	1987	1992	1997
Agriculture	32.7	36.3	40.1
Structural funds	9.1	18.6	29.3
Internal policies	1.9	4.0	6.9
External action	1.4	3.6	7.2
Administration and repayments to members	5.9	4.0	4.0
Total	51.0	66.5	87.5
Total as % of GNP	1.05	1.15	1.34
Ceiling as % of GNP	none	1.20	1.37

Note: annual average GNP growth 1987–92 3.1% (actual).
                                      1992–97 2.5% (projected).
Source: European Commission.

had drawn up a programme for meeting the convergence criteria laid down in the Maastricht Treaty on budget deficits. Later that year, at the Edinburgh Summit, the planning period was extended to cover 1993–99 inclusive, and it was agreed that the own resources ceiling would rise gradually to 1.27 per cent in 1999. Despite falling below the Delors II figure, this still implied a rise in appropriations to ECU 80.1 billion in 1999. The Cohesion Fund would rise to ECU 15.15 billion, effectively doubling the structural Funds overall.

It is worth observing that if the relatively wealthy Swedes, Norwegians and Austrians join the EU they will end up as net contributors to the Budget, so there will be rather more money available than these figures indicate. As things stand, the own resources are already equivalent to 4p on the basic rate of income tax in the UK, and it is understandable that the UK Government was, as a net contributor, less happy than most with Delors II, which not merely included a new Cohesion Fund but continued with huge subsidies to farmers and significant, albeit smaller, subsidies to inefficient EU industries.

It took 14 months to get agreement to Delors I. The final decision on Delors II is awaited. Meanwhile, in April 1993, the Commission has approved the first draft of the 1994 Budget, pencilling in a 7 per cent rise in spending to ECU 70.1 billion. The calculation of the initial allocation of the Cohesion Fund indicated, to general embarrassment, that the UK was eligible even though it was a net contributor to the Budget, not that the UK wished to stake a claim! However, by taking a longer timespan for the calculation the UK could be shifted out of the net.

7.4 The European Monetary System (EMS)

In the Treaty of Rome, which originally set up the European Economic Community (EEC) in 1957, a target of 12 years was set by which all time all tariffs and quotas were to be removed between members. This proved to be more than a little unrealistic, since it became clear that individual countries were in no rush to give up their national sovereignty. However, an attempt was made to take a major step forward with the publication of the Werner Report in 1970, which proposed the setting up of a European Monetary Union. Initially, this took the form of a narrowly constrained adjustable peg mechanism linked to the existing adjustable peg based on the dollar.

The widening of the dollar-based peg in 1971 resulted in the European Monetary Union taking the form of the **'snake in the tunnel'**, whereby each EMU member's currency was allowed to fluctuate only narrowly around its own par value, thereby restricting the gap between the strongest and weakest currency to no more than 2.25 per cent, while the European Monetary Union currencies **taken as a whole** were permitted to fluctuate against the dollar within a 4.5 per cent band.

The European Monetary Union , operated by the original six EEC members from the beginning of 1972, and also by the UK for one month in May 1972, quickly fell apart at the seams. In part this reflected the continuing precedence of national interests over monetary union, but the European Monetary Union also, by chance, coincided historically with the demise of the adjustable peg system (the UK dropping out of both when it

floated in June 1972). Other European Monetary Union members either withdrew permanently or moved in and out of the system, and by the mid-1970s it was regarded as terminated in practice even if not in principle.

The idea of monetary union was resurrected at the Bremen Summit in July 1978, which resulted in the setting up of the EMS in March 1979. The idea behind the EMS, apart from the longer-term objective of EMU within the Community, was first to promote economic convergence in the Community by inducing member governments to adopt the sort of policies being implemented by its most successful member, West Germany, and in particular to bring inflation down to the West German level, and second to create a 'zone of monetary stability' which would facilitate trade between members while providing insulation against the erratic behaviour of the dollar.

7.4.1 The European Currency Unit

The major innovation of the EMS was the introduction in 1979 of a new **European currency**, the European Currency Unit (ECU). This is a weighted average of the EMS currencies (and therefore has to be recalculated when new members join), where the weights are calculated according to the relative importance of the individual currencies in terms of key indicators such as national output and the volume of trade with other members. The contribution of different currencies to the ECU is shown in **Table 7.4**. It should be noted that there are normally eleven contributing currencies as Belgium and Luxembourg are treated as a single entity. As can be seen, the DM dominates the ECU, with the franc also a significant contributor, whereas the Portuguese, Greek and Irish currencies are insignificant. The 'official' ECU performs the function of unit of account to the ERM described below, and also provides a currency which can circulate between central banks throughout the EU. In recent years, a separate private market for securities denominated in ECU has come into being but, as noted

Table 7.4   *The Composition of an ECU*

	Amount of each currency in basket[1]	Weight % of currency in basket[2]
Deutsche Mark	0.6242	30.1
Sterling	0.08784	13.0
French franc	1.332	19.0
Italian lira	151.8	10.15
Dutch guilder	0.2198	9.4
Belgian/Luxembourg franc	3.431	7.9
Danish krone	0.1976	2.45
Irish punt	0.008552	1.1
Greek drachma	1.440	0.8
Spanish peseta	6.885	5.3
Portuguese escudo	1.393	0.8

Notes:
[1] Fixed for a five year period on 20 September 1989.
[2] The currency amounts in the ECU must be reviewed every five years, or on request if the weight of any currency has changed more than 25% since the last revision. Weights change with exchange rate movements of component currencies.

previously, this has yet to form more than a marginal part of the total Eurocurrency markets.

The most recent five-yearly recomposition of the ECU took place in September 1989. The European Commission decided in June 1989 that the currencies of members admitted since 1984, namely Spain and Portugal, should be included in the constitution of the ECU; they also discussed the weight which was to be assigned to them and from which other currencies to transfer it. Clearly, this was as much a matter of political infighting as straightforward assessment of relative economic strength. The 1984 recomposition gave rather too much weight to the DM and guilder, and rather too little to the lira, in relation to their relative economic strength at the time, and the weight of the DM should in principle have been reduced to roughly 24 per cent in order to make way for the new currencies and also to adjust for slow growth in the West German economy. This proved objectionable to the West Germans, so the adjustment was in practice rather more modest. It is also the case that since bonds issued in each ECU contributor's own

currency yield different interest rates, altering the balance of the ECU necessarily also affects the yield of bonds denominated in ECU. Considerable instability in the ECU bond market will therefore result from a major restructuring of the ECU, and this is always likely to operate to keep any restructuring within modest bounds.

7.4.2 The Exchange Rate Mechanism

The second element of the EMS is the **exchange rate mechanism** (ERM). Sterling joined the ERM on **8 October 1990** and departed from it on **16 September 1992**. Members of the EMS can contribute to the ECU without being members of the ERM, as is the case for the UK, Italy, Portugal and Greece. The ERM is a dual mechanism similar to, but more complex than, the old-style adjustable peg. In the first place, the member countries are slotted into a **parity grid** which summarises the bilateral central and intervention rates. Each currency was originally permitted to move bilaterally against any other currency in the grid by up to 2.25 per cent in either direction (the narrow band), although certain currencies could be given a dispensation to widen this movement to 6 per cent in either direction (the wide band). Currently, all ERM currencies are permitted a 15 per cent movement in either direction with the exception of the DM/Guilder link (see **p. 257**). It is important to note, however, that a currency must stay within its permitted band against **all other currencies simultaneously**. In other words, the strongest currency can never be more than 15 per cent above the weakest currency. The **effective limits** in relation to all other currencies are accordingly less than 15 per cent.

When any two currencies reach their compulsory intervention rates against each other the two central banks concerned are obliged to meet all bids/offers made to them at the relevant limit rate. In principle, currencies should not reach their effective limits because of the existence of the **divergence indicators**. Whenever a currency 'diverges' by more than 75 per cent from its central rate against the ECU (the divergence threshold) it is supposed to act as an early warning device which sets in motion a change in the way in which the country in question is conducting its economic policy. Where the divergence is below the central rate a suitable response might be a tightening of interest rates, and where it is above the central rate it might be a relaxation of fiscal policy. It should be noted that the permitted divergences are all different. This is because, when a currency's central rate moves, it also alters the value of the ECU.

If the early warning system is effective it should prevent the currency running up against its upper or lower limit on the parity grid, although the speed of response to signs of excessive divergence has in practice been too slow to achieve much in this respect. Hence there have been a number of occasions when currencies have run up against the limits of the parity grid without either adjustment of domestic policies or intervention by central banks proving sufficient to prevent these limits being breached. As a consequence, both devaluations and revaluations have occurred, as set out in **Table 7.5** (which covers the period culminating into September 1992).

Given that remedial action was expected to be taken at two prior stages, a currency realignment was intended to be a last-resort operation, and a total of 11 realignments over as many years may, therefore, appear superficially to represent a rather excessive use of this ultimate remedy. However, as **Table 7.5** shows clearly, prior to 1992 realignments mostly took place in the early days of the EMS when it was moving towards a longer-term equilibrium, and the system was much more settled (perhaps excessively so) between 1983 and 1992. As explained above, it was a characteristic of the adjustable peg that currencies were almost always devalued rather than revalued, whereas there were more revaluations than devaluations under the EMS between 1979 and 1992. This reflected, in particular, a general tendency for the DM to rise, mirrored by the guilder, and for the French franc and the lira to decline.

It has nevertheless been argued that the weaker members of the ERM have borne most of the burden of adjustment because bilateral parties with the DM rather than the ECU have been crucial, and in order to dampen pressure for realignment weaker currency countries have had to adjust their interest rates relative to the German rate.

7.4.3 European Monetary Co-operation Fund

The other major component of the EMS is the EMCF, the purpose of which is to provide funds to assist with the stabilisation of exchange rates. At the inception of the EMS, members were required to deposit 20 per cent of their gold and dollar reserves with the EMCF (which the UK does also), in return for which they received a credit in ECUs which they could then use to settle indebtness with other members or for intervention purposes. It was originally anticipated that this would evolve into a fully-fledged European Monetary Fund as a major step on the path to monetary union, but this never developed as intended. The EMCF uses funds deposited with it to offer a range of credit facilities, responding to requests by individual countries rather than to policy adjustments jointly agreed by all members. Virtually unlimited funds are available on a very-short-term basis. The very-short-term financing (VSTF) facility has been available since the advent of the Basel–Nybord Accord in November 1987. However, only modest amounts, measured in ECUs, can be provided on either a short-term (up to nine months) or medium-term (2–4 years) basis. In the case of the UK these latter credit facilites are virtually an irrelevance, in the first place because the UK has not borrowed from an international institution since 1977, and in the second place because it already has much larger credit facilities lying untouched at the IMF.

7.4.4 The EMS in Operation

It is possible to interpret the pattern shown in **Table 7.5** as indicating that in the early stages of the EMS there was a hard currency option offered

Table 7.5　*Central Parity Realignments[1] within the EMS, 1979–90 (%)*

	September 1979	November 1979	March 1981	October 1981	February 1982	June 1982	March 1983	July 1985	April 1986	August 1986	January 1987	January 1990
Deutsche Mark	+2.0			+5.5		+4.25	+5.5	+2.0	+3.0		+3.0	
French franc				−3.0		−5.75	−2.5	+2.0	−3.0			
Guilder				+5.5		+4.25	+3.5	+2.0	+3.0		+3.0	
Lira			−6.0	−3.0		−2.75	−2.5	−6.0				−3.7[2]
Belgian/ Lux. franc					−8.5		+1.5	+2.0	+1.0		+2.0	
Krone		−5.0			−3.0		+2.5	+2.0	+1.0			
Irish £							−3.5	+2.0		−8.0		

Notes:
[1] + indicates a revaluation, − indicates a devaluation.
[2] When Italy moved from the wide band to the narrow band in January 1990, it moved the central parity down towards the existing lower limit, thereby subtracting 3.75% (6%−2.25%) from its value. Technically, this does not count as a realignment.
Source: European Commission.

by the West German Bundesbank, and a soft currency option offered by the Banque de France (Weber, 1991). The guilder stayed with the DM, whereas the other currencies first devalued against the DM and then interspersed devaluations with periods of stability from 1983 onwards (except the lira, which fell continuously relative to the DM until 1990). What this suggests is that the latter countries, by effectively adopting an adjustable peg against the DM, chose to forgo the tough anti-inflationary stance of West Germany in favour of the less rigorous approach espoused by France. For this reason, although there was a tendency for inflation to fall in all EMS countries during the early 1980s, convergence on the German rate was quite slow and unsteady until 1985.

It is interesting to compare the abrupt and rapid fall in inflation in the UK and USA after 1980 with the much slower fall in other EMS countries. However, after 1985 the hard currency option offered by the Bundesbank became the dominant influence, and disinflation in the EMS continued with noticeable convergence upon the German inflation rate. This was by no means a costless experience for all participants. In France, for example, unemployment remained at a very high level throughout the 1980s whereas, as shown in Chapter 8, it fell steadily in the UK from 1986 to 1990. Indeed, it should be clearly understood that if an EMS participant has an above-average inflation rate and is thereby becoming uncompetitive, the burden of adjustment must fall upon real wages and employment precisely because it cannot be borne by the exchange rate.

The general tendency for inflation rates among ERM countries to converge was constantly reiterated as a major potential benefit of UK membership of the ERM once inflation in the UK began to rise again in the late 1980s. Nevertheless, it has never been proved satisfactorily whether this convergence was specific to ERM **arrangements** or whether it was a general feature of the **period** during which both ERM and non-ERM countries such as the UK and USA committed themselves in their macroeconomic strategies to conquering inflation (see Haldane, 1991, and Weber, 1991). It is also notable that the anti-inflationary anchor provided by Germany has slipped in recent years,

especially in the period since July 1990 when monetary union between East and West Germany took place. Indeed, it would appear that the inflation rate in Germany rose above that in France in June 1991, and that it is currently higher than in several other member states including the UK.

As noted in Haldane (1991) and Artis (1991), there is evidence to support the argument that the ERM helped to stabilise both nominal and real intra-ERM bilateral exchange rates, but it had much less effect upon the stability of members' global EERs. The recent sharp fluctuations of the dollar is an obvious case in point since the dollar has not moved consistently against all ERM currencies.

A related issue is whether lower intra-ERM exchange rate volatility was achieved at the cost of greater short-term interest rate variability. It would appear to be the case (Weber, 1991, p. 82) that, during the early EMS period (1979–83), highly volatile movements at relatively high levels of interest rates corresponded to speculative attacks upon the currencies which were devalued. Disinflation, capital controls and policy adjustments in the following period (1983–87) reduced this volatility markedly, while also exerting downwards pressure on interest rates generally. The period from 1987 to 1991 saw rates move or less in line, but mostly in an upwards direction. Here again, the influence of Germany appeared to be crucial.

The decision to remove all capital controls is often held to have heralded the coming of the 'new EMS' (Haldane, 1991). Because speculative capital flows had been such a destabilising force under the adjustable peg, steps were taken under the Basel–Nyborg Agreement in September 1987 to offset these through, for example, the introduction of the VSTF facility. Furthermore, realignments of ERM currencies were put into effective abeyance as the message was sent out to the financial markets that the ERM countries would act in concert to maintain exchange rate stability and to base their macroeconomic policy upon that in Germany.

So successful was this policy that the paradox of **excess credibility** became apparent. High inflation countries such as Spain and Italy, needed to maintain high interest rates to keep inflation under control. As noted previously, inflows of hot money, attracted by these interest rates, would normally be discouraged by the exchange rate risk involved (see **p. 219**), but this risk was no longer serious for ERM currencies, especially those in the narrow band. Hence, hot money flooded into Spain and Italy, driving the lira and peseta perversely to the top of the grid.

☐ 7.4.5 Sterling and the ERM

In the course of the first edition we discussed at length whether the UK should join the ERM. That discussion could be said to have once again become relevant in that the UK is currently outside the ERM, but the circumstances surrounding the question of re-entry warrant a different approach in the discussion which follows. However, one issue which will inevitably resurface concerns the appropriate entry value for the pound.

There was considerable controversy in 1988 concerning whether the pound was overvalued at entry relative to the DM. It is necessary to adjust for inflation when seeking to address such a question, which can be done using different deflators. If unit labour costs are used as the

deflator then on that basis it would appear that the rate at entry was sustainable, as indeed it would have been had it been either slightly higher or slightly lower. However, it was subsequently counter-argued that the EER should be used rather than the DM, and that it should be deflated by export unit values. On that basis the real EER was well above its long-term average on entry, and this allegedly speeded up the descent into recession. We can expect to see this debate resurface at such time as re-entry is contemplated no matter what central rate is chosen.

It is helpful at this stage to set out the developing situation in graphical form. **Figure 7.5** illustrates the nominal relationship between the DM and sterling over the 10–year period prior to ERM entry. As can be seen, the period 1987–90 (when sterling was effectively shadowing the DM) was far less volatile than the preceding period, although there was a tendency for the rate to stay above DM3 to the pound until the latter half of 1989.

The technical arguments about the 'correct' rate of entry, which in any event fell somewhat short of proof, played little part in influencing opinion outside the Treasury. The central parity chosen, namely DM2.95 to the pound, did not appear to be particularly high taking a superficial longer-term perspective as in **Figure 7.5**. Never-

Figure 7.5 *DM per £, 1980–90*

Source: CSO.

theless, the rate had been somewhat lower during the first half of 1990, and there were many who felt that the UK should have entered at a lower rate simply in order to give industry a competitive advantage. The period commencing with the Autumn of 1990 is covered in **Figure 7.6**. An added feature of **Figure 7.6** is the sequential reduction in the banks' base rate which occurred post-ERM entry. The pattern is significant because, as can be seen, the sharp rise in the £/DM rate at the time of entry drove sterling to the upper limit of its parity grid and thus permitted base rates to be cut by 1 per cent without seriously undermining its value. Nevertheless, sterling rapidly turned down, and remained below its central rate against the DM until April 1991. On 1 February 1991 sterling became the weakest currency in the ERM. The authorities understandably felt unable to make any further dramatic cuts in interest rates, but rather chose to engage in a succession of half-point reductions as sterling rose steadily from mid-February to May. Given the strength of the recession this may be viewed as ultra-cautious, especially as, in practice, sterling was not adversely affected by each sequential reduction. In order to understand what happened after the end of 1991, it is first necessary to discuss EMU and European Political Union (EPU).

▌ 7.5 Economic and Monetary Union (EMU) and European Political Union (EPU)

▢ 7.5.1 Economic and Monetary Union

The EMS is seen in many quarters as simply a necessary step on the road to a 'United States of Europe', incoporating a single European currency in an EMU structure. The SEA refers to EMU as '**cooperation** in economic and monetary policy' and talks about 'EMU's progressive realisation'. These are sentiments with which even Mrs Thatcher was happy to comply.

EMU involves two rather different concepts. **Economic** union is essentially concerned with the SEM: that is, a common market with an element of economic policy coordination between member states. **Monetary** union is essen-

Figure 7.6   *DM per £, 1990–91*

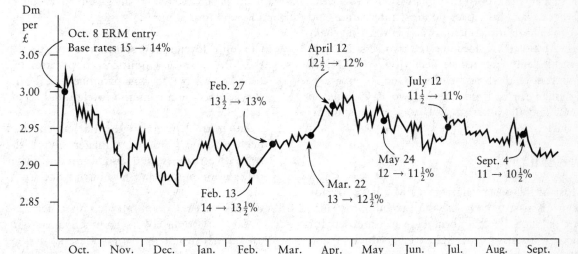

Source: Daily rates posted in *The Times*.

tially concerned with a single currency area with a common monetary policy.

The **Delors Committee** was set up in 1985 to recommend how best to proceed towards eventual EMU. It proposed a three-stage process leading to irreversible fixity of EU currencies and at some point a single currency, possibly the ECU, to replace national currencies. At the Madrid Summit in June 1989 an attempt was made to set a rigid timetable for the full implementation of EMU. However, Mrs Thatcher managed to delay matters, which led in part to her loss of office and replacement by Mr Major, who espoused a more pro-European stance.

7.5.2 The Maastricht Inter-governmental Conferences (IGCs)

In December 1991 there was a double IGC held at Maastricht under the auspices of the Dutch presidency of the EU. These IGCs were instigated at the Rome Summit in December 1990. The French were very keen to introduce EMU in order to offset what they saw as the dominant role of the DM and the Bundesbank. In return, the Germans persuaded the French that this would work better if there was also closer political integration and more democratic control over EU decision making. Afraid that combining the two sets of issues would delay his pet project of EMU, Delors insisted that they be discussed separately, although for convenience the two IGCs, one on EMU and the other on EPU took place simultaneously.

The EMU IGC

Most of the issues relating to EMU have already been discussed above. At the Luxembourg Summit in June 1992, a formula was proposed for further discussion at Maastricht which would allow the UK to postpone a decision on whether to join a single currency. This formula contained three safeguard clauses:

a no country would be able to prevent its partners from establishing a single currency if they had met certain criteria for the convergence of their economic performance;
b no country which had met these criteria could be excluded;
c no country could be compelled to join.

This formula was an advance on previous negotiations in that it met Mr Major's demand that any changes to the Treaty of Rome must not result in the imposition of a single currency without a separate decision by the British Parliament. At the same time, it did not refer explicitly to a two-speed EMU with the UK as a laggard. However, it also prevented the UK from vetoing the entire proceedings.

The Political Union IGC

The previous IGC led to the 1985 SEA. The 1991 IGC was unlikely to be as dramatic, but it was once again to consider the relationship and the balance of power between the Council, the Commission, the Parliament and the Court of Justice. The outcome was to be a Treaty similar to the SEA, containing some amendments to the Treaty of Rome, plus a number of agreements outside the Community Treaties proper. There were four main areas of discussion, all given an airing at the Luxembourg Summit.

1 **Common foreign and security policy** (CFSP): the SEA enshrines political cooperation on foreign policy; it was proposed that this should become a common foreign and security policy.
2 **Democratic legitimacy**: the Parliament had been pushing hard for a bigger say in the legislative process, and also wanted a bigger role in appointing and monitoring the Commission.
3 **Extension of Community competence**: the Treaty of Rome covers commercial activity in a fairly non-specific manner, so it was proposed that it be amended specifically to include new areas such as telecommunications and consumer protection.

4   **Efficiency of Community institutions**: it was proposed that qualified majority voting be extended to matters which at the time required unanimity.

It may be noted that the above discussion omits any reference to **social policy**, which is discussed at the end of Chapter 9.

☐ 7.5.3 Federalism

In a draft preamble to a rewritten Treaty of Rome drawn up by the Luxembourg presidency the phrase 'a union with a federal goal' appeared for the first time as a description of the EU. The UK Foreign Secretary, Douglas Hurd, promptly rejected this on the grounds that while the world 'federal' might mean different things to different nationalities: 'it has come to mean something tight and integrated in English'. Curiously, the term 'federal' means **decentralisation** in some countries even though it means **centralisation** in English. Denmark and Portugal were also less than keen on the term, so it needed to be written out of the new treaty.

Given the unfortunate recent history of such federations as the USSR, Yugoslavia and India, the UK's objection was not altogether surprising. However, the Treaty of Rome already commits the UK to 'an ever closer union', which in theory at least commits the UK to forge more and more links with other EU members, so a federal structure in which the UK's sovereign rights are more or less permanently defined might even seem to be the lesser of two evils.

☐ 7.5.4 The Maastricht Treaty

The EMU sections began by stating that:

The activities of the member states and the Community shall . . . include:

*   the irrevocable fixing of exchange rates leading to the introduction of a single currency, the ECU.

*   the definition and conduct of a single monetary policy and exchange rate policy the primary objective of both of which shall be to maintain price stability.
*   and, without prejudice to this objective, to support the general economic policies in the Community in accordance with the principle of an open market economy with free competition.

It then went on to state that:

A European System of Central Banks (ESCB) and the European Central Bank (ECB) shall be established in accordance with the procedures laid down in this Treaty . . . The basic tasks to be carried out through the ESCB shall be:

*   to define and implement the monetary policy of the Community.
*   to conduct foreign exchange operations consistent with the provisions of Article 109.
*   to hold and manage the official foreign reserves of the member states.

The ESCB shall be composed of the ECB and of the central banks of the member states.

The ECB was to be established before the end of 1992. The ECB, the ESCB and individual central banks were not to seek or take instructions from Community institutions or bodies, or from any government of a member state, thereby guaranteeing independence.

The core of the treaty concerned the path of EMU. This was expressed in terms of 'a high degree of sustainable convergence' which itself required the following criteria to be satisfied:

*   that a currency should have kept within the normal fluctuation margins of the ERM for at least two years without severe tensions.
*   that the consumer price index should not exceed by more than 1.5 per cent that of at most the three best performing member states in terms of price stability over the past year.
*   that the planned or actual government deficit should not exceed 3 per cent of GDP at market prices, unless either the ratio has declined sub-

stantially and continuously and reached a level that comes close to 3 per cent or the excess is only exceptional and temporary.

- that the ratio of general government debt to GDP at market prices should not exceed 60 per cent unless the ratio is sufficiently diminishing and approaching 60 per cent at a satisfactory pace.
- that over the past year the average nominal long-term government bond rate should not exceed by more than 2 per cent that of at most the three best performing member states in terms of price stability.

It should be noted that the first stage of EMU relates to membership of the ERM in the narrow band, so the UK is temporarily not even at stage one. Prior to the second stage of EMU, commencing 1 January 1994, all EU members will be obliged to abolish all restrictions on the movement of capital and set their economic houses in order. Once stage 2 begins a European Monetary Institute (EMI) will be set up to:

- strengthen co-operation betweeen central banks.
- strengthen co-ordination of monetary policies.
- replace the EMCF.
- monitor the functioning of the EMS.
- facilitate the use of the ECU.

By the end of 1996 the EMI will be obliged to specify the regulatory, organisational and logistical framework for the ESCB.

During stage 2 the European Commission will monitor the progress towards convergence of each country and, if the Council of Ministers so recommends on the basis of a qualified majority, on a date no later than 31 December 1996 the European Council (composed of Heads of State or of Government) will be obliged to consider:

a   whether a majority of the member states fulfils the necessary conditions for the adoption of a single currency;
b   whether it is appropriate for the Community to enter the third stage of EMU, and if so, when.

If the date for the commencement of stage 3 cannot be agreed before the end of 1997 then it will automatically begin on 1 January 1999. The Council's decision will be by qualified majority, as will be the decision concerning which countries will be permitted to proceed to full EMU, and which are to be given a derogation. At least once every two years, or at the request of a member state with a derogation, the Commission and the ECB will recommend to the European Council whether other countries have met the convergence criteria.

At the beginning of stage 3, all member states which qualify for full EMU will adopt the conversion rates at which their currencies will be irrevocably fixed in terms of the ECU, which will then become a currency in its own right.

It is worthy of note that it is not essential that a country meets all of the five convergence criteria simultaneously since it would appear to be possible for the European Council to bend the rules somewhat in practice when deciding which countries qualify. This is probably just as well in view of the fact that only Luxembourg currently meet all five criteria, as shown in **Table 7.6**, although there is some doubt over the inflation criterion even in this case.

It is a touch ironic that Germany is not currently ready for full EMU. It is frankly doubtful

Table 7.6   *EMU Convergence Criteria, 1993*[1]

	Exchange rate[2]	Price index	Budget	Public debt	Bond rate	Score
L	Yes	Yes	Yes	Yes	Yes	5
F	Yes	Yes	No	Yes	Yes	4
DK	Yes	Yes	No	No	Yes	3
UK	No	Yes	No	Yes	Yes	3
D+	Yes	No	No	Yes	Yes	3
B	Yes	Yes	No	No	Yes	3
NL	Yes	Yes	No	No	Yes	3
IRL	No	Yes	No	No	No	1
S	No	No	No	Yes	No	1
IT	No	No	No	No	No	0
GR	No	No	No	No	No	0
P	No	No	No	No	No	0

Notes:
[1] Author's estimate as of 1 September 1993.
[2] The widening of the 'narrow' band to ±15% casts some doubt upon the interpretation of this criterion.

whether Italy, Greece or Portugal ever will be. As for the UK, it insisted on an 'opt-out clause' to the effect that: 'The UK shall not be obliged or committed to move to the third stage of economic and monetary union without a separate decision to do so by its government and Parliament.'

If the UK does opt out then it will not count when calculating the majority needed to proceed to full EMU.

The EPU sections began by stating that: 'By this Treaty, the High Contracting Parties establish among themselves a European Union . . . This Treaty marks a new stage in the process creating an ever closer Union among the peoples of Europe, where decisions are taken as closely as possible to the citizens.'

The preamble then goes on to refer to the issue of **subsidiarity** which is defined for the first time in article 3b as follows:

> the Community shall take action . . . only if and insofar as the objectives of the proposed action cannot be sufficiently achieved by the member states and can therefore, by reason of the scale or effects of the proposed action, be better achieved by the Community . . . Any action by the Community shall not go beyond what is necessary to achieve the objectives of this treaty.

The concept of subsidiarity is causing considerable difficulties of interpretation. It may be asked, first, whether it is more **effective** to take a decision at the centre, and second whether it is **necessary** for that decision to be taken centrally. These are independent issues insofar as it is possible to argue that whereas a decision can be taken more effectively at the centre, it is unnecessary to do so because it can be taken perfectly satisfactorily at a national level. The UK's preference has always been to interpret subsidiarity such as to minimise the powers of the Commission. Initially, this approach was poorly supported but, in recent months, as public opinion has swung against ratification, the Commission has become a convert to the virtues of national decision making, (at least for the time being).

The new treaty nevertheless both amends and extends the list of activities as set out in the Treaty of Rome and the SEA which fall within the competence of the Commission. This encompasses:

- the strengthening of economic and social cohesion.
- measures concerning the entry and movement of persons in the internal market.
- a policy in the sphere of the environment.
- the promotion of research and technological development.
- measures in the spheres of energy, consumer protection, civil protection and tourism.
- contribution to the attainment of a high level of health protection.
- contribution to education and training of high quality, and to the flowering of the cultures of the member states.

As noted above, cohesion essentially means a transfer of resources from North to South, which will be costly for the UK as a net contributor to the Community Budget. It is also worth observing that this extension of powers will make it harder for aspiring members to reach EU standards unless, like Austria, they already meet most of them.

Readers will, perhaps, be pleased to learn that they have become 'citizens of the Union', a title awarded in the treaty to all EU nationals who 'shall have the right to move and reside freely within the territory of the Member States'.

The treaty enhances the powers of the European Parliament. Whereas, as shown in **Figure 7.1**, the Parliament currently needs the Commission's backing to get its amendments through the Council, it will now have the right, as from 1 January 1995, to negotiate directly with the relevant ministers the changes that it wants to make, and to reject any proposed legislation that does not contain them. This was originally to be called the 'co-decision' process, but this was vetoed by the UK on the grounds that it smacked of loss of sovereignty, and it will instead be known as 'the procedure laid down in Article 189b'! It covers laws on the internal market; consumer protection; the free circulation of labour; the right of individuals and companies to establish themselves in other member states; the treatment of foreigners;

vocational training; public health; and trans-European infrastructure.

In respect of foreign policy the Parliament will also have to give its assent to such matters as the objectives of the structural Funds and the rights of citizenship created by the treaty.

☐ 7.5.5 *Events Post-Maastricht*

The period since the Maastricht IGCs has been so volatile that it is helpful to begin by providing a chronology of major events.

1992

5 Jan.	Norman Lamont, the then Chancellor of the Exchequer states: **Realignment is another word for devaluation. We are not going to devalue the pound.**
7 Feb.	Treaty is signed.
6 April	Portuguese escudo joins ERM in wide band.
3 June	Danish referendum on treaty. Treaty is rejected 50.7% to 49.3%. France announces it will also hold a referendum on 20 September.
11 June	UK Government postpones parliamentary debate on treaty until the Autumn.
18 June	Irish referendum on treaty. Vote is two-to-one in favour.
10 July	Lamont states: **Leave the ERM, cut interest rates and let the pound find its own value . . . it's the cut-and-run option. The credibility of our anti-inflationary strategy would be in tatters. And quite soon interest rates would have to go back up again.**
20 Aug.	Sterling breaches ERM divergence indicator for first time since entry to ERM.
1 Sept.	Sterling rises above $2, but is at lowest level against the DM since May 1990.
3 Sept.	UK Government arranges ECU 10 billion borrowing facility to support sterling, of which ECU 5 billion to be converted initially into DM and then sold for sterling.

	Lamont states: **Devaluation . . . would lead to a collapse in market confidence and a damaging rise in interest rates. Withdrawal from the ERM . . . would see a huge fall in the pound and an explosion in inflation.**
8 Sept.	Finland abandons ECU–markka peg.
10 Sept.	Major states: **[ERM] membership was no soft option. The soft option, the devaluer's option, the inflationary option would be a betrayal of our future.**
12 Sept.	Decision taken to devalue the lira by 7% against all other ERM currencies.
16 Sept.	Lamont states: **[Britain] will take whatever measures are necessary to maintain sterling's ERM parity.** MLR raised from 10% to 12%. MLR later raised to 15%. Lamont states: **Britain's best interests would be best secured by suspending our membership of the ERM.** Sterling suspended from ERM. MLR reduced to 12%.
17 Sept.	Lira suspended from ERM. Peseta devalued by 5%. MLR reduced to 10%. Sterling falls to DM2.64. Ireland reinforces exchange controls.
18 Sept.	Lamont states: **We are floating and we will set monetary policy in this country . . . It will be a British economic policy and a British monetary policy.**
20 Sept.	French referendum vote 51.05% in favour of treaty.
22 Sept.	MLR reduced to 9%, bringing rate below that in Germany for first time in 11 years.
23 Sept.	Spain reimposes exchange controls.
30 Sept.	Kohl rejects the idea of 'two-speed' Europe. The Bundesbank reveals that it had spent DM44 billion (£17.3 billion) defending the £ and lira.
5 Oct.	Spain partially lifts exchange controls. Lira depreciates by 5%.
6 Oct.	Lira depreciates by 6% then appreciates by 8%. Sterling rises from DM2.37 to DM2.45.

2 Nov.	Sterling falls to $1.53 and the EER to 77.7.
5 Nov.	Major reveals that Parliament will not complete ratification of treaty until after Danes hold a second referendum. Denmark pencils in May 1993 and demands opt outs to the effect that it should be free not to participate in European defence policy; not to implement stage 3; not to implement cooperation on police and legal matters on a supranational basis; and not to be committed to introduce union citizenship.
19 Nov.	Sweden abandons ECU–krona peg.
22 Nov.	Peseta devalued by 6% but Spain lifts controls of 23 Sept.
	Portugal devalues escudo by 6%.
11 Dec.	Norway abandons ECU–krone peg.
16 Dec.	Portugal lifts exchange controls.

1993

1 Jan.	Ireland lifts exchange controls.
30 Jan.	Ireland devalues pound by 10%.
12 Feb.	EER falls to 75.7.
24 Feb.	Sterling falls to DM2.31
13 May	Spain devalues peseta by 8%.
	Portugal devalues escudo by 6.5%.
18 May	Second Danish referendum produces 56.8% yes vote.
19 May	Police open fire on Danish demonstrators against treaty.
1 June	European Commission says UK right to withdraw from ERM.
22 July	Government suffers defeat in vote on Protocol on Social Policy (see below) when 23 backbenchers rebel.
23 July	Government tables vote of confidence to retain the Protocol, and has a majority of 40 in favour of ratification of the treaty as negotiated.
	High Court rejects Lord Rees-Mogg's application for judicial review of the treaty, and he decides not to appeal.
29 July	Bundesbank leaves discount rate unchanged
	Massive intervention is needed to keep

	the franc and other ERM currencies within their trading limits.
1 Aug.	Announcement that ERM currencies to trade within $+/-$ 15% of central rates (although the guilder/DM link stays unchanged).
	It is estimated that the Bank of France liquidated its entire foreign currency reserve supporting the franc.
2 Aug.	German Finance Minister insists that ECB must be located in Frankfurt if EMU is to go ahead (that is, on German terms or not at all).
	The UK officially ratifies the treaty.
12 Oct.	German Constitutional Court rules in favour of treaty.
8 Nov	European Union offically comes into being.

☐ 7.5.6 *Black or White?*

It is still too early, at the time of writing, to be certain of the consequences of the events of September 1992 since, although output has subsequently risen and inflation has fallen, the uncertainty over the length of time lags leaves open the possibility that these effects can be at least partly ascribed to earlier policy decisions. Certainly, that is the view taken by Norman Lamont who lost his job as Chancellor in the fallout from the events of 16 September, a date most frequently referred to as 'Black' Wednesday, but known in some circles as 'White' Wednesday.

The distinction is straightforward. Those who believe that participation in the ERM, and eventually in stage 3 of EMU, is essential for the long-term health of the economy regard the events of 16 September as a disaster. The government was initially to be counted among these. However, those who believe that the ERM was a straitjacket resulting in the imposition of inappropriate Germanic policies upon the UK are happy to see the exchange rate trading at well below DM2.95, and hope that the UK is now entering a period of export-led growth. The government is currently to be numbered among these, a U-turn of truly noble proportions.

Indeed, Black or White, Wednesday 16 September tells us a great deal about the ineptness of those who govern us, although constraints on space prevent too deep an examination of this issue! Suffice it to say that the government appears to believe that they made no errors of judgement; and not just the government, since the then governor of the Bank of England, Robin Leigh-Pemberton, stated that, 'Having joined [the ERM], we were right to endeavour to stick with it; and, in the circumstances which evolved, we were also right to withdraw.'

True or false? It is reasonably clear that the ERM collapsed under a combination of pressures. Arguably the most important was the decision at the time of German (re)unification to exchange one Ostmark for one DM and to promise West German wage levels to much less productive East German workers, combined with a promise not to raise West German taxes. The response of the Bundesbank to the inflationary pressure this stoked up was to raise interest rates at precisely the point in time when the rest of the EU, and especially the UK, needed to lower theirs.

Second, although the Basel–Nyborg agreement specified to the contrary, the French in particular treated stage 1 as though it required fixity of exchange rates, and they were unwilling to countenance any realignments prior to the French referendum which had itself created tensions within the ERM, given the possibility of a 'no' vote.

However, as sterling fell to its floor against the DM the UK government was unwilling, and felt unable for political reasons for fear of providing ammunition to Euro-sceptics, to raise interest rates in order to bolster the pound. Slightly oddly, perhaps, the Bank of England took the view that this failure to act in good time was beneficial, since speculators could not expect to make money selling a currency which was already at its floor value, given the oft-repeated determination of the UK Government to defend sterling at all costs.

Unfortunately, the markets realised that it would be the Bundesbank rather than the Bank of England that would have to buy sterling in exchange for DM, and that it would be dismayed by the fact that this would pump up the German money supply as the DMS were put into circulation. Furthermore, the constant bickering between finance ministers and central bankers at meetings earlier in 1992 had created the impression that, for example, the Bundesbank would not feel all that enthusiastic about requests to defend sterling. In this respect much was made of comments by Helmut Schlesinger, in the course of an interview on 15 September, to the effect that he believed sterling to be vulnerable. It must also be borne in mind that the devaluation of the lira during the previous weekend, while compatible with Basel–Nyborg, was a further indication to the markets that a concerted attack upon a currency rendered vulnerable as a result of an unremedied lack of competitiveness in the relevant economy would drive it below its floor in the ERM.

Finally, it should be remembered that virtually all exchange controls within the EU had been lifted by September 1992. The stability of the ERM in previous years had tended to obscure the fact that this had removed a potential final line of defence in the face of a concerted attack upon a currency.

☐ 7.5.7 Consequences

There can be no doubt that in the Autumn of 1992 something had to give. The US economy, despite very low interest rates, was not growing at all strongly. Meanwhile, most of the EU was subsiding rapidly into recession. With unemployment high and growing, a balance of trade deficit in a recession and a rapidly expanding fiscal deficit, the UK desperately needed to find a way out of its difficulties; and it was plain that its trading partners were not going to put themselves out to be of assistance.

There is little point in agonising over precisely how much help the Germans, for example, could or should have provided. At the end of the day, the UK Government made its own decision about the entry rate when joining the ERM, despite German disapproval, and its own incompetence contributed to the scale of the recession post-1989.

Insofar as the UK's suspension of ERM membership appeared to provide the logical escape hatch to possible prosperity, it is possible to argue that the extent of Euro-scepticism was a contributory factor since the markets were aware that failure to remain in the ERM would allow the UK to opt out of stages 2 and 3 by the back door.

The government has reiterated its intention to stay out of the ERM until the EU as a whole has regained its stability. It accordingly looks increasingly likely that the UK will not be eligible to participate in stage 2 at the appointed time. It is possible that the EMS will anyway by then be in a state of total disarray (there are those who claim it is dead already, although that is technically untrue). In any event, it is instructive to remember that from 1979 to 1987 the franc fell by 31 per cent against the DM whereas the pound, outside the ERM, fell only by 20 per cent. Between 1987 and 1990 the pound rose against both the DM and franc, and only weakened perceptibly after it joined the ERM. As recent experience has shown, the pound may regain a good deal of the ground lost since its ERM suspension irrespective of any official commitment to rejoin, and there are those who argue strongly (see, for example, Minford, 1992) that the optimum solution is to move towards an EU-wide float, combined with coordination of monetary policies.

In conclusion, although it is difficult to pin down the precise commencement of economic recovery, it is evident that life post-ERM is generally quite pleasant and disaster-free. The exchange rate has recovered a significant part of the initial losses, as shown in **Figure 7.7**, which also lists base rate changes; it is even alleged that it is becoming undesirably strong. Certainly, it is interesting that the Bank of France replenished its reserves with sterling on the grounds that it was an appreciating currency. More importantly, this has helped to offset some of the inflationary pressure which was the inevitable consequence of rising import prices, and as we noted in the previous discussion on inflation, inflation has been very subdued in the past year.

The oft-expressed fear that interest rates would have to rise on account of increased uncertainty in a post-ERM world has been demonstrated to be untrue (although real rates remain high), just as it has become clear that floating has been beneficial for growth. On balance, therefore, there seem to be good reasons for preferring the 'White' to the 'Black' version of Wednesday 16 September 1992.

☐ 7.5.8 The Ratification Muddle

The document which had to be ratified in the UK was the **European Communities (Amendment) Bill**. This amended the **European Communities Act 1972**, effectively by adding to it the relevant parts of the Maastricht Treaty. It also required, as

Figure 7.7 *Sterling against the DM (DM per £)*

Source: Daily rates posted in *The Times*.

noted previously, that stage 3 of EMU could not be embarked upon without passing an Act through Parliament to that effect.

The Bill contained a mere three clauses, of which one gave the title of the Bill. Clause 1 incorporated the Protocols (appendixes), including the Protocol on Social Policy which itself incorporated the Agreement on Social Policy (Social Chapter).

The UK, having opted out, was specifically exempted from the terms of the Protocol on Social Policy. However, in February 1993, Amendment 27 to the Bill (there were 450 altogether) was proposed to the effect that the words 'with the exception of the Protocol on Social Policy' be added to the Bill. The rationale for this Amendment (which was odd in that it was proposed by anti-treaty groups, even though it sought to exclude rather than include the Protocol) was that the removal of the Protocol would simultaneously remove the opt-out clause, thereby theoretically forcing the UK to renegotiate the treaty.

Just exactly what all this **really** meant became irrelevant when early in March, the deputy speaker ruled the Amendment out of order. However, the government was defeated for the first time in three years only a few days later on a Labour amendment which forced the Bill to go to the 'report stage', thereby delaying ratification. Subsequently, Amendment 75 was tabled which would have the effect of preventing powers being transferred to European institutions under the legislation until the Commons had decided whether the Protocol on Social Policy should apply to the UK. The purpose here was to try to force the government at the last minute (post-royal assent) to choose between a treaty containing the Social Chapter and no treaty at all, although this did not appeal to the Tory rebels who had absolutely no desire to force the former choice on the government.

Early in May, faced with another likely defeat in the Commons, the government was forced to accept Amendment 2, which called for the Protocol on Social Policy (opt-out included) to be deleted from the version of the treaty to be enshrined in UK law. This did not, however,

remove the opt-out from the version of the treaty to be ratified by the UK.

On 22 July, as noted above, the government was defeated in a vote on Amendment 75, and the following day invoked a vote of confidence in respect of the treaty, including the opt-out, which it duly won. On 2 August the ratification process was completed ahead of schedule.

☐ 7.5.9 Meanwhile in Germany

The UK did not have a monopoly on constitutional conundrums. By May 1993 the German constitutional court in Karlsruhe was considering 18 challenges to the treaty. The key issue to be addressed was whether the treaty would affect fundamental constitutional rights safeguarded in Germany's Basic Law insofar as the treaty involved the transfer of sovereignty to the Community in respect of, for example, monetary matters. It was also alleged that the Community was not democratically controlled because the European Parliament lacked adequate powers, and hence that controls exercised in Germany would not be properly exercised in the Community. While the court unltimately upheld the validity of the treaty, it did so only subject to a long list of reservations whic may yet cause problems on the route to full EMU (see *The Economist*, 16 October 1993).

■ 7.6 The Demise of Free Trade?

Government policies in all the OECD countries have been moving in a market-oriented direction in recent years. There is, however, one rather notable exception to this general trend, namely international trade. The trade regimes of most OECD countries are currently less liberal than they were 10 years ago. In a survey carried out by the *Harvard Business Review*, some 11 700 managers in 25 countries proved themselves generally to be as two-faced about free trade as politicians (cause and effect?). For example, 83 per cent of British managers supported the idea of free trade along with minimal protection for domestic firms, but 80 per cent went on to support the idea that governments should actively assist domestic firms in international markets (see *The Economist*, 11 May 1991, p. 96). South Koreans, however, were all in favour of protection whereas the Japanese claimed to be much more in favour of free trade than managers in the USA and the EU!

Free trade is easy to justify, even if one's trading partners do not consider it to be to their advantage. Suppose, for example, the Japanese refuse to buy UK products but have themselves developed a life-saving drug. Should the UK refuse to purchase it on a tit-for-tat basis? Clearly, welfare in the UK will be enhanced if the drug is bought **no matter what the Japanese choose to do.** Bilateral free trade is better than unilateral free trade, but unilateral free trade is much better than no trade at all.

Once upon a time there was an enormously strong trading nation called Great Britain which considered that its best interests were served by free trade, and thrived mightily on account of it. But when the Germans and Americans began to take over its markets it began to wonder whether it was such a good idea after all. After the recession of the 1930s, when the collapse of trade was instrumental in prolonging and worsening the recession, another great trading nation, the USA, considered that its best interests were served by free trade. Because of its economic strength it was able to impose its will upon other, less enthusiastic, nations, but all came to appreciate that removal of trade barriers would be in their **mutual** best interests.

Even the oil shocks of the 1970s failed to push the USA off course, but its confidence was steadily being damaged by the rapid progress of Japanese trading. In this respect, democracy can be flawed. Free trade provides benefits to all of society, but these benefits are hard to quantify. If import barriers are erected they bring large benefits to small groups who accordingly lobby endlessly for their introduction. If introduced, they affect individual consumers so little that they rarely complain. The die is accordingly cast in favour of protection, and governments must show determination to set their faces against the lobbying.

Two issues about free trade need to be understood. In the first place, few businessmen and politicians appreciate that the classical case for free trade emphasised the merits of **unilateral** free trade. During the postwar period the USA promoted free trade primarily by promoting the idea of an **exchange of concessions** through the GATT. In the modern world, countries **expect to be compensated** for removing barriers to trade.

Second, it is evident that free trade is not universally the best solution, and even the classical economists admitted as much. For example, the need to protect 'infant industries' is an idea dating back to Adam Smith which is probably familiar to most readers (see Crook, 1990). A brief summary of the pros and cons of protection is set out in the box below. The important point to bear in mind, however, is that while new theories of trade which emphasise imperfect competition and externalities do provide some justification for export subsidies and tariffs, they do so in **only a limited number of cases,** and not as a general rule.

Managed trade should not, therefore, be dismissed out of hand. It must also be borne in mind, however, that if it is to be managed then its management must be in the **interests of society as a whole.** Needless to say, this is not what happens in practice, and it was the usurping of the intellectual defence for managed trade by lobbyists in the USA, as it progressively lost its markets to Japanese and other products, that lies at the root of the current malaise in trade affairs.

Unfortunately, as anyone who has read about the 1930s will know, this is no laughing matter. In most years, recessions excepted, the increase in the volume of merchandise trade provides a major driving force promoting the growth of world output, as shown in **Figure 7.8.** In recent years, the USA and (West) Germany have vied for the title of the world's greatest exporting nation, while Great Britain sits a comfortable fifth in the list and consequently has much to lose through a decline in world trade.

The world is divided up into four main trading groups. In practice the 'rest of world' group is disparate and unwieldy whereas the other three are busy forming strong internal alliances. The

PROS:
1 If cheap foreign imports are destroying domestic industries, they must be kept out to preserve domestic jobs and acceptable levels of domestic wages
2 If goods are being 'dumped' in the domestic market, they must be kept out to preserve output and jobs in what may be efficient domestic businesses
3 If other countries are introducing protectionist devices, retaliation is necessary to level the playing field
4 Protection is needed for 'infant industries' until such time as they are of a sufficient size to compete in international markets
5 Protection is a legitimate device to prevent the sudden collapse of an industry and to enable an orderly transfer to other activities to take place
6 Protection is justified if a country has a permanent balance of trade problem which it has been unable to resolve in more acceptable ways

CONS:
1 Since protection inevitably inspires retaliation, it causes a reduction in the volume of international trade, thereby causing damage to the economies of all nations dependent upon such trade for improvements in economic welfare
2 Because of retaliation, protection is not going to be successful anyway
3 Arguments over protection create political illwill between nations which may have ill effects beyond the trade sector

Figure 7.8 *World merchandise by Volume, Annual Percentage Change*

Source: Financial Times, 29 March 1993.

EU has its 1992 project, and the US Government, having already formed a free trade relationship with Canada, is currently discussing similar links with Mexico (the North American Free Trade Association). Meanwhile Japan, which is managing quite well on its own, is interested in links with other nations on the Pacific rim. Does this mean that, for example, **Fortress Europe** (as the EU is known by its detractors) is already a reality, a possibility in the future or a figment of other nations' imaginations? In the sections that follow we will try to shed some light on this and related matters.

■ 7.7 Protection

□ 7.7.1 Forms of Protection

Protection has become a matter of controversy primarily because of the difficulties which the US Government has had in reducing its enormous current account deficit by more acceptable means. All countries operate some protectionist policies, but it is fair to say that the UK was one of the less protectionist minded of the industrial countries throughout the 1980s. Protection is generally a negative-sum game, in that once the process is set in motion in one country its main trading partners usually respond with offsetting measures of their own, thereby causing all of them to lose out. It is therefore possible that the UK will be drawn into protection if it is instigated elsewhere on a sufficiently large scale.

Until fairly recently the commonest form of protection was the **tariff**, which is a tax imposed on imports either as a lump sum or as a percentage of their value. This drives up domestic prices, which is not particularly desirable, but the government obtains an additional source of revenue to fund its expenditure and the illusion is given that foreign exporters are suffering most because they are virtually forced to pay the tax.

Tariffs have been restricted because major industrial countries have agreed to abide by the GATT rules (see below) which greatly limit their use, but in any event their inflationary consequences are undesirable and can apparently be avoided by resort to other non-tariff barriers. Of these the commonest are **quotas**, which serve to limit the access of overseas producers to the domestic market. The quotas are generally fixed in terms of the **number** or **value** of imports to be permitted. Inflationary consequences might still arise if the importer takes advantage of the artificial shortage of the product to put up its price, in which case it is the private sector, rather than the government, which gets the extra revenue, but the government could obtain extra revenue by auctioning import licences. In recent years many countries have preferred to avoid overt confrontation by 'requesting' foreign governments to limit their exports of particular products. In the case of cars, for example, both the EU and USA have agreed import quotas with Japan during the 1980s.

Underlying such **voluntary export restraints** (VERs) is an unspoken threat of 'official' quotas if compliance if not adhered to. It is alleged that the Japanese impose unofficial quotas by requiring foreign products (such as cars) to meet specifications, for safety or other reasons, which they cannot meet without expensive modifications.

The Japanese counter-argument is, naturally, that products of 'inferior' quality simply do not sell on their domestic market.

Occasionally certain imports and/or exports are embargoed (given a **zero quota**). This is usually to 'punish' a country, such as South Africa, which is pursuing domestic polices unacceptable to the wider political community. The present UK Government has never favoured such methods of dealing with errant regimes but, irrespective of the moral issues it has to be said that embargoes are constantly being broken.

A rather more subtle procedure is to **subsidise exports**. This obviously costs the government a good deal of money, but protects jobs and hence, indirectly, the **tax base of the domestic economy**. An industry which is subsidised almost everywhere is the shipbuilding industry, which has long suffered from chronic world overcapacity. These subsidies are more subtle in the sense that they can be disguised as regional development grants (RDGs) or 'infant industry' support. The UK also operates **export credit guarantees** which insure exports against default by overseas buyers.

Finally, there is the possibility of introducing various forms of **exchange control**. Exchange controls operated in the UK until 1979. Such controls were philosophically incompatible with the free market beliefs of the new Conservative Government, and their abolition was the first major step along the path to widespread deregulation. However, there was also an underlying economic rationale to abolition. At the time, the BoP on current account was about to improve markedly as a result of North Sea oil coming on stream. This was bound to exert strong upward pressure on the exchange rate and, while the government did not wish to intervene to keep the rate down, it was realised that the abolition of exchange controls would result in a huge outflow of capital, mostly for long-term investment, and that this would help to limit the appreciation of sterling. Furthermore, there would be a net inflow of interest and dividends in later years.

Other major countries have followed the UK example, but there is still pressure in certain circles to reinstate exchange controls on the grounds that the capital being exported could be better used within the UK. Such controls could be reimposed in a variety of forms. In the past there have been controls both on capital inflows (for example, by suspending the convertibility of foreign currency into sterling), and upon capital outflows (for example, by routeing requests to obtain foreign currency via the central bank which has the right to refuse authorisation, or by refusing permission for private individuals to export capital other than in small amounts).

It is worth observing, by way of conclusion, that most of the forms of protection discussed above were developed during the era of fixed exchange rates. Obviously, if exports are uncompetitive, the simplest ways to deal with the problem where the exchange rate can float are to allow the currency to depreciate or to devalue. This is much less likely to invite retaliation, although competitive depreciation is by no means unknown, but it has to be said that this policy can help only those industries which were close to being competitive at the higher exchange rate. Where an industry, such as shipbuilding, is regularly being undercut by up to 50 per cent, selective assistance, whatever its merits, is the only solution if it is to survive.

□ 7.7.2 Effects of Protection

In a major review the OECD (1985) concluded that non-inflationary growth was being impeded by protection. The simple Keynesian model indicates that if one country refuses to buy the exports of another country, then the latter will suffer a reduction in NI and hence reduce its own imports. The original country thus protects jobs in its industries previously losing out to import substitution, but suffers job losses in industries dependent upon exporting. One might have thought that this lesson was learned in the 1930s following the US Smoot–Hawley Tariff of 1930, but regrettably this is not the case. In the first place, the jobs saved by protection are more immediate and more visible than the jobs lost as exports subsequently suffer. Second, as noted previously, it is easy to organise a combined lobby of politicians, businessmen and trade unions to support an endangered local industry.

The GATT regulations on trade barriers are based upon 'reciprocity'. **First-difference reciprocity** aims to reduce trade barriers through the requirement that a country provides a tariff reduction **comparable in value** to that introduced by a trading partner. In the USA, however, there has recently been a movement towards the principle of **full reciprocity**. This requires **equal access**, which is measured by the balance of trade overall and/or in specific sectors. A trade deficit is taken to be evidence of unequal access and to justify retaliation. The worst offender is, as usual, claimed to be Japan. It is, perhaps, naive to point out that bilateral trade balances are rarely in equilibrium in the normal course of events, because even if the UK is in overall equilibrium it will almost certainly be in surpus with, for example, the USA while simultaneously in deficit with, for example, Japan. Indeed, the principle of comparative advantage should bring about precisely such an outcome.

■ 7.8 1992 and EU Trade

In principle, all border restrictions on trade between member countries of the EU were discarded at the end of 1992. In principle, goods and services, labour and capital flow freely across national borders. However, this is not exactly the case in practice. There are, **inter alia**, a host of protectionist agreements involving individual EU members and non-EU countries. There is, for example, a quota regulating the importation of Japanese cars into the UK.

From the viewpoint of consumers there is a clear gain where the common external tariff (CET) is lower than that ruling prior to 1992, since prices on the domestic market will be lower. On the other hand, the reverse will be true where the new CET provides a higher degree of protection than before. The issue of subsidies is especially critical in this respect, since countries which have been unhappy with lower trade barriers have tended to respond by introducing a substitute protection in the form of subsidies.

■ 7.9 Subsidies

According to the European Commission the average level of subsidies fell slightly during the 1980s. The EC 10 averaged roughly ECU 89 billion during 1981–86 and the EC 12 roughly ECU 82 billion during 1986–88. Of this sum ECU 11 billion was accounted for by agriculture, ECU 13 billion by coal, ECU 26 billion by railways and the rest by industry.

These figures appear to be very high when compared to OECD data which, while it is consistently defined and illustrates a similar pattern during the 1980s, covers only direct grant aid. If other forms of aid are included the pattern changes considerably for industrial countries. It is very unlikely that, despite years of research, the Commission has managed to unearth the most opaque forms of assistance. Were it to do so, the position of the UK would look even more favourable since its subsidy policy is relatively transparent. During the 1980s the Thatcherite approach was to reduce aid to 'lame ducks' and

to cut back severely on regional policy. Independent estimates by the Kiel Institute and others suggest that 4 per cent of GNP in pre-unification West Germany was devoted to subsidies (financed by commensurately high levels of taxation). The situation is likely to deteriorate rapidly now that the former, hopelessly inefficient, industrial sectors of East Germany have been drawn into the fold, and even Italy will have to look to its laurels as the EU's subsidiser-in-chief, as shown in **Table 7.7** which compares 1986–88 with 1988–90, the latest available period.

Under the circumstances, the key issue is whether or not the EU competition commissioner can stem the tide, based on the premise that an illegal subsidy is one which involves any action whereby the State, as owner, acts differently from a private investor. The awkward problem this raises is that State ownership becomes pointless if the State must run its firms as though they were private. Unlike the UK, France has as yet failed to privatise in a meaningful way, which is why the current spate of investigations involves

Table 7.7   *State Aid to the Manufacturing Sector: Annual Averages, 1988–90 and 1986–88 (in brackets)*

	In per cent of value added		In ECU per person employed		In mio ECU[1]	
	(1986–1988)	*1988–1990*	*(1986–1988)*	*1988–1990*	*(1986–1988)*	*1988–1990*
Belgium	(4.3)	4.1	(1 606)	1 655	(1 175)	1 211
Denmark	(1.9)	2.1	(593)	634	(316)	333
Germany	(2.7)	2.5	(994)	984	(7 869)	7 865
Greece	(24.3)	14.6	(2 983)	1 502	(2 074)	1 072
Spain	(6.8)	3.6	(1 749)	936	(4 491)	2 499
France	(3.8)	3.5	(1 437)	1 380	(6 479)	6 106
Ireland	(6.4)	4.9	(2 114)	1 734	(447)	368
Italy	(6.2)	6.0	(2 139)	2 175	(10 760)	11 027
Luxembourg	(2.3)	2.6	(988)	1 270	(37)	48
Netherlands	(3.1)	3.1	(1 215)	1 327	(1 101)	1 225
Portugal	(2.2)	5.3	(302)	758	(245)	616
United Kingdom	(2.6)	2.0	(770)	582	(4 101)	3 133
EUR 12	(4.0)	3.5	(1 325)	1 203	(38 835)	35 503

Note:
[1] 1986–88 averages in 1989 prices.
Source: Commission of the European Communities (1992a) *Third Survey of State Aids in the European Community in the Manufacturing and Certain Other Sectors* (Brussels: CEC), Table 3.

so many French companies. It is probable that it will be problems with balancing budgets that will stem the subsidy tide rather than any overt desire to bend to the will of the Commission in this respect.

7.10 The General Agreement on Tariffs and Trade (GATT)

The GATT was originally signed in 1947 by 23 countries (currently 111) determined to avoid a repetition of the worst consequences of protection evidenced during the 1930s. Its aims were to reduce existing barriers to free trade (but excluding agriculture and services, which are not covered), to eliminate trade discrimination and to curb the reintroduction of protectionist measures by requiring member countries to consult together prior to such action. A critical principle was the **'most-favoured-nation' clause**, whereby any member country offering a tariff reduction to another country was obliged to offer the same reduction to all other member countries.

It may be argued that the oddest thing about the GATT was the need for anyone to join. Given that members already accepted the principle that more trade was better than less trade, it had to be in their mutual self-interest to lower tariff barriers. The necessity to treat a tariff reduction as a concession requiring reciprocity would seem to be redundant when self-interest dictates that tariff reductions should be pursued anyway, since bilateral tariff reductions should be taking place in the absence of reciprocity conditions. However, as discussed above, the economic virtues of free trade are not always self-evident to interest groups when domestic industries are being 'destroyed' by imports, so governments needed to counteract this by reference to their obligations to maintain GATT rules. In any event, governments have always been afraid of appearing to be weak when allowing competitors free access to their markets in the absence of publicly-stated reciprocity. In this respect the attitude of the present UK Government is interesting since it continues to play the reciprocity game even

though, according to its economic philosophy, reciprocity cannot be a pre-condition for trade.

The GATT therefore exists as a precaution against the facile adoption of the 'imports are bad, exports are good' creed, a creed which is intuitively appealing to the proverbial man-in-the-street. A virtue of the most-favoured-nation clause in this respect is that if a tariff is raised against one competitor it has to be raised against them all, thereby greatly increasing the risk of retaliation (an argument whch the government can fall back on when pressed to protect a specific bilateral trade). This is bolstered by the principle of reciprocity, since it becomes possible to counter the argument that tariff reductions will damage domestic industries with the claim that benefits of equal value will accrue to exporting industries.

7.10.1 The Tokyo Round

The seventh, Tokyo Round began in 1973 (see List of GATT rounds below). New or reinforced agreements called **codes** were established in respect of subsidies and countervailing duties; government procurement; technical standards; import licensing procedures; customs valuation; and anti-dumping.

The code on subsidies and countervailing duties prohibits direct export subsidies other than in agriculture. Given the widespread use of subsidies, a distinction is made between domestic and export subsidies. A domestic subsidy that treats domestic and export sales in a neutral way is normally permissible under GATT rules. However, a tariff designed to offset an export subsidy given to a foreign supplier – known as a **countervailing duty** – is prohibited unless domestic pro-

Geneva	1947
Annecy	1948
Torquay	1950
Geneva	1956
Dillon	1960–61
Kennedy	1964–67
Tokyo	1973–79
Uruguay	1986–9?

ducers can be shown to have suffered (or are expected to suffer) 'material' injury as a consequence. In addition, a country can seek redress against another when the latter's subsidised exports have replaced the former's sales in a third country.

The code on government procurement states that in respect to qualifying non-military purchases, governments and organisations under their control must treat domestic and foreign producers in the same way.

The anti-dumping code sets out rules for anti-dumping investigations, the imposition of anti-dumping duties and the settlement of disputes. A method for assessing the degree of injury sustained is set out. Developing countries are expected to be given preferential treatment by developed countries.

7.10.2 The Uruguay Round, 1986–9?

The oil price shocks and inflationary conditions of the 1970s, followed by the 1980–81 recession, made trading conditions problematic for many countries. Understandably, no country, least of all the USA which had been instrumental in using the GATT as the vehicle for liberalising world trade, wished to flout GATT rules in an open manner. Thus the favoured tactic was to 'bend' the rules in such a way as to offer some degree of protection to domestic industries threatened by imports, particularly those originating from Japan. In place of the **multilateral** agreements previously negotiated in the GATT, the USA and the EU began increasingly to negotiate **bilateral** arrangements, many of which took the form of VERs. By and large the Japanese were happy to go along with this arrangement since it enabled them to concentrate on selling top-of-the-range, high-value-added products which could be sold very profitably in competition with high-priced, uncompetitive domestic products.

Governments also resorted increasingly to **subsidies** which they alleged did not infringe the rules of the GATT, and the tactic grew up during the

1980s of imposing **anti-dumping duties** on manufactured products, especially those originating in Japan and the Far East, on the alleged grounds that they were being sold for less than was being charged on the exporter's home market.

In some ways this behaviour was not altogether unexpected given that tariffs on the importation of manufactured goods had fallen to an average of less than 5 per cent (see **Figure 7.9**), thereby offering inefficient domestic producers very little protection against imports. The proliferation of restraints on trade, which could be said to be compatible with the rules of the GATT only by exercising a good deal of imagination, nevertheless posed a severe threat to its continued role as the instrument for trade liberalisation.

Furthermore, the Japanese and West German onslaught had served in part to reduce the dependence of other countries, and especially of the USA, upon domestically produced manufactured goods. The service sectors which grew up in their place did not fall under the rules of the GATT since they were traditionally regarded as domestic rather than suitable for international trade. However, they were increasingly becoming the driving force underlying economic growth in countries such as the USA, and these countries wished to

Figure 7.9 *Industrialised Countries, Average Tariffs (%)*

Notes:
[1] Forecast.
Source: Centre for International Economics.

exploit their comparative advantage in the service sectors in international trade in return for making further concessions with respect to manufactures.

Other deficiencies in the GATT also became increasingly evident. There was, for example, the issue of the sectors which, for various reasons, had been given special dispensations from the rules of the GATT. Of these the **Multi-Fibre Arrangement** (MFA) covering textiles and clothing was a particular irritant to developing countries whose access to the markets of advanced countries was limited by quotas. More importantly, there was the **agricultural sector** which was not covered at all by the rules of the GATT. Up until the end of the 1970s this had posed few problems since the EU had been a net importer of agricultural porducts, thereby allowing the USA to export its surpluses to everyone's mutual advantage. However, once the EU became a major net exporter in its own right, the agricultural sector became the battleground between the three dominant trading blocs – the EU, USA and Japan – without there being a set of GATT rules to determine fair conduct in the field.

The other outstanding areas of the Uruguay Round are set out below. Given the proliferation of disputes, especially those relating to dumping, the inability of the GATT disputes settlement mechanism to act swiftly and to impose penalties with sufficient deterrent value to discourage deliberate abuse of the rules has also become of key importance. Equally, the expansion of the role of GATT not merely to cover trade in **services** but also **intellectual property rights** (IPRs) has come to the forefront of debate about the role of the GATT, because in current circumstances it is too much to expect any country or trading bloc to make unilateral concessions.

The advanced nations are anxious that developing countries should open their markets to imports of services, and that they should honour intellectual property rights rather than turn a blind eye to outright piracy of patents and copyrights. In their turn, the LDCs want the advanced nations to open their markets to imports of textiles, clothing and agricultural commodities. Japan is unwilling to do anythng much about its so-called 'structural impediments' to trade (for

OPENING MARKETS
Tariffs
Non-Tariff barriers

Natural resource-based products
Tropical products

Agriculture
Textiles and clothing

IMPROVING GATT
Amending GATT articles

GATT codes

Safeguard measures

Subsidies
GATT dispute settlement
Functioning of GATT

EXPANDING GATT
To cover intellectual property rights

Trade-related investment
Trade in services

example, by allowing foreign firms to bid for public procurement contracts) unless the USA and the EU agree to curtail the stream of anti-dumping actions aimed at Japanese products. Almost everyone wants to stop the USA using the **super-301 provisions** of the 1988 Trade Act to take punitive action against them without recourse to the GATT, and so forth. Because no country is prepared to make concessions without first securing the desired **reciprocity** from other countries, the Uruguay Round has dragged on for over six years.

7.10.3 The GATT and Protection

The move towards increased protection discussed above obviously threatens the foundations on which the GATT is built. For several years now many countries have been busy negotiating bilateral agreements, to the detriment of excluded countries. The Uruguay Round has done little to stem the tide. One obvious difficulty is that the GATT secretariat has no resources to dispose in order to support its powers of persuasion, or indeed any real sanctions other than adverse publicity, so it is obliged to fall back upon its stature as a body which exists to foster free trade without favour to any individual country. The trouble then, however, is that too-overt criticism of countries which are abusing the rules is likely to send their representatives scuttling home claiming unfair discrimination.

The most tricky question concerns bilateral agreements which are advocated on the grounds that they promote free trade between the signatories. A recent example is the agreement signed between the USA and Canada in 1988. The outcome is that the USA is buying certain products from Canada which were previously acquired from more expensive domestic sources. However, there is no most-favoured-nation clause which requires the treatment accorded to the most favoured trading partner to be made available to others, and it therefore follows that other products will be bought from Canada rather than, say, the UK, since they will now be cheaper from the former source on a tariff-free basis. This simply serves to **divert** trade rather than to **create** it, and indeed may result in the purchase of tariff-free products from an inefficient source being substituted for tariff-bearing products from a more efficient source.

The US–Canada trade zone is, fortunately, not dissimilar in its effects to the EU which has served more to create trade than to divert it, and it keeps to most of the GATT rules insofar as it covers 'substantially all trade' and does not result in the raising of tariff barriers against other countries. At the end of the day, it all comes down to whether or not the US–Canada agreement is to be regarded as a special case. If the USA were to extend this type of agreement to other parts of the world, which it clearly has the economic muscle to do, then trade-diverting agreements may become the norm, with the destruction of the GATT an almost certain consequence.

☐ 7.10.4 *Anti-dumping Suits*

Faced with breaking GATT rules if they are overtly protectionist, both the EU and the USA have resorted increasingly to a subtle, but no less effective, method of curbing Japanese and South Korean imports. This method is to threaten to take the exporters to court in an **anti-dumping suit**. Under the GATT's anti-dumping code, **dumping** is held to occur when a good is sold abroad at a price lower than that charged by the exporter for the same good in his or her home market, and it is permissible to impose penalties where deliberate underpricing is causing, or threatening to cause, **material injury** to producers in the importing countries.

By writing rules to regulate anti-dumping duties into the GATT during the Tokyo Round these duties were effectively legitimised, and have proliferated in a manner that was never the GATT's intention. In particular, anti-dumping suits are brought against specific countries in a deliberately discriminatory manner, and are often instigated with the intention of eliciting a voluntary restraint from the defendant.

The common rationale for an anti-dumping suit is that the exporter is engaged in predatory pricing which is designed to drive the domestic supplier out of the business. Nevertheless, for some unaccountable reason, most EU anti-dumping suits are actually brought against exporters with a small share of the EU market! All the complainant has to demonstrate is that the exporter is either making a loss or selling a price at below that in the exporter's home market, and that this is not helpful to the complainant.

Once a complaint has succeeded it becomes necessary to calculate the **dumping margin**: the difference between the price of a good in the exporter's home market and its price when exported. Both the EU and the USA are past masters at calculating preposterously high margins. Adding insult to injury, the USA has proposed that the GATT code be amended to include products which might exist if dumping were not taking place, while the EU's proposal is that if a rise in imports coincides with a fall in domestic production this should be taken as 'proof' of successful dumping.

In August 1988 the European Commission imposed duties on imported video-cassette recorders on the grounds that unless the Community could remain conversant with the technology it would lose the ability to develop new high-technology products. Whereas this could be construed as a legitimate aim of industrial policy, it is hardly surprising that the Japanese, who traditionally dislike airing trade disputes in public, felt compelled to complain to GATT's anti-dumping committee that it could be regarded as evidence of dumping only by stretching GATT rules well beyond breaking point.

Much the same could be said about duties levied in April 1988 on typewriters and scales actually assembled in the EU by Japanese companies, which the European Commission claimed was simply a device to dodge the duties. The EU was particularly fond of the **screwdriver plant** ploy at this point in time, especially in respect of cars. The idea was that any imported components of Japanese products made in the EU could be saddled with anti-dumping duties unless more than a certain proportion of the total value of the end-product was added in the EU. Not surprisingly, most Japanese manufacturers adopted the line of least resistance and increased value added in the EU. Nevertheless, a complaint to the GATT resulted in this rule being outlawed in 1990.

Undeterred, the Commission applied anti-dumping duties to Japanese audio-cassettes even though a substantial proportion were made in the EU and the share taken by the imports from Japan was falling. Furthermore, the Japanese products were actually more expensive than those made by EU companies. Indeed so, argued the Commission, but that was because the Japanese had 'forced the Community industry to undersell to hold its market share'.

The 'offending' Japanese producers have typically responded to these duties by holding prices constant and reducing profit margins. As what the Commission really wanted was for import prices to rise, they decided to introduce additional penalties where the duties are not added to the price. The reader may by now be beginning to wonder just how all of this benefits the consumer, but there really is no need to wonder: it does not! However, lest 'Fortress Europe' be taken too readily to be a fact of life, it is worth noting that, as shown in **Table 7.8**, the situation has not become materially worse since the introduction of the 1992 programme.

Table 7.8 indicates the scale of anti-dumping and countervailing duty cases lodged with the GATT since 1980. According to a forthcoming report by the World Bank, average tariffs in the entire US manufacturing sector would be 23 per cent currently as compared to the official 6 per cent if they were adjusted to take account of the cost of dumping duties on imported steel, textiles

Table 7.8   *Anti-dumping and Countervailing Duty Cases*

	Jan. 80 to Jun 80	80–81	81–82	82–83	83–84	84–85	85–86	86–87	87–88	88–89	89–90	90–91	91–92	92–93
Australia	36	61	54	71	70	63	54	40	20	19	23	46	76	61
Canada	26	48	64	34	26	35	27	24	20	14	15	12	16	36
EC	17	37	39	26	33	34	23	17	30	29	15	15	23	33
US	37	24	51	19	46	61	63	41	31	25	24	52	62	78
Other developed countries	1	3	2	0	1	0	2	5	9	12	5	9	21	8
Developing countries	0	0	0	0	0	0	3	4	13	14	14	41	39	38
Total	117	173	210	150	176	193	172	131	123	113	96	175	237	254

Source: Financial Times, 15 December 1992 and 26 November 1993.

and cars. In other words, many of the apparent gains from the GATT are illusory.

Australia and the USA are currently competing to be the worst offender in respect of anti-dumping actions, although there has been a notable upsurge in actions taken by the developing countries since 1990. Japan and India initiated actions for the first time in 1992. It has been observed that anti-dumping actions have served primarily as a means to delay restructuring of uncompetitive industries, and hence that the original problem has rarely disappeared over time.

□ 7.10.5 *The Future of the GATT*

Officially, time ran out on the Uruguay Round at the end of 1990, but it did not expire altogether. In the USA, the **fast track** authority, which requires that legislation implementing trade pacts be voted on by Congress as a package without amendment, was introduced at the beginning of the Tokyo Round. Its original expiry date for the Uruguay Round was March 1991, at which point there was supposed to be a vote on the entire GATT package. In practice, there was no package because of the ongoing disputes about matters agricultural.

In principle agriculture, which accounts for only some 13 per cent of world trade, does not seem of sufficient importance to destroy the entire Round, but in practice many of the concessions which have been proposed in other areas are a quid pro quo for agricultural reform. The reasons for the agricultural disputes are discussed subsequently, but even though they remain unresolved the US Congress chose to extend the fast track authority to 15 December 1993 in the hope of seeing the Round through to a successful conclusion.

US trade negotiators are thus much better placed than those representing the EU. The EU's position in each area inevitably reflects a series of compromises among its members, and hence its negotiators feel unable to budge from the agreed positions lest individual members withdraw their support. To other countries this smacks of intransigence and a 'Fortress Europe' mentality.

The most recent manifestation of alleged EU intransigence relates to the dispute with the USA over Article 29 of the EU utilities directive which came into force on 1 January 1993. This law gives a 3 per cent preference to EU bidders for any government contract, and allows for bids to be ignored if the EU content is less than 50 per cent. The USA responded with an embargo on EU companies seeking public contracts in America, to which the EU responded in its turn with sanctions against US exports.

Despite this and other aggravations the Quad group of countries did manage to come up with a tariff-cutting 'market access' pact in Tokyo in July 1993. However, this was restricted to manufactures, and was subsequently referred to as an agreement over a formula by which to achieve a deal rather than a specific set of tariff cuts. In any event, the pact will need to be agreed by non-Quad countries, and there remains the resolution of disagreements over agriculture, textiles, services and other matters, yet the end-1993 deadline is ominously close at the time of writing.

■ 7.11 Agriculture

Although agriculture is a domestic industry, and could therefore be discussed in the context of Chapter 8, most of the issues which it raises are concerned with relationships both within the EU and between the EU and other trading blocs. It raises issues of protection and involves the GATT, and this section has, therefore, been placed in its entirety alongside the sections which deal with the latter topics.

The markets for agricultural products operate poorly in the absence of intervention. Demand tends to grow slowly over time, both because population growth in developed countries is very low and because, as incomes rise, the extra money does not get spent on agricultural produce. Supply, on the other hand, grows rapidly as a consequence of mechanisation, improved crop strains and the intensive use of fertilisers. In a free market these forces would in any case tend to drive down prices – and hence also farmers' incomes – but the situation is further compounded by the unpredictable effects of climatic conditions and the small size of individual farms in relation to total supply, which conspire to leave farmers with very little control over the prices of their products.

☐ 7.11.1 Rationale for Intervention

In practice, the governments of developed countries have, with few exceptions, been unwilling to let agricultural prices be determined by the forces of the free market during the postwar period. The rationale for intervention has taken a variety of forms, including the contribution of the sector to employment and to the balance of payments, the need for security of food supply in the event of external aggression, the need to protect the rural way of life and the need to ensure delivery of the rural vote. Although many of these justifications currently have an archaic ring about them, it must be recognised that, once a pressure group has been built up to keep them in the public eye, it becomes very difficult to persuade the public that they are no longer relevant.

Broadly speaking, farmers in any single domestic market, such as the UK, can be protected against the forces of the free market either by paying them subsidies or by erecting a wall around the domestic market through which imports cannot pass at prices which undercut domestic suppliers. Given that the UK had traditional obligations towards the Commonwealth, which included the freedom for Commonwealth countries to export to the UK, the widespread use of tariff barriers or quotas was considered to be inappropriate, and those UK farmers who could not match import prices were therefore paid a subsidy known as a **deficiency payment**. The burden of financing such a payment fell upon the taxpayer, and not upon the consumer who paid a shop price based upon the costs of the cheapest world suppliers. As agricultural productivity rose, and agricultural prices accordingly fell, the deficiency payments scheme became increasingly burdensome, and the government began to toy with the use of tariffs and quotas.

The supremacy of the latter form of protection came with the devising of the CAP in 1958 by the original six members of the EEC. At the time UK agriculture was considerably more efficient than its continental counterparts, in good part because the system of inheritance whereby land had been handed down to the eldest son, rather than dispersed among all male children as was the custom in, for example, France, had kept land holdings intact. Furthermore, UK farmers were used to competing in the open market unprotected by tariffs. As a consequence, a much smaller proportion of the UK population was employed in agriculture in 1960 than in continental Europe.

The objectives set out for the CAP under Article 39 of the Treaty of Rome were not, of themselves, incompatible with the objectives of UK agricultural policy. They were:

a   to increase agricultural productivity by promoting technical progress, and by ensuring the rational development of agricultural production and the optimum utilisation of the factors of production, in particular labour;
b   to ensure a fair standard of living for the agricultural community, in particular by increasing the individual earnings of persons engaged in agriculture;
c   to stabilise markets;
d   to guarantee the availability of supplies;
e   to ensure reasonable consumer prices.

However, their implementation over the ensuing decade did create certain incompatibilities with UK practice, in particular the much greater emphasis upon import controls and, as a consequence, the payment by the consumer in the shop of a price sufficient to cover the full costs of operating the CAP.

It should be borne in mind that at the time of its inception the CAP was not expected to generate huge surpluses with their attendant difficulties. The reason for the rather dreadful mess in which it currently finds itself is that the Community sought to respond to the developing crisis of overproduction in a piecemeal way. No-one ever sat down and tried to rethink the CAP from first principles in the light of the changes which had occurred in agricultural markets during the 1970s and 1980s. Hence reform has always been too little, too late.

Since 1958 the EU has acquired a further six members, amongst them the UK. Not surprisingly, the history of agriculture in the UK has created major disparities between the UK and other members, especially the most recent who have not as yet implemented the attempts at restructuring directed at the original six.

7.11.2 Overview of EC Agriculture

The Utilised Agricultural Area (UAA) is slowly but steadily decreasing as a proportion of total land use in the EU (excluding the former East Germany). It dropped below 60 per cent during the late 1980s and may well drop as far as 50 per cent during the 1990s. The proportion is unusually high in Ireland and the UK. Approximately one-half of the UAA is arable land which is tilled and cultivated annually; some 40 per cent is grassland; and the other 10 per cent consists of permanent crops (orchards, vineyards and olive groves which are prominent in Southern Europe and almost non-existent in the North).

It is obvious from the above that there is considerable diversity in the patterns of agricultural output between different EU members, and that the addition of recent members has shifted the balance somewhat towards permanent crops and away from arable land. This has also served to reduce agricultural productivity, which was already relatively poor. Employment in agriculture provides 6 per cent of all jobs in the EU, but these workers contribute less than 3 per cent of GDP. In the UK the proportions are both very low, whereas in Southern countries the proportions both tend to be much higher.

The number of farms in the EU has fallen sharply over the past two decades to stand currently at a total of roughly 6.9 million. In Italy, Greece and Portugal there are almost as many farms as there were in 1970 and, predictably, as shown in **Table 7.9**, these countries currently have average farm sizes significantly smaller than other EU members. By comparison, fewer than 60 per cent of farms in Belgium and Luxembourg have

survived since 1970, and fewer than two-thirds in Denmark, France and West Germany.

The typical EU farm has a UAA of 14 hectares (roughly 35 acres). On average, those in Denmark, Luxembourg and France are twice this size, but they in turn are half the size of the typical farm in the UK where in excess of 30 per cent of all farms have a UAA of at least 50 ha. Farms of this size are almost non-existent in Italy, Portugal and Greece where, as in Spain, farms of less than 5 ha predominate. It does not take much imagination to realise that this great diversity in farm sizes, combined with very different patterns of land use, represents a major difficulty in drawing up a common agricultural policy.

Between 1970 and 1987 the agricultural population in the Community fell by roughly one-quarter, with individual member variances ranging from a few per cent in the Netherlands to nearly 40 per cent in Luxembourg. There are currently roughly 8 million agricultural workers in the EU, of whom perhaps one-quarter work full-time.

In part this reflects the age structure of the agricultural population. Nearly half of all agricultural workers are aged 55 or over, which in turn reflects a clearly expressed preference by younger generations to head for the towns and cities. It follows that in the course of time the retirement of large numbers of farm workers will create a much more efficient farming structure in many EU countries.

7.11.3 Price Support

The system of price support has two distinct strands, one applicable to EU products and the other to imports, as illustrated in **Figure 7.10**. At the apex of the price pyramid for EU products sits the **target price**, which is the notional market price negotiated annually by the Council of Agricultural Ministers for the place where a product is in shortest supply. For certain products the terms 'guide', 'norm' or 'basic' price are also used. In practice, a product's price will rise to its target level only at a time of great shortage, so target prices have little operational meaning. Of greater importance is the **intervention price**, which is the

Table 7.9 EU Agricultural Statistics, 1991

	EUR 12	B	DK	D+[1]	GR	E	F	IRL	I	L	NL	P	UK
UAA[2] (million ha)	192.5	1.4[3]	2.8[4]	16.9	5.7[5]	27.1[5]	30.6[4]	5.7[5]	17.2[3]	0.1	2.0[5]	4.5[5]	18.4[4]
Arable (%UAA)[3]	52.9	52.2	91.7[5]	n/a	50.9	57.4[5]	57.5	18.1[5]	52.1	44.3	44.4[5]	64.1[3]	38.1
Grassland (%UAA)[3]	n/a	45.1	n/a	n/a	n/a	24.6[6]	37.8	81.9	28.1	54.5	n/a	16.8[5]	63.4[5]
No. of farms (000)[6]	6929	79	86	671	704	1540	912	217	1974	4	117	384	243
1–5 ha (%)	49.2	27.7	1.8	29.4	69.4	53.3	18.2	16.1	67.9	18.4	24.8	72.4	13.5
> 50 ha (%)	6.8	5.9	17.2	6.1	0.8	6.0	18.1	9.0	1.9	26.3	4.4	1.9	33.3
Av. size (ha)	n/a	17.3	32.5	17.6	5.3	16.0	30.7	22.7	7.7	33.2	17.2	8.3	68.9
Persons employed[7] (000)	8242	99	144	927	786	1345	1257	154	1823	6	293	848	560
% employed working population	6.2	2.7	5.5	3.3	21.6	10.7	5.8	13.8	8.5	3.1	4.5	17.5	2.2
Value of output (ECU million)[4]	202.1	6.1	7.0	27.6	7.5	26.6	48.1	4.2	36.6	0.2	15.7	3.8	18.7
Share of agriculture in GDP (%)[4]	2.9	2.1	3.7	1.5	13.9	4.6	3.3	9.5	3.6	2.2	4.0	5.3	1.4

Notes:
1 Unified Germany.
2 Utilised Agricultural Area.
3 1989.
4 1990.
5 1988.
6 1987.
7 Includes all persons working for remuneration or self-employed, plus unpaid family workers; persons employed in more than one economic sector are counted only in the sector in which they mainly work.
Source: Commission of the European Communities (1993).

Figure 7.10 *Prices in the CAP*

lowest level to which product prices are permitted to fall before the relevant intervention agency is obliged to buy in all surplus supply. This price is fixed annually as a percentage of the target price by the Council of Ministers on an individual product basis. Payments are delayed to discourage selling into intervention. Should producers be willing to export, they are paid a subsidy, equal to the difference between the world price and the EU market price, in the form of an **export restitution**.

The position for imports is that, almost without exception, they must be sold in the EU at a **threshold price** which is equivalent to the target price adjusted for transport and storage costs. The minimum price at which non-EU products can be imported into the EU is known as the **reference** (or sluice-gate) **price**, and to this is added a **variable levy** in order to bring the actual import price (which may exceed the reference price) up to the threshold price (see **Figure 7.10**). All proceeds from the variable levy are paid into the EAGGF, often identified by its equivalent French initials as FEOGA, which uses roughly 95 per cent of the proceeds in order to fund intervention buying and export restitution payments (**guarantees**). The remaining 5 per cent is spent on **guidance**, largely to finance structural improvements. Guidance spending is discretionary, and EU funds usually have to be matched by recipient countries.

Since the inception of the CAP, the proportion of agricultural produce which has attracted some degree of price support has risen inexorably, and currently stands at roughly 90 per cent. However, it is significant that half of all price support expenditure goes upon milk, cereals, beef and veal, and that oils attract almost a further 20 per cent. This arises because all of these products are automatically bought into intervention. They represent almost 50 per cent of all output. The other 50 per cent attracts much less support spending and certain products, such as potatoes and flowers, are assisted only by the existence of the variable levy. Intervention buying applies predominantly to products originating in Northern Europe, and although guidance expenditure is directed largely to the more southerly members, the disparity between the guarantee and guidance funds represents a strong bias in favour of Northern members.

☐ 7.11.4 *Agri-money*

At the inception of the CAP it was intended that agricultural produce should have a common price throughout the EU. In a world of fixed exchange rates and zero inflation it is clearly possible to fix the price of, for example, wheat in several currencies, and to keep those prices constant for evermore. However, where exchange rates are subject to adjustment, and where different countries suffer different rates of inflation, common prices can be maintained only through the introduction of a complicated adjustment mechanism.

Agricultural products in the EU are priced in ECUs. These are converted into a number of units of a national currency at the prevailing exchange rate between that currency and the ECU, and the farmer then receives as payment the appropriate amount of his or her domestic currency. But if that currency is devalued against the ECU, then the farmer ends up with more of his domestic currency than before (less in the case of a revaluation) even though the price in ECUs has not altered. It was in order to avoid this outcome that 'green' currency was introduced.

Green currency has been in existence since 1969 when the French franc was devalued and the DM was revalued. The French were unhappy that this would cause the price of food to consumers to rise and the Germans were unhappy that this would cause the incomes of farmers to fall. It was accordingly agreed that currency changes should be introduced only gradually for agricultural products, and that during the adjustment period artificial exchange rates would apply, to be known as representative (or **green**) rates.

This practice of using artificial exchange rates for agricultural products subsequently became institutionalised within the CAP. When a currency rose against the ECU it was the custom to leave the green rate unchanged in order to protect the incomes of farmers. This was called the 'switch-over' mechanism. Hence the adjustment which involved monetary compensatory amounts (MCAs) in order to prevent consequent distortions of intra-country trade operated such that: Green rate = Offical rate **less** MCA. The MCA was thus **positive** and took the form of a subsidy to that country's exports and a levy on imports from other countries.

On the other hand, if a currency fell against the ECU, but the green rate either stayed unchanged or was devalued by less, the adjustment which involved MCAs in order to prevent distortions of intra-country trade operated such that: Green rate = Official rate **plus** MCA. The MCA was thus **negative** and took the form of a levy on that country's exports and a subsidy to imports from other countries.

It was recognised that a system which had been introduced originally in order to permit an orderly movement towards offical exchange rates had ended up, inevitably, as a permanent system of dual exchange rates, so the EU decided to bring the process of fixing an annual green rate for each currency to an end at the end of 1992. This partly reflected the fact that there was a good deal of cross-border smuggling in order to avoid MCA levies, but primarily it was a response to the fact that the concept of the SEM was incompatible with a system of dual exchange rates. Although it was frequently alleged that the CAP was the only element of the EU which could truly be called a common market, this was demonstrably untrue in reality since the common currency, the ECU, had two values, one official and one green, in respect of each currency.

Under the floating green rate system introduced in January 1993, the sharp falls in a number of EU countries' exchange rates in the latter part of 1992, and the subsequent widening of the narrow band of the ERM, have had significant implications for the prices of agricultural products traded within the EU. For example, farmers in the UK have been able to take advantage of lower export prices while enjoying higher domestic prices as a result of a devaluation of the green pound introduced in November 1992, although the relative buoyancy of the pound in recent months has reduced that advantage.

☐ 7.11.5 Mountains and Lakes

In the UK, between 1975 and 1985, disposable incomes, prices in general and processed product prices in particular rose at an almost identical rate. However, starting in 1978, farm-gate prices began to lag behind. This meant that the only way for farmers to maintain their incomes was to raise their output, which in turn meant more intensive use of fertilisers. However, the latter rose in price much faster than end-products, partly because of their oil-based content, and the ratio of producer prices to input prices fell sharply, both in the UK and in the EU as a whole.

This had a number of consequences. In the first place, **farmers' incomes**, as officially recorded, failed to keep pace with incomes in other sectors. However, it is important to note in this respect that very few studies have ever been done on agricultural incomes, so there is great uncertainty about the validity of income comparisons. Those studies that exist indicate that farmers' incomes (though not those of their labourers) were usually well above the average for the whole economy before 1980 (although a large part of these incomes was a return on the ownership of land rather than on the farming of the land), and that the cost-price squeeze served merely to reduce this differential somewhat; that the indiscriminate nature of price support means that large-scale farmers never have been, or are likely to be, near the breadline (on average, the wealthiest 25 per cent of farmers receive nearly ten times as much in subsidies as their poorer counterparts); and that while small-scale farmers may earn only modest incomes from their farms, they generally have other sources of income, and in many cases farming is a secondary rather than a primary occupation. Although some farmers clearly have little to show for their labours, it is also the case that no one really knows how to identify which farmers genuinely need help and which could survive quite happily with a reduced level of price support, or even with none at all.

In the second place, there is the problem of **vast overproduction**, which is illustrated in Table 7.17 for both the UK and EU. In 1988, for example, the UK held 104 days' supply of cereals, but although that has now shrunk to a mere 38 days' supply the situation elsewhere in the EU has become much worse. In 1987 the UK and EU each held the better part of a year's supply of butter, stocks of which rose sharply again in 1991. This in turn created a major problem of storage. In practice, these stocks could be disposed of, but only at prices well below those paid to buy them into intervention, and this difference was an immense strain upon the EU Budget.

☐ 7.11.6 Direct Income Aid

Partly as a response to pressure exerted by the USA during the Uruguay Round to switch agricultural support on to a production-neutral basis, the EU farm ministers agreed in January 1989 to the use of direct income aids to farmers. This scheme was strongly supported by Jacques Delors, although it was clear from the start it would have to be introduced on a purely voluntary national basis.

A number of objections were raised, in particular by the UK. It was argued, first, that adequate and universally applicable social security systems already existed throughout the EU, so there was no need for a special scheme for farm-

ers, especially one which would have to be paid for out of national taxation receipts. In any event, farmers themselves would prefer not to be singled out for special payments for fear of attracting further adverse publicity. It was also felt that the scheme could turn out to be yet another open-ended commitment, although this point was dealt with in practice by ring-fencing the scheme. The key elements of the scheme which became operational in 1991 were as set out below:

1   It was voluntary. If offered, any national scheme had to be approved by the European Commission and had to meet rules concerning eligibility and the level of funding.
2   Eligibility required that a 'significant' (ill-defined) part of household income was derived from agriculture and that the total income was low relative to national **per capitum** GNP.
3   Payments could be made for no more than five years to any individual, commencing no later than four years after the scheme's inception.
4   Payments could not exceed ECU 2500 per individual per year.
5   The EU contribution to the total paid was limited to 70 per cent of the total for the least developed member states and to no more than 25 per cent for the remaining member states.
6   Recipients were to receive decreasing amounts of aid each year, with the EU's contribution to be reduced by 15 per cent during each successive year of payment.

The EU capped the scheme at ECU 16.8 million in 1994.

☐ 7.11.7 Producer and Consumer Subsidy Equivalents

The purpose of farm support is to transfer income from consumers to producers. The particular instruments chosen to effect that outcome are, however, inefficient and create a huge waste of

Table 7.10 *UK and EU Intervention Stocks*

	1987[1]	1988[1]	1989[1]	1990[1]	1991[1]	1992[1]	1993[1]	1994[1] provisional estimate	1995[1] provisional estimate
Cereals									
UK stocks (000 tonnes)[2]	2 199	1 737	706	562	653	679	644	366	73
Value (£ million)	259	124	44	17	22	28	28	16	3
Equivalent supply (days)[3]	40	104	44	34	39	42	38	22	4
EC stocks (000 tonnes)[2][4]	13 765	10 952	8 963	12 030	17 550	24 316	n/a	n/a	n/a
Equivalent supply (days)[3]	39	32	31	67	167	231	n/a	n/a	n/a
Beef									
UK stocks (000 tonnes)	61	32	8	42	122	153	156	160	161
Value (£ million)	123	49	9	32	107	143	180	181	176
Equivalent supply (days)[3]	23	15	4	15	52	9	67	81	81
EC stocks (000 tonnes)[4]	625	670	151	305	741	641	n/a	n/a	n/a
Equivalent supply (days)[3]	38	42	7	23	43	38	n/a	n/a	n/a
Butter									
UK stocks (000 tonnes)	192	49	9	20	33	10	0	0	0
Value (£ million)	377	76	12	11	21	6	0	0	0
Equivalent supply (days)[3]	275	76	12	36	61	17	0	0	0
EC stocks (000 tonnes)[4]	1 058	221	32	188	390	353	n/a	n/a	n/a
Equivalent supply (days)[3]	238	50	7	47	100	80	n/a	n/a	n/a
Skimmed milk powder									
UK stocks (000 tonnes)	8	5	–	7	10	2	1	1	1
Value (£ million)	8	–	–	4	5	2	1	1	1
Equivalent supply (days)[3]	28	–	–	12	18	3	2	2	2
EC stocks (000 tonnes)[4]	722	14	5	340	491	93	n/a	n/a	n/a
Equivalent supply (days)[3]	167	4	1	86	126	21	n/a	n/a	n/a

Notes:
[1] The years indicated refer to EAGGF accounting years for intervention activity (to 30 September).
[2] UK stock mainly barley and wheat: EC stocks include other cereals such as durum.
[3] Calculated using EC Commission figures for consumption.
[4] Figures derived from the Financial Reports on the EAGGF Guarantee Section published by the Commission.
[5] UK holding only 40 tonnes.
n/a = not available.
Source: Ministry of Agriculture and Fisheries, *Cmnd 2203*, February 1993, Table 21.

resources. Hence, the policy-induced increase in the cost of food and taxation is much greater than the corresponding increase in farm incomes. There is a further distributional inefficiency insofar as a disproportionate share of payments to farmers goes to the largest farm units.

The OECD calculates the effect of agricultural programmes on producers and consumers by recourse to **Producer Subsidy Equivalents** (PSEs) and **Consumer Subsidy Equivalents** (CSEs). A PSE is defined as 'the payment that would be required to compensate farmers for the loss of income resulting from the removal of a given policy measure. Expressed as a percentage, it represents that part of the value of output accounted for by assistance of various kinds.' A PSE cannot, however, incorporate intervention in the form of, for example, quotas which have no budgetary cost. A CSE corresponds to the implicit tax on (or subsidy to) consumption food prices and of taxes required to maintain farm incomes.

If we start by looking back at the position a decade ago (OECD, 1987) then the evidence shows clearly that Japan was much the worst offender in PSE terms, especially in respect of cereals. The EU also came out badly, its highest PSE being for dairy products. The USA came out well for all non-dairy products, although the PSE for sugar was surprisingly high.

CSEs for dairy products were almost identical in every case, indicating that consumers everywhere were paying one-quarter more than they would have done in a free market. The fact that the Japanese paid 45 per cent extra for their rice and 30 per cent extra for their beef was especially noteworthy. In the case of the EU the burden on consumers was fairly well spread out over different products, but was especially high for sugar (expensive domestically produced beet rather than cheap imported cane) and for coarse grains.

During the 1980s the situation worsened considerably. The OECD's calculation of PSEs for 1984–86 indicated a Japanese PSE of close to 70 per cent and a PSE for the USA up sharply to 28 per cent. The only exception was the EU, where the PSE rose only by a few percentage points. A study by Tyers and Anderson (1988) concentrated upon the ratio of producer (domestic) prices to border (international) prices, as shown in **Table 7.11**. The ratio rises in line with policy-induced distortions to trade and, as can be seen, the ratio for all industrial economies changed from a situation where domestic prices were on average 40 per cent higher than international prices in 1980–82 to a situation where they were twice as high in 1988.

The figures largely speak for themselves, but the marked deterioration in respect of wheat, rice and sugar is especially interesting. The study confirms the OECD's own conclusions, which are summarised in **Table 7.12**. According to OECD (1991), after a run of good years, for reasons discussed in the previous section, the EU's net percentage PSE rose back almost to the 1987 level, whereas the USA managed to keep its PSE under control at a rate typical of the early 1980s and Japan managed a further reduction, albeit from a very high base. Lest it be assumed that PSEs must be a fact of life, a comparison with Australia is also included. The OECD also noted that CSEs were increasingly taking the place of

Table 7.11   *Effect of Agricultural Programmes on Domestic Farm Prices, 1980–82 Average and 1988 (Ratio of Producer to Border Prices)*

	United States		EC		Japan		All industrial economies	
	1980–82	*1988*	*1980–82*	*1988*	*1980–82*	*1988*	*1980–82*	*1988*
Wheat	1.15	2.20	1.40	3.40	3.90	8.00	1.25	2.45
Coarse grains	1.00	1.60	1.40	2.40	4.30	11.65	1.15	1.75
Rice	1.30	1.85	1.35	2.40	3.35	8.20	2.50	5.65
Beef and Veal	1.10	1.30	1.95	2.75	2.80	5.40	1.50	2.05
Pork and poultry	1.00	1.00	1.25	1.60	1.50	1.90	1.20	1.40
Dairy	2.00	2.20	1.75	2.50	2.90	5.55	1.90	2.55
Sugar	1.40	2.05	1.50	2.80	3.00	7.10	1.50	2.60
Weighted average, all commodities	1.20	1.50	1.55	2.25	2.35	3.80	1.40	2.00

Source: R. Tyers and Anderson K. (1988) 'Liberalizing OECD Agricultural Policies in the Uruguay Round: Effects on Trade and Welfare', *Journal of Agricultural Economics* (May). Table 1.

Table 7.12 *Producer Subsidy Equivalents*

	1987	1988	1989e	1990p
AUSTRALIA				
Net total PSE $ bn	1.10	1.23	1.25	1.30
Net percentage PSE	11	9	10	11
EUROPEAN COMMUNITY				
Net total PSE $ bn	72.95	70.48	61.49	81.62
Net percentage PSE	49	46	41	48
JAPAN				
Net total PSE $ bn	35.15	36.52	33.67	30.86
Net percentage PSE	76	74	71	68
UNITED STATES				
Net total PSE $ bn	45.07	37.21	33.42	35.93
Net percentage PSE	41	34	29	30
OECD				
Net total PSE $ bn	176.78	167.91	151.01	175.54
Net percentage PSE	50	46	41	44

Notes:
e: estimate
p: provisional
Source: OECD (1991).

PSEs. Given the total cost of subsidies, it is hardly surprising that so much attention has been focused upon agriculture in the Uruguay Round.

The cost of subsidies can be seen first of all in respect of **Figure 7.11**. There has been some prior discussion of EU spending on agriculture in the section on the EU Budget, and the current share of the Budget, at 50 per cent, is indeed much reduced from the share in 1979. Nevertheless, the global sum involved has grown considerably, and this disregards the payments made by individual member states and import duties.

For these reasons it is more illuminating to consider the data in **Table 7.13**, which shows that for the EU as a whole agricultural subsidies amounted in 1992 to £88 billion, an increase of 6 per cent on 1991. The equivalent figure for the USA was £52 billion. The amount of support in the EU was equivalent to £10 000 for every full-time farmer and £634 for every hectare of farmland, nearly four times the OECD average.

Table 7.13 *Government Support for Agriculture, 1992.*

	$bn total	$ per head of population
Australia	1.6	89
Austria	4.2	530
Canada	9.1	330
EC	155.9	450
Finland	4.5	910
Japan	74.0	600
New Zealand	0.1	15
Norway	4.1	970
Sweden	3.2	370
Switzerland	5.8	840
US	91.1	360
OECD Total	353.7	440

Source: OECD.

Figure 7.11   *EU Spending on Agriculture*

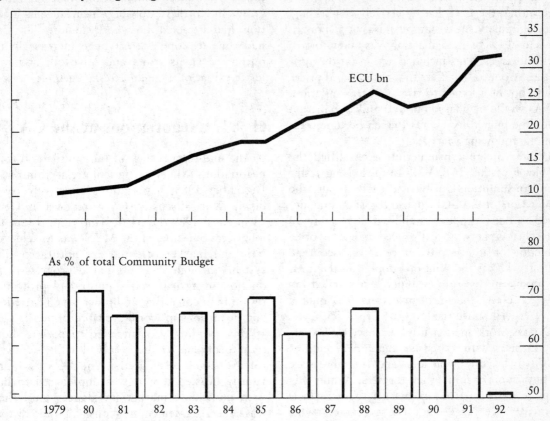

Source: European Commission.

☐ *7.11.8 Refining the CAP: 1968–87*

The CAP has been in a constant state of flux since its inception. Various reforms have been set in motion, but these have been wholly insufficient to prevent the current crisis during the Uruguay Round. The Mansholt Plan of 1968 was an early attempt to reform the CAP which recommended a reduction in land use for farming with the remaining land reorganised into fewer farms, thereby reaping economies of scale. The resultant unemployment would be resolved by finding new jobs for ex-farmers.

Disagreements among member states, combined with a poor economic climate, put paid to the Mansholt Plan, and it was not until 1981 that major reforms returned to the Community agenda

with the publication of *Guidelines for European Agriculture*. This proposed that prices should eventually be brought down to world market levels, and pointed out that 'it is neither economically sensible nor financially possible to give producers a full guarantee for products in structural surplus'. Subsequently, price support was limited to pre-determined levels of production which, if exceeded, would cause a response in the form of, for example, a quota for sugar; a co-responsibility levy for milk, which taxed production in excess of quotas in order to help pay for its disposal; or a reduction in the intervention price for cereals.

Unfortunately, these restrictions were nothing like tough enough to prevent the piling up of surpluses, and the cost of financing these grew to the point at which, despite some creative accounting, the CAP had effectively bankrupted the Community. At a summit meeting at Fontainebleau in 1985 remedial action was taken to deal with this crisis. This included action on the agricultural front to the effect that agricultural prices would not be allowed to rise as fast as inflation, MCAs would be phased out and milk production would be limited by quotas (which became tradable the following year).

Quotas on milk production exemplified the problems of the CAP. With output rising faster than consumption during the early 1980s, the proportion of EAGGF guarantee spending devoted to dairy products stabilised at roughly 30 per cent. What was really needed was a price reduction of at least 10 per cent to discourage output, whereas the solution adopted in the form of quotas and co-responsibility levies failed utterly to resolve the problem because the quotas were set well above the level of self-sufficiency.

Quotas work inefficiently because, for example, farmers with expensive machinery cannot afford to leave it lying idle, and therefore seek to buy quotas from other farmers. While this helps to unfreeze arbitrary market shares, which ironically are largest for those farmers who started with the largest supplies, it often results in a farmer's milk quotas becoming more valuable than the land itself. Furthermore, cows no longer wanted for their milk will be slaughtered for beef, thereby adding to the beef mountain.

Although the initial quotas achieved very little, a tougher set, introduced in December 1986, combined with harsher penalties on overproduction, effected a noticeable improvement. In the UK, farmers offered to pay up to 50 pence per litre for unused quotas in order to avoid the penalties. Nevertheless, the cost of supporting dairy and other surpluses remained excessive, and the political unwillingness by member states to allow their domestic farmers to suffer (while simultaneously extolling the virtues of austerity) once again left the CAP in a state of crisis in 1987.

The accession to the Community of Spain and Portugal in 1986 was a contributory factor in this respect, given that they had inefficient agricultural sectors by Community standards and produced a range of products somewhat different from those grown in Northern Europe which, since its inception, had attracted most CAP support. The CAP had thus to cope with a huge increase in the output of citrus fruits and olive oil, and to a lesser extent of wine and fresh vegetables.

■ 7.12 Negotiations at the GATT

At the mid-term review of the multilateral trade negotiations (MTN) on agriculture at Montreal in December 1988, negotiations effectively broke down. When discussions were renewed in Geneva in April 1989 the participants agreed that the long-term objective of the MTN was to achieve a 'fair and market oriented agricultural trading system' through the 'substantial progressive reduction in agricultural support and protection resulting in correcting and preventing restrictions and distortions in world agricultural markets'.

This wording was intended to permit short-term problems to be resolved while working towards long-term goals. The USA had previously insisted that it was unprepared to deal with immediate market imbalances until there was general agreement to abolish all trade-distorting policies. This latter objective was total anathema to the Community, which wanted to make some immediate progress by instituting a freeze on subsidies of all kinds. By agreeing 'substantial progressive reduction' it was possible for all parties to maintain that their own positions were still fully operative.

The USA submitted the first detailed proposal for agricultural reform in October 1989, which it then refined progressively during 1990. In effect, the amended proposal required the phasing-out of all trade-distorting government interventions, whether domestic or foreign. The key element in the proposal was **tariffication**. This meant that all non-tariff barriers to imports would be converted into tariffs and cut over 10 years to zero or very low rates. Tariffs would be 'bound', meaning that once introduced they could not be raised again. However, 'minimally trade distorting policies' would be permitted, as would direct supports not linked to production or marketing.

Tariffication was most obviously directed both at the variable import levies used under the CAP and VERs. A special **safeguard mechanism** would protect countries against import surges during the 10–year transition period. Governments would be permitted to revert to a higher level of tariff protection for the remainder of a year if imports exceeded specified proportions of the previous year's domestic consumption.

The USA proposed, second, that all **export subsidies** should be subjected to cut-backs. Policies such as government-administered pricing policies, income supports linked to production or marketing, transport subsidies and any investment subsidy provided to producers and processors other than on an equal basis would be **prohibited** at the end of the 10-year adjustment period. By way of contrast, income supports not linked to production or marketing, enviromental and conservation programmes, bona fide disaster assistance and other minor items would be **fully permitted**. Finally, anything not covered by these two categories would be **subjected to GATT rules** designed to prevent them being used in ways that would cause prejudice or material injury to another country.

A key aspect of the US proposal was that its scope would encompass the USA's own non-tariff barriers in the sugar and dairy sectors, its export enhancement programme and possibly its deficiency payments scheme for grain farmers, although the latter were seen essentially as internal supports which did not distort trade. By and large the US proposal was unacceptable to the Community. The Community did not waver from its position that agriculture was a special case where the utopian level playing field, which would exist were all trade-distorting policies to be abolished, would do more damage than good. It much preferred to take an overall view of these policies, as reflected in an **Aggregate Measure of Support** (AMS) covering the first three elements of the US proposal – to be called a Support Measurement Unit (SMU) – which all parties would agree to reduce gradually over time. This would not rule out tariffication **per se**. Partial tariffication would be acceptable provided it encompassed UK-style deficiency payments, but

only one element of such a tariff would be fixed, which would be the part reflecting the difference between domestic and market prices. There would also need to be a flexible element (known as a 'corrective factor') which would take into account such factors as currency fluctuations and serious market disturbances. In return for its agreement to partial tariffication the Community insisted that '**rebalancing**' be allowed. This meant that provided the overall trend was downwards, some subsidies could be increased at the same time as others were reduced.

The view in Brussels was that the US proposal was designed primarily as an attack upon Community export subsidies. The Community, however, was concerned about inroads being made into the animal foodstuffs market by cereal substitutes such as manioc and corn gluten feed, and hence wanted to **balance concessions** on lowering export subsidies on gains against increased protection for cereal substitutes.

With the divide between the Community and US proposals apparently unbridgeable, and with the Japanese continuing to insist that food security was of paramount importance, hopes faded of any resolution of the agricultural sector's problems by end-1990 when the Uruguay Round was due to come to a close. Suddenly, and without any prior discussion with, let alone the approval of, Community farm ministers, the then Community Farm Commissioner, Raymond Mac-Sharry, announced on 31 July 1990 that he would cut Community support to farmers. Under his proposal Community farm support would be reduced by 30 per cent over a 10–year reference period **commencing in 1986**. The programme of reductions would be retroactive so that the Community could claim credit for cuts already implemented since 1986. In the case of cereals these were alleged to amount to 10 per cent, and to amount to 15 per cent in respect of meat and dairy products.

Mr MacSharry insisted, however, that the Community would never make specific commitments to cut support in the separate areas of domestic support, import barriers and export subsidies, but would continue to insist upon recourse to the AMS. In mid-October the US Agriculture Secretary, Clayton Yeutter, formally tabled a new proposal which called for reductions of 90 per cent in export subsidies and of 75 per cent in import levies at borders and in internal supports for specific commodities (with an overall ceiling of 30 per cent in the latter case). The timescale for these reductions was a period of 10 years, **commencing in 1991–92.**

Both the USA and the Cairns group of major food-exporting countries supported tariffication of non-tariff barriers followed by an overall tariff reduction of at least 75 per cent over 10 years, with no individual product permitted to carry a tariff in excess of 50 per cent at the end of the period. The adjustment period would be stretched to 15 years for LDCs, by which time they would be expected to have achieved an average tariff reduction of at least 45 per cent of that of the developed nations.

In order to protect farmers against sudden changes in prices or exchange rates the USA proposed, first, that governments would be permitted to levy a tariff surcharge if the volume of imports of a product exceeded 120 per cent of the imports of that product during the previous year. Second, governments would be able to impose a surcharge if the import price of a product fell below 75 per cent of the average import price for the product over the three preceding years.

In the face of these proposals, the Agriculture Council began to exhibit serious internal disarray. In certain quarters, most notably France and Germany, Mr MacSharry's proposals were considered to be overly harsh (the US proposals were simply regarded as beyond the pale!).

With the Uruguay Round officially at an end, the negotiations in all other areas under discussion in abeyance pending the resolution (or otherwise) of the crisis in agriculture, the Community generally regarded as the main villain of the piece and agricultural spending in the Community forecast to exceed its 'guideline' unless remedial action was taken, Mr MacSharry had little choice but to opt for a radical shake-up of Community farming.

In effect a three-stage process was required: (a) keeping within the 1991 Budget's 'guideline' for CAP spending; (b) getting agreement by farm ministers to a reform package; (c) getting this package agreed in the GATT. Attempts to avoid (a) by raising the guideline were frustrated by the UK and Dutch farm ministers but, by going to the limit of the guideline, combined with a little fiddling of the accounts, the immediate crisis was resolved. Mr MacSharry's proposal for the longer term was, first, that cereal prices would be cut by 35 per cent over a three-year period, with compensatory income support paid on a sliding scale. This compensation would be geared to a **set-aside** programme such that arable farmers with less than 20 ha would be exempt from set-aside; those with 20–50 ha would have to set aside 15 per cent of their land to qualify for compensation but would also be compensated for the set-aside; those with in excess of 50 ha would be compensated only for a 15 per cent set-aside which did not attract further compensation. This was opposed by the UK on the grounds that it discriminated against relatively large UK farms, that the effect over the period to 1995 would be to bump up the cost of running the CAP (although savings might eventually emerge) and that the proposal was biased against Northern farmers.

The proposed price reduction for beef was 15 per cent, and it was further proposed that the emergency safety net be abolished. In principle this could lead to the cessation of intervention buying of beef. Dairy farmers would face 4 per cent reductions in milk quotas, but the smallest producers would be exempt. Prices would also be cut for other products, such as sugar and tobacco.

Throughout 1991 and early 1992 farm ministers fought over the MacSharry plan. In May 1992, it was agreed that the proposed price cut for cereals should be reduced from 35 to 30 per cent over three years, but with less compensation. A ceiling on stockpiles of beef was agreed at 800 000 tonnes in 1993, descending gradually to 300 000 in 1997. The beef safety net would have its price trigger lowered from 72 to 55 per cent of the intervention price, itself set 15 per cent lower. The price of butter would also be reduced by 5 per cent over two years, and milk quotas cut by 1 per cent in 1993 and 1994. The minimum threshold for set-aside was fixed at 92 tonnes, which penalised UK farms given their relatively large size. About 54 per cent of UK farmers were expected to apply for set-aside of £88 per acre compared to an 11 per cent average for the entire EC, in the process taking 16.5 per cent of cereal land out of production. However, given the need to rotate set-aside land, it was difficult to see how the fallow land could be used for long-term environmentally-friendly activities.

Although farm ministers felt these developments to be worthy of self-congratulation, it was observed that they would only serve to reduce food prices overall by 2 per cent over three years even assuming supermarkets passed on the benefits. In either event, the cost of the CAP would rise initially because of the additional compensation.

Unimpressed, the USA decided to force the Community back to the Uruguay Round bargaining table by threatening to dump 29 million tonnes of heavily subsidised wheat on world markets. Meanwhile Greek farmers took more than half their peach crop straight from the orchard to the dump, and the Court of Auditors published a 1100 page report on mismanagement and fraud in the CAP thought to total up to £4 billion.

In mid-November 1992 the USA and the Community signed the so-called Blair House Accord, which served first to resolve the five-year dispute over the Community's subsidised production of oilseeds. The Community agreed to limit production to 5.13 million hectares, equivalent to a reduction from 13 million to between 8.7 and 9.5 million tonnes, and agreed to binding arbitration if it exceeded the upper limit. This forestalled the imminent trade sanctions against white wine exports to the USA. The Community also agreed to cut its volume of subsidised farm exports by 21 per cent over six years. This was well below the original reduction demanded by the USA, so the Community agreed further to make permanent two-thirds of the land taken out of production as part of its set-aside scheme. Finally, subsidised Community beef exports to Asia were outlawed. In return, by way of 'rebalancing', the USA undertook to monitor exports to the Community of its cheap cereals substitutes such as corn gluten.

France, the major cereals exporter in the Community, was unhappy with the Accord, which it had nevertheless signed, and demanded further concessions. In May 1993 the compensation for set-aside was accordingly raised in order to persuade France to accept the deal on oilseeds, but it continued to threaten to veto the rest of the Blair House Accord. In early September the set-aside for cereals-producing land was raised again from ECU 45 to ECU 57 per tonne, farmers were permitted to set aside more land than the statutory minimum with full compensation; and three-year rotation was substituted for six-year, provided 20 per cent of the land was set aside. In spite of these concessions French farmers once again took to the streets, doing their best to imperil the completion of the Uruguay Round by demonstrating that the Community would be unable to negotiate on behalf of one of its largest members.

Notes

1. A **directive** states the result that must be achieved within a stated period. It is left up to each member state to introduce or amend laws to bring about the desired effect. Failure to implement a directive may result in the Commission referring the matter to the European Court of Justice. This can be compared with a **regulation**, which automatically applies to member states and hence does not need to be ratified by national parliaments. Regulations take precedence over national laws.

2. In Bruges, attending the European Summit of September 1988, Mrs Thatcher caused something of a stir by stating:

We have not successfully rolled back the frontiers of the State in Britain only to see them reimposed at a European level . . . The Treaty of Rome was intended as a charter for economic liberty . . . Our aim should not be more and more detailed regulation from the centre: it should be to deregulate, to remove the constraints on trade and to open up.

She added that 'To try to suppress nationhood and concentrate power at the centre of a European conglomerate would be highly damaging.' Such opinions did not altogether project the image of the good European in the style of Mr Heath. On the other hand, Mrs Thatcher expressed reservations which other European leaders were afraid to voice in public because they were reliant upon coalition support to remain in power.

Bibliography

Adams, J. (1990) 'The Exchange Rate Mechanism of the European Monetary System', *Bank of England Quarterly Bulletin* (November).

Ackrill, R. (1992) 'The Common Agricultural Policy – Its Operation and Its Future', *Economics* (Spring).

Artis, M. (1991) 'The European Monetary System', *Economics* (Spring).

Barrell, R. (1990) 'Has the EMS Changed Wage and Price Behaviour in Europe?', *National Institute Economic Review* (November).

Bhagwati, J. (1990) 'Multilateralism at Risk. The GATT is Dead. Long Live the GATT', *The World Economy* (June).

Canberra Centre for International Economics (1988) *Macroeconomic Consequences of Farm Support Policies* (Canberra: Centre for International Economics).

Carr, E. (1992) 'The New Corn Laws', *The Economist*, 12 December.

Cmnd 88 (1985) *Decision of the Council of the European Communities on the System of the Communities' Own Resources* (London: HMSO, 7 May).

Cmnd 419 (1988) *Decision of the Council of the European Communities on the System of the Communities' Own Resources* (London: HMSO, 24 June).

Commission of the European Communities (1992a) *Third Survey of State Aids in the European Community in the Manufacturing and Certain Other Sectors* (Brussels: CEC).

Commission of the European Communities (1992b) *Seventh Report of the Commission to the Council and the European Parliament Concerning the Implementation of the White Paper on the Completion of the Internal Market. COM (92) 383* (Brussels: CEC, 2 September).

Crook, C. (1990) 'A Survey of World Trade', *The Economist*, 22 September.

Curzon, G. and V. Curzon (1989) 'Non-Discrimination and the Rise of "Material Reciprocity"', *The World Economy* (December).

Ford, R. (1990) 'The Cost of Subsidising Industry', *OECD Observer* (October/November).

Franklin, D. (1993) 'The European Community: Back to the Drawing Board', *The Economist*, 3 July.

Giles, M. (1991) 'Business in Europe', *The Economist*, 8 June.

Haldane, A. (1991) 'The Exchange Rate Mechanism of the European Monetary System: a Review of the Literature', *Bank of England Quarterly Bulletin* (February).

Harrison, B. (1992) 'EMU: Progress, Problems and Prospects', *Economics* (Winter).

Main, D. (1991) 'Regional Policy Initiatives from Brussels', *The Royal Bank of Scotland Review* (March).

Mayes, D. (1992) 'The Realities Behind the European Single Market', *Business Economist*, 23(2).

Minford, P. (1992) 'What Price European Monetary Union?', *Economics* (Autumn).

OECD (1985) *Costs and Benefits of Protection* (Paris: OECD).

OECD (1987) *National Policies and Agricultural Trade* (Paris: OECD).

OECD (1991) *Agricultural Policies, Markets and Trade. Monitoring Outlook, 1991* (Paris: OECD).

Tyers, R. and K. Anderson (1988) 'Liberalizing OECD Agricultural Policies in the Uruguay Round: Effects on Trade and Welfare', *Journal of Agricultural Economics* (May).

Weber, A. (1991) 'Reputation and Credibility in the European Monetary System', *Economic Policy* (April).

Wolf, M. (1989) 'Why Voluntary Export Restraints? An Historical Analysis', *The World Economy* (September).

Zis, G. (1990) 'European Monetary Union: Policy and Institutional Implications', *Economics* (Autumn).

■ Chapter 8 ■

Employment and Unemployment

Peter Curwen

■ 8.1 Introduction

The purpose of this chapter and of Chapter 9 which follows is to examine the workings of the labour market in the UK. This divides into three main issues. First, there is the need to discuss **employment and unemployment** and the changes which have taken place in both, primarily in the period since 1979. Second, there is the need to examine the role played by the **trade unions** and to assess how they have fared since 1979. Third, there is the need to assess the record with respect to **education and training**, the latter of which has been a central policy issue only since the early 1980s. Inevitably, all of these issues have something to do with the rewards to labour, and so we will need to say something about that also. However, wider issues concerning the distribution of income are left until Chapter 10.

The Thatcher era was undoubtedly one which has been closely associated in people's minds with attempts to improve the workings of the labour market although, as we will discover, not all such attempts were successful and hence we need to examine why this was so. Certainly, the 1980s witnessed many changes in the laws controlling the labour market, and these are set out below. Nevertheless, the first Thatcher government had largely to live with the labour market as it found it in 1979, and a few remarks about the market prior to 1979 are therefore in order.

In the first place, there is the obvious contrast between the period of Keynesian 'full' employ-

ment which lasted for over two decades after the end of the Second World War, and the period of protracted unemployment, even in years of buoyant demand, which began in the late 1970s and which looks to be a permanent feature of the UK economic life for the foreseeable future. These days few economists believe that governments can maintain full employment using predominantly fiscal instruments in the textbook Keynesian manner. Instead, they view the government's role as one of creating the appropriate climate for **sustained investment by the private sector**. The traditional method for achieving this was to declare that the government would do everything in its power to maintain full employment. In response to this, firms were willing to invest to make goods and to provide services since they were assured that there would be no shortage of customers with incomes from employment to be spent. But the investment itself created jobs and incomes which could be spent on consumer goods, and so the expectation of buoyant demand became a self-fulfilling prophecy.

The housing market was also important in this respect since most people who buy a house take on a very long-term commitment in the form of a mortgage, and hence need to be fairly certain of remaining in constant employment while paying it off. Equally, the mortgage provider needs to believe that this will be so before making the loan, in order to avoid defaults. The expectation of full employment thus leads to buoyant demand for housing and creates demand, and hence jobs and incomes, in the construction sector, which again helps to ensure that full employment comes about.

The main drawback to this virtuous circle was that the trade unions ceased to fear the spectre of unemployment which had haunted them during the 1930s, the more so as the old-time union leaders faded away and were replaced by individuals who had never experienced anything other than an era of full employment. Wage demands accordingly began to escalate, accompanied by the threat of strike action, and employers generally gave in quickly, hoping to be able to pass on higher wages into higher prices. Full employment thus became a pre-condition for inflation, and also led to a deterioration in manufacturing standards because of the belief that there would always be ready buyers, even for poor quality products. The Japanese and West Germans were happy to disprove this hypothesis, in the process creating unpleasant problems for the UK's balance of payments.

Although there were various ways in which this combination of problems could have been tackled, Mrs Thatcher's chosen solution after being elected in 1979 was to discard any commitment to full employment and to engineer a recession which demonstrated that this was not mere bluff. The consequences of this changed approach form a unifying trend in the discussion which follows.

There was also the matter of **workers' rights**. By and large, the tradition in the UK up to the 1970s was to limit workers' rights to those who held specified types of jobs and who worked full-time. Compared to those available in other advanced countries, these rights were patchy at best.

During the 1970s the situation was to a considerable extent remedied. A series of Acts of Parliament extended to workers the rights to a contract of employment; to notice before termination of contract; to appeal against unfair dismissal; to redundancy payments; to maternity leave; to protection against discrimination; and to participation in union activities.

Whenever possible, employers responded by taking on workers who fell outside the limits fixed for access to these rights, resulting in an upsurge in female part-time labour. But for the purposes of our discussion below the key factor was that the Thatcher government set about limiting some of these rights. To some extent, as detailed below, this has come up against supranational EU laws in recent years, but there can be no doubt that the balance of power has shifted from workers to employers during the past decade.

■ 8.2 Employment

□ 8.2.1 The Working Population

Table 8.1 illustrates that the total population of the UK grew steadily from 1951 to 1971 but has since grown much more slowly. The 1990s are expected to exhibit a modest quickening of growth, but this is expected to fall off again early in the next century.

The number of children under 16 increased in the UK by over 1 million between 1961 and 1971, but this was followed by a decline of just under 3 million, to 11.5 million, in 1989 (*Social Trends*, 1993, Chart 1.4). However, during the period 1971–90 the younger adult (16–39) and pensioner

Table 8.1 *Population, UK, 1951–2011 and Great Britain, 1971–2001 (million)*

	1951	1961	1971	1981	1985	1989	1991	1996	2001	2011
UK	50.3	52.8	55.9	56.4	56.6	57.2	57.5^1	58.5^1	59.2^1	60.0^1
Britain	–	–	40.6	42.7	43.7	44.5	44.7^1	44.9^1	45.4^1	–

Note:
[1] Projections.
Source: Social Trends, 21 (1991 edn), Table 1.2; *Employment Gazette* (May 1991), pp. 272–3.

(65 and over) age groups grew by 3 million and 1.6 million respectively. Between 1991 and 2011 the number of children is projected to rise once again to a peak of 12.6 million, whereas the number of younger adults is projected to fall back by 2 million. By way of contrast, the number of pensioners is expected to rise by a further 40 per cent to 14.6 million by the year 2031 (**Social Trends**, 1993, Chart 1.5).

From the total population can be extracted a summary statistic known as the **population of working age**, which by convention encompasses all those who might work and excludes those at school or in retirement. However, parts of the population of working age are economically inactive. Some are engaged in further and higher education, some in raising children and some are physically unable to work. On the other hand, by no means all who retire officially are economically inactive. By adjusting for those factors a further summary statistic is arrived at which is called the **labour force** (or the **civilian labour force** if those in the armed forces are excluded), comprising those willing and able to work.

The civilian labour force in **Great Britain** was 24.9 million in 1971 and 26.2 million in 1981. However, it fell back to 25.9 million by 1983, before rising once again to 28.2 million in 1990. It has subsequently fallen slightly and is not expected to rise back to 28.2 million until 1995 with 29.0 million forecast only in 2002 (see **Employment Gazette**, April 1993, **p. 145**). The population of working age is driven primarily by variations in the birth rate, which surged immediately after 1945 and hence created a cyclical effect approximately every two decades. However, it is also driven by retirements, which are dependent upon the birth rate six to seven decades previously. In its turn, the civilian labour force reflects changes in the **population of working age**.

However, as shown in **Figure 8.1**, this relationship has been fairly weak. Between 1951 and 1989 the civilian labour force grew by 3.1 million, considerably faster than the population of working age. Furthermore, whereas the latter grew at much the same rate for males and females, almost 90 per cent of the growth in the civilian labour force was made up of females. This trend is projected to continue. During the current decade the number of males in the civilian labour force is expected to remain static at around 15.9 million, while the number of females is projected to increase by 0.7 million to reach 12.9 million by the year 2000, at which point women will constitute 45 per cent of the civilian labour force.

Figure 8.1 *Civilian Labour Force of Working Age and Population of Working Age by Sex, Great Britain*

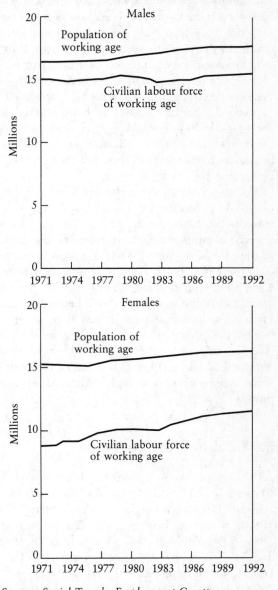

Source: Social Trends; Employment Gazette.

In the early 1980s, as can be seen, a fairly large number of workers dropped out of the labour force, and the Labour Force Survey (LFS)[1] estimated that 340 000 workers in total had become discouraged because they did not expect to get a job even if they tried hard to do so. International Labour Office (ILO) estimates indicate 220 000 a year were discouraged during 1984–86 and 110 000 a year during 1988–90.

The notion of 'discouragement' is somewhat ambiguous since some discouraged workers will have jobs in the unofficial (black) economy. They may not, however, be as numerous as is often made out in the media since, on the whole, those who are unemployed and who have lost their jobs either because the economy is in recession, or because their particular skills are no longer needed, are unlikely to be much in demand in the black economy either. On the other hand, those with skills in the official economy such as television repairers, will also find their skills in demand in the black economy.

The desire to work in the black economy is obviously influenced by taxation, and the reduction in tax rates during the 1980s may have induced a transfer of activity from the unofficial to the official economy. What is certain is that in 1989 there were twice as many people, at just over 1 million, who declared themselves to have a second job compared to 1981. From 1981 to 1985 more men had second jobs than women, but by 1987 this had reversed itself quite sharply (see *Social Trends*, 1991, Chart 4.15). Of those with second jobs in 1989, two-thirds of those jobs were as employees and one-third were self-employed.

☐ 8.2.2 Self-employment

In 1971 there were 2 million self-employed in Britain. By 1979 this figure had fallen to 1.9 million. However, numbers surged during the 1980s, to 2.2 million in 1981, 2.7 million in 1986, 3.0 million in 1987, 3.4 million in 1989 and 3.5 million in 1990 (see *Employment Gazette*, June 1992, pp. 269–92 and *Social Trends*, 1993, Chart 4.10). In 1993 there are probably no

more than 3.0 million as a consequence of the recession. Between 1981 and 1990 the net increase was 59 per cent overall (52 per cent for men as against 87 per cent for women, although there were well under 1 million self-employed women even in 1990). The net increase was the difference between very large numbers entering and leaving self-employment each year. Two-thirds of the self-employed worked by themselves.

This increase in Britain was very much greater than in other EU member states, the USA and Japan, although the UK had proportionately fewer self-employed outside agriculture in 1979 than any of the other countries. As a result, the UK self-employed rate is currently close to the EU average. More than 60 per cent of the self-employed are in services. The largest number work in distribution, catering and repairs, followed by construction, other services and banking, finance and insurance. In many sectors, such as other services, there was roughly 100 per cent growth in numbers between 1981 and 1990, but the overall average growth was only roughly 50 per cent because numbers were static in agriculture and forestry and grew only very modestly in distribution, the largest sector (where they fell after 1986). Whereas many self-employed persons struggle to make a decent living, it is equally the case that many highly-skilled individuals have prospered as a result of setting themselves up as suppliers of business and financial services.

The rapid growth in self-employment is partly accounted for by the 1980–81 recession, which created a large pool of unemployment from which large numbers of individuals chose to emerge as self-employed. Previously, self-employment was much higher in countries with extensive job protection and high social security charges, where employers preferred not to offer full-time jobs. In addition, the government has fostered self-employment both through changes in the fiscal system and by its promotion of the joys of self-reliance. Start-up capital has also become more readily available. Needless to say, the failure rate among the self-employed is high, so the significant overall growth in numbers does indicate that the switch to self-employment is more than just a flash-in-the-pan consequence of the

1980–81 recession. However, now that the UK has caught up with the EU average, the situation is likely to remain far less changeable than during the 1980s.

☐ 8.2.3 Activity Rates

The proportion of the resident population who are in the civilian labour force is usually referred to as the **economy activity rate**. Activity rates have always been very different for males and females, but have been converging steadily during the postwar years. In the case of men the activity rate has been falling since the 1930s. In part, this has been due to an increase in the numbers staying on in further and higher education, although that factor was probably most important in the 1960s. More recently, the decline has been due to earlier retirements, stemming from improved pensions, and to the 'discouraged workers' effect.

In 1971, the activity rate in Britain for males of all ages was 80.5 per cent. Subsequently it fell to 74.2 per cent in 1983 before rising back to 74.5 per cent in 1984, at which point there was a definitional changeover to the ILO/OECD system. On the latter basis, the male activity rate stood at 74.2 per cent in 1990 and is projected to fall back to 72.5 per cent by the year 2001.

The female activity rate in 1971 was only 43.9 per cent, but in spite of a set-back during 1981–83 it had risen to 52.8 per cent in 1990, and is projected to rise further to 55.1 per cent by the year 2001. This increase in female activity rates has largely been due to the switch over to service sector employment, to an increase in the availabilty of part-time jobs and to other economic and social changes encouraging women into the labour force.

Figure 8.2, which presents the data for the UK as a whole in a somewhat different format which excludes those over the age of retirement, reveals a notable difference in the pattern between the activity rates of married and unmarried women. Activity rates for unmarried females have been reasonably constant since 1971, although the 1990–92 recession has recently caused the activity rate to fall away somewhat. Among the younger age group there has been an increased tendency for females to stay on in further and higher education, and a sharp upturn in the number of single-parent families living off state benefits. Married women, on the other hand, have become increasingly active in the labour market, even through the recession. Clearly this has much to do with the modern tendency to delay having a family and to have fewer children, together with the economic necessity to supplement family earnings, especially when the husband is out of work, and the widespread social acceptance of women working outside the home. In addition, the widespread introduction of labour-saving devices in the home has eased the burden of housework.

The most significant change in recent years has been in the proportion of women with a dependent child under 5 years of age who work. In 1984 this stood at 27 per cent, whereas by 1989 it had risen to 40 per cent. This is the cause of some unease about the structure of modern society, but this goes beyond the scope of our present discussion. A summary of the role of women in the labour market is contained in the box below.

Among the countries of the EU in 1990, as shown in **Table 8.2**, the UK had the second-highest economic activity rate behind Denmark, and this applied for both males and females. The difference between the sexes in Denmark was only 14 per cent, much smaller than in the UK, so there is some reason to expect the gap to narrow further in the UK over the coming decade. It would appear from this evidence that UK residents are relatively keen to work. Unfortunately, that does not necessarily mean that their time is used productively.

☐ 8.2.4 Population and Activity Rate Effects

The 'population effects' represent the changes which would occur if activity rates stayed the same and only the size and age distribution of the population changed, whereas the 'activity rate effects' represent the changes in the proportion of the population which is in the labour force.

Figure 8.2   *Population of Working Age, by Sex and Economic Status,[1] UK (%)*

Males aged 16–64[2]   Females aged 16–59[2]

Notes:
[1] UK labour force definitions for 1981, ILO/OECD definitions for 1986 and 1992.
[2] Figures for 1971 relate to persons aged 15–59/64 (the school leaving was raised in 1972).
[3] Includes those on government schemes. In 1992 unpaid family workers are also included.
Source: Social Trends, 23 (1993 edn), Chart 4.3.

According to analysis of the 1991 LFS for Great Britain:

- Over 70 per cent of women of working age were active in the labour market in Spring 1991
- Between 1979 and 1991 the number of women in employment grew by just under 20 per cent
- In Spring 1991, 43 per cent of employed people of working age were women; of these, just over 40 per cent worked part-time and a third had dependent children
- There were 740 000 self-employed women in Spring 1991, more than double the number in 1979
- In Spring 1991 the unemployment rate (on the ILO definition) among women of working age was 7 per cent, compared to 9 per cent for men
- 0.68 million women returned to the labour market between Spring 1990 and Spring 1991
- 82 per cent of working women had jobs in the service industries in Spring 1991 compared with 54 per cent of men

Source: Employment Gazette (September 1992), pp. 33–59.

In every year since 1971, and up to 2001 according to projections, the overall changes in the labour force are more positive (or less negative) for women than for men. The population effects are nearly always positive for both women and men. They rose during the 1970s to reach a peak

Table 8.2 *Economic Activity Rates[1]: By Sex, EC Comparison, 1990 (%)*

	Males	Females	All
United Kingdom	75.6	53.2	64.0
Belgium	62.0	37.1	49.1
Denmark	75.8	61.9	68.7
France	67.1	47.5	56.8
Germany (Fed Rep.)	72.9	45.9	58.7
Greece	67.0	36.0	50.8
Irish Republic	72.6	36.3	54.4
Italy	66.8	35.5	50.5
Luxembourg	68.7	34.1	50.7
Netherlands	71.0	44.1	57.3
Portugal	72.8	47.9	59.6
Spain	67.7	33.3	49.7

Notes:
[1] The civilian labour force aged 16 years and over as a percentage of the population aged 16 and over.

Source: Social Trends, 23 (1993 edn), Chart 4.7.

around 1983 but, despite declining subsequently, they are projected to remain positive from now until 2001.

Activity rate effects are typically larger, and much more variable, from year to year. It is these, rather than in population effects, which explain both the fall in the labour force which occurred (even for women) between 1981 and 1983, and the large rises in 1983–84 and 1988–89. In most years they are positive for women but negative for men, on occasion to such an extent as to outweigh the population effect and result in falls in the male labour force.

☐ 8.2.5 Working Hours

Data on working hours are produced on a national basis and also on an internationally comparative basis by the EU and OECD. As a result of differences in definitions the data are not fully compatible, although the trends revealed are clear-cut. Since the mid-1980s there has been a steady downwards trend in the number of hours worked in the UK, superimposed upon which has been a pro-cyclical pattern. The trend line is readily explained by the substitution effect: that is, the tendency for increasing numbers of workers to substitute leisure for working hours as their real incomes rise over time.

The tendency for hours worked to rise during booms and to fall during recessions essentially reflects the volume of work on offer, and is much more marked in the manufacturing sector as compared to services, and among males as compared to females.

It is estimated from the Spring 1991 LFS that four out of five male employees had basic weekly hours (that is **excluding** meal breaks and overtime) of between 35 and 45. Those at the lower end were mostly in manual jobs in manufacturing, energy and transport. Half of all female employees worked for less than 35 hours per week, and over two-thirds for between 35 and 40 hours. For both sexes the self-employed worked longer hours than employees.

The official dividing line for part-time work is set at 30 hours per week. Women who work fewer hours invariably describe themselves as part-timers, but surveys reveal that 20 per cent of men who work fewer hours nevertheless describe themselves as full-time employees.

In 1979 the engineering working week was cut from 40 to 39 hours, and within three years a further 6 million workers had won a similar reduction. In 1989 more than 600 000 manual workers in the engineering and water industries won the promise of a 37.5-hour week, and by the end of 1992 this applied to the majority of manual workers. There has been considerable reluctance in other industries to follow suit but, in February 1992, for example, British Nuclear Fuels negotiated a 35-hour week, subject to improved working practices which made the deal self-financing.

International comparisons must be treated with care. Average weekly hours worked fell during the 1980s in most OECD countries, although Americans worked slightly longer and the Japanese exactly the same. Given the general tendency for the statutory working week to be shortened, and for official holidays to be extended, this is not particularly surprising. What is surprising is the enormous disparity between the 36–hour Dutch working week and the 47–hour Japanese working week. This is, however, something of an illusion because the incidence of part-time relative to full-time work biases the data and Holland, for example, has proportionately twice as many part-timers (at 25 per cent of the workforce) as Japan. Equally, the Japanese holiday entitlement (typically at 2 weeks) is very low compared to that in Europe. Combining annual leave with public holidays yields 40 days' holiday for Germans, 36.5 days for the French, 33.5 days for Italians but 31 days for UK citizens (only the Irish get fewer, at 28).

The latest year for which hours worked data are available officially for the whole of the EU is 1990 (see **Table 8.4**), and it should be noted that these data **include overtime**. On average, men in the UK worked longer hours than their European counterparts, whereas women worked fewer hours than elsewhere in the EU apart from the

Netherlands. If hours worked are combined with holiday entitlement it becomes evident that Danes work far fewer hours per year than the Portuguese, and that UK citizens work many more hours than the French. While this does not make much difference in any one year, it makes a huge difference over a 45-year working life. The combination of extended overtime working, together with a heavy reliance upon part-time workers sets the UK aside from most comparable countries. In theory, at least, it suggests that the UK has a flexible labour market. Furthermore, there has been a noticeable tendency for firms to cease to do many jobs in-house and to sub-contract them to outside bodies as and when they are needed. This is a significant factor in explaining the switch from manufacturing to services in the national accounts, since a service provided in-house by a manufacturing concern is listed as a manufacturing activity, whereas the instant it is sub-contracted out it becomes listed as a service activity, even if it involves the identical group of workers performing identical tasks.

From an economic perspective these developments obviously make sense for large companies, which thereby need to incur relatively low overheads and which can flex in line with the economic cycle. On the other hand, sub-contractors are increasingly vulnerable to economic downturns, and this helps to account for the exceptionally high number of bankruptcies during the 1990–92 recession.

The government has attempted through its own policies to foster **increased flexibility** in the workplace, in particular via the attack upon restrictive practices contained in the series of Employment Acts during the 1980s. The Employment Act of 1989 was also notable for removing restrictions on the hours of work of young people, and for abolishing most of the remaining legislation concerned with sex discrimination.

New contractual agreements introduced by Japanese companies are also of interest given their relative success in manufacturing. At the Nissan car plant in Sunderland the collective agreement specifies that 'there will be complete flexibility and mobility of employees', and also that 'to ensure flexibility and change, employees

Table 8.3   *Average Hours Usually Worked[1] per Week,[2] by Sex, EC Comparison, 1990*

	Males	Females	All Persons
United Kingdom	44.0	30.5	37.8
Belgium	38.1	32.1	35.8
Denmark	37.0	31.7	34.5
France	39.8	34.7	37.5
Germany (Fed. Rep.)	39.6	32.8	36.8
Greece	40.5	37.8	39.5
Irish Republic	41.0	35.1	38.6
Italy	39.5	35.3	38.0
Luxembourg	40.3	35.6	38.7
Netherlands	35.8	25.9	32.1
Portugal	42.9	38.7	41.1
Spain	40.9	37.2	39.7
EUR 12	40.4	33.1	37.4

Notes:
[1] Employees only.
[2] Excludes meal breaks but includes paid and unpaid overtime.

Source: Social Trends, 23 (1993 edn), Table 4.15.

will . . . undertake training for all work as required'. Despite union resistance elsewhere, these kinds of agreement are likely to become commonplace. Nevertheless, as demonstrated subsequently, the government (and its predecessors) have much to answer for in terms of their failure to create a system of education and training appropriate to the needs of the rapidly evolving labour market.

☐ 8.2.6 The Demand for Labour

Changes in the size of the labour force and in activity rates are aspects of the supply of labour, although employment in total clearly has to do with the balance between supply and demand. Once the analysis turns to **unemployment**, the demand side comes more into its own. Unemployment is associated in the Keynesian model with deficient demand for the goods and services in the production of which labour is used. A particular issue to which we will be referring below is the switch away from manufacturing and into services during the past two decades. This transfer has been common to all advanced economies, and indeed has proceeded much more rapidly in the USA than in the UK.

It was inevitably going to accelerate in the UK in the face of rising energy prices after 1975 and the exploitation of North Sea oil and gas which subsequently followed. The former produced a move away from energy-intensive manufacturing and towards services which were economical on energy use. In the latter respect, it is often held that the benefits of North Sea oil were traded off (unwisely) in exchange for manufactured imports and an expansion of the internationally uncompetitive protected sectors of the economy.

The transfer of demand caused large numbers of jobs to be lost in manufacturing, as can be seen in **Table 8.4**, which analyses **employees in employment** by industry. Prior to 1979 the transfer from manufacturing to service sectors was proceeding fairly smoothly, but the 1980–81 recession bit deeply into the manufacturing sectors without making any real dent in service employment. By 1988 the total number of jobs stood once again at

precisely the level of 1971 (and hence still well short of the 1979 aggregate). However, the manufacturing sectors employed exactly 3 million less than in 1971 (5.2 million) and the service sectors 3.5 million more (15.2 million). The reduction in each of the three manufacturing sectors was almost identical at 30 per cent, but the changes in the four service sectors were quite different, varying from a reduction of 12 per cent for transport to an increase of 85 per cent for banking and finance. The missing 0.5 million were lost in agriculture, energy and construction. Although this reduction was small in absolute terms, it represented a reduction of over 40 per cent in the energy sector.

It should be noted that the data on employees in employment undergo periodic revisions. The Census of Employment provides 'benchmark' figures on which to realign the estimates of employees in employment derived from the quarterly sample surveys of employers. The most recent revision for Great Britain, based upon the 1991 Census of Employment, was presented in *Employment Gazette* (April 1993).

An alternative approach is to conduct the analysis by splitting the workforce between **private** and **public** sectors (see *Economic Trends*, January 1993 and *Financial Times*, 8 February 1993 and 8 June 1993). The peak employment in the public sector (general government plus public corporations) occurred in 1979, but employment in general government remained constant from 1976 to 1989 and was untouched by the 1980–81 recession. The entire reduction of well over 1 million during 1979–89 took place in the public corporations, initially as a consequence of recession and subsequently as a consequence of the privatisation programme. Employment in the private sector peaked in 1979, fell sharply, recovered to the 1979 level in 1986 and subsequently grew very strongly. As a consequence, the public sector accounted for 30 per cent of the workforce in 1981, but had fallen back to 23 per cent by 1989.

Since 1990 a further quarter of a million jobs have been lost in the public sector, but this time around the losses have been in central government. Losses due to privatisation have come to a halt, although they may recommence with the

Table 8.4   ***Employees in Employment, by Industry, UK (000)***[1]

	1971	1979	1981	1986	1990[2]	1991	1992
Manufacturing							
Extraction of minerals and ores other than fuels, manufacture of metal, mineral products, and chemicals	1 282	1 147	939	729	721	657	635
Metal goods, engineering, and vehicle industries	3 709	3 374	2 923	2 372	2 310	2 139	2 030
Other	3 074	2 732	2 360	2 126	2 106	1 997	1 924
Total manufacturing	8 065	7 253	6 222	5 227	5 137	4 793	4 589
Services							
Distribution, hotels, catering, and repairs	3 686	4 257	4 172	4 298	4 822	4 686	4 605
Transport and communication	1 556	1 479	1 425	1 298	1 382	1 349	1 324
Banking, finance, insurance, business services, and leasing	1 336	1 647	1 739	2 166	2 744	2 687	2 639
Other	5 049	6 197	6 132	6 536	6 996	7 022	7 076
Total services	11 627	13 580	13 468	14 298	15 944	15 744	15 644
Agriculture, forestry, and fishing	450	380	363	329	298	291	283
Energy and water supply industries	798	722	710	545	449	439	403
Construction	1 198	1 239	1 130	989	1 070	962	839
All industries and services	22 139	23 173	21 892	21 387	22 899	22 229	21 758

Notes:
[1] As at June each year.
[2] The effect of revisions undertaken in 1991 impacted primarily on the 1989 and 1990 data.
Source: Social Trends, 23 (1993 edn), Table 4.9; *Employment Gazette*.

sale of British Coal, the Post Office or the railways. The public sector has continued to account for roughly one-quarter of all employment.

The UK currently has almost exactly the same proportion of the workforce in government employ (at 20 per cent) as two decades ago. This is also approximately the case for the USA (at 15 per cent) and Japan (at 6 per cent). Elsewhere in Europe it is typically both higher and well above the proportions of two decades ago (*Financial Times*, 15 March 1993). It is significant to note that whereas both the EU and North America have created a little over 5 million public sector jobs since 1974, the EU has created only 3.1

million private sector jobs compared to 29.8 million in North America.

Finally, it is possible to break employment down by **occupation** (see *Employment Gazette*, April 1991, p. 186). According to the 1990 LFS 48 per cent of men and 69 per cent of women were in non-manual occupations. The main difference between the sexes was that 31 per cent of women were employed in clerical and related occupations compared to only 6 per cent of men, whereas 25 per cent of men were employed in craft or similar occupations compared to only 4 per cent of women. These percentages changed little during the 1980s as a whole.

8.2.7 Part-time and Temporary Work

We have already referred to the prevalence of part-time work by females in the UK, and this can be seen more clearly by reference to **Table 8.5**. The recent recession has understandably induced more males to take up part-time jobs, although these represented only roughly 5 per cent of all male jobs in more normal years in the 1980s. By contrast, they have not represented less than 40 per cent of all female jobs for many years. It is reasonable to conclude from this that there are forces involved which will continue into the longer term, such as the switch from manufacturing into services, and further that these forces will significantly affect full-time job opportunities for males. A plausible forecast is set out in **Figure 8.3**, covering the period to the end of the decade.

There has been a protracted debate about the reasons for the switch to 'non-standard' or 'flexible' labour, which in the UK primarily refers to part-time jobs. This is discussed fully in the *Employment Gazette* of May 1992. The evidence from the Employers Labour Use survey indicates very strongly that firms employ part-time workers for tasks that require a limited time for their completion and, to a lesser degree to match staffing levels to patterns of demand. Other factors – such as cost savings, avoidance of unionisation and less employment protection – are ultimately much less important.

The switch from full-time to part-time jobs and associated gender effects have resulted in nine counties and two Scottish regions having more female than male employees. Ironically, recent figures from the Equal Opportunities Commission revealed that 40 per cent of complaints now come from men fighting employer assumptions about the female nature of certain jobs. There can be no question but that UK employment laws and welfare regulations remain geared to a standard full-time working week, even though that is becoming increasingly uncommon. This raises important issues about rights for part-timers, but it also indicates that something needs to be done urgently to make it more worthwhile for men to take up part-time work without excessive loss of benefits.

There is nevertheless an important distinction to be made between part-time and temporary work in the context of the EU at the present time. The prevalence of part-time work for females in the UK is, at least according to most of the evidence (see, in particular, *Employment Gazette*, May 1993) largely a voluntary phenomenon which is mutually agreeable to both employer and employee.

Figure 8.4 reveals, however, that there are relatively few temporary workers in Britain. At present, seven EU countries have minimum wage laws which discourage full-time employment. Social security costs are also often much higher than in the UK. The most important factor is, however, the cost of firing rather than of hiring. It is relatively easy to fire full-time workers in the UK but extremely difficult in Spain where, unsurprisingly, employers have responded by putting one-third of the labour force on to temporary contracts.

Table 8.5 *Employment:[1] by Sex and Full/Part Time,[2] UK (thousands)*

	Males		Females	
	Full-time	Part-time	Full-time	Part-time
1986	13 430	647	5 662	4 556
1987	13 472	750	5 795	4 696
1988	13 881	801	6 069	4 808
1989	14 071	734	6 336	4 907
1990	14 109	789	6 479	4 928
1991	13 686	799	6 350	4 933
1992	13 141	885	6 244	5 081

Notes:
[1] At Spring each year. Includes employees, self-employed, those on government training schemes and status not stated for 1986–91 and unpaid family workers for 1992.
[2] Full/part-time is based on respondents self-assessment. They exclude those who did not state whether they were full or part-time.

Source: Social Trends, 23 (1993), Chart 4.16.

Figure 8.3   *Trend to a Part-time Labour*

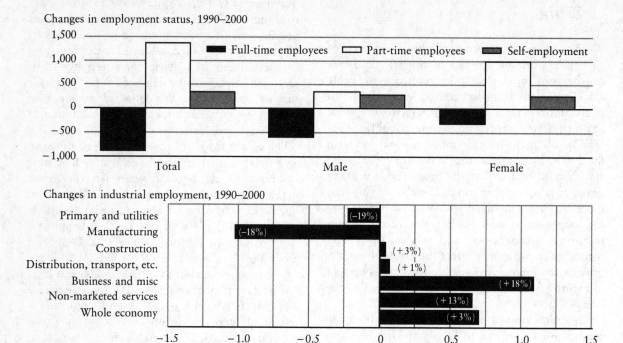

Changes in employment status, 1990–2000

Changes in industrial employment, 1990–2000

Source: Financial Times, 8 January 1993.

Figure 8.4   *Temporary Workers, % of Total Employment, 1991*

Source: The Economist, 28 August 1993.

■ 8.3 Unemployment

The most important measure of the demand for labour is unemployment. This represents the difference between the **workforce in employment**, which consists of employees in employment, the self-employed, Her Majesty's Forces and participants on work-related government training schemes, and the **workforce**[2] which also includes those people claiming benefit at Unemployment Benefit offices. This is illustrated in **Figure 8.5**, where the data have been adjusted to take account of the downwards revision referred to earlier with respect to employees in employment.

The trend in the number of unemployed can be seen more clearly in the form of **Figure 8.6**, which also includes the number of vacancies notified to Job Centres. Unemployment is here measured according to the monthly claimant count (as reported in the newspapers, but see section on measuring unemployment below). The total num-

Figure 8.5 *Workforce and Workforce in Employment,[1] UK, Seasonally Adjusted (million)*

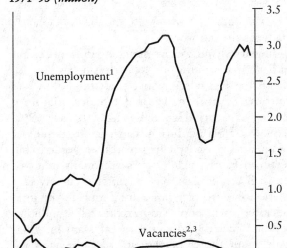

Note:
[1] As revised (see *Employment Gazette*, April 1991, p. 1991).
Source: Social Trends, 23 (1993 edn), Chart 4.2, *Employment Gazette*, Table 4.1.

Figure 8.6 *Unemployment[1] and Vacancies,[2,3] UK, 1971–93 (million)*

Notes:
[1] Seasonally adjusted unemployment (claimants aged 18 and over).
[2] About one-third of all vacancies are notified to Job Centres.
[3] Vacancy data prior to 1980 are not consistent with current coverage.
Source: Employment Gazette.

ber of unemployed on this definition reached 1 million in December 1975 , 2 million in March 1981 and 3 million in February 1985. The peak figure was 3.12 million, recorded in July 1986. Subsequently, the number unemployed fell for 44 successive months, reaching a low point of 1.60 million in March 1990, after which it grew rapidly to reach almost exactly 3 million in January 1993. It has subsequently fallen slightly, which is somewhat surprising given the much longer build-up to the previous peak in 1986.

Particular attention should be paid to the fact that the low point of each successive cycle lay above the preceding one. If that pattern is repeated, unemployment can be expected to remain at or above 2 million even at the end of a period of strong growth in the 1990s.

An alternative way to express unemployment figures is as a rate, where the numbers in **Figure 8.6** are divided by the total workforce. This appears on an annual average basis in **Figure 8.7**, which also contains the unemployment rate for males and females separately. The most notable features of **Figure 8.7** are, first, the very sharp upturn for males in 1980–81 (the rate for females rose to a much lesser degree) and in 1990–91, and second, the sharp downturn from the 1986 peak for both males and females. The rate for females

Figure 8.7   *Unemployment Rate,[1] Annual Averages, UK (%)*

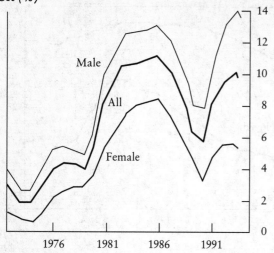

Figure 8.8   *The Unemployment Pool*

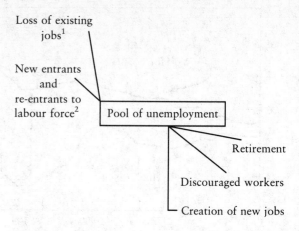

Note:
[1] The estimates use the seasonally adjusted series and are consistent with the current coverage of the claimant count.

Source: Department of Employment.

Notes:
[1] Loss of existing jobs can be voluntary or involuntary.
[2] New entrants and re-entrants consist of school leavers and college graduates; housewives; immigrants; the long-term sick and disabled; and those who do not wish to work.

may well be understated in practice since many among them do not accumulate the necessary NICs to qualify for unemployment benefit. Furthermore, unemployed women are less likely than men to say they are immediately available for work both because they often have to make arrangements for child-care and also because they may not perceive themselves to be unemployed when actively doing housework.

☐ 8.3.1 Stocks and Flows

The total number of persons who are unemployed is counted at a point in time, and thus represents a stock which we can call the **unemployment pool** (see **Figure 8.8**). It is, however, important to remember that even if the unemployment pool remains unchanged in size from one point in time to another (conventionally one month later), this does not mean that the **same people** are continuously unemployed. In the course of a year a very large number of people move in and out of employment, yet the unemployment pool will

remain constant provided the inflow exactly matches the outflow.

In general, such exact matching does not occur either on a monthly or longer-term basis as indicated in **Figure 8.9**, which plots the inflow and outflow of both males and females combined during the period commencing February 1992. This was a period during which the total number of unemployed people first rose, then began to fall again in February 1993 on a seasonally adjusted basis. It can be seen that the numbers involved in these flows are very large in relation to the total unemployment pool of approximately 3 million.

What **Figure 8.9** does not reveal is any information about the **characteristics** of those who entered and exited from the pool, or the **reasons** why they did so. Neither does it tell us anything specific about the **duration of unemployment**, since it might be the case either that the outflow during the period comprised almost entirely those flowing in, in which case most of those unemployed at the beginning of the period would still be unemployed at the end, or that the outflow comprised almost entirely those unemployed at the beginning of the period, in which case the

Figure 8.9 *UK Unemployment Flows, February 1992–July 1993 (thousand)[1]*

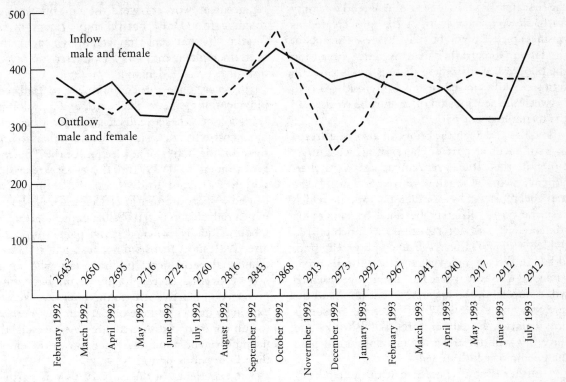

Notes:
[1] Not seasonally adjusted, standardised to $4\frac{1}{3}$-week months.
[2] Number of unemployed, seasonally adjusted (thousand).

Source: Employment Gazette, Tables 2.19 and 2.1.

average duration of unemployment would be dropping rapidly.

There are two categories of people who enter the unemployment pool. First, there are those people who have lost a job previously held, either voluntarily by giving notice or involuntarily by being made redundant. This constitutes 55–65 per cent of the total. Second, there are those people who are either entering the labour force for the first time or re-entering after a gap and who have no job to go to directly. This latter category has a number of distinct elements, namely school leavers and college graduates (normally about 15 per cent of the total); those, most commonly housewives, who have been engaged in economic activity not recognised in official statistics as 'employment' (normally about 20 per cent of the total, but nearly half of all females); immigrants; the long-

term sick and disabled; and those not wishing to work.

It is immediately evident that the unemployment pool cannot be held constant simply by creating a new job for each person who loses one. In order to achieve that objective the total outflow must equal the total inflow, including those who have never previously been employed. In effect, jobs must be created much faster than they are being lost if the unemployment pool is not to grow. There are, admittedly, devices open to a government to mitigate this problem, such as the obligation that a school leaver enter a training scheme, but the general proposition remains valid. It is, therefore, understandable that a recession causes the number of unemployed to rise sharply, since the unemployment pool is filling up both with those who have lost their jobs and with those who wish to enter the labour force for the first time. Equally, the pool will tend to empty fairly slowly, since many of the jobs created as business picks up will be filled by new entrants to the labour force rather than by those already in the pool, especially where there is a mismatch in terms of skills, location, flexibility and so forth between the new jobs on offer and the workers in the unemployment pool.

The flow through the pool can also be affected by retirement of part of the existing workforce, either at the official retirement age or earlier. When a worker reaches retirement he or she may be replaced by another person, in which case the post will either be filled by employing someone who is not registered as unemployed (which will not affect the unemployment pool although the unemployment **rate** will fall) or by someone who is registered as unemployed (which will reduce both the unemployment pool and the unemployment rate). Where a retired person is not replaced the labour force will shrink, and since this will not affect the unemployment pool the unemployment rate will rise.

A further issue is concerned with the tendency of certain workers who end up in the unemployment pool, or prospective workers who go straight into the pool without ever having had a job, to become **discouraged** by this experience. Under such circumstances they might decide not to continue to search for work, and thereby to cease to be qualified according to the rules as an unemployed person. While this would cause the unemployment pool to shrink, it would do so in a way which disguised the full extent of the unemployment problem.

We would expect the unemployment pool to empty fairly slowly were employers to decide, as a consequence of a recession, to alter their hiring practices. During the period of 'full' employment, essentially the 1950s and 1960s, labour was in short supply and hence employers were reluctant to shed labour in the face of a downturn in demand. In effect, they expected downturns to be short-lived because of governments' commitment to the principles of Keynesian demand management, and although some savings would be possible were workers to be laid off, these would

be offset by any additional costs of training replacement workers were the laid-off workers to have found alternative employment in the interim. In that sense underemployment, rather than **unemployment**, was a characteristic of periods of depressed demand.

However, once the commitment to 'full' employment has gone by the board, and a prolonged recession becomes a realistic scenario, it becomes more cost-effective to lay off workers than to hold them on the books. The election of the Thatcher government in 1979 and the severe recession which followed understandably, therefore, caused a sharp upturn in official unemployment, which reflected in part a decline in the hoarding of labour. Equally, when demand picked up again after 1981, most firms did not rush out to take on additional permanent full-time staff who might not be needed in the longer term, but rather preferred either to increase the hours worked by existing workers, to take on part-time workers or to sub-contract certain activities. As a result, the unemployment pool was much slower to empty than in previous periods.

The experience of the early 1990s was partly a consequence of the experience of the 1980s. There is good reason to believe that firms responded much faster to the 1990–92 recession than the previous time around, but in so doing they almost certainly overreacted, laying off so many employees that they could not cope with improved order books when demand began to pick up again. As a result they were obliged to rehire some of those who had been made redundant, in the process bringing the rise in the numbers unemployed to a halt much earlier than could have been predicted on the basis of prior experience.

There is one other factor of particular interest when comparing the recession of 1990–92 to its predecessors. Manufacturing once again lost the great majority of jobs, but whereas previously the same 10 to 15 per cent of the workforce moved in and out of employment, unemployment in 1990–92 extended much further both occupationally and regionally. As a result, roughly 25 per cent of the workforce became unemployed at least once during the latter period, which in turn affected confidence much more severely than had previously been customary.

☐ *8.3.2 Measuring Unemployment*

Unemployment can be measured in different ways, but there are two basic approaches to collecting the information; first, using surveys of individuals by asking about whether they have a job or would like work, and the steps they have taken to find work, and second, by counting people recorded as unemployed at government offices.

In Great Britain the main survey is the LFS, the results of which were published annually from 1984 to 1992, and are now quarterly. The annual series commenced in 1984, whereas from 1973 to 1983 it was conducted only every second year. Since 1984 the definition of unemployment used has been made compatible with that of the ILO, and comprises people who:

a   are without a paid job;
b   are available to start in the next fortnight;
c   have either looked for work at some time in the previous four weeks or are waiting to start a job already obtained.

The ILO definition is used both by the OECD and the US Bureau of Labor Statistics, and hence provides a standardised basis for international comparisons of unemployment. The ILO's unemployment rate is expressed as a proportion of the corresponding estimate of economically active people (employed **plus** unemployed).

Since, however, surveys are expensive and take time to process, the UK, in common with most EU countries, uses as its main monthly indicator of unemployment the count of those registered as unemployed. Since October 1982 the monthly figures have been based directly on the number of people claiming benefits at unemployment benefit offices, known as the **claimant count**. It is the frequency with which results are available that makes the monthly count the most widely quoted measure of unemployment.

'Claimants' include those people who claim Unemployment Benefit, Income Support and National Insurance Credits. They are counted in mid-month. Unemployment rates based on the claimant count are expressed as a percentage of the corresponding mid-month estimate of the workforce (the sum of claimant unemployment, employees in employment, the self-employed, Her Majesty's Forces and participants in work-related government training schemes). These rates are available on a seasonally-adjusted basis going back to 1971 in a series which is consistent with the current coverage of the count.

The latest LFS which has been fully analysed at the time of writing is that for Spring 1991. This indicated that there were 2.08 million people unemployed in Great Britain (as against the UK). In order to reconcile this number with the claimant count, unemployment must be confined to those aged 18 and over, because in September 1988 a guaranteed place on a Youth Training scheme (YTS) was offered to all 16 and 17 year olds, which effectively removed them all from the claimant count. The LFS/ILO figure accordingly needs to be adjusted down to 2.30 million.

The link between the two series is more complicated than might be expected, given the proximity of the figures for Spring 1991, and is illustrated in **Figure 8.10**. As can be seen, there were 660 000 claimants not classified as unemployed on the ILO measure, whereas there were 890 000 who were unemployed according to the ILO measure but who were not claiming benefits. The difference of 230 000 represented the difference between the two aggregate figures. Of the 400 000 economically inactive claimants, 140 000 did not wish to work (the men mostly because they were sick, disabled or retired and the women because they were looking after their family or home). A further 150 000 were temporarily unavailable for work and 110 000 were available but not looking for work. These are described as 'discouraged' workers if they express a belief that no work is expected to be available even if they look. The number of discouraged workers stood officially at 220 000 during 1984–86 before falling steadily to a one-third of that number in 1990, since when the number has begun to rise again (*LFS Quarterly Bulletin*, March 1993, p. 11 and Gregg, 1992, p. 10).

Figure 8.10 *The Monthly Claimant Count Compared with the ILO Measure of Unemployment,[1,2] Spring 1991, Great Britain*

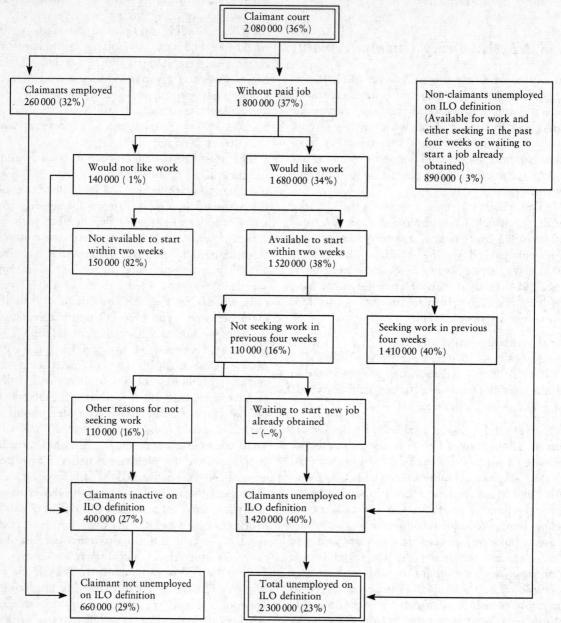

Notes:
[1] % changes since Spring 1990 are shown in brackets.
[2] The figures refer only to those aged 18 or over. This reflects the change in eligibility conditions for unemployment-related benefits for under-18 year olds in September 1988 which resulted in very few under-18 year olds remaining in the claimant court.

Source: Employment Gazette (July 1992), p. 349.

Most of the claimants who said they were employed were doing so little work that they were still entitled to claim benefits, although a number were personally active in the black economy. On the other hand, the great majority of the 590 000 unemployed who were not claimants were women, almost all married. Part-time and temporary workers do not pay unemployment insurance premiums unless their earnings reach a certain level, and hence cannot claim benefits. It was notable that a majority of the unemployed non-claimant women were specifically seeking full-time work.

It is possible to make comparisons between the two measures over the period 1984–92, as shown in **Figure 8.11**. **Figure 8.11** shows that the claimant count carried on rising to Spring 1986, in total by 220 000. During the same period the ILO measure fell from its Spring 1984 peak by a total of nearly 130 000. However, almost all of this sharp divergence took place during 1984–85. During the period Spring 1986 to Spring 1989 the claimant count fell rapidly, by 1.23 million in total, whereas the ILO measure fell by only 0.99 million during the same period.

During 1987 and 1989 the numbers ceasing to search for work according to the ILO definition were heavily outweighed by the numbers ceasing to claim benefit. Preliminary estimates indicate that the claimant count fell by 240 000, whereas the ILO measure fell by only 110 000.

During 1988 and 1989, as shown in **Table 8.6**, there was a surge in the number of people taking up new full-time jobs. When a claimant takes up employment he or she necessarily forgoes benefits. There is accordingly little financial advantage in taking up a part-time job. A drop in the number

Figure 8.11 *Comparisons of Alternative Measures of Unemployment, UK*

Notes:
[1] Unadjusted.
[2] Seasonally adjusted.
Source: LFS; Employment Department.

of claimants is therefore likely to be associated with growth in full-time rather than part-time jobs, and as shown above the number of claimants did fall sharply in 1988 and 1989. The more modest reduction in the ILO data is unsurprising given that most of those searching but not eligible to claim will be women looking for part-time jobs, and these grew more slowly than in previous years from 1988 to 1990.

As can be seen, significant discrepancies between the different measures largely disappeared as they were progressively put on to a standar-

Table 8.6 *Growth of Employment, 1984–90*

	Average increase 1984–88	Average increase 1984–90	Estimated increase 1988–89	Estimated increase 1989–90
All persons in employment	424 500	397 300	877 000	206 000
All full-timers	115 250	159 900	521 000	137 000
All part-timers	127 000	96 700	11 000	58 000

Source: Employment Gazette (April 1991), p. 179.

dised basis, but the gap apparently opened up again during 1990 before disappearing completely in 1992. It is doubtful that the definitional issue will ever be fully laid to rest. Critics on the far right of the political spectrum argue that the unemployed should exclude all those who could be in education and training; all those who could have retired early; all women, or at least all who are married; and all those who have been unemployed for less than six months. On their reckoning, therefore, unemployment is largely an illusion. Critics on the far left argue, however, that unemployment is not merely real but understated. This is because many people do not choose to register as available to work, and also because the government deliberately distorts the official figures.

There can be no doubt that the government has changed the methods of recording unemployment statistics since it was first elected in 1979. **Table 8.7** offers one version of the most significant of these changes. In every case except one the redefinitions caused the numbers of unemployed to fall, so it is understandable that the government was constantly being accused of 'fiddling' the

statistics. In point of fact, many of the changes resulted from a desire to improve accuracy and to bring the statistics into line with international practice, and the charges of fiddling the numbers have largely lost their force. It has anyway to be borne in mind that even if the official figures are indeed understated, no account is taken of those who, despite being officially unemployed, are economically active in the black economy.

There are accordingly grounds for expecting the official figures to be simultaneously both overstated and understated. Assuming these effects cancel out to a considerable extent, this still leaves open the question as to how much of any reduction in unemployment is the result of government policy and how much is due to statistical chicanery. According to the Unemployment Unit there were 30 changes in the way unemployment was measured between 1979 and 1991. According to the government there were only eight changes of any significance, of which two were concerned with **redefining** unemployment **per se** while the other six were concerned with the **rules that govern benefit entitlement** and thereby the number of people registering as unemployed (see

Table 8.7   *Changes in the Methods of Recording Unemployment Statistics, 1979–89*

Date	Change	Effect on numbers
Oct. 1979	Fortnightly payment of benefits	+20 000
Nov. 1981	Men over 60 offered higher supplementary benefit to leave the working population	−37 000
Oct. 1982	Registration at Job Centres made voluntary	
	Computer count of benefit claimants substituted for clerical count of registrants	−190 000
Mar. 1983	Men 60 and over given National Insurance credits or higher supplementary benefit without claiming unemployment benefit	−162 000
Jul. 1985	Discrepancies in Northern Ireland count corrected	−5 000
Mar. 1986	Two-week delay in compilation of figures to reduce overrecording	−50 000
Jul. 1986	Inclusion of self-employed and HM Forces in denominator of unemployment percentage (now working population)	−1.4%
Jul. 1988	Inclusion of those on work-related government training schemes in the denominator of unemployment percentage	n/a
Sept. 1988	Removal of all under 18s who have left school and not found a job but guaranteed a YTS place	−40 000
Jul. 1989	Changes in conditions of the Redundant Mineworkers Payment Scheme	−15 500

Sources: Employment Gazette (September 1982), (December 1982), (July 1985), (March/April 1986), (December 1988), (December 1990).

Employment Gazette, December 1990, **p. 608** for details).

The first official redefinition took place in October 1982 for two connected reasons. At this time the old system of registering at an unemployment centre for both benefits and another job was abolished. Under the old system, an unemployed worker would receive benefits and might be offered a choice of three jobs from which to pick one. If he or she refused the job offers and could not find alternative work then he or she might forfeit benefits. The system thus contained an incentive to find work and not to stay unemployed unnnecessarily. What the new system did was to split the payment of benefits (which was handed over to the DHSS, or Department of Health and Social Security) from the problem of finding a job. The argument for the changes was that it would improve efficiency by enabling the staff at Job Centres to concentrate on trying to fit workers to suitable jobs. However, the split meant that there was no compulsion to register at the Centres, and the effect was to decrease measured unemployment.

The second official redefinition took place in March 1986 when the production of the monthly figures was deferred by two weeks to take place three weeks (instead of one week) after the specified count date. The change was necessary to take account of those who had already ceased to be unemployed on the count day but had not yet been removed from the register.

According to the government there have only been six significant changes to the **rules** concerned with benefit entitlement. These are listed in **Table 8.7**. These six, plus the other two definitional changes, are accommodated in the consistent (seasonally adjusted) claimant count which goes back to 1971, and which, it is claimed, offers a distortion-free comparison over time. There have also been two changes to the way in which unemployment **rates** have been calculated. In July 1986 the denominator of the equation was expanded, in particular to take account of the much enlarged number of self-employed. This, given an unchanged numerator, inevitably caused the rate to fall. The denominator was expanded further in July 1988 with the

inclusion of those on work-related government training schemes. However, this followed their inclusion in the statistics of the employed workforce and had very little effect on the rate of unemployment. These changes in the way unemployment rates have been calculated have not affected the **numbers** included in the unemployment count.

Many of the other changes cited by the Unemployment Unit (see Gregg, 1992, Table 2) are too insignificant to warrant further attention and are themselves rather suspect (Gregg, 1992, p. 8). Insofar as the accusation of fiddling the numbers can be made to stick it relates, first, to the introduction of the 'Restart' programme (see **p. 327**) and, second, to the introduction of tighter 'availability-for-work' tests in 1986 and in the Social Security Act 1989. These changes can be justified insofar as they weeded out people who should not have been on the unemployment register in the first place. They are excluded from **Table 8.7** because, effectively, they involved neither a change in rules nor a change in the coverage of the count. Nevertheless, they accounted for a reduction in the official count of the unemployed, and therefore created the reasonable suspicion that the government was trying simultaneously to claim credit both for generating a huge fall in unemployment and for cleaning up the statistics.

8.3.3 Unemployment by Age, Duration and Sex

The overall position as of April 1993, when there were 3 million unemployed according to the claimant count, is shown in **Figure 8.12**. In each case the unemployed are broken down into three age groups, (namely 18–24, 25–49 and over 50 respectively), and also according to the duration of unemployment (namely up to 25 weeks, 26–52 weeks and over 52 weeks respectively). Each sub-section thus represents a combination of a specific age group and duration. The proportion of all those who fell into each sub-section who

Figure 8.12   *Unemployment by Age, Duration and Sex, April 1993 (000)*

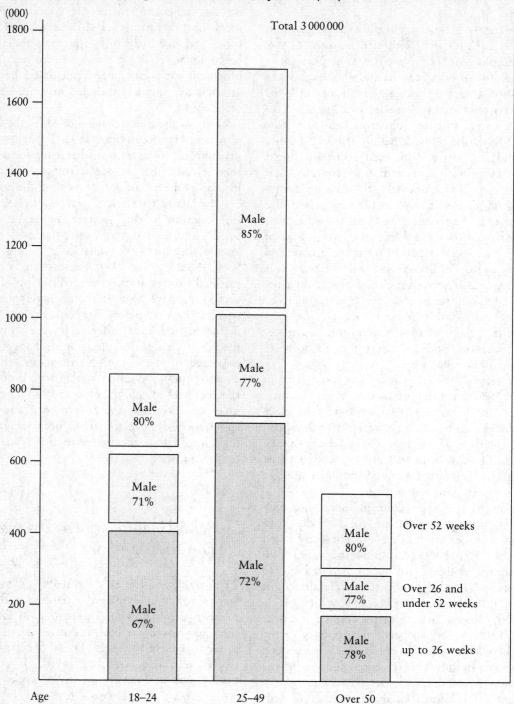

Source: Employment Gazette (August 1993), Table 2.5.

were male is also specified (and hence by subtraction from 100 per cent the proportion who were female can be deduced).

If one compares the situation in April 1987 when total unemployment stood at 3.1 million, it is interesting to note that the relationship between age and unemployment was very similar despite the sharp drop in unemployment during the interim period. In 1987 there was a little less unemployment in the 25–49 age group and a little more in the others. Of greater importance was the change in duration. Whereas 38 per cent of the unemployed were unemployed for up to 26 weeks in April 1987, this had risen to 42 per cent in April 1989 and to 57 per cent in July 1990. However, by 1993 it was only back to the 1989 figure rather than to that of 1987. The most significant fall occurred among those unemployed for over one year, where the percentage fell from 42 per cent in April 1987 to 40 per cent in April 1989 and then to 31.5 per cent in July 1990. By 1993 the percentage had risen back only to 34 per cent.

This clearly demonstrates that **unemployment becomes increasingly transient** during a period of economic growth. Unfortunately, it also demonstrates that long-term unemployment is both far more pervasive than it was during the period of 'full' employment after 1945 and also that it is likely to stay that way in spite of the improvement during the late 1980s. Nevertheless, compared to other advanced economies, the UK's record is by no means one of the worst, as shown below.

Figure 8.12 also contains information on the relative incidence of unemployment on males and females. Most of the percentages fall within the 70/30–80/20 range, but it is notable that, first, females are disproportionately likely to be unemployed in the 18–24 age bracket and disproportionately unlikely to be unemployed in the 25–49 age bracket for periods in excess of one year. The fact that, as a general rule of thumb, males are three times as likely to be unemployed as females, irrespective of age or duration of unemployment, is clearly less to do with aggregate numbers (see the earlier discussion on activity rates) than with the particular sectors in which redundancies have occurred and with the willingness of females

to take up part-time jobs which may be plentiful but are nevertheless shunned by most unemployed males.

The relatively low number of those who are officially unemployed at the age of 50 or over is almost certainly deceptive. According to the OECD, formal employment for men and women aged 55 or over is going out of fashion in the industrialised world. The latest figure for males in the USA is 37 per cent, compared to 33 per cent in the UK, 28 per cent in France and 11 per cent in Italy. The figures for females are at roughly half these levels. Two decades ago the figures were typically 60–70 per cent higher. The sum of those of working age who are either unemployed or inactive is referred to as 'non-employment', and this is estimated to apply to 25 per cent of men and 50 per cent of women over 50 throughout the OECD.

The OECD blame these high figures on social security rules, occupational pension schemes and a large increase in the number of people covered by sickness and invalidity schemes. In the UK roughly the same number of people were claiming sickness and invalidity benefit in 1986 as in 1980, whereas by 1990 the number of male claimants had risen by 25 per cent and of women claimants had more than doubled.

□ 8.3.4 Long-term Unemployment

Just as employment becomes more transient for individuals in booms, so it becomes increasingly drawn-out in recessions. **Table 8.8** illustrates the position in respect of the proportion of total unemployment which was in excess of 12 months' duration from April 1990 to January 1993. In the latter month the total was almost 1 million, a disturbingly high figure. Not surprisingly, given the 1990–92 recession, it was twice as high as three years earlier. The effects upon those unemployed for more than two years obviously reflects the lagged effect of turning points in the cycle.

A number of EU countries nevertheless normally have a far worse record if the long-term un-

Table 8.8   *Long-term Unemployment in Great Britain*

Duration of unemployment	January 1993 (thousands)	Percentage change since April 1990	January 1992
Over 1 year	974	100	40
Over 18 months	646	75	55
Over 2 years	419	39	46
Over 3 years	202	−9	13
Over 4 years	132	−25	0
Over 5 years	98	−29	−5

Source: Department of Employment.

employed are represented as a proportion of the total unemployed, especially Ireland, Spain, Italy and Belgium. These can be compared with the far lower proportions in the USA and Japan, and also with those European Free Trade Association countries such as Norway and Sweden which devote considerable resources to the prevention of long-term unemployment.

It is notable that far more Americans lose their job every month (roughly 2 per cent) than workers in the EU (roughly 0.3 per cent in France and Germany), yet they remain unemployed for an average of only 2.5 months, much less than is typical in the EU. This reflects the very fluid labour market in the USA where workers move rapidly from one relatively low-paid service sector job to another and where, for example, there is a tradition of working one's way through college. This has helped to keep the US unemployment rate below that in the EU, where the immovable block of the long-term unemployed creates a base level of 3–4 per cent unemployment even at times of growth.

In most EU countries the problem of long-term unemployment got worse during the 1980s, in some cases (such as Ireland and Greece) markedly so. Only in Britain, where the Spring 1984 rate was relatively high at 47 per cent (though by no means absolutely the highest), did the problem improve noticeably after 1984 as the government began to address itself more seriously to the issue. A key issue is that the long-term unemployed must have an incentive to maintain active job status. In the early 1980s no such incentive ex-

isted, and numbers grew rapidly. The introduction of Restart interviews and tougher availability for work testing were crucial in accounting for the speed of the subsequent fall (to 27 per cent in Spring 1991). However, toughness alone is clearly insufficient, and high quality training and job search programmes are also needed.

The relatively high incidence of short-term unemployment in the UK in recent years is probably a key factor in explaining why unemployment has had an unusually depressive effect upon wages.

8.3.5 Unemployment and Qualifications

Over the past decade the unemployment rate has been higher for people with lower levels of qualification than for well-qualified people. Approximately 12.6 per cent of economically active people with no formal qualifications were unemployed in Spring 1992, whereas among graduates and others with qualifications above GCE A-level or equivalent the unemployment rate was only 4.3 per cent (see *Employment Gazette*, June 1993, p. 288).

Qualification levels are closely related to age, with younger people tending to have higher levels of qualification. Those with higher levels of qualification tend to have been out of a job and looking for work for shorter periods than those with lesser or no qualifications.

8.3.6 *Regional Dispersion of Unemployment*

Figure 8.13 illustrates the changing pattern of the regional dispersion of unemployment since 1979, measured as the difference between the rate in each of the 11 regions of the UK and the UK average. By the standards of many other EU countries, such as Italy, the regional disparities in the UK have never been particularly severe, and it is reasonable to treat Northern Ireland as something of a special case, permanently marooned at the top of the unemployment pile. As an approximation, excluding Northern Ireland, the region with the highest rate of unemployment suffered twice as much unemployment as the region with the lowest rate from 1979 to 1991, irrespective of the stage in the trade cycle.

Prior to 1979 the gap between lowest and highest had closed somewhat due to regional policy, but this was largely allowed to wither away after 1979. Despite this, the gap closed again at the end of the 1980s, and did so very rapidly after 1989, in which year the rate was 10.2 per cent in the North and 3.6 per cent in East Anglia. In 1992 the rate was 11.3 per cent in the North but 7.8 per cent in East Anglia, indicating clearly that the gap had tended to close from below.

The same regions have, with the very recent exception of the South-East, appeared consistently at the top and bottom of the distribution. From 1979 to 1991 the same regions also appeared consistently above and below the UK average.

Figure 8.13   *Regional Unemployment*

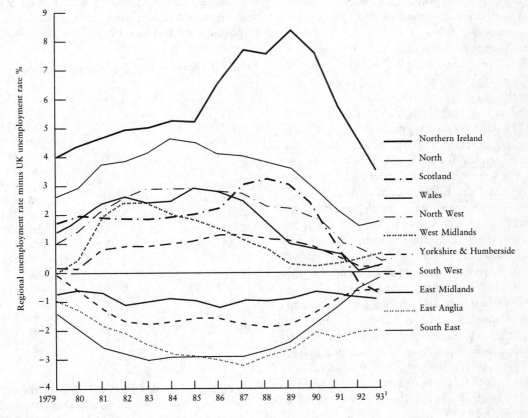

Note:
[1] Forecast.
Source: Employment Gazette.

One region's experience since 1979 is nevertheless of particular note. In 1979 the West Midlands was still very prosperous, but the 1980–82 recession caused it to suffer a disproportionate rise in unemployment (up from 5 per cent in 1979 to 12.5 per cent in 1984). However, it improved markedly after 1986, is currently once again very close to the UK average (and even fell below it briefly early in 1991). Interestingly, East Anglia (with its small working population) has for the past six years had less unemployment even than the South-East, partly as a result of improved communications.

Northern Ireland excepted, it would appear that the improvement in the employment situation to mid-1990 was fairly evenly dispersed. In contrast, whereas unemployment rose everywhere after the first half of 1991, the rate of increase was less severe in regions which were manufacturing for export than in the South-East and South-West, which were far more dependent upon non-exportable services.

The evidence from the data is that unemployment fans out along a North-South axis. For the UK as a whole, unemployment first began to fall during the third quarter of 1986, whereas this occurred one quarter later in the case of Scotland. The UK average turned up again during the second quarter of 1990. In the South-East and East Anglia, unemployment bottomed out during the fourth quarter of 1989 and one quarter later in the South-West. By way of contrast it had not bottomed out until the third quarter of 1990 in the North-West and it was still falling in Scotland and Northern Ireland at the end of that year. The only real puzzle is that the first region to exhibit a reduction in unmployment was the North, a whole year earlier than in Scotland.

The consistency of the pecking order in terms of regional unemployment is a feature common to EU countries and Japan (with the UK exhibiting the most consistent order of all) but not to the USA. This suggests that it has its roots in labour immobility, and hence that it remained a feature of the UK economy in the absence of local wage bargaining and in the presence of wide regional house price differentials. The latter, at least, have been eroded significantly over the past two years

and as shown in **Figure 8.13**, eight of the eleven regions currently have remarkably similar rates of unemployment. Such circumstances do not indicate any urgent need for regional policy measures, but rather a need to focus upon specific unemployment blackspots, such as towns where the main industry has gone into terminal decline and the inner areas of large cities, irrespective of where they are located.

8.3.7 International Comparisons of Unemployment

It is possible to make international comparisons of unemployment using either national (but mostly incompatible) data or standardised data published by the OECD (see **Employment Gazette**, September 1992, pp. 421–31). **Table 8.9** presents the latest comparative standardised data for a selection of developed countries. Whereas the

Table 8.9 *Standardised Unemployment Rates[1]*

	% rate	Latest month
Spain	21.1	Feb. 1993
Finland	17.1	Apr. 1993
Ireland	16.9	May 1993
Canada	11.3	May 1993
France	10.9	Apr. 1993
Australia	10.7	May 1993
United Kingdom	10.4	May 1993
Italy	9.1	Jan. 1993
Belgium	8.9	May 1993
Sweden	8.5	May 1993
Netherlands	8.0	Apr. 1993
United States	6.8	May 1993
Norway	5.9	Feb. 1993
Germany[2]	5.8	Apr. 1993
Portugal	4.8	Feb. 1993
Japan	2.3	Apr. 1993

Notes:
[1] Seasonally adjusted, OECD standardised rates.
[2] There are no reliable figures available for a unified Germany. The rate quoted is for the former West Germany.
Source: Employment Gazette, Table 2.18.

Figure 8.14 *Unemployment Rates, International Comparisons, 1972–93 (%)*

Notes:
[1] Germany unification took place at the end of 1990. Separate data is available from 1992.
[2] Germany, France, UK, Italy, Belgium, Netherlands, Portugal and Spain.
[3] Forecast.
Source: Social Trends, 23 (1993 edn), Chart 4.2.3; *Employment Gazette*.

UK rate is on the high side, it nevertheless looks fairly reasonable compared to that in Spain and Ireland.

The data at one point in time can, however, be deceptive. **Figure 8.14** accordingly plots the OECD data over the past two decades for five major industrialised countries and for 8 members of the EU taken as an average.

There are, as ever, certain reservations that need to be borne in mind when interpreting the data. High unemployment, as in Spain, can be attributed to slow growth. Low unemployment, as in Portugal, does not, however, necessarily have anything to do with rapid growth. In fact it results from very low productivity. Activity rates are highly divergent, as are rates of youth and female unemployment and rates of self-employment (these matters have been addressed else-

where). Hence it is important to compare like with like in assessing the performance of the UK in respect of unemployment. On that basis, as can be seen in **Figure 8.14**, the UK's record was undoubtedly satisfactory until 1974, and, in relation to countries other than West Germany and Japan, no worse than average until 1980 when the recession began to bite in earnest. Between 1979 and 1983 the UK's rate more than doubled, but this was less out of line with experience elsewhere in the EU than is generally believed to be the case. The rate in Spain, for example, also doubled from 8.5 to 17.2 per cent, and indeed continued to rise to a peak of 21.4 per cent in 1985. Partly as a consequence (the rates in Ireland and the Netherlands were also very high by 1983), the rapid fall in the rate in the UK after 1986 (the turning point measured using national data) brought it down below the EU average and indeed very close to the rate being experienced in West Germany. In France, after rising continuously from 1974 to 1987 (a fourfold rise overall), the rate remained stubbornly high, registering 9 per cent in July 1990. At that time the rate in Ireland was 14.7 per cent and in Spain 16 per cent, compared to 6.2 per cent in the UK.

It would appear, therefore, that countries in the EU which chose not to engineer such a severe recession as was suffered by the UK during 1980–81 had initially made the wiser choice. However, the UK appeared to be reaping benefits in the longer term once unemployment began to fall after 1986. Countries elsewhere in the EU, which preferred to protect jobs rather than re-structure their economies during the early 1980s, discovered that their problems did not go away, and that the need, as in the case of France, to bring inflation down to West German levels in order to stave off devaluation in the EMS meant maintaining tight control on demand and hence high rates of unemployment.

When the UK also found itself under a similar constraint through joining the ERM, the UK rate rose back through the EU average. Now that the UK has departed from the ERM the UK rate is set to decline even though it is set to rise almost everywhere else in the EU. The gender consequences of these divergent trends should prove interesting since over the past decade the UK has consistently been the only member state where the unemployment rate for women has been lower than that for men (Commission of the European Communities, 1992, Chart 6).

The data indicate clearly that unusually high rates of unemployment by historical standards are not a peculiarly British affliction. What is parti-cularly interesting is why they do not affect Japan. Part of the answer is, as usual, a matter of statistical definition since it is far less common for part-time workers who lose their jobs in Japan to be recorded as actively seeking a new job than it is in the EU. More important, in terms of potential lessons for the UK, is the degree of **wage flexibility** in the Japanese labour market.

In Japan a significant element in the total wage bill consists of bonuses, which are cut sharply during times of recession. This reduction in wages makes it possible for Japanese employers to keep their employees in work, and indeed in many cases to offer a virtual guarantee of life-long employment. In effect, rising wages are traded off against job security. Unfortunately, such an idea is alien to the culture of the UK labour market, although the 1990–92 recession has seen some Japanese-style agreements. So long as workers in the UK regard an annual pay rise as their inalien-able right, and furthermore a rise as large as that awarded to 'comparable' groups of workers, the UK's rate of unemployment will remain stub-bornly high by Japanese standards.

☐ 8.3.8 *Labour Market Flexibility*

The UK labour market appears to have become more flexible during the 1980s given the evidence of increased overtime working, part-time working and self-employment. Nevertheless, such a con-clusion is by no means self-evident.

In the first place, it can be argued that tempor-ary work may indeed be precisely that, and may lead subsequently to a (further) period of unem-ployment rather than to a permanent job. Second, part-time jobs, mostly undertaken by females, neither utilise properly such skills as the work-force possess nor offer many opportunities for skill acquisition and advancement. Third, self-employment is partly a response to unemploy-ment and utilises such skills as already exist with-out offering many opportunities for skill enhance-ment. In view of these factors it may be argued that the labour market has become more inflex-ible rather than the opposite.

Clearly, a flexible labour market requires skills to be acquired **in advance** of their being needed, so that skill shortages do not automatically ap-pear as soon as demand picks up. Furthermore, skills that are acquired must be **transferable**, rather than occupation- or firm-specific. During the 1980–81 recession, when training was predo-minantly privately funded, it mostly went by the board. This situation should not recur to the same degree given the public funding of training pro-grammes, but there is a good way to go before there is a smooth transition between such pro-grammes and full-time employment.

It may anyway be argued that the key issue for the UK is that what is needed is more flexibility with respect to pay rather than to jobs. During the 1980–81 recession wages remained too high and the recession manifested itself via a sharp upturn in unemployment. As noted already, this is not what happens in Japan, where bonuses rather than jobs are cut when demand falls back.

Much of the problem lies with the fact that in the UK higher productivity is typically passed on as higher wages instead of lower prices combined with job security. Whilst this can be justified for the individual firm, it is an undesirable outcome for the economy as a whole. This is, first of all, because higher wages inevitably leak into sectors where productivity is not rising, and therefore cause rising prices in these sectors. Second, it is preferable that the real wage of workers should be increased by combining modest wage rises with constant or falling prices, rather than by combin-ing much higher wages with somewhat more slowly rising prices. Such a conclusion does not need to be spelled out in competing countries, but even a decade of Thatcherism appears largely to have failed to get the message through in the UK. The longer-term effects of the 1990–92 recession may well prove to be more positive in this respect, but we must wait to see what happens when output picks up more rapidly before drawing any conclusions.

□ 8.3.9 Types of Unemployment

It has become customary to divide unemployment up into four main types:

- **Frictional unemployment:** consists mainly of people temporarily out of work as they move from one job to another
- **Structural unemployment:** arises when there is a mismatch of skills and job opportunities when the pattern of demand and output changes
- **Demand-deficient unemployment:** otherwise known as Keynesian unemployment, this arises when demand falls and wages and prices have not yet adjusted to restore full employment
- **Classical unemployment:** arises when the wage level stays above that at which the labour market will clear, possibly as a result of the exercise of union power or the existence of mini-mum wages legislation.

Unemployment can also be seasonal, but the unemployment data is normally 'seasonally-adjusted' to prevent this from showing up inde-pendently.

However, the current debate about unemploy-ment is usually conducted in terms of whether it is **voluntary** or **involuntary**, although the distinction is not as clear-cut as it might seem at first sight. Unemployment is 'voluntary' if a worker is of-fered a job but is unwilling to accept it at the real wage on offer. Clearly, frictional unemployment is voluntary because the workers concerned have chosen to be temporarily unemployed while mov-ing from one job to another (and it is evident in any case that such unemployment does not merit a policy response by the government to eliminate it; indeed, if it did not exist the economy could not evolve to meet changing patterns of demand). Structural unemployment can also be regarded as voluntary insofar as any worker who has become unemployed in one industry or occupa-tion refuses to accept a job which is on offer in another occupation. The fact that the worker may find the job unappealing, or may consider the wage on offer to be lower than is acceptable, does not detract from the fact that such beha-viour is voluntary.

Classical unemployment is also voluntary inso-far as it occurs when a worker – or more likely a group of workers organised in a trade union – refuses to accept the wage on offer for existing or potential jobs. However, this is strictly true only if the trade union has been mandated by the work-force to seek a wage higher than the firm is willing to pay while keeping them all in employment. If an individual worker who is willing to work for a lower wage rather than become redundant is prevented from so doing through the behaviour of a union which he or she does not support, then that person can be said to be 'involuntarily' unemployed. Nevertheless, **involuntary** unemployment is **predominantly caused by a deficiency of demand** such as occurs during the downswing of the economic cycle.

Given the above distinction, it is possible to envisage the labour market when unemployment is purely **voluntary**. In other words, the level of demand is sufficiently high to provide a job for everyone who is willing to work at whatever real wage results from the equilibrium between the demand for, and supply of, labour in the labour market. In such circumstances it is reasonable to consider employment to be 'full'. However, this does not mean that, as was true during the 1950s when voluntary unemployment was predominantly frictional, fewer than 500 000 workers would currently be unemployed if demand was not deficient because, for various reasons, the numbers of those unwilling to work at the mar-

ket-clearing real wage may have increased substantially.

The gap between the rate of unemployment which would exist were the labour market to be in equilibrium, and the rate which actually exists at any point in time, is known as the **natural rate of unemployment**. The natural rate cannot, by implication, be eliminated through a policy of generating additional demand. It is a problem which is created on the supply side of the economy and hence can be tackled only using **supply-side** measures.

8.3.10 Why is Unemployment so High?

At the beginning of the 1980s unemployment was approximately ten times as high as it had been two decades earlier, and it has remained very high by postwar standards for the past decade. In many ways it is easier to explain what did **not** cause this long-term adjustment to happen than to explain what did.

Table 8.10   *The Causes of Male Unemployment in the UK*

	Effect on Unemployment Rate (%)		
Changes In	1956–66 to 1967–74	1967–74 to 1975–79	1975–79 to 1980–83
Employers' labour taxes	0.25	0.38	0.44
Unemployment benefit	0.54	−0.09	−0.10
Trade union power	1.18	1.17	0.80
Real import prices	−0.58	1.47	−0.93
Mismatch of skills	0.16	0.20	0.49
Incomes policy	–	−0.36	0.49
Demand factors	0.12	0.54	6.56

	1956–66	1967–74	1975–79	1980–83
Estimated 'natural' rate of unemployment	2.0	4.2	7.6	9.1
Actual rate of unemployment	2.0	3.8	6.8	13.8

Source: Layard and Nickell (1986).

For example, it had little to do with the **growth in the labour force**. In the short term, an increase in activity rates or in the number of school leavers can create an excess supply of labour, but past experience in the UK as well as experience overseas demonstrates that demand adjusts to supply changes within a few years. Nor was **insufficient investment** to blame. It is evident that a given stock of capital can be combined with a variable number of workers by working it for longer hours. In any event, when capacity becomes scarce there is typically a surge in investment to enhance the capital stock, as in 1988. It is also very difficult to demonstrate that **machines replace labour**, although new technology does cause temporary structural unemployment. If, for example, the typewriter was supposed to destroy the jobs of all those clerks inefficiently wielding quill pens, where did all the clerical jobs come from which the advent of the computer was subsequently supposed to destroy? As information processing speeds up, so more information gets processed!

On a more positive note, Layard and Nickell (1986), examining male unemployment from 1956 to 1983, concluded that there were seven major contributory reasons for the upturn in unemployment, as shown in **Table 8.10**.

There was considerable variation in the contribution made by each factor cited, and during sub-periods several appeared to have had the effect of reducing unemployment. During the period up to the early 1970s the second-strongest influence was exerted by unemployment benefit. In other words, as the **replacement rate** – the ratio of unemployment benefit to wages – rises, so workers become more selective about the jobs they are prepared to accept. However, it is notable that from the mid-1970s onwards this ceased to be a factor in rising unemployment because benefits ceased to rise relative to wages. Until 1974 only trade union power exerted a stronger influence, and one that remained constant up to the end of the decade, although by then it was making a proportionately smaller contribution to the higher level of unemployment. During the early 1980s, however, it became much less significant, which was to be

expected given the effects of the recession and the attack on union powers and privileges by the Thatcher government.

Throughout the period employers' labour taxes remained a positive factor contributing to unemployment. This was only to be expected given that labour taxes have the effect of raising the marginal cost of employing additional workers. The mismatch of skills also continued to exert a positive influence which grew modestly throughout the period, but which in aggregate accounted for well under 10 per cent of male unemployment. Incomes policies made little contribution in any sub-period, and were neutral taking the period as a whole.

During the middle sub-period the biggest contribution was made by rising real import prices. In the face of the quadrupling in the price of oil and sharp increases in other commodity prices, many firms responded to the consequent costs by laying off workers. However, real import prices also tend to fall significantly at times, and as can be seen reductions in real import prices were a factor – much the most significant factor – contributing to the maintenance of employment during the other sub-periods. Hence, in the long term it is not to be expected that real import prices will exert a strong uni-directional force upon unemployment.

Prior to the latter part of the 1970s demand management was used primarily to sustain employment, although to increasingly less effect as inflation came progressively to be regarded as a more important policy objective. By the end of the decade it had effectively been discarded as a means to maintain employment, and it was viciously reined back by the incoming Thatcher Government. As **Table 8.10** shows, this swamped out all other factors contributing to the rise in unemployment at that time.

As can be seen in the lower part of **Table 8.10**, there was little difference between measured unemployment and estimates of the natural rate until the end of the 1970s. In other words, the slow but almost continuous rise in measured unemployment had little to do with a deficiency of demand, and could largely be explained by

Table 8.11 *NAIRU Estimates for the UK (claimant definition)*

	Period within which the estimates fall:			
	1969–73	1974–80	1981–87	1988–90
NAIRU range	1.6%–5.6%	4.5%–7.3%	5.2%–9.9%	3.5%–8.1%
Actual U rate	2.5%	3.8%	10.1%	6.8%
Number of estimates	11	13	15	5

Source: Bank of England Quarterly Bulletin (May 1993), Table 4.A.

supply-side factors. These factors also served to maintain the rise in unemployment during the early 1980s but were temporarily swamped by a massive dose of deflation, so it is hardly surprising that unemployment followed the pattern illustrated previously.

The natural rate is by its very nature a difficult concept to measure accurately, and there is no unanimity about Layard and Nickell's calculations (see Dawson, 1990). Nevertheless, the natural rate almost certainly began to fall after 1983, and there was subsequently, as we have seen, a four-year period during which measured unemployment fell continuously. The gap between the natural rate and actual unemployment is important because if actual unemployment exceeds the natural rate, then the gap can be bridged by expanding demand without setting off an inflationary spiral, whereas if there is no gap an expansion of supply must precede any increase in demand if an inflationary spiral is to be avoided.

The relationship between inflation and unemployment can be used as an alternative means to identify the natural rate. When actual unemployment is less than the natural rate and there is excess demand in the labour market, inflation will tend to **accelerate**: in other words, it will be higher in any one time period than in the preceding period, irrespective of what the rate was in the earlier period. Equally, when actual unemployment is greater than the natural rate, and there is excess supply in the labour market, inflation will tend to **decelerate**. When the two rates are

identical, and the labour market is in equilibrium, inflation will consequently **remain steady at whatever rate exists at the time**. This is known as the NAIRU: **the non-accelerating inflation rate of unemployment**. Thus, in principle, the natural rate can be identified by the fact that the rate of inflation is neither rising nor falling.

In practice, this may not be easy to pin down. What is certain is that the natural rate shifted considerably during the 1980s as the supply conditions of the economy evolved under a variety of pressures, as shown in **Table 8.11**. A number of these are discussed in Chapter 9, such as the concerted attack upon trade union power and the insider–outsider distinction. Others were referred to in the earlier section on supply-side economics.

If the supply-side measures have been successful then the natural rate should be permanently lower in the 1990s compared to the 1980s. Nevertheless, one problem which has, if anything, become harder to resolve is the mismatch between job-seekers and vacancies. While this could have something to do with increasing choosiness about jobs by those out of work, this is unlikely given the increasingly tight rules to qualify for unemployment benefit. It is much more likely to be due to imperfections in the housing market where there are big differences in house prices in different regions, and where jobs are normally most plentiful in areas where house prices are relatively high. The reduction in private sector rentals and the difficulties of exchanging council houses only make the problem worse.

8.3.11 Unemployment and Real Wages

During the 1980s real wages rose exceptionally fast in the UK although they fell in the USA. However, this may simply have reflected relative productivity. Rising real wages which are wholly offset by rising productivity do not eat into profits, in which case there should be no need for firms to shed labour.

We have examined the trend in productivity in Chapter 3 (see **p. 69**), but what exactly is the link to real wages and jobs? Poret (1990) seeks to answer this question by setting real wages against productivity. Real wages are defined as nominal wages deflated by the private consumption deflator, while labour efficiency is defined as output per employee adjusted for the replacement of workers by increased capital investment. Poret divides the former by the latter and expresses this ratio as an index, with the average value of the ratio for 1960–89 set at 100.

The ratio fell during the 1980s in virtually every OECD country. In 1989 the ratio was below its 1960–89 average with very few exceptions, among which the most prominent was Britain. From 1983–87 the ratio remained steady in Britain at around 95, but in 1989 it rose back up to 100 where it had previously been in 1981. Why was Britain so different?

The OECD study discovered that the biggest single factor in explaining the slower growth in real wages during the 1980s was basically the higher unemployment sustained during that decade. The study measured this using the gap between actual unemployment and the NAIRU (defined as the level at which unemployment exerts neither upwards nor downwards pressure on real wages relative to labour efficiency). As a proxy measure for this gap, the study used a measure based on a moving average of actual unemployment.

After 1982 the gap opened up throughout the OECD. In 1989 it still existed in France (where, as we have noted, unemployment grew steadily during the 1980s), whereas in Britain, by 1989, the gap had become negative (actual unemployment less than the NAIRU, which was calculated at the time as 8 per cent) by two percentage points. This was the largest negative gap anywhere in the OECD. What this indicates is that unless unemployment is allowed to rise to at least the NAIRU then real wages in Britain are likely to exceed what is warranted by productivity. Supply-side reforms do not appear, on this evidence, to have made any difference to what has been a long-standing relationship.

8.3.12 The Reduction of Unemployment

The problem of unemployment is complex, and there cannot accordingly be any simple nostrum to make it disappear. What we have established so far is that sharp, short-term changes in unemployment are normally demand-driven, whereas the medium- to long-term adjustment takes place on the supply side.

The use of demand management, when demand is deficient in the short term, is appropriate where the initial unemployment rate exceeds the NAIRU. For obvious reasons, it is undesirable to use it if there is subsequently going to be an inflationary spiral. Hence, insofar as additional demand is to be created, it must be targeted towards those parts of the economy where there is the greatest excess supply. Clearly, however, whenever the actual unemployment rate remains below the NAIRU, the appropriate response must be to improve supply conditions in the labour market.

The range of possibilities is too great to warrant detailed coverage in this section. Some, like incomes policy, are popular in certain quarters, although only in a more flexible form than has been customary in the past. It is unlikely, however, that they will ever find favour in Conservative Party circles. Others, like training vouchers, are too new to be assessed (but see the discussion in *Economic Affairs*, April 1991, pp. 16–18). Another possibility is to reduce taxation or – perhaps more appropriately, given the need to reduce labour costs – to reduce NICs, either for all workers in regions suffering severe unemployment or for all very low-paid workers. The payment of a working wage combined with minimal NICs is to be preferred to a policy of low wages combined with income support measures, although both may need to be used in practice.

Jobs can be increased by providing subsidies, although an awkward problem in practice is to ensure that subsidies are not offered to an employer to provide jobs which he or she intended to fill in any case (see **p. 334**). Equally, subsidies should be directed only towards the provision of the kind of high-skill jobs which are comparatively rare in the UK compared to its main competitors. Furthermore, subsidies should not be provided simply to deal with short-term problems, but should be associated with the provision of jobs which will be needed over the longer term.

Given that the low skills ethos in much of British industry has something to do with the influx into the labour market of ill-prepared 18 year olds and part-time women workers, it is evident that something needs to be done to improve the long-term career aspirations of these groups. One of the key issues here is to ensure that the basic education, whether academic or vocational, provided both for school children and for those who re-enter the education system as mature entrants, is comparable to that provided by successful competitors such as Germany.

All of this may appear rather grandiose in relation to the apparent inability of governments to reform UK institutions in the past. For this reason there are those who believe that the best solution which can be effected very quickly is to introduce a harsher regime for those who are out of work. In fact, as we have noted, the rules relating to eligibility for benefit were tightened up considerably during the 1980s, and the replacement rate, which stood at nearly 70 per cent in 1970 and remained well above 60 per cent until 1978, fell sharply to 59 per cent in 1979 and to only 41 per cent in 1982. It is currently even lower, and it seems unlikely that 'living off the dole' is any longer a comfortable prospect. Whether the unemployed should be 'forced' to do some kind of 'work' if they are to be entitled to any help from the State at all is even more controversial (for a discussion of 'workfare', see **p. 334**).

It is also of crucial importance that information about the availability of jobs is circulated as efficiently as possible. During the 1970s, as disclosed previously, the provision of information about jobs was divorced from the payment of benefits. Job information came to be provided by the Job Centres, which at that time were responsible to the Manpower Services Commission (MSC), and the payment of benefits was handed over to the DHSS. On the face of it, the Job Centres were very efficient: 40 per cent of vacancies were filled within one day and 68 per cent were filled within two weeks. However, employers notified only those vacancies to Job Centres which they thought they could deal with efficiently and, as previously noted, only about one-third of all vacancies are notified to Job Centres.

Information is available on the job search methods of the unemployed from the LFS (see *Employment Gazette*, June 1993, p. 271). In Spring 1992, visiting a Job Centre or government employment office was a method of job search especially favoured by males and non-married females, whereas married females relied primarily upon studying situations vacant columns in newspapers. Answering advertisements, using personal contacts and making direct approaches to firms and employers were less popular. Private agencies were used by only a small minority.

Job Centres are favoured particularly by younger job seekers, whereas the use of situations vacant columns increases with age. Job Centres are used most frequently by the unskilled. As workers grow older and acquire some skills, they turn increasingly to the newspapers. In effect, the State appears to provide a subsidised information service for low-imcome groups.

During the 1970s and well into the 1980s, Job Centres were ill-equipped to deal with the unemployed. One reason for their failure was the divorce of information transmission from both the provision of training and unemployment benefits. In an ideal system, these three functions would be brought together in an effort to assist the unemployed because the three functions address four issues: namely, the matching of an unemployed person with a vacancy; the length of time that a job is likely to last; the savings to the community of a person being permanently employed or placed on a training programme; and the costs to the community of a person being permanently unemployed. Unfortunately the issues became separated in the 1970s, when the payment of unemployment benefit was handed over to the DHSS and there was no compulsion on the unemployed to use Job Centres. Moreover, when attempts were made to improve the efficiency of Job Centres by cutting costs, the Centres reacted by reducing the amount of assistance to the long-term unemployed, and as a result many of the costs of unemployment were transferred to the DHSS. In 1987, an attempt was made to improve the efficiency of Job Centres by linking advice and assistance through the Job Restart Scheme, which was introduced to do something for the long-term unemployed. Nevertheless, there is room for further improvement in methods of information dissemination in the labour market.

Finally, it is worthy of note that reducing the level of unemployment can be made more difficult by legislation introduced for other purposes. For example, the incentive to work has been affected adversely by the Social Security Act 1988. In the housing market the philosophy has been to allow rents to be set at market-clearing levels, both in the private and public rental sectors, and to target subsidies more narrowly upon those **families** unable to afford these rents, rather than to offer subsidies on all rented **houses** via, for example, rent controls. Under the 1988 Act, rent is determined by family income and circumstances, and hence when it rises so does housing benefit paid to eligible families. As a consequence, recipients of benefit have no incentive to quibble over rent increases. More importantly, the loss of benefits as income rises obviously creates a severe poverty trap even where incomes are reasonably high if, as in London, rents are also very high.

In conclusion, certain basic facts need to be faced. Since 1979 there have been dramatic changes in the labour market, some of which are discussed more fully in the chapter which follows. The labour market has been extensively deregulated, making it easier to hire and fire workers and encouraging the switch from male to female employment. The power of trade unions has been eroded with a consequent reduction in strike activity. The desirability of living off State benefits has been eroded. In addition, newly industrialised countries have increasingly taken over markets for manufactured products.

All of these factors have combined to diminish the job prospects of the low-skilled, poorly-educated male who wants a decently-paid, full-time job in manufacturing in the old industrial heartlands of the UK. So much for the problem. Given a world in which, for example, the European Commission is seemingly determined to impose ever higher costs upon EU manufacturers, the solution may yet be many years away.

Notes

1. The LFS is a survey of around 65 000 private households throughout the UK, conducted in Spring every year. The Survey was conducted once every two years between 1973 and 1983, and annually thereafter.
2. The definition of such terms as 'unemployed', 'workforce', 'employees in employment' and so forth can be ambiguous. If their meaning is insufficiently clear in the text, a list of official definitions is to be found in the *Employment Gazette*.

Bibliography

Blanchflower, D. (1984) 'Union Relative Wage Effects', *British Journal of Industrial Relations*.

Blanchflower, D., M. Stevens and A. Yates (1991) 'Unionisation and Employment Behaviour', *CLE Discussion Paper 339*.

Brown, W. and S. Wadhani (1990) 'The Economic Effects of Industrial Relations Legislation Since 1979', *National Institute Economic Review* (February).

Campbell, M. and M. Daly (1992) 'Self-Employment into the 1990s', *Employment Gazette* (June).

Central Statistical Office (1993) 'Employment in the Public and Private Sectors', *Economic Trends* (January).

Commission of the European Communities (1992) *Employment in Europe – 1992*, COM(92) 354.

Confederation of British Industry (1988) *The Structure and Processes of Pay Determination in the Private Sector* (London: CBI).

Dawson, G. (1990) 'Interpretation of the Natural Rate of Unemployment', *Economics* (Summer).

Department of Employment (1993) *The Government's Expenditure Plans 1993–4 to 1995–6*, Cmd 2205 (London: HMSO, February).

Disney, G. (1990) 'Trade Union Membership', *British Journal of Industrial Relations* (July).

Freeman, R. and J. Pelletier (1990) 'The Impact of Industrial Relations Legislation on British Trade Union Density', *British Journal of Industrial Relations* (July).

Gregg, P. (1992) 'Out for the Count Again? A Social Scientist's Analysis of Unemployment Statistics in the UK', *National Institute Discussion Paper No.25* (October).

Kelly, J. and R. Bailey (1989) 'British Trade Union Membership, Density and Decline in the 1980s', *Industrial Relations Journal* (Spring).

Lawlor, J. and C. Kennedy (1992) 'Measures of Unemployment: the Claimant Count and the Labour Force Survey', *Employment Gazette* (July).

Layard, R. and S. Nickell (1986) 'Unemployment in Britain', *Economica*, 53 (Supplement).

Layard, R., S. Nickell and R. Jackman (1991) *Unemployment: Macroeconomic Performance and the Labour Market* (Oxford University Press).

Machin, S. and S. Wadhani (1989) 'The Effects of Unions on Organizational Change, Investment and Employment', *CLE Discussion Paper 335*.

McGregor, A. and A. Sproull (1992) 'Employers and the Flexible Workforce', *Employment Gazette* (May).

Metcalf, D. (1991) 'British Unions: Dissolution or Resurgence?', *Oxford Review of Economic Policy*, 7(1).

Nickell, S. and S. Wadhani (1989) 'Insider Forces and Wage Determination', *Economic Journal* (June).

Poret, P. (1990) 'The "Puzzle" of Wage Moderation in the 1980s', OECD *Working Paper*, 87 (Paris: OECD).

Taylor, A. and C. Lewis (1993) '1991 Census of Employment Results', *Employment Gazette* (April).

White, A. and J. Leyland (1993) 'How Unemployment is Measured in Different Countries', *Employment Gazette* (September).

Chapter 9

The Labour Market

Peter Curwen

■ *9.1* Education and Training

In the UK there is continuous public debate about how to improve the quality of education and training, and about how to transform it into something suitable for the future. However, interest in the topic tends to ebb and flow, with surges in interest usually triggered by the unearthing of some piece of evidence to the effect that the UK is either falling further behind, or failing to catch up with its competitors. Technological change has the awkward habit of speeding up rather than slowing down, and as a consequence no industrialised country can afford to go without a well-educated, well-trained workforce. Unfortunately, although it is generally possible to demonstrate that deficiencies exist, it is by no means easy to identify the precise reasons why this is the case, and hence what should be done to resolve it.

□ *9.1.1 Education*

Up until the age of 16 education is **compulsory**. The school-leaving age is currently at its highest-ever level, partly in order to keep down the numbers of unemployed. Education is primarily provided by public sector institutions which for older children conform with few exceptions to a common pattern known as the comprehensive school. The growth of the independent, private sector and pressure to restore the grammar school

attest to widespread dissatisfaction with the quality of primary and secondary education. At the beginning of 1991 Her Majesty's Inspectors of Education reported that the teaching of reading was 'less than satisfactory' in one-fifth of the institutions of lower learning which they had visited. In June 1993 the Adult Literacy and Basic Skills Unit published research indicating that one in five of the UK's 21 year olds was innumerate, while one in seven was illiterate.

Clearly, something has gone wrong with the state of educational provision, but what exactly, and what should be done to remedy it? It may be argued that parents do a good deal of the damage by ignoring their children's pre-school education. Certainly, although the school-leaving age is quite late by international standards, it is only very recently that the majority of children have **volunteered** to continue their education beyond the age of 16. In 1980–81, according to the Department of Employment's annual **Education Statistics for the United Kingdom**, 52 per cent of 16–18 year olds participated in post-compulsory education, whereas the 1990–91 figure was 58 per cent and that for 1992–93 was 71 per cent for 16 year olds and 55 per cent for 17 year olds. However, there are significant regional variations within these totals, with the proportions in Barnet in London at twice the level of Knowsley on Merseyside.

These figures include part-time participation, in which respect the UK has an exceptionally high rate. In respect of full-time attendance only, the

UK participation rate in 1992–93 was 57 per cent for 16 year olds, marginally above Italy but less than almost everywhere else in the developed world (compare the 100 per cent rate in Canada and 99 per cent rate in Germany). The fall-off in the participation rate post-16 was more marked in the UK than elsewhere, although there has been considerable improvement very recently.

This increase is clearly related to the sharp downturn in opportunities for employment and some disillusion with youth training programmes. Furthermore, it represents no more than a catching-up process in relation to Japan and even the USA, although the latter faces severe quality problems which the former appears able to avoid. Nevertheless, irrespective of the triggers, and some (such as the switch to GCSEs noted below) have been positive, this fondness for knowledge must be regarded as a desirable development.

Until very recently it was customary to sit either Ordinary (O)-level or Certificate of Secondary Education examinations at the age of 15 or 16. O-levels were 'academic' and seen as the test of suitability for further years spent in school whereas Certificate of Secondary Education candidates were mostly expected to move straight out into the labour market. On the whole, it was generally accepted that the latter were insufficiently educated for the needs of an advanced society.

All school children now sit a common General Certificate in Secondary Education (GCSE), but problems remain. For example, despite the great scientific and engineering traditions of nineteenth-century Britain, there has developed a strong bias towards arts subjects since the war. Compared to countries such as Germany, engineers are held in relatively low esteem and are relatively badly paid in the UK. A weakness in mathematics also goes hand in hand with a weakness in English. One often gets the impression that the inhabitants of countries (especially in Northern Europe) where English is a compulsory second language, speak better English than the British.

Stung by these kinds of criticism the government passed the Education Reform Act in 1988 which, although highly controversial, may ulti-

mately be seen as a lasting achievement. The underlying premise behind the Act was that control over teaching should not be left entirely in the hands of teachers who, in the course of applying 'fashionable' theories about education, were allegedly failing to deliver the well-educated workforce which was so desperately needed. During its first two terms in office the Thatcher government had held off from reform. Now it began the process by introducing a basic core curriculum designed to give all children skills in reading, writing and arithmetic and a passing acquaintance with science. The 10-subject core would be 'assessed' at the ages of 7, 11, 14 and 16.

An administrative apparatus was constructed, but this proved too unwieldy because of the excessive burden of assessment. In February 1990 the government accordingly began to beat a retreat, starting with a decree that at the ages of 7 and 11 the national assessments would apply only to 'key aspects' of mathematics, science and English, and that the other seven subjects would be assessed by teachers without the control of a national standard test.

In June 1990 the government promised simpler tests for 7 year olds, and in January 1991 it was announced that the full national curriculum would be taught only to children aged up to 14, with music and art as optional subjects. Later in 1991 the first national tests for 7 year olds took place, but proved to be excessively time-consuming, triggering a process of simplification of testing at all ages which nevertheless failed to mollify the teaching profession.

The first league tables of secondary schools' GCSE results were published in November 1992. These stirred up a good deal of controversy, mainly on the grounds that they failed to take proper account of the uneven quality of pupil 'inputs', and the teachers' unions voted for a programme of resistance, to include boycotts of compulsory testing. In response, the government commissioned a report by Sir Ron Dearing which was published in August 1993. This noted that the central problem was confusion over the purpose of testing. Whereas only simple tests were needed to assess pupil achievement in order to compare nationwide school performance, they had become overly complex, and required a complex curriculum to support them, because they were simultaneously seen as a means to diagnose individual pupils' needs.

The report accordingly recommended that the two purposes should be divorced, with the latter left to teachers outside the scope of national tests. Furthermore, the tests should concentrate upon English, mathematics and science. The government accepted the report without qualification, and the National Curriculum will accordingly be slimmed down to occupy less than 90 per cent of the timetable in primary schools and 75 per cent in secondary schools. Whether this will provide a recipe for peace in schools remains to be seen.

There are other controversial matters which remain unresolved, one of which concerns how to give parity of esteem to technical and vocational subjects so that even those school children intent upon further and higher education come to perceive them as more worthy of consideration. In February 1991, the government proposed that 16 year olds could leave school with vocational qualifications instead of GCSEs. Up to 70 per cent of class time beyond the age of 14 could be spent on vocational study, but this would be of equal rigour to academic study. Given that post-16 education is voluntary, there is a choice to be made between continuing in education, either taking Advanced (A)-levels in a narrow set of subjects (usually three) with a view to entry into a university, or a BTEC (Business and Technician Education Council) national diploma of a multi-disciplinary nature. The latter are provided in further education colleges and are intended as an introduction to subjects of relevance in a work environment, whereas A-levels are much less work-specific.

The decision to stay on in education is much affected by parental ambitions – graduate parents expect their children to get a degree – and by the relative pay of those who go to work at 16 and those who enter the workforce with qualifications at a later age. The amount of State and parental financial support for those who stay on is also a major factor. Unlike in the USA, there is no tradition of 'working one's way through college'. A-levels and degrees are generally done on a full-time attendance basis. The 1980–81 and 1990–92 recessions also served to drive home the realisation that unemployment typically affects the unskilled and unqualified more harshly than the skilled and those with educational qualifications.

The highly specialised nature of A-level courses is peculiar to Britain (it is broader based in Scotland than England) and is a major deterrent to those wishing to stay on at school. The proportion of the age cohort who are able to enrol on degree programmes at universities was in any event, until very recently, exceptionally low by international standards anyway. The virtue of this system was that those who took British degrees were on average superior to their counterparts almost everywhere else since excess demand was used to ration by academic quality rather than by price. In addition the system was very efficient, with a low cost per graduate, since it had a very low drop-out rate by international standards.

The drawbacks were that the system was physically constrained, overspecialised and inflexible, with the consequence that unless a school child did sufficiently well at GCSE to stand a reasonable chance of a place on a degree or BTEC course, he or she tended to drop out of education as soon as the rules allowed. Further and higher education also remained very much a middle-class preserve despite the abolition of many grammar schools and attempts to improve opportunities for children from working-class backgrounds.

The government is particularly concerned to expand the numbers of those who stay on in mathematics and the sciences. Unfortunately, most of those who stay in education are concerned about their job prospects and future incomes, and hence prefer courses in business studies and the professions. Presumably, if there really was a severe shortage of science graduates, then relative pay would rise to clear the market, but there is little sign of this happening so far. On the other hand, there is undoubtedly a need for more qualified technicians, and it may be argued that insufficient resources have been invested in further education to meet this objective.

In line with its general philosophy the government set out to make further and higher education more responsive to the market place. It released the polytechnics from the shackles of local education authority control and allowed them to rename themselves as universities, and went on to release further education and sixth-form colleges in April 1993. These changes were associated with an enormous expansion of provision. Within three years further education and sixth-form colleges are expected to increase their student numbers by one-quarter, a growth which will mirror that which has already been achieved in the university sector. Indeed, the universities have increased student numbers by 50 per cent since 1987, but staff numbers have increased by only 10 per cent (with unpredictable longer-term effects upon quality).

However, the physical capacity of the system has become a major constraint, not to mention the cost to the Exchequer. The government has adopted a policy of forcing higher education institutions to earn an increasing proportion of their income in the market place via research, consultancy and full-cost courses. Nevertheless, the cost is such that a major debate has been initiated to test public opinion on methods to replace fees paid from tax revenues by a graduate tax of some kind.

9.1.2 Government Spending on Labour-market Policies

Public sector labour-market measures encompass unemployment pay and 'active employment measures' such as training. The latter have been primarily a phenomenon of the past decade and their incidence is patchy in relation to GDP, as indeed it is outside the EU. The UK's spending on training is widely criticised domestically, but it is not unfavourable **in relation to the rate of unemployment** compared to most of the EU.

In inflation-adjusted terms spending on training roughly tripled during the decade post-1979, as shown in **Table 9.1**, which is a little surprising given the government's preference for market solutions to problems such as a shortfall in skills. However, if companies are reluctant to

instigate training programmes on a voluntary basis, and if the government is unwilling to compel them to do so, then either training is largely publicly funded or it is largely non-existent.

Traditionally, training in the UK took place 'on the job'. In the case of craftsmen this involved an apprenticeship supplemented by City and Guilds examinations. The first significant state intervention came with the Industrial Training Act 1964. This Act created **training boards**, which were to be financed mainly by levies on firms with a supplement from the State. The boards consisted of representatives of employers, trade unions and civil servants.

The justification for the levies was that, instead of training their own workers, many firms preferred to poach workers from other firms that did. The levies could be returned only to those firms that incurred training costs by way of compensation for the benefits transferred to the poachers. However, the levies were generally unpopular with employers, who argued that investment in training would be worthwhile only if the skills acquired by their workers were specific to their particular businesses, since such skills could not, by definition, be poached. Where skills were general, and hence could be used in a variety of firms and industries, it would not be sensible for an individual firm to invest heavily in training since trained workers would subsequently be able to sell their skills to the highest bidder. In effect, the investment would yield much greater benefits to the individual than to the firm.

Even if poaching could be prevented, however, it might not pay a firm to invest in training. If workers are performing well in their present jobs

Table 9.1   *Training Expenditure (£ m)*

	Cash Prices	Constant (1990–91) Prices
1975–76	171.7	620.2
1978–79	377.3	954.3
1989–90	2658.8	2871.5

Source: Employment Gazette (January 1991), p. 39.

they will often want to move on to more challenging tasks. Yet if they are trained to do them, they may simply become even more anxious to move on to even more demanding jobs, which are unavailable unless the workers move to other firms. The lack of transferable skills may be the only thing which keeps workers from leaving many firms.

It may be argued that any workers who realise that the acquisition of skills will result in a much higher wage will finance skills acquisition themselves. However, this will often be successful only if their firms allow them time off to train, if the unions lend their support and if there are readily available funds for this purpose. Government help to overcome these potential hurdles may thus be more sensible than trying to browbeat reluctant employers into policies which they do not perceive as self-serving.

Given the attitude of many employers, it is hardly surprising that the shortage of trained workers proved to be persistent, and the decision was taken in the early 1970s to create a national training programme under the umbrella of the MSC, a semi-autonomous body set up separately from the Department of Employment in 1973. The MSC operated a corporatist strategy in that it tried to obtain a consensus view about what the problems were and what should be done about them, rather than attempting to force its own strategy upon reluctant employers and unions. The system it created was inherited by the Thatcher government in 1979.

The history of labour-market measures from 1975 to 1993 is summarised in **Table 9.2**. Most of these measures have been terminated, and space does not permit a detailed discussion of their contents (but see Gregg, 1990, pp. 49–52).

From 1974 to 1979 the Labour government concentrated upon the traditional approach of creating more demand for labour, especially for specific groups of workers and in specific locations. Subsidies such as the Temporary Employment Scheme, Youth Employment Subsidy and Small Firms Employment Subsidy were the primary instrument to achieve this, with a little help from the Job Release Scheme on the supply side. The use of training-based schemes was very mod-

est until the **Youth Training Scheme** (YTS) was initiated in 1983.

The Thatcher government largely forsook the traditional approach, which raised the demand for labour at the existing wage, in favour of wage flexibility designed to match supply and demand at an acceptable level of employment. This initially involved the Young Worker's Scheme, followed by the New Worker's Scheme. From 1983 onwards it placed considerable emphasis upon training-based schemes, primarily the YTS, but also for adults after the inception of the Job Training Scheme in 1986.

Coupled with Restart and benefit regulations that require active job search, as noted by Gregg (1990), 'it produces a consistent policy response if the problem of unemployment persistence is too high reservation wages and too little job search by the unemployed, coupled with growing problems with skill acquisition by the young, skill maintenance when unemployed and a skills mismatch'.

The **Restart Programme** was introduced in 1986, and was aimed at the long-term unemployed. Initially, anyone unemployed for one year or longer was invited to an interview at a Job Centre and offered opportunities designed to help him or her back to employment. In 1987 coverage was extended to anyone unemployed for six months or longer. Currently, the opportunities on offer include an interview for a job; a place on Training for Work; a place on a Restart Course; a Jobstart Allowance; a place on an Enterprise Allowance Scheme (EAS); or a place in a Jobclub. **Jobclubs** aim to help people who have been unemployed for six months or more by providing help in finding jobs and free facilities, such as telephones and stationery.

Throughout 1989–91 an evaluation of Restart was carried out in the form of the **Restart Cohort Study** (see *Labour Market Quarterly Review*, November 1992). This indicated that Restart helped individuals to leave unemployment more quickly than they would otherwise have done, and made a significant difference to the amount of time during the study period for which they were claiming benefit. It also significantly increased the average amount of time spent by participants on Employment Training (see be-

Table 9.2   *Employment and Training Schemes, Great Britain, 1975/76 to 1992/93*[1]

Scheme	Incentives for employers to maintain current employment	Incentives for employers to raise employment	Direct employment by government or its agencies	Work sharing or reducing labour supply	Training-based schemes	Other	Initials	Introduced in	Phased out in	Replaced by
Restart Interviews						✓	RI	86/87	Live	X
Employment Training Scheme					✓		ET	88/89	93/94	TFW
Job Training Scheme					✓		JTS	85/86	88/89	ET
Youth Training Scheme					✓		YTS	83/84	Live	X
Work Experience Programme					✓		WEP	76/77	78/79	YOP
Jobshare				✓			JS	87/88	Live	X
Job Release Scheme				✓			JRS	76/77	Live	X
Community Programme			✓				CP	82/83	88/89	ET
Community Enterprise Programme			✓				CEP	81/82	82/83	CP
Special Temporary Employment Programme			✓				STEP	78/79	81/82	CEP
Job Creation Programme			✓				JCP	75/76	78/79	STEP
Jobstart Allowance		✓					JA		Live	X
Enterprise Allowance Scheme		✓					EAS	82/83	Live	X
New Workers Scheme		✓					NWS	86/87	88/89	X
Young Workers Scheme		✓					YWS	81/82	86/87	NWS
Small Firms Employment Subsidy		✓					SFES	77/78	80/81	X
Youth Opportunities Programme		✓					YOP	78/79	82/83	YTS
Youth Employment Subsidy		✓					YES	77/78	78/79	YOP
Recruitment Subsidy for School Leavers		✓					RSSL	75/76	76/77	YES
Temporary Short-Time Working Compensation Scheme	✓						TSTWC	78/79	84/85	X
Temporary Employment Scheme	✓						TES	75/76	78/79	TSTWC

Note:
[1] This is not by any means a complete version; see, for example, *Training Statistics 1990* (London: HMSO), p. 35.
Source: Department of Employment; P. Gregg (1990) 'The Evolution of Special Employment Measures', *Royal Bank of Scotland Review* (September).

low) and other government programmes, and reduced the average time taken to enter such programmes.

The particular problems of **youth unemployment,** which arose in the late 1970s, led initially to the Youth Opportunity Programme (YOP). In 1983 this was replaced by the YTS and was expanded to cover almost all 16 year olds not in education. The YTS placed greater emphasis upon training at employers' premises. In 1986 the YTS was itself expanded to provide a two-year structured period of training and work experience for 16 year old school leavers. Subsequently, benefit entitlement was withdrawn for those who did not participate, effectively compelling all those eligible to join. All trainees who are not employed receive a minimum weekly allowance, currently £29.50 for 16 year olds and £35 for those aged 17 or over. In every year since 1990–91 the YTS has cost roughly £850 million to administer.

In 1990 the YTS comprised the largest of the three main strands of government policy in the labour market. The second was the **Enterprise Allowance Scheme** (EAS), first introduced on a national scale in 1983 to help those setting up their own business. It provides a weekly subsidy for up to a year for a claimant who must invest modestly in his or her own business. About half of EAS ventures last six months beyond the termination of the subsidy.

The dominant adult scheme in usage until 1993 was **Employment Training** (ET), introduced in September 1988 with the slogan 'Training the workers without jobs to do the jobs without workers'. ET replaced 34 pre-existing schemes, but only two were nationally significant, namely the Community Programme and the Job Training Scheme. Its objectives were, first, to give the long-term unemployed the skills which they needed to get and keep jobs and, second, to guarantee a training opportunity for all those aged 18–24 who had been unemployed for between six and twelve months and for all those aged 18–50 who had been unemployed for more than two years. The scheme normally ran for six months, and occasionally for twelve, so the 300 000 places were expected to handle roughly 550 000 people a year.

The unemployed were allocated to training agents (who could be employees' or employers' organisations), and while on ET they continued to receive benefits as though they were unemployed together with training allowances and, if eligible, Income Support and travelling expenses. In addition, training managers were allowed to make discretionary payments without affecting benefits or liabilities for tax. As noted previously, ET was closely tied up with the Restart Programme. Of the 890 000 interviewed in January 1991, the largest proportion of those (roughly 75 per cent) who took up an offer of some kind ended up in ET.

The MSC subsequently evolved into the **Training Commission.** In 1987 the government proposed a New Training Initiative which the unions objected to on the grounds of underfunding. As a result, the government decided in September 1988 to absorb the former MSC within the Department of Employment under the umbrella of a new **Training Agency.** This Agency would operate in tandem with the **Employment Service,** formed in 1987, to bring together unemployment benefit, Job Centre and other services centred on the unemployed.

In the White Paper on training (*Employment for the 1990s*, Cmnd 540, 1988) the government went a stage further by setting in motion a restructuring of training through the establishment of 82 locally-based, employer-led **Training and Enterprise Councils** (TECs) in England and Wales, together with 22 Local Enterprise Companies in Scotland. The Department of Employment then invited local groups of employers to submit proposals for setting up the TECs which were given responsibility for drawing up local training programmes, arranging for their delivery by signing up providers including voluntary organisations, stimulating enterprise and building better industry/education links. TECs started off by signing a contract with the Training Agency. All 82 TECs were contracted up by October 1990, with 31 fully operational and 51 in the development phase, some two years ahead of schedule. At least two-thirds of a TEC Board of Directors must be top private sector business leaders with the balance drawn from local authorities, trade unions, the voluntary sector, education and others.

TEC directors were unenthusiastic about using up their funds, at a time of rising unemployment, solely on managing anti-unemployment schemes such as ET and YTS. On the other hand, few felt themselves to be in a strong position to raise private finance for innovatory programmes. Given that one-quarter of TEC income was to be related to the gaining of qualifications, fears were expressed that TECs would concentrate upon the provision of intensive courses for people who are easy to train, and largely ignore the needs of the handicapped and ex-prisoners who need basic, expensive education if they are to become employable.

On 1 April 1991, the Department of Employment handed over control of its training budget to the TECs. It simultaneously (27 March, 1991) launched a £120 million scheme to give 10 per cent of school leavers training vouchers called **Training Credits**, worth from £500 to £5000, to spend on an approved training scheme of their choice. Six additional schemes became operational in 1993, and the scheme is currently known as **Youth Credits**.

In May a White Paper was published, entitled *Education and Training for the 21st Century*. A key proposal was to extend the provision of Training Credits to every 16 and 17 year old by 1996. It also proposed the extension of the use of the National Record of Achievement for school leavers.

In July the Employment Secretary announced a new package of measures to help the unemployed. A new programme called **Employment Action** was created, commencing in October 1991, to offer up to 60 000 long-term unemployed people in a full year the chance to keep their skills up to date by work experience on local projects. It paid state benefits plus £10 a week, and was administered by the TECs. Taken in conjunction with ET, the annual cost was approximately £1 billion in 1990–91, falling to roughly £900 million in subsequent years.

In December 1991 a new Employment Service scheme called **Job Review Workshops** was initiated to help up to 50 000 unemployed executives

and managers back into work or further training. The workshops consist of 12 people who have been unemployed for roughly 13 weeks working together with a leader.

A White Paper, *People, Jobs and Opportunity* (Cm 1810, February 1992) announced TEC-delivered pilots to test **Open Learning Credits** for unemployed people to purchase open learning materials and support. It also announced the **Skill Choice** initiative (commencing April 1993) whereby individuals are offered credits to buy the guidance and assessment services of their choice.

However, these initiatives were dwarfed by that announced in the Autumn Statement of 1992, the main elements of which were as set out below:

1   A new programme, **Training for Work**, would replace Employment Training and Employment Action from April 1993. Delivered through TECs, Training for Work would provide 320 000 adults with an opportunity to improve, update and learn new skills or do work of benefit to the local community. Those eligible would include people unemployed for 6 months or longer, people with disabilities and returners to the labour market who had been out of the labour market for two years.
2   All people who had been unemployed for a year, and who did not take up other offers of help, would be required to attend a **Jobplan Workshop**.
3   The Jobclub and Job Interview Guarantee Schemes would be expanded, together with a major expansion of work trials with employers for the unemployed.
4   Additional places would be provided in Job Review Workshops.
5   Additional Career Development Loans (first introduced in July 1988) would be provided to help both employed and unemployed people to take the training course of their choice.

Further measures were introduced in the Spring 1993 Budget which, though modest in scale, showed a more innovatory approach. In particular, there was an acceptance of the principle of job subsidies to employers who take on the unemployed, an idea previously resisted by the Treasury. The initial tests in four **Workstart Pilot** areas, two run by TECs and two by the Employment Service and involving 1000 people at a cost of £2.6 million, will be based on the Benefit Transfer Programme concept proposed by Dennis Snower. The government's version will be open to those unemployed for more than two years, and will provide a one-year subsidy to the employer of £60 per week, taken from benefits which would have been paid. The unemployed person will get a normal wage, and the subsidy will taper off as the period of employment progresses. Employers will be prevented from using the subsidy to displace existing staff.

There will also be a **Community Action** programme which will provide benefit plus £10 a week for 60 000 people who are willing to work part-time on projects run by voluntary organisations while receiving help with job hunting during the rest of the week. While this will be similar to **Employment for Work**, it will be run by the Employment Department rather than the TECs (thereby, in principle, permitting it to be treated as a form of 'Workfare').

Some £67 million will also be made available to provide up to 300 000 places on vocationally-related, full-time courses for people unemployed for over 12 months under a **Learning for Work** scheme, and an additional £21 million to supplement the TEC-run Business Start-Up scheme. Finally, TECs will be invited to bid for £25 million in a TEC Challenge scheme to develop and run innovatory ways to tackle unemployment.

The Autumn 1993 Budget introduced yet further changes. Benefits for the unemployed were rationalised around a new **Jobseeker's Allowance** (JA), to commence in April 1996. In its basic form the JA will last for only six months as compared with one year for the current unemployment benefit, and recipients will have to prove that they are genuinely seeking work. Claimants will be expected to enter into a Jobseeker's Agreement which sets out in advance the steps they intend to take to find employment.

Three new pilot schemes aimed at long-term unemployed people seeking work were also an-

nounced. A Jobfinder's grant will provide assistance for people who have been out of work for more than two years when they start a job; new job search and assessment courses will be available for 18–25 year olds who have been unemployed for more than a year; and a further scheme for 18–25 year olds will test the value of giving unemployed young people their own case workers to help them plan paths out of unemployment.

☐ *9.1.3 Assessment*

It is clear from the above not merely that the government is concerned about training but also that it has devoted an enormous amount of money and energy into devising programmes. As a consequence, as shown in **Figure 9.1**, roughly 15 per cent of all employees in Britain are being trained at any point in time. Unfortunately, however, this does not necessarily imply that the training achieves anything worthwhile either for the trainee or for the long-term health of the economy.

In the first place, it may be argued that expenditure on training is, if anything excessive (see Shackleton (1992) for a detailed analysis of this proposition). The figures for expenditure in **Table 9.1** above are deceptive in that they do not include individuals' loss of earnings while learning on the job or expenditure by firms. Adding these in produces total expenditure on training roughly equal to 10 per cent of GDP. This would be justifiable if there was a clear proven link between the amount of expenditure and economic growth, but as yet this does not exist. What this highlights is the danger of concentrating training upon non-transferable skills and, less directly, the danger inherent in creating vested interests in the provision of training.

It should be emphasised that even those most sceptical about the virtues of training are not arguing against training as such, but rather against its scale and its particular formats. We have previously commented briefly, and favourably, about Restart, but it has been argued that this success has been based in part upon the diversion of people to the kinds of benefit sup-

Figure 9.1   *Employees¹ Receiving Training²*

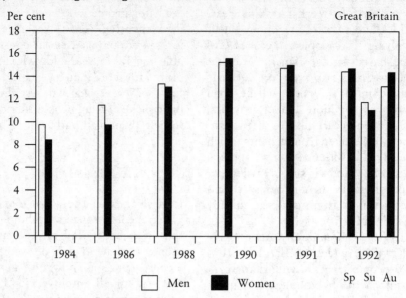

Notes:
[1] Employees of working age (16–64 for men; 16–59 for women).
[2] Job-related training received in the four weeks prior to the survey.
Source: LFS.

port, such as disability benefit, that take them off the unemployment register.

The key programmes are what is now Employment for Work and Youth Training. A review of Employment for Work is contained in **Table 9.3**. Between September 1988 and March 1993, its predecessor (ET) dealt with roughly 1.4 million joiners. Of those who left the programme between July 1991 and June 1992, 31 per cent obtained employment within three months and 33 per cent gained qualifications (see *Labour Market Quarterly Review*, May 1993).

An analysis of the effectiveness of ET, based upon a sample taken in 1989 and reported in the same journal, indicated that participation in ET had the effects of reducing time as a claimant and increasing time spent in employment. However, the study was too limited to be generalisable to all ET/Employment for Work participants. It is also argued that the Employment Service counselling service has a higher success rate even though it costs only £275 per job placement compared to £10 000 for ET.

At the end of January 1993, there were roughly 300 000 young people on Youth Training (including Youth Credits) in Britain. Of these, one half took up employment (see *Labour Market Quarterly Review*, May 1993), but this represented a significant deterioration compared to the 68 per cent recorded in 1989. It has been noted that, because of the recession, increasing numbers of young people have never had a job, and have lost any sense of discipline. This may render them virtually unemployable in the longer term even if the labour market picks up.

The main criticisms that have been directed at TECs relate first to the possibility that they overconcentrate on short-term concerns, and second that they overconcentrate upon industry-specific needs (Mawson, 1992). Recent evidence indicates that, albeit with widely differing performances, TECs are getting better at placing young people in training schemes, where they are gaining improved qualifications, and are equipping more unemployed adults with vocational qualifications. However, the TECs have always claimed

Table 9.3   *Training for Work: Expenditure and Performance, England*

	1990–91[1] outturn	1991–92[2] outturn	1992–93[2] estimated outturn	1993–94[3] plans	1994–95[3] plans	1995–96[3] plans
Expenditure (£ million)	915	710	746	790	811	839
Number of starts (000s)	306	252	246	270	277	278
Average number of participants (000s)	157	117	126	126	126	127
Cost per participant (£)	5 827	6 051	5 918	–[4]	–[4]	–[4]
Average length of stay (weeks)	24	–[5]	–[5]	24	24	24
Percentage of leavers gaining positive outcomes (jobs, further education or training)	37	34	30	30	35	40
Cost per positive outcome (£)	7 234[6][7]	7 640[6][7]	10 000[6]	9 718	8 451	7 548
Percentage of leavers gaining qualifications (including non-vocational ones) or a credit towards a qualification	28	32[6]	30[6]	35	40	45
Cost per qualification (£)	9 559	8 118[6][7]	10 000[6]	8 330	7 394	6 710
Percentage of leavers gaining non-vocational qualifications levels 1 to 4	N/A	N/A	20	25	30	35

Notes:
[1] ET only.
[2] Includes Employment Action, which began in October 1991.
[3] Training for work, which begins in April 1993.
[4] Figures are only available for past years. Planned figures will depend on the numbers and targets agreed in annual TEC business plans prior to the start of the operating year.
[5] Cannot give outturns until every participant has left programme.
[6] Applies to ET only, as Employment Action is not measured by positive outcomes and not intended to lead to a qualifications.
[7] Estimate derived from GB figures.

Source: Department of Employment (1993), Table 5.

that it is the government that has prevented them from doing more to promote enterprise through, for example, attracting inward investment and setting up loans for firms.

In September 1993, no doubt taking advantage of scepticism about the effects of training programmes, the Department of Employment called for Youth Training to be cut back to the bone. Pointing out that there were only 220 000 left on the scheme as a result of a significant increase in numbers enrolled in further education, the Department advocated that the latter be expanded rapidly at the expense of Youth Training. The effects of such a move for the TECs would be far-reaching, but it is not possible at this juncture to forecast how the government will respond.

☐ 9.1.4 Workfare

The government has for some time been toying with the introduction of increased compulsion in unemployment schemes. Whereas Restart questions people after two years of being unemployed, and Jobplan Workshops after one year, a pilot scheme announced in April 1993, called North Norfolk Action, will question participants each week about their progress in looking for work. The scheme offers temporary part-time work on community projects for 100 people who have been unemployed for more than six months. However, this type of scheme has been widely criticised on the grounds that it is inferior to temporary work with a regular employer at standard rates of pay. It is also alleged that it will push increasing numbers of young people into the black economy and crime (as in the USA).

For these reasons there is much advocacy of recruitment subsidies, but the government's Workstart scheme (referred to above) has itself been criticised on the grounds that there are no plans to monitor employers' assurances that they will not use the subsidy to displace existing employees, or any sanctions to apply where they do (see Snower in *Financial Times*, 23 February 1993 and 19 May 1993).

☐ 9.1.5 Skill Shortages and their Consequences

The only long-standing and consistent indicator of skill shortages comes from the CBI *Quarterly Industrial Trends Survey* which covers Great Britain. What this showed, as in **Figure 9.2**, was that as unemployment rose rapidly during the first half of the 1980s so, perversely, did shortages of skills. In 1982 roughly 2.5 per cent of manufacturing companies cited skill shortages as a constraint on output. By October 1988 this figure had risen to 28 per cent. By this time unemployment was falling progressively, yet in January 1991 the figure had fallen back to 6 per cent and remained at or below that level during the following period.

The Department of Employment has also published three surveys on skill needs in Britain (see *Labour Market Quarterly Review*, November 1992) covering 1990–92. These confirm that recruitment difficulties remained at a low level during this period, partly because recruitment had fallen off during the recession.

Skill shortages are location-specific, and are understandably most acute in newly-established high-technology companies. In the face of an inflexible supply of qualified personnel, companies respond either by bidding workers away from one another, which is something of a zero-sum game (the main consequence of which is to escalate wage inflation), or by resorting to extensive overtime. If the response of the government to such upwards pressures on wages is to curb demand to the point of generating widespread unemployment, then skill shortages can be viewed as a primary cause of the deterioration in the unemployment/inflation trade-off previously discussed.

What is evident is that, first, the disappearance of skill shortages during the period 1988–93 did not result in any downwards pressure on earnings growth. Second, the high of 28 per cent in 1988 was nevertheless well below the peaks recorded in the 1960s and early 1970s, while the 1991 low was comparable to that recorded in July 1980. Given that July 1980 and January 1991 represented

Figure 9.2 *Expectations of Skill Shortages,*[1,2] *Great Britain, 1975–92*

Percentages

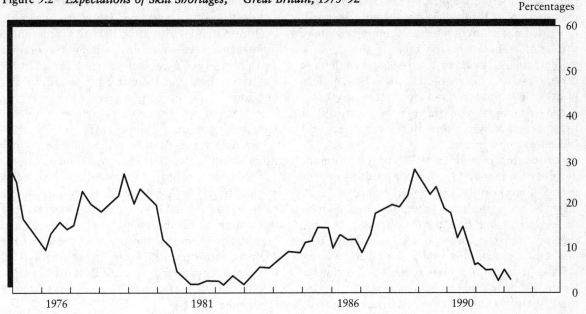

Notes:
[1] % of manufacturing firms expecting skill shortages to limit output over the next 4 months.
[2] The survey is carried out in January, April, July and October of each year.
Source: CBI *Quarterly Industrial Trends Survey.*

almost identical points in successive economic cycles, it is evident that the pattern of skill shortages is consistent over time and cannot accordingly have had more than a marginal impact upon the unemployment/inflation trade-off. It would therefore appear to be the case that this trade-off will not be improved other than marginally through improved training.

It is alleged that the UK's relatively poor long-term productivity performance can be blamed, in good part, upon the shortage of skills. This is a highly contentious matter since there must inevitably be considerable uncertainty over the boost to productivity to be expected from a given programme of education and/or training. This is not to downplay the virtues of education and training; rather, it is to remind ourselves that they cannot provide a miracle cure for the economy's ills in isolation. If they are combined with a German system of collective bargaining then the effects are going to be rather better than where they are combined with the system in the UK.

■ 9.2 Trade Unions

In their manifesto of 1979 the Conservatives stated that 'a fair balance between the rights and objectives of unions, management and the community in which they work is essential to economic recovery'. By this, they meant that the balance needed to be tilted away from the unions and towards management and the community. As the manifesto went on to say: 'We cannot go on, year after year, tearing ourselves apart in increasingly bitter and calamitous industrial disputes. In bringing about economic recovery, we should all be on the same side.'

It is not difficult to discern why the manifesto inferred that everyone was not on the same side in 1979. Trade unionism is essentially a twentieth-century phenomenon. Illegal prior to 1824, unions spent the first 50 years of their legal existence primarily as organisations of craft workers. Hence membership grew slowly despite the widespread onset of industrialisation. At the turn of the century, where we pick up the data on union membership in **Figure 9.3**, membership was still modest, but the unions were beginning to make their voices heard in the face of the adverse trading conditions faced by the UK economy at the time. The erosion of the UK's pre-eminent position as a producer and exporter of manufactures, combined with the massive transfer of workers out of agriculture, depressed wages and caused unemployment.

During the period 1906–13 the government granted immunities to unions from damages incurred in contemplation or furtherance of trade disputes and introduced minimum wage legislation. After 1914 unionism spread rapidly into the transport, energy and iron and steel industries, and unions secured a political power base by putting their voting power behind the newly-formed Labour Party. During the 1920s unions flexed their muscles, as in the General Strike of 1926 which, while it was a failure, established the political power of organised labour.

During the decades after 1945 the trade union movement grew enormously in both economic and political strength such that, by the 1970s, it effectively held the Labour Party in thrall and demanded a say in the governing of the country. The attempt by the Labour Party to meet the conditions imposed by the IMF in 1976 eventually led to the 'Winter of Discontent' which ushered in the first Thatcher government.

This government had no intention of allowing the unions any say in the political process. On the other hand, it could do little immediately to strip the unions of their accumulated privileges and immunities. A more immediate weapon was the 1980–81 recession which cost large numbers of union members their jobs, causing union membership to fall away progressively from its 1979 peak (see **Figure 9.3**).

Figure 9.3   *Trade Unions: 1900–91*

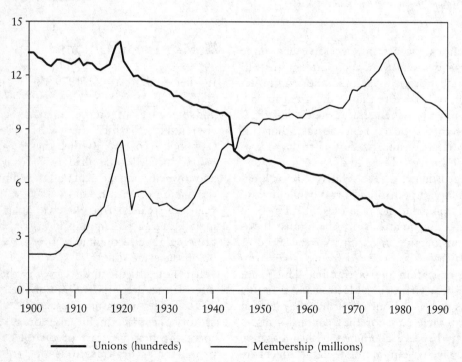

Unions (hundreds) ——— Membership (millions)

Source: Employment Gazette, May 1993.

During the 1980s the succesive Thatcher governments put in place a new legislative framework which redefined, in a cumulative fashion, the role of unions in the economy. There were six main pieces of legislation.

The Employment Act 1980

1 Employers were given the power to take legal action where strikers sought to disrupt business at a workplace other than their own (known as **secondary picketing**).
2 They were also empowered to take legal action if their employees disrupted their business in order to assist the employees of a separate organisation in the pursuit of a dispute which did not concern them directly.
3 Employees could opt out of union membership, even where a closed shop existed at their place of work.
4 Industrial action could no longer be taken on the basis of a show of hands, but required the backing of a postal ballot for which the government would provide funds.
5 There was no longer to be a statutory obligation upon employers to recognise the rights of unions at their workplaces.

The Employment Act 1982

1 Whereas previously employers could cite only individual union organisers when taking legal action in respect of disruptions to their businesses, they could now take action against the union itself.
2 Where a strike was **political** – that is, it involved neither employment matters nor a dispute between an employer and his or her own employees – an employer could seek redress from the striking employees.
3 Any contract which sought to enforce the exclusive use of union members would be deemed to be illegal.
4 Where a closed shop had not been approved by an overwhelming majority of the workforce, its provisions could not be legally enforced upon either an employer or dissenting employees.

The Trade Union Act 1984

1 All elections for senior union posts would have to be by secret (generally postal) ballot.
2 Unless a stike ballot was held by means of a secret vote, an employer could sue the organising union for damages.
3 A union would be required to ballot its members every 10 years if it wished to maintain a fund for political purposes.

The Employment Act 1988

1 Industrial action to enforce closed shops became illegal.
2 If a union member refused to participate in an industrial dispute, and the union subsequently sought to discipline him or her, he or she could take legal action against the union.
3 A union member could take out an injunction to prevent his or her union engaging in industrial action without a prior ballot, or engaging in such action before the ballot showed a clear majority in favour.
4 All union presidents and general secretaries could be elected only where the ballot was fully postal and supervised by an independent body.
5 The use of union funds was to be limited to certain purposes, and members were to have access to their union's accounts.
6 A Commission for Union Affairs was to be established in order to finance union members wishing to take legal action against their union.

The Employment Act 1989

The 1978 Employment Protection (Consolidation) Act was amended to limit the duties in respect of which an employer was required to allow officials of a recognised trade union time off with pay. The Act was also amended to ease other burdens on employers.

The Employment Act 1990

1 It became unlawful to refuse to employ a person because he or she is, or is not, a trade union member, or because he or she will not agree to become or cease to be a member, and that any person refused employment for such a reason may complain to an industrial tribunal.

2 It removed the immunities under section 13 of the Trade Union and Labour Relations Act 1974 for acts in contemplation or furtherance of trade disputes involving calling for, or otherwise organising, 'secondary' action unless made in the course of peaceful picketing as the law allows.

3 It extended section 15 of the Employment Act 1982, which prescribed circumstances in which a union is legally responsible for organising industrial action. In particular, if any union shop steward calls for industrial action, his or her union will be liable unless and until it effectively repudiates what the shop steward has done as soon as reasonably practicable.

4 It gave employers greater freedom to dismiss employees taking part in unofficial action.

So far, the 1990s have seen one further major piece of legislation in addition to **The Trade Union and Labour Relations (Consolidation) Act 1992**, which brought together much of the legislation set out above.

The Trade Union Reform and Employment Rights Act 1993

This Act, which largely came into force on 30 August 1993, departed from earlier legislation in two respects. First, it contained detailed regulation of the daily running of unions, and second, it reversed the long-standing assumption that collective bargaining is to be encouraged. Specifically it granted the following (for details see *Employment Gazette*, August 1993).

1 It gave employees the right, when pregnant, to a minimum entitlement of 14 weeks' maternity leave, and enhanced protection against dismissal on maternity related grounds.

2 It gave employees the right to receive explicit written details of hours, pay and holiday entitlement.

3 It gave employees the right to protection against being dismissed for exercising statutory employment rights.

4 It gave individuals greater freedom to belong to the union of their choice.

5 It gave trade union members the right not to have union subscriptions deducted from their pay except with their written consent, which is to be subject to periodic renewal.

6 It required union industrial action ballots to be conducted by fully-postal voting only, and to be independently scrutinised.

7 It required unions to provide employers with at least seven days' notice of official industrial action.

8 It created a new 'Citizen's Right' to restrain unlawfully organised industrial action.

9 It abolished the remaining Wages Councils and their statutory minimum pay rates.

☐ *9.2.1 Trade Union Membership*

A list of trade unions is maintained by the Certification Office of Trade Unions and Employers' Associations in accordance with section 8 of the Trade Union and Labour Relations Act 1974. Section 28 contains the definition of a union, primarily in terms of a requirement that it is an organisation of workers which has the regulation of relations between workers and employers as one of its principal purposes. All listed and unlisted unions are required under section 11 to submit annual returns, which include membership figures, to the Certification Officer.

The number of unions recorded by the Certification Office is somewhat different from that recorded by the Employment Department (which are used below) because the latter counts only 'parent' unions such as the National Union of Mineworkers, and includes unions with their head office in Northern Ireland.

Figures for union membership are those provided by the Employment Department, which are compatible with those of the Certification Office for the UK as a whole. However, membership figures which are also now available, as a result of a question included for the first time on the 1989 LFS, are calculated in a manner which results in a lower membership figure when compared to the Employment Department's figure of 9.6 million for Spring 1991. The discrepancy arises because the LFS count excludes those who were unemployed, wholly retired or overseas at the time of counting. In addition, the LFS counts individuals in membership rather than individual memberships, whereas the Certification Office counts the number of memberships even if individuals belong to more than one union.

Figure 9.3 illustrates the long-term membership trend. As can be seen, although membership slumped during the 1920s for reasons indicated in Chapter 1, it rose steadily from the early 1930s to a peak of 13.3 million in 1979. Subsequently, it

has been downhill all the way, with the 1993 figure standing at an estimated 9 million, a reduction of nearly one-third from the peak figure.

Figure 9.3 provides data for both union membership and the number of unions. The sharp downturn in membership during 1981 and 1982 comes as no surprise given the severity of the recession at the beginning of the decade, but it is surprising to observe that the previously noted upturn in employment from 1986 onwards failed to reverse the downwards trend. This can be seen more clearly in **Figure 9.4**, which also matches up membership changes to changes in employees in employment.

In part, this can be attributed to inefficient practices among the unions themselves. Workplaces where unions are recognised encompass roughly 60 per cent of the workforce, yet one-third of these workers are not union members. Under such circumstances it is easy to give up union membership without the expectation of disapproval by fellow workers. It is also the case

Figure 9.4   *Year on Year Changes in Employees in Employment and Trade Union Membership*

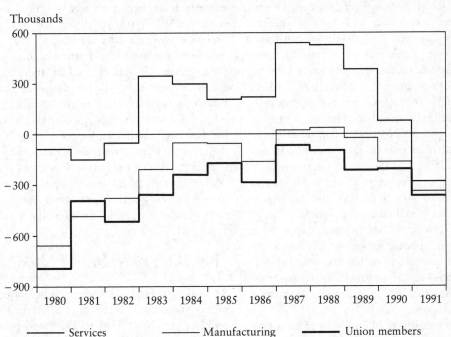

Source: Employment Gazette, May 1993.

that entrepreneurial (and, often, medium-sized) firms are neglected by union officials who prefer to service existing agreements with larger companies. The old-style bargaining methods utilised by male officials are also unlikely to strike a sympathetic chord in a modern factory full of female part-time workers.

It is reasonable to argue that the growth of female part-time workers and of small companies would have caused some erosion of union membership even if officials had tried harder to recruit in non-traditional ways. Nevertheless, there is evidence to suggest that the attitude towards unions in different types of workplace is a more critical factor. In general, managers in large companies with full-time workforces are happy to foster union membership in order to simplify bargaining arrangements. Where the employers in small companies also seek to encourage unions there is typically an equally high membership ratio. Where, however, such companies – almost all of which operate in the private sector whereas many of the largest employers operate in the public sector – discourage membership, it is typically only one-third as high.

It is often believed that workers are much more likely to join unions in the traditional manufacturing regions as compared to the South-East. However, the significant switch of employment to the South-East does not, of itself, seem to have had much effect upon union membership. Rather, the explanation is to be found in the points outlined above, namely that the type of company shedding labour in the North is much more likely to encourage membership than the newer companies taking on labour in the South-East.

Furthermore, there is no reason to attribute the decline in membership to the switch from unskilled to relatively skilled and managerial occupations. If anything, the latter group appear to have a more favourable image of unions than their unskilled counterparts. On the other hand, as suggested above, the unions themselves may show less enthusiasm for recruiting among their ranks.

A number of highly-publicised confrontations have given the impression that attempts by employers to derecognise unions have accounted for

a major decline in membership. Such incidents, however, have been relatively rare and the effects of derecognition correspondingly insignificant. Indeed, a recent survey indicated that falling union membership was one of the most common reasons employers gave for derecognition.

It would appear, therefore, that the switch from public sector to private sector employment, from manufacturing to services and from male to female employment have been instrumental in loosening the grip of unions on the workforce, and that the unions themselves have done little to counteract these trends. It should also be noted that the unions are not perceived by their members as delivering a satisfactory service. Only about one in ten workers, whether unionised or not, believes that unions are successful in defending the rights of workers. Nevertheless, this does not appear to make workers feel hostile towards unions, and neither does it appear to explain why more than a modest proportion – roughly 15 per cent according to a 1989 Nuffield College study – give up their membership.

In conclusion, it would appear to be the case that, as the industrial structure has evolved, employees have become increasingly disenchanted with traditional trade unionism and that the unions have failed to respond to the challenge. At the same time, the stream of industrial relations legislation has created an increasingly hostile environment for the union movement, and the relatively high levels of unemployment – together with, until very recently, rapidly rising wage levels for full-time male employees – have also had a depressive effect upon membership. The clause in the 1993 Act whereby union dues cannot be deducted from an employee's pay packet without his or her consent is particularly likely to affect membership adversely commencing in 1994.

☐ 9.2.2 Trade Union Numbers

As shown in **Figure 9.3**, the number of unions has fallen from 500 in 1975 to 275 in 1991. The number peaked at 1384 in 1920, and numbers fell steadily thereafter with the exception of 1973 and 1977 when small increases were recorded. In fact, new unions are constantly being formed – there were 10 in 1988 – but mergers and transfers of membership have been the dominant factor throughout the period.

Even today most unions are small. In 1991 almost half of all unions had fewer than 1000 members, accounting for 0.6 per cent of total membership. By way of contrast the 22 largest unions, each with more than 100 000 members, accounted for 81 per cent of total membership and the 10 largest unions, each with more than 250 000 members, accounted for 60 per cent of total membership. The most recently available data are presented in **Figure 9.5**.

☐ 9.2.3 Trade Union Finances

Falling memberships, coupled with a failure to raise subscriptions as a proportion of members' earnings, have resulted in a steady decline in the primary source of income for virtually all unions.

Whether this creates severe financial problems depends, however, upon their expenditure. Where unions take on large numbers of full-time officials and push for expansion, as in the 1970s, spending tends to outrun revenue and causes a reduction in real net worth (which almost halved for registered unions between 1965 and 1980). Although real net worth rose by over one-quarter during the 1980s, this reflected in part (as noted previously) the failure by the unions to engage in an aggressive membership drive in smaller work-places where, due to lack of cooperation by management, recruitment was costly.

Unions have sought to save costs by merging, in several recent cases thereby creating 'super-unions' (as shown in **Table 9.4**), but this has often been a financial disaster due to inaccuracies in the accounts of smaller unions and their tendency to exaggerate their memberships and hence their subscription income. The salaries of officials also tend to be boosted as a consequence of mergers. During the 1980s the careful investment of accu-

Figure 9.5 *Membership and Number of Unions, by Size, 1991*

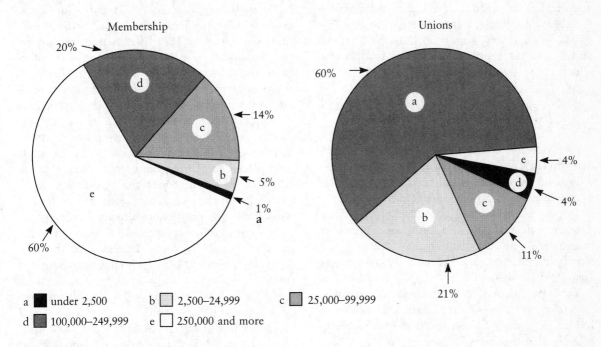

a ☐ under 2,500 b ☐ 2,500–24,999 c ☐ 25,000–99,999
d ☐ 100,000–249,999 e ☐ 250,000 and more

Source: Employment Gazette, May 1993, p. 191.

Table 9.4   *Major Union Mergers*

Merged union	Partners	Date of merger	Current membership
Manufacturing Science Finance	ASTMS/Tass	February 1988	604 000
Amalgamated Engineering and Electrical Union	AEU/EETPU	April 1992	980 000
Unison	Nalgo/Nupe/ Cohse	July 1993	1.51m
?[1]	TGWU/GMB	Mid 1990s	1.98m
Total TUC affiliation			7.76m

Note:
[1] Subject to negotiation.

mulated reserves helped to offset these costs, but many unions, even such giants as the Transport and General Workers' Union, find it hard to avoid operating at a loss and hence eating into those reserves. As a consequence, the unions have been obliged to pull in their horns during the 1990s, and this has restricted their ability to enlarge their membership, although there are exceptions, (typically in the public sector) such as the National and Local Government Officers' Association, which are still very prosperous.

☐ 9.2.4 Union Density

'Union density' is simply the number of individuals in each category who are members of either a trade union, staff association or both, expressed as a percentage of all individuals in that category. It is possible to obtain data using this 'tight' definition through the LFS, although alternative measures are also available using somewhat different definitions (see *Employment Gazette*, August 1990, p. 413).

Table 9.5 summarises the data on union density in Spring 1991 for Great Britain and Northern Ireland separately. The overall density for employees in Britain was 37 per cent. It was 47 per cent for Northern Ireland, where the higher percentage can most easily be explained by the relatively large public sector (which tends to be highly unionised) compared to Britain.

Density was higher among males than among females, and among manual workers compared to non-manual. Full-time workers were twice as likely to be union members as part-time workers. All these findings were closely in line with previous research. The difference in density between workers in manufacturing and non-manufacturing was negligible in Britain. However, sharp differences in density were found according to the number of employees per workplace.

Roughly half of all workers in workplaces employing 25 or more employees were union members, twice the proportion to be found in workplaces employing between 6 and 24 workers, and over four times the proportion to be found in workplaces employing fewer than 6 workers. In the smallest workplaces male density rates were $1\frac{1}{2}$ times greater than those for females, but the overall density is depressed by the relatively high proportion of females who work in small workplaces. The only density rate which was found to be lower was, predictably enough, among the self-employed.

The LFS estimates revealed (*Employment Gazette*, January 1993) that female part-time employees were roughly twice as likely as their male

Table 9.5   *Union Density in the UK, Spring 1991 (%)*

	Great Britain	Northern Ireland
Male	42	50
Female	32	44
Non-manual	35	49
Manual	41	46
Manufacturing (2–4)	38	52
Non-manufacturing (0, 1, 5–9)	37	46
Full-time[1]	42	52
Part-time[1]	22	24
Size of workplace:		
Under 6 employees	11	} 25
6–24 employees	23	
25 or more employees	47	62
All employees[2]	37	47
Self-employed[3]	10	[4]
All in employment[3]	33	40

[1] The definition of full-time and part-time is based on the respondent's own assessment, not on the number of hours usually worked.

[2] Includes those who did not provide information on one or more of the dimensions reported in the table.

[3] Includes those on government employment and training programmers and those who did not report their employment status.

[4] Sample size too small for reliable estimate.

Sources: 1991 LFS estimates; *Employment Gazette* (January 1993), p. 676.

counterparts to be union members. This appeared to arise because these females were predominantly middle-aged married women who stayed with the same employers for long periods of time, whereas the part-time males tended to be either relatively young or relatively old and treated their jobs in a much more transient manner. The LFS estimates also revealed that whereas West Indian/Guyanese males and females were noticeably more likely to be union members than their white counterparts, the opposite held true for most other ethnic origins.

According to the LFS, a significantly greater proportion of those aged 30 years of age or older in 1991 were union members as compared to the proportion in employment, whereas the opposite held true for those aged under 25. Density also increased with length of service, and half of all employees who had been in their current job for 10 years or more in 1991 were union members.

Interestingly, in 1991 less than one-fifth of all union members (who were employees) were skilled craftsmen, whereas 30 per cent were in managerial and professional occupations. In part, this reflected the high proportion of women in the latter groups (almost 50 per cent) who were members, a higher density both compared to their male counterparts and especially compared to females in manual occupations.

Looked at from an occupational perspective, union densities varied enormously: for example, registering 70 per cent among education professionals but only 11 per cent among those engaged in selling. Nevertheless, the union movement still consists predominantly of workers in occupations such as clerical and catering where union densities are relatively low. A final factor is region of residence. In 1991 union density was highest in the North (46 per cent) and lowest in East Anglia (25 per cent).

It is possible to take a more sanguine view of the decline in density when account is taken of the somewhat lower densities in most other EU member countries, and of the overall density of 16 per cent in the USA. It is significant, however, that 60 per cent of US union members work in the private sector whereas the comparable figure for Britain is probably only 27 per cent. Clearly, the unions in the UK need to recruit amongst workers in the private sector, yet that is harder than in the public sector. On the whole, the evidence indicates that in the private sector non-union plants are more productive and more profitable than their unionised counterparts. Hence non-union workers tend to be better rewarded and to enjoy better relations with management. Their employers understandably often refuse to recognise unions, and derecognition may occur. Unless statutory recognition is introduced, which is Labour Party policy, the union movement is likely to concede further ground. Certainly, it is notable that there are currently virtually no disputes about union recognition.

□ 9.2.5 *Industrial Disputes*

Table 9.6 contains data on industrial disputes in the UK covering a period of two decades. As can be seen, there are various ways of measuring the incidence of disputes and the various series tell a somewhat different story. For the purpose of making international comparisons it is customary to use the number of working days lost per 1000 employees, although there are definitional ambiguities (for example, only the UK and USA exclude data on political stoppages: see *Employment Gazette*, December 1990, p. 610).

What the data show fairly unambiguously is that the number of stoppages has fallen noticeably since 1979. Excluding the Winter of Discontent in 1979–80, which effectively preceded the Thatcher government, the number of working days lost per 1000 employees has also tended to be lower during the 1980s, with the exception of

Table 9.6   *Stoppages[1] in Progress, UK, 1970–92*

Year	No. of Recorded Stoppages in Progress	Workers involved in Period (000)	Working Days Lost (000)	Working Days Lost per 1000 Employees[2]
1970	3 943	1 801	10 980	489
1971	2 263	1 178	13 551	612
1972	2 530	1 734	23 909	1 080
1973	2 902	1 528	7 197	317
1974	2 946	1 626	14 750	647
1975	2 332	809	6 012	265
1976	2 034	668	3 284	146
1977	2 737	1 166	10 142	448
1978	2 498	1 041	9 405	413
1979	2 125	4 608	29 474	1 273
1980	1 348	834	11 964	521
1981	1 344	1 513	4 266	195
1982	1 538	2 103	5 313	248
1983	1 364	574	3 754	178
1984	1 221	1 464	27 135	1 278
1985	903	791	6 402	299
1986	1 074	720	1 920	90
1987	1 016	887	3 546	164
1988	781	790	3 702	166
1989	701	727	4 128	182
1990	630	298	1 903	81
1991	369	176	761	34
1992	253	148	528	24

Notes:
[1] The statistics relate to stoppages of work in the UK due to industrial disputes between employers and workers, or between workers and other workers, connected with terms and conditions of employment. Work to rules and go-slows are not included; neither are stoppages involving fewer than ten workers or lasting less than one day unless the total number of workers' days lost in the dispute exceeds 100. The statistics include lock-outs and unlawful strikes (see *Employment Gazette*, July 1989, p. 359).
[2] Based on the latest available mid-year (June) estimate of employees in employment.

Source: Employment Gazette.

1984 due to the miners' strike discussed below and, less obviously, 1986 where the printers' strike does not show up in the data.

9.2.6 Key Disputes and Data Distortion

In interpreting the data care has to be exercised in respect of the two key disputes during the 1980s. The first of these, the miners' strike of 1984–85, caused an enormous increase in the number of days lost through strikes in 1984 even though the number of stoppages was relatively modest. By way of contrast, the print union strike of 1986–87, which was almost comparable in its intensity, does not show up at all in the data for days lost because the workers involved had lost their jobs, although the company (News International), carried on production.

It is interesting to relate these disputes to the union law then in existence. In the case of the miners, their defeat can most obviously be ascribed to a determined government, astute planning by the Coal Board and an unsympathetic public, rather than to the use of new laws which were largely ignored. On the other hand, it is possible that the failure of the National Union of Mineworkers to involve other unions in the dispute may have had something to do with the law on secondary picketing and fear of having funds sequestered.

In the case of the dispute between News International and the National Graphical Association and the Society of Graphical and Allied Trades (SOGAT) 82, the dismissal of the strikers took place under the terms of pre-1979 legislation, but injunctions were also taken out to prevent secondary picketing and secondary action by other union members disrupting the company's business. Perhaps the crucial matter arising out of these disputes is that certain unions – whether newly-formed in the case of the Union of Democratic Mineworkers or long-standing in the case of the EEPTU have now decided to act wholly in accordance with the new laws and to use this as a lever to gain recognition in place of other unions,

such as the National Union of Mineworkers and SOGAT, which are wholly opposed to them. The new Acts have, therefore, served to weaken the union movement primarily by dividing it from within.

9.2.7 Are Strikes a Thing of the Past?

In 1992 the number of stoppages in progress was the lowest for more than 50 years, as it had been in the previous three years, although the exclusion of some of the smallest stoppages from the recorded data during this period casts some doubt over this conclusion. The number of working days lost showed a broadly similar pattern, although it rose slightly for four successive years from 1985 before falling back sharply in 1990. This phenomenon was also manifested in other advanced economies, so The UK's relative position in terms of working days lost per 1000 employees has remained virtually unchanged.

Throughout the 1980s four sectors of industry were especially prone to disputes, namely mining and quarrying, manufacturing, construction, and transport and communication, both in the UK and elsewhere (although the UK in particular suffered relatively due to the 1984–85 miners' strike: see *Employment Gazette*, December 1990, p. 611). In other sectors strikes are therefore of little economic significance, and even in the more troublesome sectors the period 1985–92 was a huge improvement compared both to 1980–84 and to 1970–79.

On the whole, bearing in mind that the 1980s were a decade during which there was a good deal of disruptive restructuring, there is reason for a cautiously optimistic response to the above question in the sense that, whereas industrial disputes will always remain with us, their incidence and economic effects do seem to have reached an equilibrium at an acceptable level.

It is worth observing, however, that the absence of strikes may reflect a cowed workforce as well as a contented one. A strike has two basic elements: both an unsatisfied grievance and an ability to strike. Hence, a reduction in strike activity must reflect a decline in unsatisfied employee grievances and/or a decline in the ability to strike. It is noticeable that so far in 1993 there has been a major confrontation at the Timex electronics plant at Dundee, as well as significant unrest on British Rail and the buses, and in the pits and schools, so there does not appear to be a shortage of grievances.

The data on overtime also indicate that, at least in the private sector, overtime bans were twice as likely to occur as strikes during the 1980s. Interestingly, techniques such as just-in-time deliveries have made the overtime ban an increasingly effective weapon, and fear of unemployment is more likely to discourage strikes than overtime bans. In any event, it is worth noting that absenteeism in 1992 caused the loss of 400 times more working days than did strikes, so it may be inappropriate to devote so much effort to the latter problem.

9.2.8 Effects of Legislation Upon Union Behaviour

It is generally believed that the huge improvement in corporate performance after the end of the 1980–81 recession can be ascribed, at least in part, to the stream of anti-union legislation emanating from the various Thatcher governments. It is difficult to 'prove' the precise form of the relationship between the two, but such evidence as exists (in particular the work of the Centre for Labour Economics at the London School of Economics) lends little support to the popular view that unions deter investment and hold back productivity growth, thereby creating unemployment (their effects upon wage differentials are discussed separately below).

What the studies show is that the 1980–81 recession would have created a positive climate for change even in the absence of supporting legislation, since it threatened union members with unemployment and companies with bankruptcy unless they rapidly improved their performance. What it is certainly fair to say is that there was a great deal of potential for such an improvement at the turn of the decade, and that the conservative

attitudes of unions during the 1970s in resisting change had a great deal to do with this fact.

The British tradition was that in a bargaining situation the union was concerned only with pay and job security, whereas management was concerned with efficiency and productivity. One obvious consequence was the debilitating miners' strike of 1984–85 which was fought in order to preserve jobs in arguably the least-pleasant occupation on offer, rather than to ensure that miners' sons could be found something else to do of a less arduous kind.

Irrespective of cause, however, the studies showed that unionised companies seemed to have more organisational change, higher investment and higher productivity growth after 1981 without the unions seeking to oppose these developments. The comparison of productivity growth between highly-unionised companies, with more than half the workforce in a union, and companies with little or no union representation is especially interesting. Throughout the 1970s neither group held the ascendency for other than short periods, and each held it for roughly half the period. From 1981 to 1985, however, the highly-unionised group performed much better, especially from 1983 to 1985. Unfortunately, it is as yet unclear whether this trend, which came to an end during 1985, was simply a one-off response to the recession or is a more permanent feature of the industrial landscape.

Insofar as the government chose to believe that their anti-union legislation was responsible for this improved performance, it is understandable that they chose to introduce several more Acts, set out above, during the latter part of the decade. The interesting question is, therefore, whether this legislation is mere overkill, although it is certainly electorally popular, which may ultimately prove to be its main justification.

9.2.9 The Closed Shop

Closed shops come in two varieties: pre-entry, whereby a worker cannot be hired unless he or she is already a member of a union with negotiating rights at the workplace where employment is sought, and post-entry, whereby it becomes a condition for being hired that a worker joins an appropriate union as soon as possible after being given a job. It is argued that closed shops are only fair because otherwise non-members will be able to 'free-ride' on the backs of members and secure the same improvements in terms and conditions which the members pay for via their subscriptions to the union.

It is also the case that closed shops typically come into existence only when union density has reached a high level, and that many employers look upon them with favour, particularly in the public sector, because they find it much easier to enter into collective agreements with a specific union. During the 1960s and 1970s closed shops became increasingly popular, and at their peak in 1978 they covered in excess of 5 million workers. Subsequently, however, partly as a result of the Thatcher government's labour legislation and the effects of the 1980–81 recession, numbers employed in closed shops fell away sharply to a total of roughly 3.5 million in 1985, of whom about 500 000 were covered by a pre-entry shop according to the *Workplace Industrial Relations Survey* (WIRS).

Further research by the government undertaken as a prelude to the Employment Act 1990 indicated that there were only 2.6 million workers in closed shops in 1989, although rather more than had been thought appeared to be in pre-entry shops. The closed shop, therefore, appeared to be fading away without any further assistance, but the 1990 Act, as we have seen, nevertheless made it illegal to refuse to employ a worker who neither was, nor wished to become, a union member. This arose largely because, prior to the Act, a worker who believed that he or she had been refused a job simply because he or she was not a union member could obtain no redress against the company in question. The European Court of Justice has also ruled that it is unfair to dismiss workers who refuse to join a union.

☐ 9.2.10 The Union Mark-up

In an ideal world the success or otherwise of a union can be judged by its ability to raise the pay of its members above levels ruling for non-union members while simultaneously maintaining full employment for its members. In certain industries and during certain periods this happy combination (from the union's perspective only, since it is unlikely to be conducive to improved profitability) was achieved.

In general the 1970s were a good decade for the unions, with incomes rising at the expense of profits and with the incomes of union members rising faster than those of non-union members. A comparison of unionised sectors with non-unionised sectors during the period 1964–79 by Minford indicated an enormous differential in favour of union members. However, it is more customary to treat the mark-up as the difference in pay for two workers doing exactly the same kind of work, but where one belongs to a union and the other does not. Defined in this way the mark-up appears to have risen, on average, only from roughly 5 per cent to 10 per cent during this period, but also to have shown considerable variability as between different occupations and industries. One study (Blanchflower, 1984) reached the somewhat surprising conclusion that whereas the mark-up was only approximately 1 per cent for skilled workers in 1980, it was roughly 10 per cent for semi-skilled manual workers (for a summary of other studies see Brown and Wadhwani, 1990, pp. 65–8).

Intra-industry variability is to be expected because of significant differences which exist in product markets. By and large, unions cannot establish much of a differential where there is intense product market competition, especially from foreign companies, whereas a protected home market combined with a closed shop necessarily greatly strengthens the union's hand. For our purposes the most interesting questions are whether the 1980–81 recession eroded differentials, and whether these were restrained further by anti-union legislation.

The initial impact of the recession was undoubtedly minor. Faced by the choice between taking a reduction in pay or accepting the loss of jobs which could no longer be justified at existing wage levels, unions almost invariably preferred the latter to the former. Eventually, the sheer scale of job losses, wholesale plant closures and the onset of legislation ate significantly into differentials, but the buoyant employment situation during the latter part of the decade served to restore part of what had been lost, except in circumstances where either closed shop arrangements had been removed or unions had been derecognised (Gregg and Machin, 1992). When compared to the effect exerted by changing market forces, the effect of anti-union legislation appears to have been minor (Brown and Wadhwani, 1990 and Gregg and Machin, 1992).

☐ 9.2.11 Insiders and Outsiders

The sluggish response of differentials to the rapid rise in unemployment during the early 1980s – and, indeed, their continued existence, albeit at somewhat reduced levels, at a time when between 2 and 3 million people were unemployed – is something of a puzzle. Clearly, the labour market is imperfect in its operation, and an explanation for why that is so can be found by reference to the distinction between **insiders** and **outsiders**.

'Insiders' comprise those people who are either in work or who have recently lost their jobs but who retain valuable skills. A significant proportion among them will belong to unions. 'Outsiders', by way of contrast, comprise those people who have lost their jobs recently but whose skills are largely non-transferable, those who lost their jobs more than a year ago (the long-term unemployed) and those who have never held a job at all (school leavers and housewives).

Outsiders may become very numerous, but they may nevertheless have little effect upon the labour market. In the first place, unions may be more concerned with protecting the position of their members who are still employed than with the interests of the unemployed (who will tend to let their membership lapse). Second, employers will not be interested in taking on workers with either redundant skills or none at all, unless absolutely necessary. Third, some outsiders will be content to live off social security, at least for a time. Under these circumstances an upturn in demand is likely to lead to overtime working and the re-employment of skilled workers only recently laid off. As

a consequence, wages will continue to rise despite the existence of a large pool of unemployed workers. This becomes even more probable where there is a geographic imbalance between the places where the unemployed reside and the places where demand is growing.

In general, it is fair to say that any convincing analysis of how the labour market works must contain some elements of the insider–outsider dichotomy. Nevertheless, it is also fair to say that it explains persistently high unemployment more easily than changes in unemployment.

☐ 9.2.12 Political Levies

It is hardly surprising that the Thatcher Government heartily disliked union political funds since they provided the main source of revenue for the Labour Party. What rankled above all else was the fact that large numbers of union members were voting for the Conservative Party, whereas the unions' political funds were being passed in their entirety to the Opposition. Allowing members to 'contract out' of making payments into a political fund was an step in rectifying this anomaly but inertia, combined with a preference not to be at logger-heads with fellow workers, meant that relatively few took up this option.

The government accordingly made it obligatory under the Trade Union Act 1984 for unions to hold a ballot on the question of whether or not to have a political fund. However, much to the government's annoyance, the answer in almost every case was in the affirmative.

▌ 9.3 Recent Labour Market Controversies

☐ 9.3.1 Equal Pay

The Equal Pay Act 1975 required that women who performed similar tasks to men should be treated equally. The Sex Discrimination Act 1975 further required that men and women should be guaranteed equality of opportunity. In 1970, women's hourly earnings relative to those of men, as calculated from data in the annual New Earnings Survey, stood at 63.1 per cent. In 1975 the comparable figure was 72.1 per cent and in 1976 it was 75.1 per cent. It is reasonable to attribute most of the increase to the existence to these Acts. All alternative explanations, such as the existence of flat-rate incomes policies, an upturn in the demand for female labour or a reduction in the supply of female labour lack explanatory power because they did not happen (the reduction in supply); or because they were not permanent, yet there was no reversal of the relative earnings ratio when they ceased to apply (incomes policies); or because they were permanent (the increased demand for female labour) yet the earnings differential ceased to narrow after 1977.

In fact, the differential has yet to return to its peak value achieved in 1977. On the other hand, it has never subsequently fallen back below 73 per cent. This suggests strongly that it was the pre-1977 changes which were critical. Nevertheless, the obvious lack of progress since 1977 is an indictment of government policy in this respect.

Some actions to improve things have, however, been taken. In 1983, for example, the European Court of Justice ruled that the UK was in contravention of EU legislation which defined equal pay in terms of equal value. The Equal Pay (Amendment) Regulations were speedily enacted to bring the UK into line with this ruling. Unfortunately, this did not resolve the precise meaning of the term 'equal value', and a body of case law has had to be accumlated for this purpose.

In the case of *Hayward* v. *Cammell Laird Shipbuilders* (1980), for example, the House of Lords eventually ruled that equal pay literally meant equal money wages, and chose to disregard differences in perks. In June 1989 a woman records assistant employed by Northern Ireland Electricity was awarded equal pay with a male manual worker by a Belfast tribunal in the first case in which parity was established between white-collar and blue-collar jobs. An important current case revolves around a claim first lodged in 1985 by a district speech therapist against Frenchay District Health Authority, claiming parity with hospital pharmacists. The initial ruling

that the speech therapist had no case was upheld by an appeals tribunal in January 1991.

This judgement meant that separate collective bargaining arrangements which result in unequal pay between men and women cannot be challenged under equal pay laws unless it can be shown that the arrangements are **directly** discriminatory, whereas cases are typically based on claims of **indirect** discrimination. However, an appeal to the European Court of Justice resulted in a ruling in October 1993 to the effect that employers must justify any differences in pay between groups of men and women doing jobs of equal value, even if the differences result from collective agreements which do not appear to be discriminatory (see *Financial Times*, 2 November 1993).

☐ *9.3.2 Pension Equality*

The key case involved a gentleman called Mr Barber who was made redundant by the Guardian Royal Exchange Assurance at the age of 52. Under the GRE severance scheme, men and women made redundant 10 years before the scheme's normal retirement ages would be treated as taking early retirement, thus qualifying for an immediate pension. Mr Barber received a deferred pension and redundancy compensation, whereas a woman of the same age would have received an immediate pension. Mr Barber made a claim on the grounds of sex discrimination to an industrial tribunal and the Employment Appeal Tribunal, but both dismissed his claim.

On appeal, the Court of Appeal referred the case to the European Court of Justice to give a ruling as to whether the benefits received in connection with compulsory redundancy in the circumstances of the case consititued 'pay' within Article 119 of the Treaty of Rome, and accordingly whether they had to be equal for men and women.

The UK government argued that the benefits paid from a pension scheme fell with Articles 117 and 118, not Article 119. The Court of Justice gave a judgement on 17 May 1990, ruling that (a) the benefits paid by an employer to a worker in connection with redundancy fall within Article 119; (**b**) pensions paid under occupational pension schemes, including contracted-out schemes, fall within Article 119; (**c**) equal treatment must apply to each component part of remuneration including components of a pension; (**d**) Article 119 has direct effect and does not apply to State social security benefits.

The situation was further complicated by a case involving former employees of Coloroll, a home furnishing company which had gone into liquidation. At the end of April 1993 the Court of Justice delivered a preliminary opinion to the effect that equal treatment applied to periods prior to May 1990 only where the claimant had initiated proceedings before that date. This forestalled enormous additional claims on pension schemes, but simultaneously induced the great majority of UK employers to respond by equalising the age of eligibility for all members of their occupational schemes, in order to be able to finance claims for the period beyond 1990.

A second issue on which the Court ruled simultaneously concerned lump-sum retirement benefits, in respect of which it was held that employers must not take into account that women live longer than men and hence require a larger lump-sum on retirement to provide them with monthly income for the rest of their lives.

Although EU law allows member states to keep different pension ages for men and women, at present men in the UK have to pay contributions for at least 44 years to qualify for a full state pension compared to 39 years for women. Even if a man has paid contributions for 44 years, he still has to continue making contributions until he retires or reaches 65, whereas women stop paying at 60. At the time of the November 1993 Budget the Chancellor conceded the need to equalise the age of eligibility for state pensions. For the male retirement age to be lowered to 60 would have been hugely costly. The Chancellor accordingly chose to raise the retirement age to 65 for women even at the risk of political damage, but this ruling will only apply to women aged under 44 at the time, being phased in over 10 years commencing in the year 2010.

☐ 9.3.3 The Child Care Debate

In the course of the 1990 Budget the then Chancellor, John Major, stated that 'it is not for the government to encourage or discourage women with children to go out to work'. This did not, however, prevent him from exempting workplace nurseries from taxation as a benefit in kind.

The underlying presumption behind the offering of a subsidy is that it is necessary if a problem is to be overcome. The problem in this case is that there is allegedly going to be a shortage of labour due to the reduction in the number of young people entering the labour market; that this needs to be overcome by attracting married women with young children to fill the employment void; and that this is best achieved by providing better child care facilities.

Certain commentators find this argument unappealing because, for example, they see little point in attracting more women into the labour market when the female activity rate in the UK is already the second highest in the EU. In response, it is alleged that the lack of child care facilities is instrumental in preventing women from working full-time, and hence in preventing them from realising their true potential. Unfortunately, this does not accord with the facts. According to the 1991 LFS, fewer than one in 20 married women and one in 8 single women were working part-time because they could not find a full-time job. For the great majority, part-time work was the preferred alternative.

■ 9.4 The European Dimension

It would go beyond our immediate purpose to examine in detail the implications of the SEM for the UK labour market. Nevertheless, a number of comments are in order.

In the first place, the SEM is likely to have consequences for union structures. The idea of pan-European unions in specific sectors must inevitably hold some appeal for unions which are facing an adverse climate in the UK. However, this may prove difficult to realise in practice because, for example, most other EU countries are less highly unionised; the industries in decline in the UK are generally also in decline elsewhere; there are political and cultural differences to overcome; and there is the small matter of linguistic difficulties, at least for UK union leaders.

Second, there are implications for the structure of wage bargaining. Those EU countries, including the UK, where unions are big enough to influence wages but too small to care about their effect on the whole economy, have generally performed worse than countries where either bargaining is centrally organised, and hence unions have to take into account the effects of their actions on the economy as a whole, or bargaining is highly decentralised and unions are too weak to affect wage levels. Insofar as the SEM will open up EU markets to greater internal competition it will weaken the power of unions, especially those in previously sheltered industries. By implication this should yield benefits for the performance of the UK economy.

Third, there is the matter of the European Community Charter of Workers' Fundamental Social Rights, better known as the **Social Charter**, which was first approved by the European Commission in May 1989. Its purpose is to guarantee the basic rights of workers in the Community and it covers, **inter alia**, employment and remuneration, living and working conditions and information, consultation and participation. It is proceeding primarily via the issuing of directives, known as the **Social Action Programme**, which must eventually be translated into national law once they are ratified by the Council of Ministers.

The Programme got fully into its stride in June 1990 with a draft directive giving the same rights, such as training and holidays, to **part-time and temporary workers** as to full-time workers. In July a draft directive appeared on working hours. Among the 12 EU members only Denmark and the UK do not regulate the maximum daily working period, but this is of little relevance since actual working hours for full-time employees are in most cases well below the maximum set. The UK is also unusual insofar as it is one of only two

countries which do not regulate overtime. This is because the ideal UK working week is seen as one where official working hours are short – the lowest in the EU in many industries – but there is plenty of overtime available at higher rates of pay.

This directive accordingly concentrates upon shift and night work. On average, 20 per cent of EU employees do shift work, with the highest rates in the UK and Spain (29 per cent). The directive sets out that every worker will be entitled to least 11 hours of consecutive rest in 24 hours and an average of one rest day a week. Night work will be limited to eight hours a day, averaged over two weeks. The directive was finally adopted in June 1993 but there will be exemptions, and the UK has a ten-year grace period before the directive needs to be fully implemented.

In October 1994 a further directive on **maternity leave** becomes operational. This sets out that women will get at least 14 weeks' maternity leave, and maternity pay will be raised to what in the UK is the higher rate of sick pay. Jobs will also be protected during this period. Women will qualify after either six or nine months with their employer. In aggregate, these and other measures are more generous than those previously ruling in the UK, because, for example, women eligible for current higher rates of maternity pay can continue to claim under existing regulations, and hence will create additional costs which someone (employers rather than taxpayers, if the government has its way) will have to meet.

There are also moves to require **worker representation** on boards of directors of companies with more than 1000 employees and where at least 100 of them work in each of two EU countries. Also, any EU company with subsidiaries in more than one country will be required to set up a 'European works council': effectively a consultative council at group level where strategic decisions will be discussed which touch on plant closures and employment contracts.

In its anxiety to turn many of these directives into European law, the European Commission put them forward as health and safety directives which can be passed by a majority vote. This was necessary if they were to be adopted because the UK Government was opposed to a good many, arguing that such matters are best dealt with at a purely national level, and that the directives will impose costs running into billions upon UK industry, with consequent serious damage to its competitiveness. The government has stated that it intends to appeal to the European Court of Justice in respect of the working time directive on the grounds that unanimity was required.

At the Maastricht IGC the UK refused to accept the inclusion of a 'Social Chapter' extending the scope of social provisions, and this accordingly had to be omitted from the new treaty even though the UK was isolated. The Social Charter will nevertheless proceed and, if the UK refuses to participate in future social legislation, the other member states intend to press ahead anyway, leaving the UK to catch up later when it comes to appreciate the error of its ways.

Meanwhile the UK Government intends to obstruct this course of action at every turn, confident that, in the face of persistently high unemployment throughout the EU, the illogic of imposing additional costs upon businesses will cause other members to reconsider their positions.

Bibliography

Bean, R. (ed.) (1989) *International Labour Statistics* (London: Routledge).

Beatson, M. and S. Butcher (1993) 'Union Density Across the Employed Workforce', *Employment Gazette* (January).

Bilsborough, M. and N. Ross (1993) 'The National Education and Training Targets – Progress Made in 1992', *Employment Gazette* (August).

Blanchflower, D.(1984) 'Union Relative Wage Effects', *British Journal of Industrial Relations*.

Brown, W. and S. Wadhani (1990) 'The Economic Effects of Industrial Relations Legislation since 1979', *National Institute Economic Review* (February).

Daly, M. et al. (1992) 'Job Creation 1987–89: Preliminary Analysis By Sector', *Employment Gazette* (August).

Department of Employment (1990) 'Provisions of the Employment Act 1990', *Employment Gazette* (November).

Department of Employment (1993a) *The Government's Expenditure Plans 1993–4 to 1995–6*, Cmnd 2205 (London: HMSO, February).

Department of Employment (1993b) 'Evaluating Training and Employment Measures For the Unemployed', *Labour Market Quarterly Review* (May).

Department of Employment (1993c) 'Membership of Trade Unions', *Employment Gazette* (May).

Department of Employment (1993d) 'The Trade Union Reform and Employment Rights Act 1993', *Employment Gazette* (August).

Gregg, P. (1990) 'The Evolution of Special Employment Measures', *Royal Bank of Scotland Review* (September).

Gregg, P. and S. Machin (1992) 'Unions, the Demise of the Closed Shop and Wage Growth in the 1980's', *Oxford Bulletin of Economics and Statistics* (February).

March, D. (1991) 'British Industrial Relations Policy Transformed: the Thatcher Legacy', *Journal of Public Policy*, 11(3).

Mawson, J. (1992) 'Training and Enterprise Councils – an Initial Assessment', *Regional Studies*, 25(2).

Nolan, P. (1992) 'Trade Unions and Productivity: Issues, Evidence and Prospects', *Employee Relations*, 14(6).

Poret, P. (1990) 'The "Puzzle" of Wage Moderation in the 1980's', *OECD Working Paper*, 87 (Paris: OECD).

Shackelton, J. (1992) *Training Too Much?* (London: Institute of Economic Affairs, Hobart Paper 118).

Turner, P. et al. (1992) 'Training – A Key to the Future', *Employment Gazette* (August).

■ Chapter 10 ■

Welfare: Inequality and Poverty

Paul Marshall

▋ 10.1 Inequality and Income Distribution

Even at the crudest level no assessment of the well-being of a society can have much credibility unless it takes some account of the distribution of income as well as its aggregate total. (Morris and Preston, 1986)

This quotation is from a study of income distribution over time. Previous editions of this chapter also started from this quotation because it captures so well the fact that the overall view of a society's 'welfare' must be informed by the way in which aggregate income is shared among its constituent members rather than by the size of the total itself. In the 1990s issues relating to concepts such as 'fairness', 'equity' and 'social justice' have returned to the forefront of public debate. Following the reforms to the Welfare State introduced by the Conservative Government in the mid-1980s, a different Conservative Cabinet embarked on a comprehensive review of social policy spending in 1993, concerned, in particular, with a public sector deficit (borrowing requirement) of £50 billion. Prior to this an Independent Commission on Social Justice had been initiated by the Labour Party, but established as independent of political parties, with a brief to investigate the relationships between economic and social factors and the need for reforms to ensure that these relationships foster prosperity coupled with fairness.

However, even for a simple economy, measuring the distribution of economic gains is very difficult; for a large, developed, mixed economy, in which both public and private sectors exert their influences on income distribution, the complications of measuring distribution patterns are endless. The study from which the quotation is taken is of income distribution in the UK and covers a period during which there were major structural changes to the economy, several exogenous shocks (including the oil price hike of the early 1970s) and major social and political upheavals, including three changes of government. Nevertheless, as the quotation underlines, if we are interested in measuring economic welfare, and its tendency to change over time, we must take account of the **distribution of the gains from economic processes** no matter how complicated or dynamic they might be.

In the case of a mixed economy like the UK, the role of government is a crucial influence upon the distribution of income and wealth and this will be emphasised in the course of this chapter, particularly in relation to government's objective of reducing inequality. Within the government spending section of the national accounts are many items which relate to programmes aimed at improvements in individual welfare. The range of such programmes is considerable, spanning subsidies to both production (for example, farm income support programmes) and consumption (for example, household income maintenance programmes). Indeed, such is the range that any overview must be selective. For present purposes the selection concentrates on issues which lie at the heart of government aims to reduce inequalities in the distribution of income and wealth, issues which are often subsumed under the heading of 'social policy'. Why governments need to finance and/or provide such programmes and to **what extent they should do so** are extremely difficult questions to answer, but we hope in the course of this chapter to shed as much light as possible on the policy debate.

So far as economists are concerned, the issues to be discussed concern individual welfare: whether welfare is maximised for everyone through the market system or whether market-determined incomes require alteration by State action and, if so, how the alteration is to be achieved. Clearly, the welfare of individuals depends upon a multitude of things and not simply on the acquisition of material goods and services; it is the search for an understanding of the characteristics of, and the influences exerted by, this multitude that forms the basis of enquiry in social science. Within social science it is Economics which has concentrated on the material aspects of well-being, but it is difficult to maintain a strict divorce between Economics and other disciplines when trying to analyse the causes of the distribution of material consumption.

☐ 10.1.1 The Efficiency/Equity Trade-off

As an analytical concept, and as an aim of government policy, **efficiency** holds centre stage throughout this book, reflecting the main preoccupation of economists. But questions of welfare relate often to **equity** as well as to efficiency, and therein lies a problem for both the analyst and the policy maker since **it is rare for an efficiency objective to be achieved without an inequality being created**. Indeed, to recognise the reality of the problem of managing a mixed economy is to see it as a search for acceptable **trade-offs** between equity and efficiency. What the trade-offs look

like is a major question for research into the evaluation of government expenditure programmes. What the trade-offs **should** look like is part of a normative debate which manifests itself in the varying policies advanced from different political standpoints. Thus, for some observers, the question of equity should be at the forefront of political debate and should be the primary consideration in the formation of government expenditure plans. This argument may stem from altruism, but it may also be based on pragmatism: if 'the system' creates too much inequality it may invite violent political upheaval. On the other hand, some observers argue that efficiency should always be the main criterion for judging public expenditure programmes since only if the economy is efficient in every respect can the income available for redistribution be maximised; in other words, reducing inequality depends upon reducing inefficiency! The issue of the trade-off will recur throughout this chapter, and is often illustrated by the characteristics of the social policies implemented by different governments.

☐ 10.1.2 The Concept of Inequality

Using the term 'inequality' in the present context is intended as a comment upon the extent to which the rewards of the market place, supplemented and modified by government tax/transfer programmes, are distributed equally throughout the population. To measure inequality in this way is very difficult both for reasons of practical computation and for reasons of principle. Practical difficulties loom large when choosing appropriate data from which to analyse distributions. In the UK, for example, official estimates of income distribution are often derived from Inland Revenue returns, whereby the definition of 'income' is that used for the purposes of income taxation. Since income defined for tax purposes may exclude some important sources of income (for example, capital gains, imputed income from home production and property ownership, fringe benefits and certain government transfers), measures of distribution based on this definition may be inaccurate.

Even if comprehensive measures of income were available and distributions were to be computed accurately, however, there remains a difficult issue of principle: namely, how to **judge** distributions as 'equal' or 'unequal'. Certainly, we know what an equal distribution of incomes looks like; it is one in which **every income unit** (individual or household) has the **same income as any other unit**. We might be tempted to say, therefore, that any distribution in which at least one income unit has more or less than each of the other units is unequal. However, this is not very helpful when looking at a world of many distributions in which the degree of inequality differs, and it is this very question of **degree** which makes the measurement problem so difficult to resolve. If we are interested in comparing distributions at a point in time, or assessing changes in inequality over time, the problem becomes acute.

The crux of the problem lies in the fact that, while it is always possible to describe different patterns of income distribution, it is often impossible to describe different patterns of **inequality** without invoking a value judgement. Suppose, for example, that a change in government policy makes the top 10 per cent of income recipients slightly better off, the next 80 per cent much better off and the bottom 10 per cent slightly worse off. Has the policy change effected a more equal distribution of income? How is the small loss suffered by the bottom 10 per cent of income recipients to be weighed against the large gain to the majority of the population? What comment can we make about a change which has made the bottom 10 per cent of income recipients worse off, while raising the incomes received by the top 10 per cent?

Clearly, for an observer to describe one pattern of income distribution as more or less equal than another, reference must be made to an accepted concept of **social justice**, a rule by which any pattern of shares may be judged. Later on we shall concentrate on **poverty** as an important manifestation of inequality, and this issue of social justice takes on more obvious relevance when we try to make judgements about govern-

ment measures to improve the relative positions of individuals or households at the bottom of the income distribution. We must not, however, lose sight of the fact that to compare distributions may involve comparisons of gains and losses – that is, altered distributional positions for different percentile groupings – in which case judgements about which is more equal (or even, perhaps, 'preferred') cannot be made on any objective criteria. The history of 'Welfare Economics' has been written in terms of a search for an objective criterion by which to judge the outcome of economic processes, but the question of social justice does not reside exclusively within the domain of academic reasoning. Indeed, the very question of a trade-off between equity and efficiency, discussed earlier and to be returned to later, lies at the heart of real-world government decisions affecting the distribution of income. Both government expenditures and methods of raising revenue affect income distribution; a government implementing policies to promote efficiency at the expense of equity will be more likely to create inequalities than a government opting to sacrifice efficiency gains for equity goals.

10.1.3 The Measurement of Inequality

The Lorenz curve is used for **comparative** analysis: for example, comparing income distributions between countries either at some point in time or between different points in time in a given country. The curve shows cumulative percentage income shares: the bottom 10 per cent of the population (income units) receive x per cent of income, the bottom 20 per cent receive y per cent, where y is greater than x, and so on. When there is perfect equality – when every n per cent of the population receives n per cent of total income – the Lorenz curve is a 45° line or **line of income equality**. Such a line thus operates as a yardstick by which to gauge the inequality in any given distribution. If there is inequality the Lorenz curve lies below the 45° line, and the more unequal the distribution the further away from the

45° line lies the Lorenz curve. **Figure 10.1(a)** shows two hypothetical Lorenz curves with the distribution in year t represented as more equal than that in year $t - 50$.

It is possible to draw unambiguous conclusions from **Figure 10.1(a)** because one Lorenz curve lies completely outside the other. But let us examine **Figure 10.1(b)** where the two Lorenz curves cross. Are we still able to judge which of the two distributions is more equal? The Lorenz curves show that for all percentile groups up to the bottom 40 per cent their share in total income was higher in year $t - 50$ than in year t, but above this point shares were higher in year t. A measure of inequality which gives a greater weight to improvements in the share of total income enjoyed by the lower income groups would register $t - 50$ as the year of greater equality; a measure of inequality which gives a greater weight to improvements in upper income group shares would yield a preference for year t.

The same problem arises when using the Gini coefficient. This numerical measure of inequality is based on the relationship between the Lorenz curve and the line of income equality; it measures the ratio of the area between the Lorenz curve and the diagonal (the line of income equality) to the total area beneath the diagonal. In **Figure 10.2** the Gini coefficient is measured as the ratio $A/(A + B)$.

It can be seen from **Figure 10.2** that when the Lorenz curve follows the diagonal, and hence incomes are equally distributed, the Gini coefficient has a value of 0 ($A = 0$). At the other extreme, when all income is held by one individual ($B = 0$), the Gini coefficient has a value of 1. Thus, for purposes of comparison, the nearer the Gini coefficient is to 0 the more equal the distribution may be considered to be. However, when two Lorenz curves cross, how can we draw an unambiguous conclusion regarding relative inequalities? Consider once again **Figure 10.1(b)**. The Gini coefficient suggests that incomes are more equally distributed in year t, but this obscures the fact that from the viewpoint of the bottom four deciles year $t - 50$ is more equal.

It would seem, then, that when measuring the degree of inequality in income distribution we cannot avoid introducing value judgements about the 'desired' state of distribution. Any two observers with different views on the weight which should be given by society to improvements in the position of the lower income groups could place two different interpretations on any de-

Figure 10.1   *Hypothetical Lorenz Curves and the Measurement of Inequality*

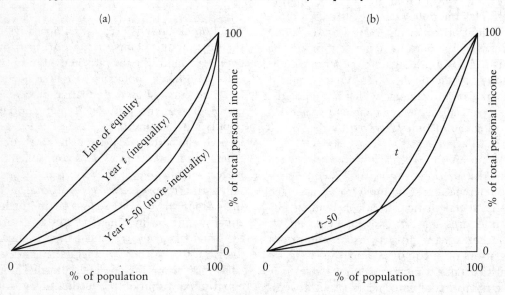

Figure 10.2 *Measuring the Gini Coefficient From the Lorenz Curve*

Table 10.1(b) *Cumulative Distribution of 'Original' (and 'Equivalised') Household Income, UK, selected years*

Quantile Groups	1977	1983	1990
Top 20%	43	50	51
Top 40%	69	73	76
Top 60%	87	90	91
Bottom 40%	14	11	9
Bottom 20%	4	3	2

Sources: Social Trends, 22 (1992 edn); *Economic Trends* (January 1993), p. 151.

crease in the value of the Gini coefficient between two points in time. Only if the Gini coefficient is used in conjunction with the original data on percentile shares is an adequate comparative picture likely to emerge.

☐ 10.1.4 The Distribution of Pre-tax Incomes in the UK

The official estimates of the distribution of personal incomes in the UK are published by the CSO and illustrate the problems referred to so far. Note that the estimates are of the **size** distribution of personal incomes. In the modern economy the distinctions between factors of production are rather blurred, and although analysing the distri-

bution of incomes among capitalists, labourers and rentiers still has its uses, it tends to be inferior to the size distribution as a summary measure of inequality.

Consider the estimates shown in **Table 10.1**. What do the data suggest? If the postwar period has been one of rising prosperity for the UK, how has this prosperity been shared out among the population? The data show clearly that pre-tax income has not been shared equally at any point in time. Insofar as pre-tax incomes reflect a market-determined set of rewards, this is to be expected. But what about shares over time: have pre-tax incomes become more or less equally shared?

The data suggest that we cannot draw unambiguous conclusions about changes in the degree of inequality over time, the main reason being that the percentile groupings at different points in the distribution have fared differently over time. We must bear in mind that the individual income units also differ within each percentile grouping at different points in time: for exam-

Table 10.1(a) *Cumulative Distribution of Personal Income before Tax, 1949–85 (selected years)*

Quantile Groups	1949	1959	1967	1975–76	1984–85
Top 1%	11.2	8.4	7.4	5.7	6.4
Top 10%	33.2	29.4	28.0	26.2	29.4
Top 50%	76.3	76.9	76.0	76.2	77.7
Bottom 50%	23.7	23.1	24.0	23.8	22.3

Sources: Diamond Commission, *Report No. 1*; Cmnd 6171, Table 15; *Social Trends,* 19 (1989 edn).

ple, the units comprising the top 10 per cent group in 1985 are not the same as those in the same percentile group in 1955. In other words, the data do not tell us anything about upward/downward mobility within the distribution. However, if we do accept that inequality is reflected in the shares enjoyed by different percentile groupings, looking at these shares over time suggests that the degree of inequality has been subjected to opposing forces, at least until the 1980s. Over the 30-year period, from the end of the 1940s to the end of the 1970s, the share of pre-tax income enjoyed by the top percentiles of income recipients fell: the share of the top 1 per cent fell from just over 11 per cent to just over 5 per cent, while the share of the top 10 per cent fell from just over 33 per cent to just over 26 per cent. This suggests that incomes were becoming more equally distributed. However, during the initial part of the period the share enjoyed by the bottom percentiles also fell, with recovery in the 1960s and early/mid-1970s proving only just sufficient to regain the share enjoyed at the end of the 1940s, suggesting that incomes did not become more equally distributed over the period.

How are we to weigh these opposing forces? It would appear that the Lorenz curves at different points of time are crossed, and that we cannot accordingly make a clear judgement about overall inequality without reference to a specific concept of social justice: the very problem discussed earlier. The only firm conclusion which might be drawn from the data is that whatever redistribution of pre-tax incomes has taken place, it has done so from the top to the middle.

Similar difficulties face us when trying to assess the changing degree of inequality after the 1970s (that is, some percentile groupings fared better than others in the overall distribution of incomes). However, the CSO estimates do suggest (see **Table 10.1(a)**) that there has been no reduction in the degree of inequality in the distribution of pre-tax incomes; indeed, the share of the top half of the distribution has increased while the share of the bottom half has decreased. The data in **Table 10.1(b)** are from an official series published since 1987, in which 'original' income replaces 'pre-tax' income and incomes are 'equiv-

alised' to account for household size and composition. 'Original' income is defined later in this chapter – effectively it is pre-tax income – and 'equivalised' incomes are calculated in acknowledgement that different household compositions create different needs and that income distribution, as an indicator of inequality, should also reflect the distribution of such needs. Not surprisingly, the data confirm the observation that before State taxes and transfers are accounted for, incomes are unequally distributed, and this inequality has worsened in recent years.

Further evidence that inequality might have increased in recent times has been offered by Jenkins (1991), who has calculated that most of the real income growth during the 1980s took place in the upper income bands, with little gain being enjoyed by those in the lower bands. According to Jenkins, 'in 1967 the richest 10 per cent had an income almost 10 times that of the poorest band. In 1978, the ratio was just more than 10, but in 1988, it was almost 18.' In his updating of the work of the Royal Commission, Stark (1990) has also added fuel to the argument that income inequality worsened over the 1980s. According to Stark, the income of the top 10 per cent increased by 40 per cent while the bottom 40 per cent suffered a decrease of up to 8 per cent.

☐ 10.1.5 Trends in Factor Incomes

To explain the causes of the observed changes in the distribution of pre-tax incomes over the period in question requires an understanding of highly complicated and inter-related forces. Not all of these forces are economic, although for present purposes we shall look in more detail at the distribution of factor market incomes. Social and demographic factors also play their part in altering income shares over time. In the 1970s the Royal Commission on the Distribution of Income and Wealth (the Diamond Commission) identified four major forces: changes in the age structure of the population; changes in the activity rates of various sectors of the population; changes in marital patterns; and changes in education patterns. Not surprisingly, the Commission concluded that alterations to the pattern of income distribution were often attributable to some combination of these separately identified factors (Diamond Commission, 1975). For present purposes we shall let the observation rest there, although we shall return to the age factor when we consider the incidence of poverty and the problem of inter-generational finance of social security arrangements. Several relevant observations on activity rates are also made in Chapter 8 (see **p. 292**).

So far as economic forces are concerned, we can usefully begin with a closer look at factor market patterns. When a mixed economy allocates resources it determines rewards to factors of production in both private and public sectors, while the State's tax-transfer mechanism provides income maintenance for those who are eligible. We shall leave the distribution of State transfers until later and concentrate first on factor incomes as an indication of how rewards are shared out on the supply side of the economy, the many determinants of this distribution being discussed in every other chapter of this book.

10.1.6 The Distribution of Factor Rewards

Whatever the nature of social and demographic changes, the distribution of rewards in a market-oriented economy must reflect the nature of markets. Thus, there are at least two important questions to address: how are the total rewards from economic processes shared out among the various factors of production and, if one type of reward dominates, what forces help to determine its distribution? The answer to the first question offers a guide to answering the second. To understand the forces which determine the distribution of incomes we need to know the dominant source of income; an increase in the share going to capital is likely to have an impact on the overall distribution which is different from that resulting from an increase in the share enjoyed by labour. Furthermore, if one component of income ac-

counts for, say, more than half the rewards in an economy, then any change in the dispersion of that component will result in a change in the overall dispersion of incomes.

As can be seen from **Table 10.2**, which shows the relative shares of the main components of total household income in the UK for the period 1971-91, the largest component of household incomes in the UK is **income from employment**. Researchers into the distribution of incomes have seen the changes in this large component as indicators of both the overall state of the economy and the prevailing degree of inequality. Lydall, for example, discerned a trend towards equality in the distribution of incomes, from the immediate postwar years until the later 1950s, and argued that this trend owed much to postwar economic expansion and the improving fortunes of labour (Lydall, 1959). According to Lydall, the sustained high level of employment during the period meant that earned income rose faster than any other form of personal income, and that such a trend would be a major force towards equality. However, as calculated by Nicholson, this pattern changed during the period 1957–63 with the rate of growth of employment income slowing down relative to that of self-employment (and, within employment income, the rate of growth of wages slowed down relative to that of salaries). During this period rent, dividends and interest became the most rapidly-growing sector of personal income. The result, according to Nicholson, was a slowing down in any trend towards equality (Nicholson, 1967).

According to official estimates, the downward slide in the share of labour income continued into the 1970s, at which point it steadied before falling again during the early 1980s, from 73 per cent in 1978 to 69 per cent by 1985, since when it has remained almost constant. Nevertheless, the trend over the long run remains in labour's favour. By itself, this long-term trend reduces inequality if the gains are equally distributed among labour units. However, over time such redistribution has not been equal. Earnings (wages and salaries) constitute the largest proportion of factor incomes, yet there are forces at work to prevent an equal distribution of earnings among earners.

Table 10.2   **% Shares of Main Components in Total Household Income, UK, 1971–91[1]**

	1971	1976	1981	1986	1991
Wages and salaries	68	67	64	59	58
Income from self-employment	9	9	9	10	10
Rent, interest and dividends	6	6	6	7	9
Private pensions, annuities, etc.	5	5	6	8	9
Social security benefits	10	11	13	13	12
Other current transfers	2	2	2	3	2

Note:
[1] Figures to nearest whole numbers.
Source: Social Trends, 23 (1993 edn), Table 5.2.

Between the sexes there is considerable inequality. In the first place, the top male earners have consistently earned more than the top female earners. Second, the difference between the highest female earnings and the lowest male earnings has been consistently less than that between highest and lowest female earnings. For example, in 1987 the gross weekly earnings figure for the highest female decile (full-time) was only about 15 per cent higher than the median for men (full-time), while the median for women was only some 70 per cent of that for men. Five years later, in 1992, this inequality had worsened with weekly gross earnings for the highest female decile only some 9 per cent higher than the median for men and the median for women only some 65 per cent of that for men. Such inequalities have persisted despite legislation on equal pay and opportunities and sex discrimination (see Chapter 9). Another significant inequality persists between manual and non-manual earners (regardless of sex), with non-manual earnings consistently outstripping manual earnings in all deciles within the two distributions. The share of personal income going to rents, dividends and interest behaved more erratically during the period from 1960. Throughout the 1960s this share fell steadily before 'hitting bottom' in the early 1970s, since when it has climbed again, particularly during the 1980s.

Looking at the shares accruing to the major components of personal income cannot by itself 'explain' changes in inequality. However, the broad categories which we have considered do give some strong indications of what is happening to the degree of inequality associated with the overall distribution of personal incomes. In particular, it is difficult to avoid the conclusion that during the 1980s the increased share in pre-tax income enjoyed by the highest percentiles in the distribution resulted, in part, from an increased concentration of earned income due to a rise in the proportions of the population who were unemployed or retired.

10.1.7 The Distributional Impact of Taxes and Transfers

(a) Income Tax

When considering how UK governments have influenced the pattern of personal income distribution over the postwar period we must concentrate on two things: the effect of progressive income taxation and the effect of Welfare State transfers. A progressive tax structure smooths out the dispersion of incomes after tax and works towards a more equal distribution. Many Welfare State benefits, in principle, are transfers of income both in cash and in kind to the poorest percentiles in the distribution and, hence, a force towards reducing inequality.

In practice, the evidence suggests that it is only the benefits side of the tax/transfer mechanism which has worked to reduce inequality. Consider first the distribution of post-tax income as shown in **Table 10.3**. Taking first the period from the end of the 1940s up to the end of the 1970s, two observations can be made: first, income tax does indeed reduce the income dispersion at any point in time; second, over time the post-tax dispersion of income alters in roughly the same directions as the pre-tax dispersion. In other words, the redistribution of post-tax income has been from the top of the distribution towards the middle rather than towards the bottom. It would thus appear to be the case that, for the period in question, income tax was progressive and a force for equality but that its progressivity altered little over time.

What about the period since 1979? The most obvious point to make is that for the first time since 1945 the share of post-tax income enjoyed by the top 10 per cent of the distribution increased. The share of the top 50 per cent of the distribution has also risen steadily during the period since 1979. For the most part, these trends are a reflection of the same patterns emerging in the distribution of pre-tax incomes. However, an additional factor is that successive governments after 1979 set out to reduce the burden of direct taxation, either by raising tax thresholds or by reducing tax rates. Raising the tax threshold takes some income earners out of the income tax net, but it does nothing positive to improve the relative positions of those whose earned incomes are initially too low to be liable for income tax. Reducing the standard rate of income tax affects only those who pay tax, and cannot be considered to be a force to reduce inequality in post-tax income distribution. It must be noted also that the 1980s saw a massive reduction in higher rates of income tax: from 83 per cent to 40 per cent on earned income.

(b) The Distribution of Incomes Post-Taxes and Benefits

The wider and more comprehensive impact of government activity on income distribution in the UK is gauged by the CSO in terms of the difference between 'original income' and 'final income'. The definitions of these two concepts and the stages between them are summarised in **Table 10.4**.

Table 10.4 *Household Definitions used by CSO in Estimates of Income Distribution*

Income Concept	Definition
Original income	Earnings *plus* Occupational pensions *plus* Annuities, plus Investment income *plus* Other income
Gross income	Original income *minus* Cash benefits
Disposable income	Gross income *minus* Income tax *minus* NICs
Post-tax income	Disposable income *minus* Indirect taxes
Final income	Post-tax income *plus* Benefits in kind (Education, NHS, Travel subsidies, Housing subsidy and Welfare foods)

Source: Economic Trends (January 1992), p. 128.

Table 10.3 *Cumulative Distribution of Personal Income after Income Tax, UK, 1949–85 (Selected Years)*

Quantile Groups	1949	1959	1967	1975–76	1984–85
Top 1%	6.4	5.3	4.9	3.9	4.9
Top 10%	27.1	25.9	24.3	23.1	26.5
Top 50%	73.5	74.8	73.2	73.4	75.1
Bottom 50%	26.5	25.2	26.8	26.6	24.9

Source: Diamond Commission, *Report No. 1*, Cmnd 6171, Table 15; *Social Trends*, 19 (1989 edn).

It should be noted that, in addition to being based on a sample of households, the figures published by the CSO are based on an assumed incidence of taxes and benefits and a corresponding imputation process. It follows that the CSO estimates are somewhat less than 'hard facts' about 'final' income distribution. However, as estimates, they do enable an informed impression to be gained about the redistributive effects of government tax/transfer programmes.

Another important feature of the CSO estimates is that in 1990 the estimates were produced using 'equivalence' scales. The figures reported that year related to 1987, and were 'equivalised' in that household incomes were adjusted for both household size and composition in order to estimate an equivalent standard of living: for example, to recognise that a household of five adults needs a higher income than a single person living alone in order to enjoy the same standard of living. It is argued that using 'equivalised income' puts all households on an equal footing regardless of size or composition and, hence, provides a better means of comparison.

'Unadjusted' Estimates

Table 10.5 shows the distribution pattern suggested for the decade 1976–86 by the CSO's 'unadjusted' (for equivalence) estimates. Such a series was not available in official publications prior to the 1970s, and this run of estimates is the culmination of CSO researches to the middle of the 1980s.

The estimates in **Table 10.5** suggest an important observation: while the combined impact of taxes and benefits works to reduce inequality at any stage, it has not prevented a widening of the gap between the top and the bottom over time. At any point in time the distribution of original income in **Table 10.5** shows a pattern which is similar to that of the distribution of pre-tax incomes, but the dispersions in the shares of disposable and final incomes are much less marked. For example, in 1986 the top fifth enjoyed 50.7 per cent of original income but only 42.2 per cent and 41.7 per cent of disposable and final income respectively, while the negligible share in original income enjoyed by the bottom fifth rose to 5.9 per cent for both disposable and final income. However, the estimates also suggest that the dispersions in both disposable and final incomes were wider in 1986 than ten years previously. In 1976 the gap in original income shares was 43.6 percentage points between top and bottom fifths, the disposable income gap was 31.1 points and that for final income was 30.5 points, whereas the respective gaps for 1986 were 50.4, 36.3 and 35.8 points.

Thus the CSO estimates suggest that, for the decade in question, despite tax/transfer arrangements softening underlying inequalities, there was

Table 10.5 *Cumulative Distribution of Original, Disposable and Final Household Income, UK. 1976–86 (%)*

Quintile Group	Original Income			Disposable Income			Final Income		
	1976	1981	1986	1976	1981	1986	1976	1981	1986
Top 20% (a)	44.4	46.4	50.7	38.1	39.4	42.2	37.9	38.6	41.7
Top 40%	71.0	73.3	77.6	62.2	63.5	66.3	61.9	62.6	65.6
Top 60%	89.8	91.3	94.0	80.4	81.2	83.2	79.9	80.5	82.6
Bottom 40%	10.2	8.7	6.0	19.6	18.8	16.9	20.1	19.5	17.3
Bottom 20% (b)	0.8	0.6	0.3	7.0	6.7	5.9	7.4	7.1	5.9
Gap (a)–(b)	43.6	45.8	50.4	31.1	32.7	36.3	30.5	31.5	35.8

Source: Social Trends, 19 (1989 edn), Table 5.18.

a trend towards greater inequality in respect of the extremes of the income distribution. This conclusion was supported by a study of the longer period from 1968 to 1983, undertaken by Morris and Preston (1986) using the raw data from the FES rather than the published group data. Using the tax and benefit model of the Institute for Fiscal Studies (IFS), which adopts income definitions similar to those of the CSO, Morris and Preston concluded that both the Lorenz curve and the Gini coefficients gave reliable results for the period studied and that there was 'a clear cut rise in inequality over the 1968–83 period'.

'Equivalised' Estimates

While it can be argued that equivalence measures offer better comparisons across households in terms of living standards, the effects on distribution patterns are not dramatic because the majority of households either stay in the same quintile grouping in the distribution or move only to the next one. However, the distribution of equivalised income is less unequal than that calculated on the unadjusted basis because in the latter there are a disproportionately high number of single person households in the bottom quintile group, and these tend to have the lowest absolute incomes. **Table 10.6** shows the 'equivalised shares' and confirms the overall pattern observed in **Table 10.5**. Once again, as with the unadjusted estimates, the dispersion at a point in time is reduced but over time the degree of inequality appears to increase (the percentage points gap between the top and bottom quintiles widens).

Following the 1991 Budget, the IFS model was used to estimate the cumulative effect of tax and benefit changes since 1979 on household disposable incomes. The model showed that while the combined changes had, on average, produced gains, the distribution of these gains was uneven and the top 10 per cent of income earners had gained a weekly rise while the bottom 50 per cent had actually lost on average over the period.

10.2 The Concentration of Wealth

In the view of many observers the distribution of wealth shares within a society gives a more accu-

Table 10.6 *Cumulative Distribution of 'Equivalised' Incomes, UK, 1977–90 (%)*

Quintile Group	Equivalised Original Income Share			Equivalised Gross Income Share			Equivalised Disposable Income Share			Post-Tax Equivalised Income Share		
	1977	1983	1990	1977	1983	1990	1977	1983	1990	1977	1983	1990
Top 20% (a)	43	51	37	37	39	44	36	38	43	37	39	45
Top 40%	69	73	76	61	62	67	59	61	66	60	61	68
Top 60%	87	90	91	79	79	83	77	78	82	77	78	83
Bottom 40%	14	11	9	22	20	18	24	23	18	23	22	16
Bottom 20% (b)	4	3	2	9	8	7	10	10	7	9	9	6
gap (a)–(b)	39	44	49	28	31	37	26	28	36	28	30	39

Source: CSO (1992) *Social Trends*, 22, Table 5.19 and CSO (1993) *Economic Trends*, No 471, January, Appendix 4 (note that the table does not include trends in final income because equivalisation is not appropriate for this measure).

rate picture of the degree of inequality, because the full extent of individuals' economic power is determined ultimately by their potential command over available resources; this must reflect ownership of assets as well as current income. It is thus held that any society which aims for social justice will be concerned about both wealth and income shares. Unfortunately, when it comes to measuring wealth shares, obstacles are met which are even bigger than those encountered in the estimation of income distributions. This is true even though wealth and income are but different dimensions of a common set of means by which individuals satisfy their wants. **Wealth** refers to the **stock** of means available, while **income** refers to the **flow** of means from the given stock. Another term for wealth is 'net worth' which underlines the fact that wealth relates to a **net stock**: the difference between a set of assets and a set of liabilities.

10.2.1 The Definition and Measurement of Wealth

Given that any stock of means is measured by the total (capitalised) value of the various items within the stock, the essential preliminary step in empirical work is to determine which assets are to be included in the definition of the wealth stock. Some researchers see the crux of the problem in the relationship between 'value' and 'ownership', the key concept being that of 'marketability'. An individual may own the right to an income flow from a given asset, yet he or she may not be able to realise the market value of that asset because it is **non-transferable**. A prime example of this is the state pension: the asset has a value to its owner because it bestows income, but the pension right cannot be traded in the market place. Should such rights be included in the calculation of a comprehensive wealth stock? Less difficult to handle in empirical work are those assets which confer income benefits upon their owner and are disposable at an **exchange price**, such as cash, bank deposits, company shares,

government bonds and dwellings. Clearly, such assets must be included in any definition of personal wealth.

Official measures of wealth distribution in the UK represent **estimates** of wealth holdings since the Inland Revenue does not undertake a regular survey of such holdings in the way that it does for personal incomes. This is because the UK fiscal system does not include a comprehensive wealth tax; it does include capital taxes but those relate to disposals or transfers of assets rather than holdings (see **p. 166**). This means that estimates of holdings are made from too narrow a definition of wealth since transfers of 'capital', as defined for tax purposes, exclude some forms of wealth. Prior to the 1960s no official estimates of wealth distribution appeared in government statistical publications, but since then such estimates have been published annually. From 1962 to 1978 the Inland Revenue published annual estimates of both total wealth holdings and the distribution of those holdings based on the 'estate multiplier' method, whereby the estates of persons who die in a given year are used as the sample base for estimating the wealth of the living in that year. From the mid-1970s the CSO published their estimates of wealth holdings based on calculations of the aggregates of assets **minus** liabilities owned by individuals: the so-called 'balance-sheet' approach. From 1978 the Inland Revenue combined these two approaches to produce a new annual series which is also published by the CSO in *Social Trends*.

Needless to say, the methods adopted by government statisticians are disputed by other researchers, and a comprehensive survey must include these alternative estimates. For present purposes we shall confine ourselves to official estimates. For estimates of wealth distribution prior to the 1960s we shall refer to the calculations of Professor Jack Revell who pioneered the balance-sheet approach, later taken up by the CSO. This was the line taken by the Diamond Commission in the mid-1970s and, following the Commission, we can present the trends in wealth concentration in two distinct periods with 1960 as the watershed. **Table 10.7** presents the various estimates of the distribution of **marketable**

wealth: that is, excluding pension rights (both state and occupational).

The patterns in **Table 10.7** suggest that over the course of the twentieth century there has been a marked reduction in the shares of marketable wealth enjoyed by the top percentiles in the distribution, although wealth remains concentrated in the hands of a minority of wealthholders. From the beginning to the end of the period – that is, by the start of the 1990s – the share of the top 10 per cent fell from over 90 per cent to just over 50 per cent; however, at the start of the 1990s, over 90 per cent of marketable wealth was still owned by the wealthiest 50 per cent of holders of marketable wealth. It should be noted also that although the rate of decline in wealth shares at the top of the distribution increased between 1960 and 1980, it slowed considerably during the 1980s. Indeed, a significant feature of the 1980s pattern is that the share of the wealthiest 1 per cent remained constant at 18 per cent, while that of the wealthiest 5 per cent increased from 36 per cent to 38 per cent between 1981 and 1986 and that of the wealthiest 10 per cent increased from 50 to 53 per cent during the same period. It should also be noted that between 1982 and 1989 the Gini coefficient for wealth rose by two percentile points, from 64 to 66, and although no firm conclusions can be drawn from such a small change it does lend support to the view that there has been little redistribution of wealth in the UK since the end of the 1960s.

The Distributional Impact of Pension Rights

The inclusion of pension rights in the definition of wealth reduces significantly the shares enjoyed by the top percentiles. The share enjoyed by the top 1 per cent is reduced considerably for the years 1976 and 1989. The shares enjoyed by the top 10 and top 50 percentiles are also reduced, but the relative changes diminish in size in moving from the top to the fiftieth percentile, suggesting that the redistributive effect of including pension rights has its biggest impact on the wealthiest percentiles in the distribution rather than across the distribution as a whole.

It should also be emphasised that not only did the share of wealth holdings, inclusive of pension rights, enjoyed by the top 50 percentiles stay above 80 per cent between 1976 and 1989, it actually **rose by three percentage points**. Indeed, the Inland Revenue estimates for 1976 and 1989 suggest that there was also an increase in the share of wealth, inclusive of pension rights, enjoyed by the top 10 percentiles from 36 to 38 per cent, only one percentage point less than the increased share, **exclusive** of pension rights, for the same percentile of wealth-holders.

One likely explanation for this trend is that since the middle of the 1970s State pensions have

Table 10.7   *The Distribution of Marketable Wealth in Great Britain, 1911–60, and the UK, 1966–90*[1]

Quantile Group	% Share of Wealth, GB			% Share of Wealth, UK			
	1911–13	*1936–8*	*1960*	*1966*[2]	*1976*	*1986*	*1990*
Top 1%	69	56	42	33	24	18	18
Top 5%	87	78	75	56	45	36	37
Top 10%	92	88	83	69	60	50	51
Top 25%				87	84	73	72
Top 50%				97	95	92	93

Notes:
[1] Figures to nearest whole number.
[2] Using 'estate multiplier' method.
Source: Diamond Commission, *Report No. 1*, Cmnd 6171, Table 41 for figures for Great Britain only; *Social Trends*, 22 (1992 edn), Table 5.20 for UK figures.

become relatively less important in the composition of aggregate wealth and, because the inclusion of State pension rights reduces the inequality of wealth distribution, this relative decline has led to some increase in inequality in the distribution of personal wealth, including pension rights (Stewart, 1991). In 1976 marketable wealth accounted for 54 per cent of aggregate personal wealth whereas in 1989 it accounted for 60 per cent, having declined steadily to 51 per cent by 1984 and then climbed back during the second half of the 1980s. Occupational pension rights rose from 10 per cent to 20 per cent between 1976 and 1986 and then fell back to 18 per cent by 1989. Over the same period State pension rights fell from 37 per cent to 22 per cent.

Other Patterns of Accumulation

(a) Property Ownership

The official estimates of wealth distribution in the UK have been required to account for the effects of the inclusion of pension rights because the growth and spread of such rights, in particular those relating to occupational and other forms of private pension, has been a significant feature of the accumulation pattern in the UK. However, pension rights have not provided the only significant change in the pattern and composition of wealth holdings in the UK in recent times. A full analysis of the determinants of accumulation requires an understanding of relative **savings functions** in the community: the relative propensities to save out of incomes generated by differing property regimes, the relative influences of earnings and profits and so on. In the space available we cannot discuss such issues in depth but we can assume that, other things remaining unchanged, an increase in the spread of property ownership over time will lead to a break-up of concentration in property incomes and, to the extent that such returns constitute a significant component of wealth holdings, should be a force to reduce inequality in wealth holdings overall.

We have already discussed the housing market in some detail in Chapter 2 (see **p. 40**). In 1971 the value of dwellings net of mortgage debt in the UK

accounted for 23 per cent of the total net wealth of the personal sector in the UK, whereas by 1989 this proportion had risen to nearly 37 per cent. The increasing importance of dwellings in the composition of total net wealth is most clearly appreciated by comparison with the trends in the proportions of total wealth held in the form of financial assets.

That a combination of increased owner occupation and rising property values will have a significant impact on the overall distribution of wealth has been recognised in official publications through separate estimations, inclusive and exclusive, of the effects of including dwellings in the calculations of wealth holdings. Taken at face value the official estimates would seem to bear out the prediction that removing the value of dwellings (net of mortgage debt) from 'marketable wealth' renders the distribution of marketable wealth more unequal than the distribution pattern which emerges when the value of dwellings is included. **Figure 10.3** depicts the comparison.

At face value the pattern suggested by **Figure 10.3** seems fairly clear, with the share of total marketable wealth enjoyed by the top percentile being significantly reduced in each of the two years on display and with the reduction increasing between the two years. Thus, by 1989, the share of the wealthiest 10 per cent is reduced by 13 percentage points if the value of dwellings is included in the estimate of marketable wealth and, while the share of the wealthiest 50 per cent is **lowered** by the exclusion of dwellings for 1976, the share is the same whether dwellings are included or excluded by 1989. However, these estimates fail to account for the slump in the property market in the early 1990s, which was unprecedented in the postwar period and which saw the emergence of 'negative equity' on a large scale. The effects of this phenomenon are the focus of much current research.

(b) Financial assets

The influence on the overall pattern of wealth ownership exerted by financial assets is rather uncertain, and it is likely that the forces of accu-

Figure 10.3 *Comparison of Wealth Distribution with and without Property Values, 1976 and 1989*

Source: *Social Trends*, 22 (1992 edn).

mulation have pulled in different directions. Between 1971 and 1986 the proportion of wealth accounted for by building society shares increased steadily, from 6.3 to 7.9 per cent according to the CSO, before falling back again, to 6.1 per cent, between 1986 and 1989. During the same period the proportion of wealth held in the form of national savings and bank deposits fell quite markedly, from 11.9 per cent to 7.9 per cent, before recovering again to 8.3 per cent between 1986 and 1989. The combined effect of these opposing trends on the overall concentration of wealth will depend upon the extent to which they represent switching among 'popular' assets, compared with changes in relative patterns of ownership.

Neither do the trends exhibited by stocks and shares suggest an obvious influence on concentration. It must be borne in mind, however, that such trends do not tell us anything about the relative values of individual shareholdings and this is essential to understanding the real impact of market shocks such as the stock market crash of Autumn 1987.

A final consideration is that neither the proportion of aggregate wealth attributed to property nor the proportion attributed to shares is the sole result of more or less widespread ownership. Each of these categories of aggregate wealth is affected significantly by relative prices. Where the trend is for house prices, for example, to rise faster than the RPI it follows that the wealth distribution will become skewed in favour of property owners, and vice versa where, as in recent years, house prices lag retail prices in general.

10.2.2 Inheritance, Wealth Concentration and Taxation

While some influences on wealth concentration might be noticeable over a relatively short time period, as in the case of changes in wealth composition, others – like certain biological, social and demographic factors – operate over very lengthy time periods. The complex set of all the relationships which ultimately determine a person's wealth are a mixture of genetic endowments, material inheritance, educational opportunities, social and economic environments, marital status and so forth. These influences are, in turn, determined in large part by social and cultural norms regarding, for example, modes of inheritance and marital patterns. Strong influences on the long-term distribution of wealth are exerted by the extent to which the rich marry the rich and the poor marry the poor and by differential fertility: if the rich have fewer children than the poor then concentration increases and vice versa. These are very important considerations, but we do not have the space here to discuss them further. However, one socio-demographic factor which we must look at more closely is that of inheritance patterns. One custom that actively discourages the dispersion of wealth is that of **primogeniture**, strictly the passing on of wealth to the first-born child (although, historically, this has been interpreted as the first-born son). If inheritance was not an important determinant of the degree of wealth concentration then such a custom would assume less importance. However, available evidence suggests that inheritance is a major factor in the self-perpetuating cycle of wealth determination (see Harbury, 1962; Harbury and McMahon, 1973; and Harbury and Hitchens, 1976).

Wealth taxation

If inheritance is such an important determinant of wealth concentration, and if the government had a serious commitment to reducing inequality, one might expect that the fiscal system would be used to discourage the concentration of inheritances. So far in the UK, however, this has not been the case. Until 1974 estate duty was the main tax on wealth in the UK. Unfortunately, estate duty was not a notable success in reducing inequalities, partly because it was never applied properly to discretionary trusts, and partly because the rules permitted exemption of gifts **inter vivos** unless such transfers took place within seven years prior to the donor's death. Perhaps the greatest fault of estate duty as a means of reducing wealth inequality lay in the principle of taxing the value of an estate rather than the value of an inheritance.

It is not large estates **per se** which perpetuate inequalities, but the fact that they are passed on as large inheritances, and the most efficient way to promote equality by taxing wealth is to tax inherited receipts. Furthermore, if its rates structure is progressive, an inheritance tax offers an incentive to donors to disperse their wealth more widely than they would in the face of an estates tax. In 1974, estate duty was replaced by the CTT. This represented an improvement in that the new tax was levied on a cumulative basis, not just on wealth at death but also on gifts and bequests **inter vivos**. However, CTT was still based on the estate principle and not levied on receipts on transfer, and thus did not provide the additional incentive to disperse wealth that is offered by an inheritance tax.

The Finance Act of 1986 brought in yet another change, with CTT being replaced by inheritance tax. As in the cases of estate duty and CTT, the new levy was hedged by a long list of wealth exemptions. Further, although the tax is cumulative, no tax is payable on the first part of the cumulative total, an exemption which is increased annually in line with the rise in the RPI. Finally, once again (despite its name) inheritance tax is levied on the value of a gift or an estate and not the amount received or inherited; the main charge under the tax arises on transfers made by an individual on death, or within seven years of death. As with its predecessors, there is no incentive provided under this tax for a wider dispersal of inheritances.

10.3 Poverty and Income Maintenance

10.3.1 'Absolute' versus 'Relative' Definitions

While the discussion of distribution and inequality referred mainly to a summary index, the Gini coefficient, important occasional use was made of the comparison between extremes in a distribution. We turn now to this question of extremes in more detail as we consider poverty as a manifestation of inequality. However, while poverty is linked to inequality, the two concepts are quite separate and have different meanings. It is a tautology to state that where incomes are unequally distributed the poorest members of the population will be found at the bottom of the distribution. It may anyway be the case that these poor individuals are rich indeed when compared with those in the bottom percentile (or even the top percentile) of the income distribution in some other population. In other words, we might judge, say, the bottom 20 per cent of any population to be 'poor', but this may be true in only a relative sense rather than an absolute one.

The issue of **relative versus absolute** makes it difficult to identify the poor. If we could rely on an absolute (objective) measure we could estimate poverty simply by counting the individuals (or the households) who do not possess the means of achieving the absolute minimum standard of living. An absolute yardstick can also be applied over time and, hence, offers the means of checking whether or not the incidence of poverty is changing. So why not rely on an absolute measure of poverty? To answer this question, we must consider carefully what exactly is meant by this term. Such a measure would attempt to define a minimum level of subsistence for the chosen income unit (individual or household) and to determine the level of income necessary to guarantee that such a minimum can be enjoyed. Thus, 'the poor' would be those units with incomes short of the minimum level.

One obvious criticism of absolute measures is that any population is likely to be heterogeneous in terms of minimum requirements. Compare, for example, the basic food requirements of an 18 year old male who is tall and heavy and whose occupation is felling trees, with those of a retired female schoolteacher who is small and light. But a more fundamental problem is that poverty is usually defined with reference to prevailing social norms and available 'life styles': that is, by comparing the differing living standards enjoyed by different units in the population. Of course this, in turn, causes further difficulties for empirical measurement. What is the minimum living standard

for the UK in the 1990s? For example, should every household be expected to own a television set? Many social observers have wrestled with the problems of defining a minimum relative living standard (and, hence, standards of 'relative deprivation') but none has yet derived a definition which has proved universally acceptable.

10.3.2 Income or Expenditure; Individual or Household?

Another difficult theoretical issue which has very serious implications for empirical work is the question of whether poverty should be defined by reference to **income or expenditure**. Some researchers argue that individuals' incomes indicate whether or not they are poor because incomes determine consumption potential. Other researchers argue that this is not the case, and that consumption is determined by expenditure which, in turn, is determined not only by income but also by wealth (past savings) and by borrowing; an individual who can dip into past savings and/or can borrow is less constrained in current spending then someone who depends solely on current income to finance current expenditure.

There is also the issue as to whether the reference unit for determining living standards should be seen as the **household** rather than the **individual**. Some researchers argue that choosing the individual as the basic reference unit loses sight of the fact that many individuals live in a household where incomes are pooled and shared, thus permitting some household members to have access to a higher level and range of consumption than that determined by individual income. On the other hand, it can be argued that households vary in size, age and gender structure, with a consequent variable network of dependants, and that such dependency must be recognised when calculating real incomes or expenditures and, therefore, real poverty.

Given the variety of approaches which might result from such differences, it is not surprising that empirical research has not used a consistent data base, or even used a consistent definition of the income unit. In their comparative study of 1953 and 1960, Abel-Smith and Townsend (1965) used the FES and based their findings on expenditure data for 1953 and income data for 1960. Since 1972, the Department of Social Security has also used the FES for its own 'official' estimates of the numbers in poverty. However, these latter studies are based upon the 'family' which usually means 'tax unit' or 'budget unit' and constitutes a narrower income/expenditure unit than that of the 'household' adopted by Abel-Smith and Townsend. Since broader units, like households, offer greater access to shared resources than do narrower definitions such as the tax unit, it is not surprising that the extent of poverty is relatively greater when measured across the narrower units.

The problems for researchers do not end here. For example, another difficult question to answer is whether or not poverty is manifested by individuals' **total** expenditure or by their **specific** expenditures (the actual goods and services purchased). Some researchers have emphasised the need to consider specific expenditures (or, strictly, consumption of specific commodities) and, historically, State welfare programmes have subsidised consumption of specific goods: for example, milk and orange juice. The difficulties for social commentators raised by such considerations are akin to those raised by the concept of **merit goods**, namely that attempts by government to subsidise specific consumption can interfere with individuals' exercise of free choice. For example, a wealthy individual might choose to eat a diet which, taken in isolation, would identify him or her as poor.

□ 10.3.3 Poverty Estimates

However, even if all empirical research were to adopt **either** income **or** expenditure and also the same definition of income or expenditure unit, they could still produce very different estimates of the scale and incidence of poverty, depending on the yardstick adopted as the 'poverty line'. Such yardsticks vary according to the degree of

'relativity' built into the measurement. The deficiencies of the absolute standard, combined with the desire to maintain a consistent yardstick, have resulted in most of the major postwar studies adopting the State's minimum standard when trying to measure the full extent of poverty in the UK.

The 'official' poverty line was the one adopted by Abel-Smith and Townsend (1965) in their survey. Their empirical investigation was based on the FES and measured poverty against 'National Assistance', the prevailing minimum available under the State's income maintenance arrangements. The investigation undertaken by Abel-Smith and Townsend was the first national survey of poverty and it produced an estimate of 3.8 per cent of the population living in poverty (that is, with incomes below the level set for National Assistance). Such a finding came as a rude shock to a nation lulled into believing that postwar prosperity, coupled with income maintenance arrangements, had eradicated poverty from the social landscape. Further empirical work by Atkinson (1969) suggested that the proportion of the population in poverty was still around 3.5 per cent at the end of the 1960s.

The pressure exerted by private researchers was not matched by any government response until 1974, when an official data series on 'Low Income Families' (LIF) was first published (covering 1972), and a comprehensive review of the empirical evidence on poverty had to await a report from the Royal Commission on the Distribution of Income and Wealth published in 1978. The official series, following the practice adopted by Abel-Smith and Townsend, measured 'low incomes' by reference to 'Supplementary Benefit' (SB) which had replaced 'National Assistance' as the State minimum. The series produced estimates relating to categories of 'low income', defined as below 140 per cent of the appropriate SB level, and it came to be used extensively by social commentators, both public and private. This series of LIF statistics was superseded in 1988 by a new one, produced biennially, based on 'average income' (the 'Households Below Average Income', or HBAI series). Estimates in the new series go back to 1981, and in addition to the difference in the definition of 'low income' they are based on the broader household rather than the family or benefit unit used by the old series. The major significance of this 1988 change is the move away from measuring poverty against the minimum standard of income established by the State's income maintenance programme (for an excellent comparative analysis of the LIF and HBAI series, see Giles and Webb, 1993).

The latest official data in the SB-based series relate to 1985, but estimates by Johnson and Webb (1991) have extended the series to 1987. **Table 10.8** shows that over the whole period covered by the series, from 1972 to 1987, both the numbers of families and the number of persons (in families) living below the SB level increased. In addition, the percentage changes during the 1980s were higher than those for the 1970s. Between 1972 and 1979 the increase in the number of families below SB was over 16 per cent and that for persons below SB the increase was nearly 20 per cent. Between 1979 and 1987 there was approximately a 20 per cent increase in the number of families below SB level and the number of persons below SB increased by almost 36 per cent during the same period. By the relative standards applying at the time, such estimates suggest that poverty has persisted stubbornly since the 1960s: on the basis of these official estimates, just over 5 per cent of the population was living below the SB level in 1987. The new 'average income' benchmark suggests also that (relative) poverty remains a significant feature of the UK's socio-economic

structure. In a detailed comparison of the 'old' and the 'new' measures, as applied to data for 1983, Johnson and Webb (1991) concluded that, on the old basis of assessing incomes, around 10 per cent of the population would have had incomes below half the average in 1983, and although the new methodology reduces this proportion, primarily due to the switch from family to household as the income unit, it remains significant at 8 per cent (see also Nolan, 1989).

10.3.4 The Origins of the Present System

For most of the postwar period, anti-poverty legislation in the UK has built on the foundations laid down in the Beveridge Report (Cmd 6404) of 1942, subject to occasional modification. There was no attempt at a comprehensive overhaul of the Beveridge system until the Conservative Government's White Paper in 1985 and the subsequent reforms embodied in the 1986 Social Security Act (implemented fully only in 1988). The primary aim of the Beveridge Plan was to eradicate all want by concentrating on its causes: loss of work through unemployment or sickness, cessation of work through retirement and the drain on household resources created by large numbers of dependants. The main instrument of the system was a comprehensive programme of social (or 'national') insurance, offering flat-rate benefits to the unemployed and the sick and flat-rate retirement pensions, financed mainly by weekly contributions from those covered by the scheme. This programme was supported by Family Allowances (later to become Child Benefits) payable on behalf of all children except the first born. As a minimum income guarantee the programme included National Assistance (later SB and then Income Supplement) for those whose needs could **not** be met by the insurance scheme. The insurance benefits were intended to be sufficient to satisfy subsistence needs, and the role of National Assistance was anticipated to be minimal.

Table 10.8 *Estimate of Numbers below SB Level, 1972–87*

Year	Families	Persons
1972	1 220 000	1 780 000
1976	1 350 000	2 280 000
1979	1 420 000	2 130 000
1985	1 830 000	2 780 000
1987	1 910 000	2 890 000

Sources: Figures for 1985 and 1987 from P. Johnson and S. Webb (1991) *UK Poverty Statistics: A Comparative Study* (IFS: Commentary, 27), Table 4, p. 50.

Social Security	*Beveridge Report* (1942)
	Social Insurance White Paper (1944): accepted most of Beveridge's recommendations
	Family Allowance Act 1945
	National Insurance Act 1946 (Based on 1944 White Paper)
	National Insurance (Industrial Injuries) Act 1946
	National Assistance Act 1948
Employment	*Employment Policy White Paper* (1944): committed government to maintaining a high (and stable) level of employment through deficit spending when necessary
Health	*National Health Service White Paper* (1944): set plans for comprehensive health care for all, free of direct user charge and financed out of general taxation
	National Health Service Act 1946 (Based on 1944 White Paper)
Education	*Educational Reconstruction White Paper* (1943): set out plans for comprehensive national system of primary, secondary and further education, primary and secondary education to be free of direct user charge and financed out of general taxation
	Education Act 1946 (based on 1943 White Paper)

The optimism underlying the anticipation of such a minimal role for National Assistance was founded on an assumption that full employment would prevail. This optimism was reflected also in the fact that Family Allowance was not to be payable for the first child in a family since the family wage in a fully-employed economy would be sufficient to support one child. It must be remembered that the Beveridge scheme was introduced at a time when government believed that management of AD would in future ensure that the evil of mass unemployment did not return. This new-found faith in demand management was to be enshrined in the famous White Paper (Cmd 6527) of 1944. It is worth remembering also that the years 1945–50 witnessed the introduction of other 'social welfare' programmes to complete a massive frontal attack on the main causes of deprivation; in particular the Education Act 1944 and the National Health Service Act 1946 were meant to add significant firepower to the state's armoury. The box below summarises the flurry of State activity in the 1940s which provided the foundations for what came to be known as the 'Welfare State'.

10.3.5 Socio-economic Changes and the Incidence of Poverty

Although not intended by Beveridge, the social security system in the UK grew steadily such that, by the 1990s, it was the largest item of public expenditure, accounting for almost one-third of the total. Over this same period the importance of social security benefits as a component of personal incomes grew dramatically, from less than 10 per cent in the mid-1950s to over 20 per cent by the mid-1980s. According to its critics, this relative growth of the social security system is further testimony to its failure, brought about by its intrinsic nature and by the fact that its basic philosophy has been interpreted differently by successive governments.

So large a scheme, covering so many categories of want through State discretion, is likely to be slow to adapt to changes in the social and economic structure. The postwar period has seen many demographic changes and, in particular, proportional increases in the dependent sectors of the population as well as changes in the scale and incidence of unemployment and changes in the occupational wage structure. One result of the many changes unforeseen by Beveridge has been the heavy dependency upon the role of the so-called 'safety net' of National Assistance/SB/Income Supplement. The Beveridge intention that the safety net would play a minimal role has not been realised. In terms of demographic and structural changes, the three most significant ones have been in the number of aged people, family composition and the level and incidence of unemployment.

☐ *10.3.6 Poverty and Old Age*

The population of the UK, like that of the rest of Europe and other parts of the developed world, has been getting older and is expected to continue doing so well into the foreseeable future. In the UK at the beginning of the 1950s, the proportion of the population aged 65 and over was just under 11 per cent, but by the middle of the 1980s it had risen roughly 15 per cent. Projections published by the OECD, and reproduced in **Table 10.9**, suggest that by the middle of the next century the elderly populations of the UK and several other developed countries will have doubled their proportional sizes.

The projections in **Table 10.9** suggest severe implications for future income maintenance arrangements (and for the health care of the elderly) in the light of their performance in the face of the ageing of the population to date.

One vivid representation of the burden placed on the system so far is that around 16 per cent of the social security budget in the mid-1980s would not have been required if the benefit at the time had been payable to the number of pensioners alive in the early 1950s (Dilnot, Kay and Morris, 1984). This is not to say that the burden of the elderly had been completely unanticipated by Beveridge. Indeed, the Report envisaged that over the 'transitional period' up to 1965, social security costs would rise by some 25 per cent due to the increasing burden of retirement pensions. However, over the course of the transitional period the cost of retirement pensions, in real terms, was twice as high as Beveridge had envisaged.

Poverty among old people is not a new feature of society, but it has been a notorious contributor to total domestic poverty over the course of the twentieth century. The famous surveys of poverty in York undertaken by Rowntree found that old age was the major cause of poverty in under 5 per cent of poor households in 1899 whereas in 1951 old age was estimated to be the cause of poverty in two-thirds of poor households. Rowntree's explanation of this trend included the increase in the relative size of the aged population and the increased tendency for the aged to live alone rather than with their families. As we have seen, the proportion of old people in the population has increased markedly since Rowntree's last survey.

Table 10.9 *Projections of the Elderly Population, UK and Selected Countries (% of Population Aged 65 and Over)*

	UK	US	Japan	Canada	France	W. Germany	Italy
1980[1]	14.9	11.3	9.1	9.5	14.0	15.5	13.5
1985[1]	15.1	11.9	10.2	10.4	13.0	14.8	12.9
2000	14.5	12.1	15.2	12.8	15.3	17.1	15.3
2020	18.7	17.2	22.9	20.0	21.2	23.5	20.7
2040	26.4	25.3	29.2	29.2	29.7	34.1	29.1
2050	28.7	29.0	33.1	33.0	34.0	36.2	31.0

Note:
[1] Actual.
Source: *Financial Times*, 6 July 1988, using OECD Demographic Data Files.

Income sources for the aged are based less on market earnings than is the case with younger age groups. Labour market activity rates for pensioner households have fallen dramatically since the beginning of the twentieth century, and retirement pensions, both State and private, have become the main source of income for such households. Some indication of how this reliance on pension income affects living standards for old people can be taken from a comprehensive survey of poverty in the early 1970s which found a 17 per cent risk of poverty for the elderly compared with only 2.5 per cent for other adults (the risk for old people living alone was calculated to be as high as 30 per cent) and that, in total, elderly households accounted for approximately 42 per cent of the poverty among the sample (Fiegehen, Lansley and Smith, 1977).

While the risk factor remains high for old people, recent government estimates suggest that old age has diminished as a factor in poverty since the beginning of the 1970s. New legislation to combat poverty introduced in the mid-1980s gave more emphasis to the burden of pensions on taxpayers than to the burden of poverty on pensioners, against the background of a fall in the proportion of pensioners in the poorest fifth of the population from 35 per cent to 19 per cent between 1971 and 1982. Nevertheless, such an estimate still suggests that roughly one in five of the poorest fifth were pensioners at the start of the 1980s.

Evidence that pensioners still figure very significantly as a low income group is provided also by the new 'average income' method of counting LIF which was, introduced in 1988. As calculated by Johnson and Webb (1991), nearly 80 per cent of individuals in pensioner households in 1983 had ('household equivalised') incomes below the average, compared with 61 per cent of all individuals. It should be noted also that despite the government's switch of emphasis in its 1985 Green Paper, in that same year 27 per cent of persons in receipt of Supplementary Benefit were in pensioner families and nearly 40 per cent of individuals with incomes below the SB level were in pensioner families (see Johnson and Webb, 1990, pp. 49–50).

☐ 10.3.7 Family Poverty

The other major component of the dependency sector of the population is children. Various surveys of poverty in the years before the Second World War had identified the number of children in a family as a major determinant of family poverty. In recent years concern has arisen again over this issue. Despite a fall in the proportion of households with dependent children from 39 per cent to 32 per cent over the period 1971–85, the proportion of couples with children, together with single parents, rose from 48 per cent to 58 per cent among the poorest fifth of the population over roughly the same period (1971–82). One estimate has claimed that between £1.5 and £2 billion of social security expenditure in the mid-1980s was due to trends in the number of children wholly or partly within the social security system's responsibility (Berthoud, 1985). The increase in the number of single parents has been a particular cause for concern. According to official estimates the rise in divorces, the increasing incidence of illegitimate births and fewer illegitimate children being put forward for adoption all contributed to the proportion of people living in one-parent families with children doubling from 2.5 per cent in 1961 to 5 per cent by 1985. It must be said that the one-parent family was a problem identified by Beveridge, but its increase on such a scale was not anticipated; by 1991 the number of single-parent families in receipt of special state assistance (one-parent family benefit and/or Income Support) had reached 1.27 million (Bradshaw, 1991).

☐ 10.3.8 Lower Earnings and Unemployment

The Beveridge Report paid a lot of attention to the problems created by unemployment, taking account of the history of the labour market and, in particular, the 1930s. However, in this one respect, the experience of the first three decades after Beveridge seemed to suggest that full employment was the norm and unemployment was, indeed, a contingency. The reality after 1970 was to shatter this illusion as unemployment rose to over 13 per cent by 1984, including a dramatic increase in the numbers of long-term unemployed which swelled the numbers in receipt of SB following the exhaustion of rights to Unemployment Benefit.

The significance of unemployment as a factor in calculating low incomes is underlined by Johnson and Webb (1990) in their survey of low incomes for the period from 1979 to 1987. They observe that the most notable change in the composition of the low income group during this period was the two-thirds increase in the number of families receiving SB, and they point out that this reflects, in part, not only the increase in unemployment over the period but also the increase in the proportion of long-term unemployed who had lost their eligibility for Unemployment Benefit. Thus, in 1979, some 50 per cent of the unemployed were receiving SB but, by 1987, the proportion had increased to 61 per cent (Johnson and Webb, 1990, p. 53).

The new official low income series also underlines the significance of unemployment: of those individuals living in households where the 'head' was unemployed in 1981, 75 per cent had incomes below 80 per cent of the average and 42 per cent had incomes below half the average; by 1985 these proportions had risen to 84 per cent and 47 per cent respectively (see *Social Trends*, 1989, Table 5.20). However, unemployment has not been the sole economic cause of poverty among families. Another problem which Beveridge failed to anticipate was the high incidence of low earnings among households in poverty after the Second World War. Beveridge virtually took it for granted that earnings in a fully-employed labour market would be sufficient to support a dependent spouse and one child, yet the general increase in living standards which has pushed up the poverty line has left behind certain groups in low-paid employment. In 1987 there were 370 000 families (940 000 persons including children) with incomes below SB level, despite the family head being in full-time employment.

10.4 The Response from the System

☐ 10.4.1 Poverty Among the Aged

How well has the system copied with these social and economic pressures? Given the numbers remaining in poverty, particularly in specific groups of dependants, the UK's social security programme has been found wanting. Some observers have blamed successive governments for failing to implement fully the Beveridge proposals, while others have emphasised that the cause of the problem lies in the nature of social insurance programmes. One important principle of the Beveridge scheme which has not been adhered to consistently is that National Insurance benefits should be at least equal to the basic poverty standard. On this principle was based the expectation that National Assistance (now Income Support) would be a genuine 'safety net'. Yet for long periods throughout the post-Beveridge years this principle was not adhered to in the categories of pensioners and children. Many pensioner households have had to rely on a flat-rate State retirement pension which has not been maintained at all times at a level above the State minimum. Hence those pensioner households totally dependent on the State retirement pension have required supplementation to their flat-rate benefit, and even in the early 1980s more than a fifth of pensioners were supported by SB.

The most important determinant of the system's response to changes in the socio-economic structure has been the fact that benefit levels and eligibility conditions have been at the discretion of government. Social security budgeting has had to take its place in the ranking of expenditure priorities, set against available government revenues. Recall that the Beveridge perception of social security was one of insurance against contingencies like unemployment and sickness, and against loss of earnings on retirement, with earmarked benefits for children and all supported by National Assistance for those not catered for within the insurance scheme. The Beveridge programme of income maintenance was thus founded on a relationship between the principles of 'contribution' for the insurance part and 'eligibility' (or means-testing) for the assistance part. This has given rise to two difficulties for governments. In the first place, social insurance is not very flexible; because its benefits depend on past contributions it reacts slowly to socio-economic change. Second, the relationship between contribution record and means-testing for supplementation is very difficult to maintain.

To try to resolve the first difficulty, successive UK governments added on several new measures to the fundamental, Beveridge-based, social security programme. Inevitably, this increased the scheme's complexity. Significant steps were taken to modify provision in the three main areas outlined earlier: retirement, family size and low earnings. The increase in the number of pensioners was to put pressure on the social security system in terms of both the increasing costs of providing Beveridge-style retirement pensions and the need to make adequate provision for pensioners as living standards rose for the population as a whole. The year 1961 saw the introduction of a graduated pension, financed by a graduated contribution (a scheme which was extended to earnings-related supplements to unemployment benefit, sickness benefit and maternity allowances in 1966). Those employees with occupational pension rights considered by the authorities to be 'adequate' were permitted to 'contract out' of the graduated pensions scheme, another significant factor leading, by the end of the 1960s, to a situation wherein the cost of benefits had risen significantly in relation to the size of the potential 'tax base'.

However, the major change in State pension arrangements was to come in the Social Security Pensions Act 1975 and its implementation in April 1978. This legislation introduced SERPS, under which retirement pensions were to comprise an earnings-related addition to the basic flat-rate benefit (once again with contracting out). The White Paper of 1986 subsequently retained SERPS with modifications designed to reduce its long-term cost.

10.4.2 Insurance or 'Pay as you go'?

The problem of the ever-increasing cost of pensions has arisen mainly because public preoccupation has been with the income maintenance aspect of pensions rather than with the principle of insurance. It is difficult to see how this could be otherwise in a State-provided scheme. To try to appreciate this point it might help to rehearse the arguments for State involvement in provisions for retirement.

Microeconomic theory depicts the individual as maximising the satisfaction which he or she derives from consuming goods (including leisure) and services, according to taste and subject to various constraints. The rational individual, interested in lifetime utility, will attach relative weights to present and future consumption levels according to the time-preference pattern of consumption, and attempt to maximise satisfaction subject to both present and expected future constraints. Given that individuals do behave in this way, a State programme of compulsory provision for old age may distort the individual's 'optimal' (from the point of view of personal time-preference) allocation of consumption between time periods. The individual with positive time preference is forced to increase future consumption at the expense of the present, and even the individual who places a greater weight upon future consumption is satisfied only if the level of State provision accords with his or her own expectations and desires.

The counter-argument is that the time preferences of most individuals are such that they make inadequate provision for old age for two main reasons: widespread myopia, intensified by the difficulties of decision making which takes account of the distant future; and a lack of means by which to plan a consumption pattern over more than one time period. Even if the State could mitigate the latter part of the problem by providing those without means with a margin of saving over current consumption, this would be fruitful only if the first part of the problem could be solved.

Thus, given that individuals are improvident, or find the calculus of optimisation concerning future income streams, investment yields, family circumstances, likelihood of employment and so on beyond their mental powers, the State assumes a paternalistic role via the compulsory purchase of annuities so as to protect the individual. If the individual does not want this protection – for example, if he or she has a very strong positive time preference for consumption – the State justifies its interference on the grounds of social costs. While concern for others might lead society to help the myopic and improvident, it does not prevent society from taking steps to ensure that the need for such aid is minimised. Furthermore, it is reasonable to expect that the working population at any point in time might wish to minimise the likelihood of their children having to support the retired population at some future date and demand that individuals be compelled to make proper provision for their retirement needs.

It must be admitted that even if a case exists for compulsory insurance, itself debatable, it is by no means obvious that this requires the compulsory purchase of State annuities. But assuming that this method of protection is adopted, should a State scheme be organised, as far as possible, on an insurance basis? The pension problem is an inter-generational one. If we accept that the sole rationale for intervention is to protect a future generation of taxpayers (the assumption we made above), then the State has a duty to organise its scheme on a funded basis: that is, to ensure its actuarial soundness. To protect current policy holders against the possibility of receipts being less than adequate to cover benefit payments at some future date, a reserve fund would be accumulated on behalf of all insured persons. To create such a reserve, premiums would be set at a sufficiently high level; if the individual wants the promise of a higher level of benefit, or more comprehensive coverage than is allowed by the original contract, he or she must be prepared to pay a higher premium. In this way, then, a reserve is accumulated for each individual, and it follows that an increase in the number of people insured must mean an increase in total reserves.

However, if we modify the rationale of intervention to one of protecting all generations, including current taxpayers, then the State has no need to organise its scheme on a funded basis (even assuming it could do so), but can make use of its coercive powers to establish the programme on a 'pay-as-you-go' basis, whereby current beneficiaries are supported by current contributions. In other words, an 'acceptable' tax/transfer plan can be devised. This argument is based on two assumptions: namely, that the scheme is financed by compulsory contributions, and that future governments maintain the compulsion. Given these conditions, we can view social 'insurance' as a form of social contract whereby the young are prepared to support the old on the guarantee that a future generation of taxpayers will do the same for them when they grow old.

What happens if the age structure of the population changes? In particular, what happens if the proportion of the retired population increases significantly? In order to maintain the same level of pension per head of the retired population, the contributory costs on the active population must rise. If this situation persists, and these costs continue to rise, the contract is very much weakened and is likely to be modified by government action. This problem appears even with real incomes growing over time if pension levels are to be determined relative to current living standards. In other words, the insurance system collapses into the government's general tax/transfer programme with a consequent burden on public finances.

The consequences of accepting the provision of income maintenance for retired people as part of a State tax/transfer mechanism are many. One important feature at the time of inception is that pensions can be paid immediately: that is, contributions do not have to grow on a funded basis before an individual enjoys the fruits of entitlement. But the most important, if obvious, consequence is that pension arrangements as part of a wider tax/transfer mechanism are decided by government and become the subject of political as well as financial constraints, a problem which has been referred to as the 'pensions time bomb'.

This can raise difficult problems in respect of inequality: what should be the 'reasonable' level for State pension benefits given the benefits enjoyed by those in receipt of occupational pensions, and how should State retirement transfers compare with, say, transfers to the temporarily sick or unemployed? For example, if the value of the State pension is maintained in relation to average earnings, then a rising 'dependency ratio' of pensioners to taxpayers will require the latter to face rising tax rates. In the UK government policy has been to allow the basic pension to grow in line with the general level of prices rather than earnings, but whereas this relieves pressure on tax rates it causes the **relative** income of pensioners to decline over time.

These questions have been discussed constantly in the debate over pensions in the UK. At the same time eligibility for retirement pension has been, and continues to be, based on contribution records. From the very start, the post-Beveridge scheme of National Insurance was not funded on an actuarial basis. Even in its early years current contributions from employees and employers comprised a very large proportion of the total current receipts of the National Insurance Fund, and by the mid-1960s this proportion had risen to 80 per cent with contributions from interest income and exchequer grants having fallen dramatically.

Clearly, the social security system has moved a long way from the insurance principles recommended in the Beveridge Report. As one research report puts it:

> in introducing full-rate pensions straight away, the Government acknowledged a funding deficiency to be met from general taxation. When the time came to pay the subsidy on any substantial scale, the pledge was abandoned and a 'pay as you go' basis adopted. The National Insurance Fund was reduced to meaningless accounting and the actuarial link between contribution and benefits abandoned. (Dilnot, Kay and Morris, 1984)

Yet, as the same report points out, 'contribution records' are still the basis of eligibility (at substantial administrative cost). Whether or not this is because governments still believe (as Beveridge did) that individuals are more willing to pay 'contributions' than 'taxes' is debatable. Of course, if governments do believe this to be so they might also believe that their capacity for raising revenue without generating too much political 'heat' is enhanced.

10.4.3 Poverty Among Families with Children

In the area of family poverty, too, there have been major changes. We have mentioned the long-term decline in the real value of Family Allowances. In 1957 child tax allowances were reintroduced (they were first used in 1909 but removed when the Family Allowance was introduced) whereby deductions could be allowed from income for tax purposes at rates varying according to the age of the child. While such allowances offered indirect help to families with children, their distributional consequences differed from those of direct benefits. To see this more clearly, consider the situation after 1968 when Family Allowances became classified as taxable income and hence subject to reclamation by the Inland Revenue (the 'clawback' principle). This clawing-back meant that the real value of the Family Allowance rose as family income fell. Tax allowances, on the other hand, increased in value as family income rose because of the rate structure of income tax. This meant that families with incomes so low as to be unaffected by income tax did not receive any real benefit from the tax allowances, and the benefits enjoyed by taxpaying families favoured the higher income groups.

Both tax allowances and Family Allowance were merged in the Child Benefit Act 1975 which introduced a **flat-rate benefit** on behalf of each child in a family which was paid at a higher rate for one-parent families, the latter in recognition of the growth in single parenthood. Child Benefit, like the Family Allowance, is a 'universal' benefit: that is, payable to every family unit with children irrespective of the income of that family unit. As such it remains a contentious issue and we shall return to it shortly when considering the vexed question of how to make social security more efficient.

The other main cause of family poverty discussed earlier was that of earnings too low to support a spouse and child, contrary to the assumption of the Beveridge Report. This problem was brought to governments' attention on several occasions by various lobbies, in particular by the Child Poverty Action Group. A response was offered by the Conservative Government of 1971 when it introduced Family Income Supplement (FIS), a means-tested benefit specifically aimed at those families where the family head was in full-time employment but whose earnings were below the 'prescribed amount'. FIS was welcomed with great optimism but its effects were disappointing, and it was replaced in 1988 by **Family Credits**.

There were many other modifications and additions to the social security over the post-Beveridge period. We cannot enter into the details of the main 'piecemeal' changes, but we should note here that help with housing costs was another major source of help offered to LIF. Rate rebates were introduced in 1968, and a national scheme of rent rebates and allowances was introduced in 1972 following years of development in local authority schemes in the 1950s and 1960s. In 1983, **Housing Benefit** was introduced to replace these earlier arrangements. By the time of the Thatcher Government's reforms of the mid-1980s the social security system offered a complex array of 30 separate benefits with differing structures and rationales which cost over £2 billion annually to administer.

□ 10.4.4 The Problem of 'Take-up'

We turn now to a question which has so far only been hinted at. While the pressures on the social security system go some of the way to explain why so many individuals have had to rely on the safety net of benefit supplementations, they do not explain why so many have fallen **below the poverty line**. The main reason why so many fall

below this line is because they are not in receipt of full income supplementations even when entitled to them. This is the infamous problem of low 'take-up' thought, by most commentators, to be due to two causes: the complexity of the social security system and the stigma which attaches to receipt of means-tested benefits. The complexity of the system was underlined earlier. Not only is there a plethora of benefits for claimants to consider, but there is also a detailed and, for many claimants, difficult application procedure. Part of the difficulty lies in the detail required in order to assess the means and needs of claimants, but this very enquiry is also considered to be degrading by many potential claimants.

A government inquiry in 1965 found that one-third of pensioners were ignorant of the availability of National Assistance, while 30 per cent of married couples and 20 per cent of single men and women indicated that pride prevented them from applying for supplementary help. FIS at the end of the 1970s was being taken up by only 50 per cent out of those eligible while, at the same time, the take-up rate for SB was around 74 per cent and that for Rent and Rates Rebates in the region of 70 per cent, all according to government estimates. In 1987, Fry and Stark published a comparison of their own estimates of SB take-up and those of the DHSS for a period covering the end of the 1950s to the middle of the 1980s (Fry and Stark, 1987). Their findings, reproduced in **Table 10.10**, underline the fact that take-up of the 'bottom line' income support for the period in question was well short of 100 per cent.

Low take-up of means-tested benefits creates two serious problems for income maintenance programmes. One obvious consequence is that income support is not being given to many of the households most in need of it. A second consequence, creating a problem for the longer run, is that low take-up rates affect the accuracy of policy planning because they influence the outcome of benefit expenditure by the government. For example, a reduction in universal benefits and an increase in selective or 'targeted' (means-tested) benefits should, in principle, result in a more equal distribution of final incomes but, if the former type of benefit has a high take-

Table 10.10   *Estimates of Supplementary Benefit Take-up*

Study	Year	Take-up rate		
		Pensioners	Non-pensioners	All
DHSS	1977	0.72	0.79	–
DHSS	1979	0.65	0.78	0.70
DHSS	1981	0.67	0.75	0.71
Fry and Stark	1984	0.87	0.81	0.83
Fry and Stark*	1984	0.66	0.78	0.74

* Estimates on 'DHSS basis'.
Source: V. Fry and G. Stark (1987) 'The Take-Up of Supplementary Benefit: Gaps in the "Safety Net"?', *Fiscal Studies* (November).

up rate and the latter a low one, the move towards equality is lessened. This is a problem we shall return to later.

10.4.5 The Social Security 'Traps'

Another reason advanced to explain high numbers remaining in poverty, even during a time of economic growth for the country as a whole, relates to the implicit taxation of earned income in a social security system which relies on means-tested benefits for basic income support. This implicit taxation arises from the interaction among means-tested benefits and between them and the income tax system. As the number of means-tested benefits rose over the decades following the Beveridge Report, this was to become an increasing problem.

The various means-tested benefits and the social security programme are, in fact, examples of the principle of 'negative (income) taxation' in the sense that principles governing the receipt of benefit include elements of tax as well as welfare payment. These separable elements emerge from both the direction of the **total** resource flow involved and the nature of the impact at the **margin** of economic activity. Taking the case of a family unit of given size, we can demonstrate

this point by assuming eligibility for weekly benefit to be determined by the amount of weekly income earned by the unit from other sources (say, from earned income). Thus, at the margin, the net flow of resources is from the private sector to the government. In other words, the family unit is being taxed on **additional earnings**. However, the total flow of resources remains in the opposite direction to that of a tax since the net overall effect of the scheme is a supplement to the income of the family unit.

We may also note at this stage that the structure of means-tested benefits, as in this example, usually bears the other hallmarks of a taxation scheme. Benefit is paid to, or withheld from, a defined tax unit (say, head of household plus dependants); is determined by reference to a defined base (say, earned income); and the benefit payable in any period depends on income received by the tax unit from the base source during that same period. There is, however, one feature of means-tested social security benefits which does set them apart from usual tax conventions: the marginal rate of tax applied to low levels of income is often very high because State supplements to income are a substitute for a lack of income from other sources within the tax base. Hence, as other income rises, the supplement is withdrawn. The rationale for this may lie in the philosophy behind the system (only those who have a genuine need for State help can receive it) and/or a lack of resources in society to permit a more generous redistribution of resources towards the lower income groups.

The propensity for claimants to incur high marginal tax rates is increased by interaction between the benefits system and the income tax. The so-called **poverty trap** usually operates when an increase in earnings offers only a small increase in final income because of simultaneous lower benefit receipt and higher taxes and/or NICs. While the withdrawal of means-tested benefits has placed claimants on high marginal rates of (implicit) tax throughout the post-Beveridge period, the piecemeal additions to the benefit system served to intensify the problem. In particular, the introduction of FIS and its resulting interaction with housing subsidies was to become the main reason for poor households facing marginal rates of tax in excess of 100 per cent: the numbers of families in this severe form of the poverty trap was estimated by the Treasury and Civil Service Committee in 1982 to have increased from 15 000 in early 1974 to 105 600 by the end of 1981.

The **unemployment trap** operates when low-earning households find that they are either financially better-off depending on State benefits than in paid employment, or that the difference in living standards offered by the two choices is so small that the incentive to find paid work is very weak. This particular problem was considered to be severe by the 1970s in the case of the short-term unemployed. It has been estimated that in 1978 about 21 per cent of the heads of working families would have received more than 90 per cent of their weekly income if, instead, they had been unemployed for a short time (Dilnot, Kay and Morris, 1984). This was probably due to the availability of earnings-related benefit supplements and the fact that tax rebates were received during unemployment of short duration. In 1982, unemployment benefit was made taxable and earnings-related benefit supplement was abolished earlier in the same year. It has been estimated that only 2.9 per cent of people would have been able to enjoy more than 90 per cent of their income in work during a short spell of unemployment (Dilnot, Kay and Morris, 1984).

10.4.6 Fairness, Incentives and Supply-side Effects

High marginal rates of tax on the poor are considered to be undesirable for reasons of equity as well as efficiency. When a tax system, like that of the UK, is based on a principle of 'ability to pay' and supported by a progressive rates structure, it is absurd as well as unfair for the tax system to combine with the social security programme and impose higher marginal rates of tax on low income groups than on higher income groups. While most observers agree about the inequity of the system's regressive rates structure, there is less agreement on the extent to which means-testing creates genuine disincentives to effort. Government preoccupation with the question of work disincentives has been a constant feature of social security in the UK, although this concern has been dressed up in different language from time to time. For example, the need to minimise the 'disincentive to effort' became an essential ingredient of supply-side economics during the 1980s.

The increasing government preoccupation with supply-side economics has encouraged several investigations by economists into household reactions to changes in the relative costs of work and leisure. These have concentrated more on changes in the marginal rate of taxation, and less on the average rate which affects disposable incomes and is more significant when considering Keynesian demand-side policy (as discussed on **p. 92**). The likely outcome to a change in marginal rates of tax is clearly an empirical question, but one which has proved difficult to answer, and research into labour supply reactions has unearthed evidence of both incentives and disincentives arising from alterations in the marginal net income of households. However, so far as the poverty trap is concerned, since the effective marginal tax rates can be so high it is difficult to assume that disincentives to effort do not exist in and around the trap, and government concern has accordingly centred on how many individuals are actively caught in the trap.

In looking at the unemployment trap, empirical work has tended to concentrate on the estimation of the **replacement rate**: that is, the ratio of net income out of work to net income in work, for various household categories. Our earlier reference to relative returns from working and living on State benefit before and after 1978 took account of replacement rates. The estimate quoted there of the proportions affected by high replacement rates was but one of several attempts to measure the supply-side disincentives of the benefit system before and after the 1978 changes. As with the poverty trap, estimation of the impact of the unemployment trap has proved difficult, and there is by no means a consensus on the issue of whether or not the benefit system has induced unemployment. In all probability both increased from 1948 to the end of the period.

10.4.7 The Conservative Reforms of the 1980s

As part of its comprehensive reappraisal of the relative roles of public and private sector in the mixed economy, and in its determination to ensure that government spending is 'efficient', the Conservative Government turned its attentions to issues of social security in the mid-1980s. A White Paper in 1985 and the resulting parliamentary debate led to the Social Security Act 1986, which introduced several major changes to the benefit side of social security arrangements, and full implementation of these reforms took place in April 1988. The main defects of the system, as identified by the 1985 White Paper, were deemed to be its complexity, its failure to give proper support to those most in need, the problems created by the poverty and unemployment 'traps' and the burden of costs on future generations of taxpayers. In addition, the White Paper emphasised the government's concern about the restrictions on individual choice on the matter of pensions.

The response to the problems identified in the White Paper was set out in the 1986 Act, and centred on changes to the income-related benefits. SB was replaced by **Income Support**; FIS was replaced by **Family Credit**; and a new **Housing Benefit** replaced the previous two-part scheme (one for recipients of SB and one for all others on low incomes). But these changes were not in name only. The new system rationalised the relationship between these three main income-related benefits and established their entitlements on the same basis for the first time. At the same time, the changes represented a shift in resources towards Income Support and Family Credit and away from Housing Benefit which, in effect, meant a **shift of emphasis in the system towards families with children and away from pensioners**. Income Support could continue to be the main benefit for those not in full-time work, offering a benefit of a personal allowance plus increases for dependants. Under the new benefit there would be no additions for specific needs, whether 'one-off' or longer term. Instead, such needs would be met out of a new Social Fund. Like its predecessor, Family Credit is designed to offer supplements to low-income families in full-time work and with children to support. It is also designed to be more extensive in its coverage than was FIS.

The issue of whether or not the provisions in the 1986 Act would be likely to achieve the objective laid down in the earlier White Paper initially provoked a mixed response. It was true that the social security system was **simplified**, but it was **not made simple**. In particular, the reforms offered no structural alterations which might improve take-up. In respect to helping those most in need, initial estimates suggested that the majority of couples with children and single parents were made better off by the reforms while about three-quarters of pensioners were either unaffected or made worse off. Finally, on the question of the social security traps, the position was ambiguous. The unemployment trap should have been eased and the extreme form of the poverty trap was virtually eliminated (no more marginal tax rates of 100 per cent or greater). However, the extension of cover offered under the Family Credit arrangements was to face many more individuals than previously with marginal tax rates around 80 per cent (Dilnot and Webb, 1988).

The reforms of the mid-1980s were aimed to combine with the income and wealth creating effects of the freer market economy encouraged by the government's general economic programme of the period following 1979, a programme which came to be labelled 'Thatcherism'. This combination should have provided a major force for the eradication of poverty: the 'trickle down' effect of wealth creation supported by a more efficient social security system. Unfortunately, the expected result was not forthcoming by the beginning of the 1990s. On the contrary, as we saw in the early section on income distribution, the signs were suggesting an increase in inequality. So far as the absolute position of the poor was concerned, researchers were unable to find any evidence of a significant improvement. According to one estimate (Jenkins, 1991) average real incomes for the poorest 10 per cent of households were about the same in 1988 as they had been 20 years previously, and were actually lower than they had been 10 years previously. Townsend was also to argue that the real incomes of the poorest two deciles had fallen over the decade 1979–89 (Townsend, 1991), and even though Johnson and Webb were to modify Townsend's findings – showing that by removing an inconsistency in Townsend's income definition the real incomes of the poorest two deciles had risen by 5 per cent – the same authors could not escape the conclusion that as far as the poorest groups are concerned 'it is clear that even on a consistent definition of income their living standards have grown only slowly over the last decade' (Johnson and Webb, 1991).

■ 10.5 A European Perspective

How does the UK poverty picture compare with that in the rest of Europe? To answer this question properly and fully would require us to reconsider all of the methodological issues raised so far in order to attempt any comments about the pattern of poverty across a population totalling more than 350 million individuals.

One attempt which caused considerable controversy on publication, but which did give rise to real concern about the UK's record on poverty vis-à-vis its European partners, was the EC report on the second anti-poverty programme, published in April 1991 (EC, 1991). The stark conclusion of this report was that in 1985 the UK had the fifth highest 'poverty rate' in Europe behind Portugal, Ireland, Spain and Greece, and that the percentage in poverty (both individuals and households) in the UK had risen between 1980 and 1985, the two reference dates used in the report. Not only did such findings give cause for concern to policy makers, but they also created considerable controversy because they were based on **relative** measures and, hence, emphasised inequalities in income distribution rather than poverty in any **absolute** sense.

Estimating for both individuals and households, the EC report measured poverty in relation to both national and Community criteria. Using expenditure, rather than income, as the guide, the report defined as poor, by the **national** criterion, any individual or household spending less than 50 per cent of the national average for any given period. Using a Community criterion, an individual or household was classified as poor when spending less than 50 per cent of average Community spending (measured by a purchasing power standard) for any given period. In each case 'adult equivalent' scales were used to take account of differences in household size and composition.

☐ 10.5.1 Using a National Criterion

The Overall Picture

The picture presented by using a national criterion was a depressing one, suggesting that in 1985 some 50 million persons in the Community (about 16 million households) were poor, and that this represented very little change in the total number of poor in the Community since 1980. The findings suggested, however, that there had been changes in the proportions of poor found in individual countries, with some faring better and some worse between the two years. **Figure 10.4** presents a clear and stark impression of the relative changes in numbers of poor persons experienced by 11 of the 12 members over the five-year period (there were no survey returns for Luxembourg) with the biggest increase in numbers seen to be in the UK.

High-risk Groups

These comprise predominantly children and the elderly. The findings of the EC report emphasised yet again that the very young and the very old are particularly vulnerable to poverty. We saw earlier how these distinct groupings have emerged time and again from UK studies, and the evidence from across Europe confirms that throughout all Community countries children and the aged form consistently high-risk groups in relation to poverty. **Table 10.11** gives data from the report which show that, with the exceptions of Greece in 1980 and Italy in 1985, the index of poverty among

Figure 10.4   *Changes in the Number of Poor Persons in the Community, 1980–85[1]*

Note:
[1] National criteria.
Source: EC (1991) *Final Report on the Second European Poverty Programme* (Brussels: Commission of the European Communities).

Table 10.11   *Poverty among Children and the Elderly in the Community*

	Children			Elderly		
	Poverty Index (National Poverty Rate=100)		Variation in the Absolute Number of Poor (%)	Poverty Index (National Poverty Rate=100)		Variation in the Absolute Number of Poor (%)
	1980	1985		1980	1985	
Belgium	113	114	−20.3	175	181	−17.7
Denmark	110	114	−5.4	238	255	12.1
F.R. of Germany	110	138	3.5	136	141	−8.1
Greece	96	103	−16.5	145	153	−2.9
Spain	106	107	−14.5	157	125	−21.7
France	108	124	−6.6	159	136	−31.2
Ireland	122	143	23.8	163	73	−50.5
Italy	114	97	−14.4	132	129	1.5
Netherlands	136	155	25.6	44	46	31.9
Portugal	112	112	−2.3	139	139	8.1
United Kingdom	138	132	12.2	163	119	−7.1

Source: EC (1991) *Final Report on the Second European Poverty Programme* (Brussels: Commission of the European Communities).

children was positive everywhere in both years and, with the exception of the Netherlands, the poverty index for the elderly was positive everywhere in both 1980 and 1985. **Table 10.11** shows also that in most countries (exceptions being Italy and the UK) the poverty index either stayed the same or worsened for children between 1980 and 1985, while for the elderly it either stayed the same or worsened in six of the eleven countries surveyed over the same period.

As a final point in relation to **Table 10.11** we should remind ourselves that insofar as the ageing of the European populations is a contributor to the large number of poor persons also being elderly persons, the problem is unlikely to diminish (as shown in **Table 10.9**).

The EC Report also highlighted the other socioeconomic groups most vulnerable to poverty, and again we can see the parallels between the UK picture, as discussed earlier in the chapter, and the rest of the Community. In particular, we can observe the prevalence of poverty among single-parent (particularly female) households and among households with low educational attainment and/or low economic activity of the household head.

10.5.2 Using a Community Criterion

Using average household, or individual, income or expenditure as the poverty yardstick for each member state produces 12 different poverty lines (only 11 in the 1991 report, given no returns for Luxembourg). What happens to the picture if we apply just one Community poverty line: that is, if poverty is defined with reference to some notion of Community average income or expenditure for households and individuals? The question is addressed in the 1991 report by referring to any household (or individual) as being poor if expenditure is less than 50 per cent of the Community average household expenditure (per adult equivalent) for the period in question. As with the measures for individual countries, this poverty line was calculated by reference to data from national family budget surveys. The survey suggests that the fundamental extent and causes of poverty changes only slightly but the distribution of Community poverty changes dramatically.

Table 10.12, taken from the EC report, suggests that, measured against an EC poverty line, overall poverty fell slightly between 1980 and 1985 and that it fell slightly also for the high-risk groups of children and the elderly across the whole of the Community. That Community-wide poverty was reduced during the period 1980–85 was welcome news for the makers of European social policy, but the size of the reduction was not impressive and begged questions about the efficiency of the Community's general social programme. We shall address some aspects of this shortly, but first we should also consider the dramatic changes in the geographical distribution of poverty which result from adopting a poverty line. **Figure 10.5** gives a very clear impression of how the geographical distribution of poverty responds to changing the poverty line from a national to a Community criterion.

From the viewpoint of the UK the initial comparison is not very favourable. Using the national poverty line as the criterion, the UK had the biggest share of the community's poor in 1985 at 23.5 per cent, with France next at about 18.3 per cent followed by Italy (17.1 per cent), West Germany (14.3 per cent) and Spain (11.9 per cent). National poverty lines obviously do not take account of relative living standards outside national boundaries and, as we saw early in this

Table 10.12 *Community Poverty Incidence, 1980 and 1985*

	1980		1985	
	%	million	%	million
Households	14.8	16.4	14.4	16.2
Persons	16.8	52.9	15.9	51.3
Children	19.7	13.5	19.4	12.3
Elderly (65+)	22.5	9.9	19.6	8.5

Source: Final Report on the Second European Poverty Programme (Brussels: Commission of the European Communities).

Figure 10.5   *Percentage of Poor Community Households Located in Each Member Country*

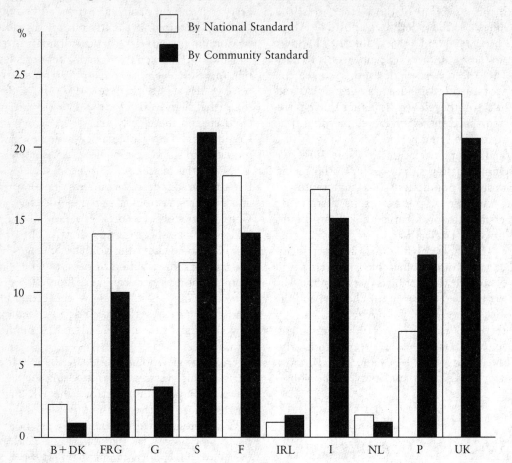

Source: *Final Report on the Second European Poverty Programme* (Brussels: Commission of the European Communities).

chapter, a cohort of poor according to a national poverty line might appear (relatively) rich according to some other nation's poverty line. So how does adopting the Community poverty line change poverty rankings? As **Figure 10.5** illustrates, the UK is overtaken by Spain but the gap is very narrow and remains potentially embarrassing for UK policy makers. The proportion of the Community's poor who are resident in the UK does fall, but it also falls in Italy, France and West Germany whereas only Spain suffers an increase (a fairly dramatic one in fact, from 11.9 to 20.9 per cent).

It could be argued, however, that measuring poverty distribution on the basis of population percentages is very unfair to countries with large populations because this increases the likelihood of larger numbers in poverty. Thus, to counteract the population effect, the EC report offered a picture of the geographical distribution of poverty that results from assuming the Community's population to be equally distributed. One obvious effect of this is to offer a picture as if some of the households from the more densely populated and more industrial countries had been relocated into previously less dense and more agrarian countries. As one would expect, the poverty percentage now rises dramatically in countries like Portugal and Ireland and falls dramatically in the UK, France and Italy.

10.5.3 Community Action to Combat Poverty

Every member state has adopted some form of the mixed enterprise economy and, in line with this, some variant of the 'Welfare State' model of social policy (whereby markets reward individuals and households according to the market value of their productivities, and the State offers income supplementation when market earnings are low and also when there are no market earnings, as in the case, for example, of children, the retired and those whose skills are obsolete). Hence, as we saw earlier in the case of the UK, researching all the reasons for a country's poverty profile requires analysis of both market patterns, State tax-transfer programmes and labour market legislation. Clearly, we cannot begin here to explore the details of each of the other eleven countries within the Community. However, we can at least offer some comment on the collective action taken so far by the Community to combat the considerable poverty in its midst.

The Community programme to combat poverty is piecemeal, but it is possible to single out three main prongs of attack on both inequality and poverty:

a   The collective commitment by member states to develop **social as well as economic policy;**
b   The European Social Fund;
c   The Anti-Poverty Programme.

The Commitment to Social Policy

Article 2 of The Treaty of Rome specifies an objective of an accelerated raising of the standard of living across the Community – that is, it makes it clear that the Community's objectives are social as well as economic. To this end, the Community has developed policies and provided finance for projects relating to unemployment; training; equal opportunities (to include policies relating to regions as well as gender); improving working conditions; families and the elderly; immigrants; handicapped people; and social security and pub-

lic health. Many of these areas have received significant funding for many years.

The European Social Fund

Many of the real commitments to the development of social policy are made through this Fund, representing a massive injection of finance, mainly into the improvement of labour market returns. The list of commitments made under the Social Fund is large but its three major categories are:

a   training and employment of young people (under 25s): about 75 per cent of the Fund's resources are put to this end;
b   helping disadvantaged regions via a geographical concentration of the Fund's activities, with targeted regions so far including all of Greece, Ireland and Portugal and specific areas of Italy, Spain and Northern Ireland;
c   helping specific adult groups: for example, the long-term unemployed; women returning to work; handicapped people who are capable of work in the labour market; immigrant workers; individuals suitable for retraining for new technologies; and persons working in the promotion of employment (for example, in vocational training and recruitment). By the second half of the 1980s the expenditure in these various areas was accounting for 7 per cent of the Community budget and covered some 2.5 million people (approximately 85 per cent of them under 25 years of age were benefiting from the Social Fund).

The Specific Anti-poverty Programme

In addition to its efforts on the supply side of the European market-based economies, the Community has also addressed the issue of poverty created by absence of any access to labour markets. There have been two major programmes launched, each one concerned primarily with the gathering of information about poverty and inequality and with measuring poverty incidence. The initial programme for the period 1975–80, very much concerned with gathering information about poverty, was superseded in 1984 by a new

Figure 10.6   *Community Anti-poverty Programme*[1]

		%
①	Disadvantaged urban districts	10
②	Impoverished rural areas	16
③	Long-term unemployed	17
④	Young unemployed	13
⑤	Elderly	10
⑥	Single-parent families	15
⑦	Second-generation migrants	7
⑧	Refugees	4
⑨	Returning migrants	4
⑩	Homeless and marginal	4

Note:
[1] Excluding Spanish and Portuguese projects selected in 1987.
Source: Commission of the European Communities, DG V.

programme of more specific Community action for the period up to 1988 coupled with further research into, and measurement of, the incidence of poverty. The EC report referred to earlier is part of the culmination of this research. The various projects under the second programme were to concentrate on testing new methods of helping the poor, on the dissemination and exchange of knowledge about the extent and incidence of poverty and on the evaluation of projects. In terms of target areas, the distribution of activities can be seen from the pie chart published by the Community in 1987, and reproduced as **Figure 10.6**.

10.5.4 Recent Debate and the Future of Social Security

What emerges from both the findings of the EC report and the nature of the categories within the Community's anti-poverty programme is an awareness of what has been labelled by some observers as the 'new poverty'. As we have seen

in previous sections of this chapter, what might be termed the 'old poverty' was concentrated mainly in two broad categories: dependent children (and their families), and old people. Both of these categories remain at the core of the poverty problem in both the UK and throughout the Community, but a new category of poor has emerged who are more diverse in nature and belong perhaps to what is regarded as society's periphery rather than its core: immigrant workers (who usually earn low wages and suffer intermittent unemployment); single parents; ethnic minorities (who might suffer the additional burdens of prejudice and discrimination); the mentally and physically handicapped; and longer-term unemployed young people. As the 'service economy' emerged throughout the 1970s and 1980s, there was rapid growth throughout the Community in both part-time working and in home-based work and small-scale self-employment, and many of these opportunities offered no more than relatively low and often temporary returns for labour.

According to one eminent poverty analyst, the sufferers of the 'old poverty' were a large proportion of the working class who were able 'to mobilise particularly through labour and socialist movements, to form alliances with the liberal middle class, and to build the defences which eventually came to be called the Welfare State' (Donnison, 1991). The same observer sees no similar socio-political solution to the problems of the 'new poor' because they are so diverse and scattered and, therefore, do not form a cohesive political lobby; indeed, they 'share nothing but their exclusion from the mainstream of society'.

Whether or not one agrees with this socio-political analysis, it is clearly being recognised to some extent in the categorisation of aid objectives within the European Social Fund. But so far as social policy in individual countries is concerned, the 'new poverty' adds yet another dimension to an already difficult policy agenda: if households or families comprise low earners who find only intermittent employment to supplement, say, one mainstream household income, then both the poverty and the employment traps discussed earlier pose severe disincentive effects unless combined incomes lift the whole family or household well above state assistance levels.

It is not surprising, therefore, to find that the issue of 'universal' versus 'selective' benefits remains at the centre of debate on social security. The UK Government has placed **efficiency** at the forefront of economic objectives, and increasingly blurred the distinctions between economic and social issues. Since universal benefits are made available to all, regardless of means, they are deemed to be a less efficient means of income redistribution than selective benefits which, by definition, are targeted on those recipients most in need. This issue underpinned the 1986 reforms, but the argument has continued and lies at the heart of the debate over social security spending which was fuelled by the 1993 review of social security spending.

Proposals for resource switching, and consequent denial of fundamental Beveridge principles such as providing a flat-rate benefit for all families with children, are seen by many as a significant denial of 'universality' as a cornerstone of the social security system. However, the 1988 reforms opened the door for 'selective' arrangements which followed soon after with the freezing of universal child benefits and renewed 'benefit targeting' of needy families (special benefit rises of up to 9.3 per cent in 1988). Future tax/transfer support of the aged could be modified along similar lines. Bearing in mind the burden on future generations of working taxpayers of providing income support to a proportionally growing retired population, many of whom will be enjoying the fruits of their occupational pension schemes, the demand by voters for more selective measures to concentrate transfers on the 'genuinely needy' within the retired population is likely to grow. Increased awareness that the UK State pension scheme has not been 'as of right' but 'pay as you go' is likely to fuel such demands.

The debate over selectivity in the social security system brings us back, full circle, to the efficiency/equity trade-off. On the one hand lies a concern for efficiency and the removal of disincentives in tax/transfer programmes, while on the other, lies a concern for the welfare of the poor. A problem for the Party image-makers in the 1980s was how to present the government as a 'caring' administration as well as one which promoted efficiency and increased incentives. The solution to the problem for the future lies in persuading the electorate that 'targeting' is 'cost-effective caring'.

To persuade the electorate of this is conditional upon achieving two related objectives: namely, finding a way to much simpler means-testing and improving markedly the take-up of available benefits. One way to reach these goals, which has received a lot of attention from economists and which enjoys a degree of consensus among political opinions, is to introduce some form of **truly comprehensive negative income tax**, which would follow the principles outlined earlier but would combine social security benefits and income tax payments in a single system of redistribution, centrally administered. To date no government has gone that far in its legislation (although a variant was proposed in a Green Paper published by the Heath-led Conservative Government of 1972), and Mr Fowler's overhaul of the mid-1980s fell a long way short of such radicalism. To date, the concept of a 'European Social Dividend' available to all (but subject to means) and across national boundaries has not appeared as a serious item on the politico-economic agenda for post-1992 Europe.

Bibliography

Abel-Smith, B. and P. Townsend (1965) *The Poor and the Poorest* (London: Bell & Sons).

Atkinson, A. B. (1972) *Unequal Shares* (London: Allen Lane, The Penguin Press).

Berthoud, R. (1985) 'Mr Fowler's Examination', *Catalyst* (Autumn).

Bradshaw, J. (1991) 'Social Security Expenditure in the 1990s', *Public Money and Management* (Winter).

Cmd 6404 (1942) *Social Insurance and Allied Services* (The Beveridge Report) (London: HMSO).

Cmd 6527 (1944) *Employment Policy* (London: HMSO).

Diamond Commission (1975) *Report No.1*, Cmnd 6171 (London: HMSO).

Diamond Commission (1976) *Report No. 4*, Cmnd 6626 (London: HMSO).

Dilnot, A, J. Kay and C. Morris (1984) *The Reform of Social Security* (Oxford: Clarendon Press).

Dilnot, A. and S. Webb (1988) 'The 1988 Social Security Reforms', *Fiscal Studies* (August).

Donnison, D. (1991) 'Squeezed and Broken on the Brink', *The Times Higher Education Supplement*, 19 April, p. 13.

EC (1991) *Final Report on the Second European Poverty Programme* (Brussels: Commission of the European Communities).

Fiegehen, G., P. Lansley and A. Smith (1977) *Poverty and Progress in Britain, 1953–73* (Cambridge University Press).

Fry, V. and G. Stark (1986) 'The Take-Up of Supplementary Benefit: Gaps in the "Safety Net"?', *Fiscal Studies* (November).

Giles, C. and Webb, S (1993) 'A Guide to Poverty Statistics', *Fiscal Studies*, 14(2).

Harbury, C. D. (1962) 'Inheritance in the Distribution of Personal Wealth', *Economic Journal* (December).

Harbury, C. and D. Hitchens (1976) 'The Inheritance of Top Wealth Leavers', *Economic Journal*, 86.

Harbury, C. and P. McMahon (1973) 'Inheritance and the Distribution of Personal Wealth in Britain', *Economic Journal*, 83.

Jenkins, S. (1991) 'Living Standards and the Diverging "Thatcher" Effect', *The Guardian*, 15 April, p. 13.

Johnson, P. and S. Webb (1991) *UK Poverty Statistics: A Comparative Study* (IFS, Commentary, 27).

Lydall, H. (1959) 'The Long Term Trend in the Size Distribution of Income', *Journal of the Royal Statistical Society* (Series A, 122, Part 1).

Morris, N. and I. Preston (1986) 'Taxes, Benefits and the Distribution of Income 1968–83', *Fiscal Studies* (November).

Nicholson, R. (1967) 'The Distribution of Personal Income', *Lloyds Bank Review* (January).

Nolan, B. (1989) 'An Evaluation of the New Official Low Income Statistics, *Fiscal Studies*, 10(4).

Social Security Select Committee (1991) *Low Income Statistics: Households Below Average Income Tables 1988*. First Report 1990–91, House of Commons.

Stark, T. (1990) *Income and Wealth in the 1980s* (London: Fabian Society).

Stewart, I. (1991) 'Estimates of the Distribution of Personal Wealth II: Marketable Wealth and Pension Rights of Individuals 1976 to 1989', *Economic Trends*, 457 (London: HMSO).

Townsend, P. (1991) *The Poor are Poorer: A Statistical Report on Changes in the Living Standards of Rich and Poor in the United Kingdom 1979–1989* (Statistical Monitoring Unit, University of Bristol).

■ Chapter 11 ■

Industry and Policy

Keith Hartley and Nick Hooper

■ 11.1 Introduction: The Policy Issues

Industrial policy has been defined in different ways, reflecting differing views about the role, extent and appropriate form of State intervention in the economy. At the one extreme, interventionists favour an active role with governments intervening throughout the economy at both the industry and the firm level. The other extreme takes a **laissez-faire** approach, leaving everything to market forces. In the UK, these alternative views about industrial policy have been reflected in continuing controversy between the major political parties.

During the 1970s and 1980s, controversy ranged over policy towards manufacturing industry and over the size of the public sector, reflecting concern about crowding-out, de-industrialisation and the decline of the UK's manufacturing industrial base. Aspects of this controversy were apparent in debates about state rescue operations for 'lame duck' companies such as British Leyland (now Rover), Chrysler and Rolls-Royce. In the 1980s, the debate focused on the decision to sell off valuable national assets (which was likenend to selling the family silver) such as British Aerospace, British Telecom, British Steel and the Royal Ordnance Factories; the sale of public utilities

(namely, gas, electricity and water); and whether the Ministry of Defence should buy British (for example, Nimrod AEW, the Westland helicopter company, tanks). On such issues, the major political parties have differed in their views on the extent and appropriate form of State intervention.

The Labour Government of the 1970s (1974–79) favoured interventionist policies in the form of an industrial strategy. This strategy was supported by an interventionist State agency (the National Enterprise Board); State ownership; planning agreements; industrial democracy; a policy of selecting the winners; and an extensive system of financial subsidies to firms, industries and regions. In contrast, the Conservative Government of the 1980s relied on market forces as its preferred industrial policy. Its emphasis has been on supply-side policies with a smaller public sector and reduced State intervention reflected in privatisation, contracting-out, deregulation; the withdrawal of industrial and regional subsidies; and more emphasis on competition policy and support for small firms. This policy aimed to replace a culture of dependency with an enterprise culture based on profitability and lower personal taxation, offering greater incentives for managers, workers, shareholders and new businesses.

The policy agenda for the 1990s is likely to depart from that of previous decades. Changes in the electorate, political parties and their leaders will mean a continued search for new solutions to the UK's economic problems as reflected in its growth, inflation, unemployment and BoP performance. The major political parties appear to be moving away from extremist solutions and returning to consensus politics, with parties offering broadly similar policies aimed at the median voter. Events in Eastern Europe and the Soviet Union during the late 1980s and early 1990s have also raised serious doubts about the performance of centralised planning and collectivist solutions to economic problems. These changes have also resulted in the end of the superpower Cold War arms race and its possible replacement with a disarmament race as nations seek a Peace Dividend. Furthermore, the European dimension is becoming increasingly important with the EU's 1992 Single Market initiative.

The Conservative Government, re-elected in 1992, is committed to the **enterprise economy** with further privatisation (for example, British Coal, British Rail and the Royal Mail), contracting-out and deregulation, the 'hiving-off' of State agencies and the introduction of a Citizen's Charter for public sector activities (for example, education, health, rail services). In an effort to achieve a Peace Dividend, UK defence spending is being reduced with the government leaving defence contractors to make commercial decisions about diversifying into civil markets.

Critics believe that such policies will fail to improve the long-run competitiveness of UK industry. They point to the need for a government industrial policy which actively supports the manufacturing base, which is seen as the 'key' sector of the economy (manufacturing is wealth-creating). Such critics of current policy stress that industry needs more investment, more R&D, a greater use of the latest technology and an improved quality of its labour force through more and better education and training.

Whilst governments have differed in their policies towards UK industry, policy performance can be assessed against some broad indicators of the trends in manufacturing, such as its productivity and its export and import record. A starting point is the changing role of manufacturing in the economy. The overall picture is of a continuing shift away from an economy dominated by industry to one based on services. As shown in **Table 11.1**, the manufacturing share of GDP has fallen from a more than a third in 1969 to well under a quarter in 1992. Over this period activity shifted towards services, with private services rising from 38 per cent to 47 per cent of total output and public services from 12 per cent to 17 per cent of GDP. Inevitably, concern has been expressed about the contraction in manufacturing industry reflected in de-industrialisation and its possible adverse effects upon the economy's investment and export performance. Various explanations

Table 11.1   *Contribution to GDP by Sector (%)*

	1969	1980	1985	1990	1992
Manufacturing	34.1	26.8	25.3	23.7	22.7
Agriculture	3.1	2.1	2.0	1.9	1.8
Energy	4.9	9.7	9.9	4.5	4.6
Construction	7.0	6.1	6.0	7.2	6.2
Private services	38.5	39.0	41.2	46.8	47.4
Public services	12.4	16.3	15.6	15.9	17.3
	100.0	100.0	100.0	100.0	100.0

Source: UK National Accounts Blue Book (CSO, 1993), Table 16.4.

have been advanced, ranging from rising government spending 'crowding-out' private sector investment to the long-run decline in the competitiveness of UK industry (as in Blackaby, 1979).

The falling share of manufacturing is reflected in steadily declining industrial employment. In 1992 manufacturing employment was 64 per cent of its 1979 level. Part of the fall in manufacturing employment over this period was due to productivity gains. Labour productivity in manufacturing grew faster than in the whole economy, as shown in **Table 11.2**. Comparative studies show that the productivity gap between the UK, on the one hand, and Germany and the USA, on the other, narrowed in the 1980s, although at the cost of a substantial 'shake-out' of Britain's man-

ufacturing labour force. Even so, in the late 1980s, German manufacturing productivity levels were over 20 per cent higher than in Britain and value-added per hour worked in the UK was 58 per cent of US levels. Nonetheless, the substantial UK productivity gains in the 1980s raise questions as to whether the Conservative Government has succeeded since 1979 in permanently reversing the UK's relative economic decline.

The changing position of manufacturing in the UK economy has been reflected internationally in the pattern and balance of trade. The manufacturing share of UK exports fell from 76 per cent in 1979 to shares ranging from 62 per cent to 67 per cent between 1981 and 1985, rising to 82 per cent by 1992. Similarly, between 1979 and 1992, the

Table 11.2 *Employment, Productivity and External Trade*

	1979	1982	1988	1990	1992
Employment					
Manufacturing	132.6	107.5	98.2	96.5	85.1
Total labour force	103.8	97.7	105.2	108.5	102.6
Productivity (output per person					
Manufacturing	81.9	84.7	116.2	122.8	130.9
Total labour force	90.8	93.1	107.5	107.9	110.2
Employees in employment, GB (000)					
Manufacturing	7 053	5 751	5 116	4 888	4 217
Services	13 578	13 117	14 853	15 602	15 186
All industries and services	22 587	20 916	21 760	22 226	20 875
External trade (£m)					
Total UK visible exports	40 637	55 538	82 098	103 691	108 298
of which manufacturing	30 870	37 316	66 194	84 165	88 672
Total UK visible imports	46 925	56 940	106 572	126 086	125 896
of which manufacturing	29 689	37 083	83 484	98 067	98 729
Index numbers 1985 = 100					

Source: Monthly Digest of Statistics; Employment Gazette.

manufacturing share of imports rose from 63 per cent to 78 per cent; and during the same period, the balance of visible trade in manufactures shifted from a surplus to a substantial deficit. Such stylised facts raise questions about the performance of UK manufacturing industry and whether public policy can improve its performance.

The contribution which economists can make to this debate about industrial policy is to subject myths and special pleading to economic analysis and critical appraisal, and to confront the arguments with the available evidence. Some of the major issues are now apparent, and we must ask whether economic theory offers any guidelines for a public policy towards industry. What, for example, are the implications of the analysis for the size, structure, location, ownership and performance of UK industries? In particular, how can economic theory be used to evaluate specific industrial policies such as policy towards competition, subsidies, privatisation and the role of government purchasing?

11.2 Theory and Industrial Policy

☐ 11.2.1 Introduction

Questions about the proper role of government in the economy dominate policy debates. In relation to industry, it has to be asked whether there are any economic arguments for government intervention and, if so, to what extent should the State intervene and in what form? For example, should the State favour British manufacturing industry? Should policy be applied to all firms or to a selected group (selected by industry or region)? Should intervention be in the form of subsidies (to firms, capital, labour or R&D); import controls; a buy-British government purchasing policy; competition and merger policy; nationalisation; or privatisation with State regulation? These are the general issues behind such specific examples as the UK Ministry of Defence decision to buy US Boeing AWACS aircraft and to

cancel the British Nimrod project; to bring Rolls-Royce into public ownership in 1971 rather than to bail out the privately-owned company through subsidies; and to replace publicly-owned enterprises such as British Telecom, British Gas and Electricity with privately-owned companies subject to State regulation.

The methodology of economic policy provides a framework for analysing industrial policy issues. The approach requires economists to seek answers to three questions:

1 **What is the policy problem** and what are governments seeking to achieve? Usually, the underlying problem worrying policy makers can be deduced from the government's stated objectives (and vice versa). For example, in 1993, the Conservative Government's DTI aimed to help UK business compete successfully at home, in the rest of Europe and throughout the world.

2 **Why is there a problem?** Economists use their theories to explain the causes of problems which are worrying governments. For example, British industry's declining international competitiveness might result from a structure of too many small firms unable to undertake the necessary R&D and thus obtain the scale economies required to compete in world markets, or it might reflect a comparative advantage in areas other than manufacturing. Alternatively, it might be due to general inefficiency reflecting the motivation and attitudes of managers and workers (a culture of dependency rather than enterprise), or it could reflect interest rate and exchange rate policy. The choice between these theories depends on which best explains the facts.

3 **What can be done to solve the problem?** Usually, there are alternative policy solutions. To improve the performance of UK manufacturing industry might require an industrial strategy; better management; the creation of labour-managed firms; or a competition policy. Private monopolies could be controlled through nationalisation, by creating contestable markets or by State regulation of prices or profits. Governments might pro-

mote technical progress through subsidising R&D, by training more scientists or placing contracts with UK firms for advanced technology equipment (such as computers, Concorde, nuclear power stations and space satellites). Theories can be used to predict the likely effects of alternative policy solutions, with governments having to choose between the options. Such choices will reflect the governing party's values and ideology, its possible interest in maximising the welfare of the community and its immediate concern with votes and re-election.

Economic theory approaches industrial policy issues from the starting point of Paretian welfare economics. It is assumed that society aims to maximise welfare by achieving an **optimum allocation of resources** (that is, a Pareto optimum occurs where it is impossible to make one person better off without making someone else worse off). In a private enterprise economy, the Paretian model suggests that properly-functioning competitive markets are socially desirable since perfectly competitive markets result in a Pareto optimum allocation of resources. On this basis, market forces determine the optimum size of the manufacturing sector. The model provides some broad guidelines for industrial policy. State intervention is required whenever markets are failing to work properly (that is, where there are substantial departures from the competitive ideal). **This approach suggests that industrial policy is a means of correcting for major market failures**. The obvious focus is on the operation of product markets, although it has to be recognised that failures can occur in markets for capital, labour, money and foreign exchange.

There are two general sources of market failure, namely (a) **imperfections** in the form of monopoly, oligopoly, restrictive practices and entry barriers, and (b) **beneficial or harmful externalities**, including public goods (for example, defence). Externalities mean that, left to themselves, private competitive markets might provide too little of some socially desirable activities (such as information, basic R&D) and too much of some socially undesirable outcomes (such as pollution, noise and traffic congestion). Here, however, economists have to be careful in distinguishing between the **technical issues** concerned with the causes of market failure, and the policy issues concerned with the choice of the most appropriate solution. For example, even if imperfections are identified as the main source of market failure, governments have to choose between such alternative policies as increased competition, reduced tariff barriers and State regulation of monopoly prices and profits. Similarly, externalities might be corrected through taxes and subsidies, public ownership or by legislative changes in property rights, allowing the courts to determine compensation for the victims of spillovers. The 1990s are also likely to see a continued and increased concern with **protecting the environment**. Worries have been expressed about the environmental impact of acid rain, ozone depletion, deforestation, the greenhouse effect, the need to preserve the natural environment and fears about the exhaustion of natural resources. Industry is seen as a major cause of pollution and environmental destruction. Profit-conscious firms seeking to minimise costs have every incentive to adopt cheap production methods and to produce outputs which might impose harm and costs on the rest of society (harmful externalities). Examples include atmospheric pollution from smoking chimneys, from petrol-driven motor cars and from cooling towers at electricity power stations; water pollution from waste disposal and oil spillages; and noise from jet aircraft. Various policy solutions have been proposed, including **market incentives** in the form of environmental taxes imposed on firms and 'harmful' products as well as tradable permits allowing firms to pollute. Alternatively, regulations can impose either limits or a complete ban on certain socially undesirable activities (for example, smoke-free zones; restrictions on airport opening hours), and governments might support basic research into new, cleaner, environmentally-friendly production methods. However, environmental problems are not created solely by industry. Consumers also create external effects, as in the case of tourism with its possible destruction of the natural environment. All of the above raise questions as to whether environment issues are the proper concern of the DTI or the Department of the Environment, or, ultimately, consumers themselves. In analysing policy issues, care must also be taken to distinguish between **efficiency issues** concerned with market failure, and **equity issues** where the outcomes are socially unacceptable. Finally, a Pareto optimum allocation of resources can be achieved through either a perfectly competitive private enterprise economy or by direct controls and commands in a centrally-planned economy.

11.2.2 The Structure–Conduct–Performance Paradigm

In examining the causes of market failure and the range of policy solutions, industrial economists use their standard tool kit, namely the structure–conduct–performance framework. This states that industrial performance depends ultimately upon industry structure where the variables in the model are structure, conduct and performance.

Structure

Structure comprises the number and size distribution of firms in an industry and the opportunities for the entry of new firms. There are two extremes – **perfect competition** and **monopoly** – with the intermediate and often typical cases of **monopolistic competition** and **oligopoly**. With this approach, industry concentration is determined by economies of scale, the size of the market (the number of firms of optimal scale it will support) and entry barriers. Perfectly competitive markets are characterised by free entry, with large numbers of relatively small firms, each operating at optimal scale.

Conduct

Conduct embraces the pricing, advertising, marketing, R&D and product differentiation aspects of firm behaviour (in other words price and non-

price competition), as well as the possibilities for collusion and restrictive agreements.

Performance

Performance is measured by technical and allocative efficiency. In this context, **a concern with a Pareto optimum allocation of resources requires that prices equal marginal cost throughout the economy.** Applied to a private enterprise competitive economy, the result would be firms which are technically efficient so that X-inefficiency (organisational slack) is absent and, in the long run, normal profits would be earned. On this basis, the efficiency of an economy's industries might be measured by such performance indicators as profitability, and by inter-firm and international comparisons of labour productivity and total factor productivity. However, the Pareto approach is static, and a society interested in growth will be concerned with the dynamic aspects of industrial performance as reflected in innovation and technical progress (see the taxonomy in **Table 11.3**).

The model in **Table 11.3** runs from industry structure to conduct to performance with the relationships depending on the assumptions about firm behaviour (that is, its objectives). The standard assumption is that firms are **profit maximisers**. On this basis, the neo-classical model shows that, for given demand and cost conditions, monopoly leads to a higher price and to a lower output than perfect competition. Also, since monopoly prices exceed marginal costs, Paretian welfare economics concludes that there will be a misallocation of resources and hence a market failure: monopoly is regarded as socially undesirable (see **Figure 11.1**). Estimates of the losses of consumer benefit due to monopoly have ranged from extremely small to up to 7 per cent of gross corporate product in the UK and up to 13 per cent of gross corporate output in the USA. However, the analysis can be modified to allow for a trade-off between the cost savings from mergers and economies of scale and the loss of consumer benefits due to monopoly. Alternative approaches have also emerged involving contestability, transaction costs, game theory and the Aus-

Table 11.3 *A Taxonomy of Industrial Policy*

Industry Features	Main Characteristics	Examples of Industrial Policy Options
Structure	Number of firms	Monopoly, mergers and restrictive
	Size of firms	practices policies in UK and EC
	Entry conditions	Tariff policy; government contracts
Conduct	Pricing	Monopoly and restrictive practices policy
	Advertising	Regulation of prices and advertising
	Marketing	Consumer protection policy
	Product differentiation	Regulation of new products and standards
	Research and development	Restrictive practices policy
	Collusion and restrictive agreements	
Location	Regional	Subsidies to firm and labour
	Towns	Location of industry policy
	Inner cities	Local authority planning controls
	Rural areas	Tourism policy; subsidies to rural
		industry and to agriculture
Ownership	Firm behaviour	Nationalisation of firms and industries
	– profit maximisation	Privatisation with or without:
	– non-profit objectives	**a** competition
		b regulation
Performance	Efficiency – technical	Monopoly, merger and competition policy
	– allocative	State regulation of profits
	Profitability	Industrial strategy; R&D and
	Growth	technology policy

trian critique, all of which are discussed in the sections which follow. Moreover, the theory of second-best shows the limited applicability of the Paretian model.

☐ *11.2.3 Trade-offs*

Let us consider a competitive industry and ask whether such an industry should be monopolised through mergers? If we assume that a merger leads to economies of scale which would not otherwise be available to a competitive industry, then a merger to monopolise a competitive industry will result in cost savings. Thus there will be a trade-off between the cost savings from scale economies and the loss of consumer benefit (surplus) due to the monopolisation of the competitive industry. Logically, the merger should be allowed to proceed if the additions to producer profits (surplus) exceed the loss of consumer benefits (surplus) as shown in **Figure 11.1**.

This trade-off analysis is not, however, without its critics. It uses a modified form of Paretian welfare function which allows a comparison of gains and losses, but distributional issues cannot be ignored so that we must ask whether the same or different weights should be attached to changes in producer and consumer benefits. Moreover, after the merger has taken place, a profit-maximising monopolist will expand output (beyond OQ_m in **Figure 11.1**) so raising producer profits and reducing the loss of consumer surplus, resulting in an even stronger case for the merger.

Figure 11.1   *Mergers, Scale Economies and Competition*

Nevertheless, the merger will continue to be associated with a misallocation of resources, with price greater than the new marginal costs. In the circumstances, consumers could in principle bribe the monopolist to produce at the new competitive price and output (Q_{c2} at P_1 in **Figure 11.1**): the monopoly would be no worse off since it would be compensated for its lost profits and consumers would be substantially better off. Such socially desirable compensation does not occur because substantial transaction costs make it too expensive to negotiate such a solution between the consumers and the monopolist. Finally, once the merger has occurred, competitive pressures will be absent allowing the firm to become technically inefficient which results in a departure from cost-minimising behaviour.

☐ 11.2.4 Contestable Markets

The concept of contestable markets represents a further modification to the standard structure–performance paradigm. A contestable market is one where there is the possibility and threat of entry by domestic and foreign firms, and therefore the **threat** of rivalry. A perfectly contestable market is one which has no entry barriers, where entry and exit are easy and costless, and which may or may not be characterised by economies of scale or economies of scope (that is, economies

which result from the range or scope of a multi-product firm's activities). In contestable markets, potential entrants are attracted by opportunities for profits. 'Hit and run behaviour' is evident since new entrants are not at a cost disadvantage compared with established suppliers, and the absence of sunk (irrevocable) costs means that exit is costless. One of the major features and policy implications of this approach is that a contestable market need not be populated by a large number of firms (as in perfect competition). In fact, a contestable market may contain only one or a small number of firms. Thus, with contestable markets, economists no longer have to assume that efficient outcomes occur only where there are large numbers of firms as in perfect competition. **Contestability rather than structure determines performance**.

☐ 11.2.5 Transaction Costs

Economic activity and exchange is a transaction process in a world of imperfect information and knowledge. Producers do not have complete knowledge of production possibilities and market opportunities. Similarly, individuals as consumers lack information on the price and quality of goods and services on offer, and as workers they will have only limited information on the wages, employment conditions and career prospects available in the labour market. Further costs are incurred in completing a transaction or doing business. For instance, after searching the market for a new car, costs are incurred in negotiating a price, and then policing, monitoring and enforcing a contract. After all, if producers and consumers were perfectly informed, and there were no transaction costs, then markets would not fail since all opportunities for mutually advantageous trade and exchange would be fully exploited.

Transaction costs have been defined as the costs of running the economic system, and include all the costs involved in planning, bargaining, modifying, monitoring and enforcing an implicit or explicit contract (Williamson, 1981, p. 1544). On this approach, the modern corporation and other economic institutions reflect efforts to economise on transaction costs rather than to pursue anti-competitive practices and create monopolies. Two assumptions are central to transaction costs, namely **bounded rationality and opportunism**. Bounded rationality recognises that economic agents have a limited capacity to handle information and to solve complex problems. Opportunism recognises that individuals will affect transactions through pursuing self-interest by hoarding valuable information, distorting data and sending misleading messages.

Transaction cost economics offers some distinctive explanations and interpretations of economic organisations:

1 Transactions will be organised in markets unless market exchange creates substantial transaction cost penalties.
   On this basis, firms will be substituted for markets if it becomes too costly to use markets compared with the costs of managing a firm.
2 It explains decisions by firms to undertake activities in-house or to buy-in, as reflected in the extent of integration.
3 It explains the internal organisation of firms in the form of hierarchies, internal government and divisions. An example is the multidivisional, or M-form, organisation which resembles a mini-capital market compared with the centralised, unitary or U-form structure. The success of the M-form was due to its ability to economise further on transaction costs.
4 It explains non-standard and unfamiliar forms of economic organisation such as conglomerates, multinationals and franchising.

This approach accepts that whilst firms seek to economise on transaction costs, they might also aim to become monopolists. However, the transactions school believes that monopolising behaviour is the exception. In advocating transaction cost economics, it has been suggested that it is the only hypothesis which is able to provide a discriminating rationale for the succession of organisational innovations that have occurred over the past 150 years and out of which the modern corporation has emerged (Williamson, 1981, p. 1564). However, critics claim that transaction costs are so general that they can be used to rationalise almost anything, and that the approach does not offer any testable and refutable predictions. The critics suggest that we have a simple proposition without any predictive content: firms are used whenever they are cheaper, all costs considered, and markets are used whenever they are cheaper, all costs considered. However, the notions of imperfect information and contestability are elements in the Austrian critique.

☐ 11.2.6 Game Theory

Many real world markets do not resemble the perfectly competitive model. Instead, many markets are imperfectly competitive, often comprising small numbers of relatively large firms. Such oligopoly industries are characterised by **interdependence**, and game theory attempts to explain how oligopolists respond to their rivals' actions. Game theories focus on equilibrium outcomes which occur when each firm selects the best strategy, given the strategy of its rivals. Examples of oligopolies include the UK brewing, car, cigarette, newspaper and pharmaceutical industries. Competition in such industries often takes non-price forms such as advertising, 'free gifts', brand proliferation, R&D and the availability of spare capacity to deter new entrants (although price wars and predatory pricing are not unknown). These developments in the New Industrial Economics use modern game theory to explain strategic competition between large firms. Whilst the approach has the appeal of being more realistic, Austrian economists are critical of its dependence on equilibrium outcomes.

☐ 11.2.7 The Austrian Critique

The Austrian economists (such as Hayek, Schumpeter and Kirzner) are critical of the structure–conduct–performance paradigm, with its underlying emphasis on perfect competition and equilibrium. They assert that actual economies consisting of real world firms and industries are never in equilibrium (that is, never at a state of rest). Instead, economies are characterised by **ignorance** and **uncertainty**, which leads to continuous change and continuous market disequilibrium. Ignorance and uncertainty create opportunities for profits, and it is the entrepreneur's task to discover these profitable opportunities. To the Austrians, competition means continuous rivalry (contestability), with entrepreneurs searching for opportunities to make money before anyone else; all of which occurs in a world of ignorance and uncertainty where there is no such thing as perfect information and knowledge. To the Austrians, trial and error price adjustments, and trial and error advertising and product variations are simply a **search and discovery process**: they are methods of trying to obtain market information in situations where knowledge is imperfect and costly to acquire. But conventional theory would regard these actions by businesspeople as evidence that they possess some monopoly power. In other words, the competitive process which we witness in the high street seems alien to our model of a perfectly competitive equilibrium. In the high street, the trial and error price cuts made by businesspeople are simply examples of the way they try to gain information on their profit-maximising price (they are searching for profits).

The public policy implications of the Austrian approach concern two major issues in particular. In the first place, they concern the role of **profits**. At any given moment, profits may seem to be monopolistic resulting from output restrictions: the monopoly problem. Austrians, however, regard high profits as temporary since rival entrepreneurs will be attracted into the relatively profitable activity. Austrians suggest that monopoly control regulations should involve an assessment of profits over the **long run** (whatever that might be). They believe that any public policy which minimises the rewards of entrepreneurship will **reduce** future entrepreneurial effort, with adverse effects on the competitive process.

Second, they concern **industrial organisation**. Austrians believe that policy makers should avoid making statements either about the most efficient form of industrial organisation or about the wastes of advertising, product differentiation and duplication. Austrians claim that no-one has sufficient knowledge and competence to judge which form of market structure is the most efficient for meeting **tomorrow's** consumer needs (given that some of today's sunrise industries will almost certainly have to be tomorrow's dinosaurs and smokestack industries). Entrepreneurs do not have perfect foresight, but they do have a greater motivation than politicians and bureaucrats to meet new and unexpected consumer demands: namely, their desire to seek out profitable opportunities. Critics, though, say that the Austrian approach ignores completely the costs and time required for an economy to adjust and respond to free market forces, and that such costs and time might be unacceptable to society and to vote-conscious governments.

11.2.8 The Theory of Second-Best

There is a further problem in using the Paretian model. It requires that all the conditions for an optimum are satisfied simultaneously throughout the whole of the economy. For example, optimality requires that all markets be perfectly competitive throughout the economy. However, consider the case where perfect competition exists in only a limited section of the economy, but not everywhere. Assume also that there is a constraint in the form of at least one private market which is monopolistic and which can never be made perfectly competitive. In these circumstances, it does not follow that policy efforts to introduce perfect competition into some, but not all, of the private markets will necessarily move the economy towards an optimum position. It might, but it might also either leave welfare and/or efficiency unchanged, or affect them adversely. Thus, given a constraint such that the rules for optimum resource allocation cannot be satisfied throughout the economy, it becomes necessary to resort to a next-best or **second-best** solution, in which efforts are expended to make the best of the existing situation. A second-best solution is likely to involve a complete departure from the conditions required for optimum resource allocation. In the example given above, the second-best policy rule might require the departure from perfect competition in those markets where it already exists. Similar examples apply to other Paretian-type, piecemeal policy recommendations involving proposals for more marginal cost pricing, more centralisation or more free trade.

Given the importance of **constraints** or **distortions** preventing the achievement of a first-best or Pareto optimum, questions arise about their nature. Constraints can be policy-created, such as a government's support for 'national champions' or domestic monopoly defence contractors, or its desire to protect newly-privatised State industries from competition. But such policy-created constraints can always be removed by changing public policy! Presumably, therefore, governments are reluctant to change policy because of the likely effects on their popularity. If so, an alternative theory of industrial policy is required which embraces voters and political parties, and which recognises the role of the political market place.

☐ 11.2.9 A Public Choice Approach

Traditionally, State intervention in an economy was rationalised on grounds of market failure. Governments and bureaucracies were assumed to formulate policies to correct such market failures. Government was regarded as a black box and was not analysed using the same self-interest, maximising and exchange concepts which had been applied extensively to households, firms and markets in capitalist economies. Instead, elected politicians and bureaucracies were assumed, somewhat simplistically, to pursue the public interest and to implement the will of the people. By way of contrast, public choice analysis is concerned with collective non-market decision making. It applies neo-classical concepts of exchange and self-interest to the political market place of voters, political parties, governments,

bureaucracies and interest groups. Voters are assumed to act like consumers and to maximise their expected benefit or utility from the policies offered by rival politicians and political parties. Similarly, political parties resemble firms and seek to maximise votes. Parties compete in market structures ranging from small to large numbers of rivals, where new parties can enter or threaten to enter the market. The majority party forms the government and obtains the entire market. Its policies will be implemented through bureaucracies which are monopoly suppliers of information and services, aiming to maximise their budgets. In the UK, the DTI has a central role in policy towards industry, including aerospace, coal, energy, shipbuilding and steel manufacture, together with support for regions, inner cities and industrial innovation. Other Departments with an involvement in industrial policy include Defence (R&D and equipment procurement); Environment (environmental protection); the Home Office (fraud); Transport (civil aviation and bus and rail services); the LAs (for example, industrial estates); and the State regulatory agencies: for example, the OFT, the Office of Gas Supply (OFGAS) and the Office of Telecommunications (OFTEL).

In the course of formulating and implementing policies, governments and bureaucracies are lobbied by pressure groups pursuing their own self-interest by trying to influence policy in their favour (so introducing contestability into the political market). With the intention of safeguarding or improving their incomes, producer groups of management, professional associations and trade unions lobby governments for contracts (to buy British), subsidies, laws to licence and restrict entry and for protection from foreign competition. Producer groups are willing to allocate resources in their efforts to persuade governments to create or protect monopoly rights (sometimes referred to as rent seeking and rent protection). For example, producers in a competitive industry will seek to obtain monopoly profits by persuading the government to introduce economic regulation of their industry, perhaps by pointing to the wastes and duplication of competition and to the fragmented nature of competitive industries. Presumably, they would be willing to invest resources in order to capture monopoly profits. At the limit, they would spend P_mBAP_c in **Figure 11.1**, so that the social cost of monopoly is the sizeable area P_mBCP_c.

It happens that not all the lobbying costs are wasted. Politicians and officials may receive payments in kind in the form of expenses-paid trips or free meals. In some cases, the market may be provided with valuable information. Nevertheless, the producer group and rent-seeking approach to government explains public policies in terms of **wealth transfers**. Government is a mechanism for promoting exchanges of wealth or rents, the aim being to take wealth from some groups and to transfer it to other groups. On this view, industrial policy is about which firms, in-

dustries and regions gain from policy and about who loses and who has to pay. Such wealth transfers and rent seeking occur in a political market place where the rules and constraints on behaviour are determined by the constitution, which is itself the result of exchanges within the political market.

When the various agents in the political market place are recognised, it is perhaps not surprising that governments often seem to ignore obvious opportunities for making people better off. Many economists are fond of advocating public policies which expand the opportunities for consumer choice by promoting competition and mutually advantageous trade and exchange both within and between nations. But if such policies are socially desirable, why do governments fre-

Figure 11.2   *Linkages[1] in the Political Market: the Example of Smoking*

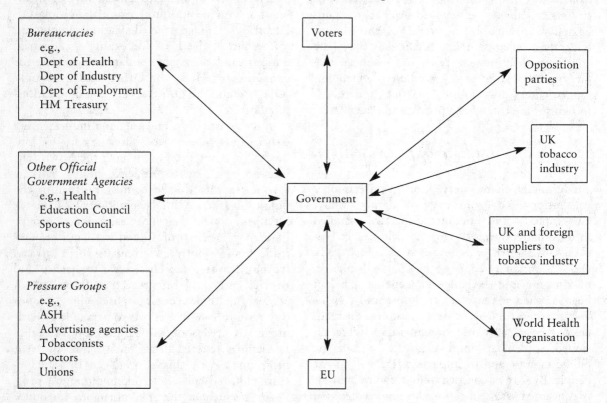

Note:
[1] For simplicity, most of the linkages shown by the arrows focus on the government. Other inter-relationships are possible.

quently ignore them? Why the use of tariffs to protect British industry, regulations to prevent entry and a preference to buy defence equipment from higher cost domestic firms? Changes and policies which appear so attractive to economists often fail to recognise the influence of the different agents in the political market place and their impact on policy formulation. **Figure 11.2** presents a framework for identifying and mapping the various linkages within the political market. It takes the example of government policy towards cigarette smoking and shows the agents which will try to influence and modify government policy in their favour.

Let us now consider the economics of politics and bureaucracies, which provides predictions that are relevant to explaining UK industrial policy (see Downs, 1957, and Niskanen, 1971).

1   In a two-party democracy, both parties agree on any issues which are strongly favoured by a majority of voters. As a result, party policies will be more vague, more similar to those of the other party (consensus politics) and less directly linked to an ideology than in a multi-party system.
2   Political parties will attempt to differentiate their policies, but movements towards the political extremes of total **laissez-faire** or complete collectivism are likely to be constrained by the potential losses of moderate voters.
3   Government is more attentive to producers than consumers when it formulates policies. Producer groups dominate both because they can afford to invest in the specialised information needed to influence government, and also because they have the most to gain from influencing public policy in their favour. As a result, government policies tend to favour producers more than consumers.
4   Bureaucracies aiming to maximise their budgets will be inefficient in supplying a given output and will overspend. Their budgets are likely to be too large as they exaggerate the demand for their services and underestimate the costs of their preferred activities. This affects the way in which information is pre-

sented to politicians. In bidding for a larger budget, a bureaucracy can stress how the funds will contribute to social benefits in the form of, say, jobs, high technology and exports.

The public choice approach shows that the form and extent of State intervention as reflected in industrial policy cannot be divorced from the motives and behaviour of politicians, bureaucracies and interest groups. The traditional market failure analysis suggested that State intervention was needed to correct market failure and to improve the operation of markets. By way of contrast, the public choice approach recognises that governments and State intervention can also fail!

These approaches to analysing aspects of industrial policy will now be applied to a set of issues which dominate current debates: should governments regulate the economy and is competition policy an effective regulatory instrument? Alternatively, should policy focus on ownership, choosing between private or public ownership? Can firm behaviour and performance be sufficiently influenced by subsidies? It should be borne in mind that governments can affect industrial performance directly through their public purchasing policies. In some cases, the absence of a policy or doing nothing is a conscious policy decision. The rest of this chapter will show how economists can contribute to these debates, all of which involve public policy towards UK industry.

11.3 The Economics of Regulation and Regulatory Policy

☐ 11.3.1 The Issues

Since 1960, there have been numerous examples of regulation. They have included employment legislation embracing contracts; employment protection; equal opportunities; health and safety at work and training and redundancy. At various times there have been controls on prices, wages and profits in such forms as minimum wages, equal pay, rent control, price regulation schemes (for example, NHS drugs), profit rules on government contracts, and price freezes for the nationalised industries. The structure, conduct and performance of industry has been regulated by monopolies, mergers and restrictive practices policy. Regulation has also taken the form of government licensing of entry as with patents, public houses, taxis, television companies, road and air transport, and new pharmaceutical products. Finally, output is regulated through such forms as pollution controls and safety standards, as in the case of food products and passenger transport (for example, speed restrictions, vehicle testing and airliner safety).

The 1980s have been characterised by a mix of both regulation and deregulation, which can be linked to a broad interpretation of privatisation (see **Figure 11.3** below). The privatisation of public monopolies such as British Telecom, gas, electricity and water has resulted in the creation of industry-specific regulatory agencies (for example, OFTEL). At the same time, the government has **deregulated** some markets, such as bus transport and financial services. All of this raises general issues concerning the rationale for regulation, the likely response of firms to regulatory constraints on their behaviour and the calculation of the costs and benefits of regulation. In addressing such issues it is useful to start with a classification system.

☐ 11.3.2 The Forms of Regulation

Regulation takes various forms, and a distinction can be made between voluntary self-regulation and government regulation via laws and regulatory agencies. The professions and the Stock Exchange, together with codes of conduct for advertisers (such as cigarette companies) and the media are examples of voluntary self-regulation. In contrast, government regulations can be general or specific. General regulations such as competition policy affect all firms in the economy, whilst specific regulations can be aimed at one sector such as telecommunications or gas, and/or relate to specific aspects of firm behaviour such as advertising, prices or profits. For example, the Review Board for Government Contracts regulates profit rates on all non-competitive government contracts, whilst the Medicines Act 1968 regulates the introduction of new pharmaceutical products into the UK market. In these various forms, regulations affect aspects of structure through entry conditions, as well as conduct (advertising, R&D) and performance (prices, profits). Whatever its form, the central issue is **why regulation is needed.**

☐ 11.3.3 The Rationale of Regulation

Economic theory suggests that regulation is a means of correcting for market failure, thereby improving the operation of markets. State regulation might, for example, be a means of controlling private monopoly power or, alternatively, a means of controlling harmful externalities. **An alternative public choice view suggests that government regulation benefits producers rather than consumers.** Firms will devote resources to lobbying governments to introduce favourable policies such as regulating entry, on the pretext of protecting consumers from cowboy operators and from cheap, inferior and unsafe foreign products. Regulators will have only limited information about producers. The possibility arises of new or existing regulatory agencies being **captured** by the industry and persuaded to act in favour of producers rather than consumers. Senior officials in the regulatory agency might seek employment in their regulated industry (for example, defence or pharmaceuticals).

Firms also have an incentive to persuade the regulatory agency that its required standards can be met voluntarily, claiming that excessively high standards will lead to bankruptcy with implications for plant closures, unemployment and a government's popularity. Alternatively, firms might accept the costs of government regulations in return for more beneficial policies elsewhere, such as restrictions on new entry. Certainly, firms are unlikely to be passive, mechanistic agents, but will seek to change regulations and to adapt to them. This in turn requires an explanation of how firms are likely to respond to different regulatory rules.

11.3.4 The Response of Firms

Regulation can take various forms such as licence requirements; certification; entry fees; inspection systems and fines for breaching regulations; the auctioning of rights; and controls on prices and profits. In choosing between these, policy makers need to know what they are trying to achieve, and how firms are likely to respond to different regulatory instruments.

At the outset, it has to be recognised that regulators do not have perfect information about producers in the regulated industry. For example, a regulator trying to enforce cost-based prices incorporating an average profit rate does not know whether a firm's costs reflect efficient behaviour or X-inefficiency. In these circumstances, regulators have to formulate incentives which will change firm behaviour in certain socially desirable directions, but some incentives can give unexpected and undesirable results. A State-determined limit on profits might, for example, induce a firm to pursue objectives other than maximum profits, so substituting expenditure on staff or other discretionary items (such as luxury offices) for profits. Alternatively, if the profit controls take the form of a maximum rate of return earned on capital, the regulated firm may use increasingly capital-intensive production methods. Regulatory controls on advertising may encourage a firm to expand its unregulated marketing inputs by employing a larger salesforce or introducing new sponsorship schemes (as with sports sponsorship), for example. In other words, firms may respond to regulatory constraints by seeking other ways of making money, thereby raising questions about the effectiveness of regulation.

11.3.5 The Desirability of Regulation

Some governments, politicians and civil servants are fond of proposing regulation; they seem to believe that all regulation is good and that more is desirable regardless of cost. However, regulation is not costless, so it is necessary to examine the likely **costs and benefits** and to assess any evidence, particularly on costs and benefits at the **margin**, in order to enable a choice to be made about the **optimal amount** of regulation.

Regulation involves substantial transaction costs in negotiating, monitoring and enforcing regulatory rules. Staff are needed by the regulatory agency, and costs are imposed on producers in responding to the regulator's requirements. For example, a monopoly inquiry involves substantial inputs by members of the inquiry team and corresponding inputs by the monopolist. Specialist witnesses will also be hired by both parties, and the monopolist might devote resources to a public relations campaign and to lobbying politicians. There are also possible indirect costs which need to be included in the analysis. For example, regulatory requirements for the introduction of new drugs into the NHS might lead to longer development periods, so delaying the introduction of new pharmaceutical products. There might also be adverse effects on innovation with fewer new drugs being marketed, and firms might shift their R&D activities to foreign locations where there are fewer regulatory restrictions. In the meantime, delays in the introduction of new drugs can have harmful effects on patients in the form of prolonged suffering and death which might have been avoided by the earlier use of the new product. Questions then arise as to whether the delays are beneficial insofar as they protect consumers from the unforeseen and possibly harmful side effects of new drugs: a classic trade-off situation.

A cost-benefit analysis of regulation must also take account of its potential benefits. Regulatory agencies which aim to remove market failures will introduce policies to correct for externalities or to change the structure, conduct or performance of markets, with the ultimate objective of improving consumer welfare. But can society assess the output or performance of a regulatory agency? Various performance indicators have been suggested, not all of which can be easily related to consumer satisfaction. For example, agencies are likely to emphasise the number of inquiries and reports; the number of licences issued; the number of inspections; the number of prosecutions; and the size of the regulatory authority. The Director-General of Fair Trading will refer to the number of monopoly inquiries; the number of merger investigations; reports issued; and the number of cases brought before the Restrictive Practices Court. Similarly, in regulating the introduction of new drugs, the Medicines Division of the Department of Health will eagerly report the number of licences awarded; the time taken to process applications; the introduction of any new testing requirements; inspection and enforcement activities; and the number of statutory orders.

The various performance indicators **appear** impressive, indicating a lively, active and vigorous regulatory authority. However, many of the indicators measure inputs or intermediate output, rather than **final output**: they do not indicate the effects on consumers and how highly consumers might value such effects. Supporters of regulation will obviously claim that it results in substantial social benefits. However, a regulatory agency aiming to maximise its size or budget will exaggerate the social benefits of its activities (such as improved product safety), and underestimate or ignore the costs of regulation. A regulatory agency will also favour independent fund-raising powers in the form of, say, licence fees which enable it to finance inefficiency, labour hoarding and discretionary activities such as luxury headquarters and offices. Some of these arguments about regulation will now be applied to UK competition policy which is a classic example of a general form of regulatory policy.

■ 11.4 Competition Policy

☐ 11.4.1 The Economic Rationale

Competition policy is a classic example of general regulatory arrangements applying to all firms in the UK economy. It embraces policy towards monopolies, mergers and restrictive practices. In this context, standard economic theory offers some clear policy guidelines, suggesting that monopoly and other imperfections result in market failure and hence are socially undesirable (see **Figure 11.1**). Theory defines monopoly as a single seller of a product with no close substitutes. This model indicates that policy-makers need to focus on structural characteristics, the resulting performance reflected in the relationship between price and marginal cost and whether excessive profits are earned in the long run. However, theory also recognises that small numbers of firms constituting an oligopoly can have market power and that groups of firms acting together through collective agreements (cartels) can behave like a monopolist. As a result, policy needs to focus on mergers creating oligopoly or monopoly situations; on the conduct of firms in relation to entry barriers (for example, advertising); and on collective agreements which restrict competition in an industry. How far have such guidelines from economic theory influenced UK competition policy?

☐ 11.4.2 UK Practice

UK competition policy is based on various pieces of legislation dating from 1948, concerned with monopolies, mergers, restrictive practices, resale price maintenance (RPM) and consumer protection. Monopolies and mergers may be referred for investigation by the MMC whilst restrictive practices including RPM are the subject of legal procedures in the Restrictive Practices Court (see **Table 11.4**). Specific reference to consumer protection was first incorporated in the 1973 Fair Trading Act.

Current policy towards monopolies and mergers is based on the Acts of 1973 and 1980. The 1973 Fair Trading Act created an Office of Fair

Trading with a Director-General, and cases **se-lected for investigation** were referred to the MMC. Where a monopoly situation appears to exist, both the Director-General of Fair Trading and the Secretary of State for Trade and Industry can refer cases to the MMC. A monopoly is defined as one firm or a group of firms acting together (called a complex monopoly), accounting for **at least 25 per cent** of the relevant **local** or **national** market. Selected mergers are referred to the MMC by the Secretary of State for Trade and Industry. Mergers **may be** investigated where they involve a 25 per cent or more market share or **at least £30 million worth of assets are taken over**. These definitions are interesting. The market share criterion contrasts with the economist's definition of monopoly as a single seller. Whilst the policy definition embraces oligopoly, it also implies that as the number of similar-sized firms declines from 5 to 4, a market changes from competition to a monopoly situation, constituting a policy-relevant imperfection. Moreover, the value of assets taken over in mergers introduces an absolute size of firm criterion into the policy definition of monopoly. This contrasts with the economist's emphasis on market share. However, an absolute size criterion allows vertical and conglomerate mergers to be investigated. It might also reflect a public choice perspective, whereby large size can create dominant producer groups capable of influencing government purchasing and regulatory policies: hence, large firms might be undesirable.

In its investigations, the MMC has to determine whether a monopoly or proposed merger operates or is likely to operate **against the public interest**. In the case of both monopolies and mergers which are contrary to the public interest the MMC can recommend appropriate action to be taken, but cannot itself enforce a remedy. Only the relevant Secretary of State can enforce remedies against monopolies and can choose to prohibit a merger or to allow it to proceed unconditionally or subject to conditions. For the first time, the 1973 Act defined the public interest to include the desirability of maintaining and promoting competition. However, the public interest definition is wide-ranging. It includes a concern with consu-

mer interests in relation to price, quality and variety; encouraging cost reductions, technical progress and new entry; a consideration of the international competitive position of UK producers; and promoting a balanced distribution of industry and employment. It is not at all obvious that some of these elements such as a balanced distribution of industry (itself an ambiguous term), are the proper concern of competition policy. Moreover, the MMC retains substantial discretion since it is allowed to take into account any factors which it deems to be relevant in determining the public interest! This is, in fact, a distinctive feature of UK policy towards monopolies and mergers.

Whilst standard economic theory suggests that competition is socially desirable, UK policy has not condemned monopolies and mergers as undesirable. **A discretionary cost-benefit approach is adopted, with each case examined on its merits**. Policy recognises that monopolies and mergers involve a trade-off between the costs of reduced competition, including X-inefficiency, and the potential benefits through scale economies and technical progress (**Figure 11.1**). Moreover, existing UK monopolies and mergers policy might be rationalised on second-best grounds. The standard welfare economics case for competition has to be modified where governments accept as policy-created constraints the continued existence of monopolies in parts of the economy. Alternatively, a public choice approach would explain current policy, with its wide-ranging public interest criterion and a reluctance to act against monopolies, as reflecting the influence of producer groups.

UK policy towards restrictive practices and RPM has taken a different approach. The Restrictive Practices Act 1976 and the Resale Prices Act of 1976 consolidated the prior legislation of 1956, 1964 and 1968. Restrictive practices legislation applies to the supply of both goods and services. It is concerned with agreements which restrict prices, conditions of sale and quantities to be supplied, and which lead firms to exchange information on prices and costs. Restrictive agreements have to be registered, and are presumed to be illegal and against the public interest unless the

Table 11.4   *Major Competition Policy Measures*

Legislation	Agencies	Features
Monopolies and Restrictive Practices Act 1948	Monopolies Commission	Monopoly = one-third or more of a market
Restrictive Trade Practices Act 1956	Registrar and Restrictive Practices Court	Restrictive agreements illegal but exemptions (gateways); if agreement passes through a gateway it still has to satisfy a public interest criterion
Resale Prices Act 1964	Restrictive Practices Court	RPM declared illegal subject to exemptions (gateways) and ultimate public interest test
Monopolies and Mergers Act 1965	Board of Trade mergers panel Monopolies Commission	Mergers to be reviewed involving one-third or more market share, or where value of assets taken over exceeded £5 million
Restrictive Trade Practices Act 1968	Registrar and Restrictive Practices Court	Amendment of 1956 Act to incorporate information agreements
Fair Trading Act 1973	Director-General of Fair Trading Monopolies and Mergers Commission Consumer Protection Advisory Committee	Replaced 1948 and 1965 Acts Monopoly = 25 per cent or more of a local or national market Mergers to be reviewed involving one-quarter or more market share or value of assets taken over exceeded £15 million (increased to £30 million in 1984) Public interest defined to include competition Reference to consumer protection
Restrictive Trade Practices Act 1976	Director-General of Fair Trading Restrictive Practices Court	Consolidated previous legislation (1956, 1968) with an extension to services Agreements registered with Director-General of Fair Trading
Resale Prices Act 1976	Director-General of Fair Trading Restrictive Practices Court	Consolidated previous legislation (1964), banning RPM

Table 11.4 *Major Competition Policy Measures (cont'd)*

Legislation	Agencies	Features
Competition Act 1980	Director-General of Fair Trading Monopolies and Mergers Commission	Deals with anti-competitive practices and extended monopoly control to public sector bodies and nationalised industries
EU Articles 85 and 86 of Treaty of Rome	Directorate General for Competition (European Commission) European Court of Justice	Applies only where trade between member states is affected Article 85 deals with restrictive practices and allows exemptions Article 86 originally applied to monopolies; but extended to prohibit mergers
EU merger regulation 1989	Directorate General for Competition (European Commission) European Court of Justice	Aggregate world-wide turnover above ECU 5 billion and other requirements

parties can establish a case for exemption before the Restrictive Practices Court. To be exempted, an agreement has to pass through one or more of eight **gateways**. For example, it has to be shown that an agreement protects the public against injury; that it provides substantial benefits to the public as purchasers, consumers or users; that it acts as a countervailing power against the anti-competitive practices of third parties; or that its removal would result in serious and persistent local unemployment or a substantial reduction in exports. Once again, some of these gateways such as the concern with employment and exports, are rather odd aims for competition policy. However, even if an agreement passes through the gateways, it still has to satisfy the tailpiece or public interest test. The Court has to determine whether, both currently and in the future, the benefits to the public on balance outweigh the detriments or costs.

The Resale Prices Act 1976 controls RPM in the same way as restrictive agreements. There is a general presumption that RPM is contrary to the public interest unless a supplier can gain exemption through one or more of five gateways. RPM would be allowed if its abolition would substantially reduce the quality and variety of goods for sale; if there would be a substantial reduction in the number of retail outlets; if there is likely to be a long-run increase in retail prices; or where there might be dangers to health or a substantial reduction in necessary point-of-sale sales or after-sales services. Once through a gateway, it is still necessary to satisfy the tailpiece whereby the Court has to consider the balance of benefits and detriments.

The Competition Act 1980 complemented existing legislation and takes a different approach from that of the 1976 Acts. It is concerned with the anti-competitive practices of individual firms supplying goods or services which have the effect of restricting, distorting or preventing competition. Examples include price discrimination, predatory pricing, exclusive supply and rental-only contracts, all of which are aspects of a firm's **conduct**. The 1980 Act also extended monopoly control to include the nationalised industries and other public sector bodies (for example, the bus companies and water authorities). The 1980 procedure requires the Director-General of Fair Trading to investigate alleged anti-competitive practices. Where such a practice exists, the Director-General can require the firm to cease the practice or it can be referred to the MMC which will apply the 1973 public interest test.

As a member of the EU, the UK is also subject to European competition law, reflected in Articles 85 and 86 of the Rome Treaty which are enforced by the Commission. Article 85 prohibits restrictive agreements and practices which prevent, restrict or distort competition within the EU and which affect trade between member states. Examples include price-fixing, market-sharing and limitations of production, technical progress and investment. As in the UK, agreements may be exempted where they improve production, distribution or technical progress, subject to the requirement that these benefits must not be outweighed by other detriments associated with reduced competition. The Commission has the power to impose **heavy fines** on the guilty parties to a restrictive agreement.

Article 86 originally applied to monopolies but was extended to mergers. It deals with situations where trade between member states might be affected by one or more enterprises taking improper advantage of a dominant position. Examples of improper practices include the imposition of inequitable purchase or selling prices, or limiting production, markets or technical developments. However, questions arise as to what constitutes a firm with a dominant position. In the case of mergers, the position is clearer. Under the 1989 regulation, the Commission can control and prohibit mergers which have a Community dimension. These are defined as mergers where the **aggregate world-wide turnover** of the firms involved is above ECU 5 billion (approximately £3.5 billion), and **Community-wide turnover** of each of at least two of the firms is above ECU 250 million (approximately £175 million), unless two-thirds of that turnover is within one member state. Such mergers must be notified and will be prohibited if they create or strengthen a dominant position so that effective competition is impeded.

All other mergers falling outside this regulation will be dealt with by national governments. Firms and member states can appeal to the European Court of Justice against decisions of the Commission. Clearly, Community competition policy and its relationship with national policy has become a more important issue with the creation of the SEM in 1992.

Three issues are likely to dominate the evolution of a Community competition policy required for achieving a genuinely free internal market from 1993 onwards. First, there is likely to be a continued concern with the Community's merger regulations and their potential conflict with national merger policy. Indeed, the 1989 Community regulation on mergers reflected unanimous voting, with some countries objecting to limits lower than the ECU 5 billion threshold. Second, the Commission has become increasingly concerned about the competition implications of State subsidies and other forms of government protectionism. An example was the Commission's requirement that the UK Government reduce the amount of State aid offered as part of British Aerospace's acquisition of the Rover Group. Third, the Commission is likely to become more actively involved in policy towards cartels and restrictive policies, particularly in the services sector and in markets dominated by state-owned industries. Indeed, for 1993–94, the EU is focusing on creating a **level playing field**, taking action against agreements, concerted practices, abuse of dominant positions, government subsidies (for example, for R&D and specific industries), dumping and mergers which are incompatible with the Common Market. In a radically changed environment (due, for example, to the SEM, recession and technical change), the Commission has to distinguish between two types of firm and group behaviour: first, behaviour which contributes to the development and restructuring of European industry (for example, co-operation and mergers which increase competition); and second, behaviour which prevents adjustment by partitioning markets and strengthening dominant positions (for example, anti-competitive behaviour; State aid and subsidies).

11.4.3 The Results of Competition Policy

Any evaluation of UK competition policy needs to focus on final output indicators in terms of the effects of policy on market structure, conduct and, ultimately, performance. Such an appraisal requires a model of structure, conduct and performance which holds constant all other relevant influences and identifies the contribution of competition policy. Other influences – such as newly-industrialising nations, international trade, membership of the EU, technical progress, oil price shocks and the general level of AD and expectations in the UK economy – cannot be ignored.

Competition policy can be evaluated against the general evidence on trends in the size of firms and industry structure in the UK economy. **Table 11.5** shows data on aggregate concentration in the form of the share of the 100 largest enterprises in manufacturing output. Aggregate concentration rose significantly from a pre-1939 figure of some 25 per cent to about 40 per cent by the late 1960s. However, since 1970, aggregate concentration has remained relatively stable, a feature which shows the uncertainties involved in predicting future trends. Interestingly, in 1987, about 10 per cent of the top 100 enterprises were the leading alcohol and tobacco companies such as BAT Industries, Grand Metropolitan, Hanson Trust (Imperial), Allied Lyons, Gallaher, Bass and Guinness. At the same time, small firms are important. By 1987, there were 2.5 million firms in the UK, with 96 per cent employing fewer than 20 people; such small firms accounted for 36 per cent of total employment.

The extent of competition in a single market is usually shown by a **5-firm** concentration ratio (CR) which measures the proportion of industry output accounted for by the five largest firms in the industry. Evidence on CRs is shown in **Table 11.5**. Following a small rise in the early 1970s, industry concentration declined up to the mid-1980s. Indeed, once the ratios are adjusted for foreign trade, industry concentration actually declined between 1970 and 1984. Interestingly, though, a number of UK manufacturing industries remain highly concentrated, with 5-firm CRs exceeding 75 per cent in 1988. Examples included asbestos, cement, man-made fibres, motor vehicles, shipbuilding, ordnance and tobacco. Inevitably, such data raise questions about the role and effects of monopoly policy.

Table 11.5 *Firm Size and Market Structures*

	1970	1974	1975	1979	1980	1984
100 largest enterprises share in manufacturing output (%)	39.3	42.1	n.a.	n.a.	40.5[1]	38.7
Unadjusted 5-firm CR[2,3] (%)	49.0	50.9	48.5	51.4	n.a.	49.1
Adjusted 5-firm CR[3] (%)	41.3	40.9	36.5	39.3	n.a.	33.8
Mergers[4]						
Number of companies acquired	793.0	504.0	534.0	–	469.0	568.0
Expenditure on acquisitions (£ bn at 1986 prices)	5.9	1.7	2.8	–	2.1	5.9

Notes:
[1] Change in definition after 1980.
[2] 5-firm concentration ratios (CR) based on a sample of 93 comparable industries 1970–9 and a sample of 195 comparable industries 1979–84.
[3] Unadjusted 5-firm CR is unadjusted for foreign trade while the adjusted CR allows for foreign trade.
[4] Mergers refer to acquisitions and mergers by UK industrial and commercial companies.
Source: DTI (1988) *Mergers Policy* (London: HMSO).

By 1993, the MMC had issued over 80 reports on UK monopoly situations. Examples included the supply of beer (tied houses); the British Gas industry; cigarettes; soap and detergents; postal franking machines; animal waste; credit card services; the supply of petrol; cross-channel ferries and travel agency services for tour operators. There have also been investigations of professional services (for example, of architects, surveyors and solicitors) and such public sector activities as British Rail commuter services, some water authorities and the National Coal Board. Various monopoly situations and practices have been found to be against the public interest.

In its judgements, the MMC assesses monopolies in terms of their policies and their effects on prices; advertising; marketing; new entrants; and, ultimately, profitability. For example, in 1989 the MMC found that certain restrictions on advertising by the professions acted against the public interest, and the Director-General of Fair Trading was asked to seek assurances that the professions would modify their behaviour. Similarly, the 1989 report on the supply of beer found that six brewers produced 75 per cent of beer sold and owned 75 per cent of all tied houses. An earlier 1969 report on the supply of beer had already concluded that the tied-house system operated against the public interest. In its 1989 report, the Commission found a **complex monopoly** situation in brewing (mainly through tied houses) which restricted competition and was against the public interest. Unusually for the Commission, it recommended a series of **structural changes** to achieve a more competitive regime. These included a ceiling of 2000 on the number of tied premises owned by a brewer; allowing tied tenants to sell a 'guest' draught beer; and also allowing them to buy non-alcoholic and low alcohol drinks as well as wines and some other drinks from the lowest-cost suppliers (Cmnd 651, 1989; also Cmnd 216, 1969).

The concern of UK monopoly policy with prices, entry, profitability and consumers has a possible economic basis in models of perfect competition and contestable markets. But such models do not provide operational guidelines for determining when prices are too high and profits

become excessive. Are prices too high if they result in abnormal profits, and, if so, how is it possible to distinguish abnormal from normal profits? Austrian economists would adopt a different approach, suggesting that market power is usually transitory and that so-called monopoly profits are the temporary reward of successful entrepreneurship. To the Austrians, an innovating monopolist generates a **social gain** represented by the firm's profits and the resulting consumer surplus: without the innovation a new product such as a microcomputer would never have been produced, so there is no question of a deadweight loss due to a departure from the perfectly competitive output. Such contrasting interpretations of monopoly makes life extremely difficult and complicated for governments who have to determine a monopoly policy!

Critics of UK monopoly policy claim that it is **slow and ineffective**. Typically, an MMC inquiry took 2–3 years, although recently inquiries have been completed in one year or less. Few reports are issued in any one year and, to date, the total number of monopoly investigations represents only a small part of the UK's monopoly and oligopoly industries (although the presence of the MMC might have a deterrent effect). Moreover, governments are often reluctant to take effective remedial action against monopolies, preferring to rely on informal undertakings, which may reflect pressure from producer groups and the possibility that the regulatory agency has been captured by producers. In addition, the remedies secured after an investigation apply only to the firms involved so that they have only limited impact on the conduct of other firms in other markets. Thus, the system has only a limited deterrent effect. The result is that UK monopoly policy has not achieved any major changes in either the structure or the conduct of monopoly industries which have been investigated.

Even the 1989 MMC recommendations for structural change in the brewing industry were modified by successive Secretaries of State. Clearly, the brewers represent a powerful producer group which lobbied the Government to modify, or not to implement, or to delay the recommendations of the MMC. In the event, the MMC's recommendations were modified, so that brewers were required to sell or place at 'arm's length' **half** of the pubs they owned above the 2000 ceiling (for example, Bass with 7300 pubs had to sell 2658 rather than 5300). At the same time, the brewers have responded to the new regulatory requirements in ways which are to their benefit and which might conflict with the aims of the MMC's 1989 report. For example, Grand Metropolitan and Courage agreed to a pubs-for-breweries exchange with Grand Met ceasing to make beer and a new jointly-owned company running the pubs. At the same time, Courage entered into an agreement to supply beer to Grand Met's pubs. In fact, a number of brewers and companies running pubs have entered into long-term supply agreements. Some brewers have stopped brewing and retained their pubs (for example, Greenalls). Elsewhere, pubs have been sold and then converted to private houses. Allegations have also been made that sales representatives of the big brewers have intimidated tenants not to take a guest beer, or have made it difficult to stock a guest beer (for example, threatening rent increases or eviction).

Cases continue to arise and the issues are not diminishing. In 1989, the Competition Act 1980 was applied to Black & Decker. The company's policy of refusing to supply retailers who sold its products below a particular price was found to be anti-competitive and against the public interest. The government's initiatives on privatisation, deregulation, contracting-out and public purchasing policy are likely to create new demands on the UK's competition agencies. An example occurred with the 1993 MMC Report on the gas industry. The Report recommended that the privately-owned British Gas should be split into two companies (separating trading from transport and storage) and that competition should be introduced over a 10-year period.

Mergers are also contributing to major structural changes in the UK economy with substantial numbers of mergers being of the horizontal and conglomerate types. Between 1964 and 1989, the annual rate of mergers within the UK varied

between 315 and some 1200 per annum, with a similar variation in annual expenditure on acquisitions of between £0.8 billion and some £22 billion at 1986 prices. Peaks of merger activity in terms of numbers and expenditure occurred in 1965, 1972–73, 1986–87 and 1989. Despite the high level of activity, relatively few qualifying mergers, typically well under 5 per cent, are actually referred to the MMC (for example, 1.2 per cent in 1987). Of those referred, not all are found to be contrary to the public interest. For example, between 1965 and 1992, there were 176 merger references, of which only 61 were declared to be against the public interest. However, by the mid-1980s, there was concern over the continued merger boom, over allegations of asset stripping and especially over the size of some acquisitions and their controversial nature (for example GEC–Plessey and Nestlé–Rowntree). As a result, the government reviewed its merger policy and published the results in 1988 (DTI, 1988).

The 1988 government review of merger policy examined two performance indicators, namely **trends in concentration ratios** and **post-merger performance**. Whilst evidence showed a substantial increase in industry concentration in the 1950s and 1960s, it seems that between 1970 and 1984 concentration ratios adjusted for foreign trade actually declined, as shown in **Table 11.5**. The 1988 review also confirmed the earlier findings of poor, disappointing or inconclusive post-merger performance (for example, with respect to profitability). Such evidence has been used to suggest that mergers were failing to provide economic benefits. Nevertheless, the government review reaffirmed its policy of leaving most merger decisions to the market: 'the vast majority of mergers raise no competition or other objections, and are rightly left free to be decided by the market' (DTI, 1988, p. 7).

The 1988 review also confirmed that the main, though not the only, factor in determining whether a merger should be referred to the MMC should be its **potential effects on competition in the UK market**. In fact, evidence from MMC merger reports between 1970 and 1990 showed that bidding firms had a significantly better chance of success if the MMC decided that competition was likely to increase or remain unchanged. However, to allow for a few exceptional cases (such as foreign ownership of UK companies or the level of any State ownership in the acquiring company), an open-ended public interest criterion was retained in the legislation. Finally, the review proposed two legislative changes to improve the speed and flexibility of merger policy. Both changes were incorporated in the Companies Act 1989. In the first place, a procedure for **voluntary pre-notification** was introduced, which is designed to obtain faster clearance of mergers involving no major public interest issues. Second, where a proposed or completed merger gives rise to concern about loss of competition, the merging parties can give a binding undertaking for the divestment of part of the merged company's business, as an alternative to a reference. The Companies Act 1989 also introduced a charging system to cover the costs of public sector merger control work. Even so, there is continued concern over mergers. Worries have been expressed about asset stripping, that foreign competitors are taking advantage of the UK's open-door policy and that industrial structure is determined by short-termism (see Peacock and Bannock, 1991).

At the Community level, a 1991 case showed how the Community's merger control regulation was applied to the creation of a dominant position defined to embrace actual and potential competition from firms located within and outside the Community. The case involved a bid by Aerospatiale (France) and Alenia (Italy) for the de Havilland Aircraft Company of Canada. The Commission found that the acquisition would have given de Havilland and ATR (the French–Italian venture) 50 per cent of the world market and 67 per cent of the EU market for 20–70 seat commuter aircraft. This would have created a dominant position, so the Commission rejected the proposed merger in 1991.

Restrictive practices legislation has been extremely effective in removing certain restrictive agreements which were the basis for the widespread cartelisation of UK industry in the 1950s. By 1988, some 6650 agreements had been registered, over 70 per cent of which were goods agreements. A substantial number of agreements have been abandoned, and many have been modified to remove any anti-competitive effects. Interestingly, it is possible that restrictive practices legislation, originally introduced in 1956, might have contributed to the high rate of merger activity in the 1960s. Nevertheless, evidence shows that the legislation resulted in new entry, increased competition, lower prices and generally contributed to its main objective of improving industrial efficiency (Cmnd 331, 1988).

Similarly, legislation was effective against RPM. In 1960 RPM applied to about 20–25 per cent of consumer expenditure; by 1979, it was restricted to net books and medicines, representing under 2 per cent of consumer expenditure. The result was improved efficiency in retailing and lower prices, although the effects were smaller than expected and some groups such as small independent retailers and their customers, had to bear the costs of the change. Nevertheless, the Resale Prices Act has made a major contribution to increased competition in retailing to the general benefit of consumers.

By the late 1980s, there were serious doubts about the effectiveness of restrictive practices legislation in tackling cartels. A government review suggested that 'the Act must now appear a relatively weak piece of legislation' (Cmnd 331, 1988, p. 29). It is criticised because potential colluders are unlikely to be detected (for example, secret price-fixing agreements amongst ready-mixed concrete companies in 1991); whether an agreement is registerable depends on its form, not upon its effect; penalties for ignoring the law are not sufficiently heavy to act as a deterrent; it catches trivia by including agreements which do not restrict competition; there are too many exemptions, and the whole registration process is costly and a waste of resources.

Instead, it was proposed that the registration system be abolished and **any agreement with anti-competitive effects was to be prohibited**. Examples of anti-competitive agreements include the price fixing of goods and services, collusive tendering, market sharing, restrictions on advertising and collective refusals to supply. Exemptions would be allowed using a broad test similar to Article 85(3) of the Treaty of Rome. The new policy was to be administered by a competition authority, as part of the OFT. The authority would have to determine whether an agreement is anti-competitive and, if so, whether it qualifies for an exemption. It was proposed that fines be imposed by the authority of up to 10 per cent of a firm's turnover. Appeals on prohibitions and exemptions were to be made to the Restrictive Practices Court, which would also have the power to impose fines above the competition authority's maximum limit (Cmnd 331, 1988). However, whilst a White Paper in 1989 was issued (Cmnd 727, 1989), none of the proposals had been incorporated into legislation by 1993. Indeed, in late 1992, another Green Paper was issued, entitled *The Abuse of Market Power: A Consultation Document on Possible Legislative Options*. The Green Paper accepts that the current policies against companies which engage in anti-competitive practices are too weak and have little deterrent effect. Three options are proposed: first, a strengthening of current legislation; second, the introduction of a prohibition system whereby abuses of market power would be unlawful and subject to penalties (for example, fines of up to £1 million); and third, a dual system combining prohibition and changes in legislation.

11.4.4 The Single European Market

In addition to competition policy within the UK market, a major change has occurred which will affect competition and contestability within the EU. Whilst there are no tariffs between member states, there were, until 1992, a number of substantial and costly non-tariff barriers. Physical, technical and fiscal barriers meant that the EU consisted of 12 fragmented national markets, separated by frontier controls, public procurement practices and different product and technical standards, all of which hindered trade in goods and services between member states. The EU aimed to remove these various barriers and to create a single internal market by the end of 1992.

It is estimated that the SEM will result in potential gains of over ECU 200 billion, equivalent to 5.3 per cent of EU GDP in 1988 (Cecchini, 1988, p. 84). Such gains will result from lower costs due to the abolition of frontier barriers, removing the barriers to entry into national markets (for example, for public procurement), exploiting scale economies and a general increase in competitive pressures in both goods and services markets. Currently, for example, cross-frontier trade is hindered by administrative formalities and border controls (red tape and delays); public procurement protects national industries from foreign competition; and divergent technical regulations, standards and certification procedures means costly market fragmentation (as in the case of financial services and telecommunications). However, the estimated benefits from abolishing non-tariff barriers will not be achieved immediately in 1993: it will take time for economies to adjust and adapt to the new market conditions, and the adjustment will not be costless.

Critics claim that the likely benefits have been exaggerated, that they are based on a simple perfectly competitive model which will never be achieved and that most of the worthwhile economies of scale have been exploited. Further gains are also available from opening up national defence equipment markets, an area currently outside the remit of the EU. Moreover, efforts to exploit any potential scale economies within the EU will probably require mergers, leading to possible conflicts with competition policy: the price of efficient scale might be monopoly which will benefit producer groups rather than consumers. Similar worries about the potential gainers and the potential losers from policy changes have dominated the debate about UK privatisation policy. Indeed, privatisation involves issues of ownership, monopoly, regulation and market competition. We must, therefore, turn to examine the relative merits of public versus private ownership and the role of ownership in enterprise performance.

■ *11.5* Ownership

☐ *11.5.1 The Nationalised Industries*

The UK economy consists of a mix of publicly and privately-owned firms and industries. Within the public sector, public corporations, including nationalised industries, are State-owned bodies accountable to government but with a substantial degree of independence, and whose activities (in the case of nationalised industries) are financed largely by the consumers of their goods and services rather than by the taxpayer. These industries have been the focal point of continuing debate between the political parties with Labour governments traditionally preferring State ownership of the means of production. Since 1945, UK industries such as aerospace, airlines, coal, gas, electricity, rail, shipbuilding, steel and telecommunications have at various times been State-owned, as too have individual firms such as British Leyland, British Petroleum, Rolls-Royce and Royal Ordnance. However, since 1979, a substantial number of nationalised industries and State-owned companies have been privatised, raising debates about whether ownership is an important determinant of enterprise performance.

Various economic arguments have been used to explain and justify nationalisation. After 1945, much emphasis was placed on the need to control private monopoly power; to plan and control the commanding heights of the economy; to include social costs and benefits in decision making, and to improve industrial relations by removing the traditional conflict between labour and capital. In the 1970s, State ownership of firms such as British Leyland and Rolls-Royce was justified as a rescue operation to save strategically and economically important companies and to prevent substantial job losses. Nationalisation, however, is not without its problems. Objectives have to be specified,

pricing, investment and financial rules are required; and performance has to be monitored. Problems have often arisen because of the lack of clearly specified objectives or because of changing and conflicting aims, resulting from the need to balance concerns about economic efficiency, technical efficiency, anti-inflationary pricing policies, social objectives and financial targets.

Economists seeking economically efficient solutions are fond of proposing **marginal cost pricing rules** for nationalised industries, requiring them to set price equal to long run marginal cost. However, 'marginal cost' has to be defined and measured, and difficulties arise where State industries are monopolies not subject to competitive pressures. In such circumstances, the lack of contestability is likely to be associated with organisational slack and X-inefficiency: marginal cost is whatever the chairman of the nationalised industry says it is! Moreover, in decreasing cost industries, marginal cost pricing will be associated with losses. In such circumstances, losses are consistent with an economically-efficient solution and are not an indication of inefficiency. However, marginal cost pricing is further criticised on second-best grounds. Where prices do not equal marginal cost throughout the economy, the appropriate second-best pricing rule for a nationalised industry is likely to require a departure from strict marginal cost pricing.

Actual pricing policies for the UK nationalised industries have varied from a requirement to break even (that is, average cost pricing), to marginal cost pricing to a requirement to act commercially. Marginal cost pricing was introduced following a 1967 White Paper. In a 1978 White Paper a further element was introduced, requiring nationalised industries to aim at a **real rate of return** on their new investment programmes of 5 per cent (8 per cent in 1993). The required rate of return is reviewed periodically and is related to the return achieved by private companies, thereby ensuring that the nationalised industries do not divert resources away from more valuable alternatives. Also, since 1976, the nationalised industries and most other public corporations have been subject to **external financing limits** (EFLs) which control the amount of finance, whether grants or borrowing, which an industry may raise during the financial year to supplement its income from normal trading.

Since 1979 the government has been concerned about the efficiency and losses incurred by the nationalised industries and has sought to reduce the size of this sector through denationalisation or privatisation. By 1989, the government's major aim for the nationalised industries was to 'ensure their effectiveness and efficiency as commercial concerns and to strengthen them to the point where they can be transferred to the private sector or, where necessary, remain as successful businesses within the public sector' (Cmnd 621, 1989, p. 62). As a successful public sector business, they are expected to minimise the burden on the taxpayer (via subsidies), earn an economic return on their assets and improve their commercial performance. In other words, the remaining nationalised industries are to act commercially. If such an objective is interpreted as profit maximisation, it will promote technical efficiency but, in the absence of competition, it will not produce allocative efficiency.

During the 1980s a substantial number of nationalised industries have been privatised. In 1979, the nationalised industries accounted for some 9 per cent of GDP and employed over 1.8 million people; by 1991, the corresponding figures were under 2.5 per cent and some 500 000 employees. During this period, the productivity of the nationalised industries increased substantially, reflecting efficiency improvements, reductions in overmanning and the incentive of possible privatisation. Between 1979 and 1992, average annual productivity growth of the nationalised industries was 3.9 per cent, exceeding that for both manufacturing (3.5 per cent) and the economy as a whole (1.9 per cent). By 1993, the remaining UK nationalised industries were British Coal, British Rail, British Waterways, Caledonian MacBrayne (services to remote islands), the Civil Aviation Authority, London Transport, Nuclear Electric and the Post Office, together with such public corporations as the BBC (British Broadcasting Corporation), the Commonwealth Development Corporation and the Urban Development Corporations. How-

ever, by 1993, plans had been announced for the privatisation of British Rail, London buses and British Coal (this last to be sold in five regions with private firms allowed to bid for one or more regions).

11.5.2 Privatisation: a Classification System

Privatisation has been a central feature of the successive Conservative governments elected since 1979. The policy has embraced denationalisation or selling off State assets, deregulation (liberalisation) and competitive tendering. Public sector assets have been sold to the private sector in the form of both offers for sale/tenders to the general public and institutions and private sales (trade sales and management buy-outs). Examples of public offers include British Aerospace, British Airways, British Gas, British Steel, British Telecom, Cable & Wireless, Regional Electricity companies, Rolls-Royce and the water companies (see **Table 11.6**). Trade sales/buy-outs have included the assets of the National Enterprise Board, the National Freight Corporation, BR hotels, International Aeradio, shipbuilding yards, National Bus, Scottish Bus, Royal Ordnance factories, Unipart, Short Brothers, Harland & Wolff and the Trust Ports. A number of markets have been deregulated, thereby reducing or removing restrictions on new entrants. Examples include short and long-distance bus services (Transport Acts 1980 and 1985), the Stock Exchange, opticians and building societies offering banking services, together with the emergence of Mercury as a rival supplier of telecommunications services. Finally, a range of services provided by central and local government, by the NHS and the Armed Forces have been exposed to rivalry through competitive tendering and contracting out. Examples include catering, cleaning and laundry services, refuse collection and the maintenance of grounds and vehicles (Bishop and Kay, 1988).

The distinction between government (public) and private finance and provision can be used to classify the different forms of UK privatisation

Table 11.6 *UK Privatisations*

		Percentage Sold[1]	Gross Proceeds (£m)		
			Company	Government	Total
Amersham	1982	99	6	65[3]	71
AB Ports	1983	49.0	56[4]	(34)	22
	1984	48.5	–	52	52
BAA	1987	95.6	–	1281	1281
British Aerospace	1981	51.6	100	50	150
	1985	59.0	188	363	551
British Airways	1987	100	–	900	900
British Gas	1986	97	(2286)[2]	7720	5434
British Petroleum	1979	5.2	–	290	290
	1983	7.2	–	566	566
	1987	36.8	1515	5370	6885
British Steel	1988	99	–	2425	2425
BT	1984	50.2	1290[5]	2626	3916
	1991	25.6	–	5240	5240
	1993	21.9	–	5335	5335
Britoil	1982	51.0	–	641	641
	1985	48.0	–	449	449
Cable & Wireless	1981	49.4	35	189	224
	1983	22.0	–	275	275
	1985	31.0	331	602	933
Enterprise Oil	1984	100	–	392	392
Jaguar	1984	99	–	294	294
National Power/PowerGen	1991	60		2186	2186
Northern Ireland Electricity	1993	96.5		362	362
Regional Electricity	1990	96		7907	7907[6]
Rolls-Royce	1987	97	283	1080	1363
Scottish Hydro/ScottishPower	1991	96	–	3481	3481[7]
Water Companies	1989	97	–	5239	5239[8]

Notes:

[1] May total more than 100% due to rights issues or less than 100% due to shares retained for loyalty bonus arrangements and/or free/matching offers for eligible employees.

[2] New debt created (unsecured debentures).

[3] Including debt repaid.

[4] Debt extinguished at time of sale.

[5] Debt written off.

[6] Including debt repayment of £2815 million.

[7] Including debt repayment of £626 million.

[8] To which should be added the introduction of debt and from which should be subtracted cash injected into the companies, to leave net proceeds of £3594 million.

Figure 11.3   *Classifying Privatisation*

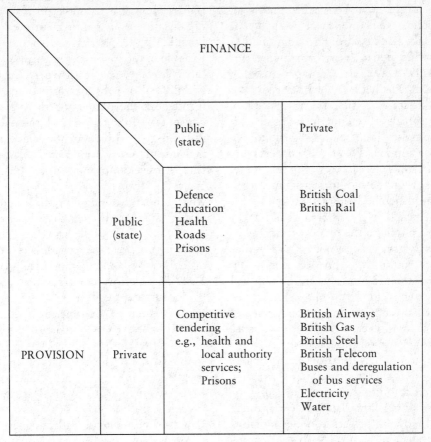

policy. Such a classification system is shown in **Figure 11.3**, which provides a useful starting point for analysis and also allows the rival advocates of private and State ownership to contemplate horizontal, vertical and diagonal movements between the boxes. Inevitably, **Figure 11.3** is only a broad classification system. For instance, State-owned enterprises selling products to private markets may also receive subsidies (British Coal and British Rail), and there are privately-owned schools and hospitals. In addition, monopolies transferred from the public to the private sector are subject to regulatory constraints. In the case of airports and the privatised utilities (namely, electricity, gas, telecommunications and water), the regulatory agencies impose a pricing rule known as RPI–X, where RPI is the retail price index and X is a percentage figure. This rule imposes a ceiling on the annual increase in a firm's prices which will always be X per cent below the general inflation rate (for example, RPI-7.5% for BT). Even so, the early 1990s financial results of the major privatised utilities led to public criticism of excessive profits and overcharging, reflecting their monopoly power. Critics have also pointed to the deliberate and substantial underpricing of some privatisations, where the beneficiaries were the financial institutions (underwriters).

11.5.3 Objectives of Privatisation Policy

Current privatisation policy has been associated with various objectives, some of which are in conflict. Consumers are expected to benefit from rivalry, more choice, greater efficiency and innovation. The policy is also aimed at reducing the size of the public sector through denationalisation, and reducing public sector borrowing (for example, by 1993, proceeds from privatisation were £50 billion). Furthermore, it has been associated with a desire for wider share ownership. Suggestions have also been made that the real purpose of the policy is to reduce the monopoly power of trade unions. There are conflicts between some of these objectives. For example, reducing the size of the public sector and maximising Treasury income from selling public assets can be achieved by transferring monopoly power from the public to the private sector without increasing rivalry. It is, of course, likely that the actual extent and form of privatisation policy will reflect the influence of agents in the political market place: namely, governments seeking votes and established interest groups (managers and workers) trying to protect their positions, especially their income and on-the-job leisure.

The debate about privatisation in its wider aspects raises the general question of whether ownership is an important determinant of economic performance. The 1980s Government claimed that following privatisation, productivity and profitability in the newly-privatised companies increased dramatically (as in the case, for example, of British Aerospace, Jaguar and the National Freight Consortium). The official explanation offered is that:

> the overwhelming majority of employees have become shareholders in the newly privatised companies. They want their companies to succeed. Their companies have been released from the detailed controls of Whitehall and given more freedom to manage their own affairs. And they have been exposed to the full commercial disciplines of the customer. Even former monopolies now face increased competition. (Conservative Party Manifesto, 1987, p. 36)

This suggests a model in which improvements in economic performance depend not only upon ownership, but also on competition and managerial freedom (for example, in respect of internal organisation and employment contracts). Others would add the external environment as a further variable in the model in the form of, for example, the Thatcher effect via Rayner scrutinies, and the withdrawal of subsidies providing a shock effect throughout the public and private sectors (Dunsire et al., 1988). Some of these complex and sometimes interdependent issues can be simplified into a two variable model showing the impact of ownership and market structure on efficiency. A framework is shown in **Figure 11.4**, where the following hypotheses on enterprise performance or efficiency can be formulated:

1 *D* is superior to *A*, where *D* represents private ownership and a competitive product market.
2 *D* is superior to *C*: neo-classical economics favours competition.
3 *D* is equal to, or superior to, *B*: does ownership matter? One review of the evidence suggests that under competition, private firms are likely to be superior (Kay and Thompson, 1986, p. 16).
4 *B* is superior to *A*, reflecting the role of competition.
5 *C* is superior to *A*, reflecting the policing role of private capital markets.
6 *B* could be superior, inferior or equal to *C* (inconclusive) depending on the relative strengths of competition and ownership.

Testing hypotheses about the effects of ownership and market structure on enterprise performance and efficiency is not without its problems. Indicators are required to measure enterprise performance and, ultimately, economic efficiency. Some crude performance indicators are readily available such as profitability, labour productivity and international competitiveness, and tests can be undertaken to determine whether performance improves following a change from public to private ownership, **ceteris paribus**. It should be borne in mind that an increase in profitability might reflect the exercise of market power by a newly-privatised monopolist, and higher labour productivity could reflect invest-

Figure 11.4 *Ownership and Market Structure: a Taxonomy*

	Monopoly	Competition
Public Ownership	A 1 Absence of competition induces technical inefficiency 2 No fear of going bankrupt 3 Government intervention distorts decision making 4 Potential for allocative efficiency (price=marginal cost)	B 1 Market forces promote greater technical efficiency 2 Still no fear of bankruptcy 3 Government intervention still distorts decision making 4 Potential for allocative efficiency
Private Ownership	C 1 Fear of bankruptcy 2 No government intervention 3 Pressure exerted by shareholders	D 1 Competition induces technical efficiency 2 Fear of bankruptcy 3 No government intervention 4 Pressure exerted by shareholders 5 Allocative efficiency

ment in new equipment. Moreover, empirical tests of performance before and after an ownership change need to allow for what would have happened without the change, and the distinct possibility that a transfer of ownership will result in the pursuit of different objectives. There are, however, alternative policies for influencing enterprise performance, with subsidies as an obvious option.

■ *11.6 Subsidy Policy*

□ *11.6.1 A Classification System*

At their simplest, subsidies are payments by government to producers which are designed to reduce prices. Such a definition can be modified to allow for payments to firms and industries to ensure their survival or to prevent contraction. More generally, subsidies are a means of affecting the **allocation and use of resources** in the economy, thereby interfering in the operation of markets. The issue is, however, whether such interference is desirable.

Over time, British governments have offered various subsidies to firms, industries, regions and to factors of production. Examples have included private firms such as British Leyland and Chrysler, private and State industries such as aerospace, computers, cotton, steel and shipbuilding, as well as high unemployment regions (namely development areas). Subsidies have been used to achieve specific policy objectives such as maintaining or increasing employment, assisting the balance of payments through export promotion and import-saving, and encouraging growth through supporting high technology. At times, the range of industrial subsidies has been bewildering, and so extensive that questions have arisen as to whether there are any economic activities in the UK which should not qualify for a subsidy!

As a starting point in analysing subsidies, a classification system is required. Subsidies can be classified in at least three related ways, as outlined below.

General and Specific Types

General schemes offer subsidies to all firms satisfying certain conditions which might relate to investment, location, employment, size of firm or type of activity (for example, agriculture, manufacturing or tourism). General schemes have been the traditional method of subsidising UK industry. They are automatic and aim to influence industry decisions and hence the operation of markets without involving substantial transaction costs. In contrast, specific or discretionary schemes are designed for an individual firm or project, with subsidies being used to prevent bankruptcy and plant closure or to promote re-organisation, re-equipment and restructuring. Or, again, specific subsidies might be offered for the development of a new high technology project, such as a supersonic airliner or a new generation of computer. In principle, specific schemes aim at fine tuning by setting the subsidy at the minimum level required to influence a firm's decisions. However, this approach involves substantial transaction costs. It requires detailed information about a firm's costs and its efficiency, and it assumes that civil servants will be motivated to negotiate the minimum subsidy. Further costs will be incurred in bargaining, monitoring and policing. Critics claim that public servants may be influenced in their decisions by the prospect of employment in industry, or that specific subsidies result in an undesirable cosiness between civil servants and the firms with which they negotiate.

The Production Function Approach

A distinction can be made between subsidies for outputs and for factor inputs. Farmers, for example, receive output subsidies. Factor inputs can also be subsidised, the aim being to encourage and increase the use of relatively cheaper (subsidised) factors. Input subsidies embrace capital, labour and technology, and examples include incentives to invest in new plant and machinery, to substitute labour for capital and to increase R&D.

The Geographic or Location Dimension

Subsidies in their general and specific forms, for inputs and outputs, can be tied to specially designated areas of the country embracing development areas, intermediate areas, enterprise zones, free ports and inner cities.

During the 1960s and 1970s, UK expenditure on subsidies increased substantially from under 2 per cent of GDP at market prices and around 4 per cent of government expenditure in 1965 to corresponding figures of almost 4 per cent and around 7–8 per cent respectively in 1975. The government since 1979 has taken a different attitude towards a general and massive subsidy policy. Indeed, **Table 11.7** shows the declining trend in government subsidies between 1987 and 1993. As a further indication of the government's industrial policy, the annual level of real spending by the DTI declined substantially during the late 1980s, whilst privatisation proceeds were much greater than the Department's budget. In view of the major contrasts between the 1970s and 1980s, questions have to be asked about the economic logic of UK subsidy policy.

11.6.2 Economic Theory and Subsidies

A **market failure approach** suggests that subsidies are required whenever there are substantial and beneficial externalities or social benefits. Alternatively, subsidies might be required to cover the **losses associated with marginal cost pricing** applied to a decreasing cost industry. Whilst a number of UK firms and nationalised industries have received subsidies to reduce losses and to prevent closure, usually these have not been associated with marginal cost pricing and decreasing costs. Instead, subsidies have more often been justified on grounds of social benefits. The argument is that private markets, if left to themselves, will provide too little of some socially desirable activities so that subsidies are required to correct this market failure. Typically, governments have used the social benefits argument to justify subsidies to protect jobs, to promote high technology and to support the balance of payments, all of which are deemed to be in the national or public interest. Economists need to assess these arguments critically, subjecting them to economic analysis and empirical evidence.

The methodology of economic policy can be applied to subsidy policy, although critics might

Table 11.7 *DTI Programmes*

DTI Expenditure[1]	1987–8	1988–9	1989–90	1990–91	1991–92	1992–93
Total expenditure (cash) £m	1491	2183	1589	1600	1401	1456
Total expenditure (real at 1991–92 prices)	1967	2685	1834	1711	1401	1396
Privatisation	5140	7069	4226	5346	7923	8000
Expenditure on major programmes (£m at current prices)						
Regional and general industrial support	684	796	719	628	582	582
Support for aerospace, shipbuilding, coal, steel and vehicle manufacture	456	1287	708	390	224	198
Scientific and technological assistance	470	545	474	521	525	541
Trade and technological support	361	366	627	696	567	512
Government subsidies	5950	4963	5296	5965	6393	6674
GDP deflator (1991–92 = 100)	75.8	81.3	86.6	93.5	100	104.3
Subsidies as % of public expenditure	3.3	2.7	2.6	2.7	2.6	2.5

Note:
[1] DTI now includes Energy.
Source: HM Treasury, *The Government's Expenditure Plans, 1993–4 to 1995–6*, Cmnd 2219 (1993).

claim that it is a counsel of perfection. The objectives of policy have to be clearly stated. The causes of the policy problem have to be identified, and it needs to be shown that subsidies are the most appropriate and efficient solution from the alternatives available. For example, with regional policy, the aim might be to increase employment in the high unemployment areas of the country. However, this might conflict with the objective of promoting a reallocation of resources from declining to expanding regions and encouraging firms to locate in their most efficient areas. Questions then arise about the causes of local unemployment. Is it, for example, due to high wages failing to reflect local labour scarcities; do firms elsewhere lack information about local labour supplies; are there infrastructure deficiencies which raise the costs to firms locating in the area; is the housing market impairing labour mobility; or is the capital market failing to finance worthwhile human investments in mobility and training? From this analysis of causes, it does not follow that subsidies to firms in high unemployment areas are the most appropriate and efficient solution. Questions have to be asked about the effectiveness of policy: has it achieved its objectives? If so, at what cost? Regional policy, which offers a variety of incentives and subsidies to firms located in high unemployment areas, is an obvious candidate for evaluation.

☐ *11.6.3 Regional Policy*

Markets are changing continuously and the results of change are reflected in the expansion and decline of different regions in the UK. High unemployment areas in northern England, Scotland, Wales and Northern Ireland are associated with the decline of the UK's traditional smokestack industries such as coal, shipbuilding, steel and textiles. Sunrise industries, such as electronics, have developed elsewhere. In the 1990s, cuts in defence budgets will mean that UK and other EU regions dependent on defence industries and bases will be vulnerable to job losses.

The regional policy problem arises because markets do not adjust instantly, and because private markets do not consider the social costs and benefits of their activities (externalities). Successive UK governments have thus intervened to correct regional imbalances by seeking to reduce the regional differentials in unemployment rates. However, problems have arisen because the objectives of regional policy are often social and political rather than economic. Budget-conscious government departments can offer schemes to solve regional unemployment which will be supported by producers likely to benefit and by governments attracted by the likely favourable effects on votes.

A new UK regional policy was introduced in 1984. This was a result of substantial economic changes which had occurred in the 1970s, with UK membership of the EU, the oil crisis and higher national unemployment. It was estimated that between 1972 and 1983, the previous regional policy created some 500 000 more jobs in the assisted areas at an Exchequer expenditure of £35 000 per job (at 1982 prices). Nevertheless, it was felt that the 1970s regional policy was not cost-effective or sufficiently selective; it discriminated against services; it favoured capital-intensive projects; and it often resulted in a transfer of jobs and a failure to emphasise job creation.

Under the policy introduced in 1984, there were two types of region or assisted area (namely, development areas and intermediate areas), together with two types of grant (namely, **Regional Development Grants**, or RDGs, and **Regional Selective Assistance**, or RSA). Firms in development areas qualified for both RDGs and RSA. RDGs were automatic and paid at 15 per cent of eligible capital expenditure subject to a cost ceiling per job or, where higher, at £3000 for each new full-time job created (at 1989 prices). In 1988–89, it was estimated that RDGs had led to some 56 000 jobs for an Exchequer outlay of £220 million. The RDG scheme was phased out in 1988.

In 1993, there were two main regional incentives, namely, RSA and **Regional Enterprise Grants** (REGs). RSA is available for investment projects which create or safeguard jobs in the assisted areas. It is not an automatic scheme and there is no fixed grant rate. RSA is negotiated as the minimum necessary for the project to proceed. By the end of 1992, RSA had supported some 134 000 jobs (for example, in 1992–93, RSA supported 15 385 new jobs and safeguarded 6062 jobs). REGs were introduced in 1988. They are available to small companies based in assisted areas and they offer limited grants for innovation and investment projects (maximum grants of £25 000 and £15 000 respectively in 1993).In addition, there is an Urban Regeneration Agency (incorporating English Industrial Estates) and UK Government support is available for inner cities, enterprise zones and free ports. Regional support is also provided through the European Community's Regional Development Fund. In 1993, the EU agreed a new initiative, known as KONVER, as part of its Regional Fund. KONVER provides funds to those areas in the EU particularly dependent on, and especially vulnerable to cuts in, defence spending. KONVER funds are available for a variety of measures to assist regional adjustment to disarmament (for example, training, innovation, conversion).

A further change occurred in UK regional policy in 1993 with the announcement of a new assisted areas map, defining those areas of Great Britain eligible for regional funds. The previous assisted areas map dated from 1984 and the new map represents the government's assessment of those areas now facing structural unemployment problems. New areas which have become eligible for regional aid include the South-East (for example, East Kent, inner areas of London, south-eastern coastal towns); coalfield areas in the Midlands and Yorkshire affected by pit closures; and areas subject to closures or manpower reductions at defence establishments or major defence suppliers. As a result, the assisted areas will cover 34 per cent of the working population of Great Britain (slightly less than in 1984).

Critics of current UK regional policy claim that it represents a move towards a free market approach, with reductions in special support for the regions and an emphasis on improving the operation of product and factor (including labour) markets throughout the economy. They claim that there will be too little government assistance and financial support to solve the regional problem, and they also assert that there is a need for more policy instruments. In particular, supporters of an interventionist policy favour **Industrial Development Certificates** (IDCs) as a means of controlling new factory buildings and extensions, thereby influencing the location decisions of firms. Originally, IDCs were used to reduce congestion in London and the South-East and to promote activity in the assisted areas, but they were no longer used after 1982.

Nonetheless, whether an interventionist or **laissez-faire** approach is preferred, there remain some outstanding issues for regional policy. Questions arise about the aims of policy and the potential conflicts between efficiency and social objectives; about whether policy is simply transferring jobs between different parts of the country; and ultimately, about the beneficiaries from the policy. But regional policy is not the only form of support for UK industry. The DTI also offers selective assistance to individual firms and industries (for example, aerospace and shipbuilding); it has a variety of measures for supporting small firms (for example, one-stop shops; consultancy; loan guarantees); it encourages business to develop a positive and competitive response to environmental issues; and there is a major programme of support for industrial innovation.

☐ *11.6.4 Technology Policy*

Government support for science, technology and R&D is designed to improve the efficiency, competitiveness and innovative capacity of the UK (Cmnd 621, 1989, p. 25). But why is State intervention required? Here, the argument is that R&D is risky, it may take a long time to produce marketable results and the benefits are likely to extend far beyond a single innovating firm. On this basis, it is argued that if left to themselves, **private markets will fail to provide the socially desirable amount of R&D** and will encourage the hoarding of valuable ideas, so resulting in too little innovation and its dissemination, with adverse effects on economic growth. Such market failure reflects at least three factors: in the first place, a belief that capital markets will fail to finance large-scale, risky and long-term projects; second, it might reflect the costs of establishing property rights in valuable ideas; third, the pursuit of profits might lead to the hoarding of valuable ideas and a failure to generate the socially desirable transfer of knowledge throughout the economy.

Persuasive though these arguments appear, they are often long on emotion and short on economic analysis, critical content and empirical evidence. For example, what might appear to be market failures in research and scientific activity might simply reflect the diversity of solutions adopted by firms to economise on transaction costs. Similarly, it is not sufficiently convincing evidence of a capital market failure to claim that it failed to provide funds for such high-technology projects as Airbus and *Concorde*. In such cases, the capital market might be working properly and judging that the projects are likely to be unprofitable. After all, the UK capital market has funded large-scale, long-term and risky projects such as the Channel Tunnel and the North Sea oilfields. Neither does it follow that State intervention will take an impartial long-term view, independent of the political market including a government's need to be re-elected. In fact, public choice analysis predicts that governments can also fail.

Once governments decide to intervene in research and scientific markets they are faced with **a complex choice set**. Decisions are needed on support for basic or applied research and technology transfer; on training the appropriate number and mix of different types of scientists and engineers; and on whether to offer support in the form of cash incentives (such as subsidies), tariff protection, patent legislation, or public procurement. Further choices are required on whether to support key high-technology industries such as aerospace, electronics and telecommunications and, if so, whether to favour **small or large firms and a competitive, oligopolistic or monopoly industry structure**. Here, the evidence suggests that an industry with many moderate-to-large firms of relatively similar size will be the most technically progressive, and that a market structure intermediate between monopoly and perfect competition would promote the highest rate of inventive activity (Kamien and Schwartz, 1982, p. 3).

Some of the results of UK government choices on science and technology policy are shown in **Table 11.8**. Defence is the largest programme, followed by the Office of Science and Technology, Education and the DTI. Within defence R&D, some 60 per cent of expenditure is allocated to the aerospace and electronics industries. Moreover, the large share of defence in government spending on science and technology led the Ministry of Defence in 1987 to admit that defence R&D may crowd out valuable investment in the civil sector, so impairing industry's ability to compete in international markets for civil high-technology products. Interestingly, though, between 1987 and 1993, there was no dramatic shift in the relative shares of government spending on military and civil technology (but see plans for 1995–96).

The DTI has a major programme of assistance for industrial innovation. In recent years, policy has changed from support for near-market R&D to support for long-term research collaboration,

Table 11.8   *Government Spending on Science and Technology*

Department	Expenditure (current prices £m)				
	1987–88	1990–91	1991–92	1992–93	1995–96 (Plans)
Defence	2 156	2 337	2 410	2 791	2 580
Office of Science and Technology*	660	914	943	1 059	1 272
DTI	560	494	480	491	449
Education	743	838	924	982	1021
Total	4 675	5 314	5 500	6 055	6 094
of which: Civil science and technology	2 492	2 888	3 094	3 302	3 589
% civil	53	54	56	55	59

* Research Councils included in office of Science and Technology.

Source: Cmnd 2219 (1993); *DTI Expenditure Plans*, 1993–4 to 1995–6, Cmnd 2204 (1993).

technology transfer and measures for small firms. The DTI has encouraged collaborative programmes, involving European firms (Eureka), as well as collaboration between government, industry and higher education. It has also promoted technology transfer where the market may be slow to adapt (for example, information technology and modern materials). In addition, the DTI has provided further support for specific sectors, namely aircraft, aero-engine and civil space research programmes, together with launch aid for civil aerospace projects. Interestingly, both the defence and DTI R&D programmes offer substantial public sector support to the UK aerospace industry. In evaluating government support for civil aircraft programmes, one study concluded that between 1945 and 1975 the net effect of aerospace launching aid has been a net loss of national welfare (Gardner, 1976, p. 149). In contrast, a 1993 Parliamentary Report recommended that the government increase its funding towards aerospace research and technology to a level which is sufficient to maintain the UK industry's technology competitiveness (HCP 563, 1993).

☐ 11.6.5 European Collaboration

The trend towards the rising costs of some advanced technology projects means that the minimum entry costs are so high that it is necessary for a number of large firms or even nations to combine. Even before the completion of the single internal market in the EU, there have been some notable examples of European government involvement in collaborative programmes. These include Airbus, *Concorde*, the European Centre for Nuclear Research, ESPRIT (an information technology programme), the European Space Agency and a series of joint defence ventures mainly involving military aircraft, helicopters and missiles such as the three-nation Tornado and the four-nation European Fighter Aircraft. For these projects, European collaboration reflects the fact that independence based on small national markets is too costly.

Europe's high-technology industries (such as aerospace, defence, electronics and telecommuni-

cations) are frequently criticised for the wasteful duplication of costly R&D and for the relatively short production runs resulting from a dependence on a small domestic market. International collaboration is often presented as the appropriate solution leading, so it is claimed, to the eventual creation of European-wide high technology industries capable of competing with Japan and the USA in world markets. Supporters of European collaboration in high technology claim a variety of benefits, as indicated below:

a   cost savings for both R&D and production.
b   the sharing of risks and costs allows projects to be undertaken which would be too costly on an independent national basis (for example, space satellites and a supersonic airliner);
c   the creation of a European industry able to compete in world markets for high-technology products, so avoiding Europe becoming a nation of metal bashers;
d   a set of general economic and political benefits in the form of domestic jobs, the balance of payments, rivalry in ideas and the creation of a united Europe through reducing national barriers and prejudice.

The simple economics of collaboration are shown in **Figure 11.5**. Consider the case of a two-nation collaborative military aircraft project based on equal sharing of R&D costs and a pooling of national orders. In the ideal case, each nation bears only 50 per cent of the development costs compared with an independent national venture and gains from the doubling of output which, through learning economies, will reduce unit production costs by about 10 per cent.

Collaboration, however, has some disadvantages and costs leading to departures from the ideal model. Where governments are involved, substantial transaction costs arise as each partner nation seeks to establish property rights in the joint programme. Bargaining between partner governments, their bureaucracies and customers (such as the Armed Forces), together with lobbying from producer groups of scientists and contractors, can lead to substantial inefficiencies. Work might be shared on political, equity and

Figure 11.5 *The Economics of Collaboration*

a   R&D Costs

b   Unit Production Costs

bargaining criteria and not on the basis of efficiency and competition. Each partner will demand its fair share of high-technology work. Also, there might be substantial administrative costs in the form of duplicate organisations, frequent committee meetings, delays in decision making and excessive government involvement in monitoring and policing international contracts. As a result, collaborative programmes involving governments might lead to higher costs and take longer to develop than a national project.

The Airbus civil airliner is often quoted as one of the successes of European collaboration. Airbus entered the Boeing-dominated market for jet airliners and achieved a market share of 27 per cent by the early 1990s; but this market penetration was at a cost in terms of subsidies. One study has estimated that the net welfare effect of Airbus

market entry is negative for Europe, suggesting that the Airbus project has actually decreased European welfare (Klepper, 1990). Government involvement in collaboration also raises wider issues of public purchasing, and we must accordingly turn to consider the likely effects of government purchasing on industrial performance.

■ *11.7* **Public Purchasing**

☐ *11.7.1 Scope of Government Procurement*

Government purchasing is big business. Government purchases range from standard items such as clothing, paper clips, furniture, motor cars, office equipment and accommodation, to more complex products such as computers, space satellites, nuclear power stations and Trident submarines. Such purchases have the potential for influencing industrial performance. Defence and Health are the major spending departments, purchasing from industries such as aerospace, electronics, ordnance, shipbuilding, pharmaceuticals and medical equipment.

Government purchasing from private and State-owned enterprises involves **choices about a product, a contractor and a contract.** Decisions are required on the type of goods and services to be purchased, the selection of a contractor and the choice of a contract. Often such choices provide scope for governments to pursue wider economic and social objectives and not simply the acquisition of goods and services. Considerations of the national interest might lead a government to purchase from higher-cost domestic suppliers so as to protect a nation's key strategic industries, its technology, jobs and the balance of payments. The pursuit of such wider ends makes it difficult for Parliament and independent analysts to determine whether public procurement is giving good value for money. However, privatisation results in the transfer of purchasing from the public to the private sector, where commercial criteria rather than wider public interest considerations dominate procurement choices.

The range and complexity of public procurement choices can be illustrated by considering two limiting models. At one extreme, the government as the buyer knows what it wants, the products exist and they are being traded in competitive-type markets. In these circumstances, the State acts as a competitive buyer, specifies its requirements, invites competitive tenders and awards a fixed price contract to the lowest bidder. Problems arise at the other extreme where the government is the only buyer, is uncertain about its requirements, and the product does not yet exist (as is often the case for high-technology products such as defence equipment and telecommunications). Moreover, the domestic market might contain only one or relatively few actual or potential suppliers. The government as the major, or only, buyer might have to select a contractor and to write a contract for a project which perhaps does not yet exist, might involve a major jump in the state of the art and where the contractor requires a cost-based contract with a substantial proportion of the risks borne by the State. Contracts for such advanced technology projects are often associated with cost overruns, time slippages and major modifications and sometimes with cancellations (for example, the Nimrod project) leading to allegations of waste, incompetence and contractor inefficiency.

Where a government department is a major buyer, as with defence equipment, the NHS, nuclear power and railway equipment, its procurement choices and contracting policies can have a decisive effect on an industry's size, structure, entry and exit, technical progress, efficiency, prices and profitability. For example, non-competitive government contracts, as with some defence equipment and pharmaceuticals for the NHS, are subject to state regulatory constraints. A Review Board for Non-Competitive Government Contracts and a Pharmaceutical Profit Regulation Scheme are designed to ensure that government contractors receive a reasonable rate of return on capital, where 'reasonable' usually means a profit rate similar to the average return earned by British industry. However, firms respond and adapt to regulatory constraints. The possibility of post-costing and renegotiation of excessive profits provides firms with an inducement to sacrifice profits for expenditures which give satisfaction (utility) to the company's managers, such as company cars, luxury offices and the hoarding of scientists.

For many years, there have been continued debates about whether coordinated government purchasing might improve industrial performance through, for example, exploiting the economies of scale associated with combining and standardising orders from different State agencies. Since 1979, the emphasis has been on achieving better value for money from public purchasing. Government departments have been subject to Rayner scrutinies, budgets have been cash limited, civil service manpower has been reduced and functions traditionally undertaken in-house have been contracted out to private firms. Also, in 1984, an official review concluded that government procurement was costing the taxpayer too much, mainly due to administration costs and because the prices paid were often higher than necessary. At the same time, defence has been the focus of a major initiative in the form of its competitive procurement policy, which was launched officially in 1984.

Evidence suggests that there is substantial scope for improving the efficiency of public procurement, not only in the UK but throughout the EU. As the only or major buyer, governments will be lobbied to buy British, thereby preventing foreign firms bidding for UK Government contracts. In fact, protection and support for domestic industries (national champions) characterises public procurement throughout the EU. The creation of the Single European Market will enable public procurement for civil goods and services to benefit from increased competition, free trade and economies of scale. It has been estimated that open public procurement throughout the EU would result in aggregate savings for the 12 member states equivalent to some 0.6 per cent of 1986 Community GDP (Cecchini 1988, p. 17). For the UK, ending protectionism and introducing open competition into public procurement at the national and local levels might produce price savings of 25 per cent in coal and 40 per cent in pharmaceuticals (Cecchini, 1988, pp. 19–20). The

UK's experience with competitive tendering further illustrates the potential gains from a more competitive public procurement policy.

☐ *11.7.2 Competitive Tendering*

Competitive tendering and contracting-out is potentially a vast area, covering the possible use of private contractors for a whole range of public sector services. Contracting-out is one element of the current government's privatisation policy. It is concerned with the central or local government **financing** of services which could be **supplied** by private contractors. By the late 1980s, it was the focus of major policy initiatives in local government, the NHS, defence and other parts of central government. Cleaning, catering, laundry, refuse collection, maintenance and security services are popular examples (see box below). With its emphasis on better value for money, government policy aims to extend the use of private contractors by public bodies where this will increase their economy, efficiency and effectiveness. By 1993, the policy had been extended to prisons and prison escort services.

Contracting-out can be viewed as an aspect of public procurement policy since it involves the public sector purchasing goods and services from private firms. As such, the debate about contracting-out is not new. For example, within the NHS, there is a tradition of buying pharmaceutical products, high-technology medical equipment and buildings from private firms. Similarly, within defence there is a long tradition of buying weapons and equipment from private firms.

Consideration now needs to be given to the basic policy problem: how do public bodies such as NHS hospitals assess the efficiency of their direct labour departments and in-house services? The starting point is that direct labour departments are usually monopoly suppliers of services, protected from possible public and private sector rivals. In the absence of competition from rival departments and from private contractors, there are no alternative sources of information and no alternative cost yardsticks to assess the efficiency of a public agency. Here, efficiency is defined to embrace two aspects. In the first place, it is concerned with the lowest-cost method of supplying a given quantity and quality of service. Second, it is also concerned with the lowest-cost

Local Authorities

1 Since legislation in 1908, direct labour organisations are required to compete with private firms for most of their construction and maintenance work
2 The Local Government Act 1988 extended compulsory tendering to refuse collection, catering, cleaning streets and buildings, the maintenance of grounds and vehicles and the management of LA sport and leisure facilities
3 Other possibilities for contracting-out might include accountancy, architectural services, careers advice, computer and data processing services, housing sales and fire protection

NHS

1 DHSS introduced competitive tendering for hospital catering, cleaning and laundry services (domestic services)
2 Other possibilities could include ambulance and transport services, the contracting-out of major surgery and patient care to private hospitals, together with hospital management, and care for the elderly, disabled and mentally handicapped.

Ministry of Defence

Current examples include catering and cleaning at defence establishments, the refitting of warships (traditionally undertaken in the Royal Dockyards), some limited aircraft servicing and vehicle repair, air transport, the management of stores and elementary flying training method of supplying **different** levels of service. This second aspect of efficiency enables a local authority or hospital to determine whether its existing level of service is worthwhile. For example, a lower level of service might be so much cheaper that the extra cost of the existing provision is deemed not to be worthwhile.

Contracting-out is offered as a solution to the problem of public sector monopolies which are criticised as inefficient bureaucracies responding to the wishes of producer groups rather than consumers. To its supporters, competitive tendering, or even the threat of rivalry (contestability) means improved efficiency and cost savings. It allows public procurement agents to recontract with different suppliers and for different levels of service. Competition between rival suppliers leads to the introduction of new ideas, the latest management techniques and modern equipment, thereby resulting in major changes in established and traditional methods of working. New equipment might replace labour; manning levels can be reassessed; and part-time workers might replace full-timers. Successful firms in a competition are also subject to the incentives and penalties of a fixed price contract so that there is no open-ended financial commitment, as can arise with in-house units.

The opponents of contracting-out claim that it leads to a poor quality and unreliable service. Examples are given of dirty streets, schools and hospital wards, and of penalty clauses being imposed on contractors. Proposals for privately-managed prisons have been condemned because of fears of lower standards and conditions in prisons, with discipline determined by profit-conscious managers who have an incentive to 'encourage' returners. Private contractors are also believed to be less reliable than in-house units. For example, it is suggested that they are less able to respond to emergencies; they are liable to default and bankruptcy; and the award of a contract to a private firm leads to industrial relations problems and strikes. On the issue of cost savings, critics claim that these are short-lived. Low bids can be used to buy into an attractive new contract and eliminate the in-house capacity, so that the public authority loses its bargaining power. As a result, it becomes dependent on a private monopoly which, in the long run, means higher prices, a lack of dynamism and a poor quality service. Competitive tendering involves substantial transaction costs which are often ignored by the supporters of contracting-out. Moreover, critics claim that any cost savings from contracting-out are achieved at the expense of the poorly-paid members of society, so that the policy cannot avoid equity issues and debates about the distribution of income. The various arguments are summarised in below.

The arguments for and against provide extensive opportunities for critical analysis and evaluation. Some of the arguments obviously represent special pleading by those interest groups most likely to gain or lose from the policy. However, many of the arguments for and against contracting-out can be resolved by empirical testing. UK studies suggest, for a given level of service, annual cost savings of some 25 per cent over a range of hospital and local authority activities and 20 per cent for refuse collection. Whilst private contractors require longer hours, shorter holidays and withdraw sickness benefits and pension rights, most of the cost savings from contracting-out reflect productivity improvements (Hartley and Huby, 1985; Szymanski and Wilkins, 1993).

If society wants improved efficiency, then privatisation and contracting-out are not sufficient: competition is also required. However, competitive tendering is likely to be associated with contractors lobbying for public sector business and for entry barriers to protect their existing markets and profits. Inevitably, there will be opposition from established interest groups likely to lose from the policy. Opponents of the policy can impose delays by insisting upon discussions with all interested parties; the timing of any change can be inappropriate; administrative time might be unavailable to prepare the tender documents and to undertake the necessary comparative studies, especially in an era of manpower cuts; and an authority might be reluctant to face a confrontation with the trade unions, leading to major industrial relations problems. There is a more fundamental worry. With competitive tendering, choices about the quantity and quality of service

The Case For Contracting-out

1   Public sector in-house monopolies are inefficient bureaucracies

2   Competition allows regular recontracting by public procurement agents

3   Competition leads to new ideas, modern equipment and charges in traditional methods of working

4   Successful firms in a competition are subject to the incentives and penalties of a fixed price contract

The Case Against Contracting-out

1   Private contractors offer a poor quality and unreliable service

2   Private contractors are liable to default, bankruptcy, and are less able to respond to emergencies

3   Contractors use low bids to buy into attractive contracts and eliminate the in-house capacity so that public authority becomes dependent on a private monopoly

4   Private contractors achieve cost savings by cutting jobs, reducing wages and worsening working conditions

provision are ultimately made by elected representatives whose preferences are unlikely to reflect the diversity of preferences of large numbers of individual consumers in properly functioning markets. The government's commitment to better value for money in public purchasing has also been reflected in its new competitive procurement policy for defence equipment.

11.7.3 A Competitive Procurement Policy: The Case of Defence

The Ministry of Defence (MoD) is the largest single customer for the products of British industry, with purchases ranging from simple items such as batteries, cars and furniture to highly complex equipment such as missiles, submarines and advanced combat aircraft. For 1993–94, expenditure on defence equipment totalled £9.9 billion. About 75 per cent of the MoD's defence equipment is purchased directly from UK industry; a further 16 per cent benefits domestic industry through its participation in collaborative programmes; and the remaining 9 per cent is imported. Within the UK, the MoD is a major purchaser of the outputs of the aerospace, shipbuilding ordnance and electronics industries. In 1992–93, the leading UK defence equipment con-

tractors, which were each paid over £250 million by the MoD, were British Aerospace (including Royal Ordnance), GEC, Rolls-Royce, Vickers Shipbuilding and Engineering and Devonport Management.

R&D also forms a substantial part of the defence equipment programme through which it can have a major impact on technical progress in specific sectors of the UK economy, particularly aerospace, electronics and shipbuilding. Also, it is often claimed that there are additional economic benefits associated with spin-offs and technology transfer from defence to the civil sector of the economy. However, the government has announced that necessary investment in defence R&D may crowd out valuable investment in the civil sector and that restraints on government-funded defence R&D spending were required to free resources for civil work. Such a proposition needs to be carefully assessed, particularly the evidence on crowding-out and whether the UK's commitment to defence R&D has adversely affected its international competitiveness. Furthermore, where there is evidence of these adverse effects, it is necessary to discover whether they have arisen because, in the past, cost-plus defence contracts have tended to reduce a firm's innovative drive, and whether the situation will change now that the MoD operates a competitive procurement policy. Issues also arise as to what happens to the resources released from defence

R&D: are they used in civil technology or else-where in the civil sector in the UK; do they remain unemployed; or do they emigrate? It is evident that, in the long run, reduced defence R&D sends out clear signals to the labour market about future employment prospects in military technology work.

Traditionally, MoD procurement policy was characterised by support for UK industry, by non-competitive cost-plus or cost-based contracts, and by contractors bearing none of the risks of the project. Defence contractors were often criticised for cost escalation, delays, labour hoarding, inefficiency and project failures. In 1984, the MoD introduced a new competitive procurement policy in an effort to change the traditional dependency relationship in which defence business was regarded as 'lucrative, not very competitive and a cosy relationship' (HCP 392, 1988, p. vi). The MoD became a more demanding customer, introducing and extending competition and encouraging new entrants, especially small firms. Risks have been shifted from the MoD to industry, with a greater use of firm or fixed price contracts rather than cost-plus contracting. In 1988, a further extension of competition occurred when the MoD announced that it was more willing to purchase equipment from overseas sources where they were likely to offer greater value for money.

The published results of the new competition policy are impressive. In 1979–80, 30 per cent of MoD contracts by value were awarded on a competitive basis and 22 per cent were cost-plus a percentage fee contracts; by 1992–93, the corresponding figures were 56 per cent and 1 per cent, respectively. At the outset of the new policy, a target was announced for achieving cost savings of 10 per cent on the total equipment budget. Some of the actual results of competition have been impressive, with cost savings ranging from 10 per cent to 70 per cent, all of which might be taken as indicators of monopoly pricing and/or inefficiency in UK defence industries. In 1987–88, for example, the median cost saving on a group of 13 equipment projects was 40 per cent, giving total savings of over £100 million. Similarly, there are examples where competition resulted in savings of over £400 million from 10 projects originally expected to cost £2.4 billion.

Competition policy as implemented by the MoD is not without its problems and it is subject to both constraints and conflicts. A potential constraint arises if the MoD or the government is unwilling to impose the ultimate sanction on poor performance by a major contractor: namely, bankruptcy. Until 1988, there was a further constraint in that domestic monopolies dominated the high technology and costly equipment programmes. These comprise British Aerospace (aircraft, missiles, ordnance and small arms), Rolls-Royce (aero-engines), Westland (helicopters), GEC (torpedoes), Vickers Shipbuilding (nuclear-powered submarines) and Vickers (tanks). However, the 1988 announcement that the MoD is willing to buy from overseas means that the threat of competition is likely to increase the contestability of those UK defence markets dominated by domestic monopolies. But conflicts arise between competition policy leading to foreign purchases and support for the UK defence industrial base which appears to offer attractive wider economic and social benefits in the form of security, independence, jobs, technology and an improved balance of payments.

11.7.4 The UK Defence Industrial Base and the Peace Dividend

The debate in 1985–86 over the future of the Westland helicopter company was a classic example of the arguments about the need for a defence industrial base (DIB). It was claimed that the UK needed a strong DIB for strategic objectives and for national economic benefits. The strategic benefits included security of supply in times of tension and war (an insurance policy), the need for equipment designed specially for national requirements and the capability to respond to emergencies (such as the Falklands crisis and Gulf conflict). There are also claimed to be national economic benefits in the form of employment, foreign exchange savings and earnings and the development of high technology, including spin-offs to the civil sector. Certainly, defence sales are a major source of industrial employment, accounting for 560 000 jobs in 1992. The result is a significant pressure group which will seek to persuade governments to spend more on defence equipment and to buy British. Large producers with domestic monopolies will use their political influence and lobbying to oppose foreign purchases (of, for example, Boeing AWACS). Stress will be placed on job losses, possibly in marginal constituencies, the loss of a vital defence capability and the dangers of depending on foreigners.

Many of the arguments for a DIB are vague and emotive and are used to rationalise and justify the status quo. Costs are ignored. Informed public choice on the appropriate or optimal size and composition of the UK's DIB needs answers to three questions. In the first place, what is meant by the DIB and why is it needed? Second, what is the minimum size and composition of the DIB? For example, should it comprise only an R&D capability in certain key technologies (which?) and what would be the costs and benefits if the current DIB were reduced by, say, 10 per cent or 20 per cent? Third, how much are the Armed Forces willing to pay for retaining key UK industrial capabilities for military objectives? Any wider economic benefits such as jobs and advanced technology should be charged to other government departments (for example Employment and the DTI). Indeed, the point has to be made that there are usually alternative ways of achieving employment, technology and balance of payments objectives.

Buying British is not costless. It can mean paying more for equipment (perhaps an extra 25 per cent or more), and waiting longer for delivery. The result is smaller defence forces and less protection. Ultimately, it is necessary to ask what the defence budget is buying: protection for UK citizens or protection for UK defence industries? Each option involves different sets of costs and benefits and, once again, choices cannot be avoided (Hartley and Hooper, 1993).

Major changes will occur in the 1990s as UK defence contractors adjust to the prospects of substantial reductions in British defence spending. Faced with a reduced demand for new equipment (fewer new projects; shorter production runs), defence firms will respond by seeking new military and civil markets at home and overseas. Mergers are likely both nationally and internationally, especially within the EU; and, of course, there will be job losses, plant closures and exits from the industry. The question then arises as to whether governments should leave the adjustment process to market forces, or should they intervene either to encourage a re-allocation of resources from declining defence industries to expanding sectors, or more directly to assist the conversion of defence plants to civil activities (swords to ploughshares)? Whichever policy option is chosen, the required re-allocation of resources from defence to civil activities will involve time and substantial adjustment costs: any peace dividend will not be an instant free gift. On this basis, disarmament can be viewed as an investment process involving short-run costs and the prospect of long-run benefits (the Peace Dividend).

■ *11.8* Conclusion

Economics is the study of choices, and industrial policy is a classic example of choices under uncertainty. Economists contribute to policy debates by focusing on policy objectives, by applying their theories and by identifying alternative policy solutions. They are also concerned about the economic welfare implications of alternative policies. Increasingly, though, it is recognised that this ideal approach to policy issues cannot be divorced from the realities of the political market; neither can it ignore the institutional framework of the economy. Moreover, many of the traditional certainties in industrial economics are being challenged. New models of the supply side are being developed and applied, all of which makes it more difficult for economists to be confident about the advice which can be offered to policy makers.

Bibliography

Beesley, M. (1993) *Major Issues in Regulation* (London: Institute of Economic Affairs).

Bishop, M. and J. Kay (1988) *Does Privatization Work?* (London Business School).

Blackaby, F. (ed) (1979) *De-industrialisation* (London: Heinemann).

Cecchini, P. (1988) *The European Challenge 1992* (London: Wildwood House).

Cmnd 216 (1969) *Report on the Supply of Beer* (Monopolies Commission) (London: HMSO).

Cmnd 331 (1988) *Review of Restrictive Trade Practices Policy*, DTI (London: HMSO) March.

Cmnd 621 (1989) *The Government's Expenditure Plans 1989–90 to 1991–92* (London: HMSO).

Cmnd 651 (1989) *The Supply of Beer* (MMC) (London: HMSO).

Cmnd 727 (1989) *Opening Markets – New Policy on Restrictive Trade Practices* (London: HMSO) July.

Conservative Party Manifetso (1987) *The Next Moves Forward* (Conservative Political Centre).

DTI (1988) *Mergers Policy* (London: HMSO).

Downs, A. (1957) *An Economic Theory of Democracy*, (New York: Harper & Row).

Dunsire, A., K. Hartley, D. Parker and B. Dimitriou (1988) 'Organizational Status and Performance', *Public Administration* (Winter).

Foster, C. (1993) *Privatisation, Public Ownership and the Regulation of Natural Monopoly* (Oxford: Blackwell).

Galbraith, J. (1992) *The Culture of Contentment* (London: Penguin).

Gardner, N. (1976) 'Economics of Launching Aid', in A. Whiting (ed.) *The Economics of Industrial Subsidies* (London: HMSO).

Gowland, D. and S. James (1991) *Economic Policy After 1992* (Dartmouth).

Hartley, K. and M. Huby (1985) 'Contracting-out in Health and Local Authorities', *Public Money* (September).

Hartley, K. and N. Hooper (1993) *The Economic Consequences of the UK Government's Decision of the Hercules Replacement*, Research Monograph Series 2 (York: Centre for Defence Economics).

HCP 392 (1988) Defence Committee, *Business Appointments* (London: HMSO) March.

HCP 563 (1993) *British Aerospace Industry*, Trade and Industry Committee, House of Commons (London: HMSO).

Kamien, M. and N. Schwartz (1982) *Market Structure and Innovation* (CUP).

Kay, J. and D. Thompson (1986) *Privatization and Regulation: the UK Experience* (Oxford: Clarendon Press).

Klepper, G. (1990) 'Entry into the Market for Large Transport Aircraft', *European Economic Review*, 34(4).

Niskanen, W. (1971) *Bureaucracy and Representative Government* (London: Aldine Atherton).

Peacock, A. and G. Bannock (1991) *Corporate Takeovers and the Public Interest* (Aberdeen University Press).

Szymanski, S. and S. Wilkins (1993) 'Cheap Rubbish? Competitive Tendering and Contracting-Out in Refuse Collection – 1981–1988', *Fiscal Studies*, 14(3).

Williamson, O. (1981) 'The Modern Corporation: Origins, Evolution, Attributes', *Journal of Economic Literature* (December).

■ *Chapter 12* ■

Macroeconomic Policy

David Gowland and Stephen James

■ 12.1 Introduction

In the course of this chapter many of the threads which run through earlier chapters will be pulled together with a view to explaining the evolution of macroeconomic policy in the UK. The purpose is both to examine the theoretical models which at various times have been adhered to with varying degrees of conviction by UK governments, and also to examine the empirical assessments of the results of using these models. This chapter necessarily contains a more wide-ranging historical perspective than most others, but in common with them it concentrates upon the evolution of theory and practice over the past two decades. In setting this discussion at the end of the book, rather than at the beginning, as is commonly the case in other texts, the problem of introducing many matters as yet unfamiliar to some readers (such as the exchange rate) is avoided. To retain the continuity of the narrative it is assumed that the reader has indeed read the previous chapters, but where necessary he or she is referred back to the discussion earlier in the book. Thus there is, for example, no attempt to replicate the discussion of supply-side economics in Chapter 3, but models such as new classical macroeconomics, which were mentioned only briefly in Chapter 1, are spelled out in more detail. However, it is necessary to emphasise that in reality policy cannot be compartmentalised in this way. It is impossible to separate a government's demand management and supply-side policy. Indeed, the belief that this was possible was probably one of the major flaws in the Keynesian consensus of the 1950s.

Virtually everything discussed in this chapter is in some way controversial. Some controversies are concerned with matters of theory, such as the debate about expectations, and some with the interpretation of the statistical data. These controversies are ongoing, and it is not the purpose of this chapter to do other than to spell out some key issues and to guide the reader through the debate. As in certain other chapters, this one ends by addressing specific controversies which are currently at the forefront of the policy debate in the UK: in particular, whether credit controls have any useful role to play as an alternative to interest rates, and the continuing debate about whether the size of the budget balance matters.

■ *12.2* Macroeconomic Policy

The phrase **macroeconomic policy** is used to describe the actions of governments when they seek to manipulate the economy so as to influence the level of inflation and unemployment. Sometimes macroeconomic policy is used to try to stimulate the level of economic activity so as to increase the level of output and employment and so reduce unemployment. These policies are usually referred to as **expansionary**, or **reflationary**. However critics of such policies point out that they sometimes lead to inflation and so term them 'inflationary policies'. On other occasions governments seek to reduce the level of economic activity in an attempt to reduce inflation. These policies are referred to as **deflationary** (or occasionally disinflationary). In the UK the government first started to pursue active macroeconomic policies in 1941. As the date suggests, this was part of their effort to manage the economy so as to win the Second World War in the most efficient and equitable manner. For most of the period since 1941 governments have frequently referred to macroeconomic policy as **stabilisation policy**. This presumed that the level of economic activity was likely to fluctuate, hence the role of macroeconomic policy was to minimise the fluctuations of output around its long-run trend level.

Logically, the term macroeconomic policy could be used to refer either to policies which sought to influence aggregate supply or to policies which sought to influence aggregate demand. In practice, however, the term was traditionally used to refer only to **demand management policies**, although in recent years there has been a revival of supply-side policies. The underlying objective of governments in formulating macroeconomic policy is to achieve the best available (that is, the optimal) combination of output, inflation, employment and other desirable objectives (such as the distribution of income, or, more generally, equity). These are also known as the goals or final targets of economic policy.

In Chapter 2 the role of instruments, intermediate targets and objectives was considered in our macroeconomic model (see **pp. 18–24**). Tinbergen's law states that a government can achieve as many objectives as it has independent instruments: with five instruments a government can achieve five objectives, **but no more**. In practice, however, due to uncertainty, it is much harder to make economic policy than Tinbergen's law suggests. Attempts to modify this approach to incorporate uncertainty and other real world complexities are called **optimal control**. A number of economists have worked on this for several years, but with little result so far.

There are two crucial issues in macroeconomic policy:

Rules or Discretion? Keynes and his followers argued that governments should actively manage the economy. This means that they should vary their instruments of policy so as to stabilise output whenever the economy suffers a shock. The alternative view, whose most famous advocate is Milton Friedman, argues that this is not possible. Instead, governments should set their instruments so as to keep an intermediate target at a constant level.

Which Target? A **rule** might be set in terms of, for example, the exchange rate, the Budget deficit or the money supply. Similarly, the government might choose to vary any of these three as part of a discretionary policy. In practice, the choice has always been restricted either to an external target (normally the exchange rate) or to an internal one, such as the money supply. This debate is totally independent of that in the issue above. Both Friedman and Keynes have taken the same side in this debate in that both have argued passionately in favour of an internal rather than an external target.

These debates were inaugurated by Ricardo in 1817. He persuaded the UK Government to return to the gold standard. This fixed exchange rate system meant that the government had accepted a **rule** and an **external** target. Most economists supported this view until the 1920s, when Keynes argued in favour of **discretion** and an **internal** target. In the 1950s, Friedman argued in favour of an internal target and a rule in the form of a fixed rate of money supply growth. The decision by the UK Government to join the ERM of the EMS in 1990 was another round in this long-running debate. Despite the preference of economists for an internal target, governments have usually preferred an external one. The only periods when clear precedence has been given to internal targets were 1931–39, 1971–90 and seemingly 1992–94.

There are various ways in which instruments can influence objectives. It is useful to group these into three forms of economic policy: direct controls; Keynesian policy (fiscal policy is the best-known form of this); and financial policy (monetary policy is one form of financial policy).

☐ *12.2.1 Direct Controls*

Direct, or one-stage, controls are so named because they operate **directly upon objectives**. For example, a government seeking to control inflation might issue an ordinance setting out maximum prices and draconian penalties for charging in excess of them (the penalty in Stalin's Russia was death). Such policies are easy to understand because it is clear to the general public how they are intended to work. However, economists believe they are generally ineffective because of the problem of **black markets**: the control creates an incentive to set up an unofficial market in which mutually beneficial exchanges can be made in violation of the control. In the UK the only direct

control used in the last 20 years has been incomes policy. The general form of an incomes policy consisted of a direct attempt by the government to reduce the level of wage settlement. It thereby hoped, through various mechanisms, to reduce not only the level of wages but also the level of prices and to increase the level of output. The Conservative Government immediately abandoned incomes policy when it came into power in 1979. However, its critics feel that this was a mistake, and the issue of incomes policy still forms one of the major issues dividing Thatcherite opinion from its opponents. It is sometimes argued that Conservative governments have in fact introduced incomes policies, but only for public sector workers. It seems better, however, to regard these as an application of the government's market power as an employer.

☐ *12.2.2 Keynesian Policy*

Keynesian policy consists of using instruments in the **goods market**: the government operates so as to change demand in the goods market. Keynesian policy thus involves two stages: the instrument is used to influence the goods market which, in turn, is used to influence the objective variable(s). For example, if the government sought to reduce inflation it would use its instruments to reduce demand in the goods market (the 'real sector') and would hope that lower demand would reduce the price level (below the level at which it would otherwise have been). Hence Keynesian policy can fail if either:

a   the government's instruments do not influence demand in the predicted fashion, or
b   the change in demand does not influence the objective variable(s), such as price or output as intended, for example because (aggregate) supply shifts.

☐ *12.2.3 Financial Policy*

Financial policy is the most indirect of the three forms of economic policy, involving three stages;

hence Milton Friedman's famous aphorism that monetary policy would operate only with a long and variable lag. The three stages are set out below:

1   The monetary authorities (an umbrella term to describe all branches of government including the Bank of England) **do something**. This disturbs the financial system in a way which can be analysed using supply and demand curves. This disturbance is often called a 'shock' because it disturbs equilibrium. This stage involves the use of a policy instrument. In the case of monetary policy, narrowly defined, this instrument is called a **technique of monetary control**.

2   The purpose of stage 1 is to change either **price** or **quantity in financial markets**. The quantity might be the quantity of money or of credit (see below). The price might be the price of borrowing (the rate of interest) or the price of foreign currency (the exchange rate). This variable is called the **intermediate target**. The arguments for the money supply being the most appropriate intermediate target are examined below.

3   The purpose of stage 2 is to influence the **real sector**, the goods or labour market. In this way a government hopes to achieve its ultimate objective.

As three stages are involved, the possibility of error is much greater than with direct or Keynesian policy. This does not mean that financial policy is necessarily less effective or less important; indeed, the contrary may be the case. It does, however, mean that greater care in its use is essential. The crucial feature of the analysis of financial policy is to examine the means by which changes in financial markets influence developments in the real sector (how stage 2 leads on to stage 3). This is usually called the **transmission mechanism** of monetary policy: the means by which developments in financial markets are passed on to (transmitted to) the real sector.

It is important to distinguish between **direct** and **indirect** transmission mechanisms since the core of the monetarist position is a belief in a direct transmission mechanism, whereas Keynesians believe in an indirect one. This means that they accept that money influences income, but only through its effect on some other variable. Young Keynesians believe that this variable is the exchange rate, whereas older Keynesians believe it is the rate of interest. All Keynesians believe that government policy should focus on these variables. Monetarists, on the other hand, believe that money has a direct impact on income and hence the government should set a monetary target (see discussion below).

12.2.4 Financial, Monetary and Credit Policy

It is important to distinguish financial policy in general from monetary policy. Narrowly used, the phrase **monetary policy** refers to control of the **money supply**. Financial policy encompasses not only monetary policy but also credit policy, interest rate policy and exchange rate policy. The latter two terms are quite straightforward. Exchange rate policy occurs when a government seeks to control the exchange rate. This policy has both micro- and macroeconomic aspects, some of which were analysed in Chapter 4. Interest rate policy is mainly concerned with influencing the level and structure of interest rates, and thereby influencing the rate of interest which firms and persons pay when they borrow to finance expenditure. This mechanism is critical in Keynesian analysis. Monetarists, by contrast, place greater emphasis on the concurrent changes in the interest received by savers and investors, and the value of their assets.

Credit policy, however, is more complicated and more controversial. The distinction between money and credit is straightforward. **Money** is an asset which a person owns, whereas **credit** is a liability which a person owes. It is not hard to tell the difference! Monetarists believe that a person's actions are largely influenced by the amount of money which he or she has: that, as the saying goes, 'money burns a hole in one's pocket'. Keynesians, on the other hand, emphasise the importance of credit. Keynesians believe that consumers' expenditure is very likely to be influenced by the cost and availability of credit to the personal sector. If the cost of borrowing falls then Keynesians expect expenditure to rise. Moreover, if individuals are allowed to borrow more, then their expenditure will rise. Such a general increase in borrowing possibilities occurred in the UK in the 1980s due to financial innovation. Keynesians believe that the availability of credit is critically important in economic analysis because they believe that individuals are rarely able to borrow as much as they would wish to. Consequently, any relaxation in credit limits is likely to lead to increased spending. Monetarists, on the other hand, usually believe that this would have little effect in itself.

In seeking to clarify the relationship between instruments and objectives, many economists and most governments believe that it is useful to introduce a further concept: the **intermediate target**. The idea is that a government should use its instruments to control the intermediate target, and rely upon the effect of the intermediate target in attaining its objectives. Economists tend to have some of their fiercest debates about the question as to which is the most appropriate intermediate target. Monetarism is defined by most authors as being belief in a monetarist target: in other words, that the money supply should be the intermediate target. It is consequently important to distinguish between a belief in the use of financial (or even monetary) policy and monetarism itself. Monetarism is a belief that the best intermediate target is the **money supply**, and that a government should sacrifice other variables such as government spending, tax rates, interest rates and exchange rates so as to ensure that the money supply performs this function.

Monetary policy is one of the means by which governments can seek to manipulate the economy in order to influence inflation and unemployment. In 1960 it was unfashionable in the UK, and regarded as of little importance. Thereafter, its importance grew steadily until 1981, especially after the adoption of monetary targets (defined below) in June 1976. After 1981, the Conservative Government played down the role of monetary policy, particularly when Mr Lawson became Chancellor of the Exchequer in 1984. Similar developments have occurred in other countries, but the extent of the controversy has been much greater in the UK. Some critics believe that the government was wrong to abandon monetary targets. In their view the price for this mistake could be seen in 1988 with rising inflation, soaring house prices and an enormous and growing BoP deficit. Their view was put eloquently by Sir Alan Walters, a close associate of Mrs Thatcher (Walters, 1986). In this view, the need to increase interest rates nine times (by 5 per cent in all) in the second half of 1988 was a belated attempt to correct for the error although perhaps too late. At the very least, the need for such strong medicine showed to monetarists the extent of the error in abandoning their nostrum. More generally, monetarists argue that both the excesses of the Lawson boom and the suffering of the subsequent depression would have been averted if the UK Government had remained faithful to monetarism.

Other critics argued that the government had been wrong to put as much emphasis on money as it had. Instead it should have sought to manage – and indeed to stabilise – the exchange rate. Many such critics believed that the attempt to control the money supply in 1978–81 led to an excessively high exchange rate and so to deindustrialisation. Some argued that membership of the ERM was the best form of exchange rate policy: keen supporters of the EU believed that it was inevitable anyway, so the sooner the UK joined the better.

They argued that the problems of the late 1980s would have been avoided if the government had joined the ERM in 1985. These arguments caused serious divisions within the Conservative Government. Nigel Lawson resigned in consequence as Chancellor in 1989. The controversy over this and related wider issues led eventually to a successful challenge to Mrs Thatcher's leadership of the Party, but even before this Mrs Thatcher had been forced to agree to UK membership of the ERM on 6 October 1990. The UK subsequently left the ERM on 16 September 1992. The behaviour of the economy in this period seemed to most monetarists to confirm their views about the undesirable effects of exchange rate targets.

■ 12.3 A Framework for Analysis

The same macroeconomic instrument may have both a direct (Keynesian) impact on the goods market, and also an indirect one through its effect on financial markets. For example, an increase of £100 million in government expenditure on currently-produced goods and services can be regarded as a Keynesian policy designed to raise the level of planned injections (exports plus investment plus government spending) at each level of income, and so to raise the equilibrium level of income. However, **ceteris paribus**, such a policy also increases the money supply permanently by £100 million – that is, by the exact amount of the spending – and is therefore also an instrument of monetary policy. In whichever way the instrument is regarded, its effect is nevertheless to **raise income**. However, the amount and duration of the change in income may depend crucially on how it is viewed. The **interdependence of policy instruments**, as it is usually called, is thus essential to understanding macroeconomic policy. It is the source of both theoretical and practical controversies in economics, because it means that it is usually impossible for a government to achieve all of its intermediate targets simultaneously. If one target variable is too high (for example, the money supply) and one too low (for example, a measure of fiscal policy), then the use of an instrument which will bring the first back on course (lower government spending) will tend to depress the other (fiscal) target still more and so cause it to move even further away from its desired value.

▯ 12.3.1 The Supply-side Counterpart Equation

It is therefore necessary to have some sort of conceptual framework both in order to elucidate this inter-relationship between variables and also to analyse their impact. The most useful such framework is the flow-of-funds or supply-side counterpart equation. This uses the orthodox definition of the change in (Δ) the money supply as:

$$(\Delta) \text{ Money Supply} = (\Delta) \text{ Currency held by the non-bank private sector}$$

$$+$$

$$(\Delta) \text{ Bank deposits}$$

This is a very general definition of money. In practice, a number of definitions of money are consistent with it; UK policy makers currently use 4, the US over 40. Until the end of July 1989 the UK definitions were M0; non-interest bearing M1 (nib M1); M1; M2; M3; M3c; M4; and M5. M1, M3 and M3c were dropped but were replaced by M4c. Then, in August 1990, M4c and M5 were replaced by data for a range of liquid assets outside M4. M3H was introduced in August 1992 in order to provide a broad monetary aggregate similar to that used elsewhere in the EU. The definitions were rationalised and clarified in December 1992. The Bank of England made it clear that many of the definitions were produced so as to satisfy outside demand (for example, from econometricians requiring consistent runs of data). Only three mattered for policy purposes: M0, M2 and M4. M0 consists almost entirely (99.5 per cent) of notes and coin. M2 is notes and coin in circulation plus private sector retail deposits, whereas M4 includes these and wholesale deposits as well. Retail deposits are relatively small and taken in at branch level, whereas wholesale deposits are large and taken by banks in organized markets. M4 is, in effect, a modernised version of £M3, reflecting institutional change. The main reason for this multiplicity of definitions is that it is not clear in practice which institutions are banks (see **p. 98**). Given that a building society is similar, but not identical, to a bank, it is treated as a bank for some definitions but not for others. The Abbey National Building Society's conversion to a bank on 12 July 1989 triggered an alteration in definitions of money because it caused a huge switch of assets from

Figure 12.1   *Relationships between the Monetary Aggregates and their Components[1]*

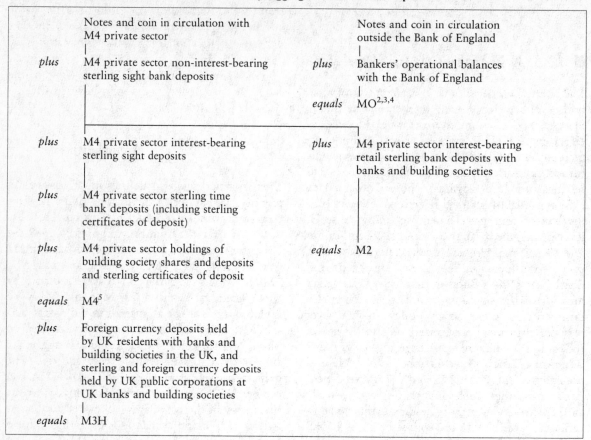

Notes:
[1] The Abbey National Building Society was authorised under the Banking Act 1987 as from the date of its conversion to a public limited company on 12 July 1989. From the end of July onwards its assets were transferred into the category of retail banks and ceased to be included in the building societies category. The amount of assets transferred (£32 billion) were such as to cause a major discontinuity in the series which included bank deposits but excluded building society deposits (namely M1, M3 and M3$_c$) and these were accordingly terminated as of June 1989. In aggregate M2, M4 and M5 were unaffected as there were equal and offsetting changes in the bank and building society contribution to each aggregate. There was a small but easy to adjust for statistical break in M0 due to the appearance of bankers' deposits at the Bank of England placed by the Abbey National, and an insignificant break in nib M1. The disappearance of M3$_c$ was compensated for by the creation of a new definition M4$_c$ which included certain deposits in currencies other than sterling placed with UK banks and building societies by the rest of the UK private sector.

The term 'non-bank private sector' is used throughout this text to refer to the sector comprising UK residents other than the public sector and banks. The increasingly blurred distinction between banks and building societies has resulted in the increased use of the term 'M4 private sector' to indicate that both banks *and* building societies are excluded.

In the light of the statistical discussion paper (Bank of England, 1990a) and the subsequent responses to it, the August 1990 *Bank of England Quarterly Bulletin* (pp. 336–7) announced the Bank's intention of replacing the monetary aggregates M4$_c$ and M5 by data for a range of liquid assets outside M4. These were also discussed in the May 1991 *Quarterly Bulletin* (pp. 263–6).

As a consequence the definition of 'broad' money is now confined to M4, and has its base 'notes and coin in circulation with the M4 private sector' as shown in the Figure.
[2] M0 is calculated on a weekly averaged basis. All other aggregates are calculated at end-months.
[3] The stock of M0 outstanding at the end of June 1991 was £18 million while that of M4 was £445 billion.

Figure 12.1 notes continue opposite

⁴ Bank of England equations suggest that a 1 per cent increase in consumption will raise M0 by 0.2 per cent in the current quarter and by 1 per cent in the long run. A permanent 1 per cent increase in interest rates will lower M0 by 0.1 per cent in the current quarter, and in the long run will lower the growth of M0 by 0.5 per cent per annum.
⁵ Over the last decade M4 deposits have grown broadly in line with total gross wealth. See *Bank of England Quarterly Bulletin* (August 1990), pp. 381–2.
Source: Bank of England.

the building society to the banking sector. This switch, however, was purely a statistical artefact with virtually no economic significance.

There are similar difficulties over the definition of a deposit. As a concept it is an 'almost perfectly liquid' claim on a bank. However, it is unclear whether a 7-day account is 'almost perfectly liquid', or indeed whether such a term can be applied to funds which can be obtained instantly, but subject only to the payment of a penalty. Different answers to these issues produce different definitions of money. It is preferable to examine a range of definitions rather than to risk being misled by a single one. The full range, both current and recent, is set out in **Figure 12.1**.

It is important to see whether different money indicators give different signals about the nature of the economy, a matter to which we will return below. The basic definition of money in **Figure 12.1** (deposits plus currency) is often used by economists to analyse financial developments, and is referred to as **demand-side analysis**. However, supply-side analysis is more common. The supply-side counterpart equation is derived by two substitutions into the definition of money:

a **the bank balance sheet equation:** bank assets are equal to liabilities so loans (assets) can be substituted for deposits (liabilities);
b **the government finance equation:** bank loans to the government are replaced by a rearrangement of the government finance equation:

PSBR = (Δ) Bank loans to the government
+
(Δ) Non-bank private sector loans to the government
+

(Δ) Non-bank private sector holdings of currency

These substitutions are merely rearrangements of accounting identities. When the government runs a surplus, called a PSDR, the relationship still holds: (−PSDR) replaces PSBR. The purpose is to derive a useful and economically meaningful relationship, which now takes the form:

(Δ) Money Supply = Public Sector Borrowing Requirement
+
(Δ) Bank loans to the non-bank private sector
−
(Δ) Non-bank private sector loans to the public sector (government)
+
Overseas effect

The supply-side counterpart is the key to the analysis of macroeconomic policy making in the UK, as explained below.

□ 12.3.2 Intermediate Targets

Many of the rival candidates for the role of intermediate targets can be identified from this equation. They are as set out below:

1 **Money supply:** this, the preferred target of monetarists such as Milton Friedman, is the sum of the four supply-side counterparts.
2 **Domestic Credit Expansion (DCE):** this is the domestic component of money creation (that

is, the first three of the supply-side counterparts). Any exchange rate fixing mechanism necessarily implies that the government should pursue a DCE target (see below, **p. 449**).

3 **Public Sector Borrowing Requirement:** Mr Lawson had a variety of targets for the PSBR. From 1985–88 his target was a PSBR equal to 1 per cent of GDP. Thereafter his target was for a substantial surplus. Budgetary policy was sharply reversed after Mr Major became Prime Minister in 1990. The government chose to run a large deficit, as shown in **Table 12.3** below. In 1993, this became a matter of concern and the government sought to constrain this deficit.

4 **Measures of fiscal policy:** the PSBR is equal to:

* Government spending (a Keynesian injection)

−

* taxation (a Keynesian withdrawal)

−

* asset sales by the public sector

+

* public sector loans to the rest of the economy

By an accounting quirk the last category includes nationalised industries' profits and losses. Losses appear as loans by the National Loans Funds to the industry concerned; a profit as a notional repayment. Keynesian measures of fiscal policy could be a weighted average of the first, second and fourth of these, reflecting the impact on net injections. For example, Musgrave's 'fiscal leverage' might be government spending −0.7 taxation +0.5 public sector loans. Moreover, Keynesians might disaggregate some components further: government spending might be divided into expenditure on goods and services and on transfers, with a higher weight given to the former.

5 **Credit:** credit, the preferred target of Ben Friedman and many other new Keynesians, is measured by the second supply-side counterpart: bank lending to the non-bank private sector.

6 **Interest rates:** the level of interest rates influences both bank lending and non-bank private sector purchases of public sector securities (National Savings and gilt-edged). Higher rates reduce the demand for bank loans and increase the demand for public sector securities. Hence the level and structure of interest rates are critical determinants of these supply-side counterparts.

7 **Exchange rate:** the overseas influence on the money supply, the fourth of the supply-side counterparts, is closely related to the balance of payments surplus; hence exchange rate policy will be reflected in monetary developments, and vice versa.

This framework can be used to analyse a large number, indeed virtually all, issues in UK macroeconomic policy. More importantly, perhaps, it has been used by policy makers in formulating their policy. Hence the use of flow-of-funds analysis is crucial to an understanding of the origins and objectives of economic policy. For example, the Conservative Government used it to devise the MTFS in 1979. The government purported to commit itself to setting the key values of economic policy for a period of four years in advance; the purpose was to give the private sector information about macroeconomic policy and to increase the credibility of economic policy. It did this by announcing its target values for the key flow-of-funds variables, especially money supply and PSBR. However, the values included in the MTFS bore no relationship to the actual outturn, as shown in **Table 12.3** below. Hence they were useless both as forecasts and as targets. Thus, while the government continued to publish the MTFS in order to avoid losing face, neither it nor its critics regarded it as of any importance. As its name implied, flow-of-funds analysis looks at flows but not directly at stocks. The next subsection is therefore designed to complement flow-of-funds analysis by looking directly at stocks.

☐ *12.3.3 Debt Deflation*

Milton Friedman differed from the Keynesian consensus by stressing stocks rather than flows. Stocks, such as wealth, can be measured independently of time. It is clear that a person worth £1 million is rich. It is not clear how well off a person with an income of £1000 is unless one knows the period of time to which it refers. If the income is £1000 per year, the person is very poor, at least by UK standards. If the income is £1000 per day, then the person is very rich. This is because income is a flow variable. All the variables in standard Keynesian models are flows; income, consumers' expenditure, and so on. Friedman argued that this was a mistake and that it was necessary to incorporate stock variables, such as wealth and the money supply. Many Keynesians have come to accept this view. Many authors, both Keynesian and monetarist, have stressed the importance of debt levels in recent years. This has led to a revival of a concept known as debt deflation. It has been widely argued that it was a major factor in both the UK and USA in recent years. In particular, it has been argued that it was a major factor in causing the onset, severity and length of the recession, from which both economies suffered.

As argued throughout this chapter, monetary policy causes a change in asset prices. Indeed most – perhaps all – of the impact of monetary policy arises in this way. For example, a higher level of the money supply leads to a higher level of house prices. This, in turn, makes it more profitable to build houses. Similarly, it has been demonstrated that higher share prices lead to greater investment by companies. Such mechanisms were very important in the UK in the Lawson boom. However, asset mechanisms can work in reverse!

The impact of falling asset prices is reinforced by the workings of the credit market. It is at this point that the analysis of monetarists (especially Congdon in the UK) coincides with that of new-Keynesian authors like Buiter and Blinder. Suppose that there is a fall in asset prices; this will directly cause a fall in expenditure. In addition, the fall in asset prices, however, may very well lead to the bankruptcy of some individuals. In particular, property developers frequently borrow to finance the construction of office blocks. A fall in the value of office blocks will cause at least some of them to go bankrupt. This bankruptcy will have direct adverse effects on economic activity. However, it is also likely to lead to a further fall in asset prices. This will, in turn, cause other property developers to go bankrupt, and so on. This is debt deflation in its simplest form. It was certainly widely observed in the UK in 1990. A more sophisticated version was even more prevalent. In many cases, both individuals and companies had borrowed on the security of real assets, especially houses and commercial property. A fall in the value of such assets meant that banks restricted further lending to these borrowers, or even called in existing loans. The borrowers were forced to restrict expenditure so as to meet these repayments. At the very least, they were forced to abandon spending plans that had previously been formulated. These decisions would involve selling existing assets, and so reducing their price, at a time when the demand for them was falling. Hence, asset prices would fall still further and the vicious cycle continued.

The analysis presented above is only a very slight modification of standard monetarist thought. It is also entirely in the spirit of new Keynesian analysis. However, it would be fair to say that this approach received little emphasis either in textbooks or in the media prior to 1988.

12.4 Methods of Monetary Control

A very useful and fruitful use of supply-side counterpart or flow-of-funds analysis is in analysing the methods of monetary control used in the UK. In presenting the range of options open to the monetary authorities textbooks frequently emphasise the reserve ratio/reserve base system, whereby a change in either the quantity of reserve assets or the reserve ratio leads to a corresponding change in the money supply. It does this by either forcing banks to lend less or making it possible for them to lend more through the workings of the credit multiplier. Such a system has never been used in the UK, though the government might have chosen to introduce it and did consider doing so in 1979–80. There have been various reserve ratios in the UK but they were neither designed to – nor did they – work in the textbook fashion. In the reserve ratio method of monetary control a bank lends whenever, **but only when**, it has the necessary reserve assets. In other words, the direction of causality runs from reserves to loans. In the UK there has been no attempt to control the volume of reserves and the direction of causality has run from loans to reserves; in other words, banks lent because they wanted to (usually because it was profitable) and then acquired the necessary reserves. This meant that the various ratios were partly prudential (to reduce the risk of bank failure) and partly devices to increase the authorities' control of short-term interest rates: an intention made clear in *Competition and Credit Control* in 1971 and repeated in *Monetary Control* (Cmnd 7858) in 1980. However, as was also made clear in the latter, these devices did not work very well. Hence neither the introduction of a 12.5 per cent minimum liquid assets ratio in 1971 nor its abolition (in stages) in 1980–81 was of much importance.

In the UK, the monetary authorities have sought to control the money supply through influencing the variables listed in the supply-side counterpart equation: bank lending and so forth. These **modus operandi** are described further below.

12.4.1 The ERM and Monetary Policy.

The UK was a member of the ERM in 1990–1992. Both its decision to join and its forced withdrawal were major developments in macroeconomic policy. Despite leaving the ERM, the government ratified the Maastricht Treaty in 1993, which committed it to rejoining the ERM at some stage and to proceeding to monetary union. It is therefore necessary to analyse the effects of, and arguments concerning, ERM membership in some detail. Controversy surrounding future UK policy towards the ERM and European Monetary Union remain central to political and economic debate in the UK.

It is necessary to distinguish the analysis of the economic effect of something from the motive for carrying it out. This is very important in the case of the ERM. It is easy to establish that many of the actors both were and are influenced by political as well as economic considerations. Indeed, this is a difference between Anglo-Saxon politicians and their continental equivalents, since the former are normally far more influenced by narrow economic considerations.

In the case of European Monetary Union, as so often, it is quite easy to agree on economic analysis but not necessarily on the consequent policy implications. For example, it is easy to agree that monetary union will lead to unemployment in some regions of Europe. Moreover national governments will be powerless to do much about this. Mrs Thatcher believes that this is an argument against monetary union. Jacques Delors argues that this is a reason for a much enlarged European Social Fund, and for greater **dirigiste** activity generally.

Some of the underlying issues raised in switching from a floating to a semi-fixed exchange rate have been discussed in an earlier chapter (see **pp. 216–20**) and do not need to be reiterated at this juncture. It is interesting to note that Keynes himself argued that adjustable parity systems were undesirable in that they deprived domestic monetary authorities of the autonomy to pursue the policy they wished. Keynesians frequently argued the case for autonomy in the 1960s. It is therefore ironic that the only remaining prominent upholder of this position is Mrs Thatcher. In many ways she is the last remaining Keynesian, arguing for political control of economic policy (discretion), rather than a rule based on exogenous discipline. Indeed, autonomy and discipline/credibility are the key elements in any analysis of the ERM. The argument about autonomy is also the argument against accepting narrower bands within membership of the ERM and against membership of a monetary union.

A monetary union exists when:

a   there are no exchange controls or other inhibitions on movements of money, and

b   when exchange rates are fixed permanently and are believed by all market participants to be fixed forever.

Within such a system, it would not seem to matter whether there were one currency or many currencies. In these circumstances, one currency is always a perfect substitute for another. If £1 is always worth DM3 then it is a matter of indifference whether it says on a pound coin '£' or 'DM3'. This was illustrated in the nineteenth century when gold coins from different countries were treated as perfect substitutes. A contemporary example is Italy, the Vatican and San Marino. These three countries form a monetary union and coins from each of the three are used in the other two. Similar considerations applied between Ireland and the UK prior to 1979. However, there are two economic reasons why the 'one currency' issue is thought to be important in addition to symbolic arguments.

1   **Seignorage,** the profit on issuing currency. This was analysed by classical economists in the eighteenth and nineteenth centuries and then disappeared from textbooks until recently. This is one of the many contexts in which it is of contemporary importance.

2   **Fixed exchange rates.** The crucial phrase in the definition of a monetary union is 'believed to be fixed forever'. Jacques Delors argues that if currencies remain distinct, then there will always be a possibility that their parity will change. Only a single currency can ensure permanent locking of exchange rates. Even this may be insufficient. Nevertheless, it is clearly much easier to break a monetary union if separate currencies remain. This is illustrated by the ease with which the Republic of Ireland broke away from its monetary union with sterling in 1979 after 58 years.

There are three pieces of economic analysis that are relevant to analysis of the UK position within a fixed exchange rate system.

Exchange Rates and the Domestic Economy

The first concerns the impact of exchange rate changes upon a small economy: that is, one unable to influence world prices. The question of whether the UK is a small economy is considered below.

The effect of a variation in the exchange rate is illustrated in **Figure 12.2**. The underlying idea behind this analysis is that most UK firms are price takers in markets (both in the UK and abroad) in which the price at which they sell is determined by the world price and the exchange rate (the world market may be competitive, or the UK producers may be relatively small firms in a market in which a foreign price leader or cartel determines the price). **Figure 12.2** illustrates this for a representative UK producer, and thus for the entire UK economy. It shows the marginal cost and revenue curves for a producer of a representative good, 'leets'. 'Leets' have a world price of $1. Originally the exchange rate is $2 = £1, so the world price expressed in pounds is 50p; this is the world price divided by the exchange rate. The UK producer faces a perfectly elastic demand and marginal revenue curve at this price. Hence his or her output of leets is Q_1 at a price of P_1 (50p).

The exchange rate then falls to $1 = £1. The world price expressed in sterling is now £1. Hence the fall in the exchange rate causes the MR curve to shift upwards to $MR = £1$. Output of leets rises to Q_2 and price to $P_2(£1)$. This can be generalised:

a fall (rise) in the exchange rate will lead domestic producers to increase (decrease) their output and prices. Hence a fall in the exchange rate increases output (and so reduces unemployment) but at the cost of higher prices (more inflation); a rise in the exchange rate will reduce inflation but at the price of more unemployment.

However, this result applies only in the short term. The lower exchange rate causes a rise in prices. This means domestic producers will face a rise in costs because:

Figure 12.2   *The Effect of the Exchange Rate on the Economy*

(a)   Short term

(b)   Long term

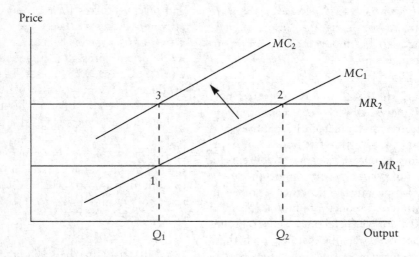

1   **Costs of raw materials and inputs have risen.** If they are imports, they obviously rise by an amount determined by the depreciation. If they are domestically produced, then their price rises in exactly the same way as the good analysed in **Figure 12.2**. British Steel raises its prices by exactly the same amount as Austin-Rover and for exactly the same reasons. Thus, the steel purchased by Austin-Rover rises in price by exactly the same amount as the price of cars.

And, much more importantly,

2   **Real wages are lower and marginal value product higher.** Hence, whatever model of the labour market is used, wages will rise.

The rise in marginal cost is shown in **Figure 12.2**. The MC curve shifts upwards from MC_1 and ultimately reaches MC_2, where output has fallen back to Q_1: that is, the economy moves from 1 to 2 to 3. **Figure 12.2** can be reversed to show the effect of an appreciation. The spirit of this model has influenced UK governments since 1974. Whenever they have wanted to reduce inflation they have sought a high exchange rate (1974–75, 1977–78, 1979–80, 1988–89). It is possible to regard the decision to join the ERM in 1990 as a further choice of a high exchange rate to reduce inflation. On other occasions they have sought a lower rate to reduce unemployment (1976, 1985). This is of considerable relevance because the UK has not got out of a depression in the last 70 years without a devaluation. Monetarist critics of ERM membership believed that the UK economy would remain in a depressed state as long as it was a member of the ERM. They therefore believed that recovery was made possible by the events of 16 September 1992.

The above analysis thus illustrates the proposition that membership of the ERM deprives a country of freedom in using macroeconomic policy. It can no longer use the exchange rate to counter unemployment and inflation. It also illustrates the other proposition about the ERM, that it leads to lower inflation. In this model, the UK price level is determined by the exchange rate and world prices. Within the ERM, world prices means German prices. If the exchange rate is fixed, then a necessary consequence is that prices are equal to world (German) ones. It is usually assumed that the other members of the ERM will move to Germany's low inflation rate. As Karl Pohl (then President of the Bundesbank) pointed out, it is equally possible that the reverse might occur.

One may argue about the precise relevance of this model. It is arguable that the UK is a medium-sized economy and that therefore one needs to use both traditional large economy models as well as this one. Certainly, however, the UK is in this sense much 'smaller' than it used to be and the model is becoming ever more relevant.

Optimal Currency Areas

The argument above is one way of illustrating a crucial problem:

Within a fixed exchange rate system, balance of payments problems show up as unemployment.

If the exchange rate is fixed, then if a random shock occurs in the above model, its impact will be to shift the *MC* curve and so cause a change in output. If this leads to a fall in output, the consequence will be unemployment. This analysis has been standard in textbooks for 30 years to explain regional unemployment. The reason that unemployment persists in, say, Scotland, is that Scotland cannot devalue its £ against the rest of the UK. The proposition is generally accepted, but the policy implications vary (see above).

This above analysis leads to a discussion of optimal currency areas. The theoretical conclusion is that an optimal currency area exists if factors are perfectly mobile within it. The world would thus be divided into optimal currency areas; goods, but not factors of production, would be mobile between these blocks; exchange rate variations could then eliminate unemployment. This analysis reappears frequently in John Major's speeches. It is cited as being a necessary condition of moving towards European Monetary Union.

It is worth pointing out that **existing** currency areas are **not** optimal. Almost certainly there should be a different currency for Scotland and England. It is arguable that the optimal currency areas are even smaller. It is also conceivable that optimal currency areas cross existing national frontiers. A half-serious study by an American Federal Reserve Bank pointed out that Scotland and Northern Ireland should be part of the same currency area as the Republic of Ireland! On the other hand, in their model Brittany was annexed by the £ sterling area, rather than the French franc.

Finally, it is worth emphasising that theoretical analysis suggests that factor mobility is as important a consideration as inflation convergence in deciding when the time is ripe for monetary union. This is one way in which the SEM is viewed as being a natural precursor to European Monetary Union.

DCE and Related Matters

One of the many virtues of flow-of-funds analysis is that it makes it possible to break down the sources of the supply of money into a **domestic** (*DCE*) and an **overseas** (*Ov*) component. The change (Δ) in the money supply is necessarily given by:

$$(\Delta)M = DCE + Ov$$

The significance of this is that a necessary condition of membership of an exchange rate fixing mechanism is that a DCE target must be maintained. The IMF have, in consequence, always preferred DCE targets. The rationale is simple. The overseas effect on the money supply is very closely related to the balance of payments surplus. Hence, when a country has a balance of payments surplus, its money supply will grow relatively quickly. In consequence, incomes will grow relatively fast and it will therefore tend to import more, which will tend to erode the surplus. Similarly, if a country has a deficit then its money supply growth will be relatively slow and so incomes will fall relative to these in the rest of the world, hence its balance of payments will improve. DCE targets are therefore stability conditions for any fixed exchange rate system.

This is one way of emphasising Minford's objection to the ERM, which is that ERM membership is inconsistent with a monetary target. Membership of the ERM necessarily involves a DCE target. Overseas flows will therefore determine short-term fluctuations of the money supply and mean that no monetary target can be met. This is reinforced by the fact that any intervention in the foreign exchange market by the government will also affect the size of this overseas influence on the money supply. Intervention must be such as to maintain the parity within the prescribed bounds. In other words, the money supply can no longer be controlled by the authorities.

From 1989 onwards the money supply grew very slowly in the UK (see **Table 12.3** below). ERM membership meant that the UK authorities were unable to take measures to increase the growth rate to a more reasonable level. The UK was also running a very large balance of payments deficit. Hence the implication of ERM membership was for even lower monetary growth so as to eliminate this. Monetarist authors, especially

Congdon, broadened the debate about monetary policy by stressing a hitherto neglected transmission mechanism: debt deflation. Debt deflation is discussed and analysed in Section **12.3.3**.

12.4.2 The Consequences of ERM Membership

Membership of an exchange rate fixing agreement involves a commitment to support one's currency. If the parity is fixed at £1 = DM3 then every time anyone presents the Bank of England with £1, it must be exchanged for DM3 (or the appropriate amount of other currencies in the ERM). This means that the UK needs sufficient foreign exchange to meet all such demands. Usually there is little problem in keeping a currency within its limits, but occasionally there is a widespread view that it is overvalued and there is an excess of sell orders. This is called a crisis of confidence.

This is an especial problem for the UK given that the pound is held internationally on a far wider scale than continental European currencies. This is why the UK Government argued that a necessary condition for UK membership (and why it argued that a wide band was necessary) was that its inflation rate be equal to that of Germany. In the latter case it is reasonable to expect the pound to maintain its value against the DM, so there is little incentive to convert pounds into DM. Were this not achieved, the government argued, membership would involve excessive heavy expenditure in buying DM in exchange for pounds which would not be successful. However, inflation convergence is not a sufficient condition to eliminate the possibility of an exchange rate crisis.

If a country does not have enough reserves on such occasions it has three options: to leave the ERM, to impose direct exchange controls or to change its economic policy in such a way that it convinces people that the currency is worth holding. This led to five arguments. These arguments were originally made as predictions by the authors of this chapter as well as by many other analysts. Experience, however, seems to bear out their relevance.

British Membership of the ERM Could Prove an Expensive Fiasco

The UK joined the previous version of the ERM in 1972 and had to leave after a few weeks because it did not have enough reserves. The effect was not only to humiliate the UK but also to set back the cause of European economic integration.

The government, in consequence, this time only joined the wide band. In August–September 1992, there was heavy selling pressure on the pound. In a rerun of 1972, the UK was forced to leave the ERM and (as in 1972) this weakened the entire system. Other countries were forced either to leave the ERM temporarily, or to devalue, or both. In August 1993, further speculative pressure forced the French Government to leave the ERM. UK membership of the ERM was therefore a victory for the pro-European camp in the short term but disastrous for their objectives.

Membership may Involve Actions that Impede European Economic Integration

To ease the problem described above, most of the members states of the EU have used exchange controls: that is, regulations which forbid some or all transactions in a foreign currency. Until 1990 Italians, for example, could not have a UK or German bank account, or any other sterling or DM asset without government permission. Hence they could not convert lira into DM without government permission, so it was much easier to support the lira's value against the DM. These restrictions impeded the EU's goal of a single market and led to the UK's requirement that the remaining members of the EU abandon their exchange controls before the UK joined the ERM. They promised to do this at Hanover in June 1988 (with a waiver for Italy until 1992 and for Portugal, Spain and Greece until 1995). Following further British pressure at the Madrid summit in 1989, France and Italy abandoned their exchange controls in the first half of 1990.

After the UK left the ERM, exchange control was reintroduced by six countries that were either members of the ERM (for example, Ireland), or that had chosen unofficial membership (for example, Sweden). There may, in other words, be a conflict between the two aspects of a move towards monetary union: permanent exchange rate fixity and freedom of capital movement.

A Country may be Forced to Change its Macroeconomic Policy so as to Remain a Member of the ERM

For example, the French Government in 1983 had to abandon a Keynesian policy of reflation adopted after the election of President Mitterrand. Usually this is regarded as a consequence of the wider proposition that the UK's membership of the ERM will cause a loss of autonomy over **domestic policy**. The exchange rate is linked to the money supply (and other domestic targets, such as interest rates). Hence if the exchange rate is fixed it becomes impossible to retain complete control over the other variables, just as a monetary target involves the sacrifice of other objectives, and the UK Government will not be able to manage the UK economy.

There was considerable debate concerning the impact of ERM membership on UK interest rates in 1990–92. In accordance with theory, UK interest rates fell relative to those in Germany, but rose substantially relative to those in the USA (see **Table 12.6** below). Different opinions prevailed as to which effect was more significant. However, the issue was resolved in 1992 as events unfolded. The then Chancellor, Mr Lamont, had to raise interest rates by 5 per cent on 16 September 1992. It was clear that yet further rises would be necessary to preserve membership, which meant that UK withdrawal became inevitable. After the UK's ignominious departure, short-term interest rates were increased dramatically by those who remained in the ERM, to over 100 per cent in Ireland and over 500 per cent in Sweden. These were only crisis reactions, but longer-term rates also rose substantially. By contrast, interest rates in the UK were reduced significantly.

The Bundesbank will Manage the UK Economy Better than UK Politicians

Many economists and people in the City welcomed the loss of autonomy. They argued that if membership of the ERM involved management of the UK economy by the Bundesbank then this could be seen only as an improvement. This argument was usually stated by saying that the Bundesbank possessed credibility.

Membership of the ERM will Increase the Credibility of UK Anti-inflation Policy

Given the importance of expectations in determining inflation, it is desirable that people expect a low rate of inflation. This means that inflation policy will work only if people have confidence in it. This is called 'credibility'. Membership of the ERM may have increased the credibility of anti-inflation policy in France. Almost all economic theories involve either an AS curve or a Phillips Curve incorporating an expected inflation mechanism (see below). Within such a model, it is desirable to reduce inflationary expectations. This makes it possible to reduce unemployment without an inflation cost. Similarly, it is desirable to stop inflationary expectations rising if there is a rise in inflation rate, otherwise there can be adverse long-term consequences following upon a short-term shock to the economy, exemplified by increases in oil prices or VAT. In effect, the argument for ERM membership was that these could be achieved. Economic agents would form future expectations of **British** inflation by reference to the performance of **Germany**.

The Bundesbank has credibility in the sense that short-term shocks do not raise inflationary expectations. The UK, it was argued, could obtain this by surrendering control of its economic policy. This is, in fact, the most common way of testing for the impact of the ERM on a country's economic management. It is hypothesised that inflationary expectations bear a growing dependence on German and a declining dependence upon domestic inflation.

The above argument can, however, be reversed. It was conceivable that German inflation would rise to British levels rather than vice versa. In other words, how can the Bundesbank retain its credibility within the ERM or in the event of European Monetary Union? Such doubts are reinforced by Pohl's resignation and by the events surrounding German reunification. The answer proposed by the Maastricht Treaty is that it is necessary to have an independent European Central Bank.

12.4.3 Economic Policy within the ERM

It is useful to go through the various aspects of economic policy and see how much, if any, scope is left to the domestic authorities.

Monetary Policy

It was argued above that it is impossible to control the money supply and the exchange rate simultaneously. The one exception is if exchange controls are used.

Interest Rate Policy

There are two problems with the use of interest rates as an instrument of economic management. The first arises if they are assigned to management of the exchange rate. It is normally presumed that if a country's currency is under pressure then its interest rate will be raised, and vice versa. However, there is a more fundamental problem: the **Walters critique**.

Walter's argument, which is generally accepted although it is not clear how relevant it is, is that given freedom of capital movements, interest rates in each country will **differ** only by the amount of **the expected change in the exchange rate**. This is necessary to ensure an equality of expected returns. If such a condition is not met, there will be capital flows until it is. Within a monetary union, exchange rates are therefore equalised. Walters goes on to point out that this is true within the ERM or any other exchange rate mechanism, at least for short-term interest rates. If no-one expects the pound to be devalued within the next six months then UK interest rates will equal German ones. This is incontrovertible and has happened to a significant extent in the ERM. However, inflation may not be the same in different countries in the ERM. Walters points out that this means that **real** interest rates will therefore be low in the countries in which inflation is high, and vice versa. However, a low real interest rate tends to be expansionary and to cause inflation to rise, and vice versa. As a consequence, the effect of interest rates will be destabilising.

Fiscal Policy

Use of fiscal policy involves manipulation of the PSBR. It is generally accepted (see above) that even the ERM requires a DCE target, of which the PSBR is a component. If one examines the three components of DCE, then either the authorities must be able to influence bank lending and debt sales (non-bank private sector loans to the public sector) or they will no longer have autonomy over fiscal policy (because they cannot determine the PSBR). It would appear to be the case that the inability to use interest rate policy or, alternatively, the fact that it will be destabilising leads to the conclusion that the implication of a DCE target may be the necessity to surrender autonomy over fiscal policy. Mrs Thatcher and Jacques Delors would agree with this, whereas Minford would disagree. The one exception to this is where it is possible to use **direct credit controls** to influence DCE. This highlights the continued relevance of the domestic debate between the Labour and Conservative Parties about whether such policy instruments are viable.

It is important to try to identify the precise scope of domestic economic management within ERM or EMU. In the light of the above discussion, there does not seem to be very much left, and this can be taken to highlight the importance of one final point, namely that:

> **Within an EMU most traditional issues of economic policy would be relevant, but would be now relevant at the level of the European Community.**

These include whether the money supply should be controlled, and if so how; how should credibility be maintained, and so forth. Within the UK, the residents of York have to accept the general price level. The price level in York is determined by the price level in the UK and by the fact that the York pound is irrevocably linked to the UK pound. The same argument would eventually apply to the UK pound within a European Monetary Union. Thus, it will be necessary to apply traditional macroeconomics at the level of the EU to see what determines its rate of inflation.

12.5 Monetary Policy in the UK, 1971–93

12.5.1 Competition and Credit Control

Instead of relying on a reserve base system the authorities sought to control the money supply through the various items of the flow-of-funds equation. The five crucial flow-of-funds variables are bank deposits (from the demand side) and the four supply-side variables: PSBR, bank lending, non-bank lending to the public sector and overseas effect. The PSBR can be influenced in a variety of ways, such as via changes in government spending, tax rates and asset sales (privatisation). The remaining variables can be influenced by either quantity controls or price devices. The latter work by seeking to induce economic agents to change their behaviour (in other words, to move along a demand curve). Quantity controls, in contrast, seek to override demand by official fiat.

Prior to 1971 monetary policy was in effect credit policy since the principal tool of monetary policy was a number of quantity controls on bank lending and other forms of credit, notably hire purchase instalment credit. However, any form of rationing or quantity control will create an incentive to evade it (the familiar 'black market' argument of elementary microeconomics). Financial markets are no exception: new institutions, notably secondary banks, grew up whose main purpose was to evade the controls. The authorities became convinced that rationing was no longer effective, and this regime of monetary control, the 'old approach', was abandoned in 1971. Its replacement was known as either the 'new approach' (1971–73) or 'Competition and Credit Control'. Its principal feature was a decision to seek to control bank lending solely by means of **interest rates**. If the money supply grew too quickly then interest rates would be raised so as to reduce the demand for bank loans and thus the money supply. This policy failed at the time, although it is still not clear why. To some extent the new approach was flawed technically since the authorities had less control over bank base rates than they had anticipated. Largely, however, the problem was a lack of political will by Mr Heath and his Chancellor, Mr Barber: they were unwilling to change interest rates often enough, or by a large enough amount.

It fell to the incoming Labour Government to devise a new regime of monetary control early in 1974. It had three instruments of control: a ceiling on interest-bearing eligible liabilities (IBELs), an aggressive debt management policy and manipulation of the PSBR for monetary purposes. The latter was accomplished by a combination of tax increases, public expenditure cuts and, after 1977, asset sales (mainly of BP shares and government holdings of private sector loans). Such policies were continued after 1979 by the incoming Conservative Government, and were largely successful as macroeconomic tools. Debt management policy was similarly successful, especially through selling National Savings Securities to the private sector. The controversial element of the package was the ceiling on IBELs (a legal term for bank deposits), often called the 'corset'. This ceiling was reinforced by a system of penalties, whereby a bank whose deposits grew faster than permitted had to deposit a proportion of the excess interest-free with the Bank of England. This interest-free deposit was termed a 'supplementary special deposit'. Initially the ceiling held, but it was later evaded on a massive scale; in other words, the black market problem was once more evident.

☐ 12.5.2 Policy After 1979

Monetary policy was reasonably successful under the 1974–79 Labour Government but the breakdown of the IBELs ceiling, and the election of a new Conservative Government in 1979 headed by Mrs Thatcher, led to a reappraisal of monetary policy. The PSBR and debt management instruments of monetary policy remained, although the latter was abandoned in November 1985. However, the IBELs ceiling was dropped in June 1980 and replaced by a plethora of new instruments.

1 A reiteration of the **interest rate weapon** as a tool to control bank lending, as in the 'new approach'.
2 Use of the **exchange rate** to influence overseas flows, especially in 1979. Later the exchange rate was an intermediate target rather than an instrument of monetary policy. The idea was that a high exchange rate made foreign assets cheaper. UK citizens and financial institutions would buy them and the resultant capital account deficit would reduce the money supply. This mechanism was the centrepiece of criticism of the government by moderate left and 'young Keynesians' who argued that the consequent high level of the exchange rate was a major cause of de-industrialisation.
3 The **abolition of exchange controls** in November 1979. This mechanism was similar to **2** in that this allowed an outflow of money from the country, which would reduce monetary growth. In 1983 the Labour Party made this the centrepiece of their criticism of the government: £100 billion of capital was exported during 1979–86 which, they argued, reduced domestic investment and hence caused unemployment to rise. The government's defenders claimed that overseas investment was a complement to, rather than a substitute for, domestic investment. Moreover, it yielded a high rate of return.

In addition the government made a number of technical changes in monetary policy in 1980–81. The most important was the replacement of MLR by the much more flexible 'intervention rate'. In all Western countries the banking system normally borrows from the central bank. The central bank uses variations in the cost and terms of such borrowing as a means of controlling the short-term rate of interest. The Bank of England has made a number of changes in this system since 1971. Their goal has been a system in which the rate at which the banking system borrowed could be changed frequently: if necessary, several times a day. They wished such changes to be viewed as normal, minor technical acts of policy rather than as major changes. In some countries, as in the UK prior to 1971, publicity is sought for such changes so as to reinforce their impact through changing expectations. At the present time the Bank prefers the flexibility of frequent unobtrusive changes.

12.6 The 1950s and 1960s: The Age of Demand Management

12.6.1 The Development Phase

This period constituted the high years of demand management in the UK. In retrospect, at least from the standpoint of the recession of the early 1990s, these years seemed to be a time when economic principles were successfully applied so as to achieve high employment, moderate growth and reasonably stable prices. Granted, the growth rate was moderate by comparison with other European countries and it gave rise to increasing concern as time wore on. Periodic balance of

payments and sterling crises and inflationary spurts required the application of the economic brakes to the extent that the booms and slumps of earlier periods became the policy-induced stop–go cycle. Nevertheless, it was a period in which unemployment never rose above 2.4 per cent, GDP grew at an average rate of 2.7 per cent per annum, and inflation – at least until the late 1960s – fluctuated in the range of 1–5 per cent per annum. **Table 12.1** gives a summary of the economic performance.

The consensus view that it was the responsibility of the government to regulate demand grew out of the inter-war experience and the development of Keynesian macroeconomics. The policy can be characterised as the short-term management of the level of demand through the use of fiscal and monetary policies in order to iron out fluctuations in the level of economic activity, thereby maintaining the economy at or near its full employment level. In the extreme the policy becomes one of 'fine tuning' whereby frequent adjustments are made to keep the economy on course. The principal instrument was to be fiscal policy, and in particular the adjustment of **tax rates**. Public expenditure was regarded as less flexible in the short term, and in any case was determined by long-term factors. Monetary policy played a subsidiary and supportive role, mainly through the use of direct control on credit. Interest rates were primarily deployed in defending the exchange rate. The economy fluctuated in a fairly regular pattern, with a cycle of around four to five years' duration (that is, from peak to peak or

Table 12.1 *GDP, Inflation and Unemployment, 1950–79, Selected Years (%)*

	1950–69	1950–59	1960–69	1970–79	1970–73	1974–79
Real GDP growth (annual average)	2.7	2.4	3.1	1.8	2.9	0.5
Inflation (annual average)	3.1	2.7	3.5	12.6	8.0	15.7
Unemployment (% of employed labour force)	1.7	1.5	1.9	4.1	3.1	4.8

Source: Economic Trends, Annual Supplements.

trough to trough). Policy was adjusted in a **counter-cyclical fashion**, becoming contractionary in times of current account deficit and rising inflation, and expansionary when unemployment rose.

12.6.2 Fiscal Policy in the Ascendant

Starting with the mid-1950s, demand management was operated primarily through **fiscal policy**, with interest rates directed towards influencing the capital account of the balance of payments. In terms of the flow-of-funds equation, the authorities relied during the period 1951–55 on the manipulation of the bank lending term, but from 1955 they relied primarily on adjustment of the PSBR term through tax changes. The failure to look at economic policy as a whole – that is, at all four parts of the equation simultaneously – handicapped policy considerably.

By the beginning of the 1960s it had become apparent that the management of demand alone was not sufficient to achieve all macroeconomic objectives simultaneously, and the authorities began to look for alternatives to supplement their fiscal instruments. On the one hand, there was an experiment with supply-side policies with a shift to planning, first with the establishment of the National Economic Development Council and later with Labour's Department of Economic Affairs and its National Plan. Attempts were made to control inflationary pressure through various prices and incomes policies, monitored from 1964–70 by the National Board for Prices and Incomes. Overall, the period 1964–1970 was, however, mostly dominated by the balance of payments and the attempt to maintain the exchange rate (Blackaby, 1978).

12.6.3 The First Wilson Government (1964–70)

On its accession to office Harold Wilson's first government faced what appeared at the time to be a major current account deficit (but one which subsequent statistical revisions have shown not to have been so bad) and initiated deflationary measures. Further restrictive action was taken in response to the three successive sterling crises (November 1964, July 1965 and July 1966) that ultimately led to the 1967 devaluation.

When devaluation finally came in November 1967, it was accompanied and followed soon after by further deflation as the current account failed to respond in the way the government had expected, and as set out in the Letter of Intent to the IMF in November 1967. Moreover, speculative pressures on sterling continued. The year 1968 witnessed the most deflationary Budget since the Second World War, which included significant cuts in public spending.

The government was now acting on three of the flow-of-funds items: the PSBR via budgetary policy, bank lending via ceilings and private lending to the government via import deposits. Compared to the 1950s and earlier 1960s the use of policy instruments was more coordinated and hence more successful. By the time of the 1970 General Election, the current account was in surplus. Internal measures of domestic performance – inflation, unemployment and growth – were somewhat worse than their postwar average, but only by small amounts.

12.7 The 1970s

The 1970s were a time of major and repeated crises in the UK economy. During this period macroeconomic policy lurched from overexpansion to crisis management as the governments of Heath, Wilson and Callaghan attempted to cope with major developments, both within the UK and in the world economy. In common with the latter part of the 1960s demand management alone proved insufficient, and during much of the period governments attempted to control wage inflationary pressures by the use of incomes policies, either as voluntary agreements or imposed by statute. Furthermore, in the desire to release economic policy from the constraint of maintaining the value of sterling, it was allowed to float from 1972 although this owed much to the developments in international monetary relations (see **p. 225**).

The period can be usefully divided into a number of sub-periods, although the division is somewhat arbitrary:

1970–71:   A short-lived market experiment, with no active demand management policy.

1971–early 1974:   An initial period of overexpansion ending in the chaos of a wage–price spiral, a major external shock to the economy and 'stagflation' (often referred to as Barberism after the then Chancellor).

Early 1974–mid-1975:   A time without major policy initiatives during a major crisis as the new Labour Government concentrated on re-election.

Mid-1975–77:   Labour's deflationist period.

1977–79:   A time of misjudgement on major policy issues.

☐ *12.7.1 The Heath Government*

Table 12.1 provides a summary of the economic performance over the decade. In the first year of the 1970–74 Conservative Government there were no major policy initiatives in managing the economy: policy was primarily aimed at reducing the involvement of government in economic life. This followed the 'Selsdon' philosophy announced by Edward Heath during his last months in Opposition. On the other hand, subsequent action would seem to imply that the government had by no means given up its commitment to maintaining high employment. As output stagnated and un-

employment rose towards the 1 million mark, the government's policy shifted from neutral to expansionary, culminating in the infamous Barber Budget in the Spring of 1972 and the Barber boom that followed.

The 1972 Budget was designed to raise the annual rate of growth of output to 5 per cent over the ensuing 18 months, and its main measures were significant tax reductions (achieved by raising allowances and cutting purchase tax) since they were faster acting than increases in public expenditure. They were also more in line with the government's philosophy. In addition, the Chancellor announced that monetary growth was to be allowed to accelerate in order to accommodate this expansion, and that an unrealistic exchange rate would not be maintained if it meant unacceptable distortion to the domestic economy. This was the first public indication that the government might permit the exchange rate to fall if the current account of the BoP constrained the growth of the economy. This Budget has often been presented as a U-turn in policy: it is probably truer to say that the U-turn best describes the shift in the government's attitude to intervention at the macroeconomic level, notably that of supporting lame ducks. It also marks the embarkation on a prices and incomes policy as a solution to the growing inflation problem.

This 'dash for growth' Budget was almost certainly misconceived. Not only had fiscal policy become steadily reflationary from mid-1971, but output had begun to rise, unemployment was expected to stabilise by the end of the year and significant underlying inflationary pressure was building up in the economy. In 1970 the inflation rate had been 6.3 per cent, but by the end of 1971 it had accelerated to 9.4 per cent. More importantly, monetary policy had become expansionary from the early Summer of 1971. The abolition of direct controls on bank lending under the new framework had led to a surge in bank lending. This was partly the result of reintermediation – that is, the re-entry into the banking system of lending that had been forced out of the officially regulated banking sector by the operation of credit ceilings – and largely as a result of the fact that banks were now able to satisfy previously frustrated demand for credit. This added directly to demand, which was stoked further by the lowering of interest rates and the ending of the agreement by which banks collectively fixed interest rates on deposits. This had restricted their ability to bid competitively for funds in order to finance lending.

Credit was made even more attractive by the reintroduction of the relief on loan interest in the 1972 Budget. In the event, the money supply expanded wildly out of control, growing by 60 per cent in 27 months. The effects of such monetary laxity soon became apparent in the inflation figures. One of the major routes for the transmission of the inflationary effects came through the **property market**, where there was an enormous speculative bubble. Between 1970 and 1973, commercial property prices almost tripled and house prices rose by an annual average of 34 per cent in 1972 and 1973. There are numerous channels through which house price inflation may be linked to more general inflation, including the wealth effects on consumption or the cost and wage inflation impact of higher property prices (Gowland, 1984, pp. 127–31). For a monetarist the experience of the period provided an almost perfect fit for the proposition that an excessive expansion in the money supply would result in accelerating inflation after a lag of about 18 months to two years.

Further inflationary twists were added by a world-wide commodity price boom and the depreciation of sterling after it had been floated in 1972. Indeed, as in previous reflations, there followed the characteristic sterling crises (in June 1972 and March 1973) and a marked worsening of the current account which went into deficit in 1973, and even more so in 1974. As if these developments were not sufficient, the 1973/74 oil crisis administered a severe supply-side shock to an already fragile economy. Whatever interpretation is put on the period – whether monetarist or Keynesian – such developments made the appearance of stagflation almost inevitable.

The authorities' response was slow in coming and may be seen as a classic case of 'too little too late' and of a misalignment of instruments and objectives. Attempts were made to hold back

wage pressure by the use of a statutory prices and incomes policy (in three stages), whilst demand was kept at a level sufficient to reduce unemployment. By the end of 1973 interest rates had been raised significantly, and in December of that year CCC was abandoned, being replaced by a new form of direct control on bank liabilities called supplementary special deposits (the 'corset'). Monetary growth did indeed fall as bank lending was reduced under the new regime, but the growth in demand was enough to raise output by 5.2 per cent, at the cost of raising inflation to 10 per cent at an annual rate by the end of the year. In early 1974 the government, now facing a rapidly deteriorating economic climate, with a three-day week and a second miners' strike, panicked, called an early election and got thrown out of office for its pains.

☐ 12.7.2 Labour Back in Power

Mindful perhaps of its tenuous position and the rapidly contracting economy during the year, the subsequent minority Labour Government took no major deflationary measure in 1974, despite four Budgets. Indeed, public spending rose in cash terms by 28.3 per cent in 1974 and by 31.4 per cent in 1975: in cash terms it was out of control. The PSBR also soared to over £10 billion in 1975 (11 per cent of GDP), although its effect on monetary growth was offset by falling bank lending and a large negative overseas impact (the result of the sizeable BoP deficit). The £M3 measure of the money supply rose by only 10.4 per cent in 1974 and by 6.8 per cent in 1975.

In mid-1975 the government finally produced a coherent policy response to the economic crisis, and this date marks a watershed in postwar macroeconomic management. There are a number of main strands to consider. In the first place, inflation became the primary policy objective. As a consequence, the commitment to full employment (to be achieved by manipulating AD) was dropped. This is best summed up in the Prime Minister's (James Callaghan) famous speech to the Labour Party Conference in 1976, when he said:

We used to think that you could just spend your way out of a recession, and increase employment, by cutting taxes and boosting government spending. I tell you in all candour that that option no longer exists, and that in so far as it ever did exist, it worked by injecting inflation into the economy.

Second, the principal instrument of policy was **incomes restraint** in the form of a notionally voluntary agreement with the trades unions: the Social Contract. Third, a major role in the attack on inflation was assigned to **financial policy**, specifically controlling and targeting the money supply and manipulating the PSBR to this end.

Even if the adoption of a money supply policy did not represent a conversion to monetarism as such, it did indicate a recognition of the importance of the money supply in the inflationary process, possibly as a way of validating inflationary pressure. There are alternative justifications for the adoption of money supply targets. One is that, **ceteris paribus**, a money supply target implies a given PSBR, and thus a given stance on public spending and taxation. Public expenditure, as a consequence, becomes politically easier to control. Another is that such targets are required to convince 'monetarist' financial markets of the government's resolve to combat inflation. A final possibility is that the targets were foisted on the UK by the IMF in 1976, after the collapse of sterling. This third explanation can be rejected as the government had shifted towards targeting before IMF involvement in the economy, whereas the other two might well have been accepted by the authorities (Gowland, 1984, pp. 154–6). Moreover the IMF put the emphasis upon DCE rather than money.

It is worth emphasising the use of the PSBR as a means of controlling the money supply. This meant that fiscal and monetary policy became inextricably linked as part of the government's financial policy, and was a major change from the earlier demand management approach of the 1950s and 1960s when fiscal and monetary policy were seen as independent instruments, with the former as the senior partner. Indeed, it was something of a role reversal. The authorities now used the flow-of-funds approach to guide policy with instruments aimed at each component. Macroeconomic or monetary policy had thus changed over 20 years, from a naive Keynesian analysis of injections and withdrawals to a financial analysis of flow of funds and an emphasis upon the money supply as a summary indicator of this.

☐ 12.7.3 The Deflationist Period

The first positive deflationary action was taken in the April Budget of 1975. There followed a pay freeze under a renegotiated Social Contract, and further rounds of public expenditure cuts throughout 1976. In addition, cash limits were introduced to control the growth of public spending. On the monetary side, the first official money supply target was announced (July 1975) and there was a tightening of monetary policy, with rises in the MLR and the reintroduction of the supplementary special deposits scheme, particularly during 1976 as sterling began to slide in the foreign exchange markets. Following the fall in sterling to an all-time low against the dollar in October 1976 – a crisis that resulted from a mismanaged attempt to float the currency down to a more competitive level – and negotiations with the IMF for a loan, the Chancellor announced a further package of spending cuts along with targets for both £M3 and DCE.

There can be little doubt that these policies achieved their objectives, at least over the short term. £M3 growth was well within its target range for 1976/77, as shown in **Table 12.2**, and DCE was some 45 per cent below its target level in the same period. Public spending growth fell to 5.8 per cent in 1977 and the PSBR was reduced to 4.7 per cent of GDP in the same year, the latter being significantly less than its forecast levels in the financial years 1976/77 and 1977/78. By mid-1978 inflation had fallen to 8 per cent at an annual rate, although unemployment remained intractably high despite the moderate growth of GDP in 1976 and 1977.

However, from late 1977 policy had become markedly more expansionary as monetary policy eased and public spending and the PSBR rose.

Table 12.2 *Monetary Targets and Outcomes, 1976–79*

Target set	Period Covered	Aggregate	Target Range (%)	Outturn (%)
December 1976	Financial year 1976/77	£M3	9–13	7.7
March 1977	Financial Year 1977/78	£M3	9–13	15.5
April 1978	Financial Year 1978/79	£M3	8–12	10.8
November 1978	12 Months to October 1979	£M3	8–12	13.1

Source: Bank of England.

This was largely a paradoxical by-product of the IMF agreement. The government, equipped with the IMF seal of approval, was less constrained and indeed was pressed by the IMF to reflate. £M3 also overshot its target range. This combination of circumstances produced a mini pre-election boom in 1978, but this was accompanied by consequent pressure on the housing market, inflation and the government's incomes policy. Indeed, it occurred just as the government was tightening that incomes policy, setting a 5 per cent guideline for settlements in the 1978/79 pay round. This was rather like trying to hold the lid on a saucepan whilst turning up the heat, albeit accidentally. Not only did the lid come off wages, which rose rapidly after the notorious 17 per cent Ford settlement in November 1978, but the government also got embroiled in the 'Winter of Discontent' which preceded its electoral defeat in May 1979. As in 1971–73, monetary expansion led to a house price explosion, a BoP problem and finally to rapid inflation.

One final aspect of policy of some importance at this time was the approach to the exchange rate: that is, the means of influencing the fourth flow-of-funds item. At first, in 1972, the exchange rate was floated in the hope that this would reduce the BoP constraint on expansion, but it subsequently became an **instrument** of demand management policy. As has been noted (Allsop and Mayes, 1985), it was argued by some economists, notably Kaldor, that the exchange rate

could be depreciated in a controlled way, inducing expansion from the export sector and from import substitution. This is the well-known 'export-led growth' policy. There would, therefore, be no need to compromise on the tight stance of domestic policy required to combat inflation. The experiment with this policy effectively came to an end with the sterling crisis in 1976: a managed depreciation was not quite so easy to accomplish in practice. Moreover, it was increasingly realised that the inflationary impact of a lower exchange rate would work faster than, and more than outweigh, the trade benefits of a lower exchange rate.

12.8 The 1980s: The Thatcher Years

During the years since 1979 discussion of economic policy in Britain has been dominated by 'Thatcherism', an economic doctrine that is wider in scope than the macroeconomy but which has particular relevance to it. While demand management is consistent with either more or less government involvement in economic life, and hence was acceptable to both Labour and Conservative governments of the 1960s and 1960s, Thatcherism is consistent only with less involvement. Indeed, the reduction of government activity – or, more graphically, 'rolling back the frontiers of the State' – is one of the central tenets of this economic outlook.

It should be recognised that the **ultimate** objectives of government policy in the 1980s have not changed: that is, the aim of achieving a high growth in living standards combined with stable prices. What is distinctive are the methods by which these are to be achieved and the costs the government, and implicitly the British electorate, are prepared to accept in their pursuit. The principal features of the approach can be identified as follows.

1. **The necessity of eradicating inflation** is of fundamental importance, not only for its own sake but because of its effects on the level of **unemployment**. In contrast to the more pragmatic policies of Denis Healey, who saw the abandonment of demand-managed full employment, and the need for higher unemployment, as a requirement for bringing inflation under control, the major proposition of Thatcherism is that inflation has to be reduced as it is a major **cause** of rising unemployment. Thus, instead of a conventional Phillips Curve trade-off, or even a Friedmanite vertical long-run Phillips Curve, the government believed in an **upward sloping one**. Traditional demand management is rejected since it can have no beneficial long-term effect on the economy.

2. The emphasis of macroeconomic policy is to provide a **stable non-inflationary** framework within which the private sector of the economy can flourish. The means to this end is to exercise control over the growth in the money supply – the government, at least in its early years, was self-proclaimed monetarist. Furthermore, the policy is to be operated over both the medium and long term. This ties in closely with the view, accepted by the government, that manipulation of policy for short-term stabilisation will have unpredictable and possibly destabilising effects on the economy.

3. **Free market supply-side policies** constitute the main long-run weapons for tackling unemployment and raising the rate of growth of output. These include tax cuts to boost incentives, privatisation and deregulation to extract the State and its agencies from the economy, and especially

a series of reforms in the labour market which have removed a number of trade union privileges (see Chapter 9). The aim of the last was both political and economic, the economic aim being to increase labour market flexibility. It is also interesting to note that the government was at pains to stress that the unions cannot cause inflation, but can 'only' price themselves out of a job and so cause unemployment.

☐ *12.8.1 Financial Discipline*

The specific details of the government's macroeconomic policy intentions were enshrined in the MTFS, first published with the 1980 Budget and detailed in **Table 12.3**. The strategy set out a declining target for £M3 over the subsequent four years as the principal mechanism for reducing inflation. The importance of the declining target lay not only in the government's attachment to a monetarist view of the inflation process, but also for the supposed effects of such targets on inflation expectations. It was believed that by committing the government to the creation of a stable environment over the medium term, **wage and price inflation expectations could be reduced.** The prime benefit was that the unemployment costs of the transition to a low inflation economy could be cut significantly. More generally, the government believed that financial discipline would change the behaviour of both the public and private sectors. Financial discipline was sought through monetary targets in the early 1980s and later through the ERM.

Monetary policy was the dominant weapon in the government's array of macroeconomic policy instruments. Particular reliance was placed on the use of interest rates, the PSBR and debt sales to contain monetary growth. Direct controls were rejected on the grounds of their distortionary impact on the banking sector; they reduced the efficiency of the financial institutions and produced disintermediation (see **p. 489**).

The use of the PSBR as an instrument of monetary control continued the subordination of fiscal to monetary policy. The government aimed to decrease the PSBR because of its direct

Table 12.3 MTFS, Target Ranges[1] and Outcomes (%)

	1979/80	1980/81	1981/82	1982/83	1983/84	1984/85	1985/86	1986/87	1987/88	1988/89	1989/90	1990/91	1991/92	1992/93	1993/94
Money Supply: M0 (% change)															
March 1984						4–8	3–7[2]	2–6[2]	1–5[2]	0–4[2]					
March 1985							3–7	2–6	1–5	0–4[2]					
March 1986								2–6	2–6	1–5[2]	1–5[2]				
March 1987									2–6	1–5	1–5	0–4			
March 1988										1–5	1–5	0–4	0–4		
March 1989											1–5	0–4	0–4	−1–3	
March 1990												1–5	0–4	0–4	
March 1991													0–4	0–4	
March 1992														0–4	
March 1993															0–4[3]
Outcome[4]	10	6½	0	3½	6¼	5½	3½	4	5	7½	5¾	2½	2¼		
Money Supply: M1 (% change)															
March 1982				8–12	7–11										
March 1983					7–11										
Outcome				11	11										
Money Supply: £M3															
June 1979[5]	7–11														
March 1980		7–11	6–10												
March 1981			6–10	5–9											
March 1982				8–12	7–11	6–10									
March 1983					7–11	6–10	5–9								
March 1984						6–10	5–9[2]	4–8[2]	3–7[2]						
March 1985[6]							5–9	4–8[2]	3–7[2]	2–6[2]					
March 1986								11–15							
Outcome[4]	16¼	19½	12¾	10	9¾	9½	14¾								
Money Supply: PSL1[1] (% change)															
March 1982				8–12	7–11										
March 1983					7–11										
Outcome				9	12⅓										
Money Supply: M4 (% change)															
March 1993														4–8[7]	3–9[3]
RPI excl. MIPs (% change)															
March 1993														1–4	1–4

Table 12.3 MTFS, Target Ranges[1] and Outcomes (%) (cont'd)

	1979/80	1980/81	1981/82	1982/83	1983/84	1984/85	1985/86	1986/87	1987/88	1988/89	1989/90	1990/91	1991/92	1992/93	1993/94
PSBR (% of GDP)															
June 1979	4½														
March 1980	4¾	3¾	3	2¼	1½										
March 1981	5	6	4¼	3¼	2										
March 1982		5¾	4¼	3½	2	2½									
March 1983			3½	2¾	2¾	2¼	2								
March 1984				3¼	3¾	3¼	2	2							
March 1985						3	2	2	1¾	1¾					
March 1986							1½	1¾	1¾	1½	1½				
March 1987								1	1¼	1¼	1	1			
March 1988									−¾[3]	−¾[3]	0	0			
March 1989										−3[3]	−2¾	−1¾	−1	−½	
March 1990											−1¼	−1¼	−1½	0	
March 1991												−¼	1¼	2	
March 1992													2¼	4½	4¾
March 1993														5¾	8
Outcome	4¾	5½	3½	3¼	3¼	3	1½	1	−¾	−3	−1⅔	−⅛	2¼	5¾	8
Money GDP (% change)															
March 1985				7¾	6¾ (8¼)[9]	8½ (7)[9]	6¾	5¾	5						
March 1986						9½ (8¼)[9]	6¾	6½	6	5½					
March 1987							6	7½	6½	6	6				
March 1988									7½	6½	6	5½			
March 1989									11	7¾	7⅛	6	6		
March 1990										8½	7⅞	6⅝	5½	5½	
March 1991											7¼	6⅝	6⅝	6¾	
March 1992												6⅛	7⅛	6¾	
March 1993														6½	4¾

Notes:
1 Targets are set for a 14-month period commencing in February.
2 'Illustrative range'.
3 'Monitoring range.' Thus also applies to years beyond 1993/94.
4 Data taken from source cited. Slightly different figures are cited elsewhere. Outcomes relate to a 12-month period commencing in February.
5 Old definition including public sector deposits.
6 New definition excluding public sector deposits.
7 2nd half only.
8 Adjusted for distortions arising from the abolition of domestic rates.
9 Adjusted for coal strike.

impact on the growth of £M3 and also because of the effect of financing a high PSBR on interest rates: the so-called 'crowding-out' effect. As a result, the MTFS and other government policy statements emphasised the need for consistency between the PSBR and monetary targets, and a series of projections (not targets) for the PSBR was announced in 1980, as shown in **Table 12.3**. It is worth emphasising that the achievement of a stable financial policy, summarised in the £M3 target, required a reduction in the PSBR if interest rates were to be prevented from rising to an excessive level because of the need to finance the deficit from debt sales. This is evident from the flow-of-funds money supply counterpart equation.

12.8.2 Conservative Policy 1979–93: An Overview

When academics analyse government policy, there is a danger that they present an overcoherent and rational account of government behaviour. Government policy is rarely as clear cut as a textbook presentation. Governments inevitably have to respond to short-term political and economic developments. It is unlikely that any one person will hold a consistent set of opinions over a period of 14 years. It is still less likely that a group of individuals (such as the Cabinet) will do so, especially when its personnel is constantly changing. However, there are equal dangers in overstating variations and underemphasising the consistency which has underlaid the policy of Conservative governments since 1979.

There have been a number of marked shifts in Conservative policy. From 1979 to 1982, the government was committed to a strict monetarist policy. From 1982 to 1985, the government could still be described as monetarist, but in a much modified and watered-down form. From 1985 to 1990, economic policy was largely set by Mr Lawson, rather than by Mrs Thatcher. His approach was very different in many respects and placed far greater emphasis on the exchange rate. From 1990 to 1992, the government was com-

mitted to ERM membership. Since 1992, policy has been more expansionary within a framework of a managed exchange rate.

Nevertheless, it is important to emphasise that there were a number of consistent themes throughout the period. Indeed, some commentators would argue that the ends and underlying approach remained constant, even though the means varied so dramatically. The government was committed throughout to a policy of eliminating inflation, with possible exceptions only in 1987–88 and perhaps since October 1992. This goal was to be achieved through the use of financial policy. The government eschewed both Keynesian fiscal policy and the use of incomes policy. The government sought by various means to impose a framework of stability which would in some sense act as a discipline on private sector behaviour. In this context, both monetarism and exchange rate stability can be viewed as alternative mechanisms designed to provide stability and discipline. These should both constrain private sector behaviour and induce the formation of favourable inflationary expectations. It is now fashionable to describe this as seeking a credible policy. The policy is credible if, and only if, private sector economic agents believe in it. This belief shows up in low inflationary expectations. In these circumstances economic agents do not revise their inflationary expectations upwards in response to a short-term shock.

Mrs Thatcher can rightly claim that she saw the benefits of credibility before the concept became fashionable in academic literature. Her various lieutenants and successors could all claim that they sought such credibility, albeit through a variety of means.

12.9 The Policy in Action

12.9.1 Overview: The First Budget

The operation of policy and the fortunes of the economy can be divided for convenience into a number of phases:

- **1979–81: A policy-induced recession** as the government set up its anti-inflation strategy.
- **1982–85:** A period during which the authorities **abandoned a single monetary target** and experimented with multiple ones; as the inflation rate fell the policy stance eased, and the economy recovered slowly but steadily.
- **November 1985–Summer 1988:** A time when the focus of monetary policy switched to the **exchange rate**; policy was relaxed and the boom in the economy intensified.
- **Summer 1988–October 1990: A tightening of policy** as the government attempted to deal with the effects of the boom.
- **October 1990–December 1993:** This period largely coincided with the initial phase of Mr Major's premiership. It was characterised by recessionary conditions and falling interest rates.

Table 12.4 summarises the performance of the economy during the first two periods. Committed to an anti-inflationary strategy from the outset, the government began to tighten both fiscal and monetary policy almost immediately after taking office. The first Budget, in June 1979, saw the announcement of some £1.5 billion cuts in public expenditure and a planned fall in the PSBR from £9.2 billion to £8.2 billion over the year, reducing it from 5.5 per cent to 4.5 per cent of GDP. On the monetary side, MLR was raised by 2 per cent to 14 per cent, and the £M3 target range of 8–10 per cent was adjusted to 7–11 per cent, although this

Table 12.4 *The Performance of the Economy, 1979–88*

	1979–88	1979–83	1984–8
Real GDP growth (average % pa)	2.3	1	3.5
Inflation (average % pa)	8	11.2	4.7
Unemployment (average % of labour force)	9.3	8.4	10.3

Source: Economic Trends, Annual Supplement 1989.

was for the 10–month period to April 1980. For the time being the direct controls on the banking system remained in place. More controversially, there was a major switch in **taxation policy**: income tax rates were reduced (the basic rate from 33 to 30 per cent and the top rate from 86 to 60 per cent), and VAT rates were raised to a uniform 15 per cent. At a time when inflation was rising, from 8.1 per cent in the fourth quarter in 1978 to 10.6 per cent by the second quarter of 1979, the policy was to a degree perverse since it added to the RPI, and thus to inflationary expectations. Some writers have dismissed such a view as confusing a once-and-for-all rise in prices with a persistent increase in the general price level. However, the impact of a once-and-for-all rise in prices on inflationary expectations can be significant, and it probably was at this time. In the event, inflation continued to accelerate, reaching a peak of almost 22 per cent by mid-1980.

The removal of subsidies to, and of price controls on, the nationalised industries was pursued vigorously. Nationalised industry prices rose by 25 per cent in 1980, by 19 per cent in 1981 and by 58 per cent between 1980 and 1982. This increased cost inflation but reduced demand inflation. To a large extent, this was a continuation of Mr Healey's policies.

Further tightening occurred during 1979, with the MLR being raised to 17 per cent as the government attempted to cope with a policy that seemed to be going awry. By the end of the third quarter £M3 was growing at an annual rate of 14 per cent, well outside its target range, and the PSBR appeared to be on course for a major overshoot. It was only the abolition of exchange controls in July which prevented the money supply from rising completely out of control: the external impact in the third quarter of 1979 was £1.7 billion alone.

12.9.2 Introducing the Medium Term Financial Strategy (MTFS)

The introduction of the MTFS in the Budget of 1980 saw the reaffirmation of the government's principal objective of attacking inflation by reducing the rate of growth of £M3. A declining target range for this broad money aggregate was announced (see **Table 12.3**). The tightening of fiscal policy was reflected in a projected PSBR of £8.5 billion to be achieved through planned cuts in public spending and increases in taxation – the raising of excise duties and the abolition of the reduced income tax band of 25 per cent. There was also a projected decrease in the PSBR as a percentage of GDP over the next four years to 1.5 per cent of GDP (see **Table 12.3**). The apparent monetary squeeze continued.

The MLR was maintained at an historically high level in nominal terms (although it was nevertheless negative in real terms) and by the end of 1980 stood at 14 per cent, having been reduced to 15 per cent in July and to 14 per cent in November. The general trend of interest rates can be seen in **Figure 12.3**. The exchange rate appreciated sharply and M1, a narrow money aggregate, slowed.

During 1980 it became clear that the economy had moved into a major downturn as output contracted rapidly and unemployment began to mount, rising to 1.7 million by the end of the year. It was to be the severest recession of the postwar period, reaching its depth in output terms during the second quarter of 1981, with GDP 7.5 per cent below its previous peak two years earlier. Manufacturing output contracted by nearly 9 per cent in 1980 alone.

The most cogent explanation of the severity of the recession is that it was the effect of the extremely tight monetary policy on the exchange rate that produced such an intense squeeze on UK industry. Not only did sterling rise to over $2.40 in 1980, but the Exchange Rate Index in the second quarter of 1981 was also over 17 per cent above the level it had been two years before (see **p. 223**). Adjusting for the surge in domestic prices and costs, the real exchange rate was even higher. Domestic producers were caught between rising costs and interest rates at home, and a major loss of competitiveness abroad. Exports held up surprisingly well; it was the **import-competing sector** that bore the brunt of the adjustment.

Other explanations of the contraction include the impact of oil on the exchange rate and the conjunction of the second oil price shock with the

Figure 12.3   *Bank Base Rates, 1979–93*

Source: *Barclays Bank Review.*

ensuing world-wide downturn in economic activity. Whilst these added to the UK's problems, some estimates suggest that North Sea oil contributed only 8–12 per cent of the real appreciation, and yet others suggest much less. With regard to the international recession, the slowdown occurred rather later, in 1980–81, than the downturn in activity in the UK.

It was against such a background that the government tightened its fiscal policy further in the 1981 Budget. This was achieved primarily through significant rises in taxation, principally increases in excise duty and the non-indexation of income tax allowances. The objective was clearly to bring the PSBR and money supply closer into line with the MTFS plans after they had increased beyond their anticipated levels and target ranges respectively in 1980–81. The PSBR overshot by about £5 billion and £M3 grew at 19 per cent. Most commentators, however, were surprised that the government was apparently ignoring the increasing evidence of the stringency of policy. In the first place, there was the fact that the PSBR would be expected to rise as the economy moved into recession. Second, it was argued that £M3 was unreliable following the ending of the corset, the 'distress' borrowing by UK businesses and the high interest rates encouraging a shift from non-interest to interest-bearing accounts (see Gowland, 1984, for a defence of the value of £M3). The reason why the government chose to maintain such a policy stance can perhaps best be explained by a desire to retain the credibility of its anti-inflation commitment. Undoubtedly the 1981 Budget was an act of considerable political and economic courage, and almost certainly it paved the way for the successes of subsequent years.

Towards the end of 1981 economic activity reached a turning point, and there were some signs of an incipient recovery in output despite the fact that unemployment rose above 2.5 million by the end of the year. The anti-inflationary policy was also beginning to show its first fruits as the annual rate fell to 12 per cent. From this time on, a number of changes in policy became apparent. One was the beginning of the disillusionment with £M3 as the proximate target for

economic policy. In the 1982 Budget, target ranges were set for M1 and a broader aggregate, PSL2. There was also an indication that some account would be taken of the exchange rate in the operation of monetary policy. The then Chancellor, Mr Howe, stated that no single indicator of monetary policy was adequate. Instead, the government would pay attention to a number of indicators, termed 'considerations' in the formulation of policy. Another change was a switch in emphasis to nominal (money) GDP as the target for economic policy, with projections set for four years ahead as part of the MTFS. The basis of the GDP target was that if inflation showed signs of reaccelerating it would not be accommodated: policy would be adjusted to keep money GDP in the target range, and output would decline until price inflation fell.

☐ 12.9.3 Emerging from Recession

A further development was that the general stance of policy was eased slightly and progressively. In fact the fiscal position can be said to have remained relatively tight despite the reflationary effects of a series of income tax cuts in the 1986, 1987 and 1988 Budgets. The rise in productivity has also been cited as a significant change from earlier booms (Minford, 1989). There has been a major and prolonged debate about the behaviour of productivity during the 1980s. Some commentators saw evidence of a Thatcher miracle, whereas others believed that productivity followed a normal cyclical pattern. This debate is reviewed above (see **p. 69**). The emphasis on reducing the PSBR continued as it repeatedly overshot its original target level set in 1980, but fiscal policy did ease a little. In the 1983 Budget income tax thresholds were raised by 14 per cent, well above the 5.5 per cent inflation rate and the National Insurance surcharge was cut. These measures were seen as mildly reflationary in some quarters, although the Chancellor of the time, Sir Geoffrey Howe, re-emphasised that such cuts were not part of a scheme of demand management. The cynic, however, might point to the election that was called in June of that year and the additional spending cuts introduced in the Autumn. On the other hand, most indicators of the fiscal stance show that it was still tight; the cyclically adjusted public sector balance suggested that there was a real structural budget surplus (Dornbusch and Layard, 1987, p. 37).

The main easing came through the monetary side, the money supply targets notwithstanding. By the Autumn of 1982 interest rates, as measured by short-term money market rates, had fallen to 9 per cent (see **Figure 12.3**) and, despite a sharp increase in the Winter of 1982–83 to prevent too fast a fall in the exchange rate, interest rates remained in the 8–9 per cent range until June 1984. It was this monetary relaxation, and the corresponding fall in the exchange rate as interest rates rose abroad, which provided some of the stimulus to growth, but the main impetus came from consumers' expenditure. This was boosted by the rise in real incomes as earnings grew faster than prices, a credit boom inspired by deregulation and the effects of falling inflation on the saving ratio via a wealth effect. At the end of 1983 the inflation rate had fallen to 4.5 per cent per annum, and GDP grew by 1.9 per cent in 1982 and 3.7 per cent in 1983.

Under a new Chancellor, Mr Lawson (1983), the monetarist strategy – though not the other elements of Thatcherism – was officially abandoned. The official date is November 1985 when it was announced that £M3 was to be downgraded from a target variable to a monitored one. Starting in 1987, M0 became the only targeted monetary aggregate. Monetary policy reverted to influencing the exchange rate; this had been evident for some time before the official abandonment of monetary targets. In June 1984, for example, the Bank of England signalled a rise in interest rates which persisted until the Autumn, while sterling fell to 76 per cent of its 1980 level. The events of January 1985 were more dramatic. At a time of increasing uncertainty over oil prices, the UK's BoP and the government's resolve to maintain its anti-inflation policy (inflation had begun to accelerate during 1984 and the government had shown increasing concern over the serious unemployment problem), sterling fell sharply. At one time it went below the $1.10

level. The government responded by reintroducing the MLR at 12 per cent for a short period, and interest rates remained high for most of 1985 (see **Figure 12.3**).

The reasons for the shift in monetary policy towards the exchange rate lay in an increasing concern that exchange rate volatility affected adversely the trade performance of UK industry, and an acceptance of the view that exchange rate depreciation was the main mechanism through which inflation was transmitted to the domestic economy. With regard to the latter, it was maintained that if the value of sterling could be tied to the currency of a stable, low inflation economy this would provide an 'anchor' for the UK's inflation rate. For this reason the government operated an unofficial exchange rate target of £1 = DM3, later amended to DM3.10 and then DM3.20. It was at this time that the appropriateness of the UK's entry into the ERM became an issue of increasing topicality.

☐ 12.9.4. Overheating

Monetarist critics of the government felt that the government pursued an excessively expansionary policy from 1986 to 1988. They believed that this was reminiscent of earlier 'go' phases of the stop–go cycle. Certainly, there are marked similarities with 1964 and 1971–3: the rapid expansion in consumer credit, a house price boom, a surge in consumer spending and the deterioration in the current account are all characteristic symptoms of overheating in the UK economy. To some extent, economic policy was influenced (excessively?) by a desire to maintain a relatively stable exchange rate: the policy of shadowing the DM.

By far the most important contributor to the boom was the continued rise in consumers' expenditure, which grew at an average rate of 6.2 per cent per year between 1985 and 1988, as shown in **Table 12.5**. In particular, the housing market once again provided a graphic indicator of the loosening of money and credit policy. House prices rose at an average of nearly 16 per cent per annum in both 1986 and 1987; by 1988 the increase had accelerated to 38 per cent per annum.

Inflation followed suit. After reaching a low of 2.6 per cent per annum in the third quarter of 1986, rising demand began to feed through into higher inflation figures during 1987, and especially in 1988 when it rose to 6.5 per cent by the year's end. The unfolding of events at this time is instructive since it reveals the government's attempt to deal with a major policy dilemma.

Policy entered a critical phase early in 1988 after interest rates had been cut in the wake of the Stock Exchange collapse of the previous October, as shown in **Figure 12.3** and **Table 12.6**. Just as the concentration on a single internal monetary target in the early years of the government led to an excessively tight monetary policy, so the emphasis on a single external target – the £:DM exchange rate – had resulted in an over-relaxation of the monetary stance.

One difference from earlier booms was that the public sector moved into considerable surplus as higher levels of economic activity increased tax revenues (see **p. 178**). On the domestic front,

however, there were signs of too rapid an expansion, yet upward pressure on sterling forced further interest rate cuts as the government attempted to hold sterling at its DM3 target. After sterling had been 'uncapped' in March 1988, it became clear that either the exchange rate target would have to be sacrificed or interest rates would have to fall further, but at the risk of fuelling further domestic demand. By mid-Summer the problem resolved itself since the evidence of over-heating had become incontrovertible as measured by any indicator of the level of economic activity, be it the current account, inflation, consumer credit, average earnings or the government's sole remaining monetary target, M0. Compared with its target range of 1–5 per cent, M0 grew by 7.7 per cent between June 1987 and June 1988. Interest rates were raised progressively through the Autumn and the exchange rate permitted to rise as the government sought to slow the pace of expansion. Base rates reached 13 per cent in November and mortgage rates followed suit.

Table 12.5   *The Lawson Boom: Selected Indicators, 1985–88*

		Real GDP Growth (% pa)	Inflation[2] (% pa)	Average Earnings (% pa)	Real Consumers' Expenditure	Consumer Credit (%)	M3 (% pa)	Current Balance[3] (£ m)
1986	I	3.2	5.0	8.3	5.0	43.0	16.9	440
	II	3.3	2.9	8.1	7.8	50.0	18.9	1 888
	III	4.3	2.7	7.4	6.2	43.1	19.1	−1 042
	IV	5.0	3.5	7.9	6.2	36.9	19.1	1 782
1987	I	4.3	3.8	7.0	4.8	12.4	19.7	323
	II	4.3	4.2	7.5	3.9	20.1	19.8	−844
	III	5.5	4.2	7.7	5.9	21.2	20.2	−1 215
	IV	4.9	3.8	8.4	6.3	29.2	22.8	−2 423
1988	I	5.1	3.5	8.9	8.6	30.4	21.0	−3 258
	II	4.6	4.3	8.2	7.3	25.0	20.1	−3 100
	III	3.6	5.5	8.7	7.2	27.9	22.5	−3 331
	IV	3.8	6.5	9.5	6.7	18.4	20.3	−5 832

Notes:
[1] All % changes are year on year.
[2] Headline rate.
[3] Seasonally adjusted.
Source: Economic Trends; Bank of England Quarterly Bulletin; National Institute Economic Review, various issues.

Table 12.6   *Representative* Money Market Interest Rates (%)*

	USA	Germany	Japan	UK		USA	Germany	Japan	UK
Annual Averages					*Monthly Averages 1992/93*				
1980	13.1	9.5	10.9	16.6	1992 August	3.4	9.7	4.1	10.3
1981	15.9	12.1	7.4	13.9	September	3.2	9.3	4.1	10.2
1982	12.3	8.8	6.9	12.3	October	3.4	8.9	4.0	8.3
1983	9.1	5.8	6.4	10.1	November	8.7	8.8	3.9	7.2
1984	10.4	6.0	6.1	10.0	December	3.6	8.7	3.9	7.2
1985	8.1	5.4	6.5	12.2	1993 January	3.3	8.6	3.9	6.9
1986	6.5	4.6	4.8	10.9	February	3.2	3.3	3.2	6.2
1987	6.9	4.0	3.5	9.7	March	3.2	7.9	3.2	6.0
1988	7.7	4.3	3.7	10.3	April	3.2	7.9	3.1	5.9
1989	9.1	7.0	4.9	13.9	May	3.2	7.4	3.2	5.9
1990	8.0	8.4	7.2	14.7	June	3.3	7.5	3.2	5.9
1991	5.9	9.1	7.5	11.5	July	3.3	7.6	3.2	5.9
1992	3.8	8.6	4.6	9.6					

* USA: 3 months' CD rate; Germany: 3-month inter-bank; Japan: Call money; UK: 3-month inter-bank.
Source: Barclays Economic Review (August 1993).

Nigel Lawson, the ex-Chancellor, emphasised on numerous occasions (for example, Lawson, 1988) that short-term interest rates were regarded as the only effective instrument of monetary policy and hence the best way of affecting demand. This clearly indicated that demand management was by no means dead; during much of the 1980s it was actively pursued. What was different was that greater importance was given, at least verbally, to the **control of inflation** rather than the regulation of employment, as in earlier decades. Furthermore, fiscal policy was ostensibly used as a supply-side instrument as well as a demand-side one.

In reflecting on the 1980s it is possible to identify two sharply contrasting ways of looking at the experience of the UK economy. The first is that because of the shake-up which had been administered by the tight anti-inflationary policy of the early years (1979–81), the prudent fiscal policy and the continuing emphasis on free market supply-side measures, the economy emerged as more robust and flexible. The consequence was that economic growth was more sustainable. The second, more pessimistic, interpretation is that in spite of the growth performance in 1986–88, much of the improvement represented a catching-up period after a time of severe recession and the result of the operation of policy in a way rather different from its original conception. Moreover, many of the inherent weaknesses still remained and would resurface given the right conditions.

However, both these views are too extreme. The period produced some positive benefits: for example, in the marked improvement in the trend growth of productivity and the competitiveness of the manufacturing sector. On the other hand, such achievements were obtained at the cost of heavy unemployment and lost output. As is the case with all economic adjustments, the costs have not been shared equally. In addition, there was ample evidence of the resurgence of some of the underlying problems of the UK economy: the current account deterioration, rising inflation and the behaviour of earnings.

☐ 12.9.5 From Boom to Bust . . . Again

Economists are justifiably sceptical of the existence of obvious symmetries in the historical development of economies. It is, however, more than just a cruel coincidence that the 1980s ended and the 1990s began with the UK economy exhibiting some of the same problems that had existed a decade earlier, and which the Thatcher Government had set out to remedy in the certainty that its approach was correct. Thus the large current account deficit of £15 billion in 1988 had worsened to nearly £20 billion by 1989 and, by the early Autumn of 1990, inflation had accelerated to just short of 11 per cent.

The policy response, that of raising interest rates progressively from Summer 1988 (when bank base rates were at a low of 7.5 per cent) to October 1990 (when base rates reached 15 per cent), was relatively slow to take effect. This was especially true on the inflation front. The inflation rate continued to rise despite the slowing of the economy, and this was irrespective of whether inflation was measured by the headline or the underlying rate (see **p. 80**). As was the case a decade earlier, inflation once again became the

principal objective of macroeconomic policy. For example, the mounting current account deficit was variously dismissed as either symptomatic of overheating, the result of unreliable statistics as indicated by the massive balancing item or a temporary phenomenon that would be self-correcting.

In the early days of the operation of the restrictive policy, much was made of the likelihood of a 'soft landing', where the economy would adjust with relatively little cost in terms of lost output and of unemployment. The reality was quite the reverse as the details in **Table 12.7** indicate. From around the third quarter of 1990 the UK entered a major recession.

ERM Entry

Of central importance to the operation of macroeconomic policy at this time was the debate – indeed split – within the government over the causes of the inflation and the related and critical

Table 12.7 *Into recession, 1989–91*

		Real GDP[1] Growth (% pa)	Inflation[2] (% pa)	Unemployment (%)	Manufacturing Productivity (% change pa)	Current Balance (£m)
1989	I	2.7	7.7	7.0	6.4	−5 039
	II	2.4	8.2	6.5	5.4	−5 262
	III	2.1	7.7	6.2	3.0	−6 323
	IV	1.4	7.6	5.9	1.5	−5 103
1990	I	1.8	7.8	5.7	1.5	−5 692
	II	1.8	9.7	5.6	2.8	−5 469
	III	−0.1	10.4	5.7	1.9	−2 796
	IV	−1.4	10.0	6.1	0.1	−3 074
1991	I	−2.4	8.6	6.7	−0.3	−2 537
	II	−3.5	6.0	7.6	−0.3	−349
	III	−1.9	4.8	8.3	2.5	−1 478
	IV	−1.1	4.2	8.8	4.1	−1 877

Notes:
[1] At market prices.
[2] Headline rate.
Source: Economic Trends.

issue of the appropriate policy response. It is a debate that led to the resignation of a Chancellor (Lawson), and the wider aspects of which brought about the departure of a Foreign Secretary (Howe) and a Prime Minister (Thatcher).

As regards the causes of the inflation, one explanation offered was that of the Thatcher–Walters camp. This view maintained that the policy of shadowing the DM from 1987 resulted in excessive monetary expansion as the authorities sold sterling on the foreign exchange markets and lowered interest rates to prevent the pound from rising above its DM3 target. For a monetarist such as Walters, the excessive money supply increases could lead only to an acceleration in inflation at some later date.

Opposing this view was Lawson and the ERM camp. Their argument was that had the UK entered the ERM at an earlier date, say in 1985, this would have provided a credible anchor for UK inflation. In brief, the policy works by tying the pound to the DM, thus not permitting faster inflation in the UK relative to Germany to be offset by a currency depreciation. As long as wage bargainers and price setters have confidence in the authorities' determination to maintain the exchange rate, expectations should adjust and the UK inflation rate should ultimately converge on the German rate. A failure of expectations to adjust, and the persistence of higher inflation in the UK, can lead to a loss of competitiveness and unemployment. Ultimately, the discipline of the ERM should force a convergence of inflation rates either through the effect of reduced competitiveness producing a rise in unemployment, or because the authorities have to raise interest rates in order to maintain the exchange rate, or both. To support their case the proponents of ERM entry cited the superior inflation performance of countries such as France and Italy.

The policy implications of the two views should be reasonably clear. In the Thatcher–Walters version, the best indicators of inflationary pressure are the **domestic monetary statistics**, especially the narrow monetary base (M0). As a consequence, policy should be targeted to maintain a steady non-inflationary growth of these aggregates. By contrast, the government settled finally upon the ERM approach, joining the wide band in October 1990 at a central rate of £1 = DM2.95. Although entry can be seen partly as a victory for the supporters of this approach to inflation control, following the disappointing response of domestic inflation to high interest rates, there were other factors at work. In the first place, the victory had in essence already been won in June 1989 when Mrs Thatcher gave a conditional commitment to join the ERM. Second, the pressure to join was intensifying following the increasing integration of the EU economies as a result of the SEM and the proposals for full monetary union.

An important aspect of exchange rate regimes such as the ERM is that they reduce greatly a government's freedom in the domestic monetary sphere. Interest rates cannot be set solely with reference to domestic developments, but must be directed to maintaining sterling within its ERM band. This provides one possible explanation of why interest rates were maintained at so high a level for so long at this time. A rapid cut in interest rates immediately after ERM entry could have undermined confidence in the government's commitment to a stringent anti-inflationary stance, and any pressure on sterling resulting in an early realignment would have eroded credibility altogether. As a result, interest rates were reduced by only 1 per cent on entry. It was not until the rate of increase in the RPI began to fall back in late 1990 and early 1991, and the severity of the downturn became evident as the level of economic activity plunged, that the government felt confident enough to cut interest rates. Base rates subsequently fell from 14 per cent in January 1991 to 11 per cent in July that year.

ERM entry alone cannot explain why the government maintained high interest rates for so long in the 1988–91 period, since the policy had operated for at least two years prior to entry. Furthermore, the downward trend in interest rates began after October 1990, albeit slowly and in line with falling inflation. One possible explanation is the previously noted slowness of the economy to respond to the monetary squeeze. A second possibility is that the government misjudged the seriousness of the recession. Even though growth had slowed down from its high levels in early 1988, and unemployment had started to rise from the low point of 1.6 million in March 1990, GDP was still growing at an annual rate of 1–2 per cent up until the second quarter of 1990. It was not until the third quarter of that year that, in the colourful language of City commentators, the economy 'fell off the edge'. GDP growth halted and subsequently fell precipitously (see **Table 12.7**). This abrupt plunge probably arose from the combination of a slump in consumer and business expectations after a protracted period of high interest rates and rising inflation, combined with high levels of indebtedness following the credit boom earlier in the decade.

Another likely explanation is that the government overcorrected, squeezing the economy too hard (a reaction to the laxity in monetary policy that had allowed the boom to run on too long in 1987–88). Faulty statistics may have had some part to play in misjudging the boom, as perhaps did a misplaced belief in the productivity 'miracle'. Nevertheless, errors of policy in the upswing of the cycle should not be used as an excuse for overreacting in the downturn.

A further, and important, aspect of ERM entry is the question of whether the UK entered at too high a level for the pound. This is a view shared by monetarist critics such as Walters and Keynesians (for example, the NIESR) alike. Both have emphasised the long-term loss of competitiveness and the consequent unemployment problems that arise from an overvalued exchange rate. It imparts a recessionary bias into the economy, a problem which may become greater in the UK unless inflation falls to, or below, the EMS average. For monetarists such as Walters, interest rates were held at too high a level throughout 1990. In their view, the monetary indicators showed that the battle against inflation had already been won and that policy needed to be relaxed significantly if a serious recession was to be avoided. As a consequence, ERM entry could only make things worse.

Political considerations notwithstanding, a possible justification for the government's decision to enter at its chosen rate is that any lowering of the rate on entry would have threatened the strict anti-inflationary stance of policy. A relatively high pound had the benefit of reaffirming this policy, possibly having a beneficial effect on expectations. Moreover, as argued above, a higher exchange rate necessarily leads directly to a lower level of inflation. ERM membership at a high exchange rate was a logical and consistent part of anti-inflation policy. It was clear, as also argued above, that this would lead to unemployment. One must presume that the government either misjudged the extent of the cost relative to the benefits or felt that the unemployment was, as Mr Lamont held, a 'price worth paying'.

Fiscal Policy

In terms of the counterpart equation outlined at the beginning of this chapter, policy during the period 1988–91 operated primarily on the credit term; interest rates were used to reduce the growth of bank and building society lending. As it had during the first half of the 1980s, the government continued the break with the earlier Keynesian tradition and did not use fiscal policy (measured by the PSBR in the counterpart equation) as a discretionary counter-cyclical measure. As a consequence, the PSBR tended to move with the cycle, and in 1989 the PSDR reached £11.8 billion. As the pace of economic activity slowed, the PSDR declined so that by the end of the 1990–91 financial year it was only roughly £0.5 billion.

The recession caused the PSBR to reappear. However, unlike the policy of the early 1980s when the government sought to cut the deficit in a recession, the intention as stated in the 1991 FSBR was to permit the deficit to move with the economic cycle. This may well provide the economy with some automatic stabilisation, although of a very limited kind.

In summary, the past several years provide a classic demonstration of a fundamental difficulty of macroeconomic policy, namely that it is rarely possible to achieve **all policy objectives at the same time**. A traditional explanation for this is that to hit more than one policy target requires more than one policy instrument. Policy during this period has been compared to a golfer using only one club. Another, less emphasised, aspect is the problem of economic dynamics: that is, the way an economy develops over time. In the first place, it takes time for a policy measure to take effect. Thus the timing of an increase or reduction in interest rates is critical to the effect of the policy on inflation and growth. Second, when an economy recovers after a period of disinflation, the level of economic activity, and especially the rate of unemployment, may remain at undesirable levels for some time. It was this latter problem that was beginning to oppress the government from about the middle of 1991.

■ *12.10* Majorism

☐ *12.10.1 Waiting for the Economy to Recover*

In theory, falling inflation can produce an automatic recovery in economic activity either because of a wealth effect on consumption, because of improved cost competitiveness of traded goods or by permitting interest rates to fall. Throughout 1991 and much of 1992, in addition to the attempts to talk up consumers' and borrowers' confidence, the government seemed to pin its hopes for recovery more or less exclusively on this automatic self-righting mechanism. This complacency had some basis in events since inflation and interest rates were on a clear downward trend. Sharp rises in unemployment had moderated earnings growth and raised productivity, so that by 1992 the growth in unit labour costs in the UK was lower than its main competitors. In the view of some commentators, the cost competitiveness of exports and import-competing products had been restored and a recovery was imminent.

The upturn, however, proved elusive and the recession of the early 1990s turned out to be the most protracted one in the postwar period. Though less deep in terms of the decline in GDP compared to the recession a decade earlier, it was of a longer duration. Unemployment rose less sharply, but from a lower base, so levels were very similar in the two recessions (statistical changes make exact comparisons impossible).

Women and younger workers suffered greater unemployment in the 1990s, as did workers in the South-East.

One of the reasons why the level of economic activity remained depressed for so long was the high level of debt in the personal and company sectors. In terms of simple Keynesian macroeconomics, the debt overhang raised savings which in turn reduced demand and output: the paradox of thrift. In the company sector the debt burden, in conjunction with declining demand, was an important cause of retrenchment in some firms – labour shedding and reining in investment – and insolvency in others. Some of the most dramatic effects were seen in those firms which had invested heavily in the commercial property market, anticipating a continuation of the late 1980s boom. The collapse of prices in this market led to some notable failures – for example, Olympia & York of Canary Wharf fame (or notoriety) – and had serious repercussions on some financial institutions as well as the construction industry.

An important contributor to the recessionary conditions was the maintenance of a relatively tight monetary policy. Base rates had fallen from their peak of 15 per cent in 1989 but, by the beginning of 1992, they were stuck at 10 per cent despite the downward trend in inflation. The reason, as noted above, was the commitment to keep the pound within its ERM band. Another popular explanation for the length of the recession was that consumer confidence had been depressed by a fear of unemployment. While this is a possibility, there is little direct evidence to suggest that this had any more of an effect in 1991–92 than in previous downturns. Moreover, the combination of debt, tight money and a high exchange rate seems sufficient to provide an explanation.

☐ *12.10.2 ERM Exit*

A fourth consecutive Conservative election victory in April 1992 coincided with some stirrings of recovery, but these failed to develop into anything more substantial. Indeed, it took until the Spring of 1993 for any real signs of an upturn, by which time there had been a number of dramatic reversals in policy that helped to stimulate demand. The key to the policy U-turn was the UK's exit (or ejection) from the ERM in September 1992, and the unfolding of events over the Summer of 1992 is a classic illustration of the impossibility of operating an independent monetary policy at the same time as targeting or fixing the exchange rate.

In the last few months of 1992, the government sought to regain credibility by various means. The government announced that it would be committed to a final target (2–4 per cent inflation), rather than an intermediate target. This marked a return to Mr Lawson's approach in a rather more formal fashion. The Bank of England was charged with monitoring the government's performance in this respect and was required to issue a quarterly Inflation Report which would analyse the prospects for future inflation and the impact of government policy. The government announced this as part of a series of measures designed to make economic policy making more open and accountable. This was an attempt to achieve by other means some of the objectives common to both ERM membership and monetary targets. One such measure was the establishment of a council of economic advisers, known as the 'seven wise men', who embraced a wide range of views.

The policy dilemma at the time can be stated in the following way. On the one hand, the failure of an economic recovery to materialise and a poor trade performance, especially in respect of imports, clearly indicated a need to ease monetary policy, via a lowering of interest rates and an associated fall in the exchange rate. On the other hand, the credibility of the government's anti-inflation policy rested on maintaining the external value of the pound, both because of the direct effect of exchange rates on the price level and because of confidence effects. An ideal solution for the government would have been to be able to cut interest rates while leaving the exchange rate unaffected, but this would have been possible only if interest rates in the rest of the EU, and especially in Germany, were falling. However, German interest rates remained high as the Bun-

desbank pursued a hardline anti-inflation policy (probably correctly, despite criticism from London). As a consequence UK interest rates needed to be high to prevent a sterling depreciation.

The balance of opinion in the financial markets was, however, that the UK's policy was unsustainable and, anticipating a devaluation of sterling within the ERM and lower interest rates, speculative pressure mounted throughout the Summer of 1992. These speculative pressures were both financial, with sterling trading close to the bottom of its ERM band, as well as of the type produced by the press and other commentators. Against such a background the government struggled to maintain the credibility of its exchange rate target. Matters came to a head on 16 September, known either as Black or White Wednesday (see **p. 257**). This produced an immediate depreciation, and after two months sterling had fallen by 13 per cent against the DM. Subsequently it recovered somewhat, such that by mid-1993 the effective depreciation was only 7 per cent.

□ 12.10.3 Policy after the ERM

Once the U-turn had been completed, the government pursued an expansionary monetary policy with some vigour. Interest rates were cut to 7 per cent by the end of 1992 and by a further 1 per cent in early 1993. In the first half of 1993 a rather sluggish recovery became evident. The policy change, however justified, has left a number of issues unresolved. First, there were some fears that a falling pound would jeopardise the gains made in respect of inflation. In practice, a recovery in the level of sterling in early 1993 abated this fear and it seemed the eventual depreciation (7 per cent) might be sufficient to stimulate without inflating. Second, and related to the first point, is that although cutting sterling free from its ERM constraints has allowed the government some freedom in monetary policy, the problem has not been solved. If a government cares about the level of its currency's exchange rate, and especially if the exchange rate is regarded as an important mechanism through which inflation is transmitted, it loses the ability to pursue an independent monetary policy.

Third, a number of commentators have argued that having suspended its membership of the ERM, the UK no longer has an effective anchor for inflation; that is, there will be a danger of acceleration once the economy moves out of recession. One solution to the problem would be to re-enter the ERM at a later date, followed rapidly by progress towards full European Monetary Union. The effect would be to force a convergence in European inflation rates. The difficulty with this path lies not only in domestic political constraints but also with the failure of the EU economies to meet the conditions necessary for European Monetary Union. For its part, the government's response has not been to set out a new policy framework in any detail, but to announce rather broad targets for growth and inflation of 2.75 per cent and 1–4 per cent respectively. In addition, the Prime Minister, John Major, signalled a shift towards growth as the main objective of policy in a speech in October 1992. The change in policy is a significant departure from the pre-announced targeting of an intermediate objective as operated in the early years of Mrs Thatcher's Government (with £M3 as the target) and from 1990 to 1992 (with an exchange rate target), and it constitutes a shift to the use of monetary policy as a discretionary instrument. Whether this and the steps taken to improve credibility are sufficient, or whether a more explicit framework is required, remains to be seen.

A fourth issue is that of the growing public sector deficit, largely due to the recession and some pre-election spending increases in 1991–92. In the financial year 1992–93 the PSBR reached £36.7 billion (6 per cent of GDP), and is predicted to rise to £50 billion (8 per cent of GDP) in 1993–94. Some old arguments about the appropriateness of a sizeable deficit have begun to resurface. On the one side there is a fear that increased sales of government debt may result in the crowding-out of private sector spending, especially investment, as interest rates are pushed up. The suggested solution is that either taxes should rise or spending commitments should be cut. An alternative view is that the PSBR problem will disappear with the recovery or require only minor tax increases, and then only when the recovery is under way. Indeed, a monetary expansion resulting from an unfunded PSBR (that is, where the PSBR is not fully financed by debt sales: see the supply-side counterpart equation on **p. 441**) at such a low point in the business cycle may be no bad thing. As ever, the government steered a cautious course, taking account both of the concerns of the financial markets (which needed to be reassured over the government's commitment to controlling public borrowing), and the possibility of stifling an upturn with premature tax increases. In order to resolve these conflicting pressures, the then Chancellor, Mr Lamont, used the 1993 Budget to announce tax increases but with full implementation delayed for up to two years so that the bulk of the increased revenue would be raised in 1994–95 and 1995–96. These tax increases amounted to £10 billion spread over three years.

☐ *12.10.4 The Supply Side*

One of the fundamental weaknesses in textbook Keynesian analysis is that it analyses demand management without consideration of the supply side. The authors of this chapter would like to stress that it is impossible to formulate any judgement about economic policy without reference to the supply side as well as to demand management. Some supply-side issues are considered elsewhere, notably in Chapter 2, and while there is no desire to replicate these, it is helpful to sketch out a few of the inter-actions between macroeconomic and microeconomic policy.

Mr Lawson chose in 1985–6 to pursue a highly expansionary policy. Such policies have failed before, and it seemed to many commentators (including the present authors) that the experiment was doomed to fail once more. However, Mr Lawson believed differently and was supported by many economists, including the editor of this volume! It is therefore necessary to examine why he acted as he did. One possibility is that he believed that it would help the Conservative Party in the 1987 General Election. This is almost certainly a part of the truth. Another explanation is that Mr Lawson believed that Conservative supply-side policy had transformed the economy such that rapid expansion was no longer dangerous. It is also possible that some of the expansionary policies were designed for supply-side reasons. This is particularly relevant to his actions concerning credit policy. Mr Lawson may have believed that liberalisation of credit markets would have desirable microeconomic supply-side effects. He may have been aware of their deleterious macroeconomic consequences, but felt that these were outweighed by the microeconomic benefits.

Similarly, it was clear to all neutral observers that ERM membership would reduce inflation at the price of increasing unemployment. The magnitude of these costs and benefits would depend upon how the labour market responded to a savage deflationary shock. ERM membership was executed by Mr Major, but long urged by Mr Lawson. It seems both reasonable and charitable to believe that they were far more optimistic about the extent of Conservative supply-side policies than the facts warranted. Monetarists felt that ERM membership demonstrated the validity of their case. New Keynesian authors felt similarly that their analysis was proved right by the behaviour of the UK economy during both the Lawson boom and the ERM deflation.

To concentrate exclusively on the demand side of macroeconomic policy is to miss one of the most important lessons of the Lawson boom and the Major–Lamont recession, which is that in the UK an expansion in demand comes up against a supply constraint at an early stage, so that inflation begins to accelerate even when unemployment is unacceptably high. Or, to put it in more technical language, the UK's NAIRU is too high. It will be recalled that a central tenet of Mrs Thatcher's economic policy in the early 1980s was that the UK's economic performance could only be improved if the supply side was overhauled. To achieve this objective the government embarked on a programme of free market microeconomic policies, known as supply-side economics, but the effects have not all been beneficial. The liberalism of the financial markets, for example, contributed both to the upsurge in demand in the credit and mortgage boom of 1988–89 and

the prolongation of the 1990s recession. On the other hand, to some the clearest evidence of the government's achievements has been the improvement in the growth rate of productivity, with output per person per hour in manufacturing in 1992 standing some 52 per cent above its level ten years earlier, and for the whole economy the rise being 19 per cent (output per person employed). In terms of international comparisons UK productivity grew faster in the period 1980–92 than productivity in the other OECD countries besides Japan. Nevertheless, the productivity performance was insufficient to overcome the supply constraints in 1988–89, and some analysts have questioned whether there has been a productivity 'miracle' at all. To the sceptics, the acceleration in productivity growth can be attributed to a once-and-for-all catching up after lagging behind in earlier decades, rather than an upward shift in the long-term trend. That is, of course, not to say that the supply-side reforms have not contributed to the improvement.

Finally, some doubt can be cast on the effectiveness of the labour market reforms (for example, the trade union legislation and changes in benefit entitlements). Designed to improve the operation of market forces in the labour market by increasing flexibility in wage-setting and the allocation of labour and to increase the incentive to work, these were ultimately aimed at reducing the NAIRU. Yet some recent estimates have put the level of unemployment compatible with stable inflation as high as 8 per cent. Some insights into why the NAIRU should have remained so high are provided by recent theoretical advances in the analysis of labour markets. Broadly speaking, these approaches suggest that the labour market cannot be treated as being akin to the market for apples or oranges: wages do not adjust to clear the market, but may remain high despite persistent excess supply. Two possible explanations lie in the existence of efficiency wages – employers pay above-market-clearing wages to motivate employees – and the division of the labour market into 'insiders' and 'outsiders' (see **p. 348**). The behaviour of wages over the recent recession provides some rather casual evidence in support of such explanations, although other interpretations are possible.

The experience of the UK economy in recent years has been a sobering one, especially for the optimists who believed that the Conservative Government's reforms begun in 1979 had transformed the backdrop against which macroeconomic policy operates. There have indeed been radical changes, but some fundamental and seemingly intractable difficulties still confront UK policy makers. On the demand side there is the question of how best to control the inflationary tendencies of the UK. Others are supply-side issues, often regarded as outside the traditional ambit of macroeconomic policy, but still central to macroeconomic performance, such as unemployment and the operation of the labour market and the non-exchange rate factors affecting competitiveness and the trade balance.

12.11 The Decline of Keynesianism

☐ 12.11.1 Self-fulfilling Beliefs

In the 1950s the average level of unemployment was about 250 000, only one-tenth of the level of the 1980s and about one-eighth of that of the 1930s. The low level of unemployment was almost universally attributed to Keynesian economic management as economists complacently congratulated themselves on having rid the world of the scourge of unemployment. Any appraisal of economic policy in the 1980s must, therefore, start by asking why the techniques that worked so well in the 1950s were not even tried in the 1980s; and whether, if tried, they would have worked.

Full employment in the 1950s and 1960s was the result of the **private sector's response** to the government policy of the time, not directly of what the governments did. In particular, because the private sector believed in full employment, it changed its behaviour and invested more. The critical act of government was to commit itself to a policy of **full employment**. Full employment implied that demand and expenditure (and hence future sales) would remain high. It would thus be profitable to invest to satisfy this demand. More-

over, a belief in full employment boosted such intangible forces as business confidence, and so caused a further rise in investment.

One category of investment does not depend in any way on expectations of future sales. This is housebuilding, which is of especial importance because some studies suggest that it was a major cause of the high levels of employment experienced in the late 1950s: that this was, in Keynesian terms, the injection which kept the economy at a high level of demand. However, the housebuilding boom depended in large apart on the enormous personal sector demand for housing which was matched by a willingness to accept long-term mortgage commitments to finance house purchases. Keynesian economists argue plausibly that the belief in full employment was at least a necessary condition for people to be prepared to do this. If someone takes out a mortgage they are committing themselves to making repayments over a period of at least 20 years. No-one would do this if they feared that they were likely to lose their job in the near future, for that matter, building societies (which had a monopoly of mortgage lending in the 1950s) would not lend to such people. Moreover, house purchasers have to consider the prospects of resale, which depend upon both the state of the economy in general and upon other people's willingness to take out mortgages in particular. Hence, the **belief** in full employment was again one of the causes of extra demand.

These Keynesian arguments can be challenged, but it is generally accepted that they have some force and that belief in the efficiency of activist government policy boosted employment in the 1950s. The reasons for its apparent failure in the 1960s and 1970s are more controversial. Keynesians cite two factors: a decline in the belief in full employment and the adverse consequences of the belief in full employment.

☐ 12.11.2 The Erosion of Belief

Belief in the continuation of full employment, and in particular of the ability of government to maintain it, declined from about 1965 because:

a the theory of demand management came under criticism from Milton Friedman; this has led some prominent Keynesians (such as Hahn) mischievously and humorously to suggest that such views should be suppressed even if they are right and Keynesianism promoted even if wrong;

b governments seemed to give less prominence to full employment as a goal of economic policy after 1964 (when the Labour Government gave priority to the BoP);

c as unemployment rose after 1965, faith in the efficiency of full employment policies declined.

The Keynesian account is thus of a **cumulative process**. Full employment would continue only so long as people believed that it would. As faith declined so unemployment rose and faith declined further, and so on **ad infinitum**.

Most Keynesian analysts, however, give much more weight to the adverse effects of a belief in full employment rather than to the decline in the belief itself. In particular, because trade union leaders believed in full employment, they ceased to believe that the threat of unemployment need constrain wage demands. Hence they asked for large-scale wage demands. Employers acceded to these demands, in part because their belief in full employment created the expectation in their minds that they would be able to pass the wage increases on as price increases, and consequent high demand. Hence the belief in full employment led first to cost inflation, and so to upward movements of AS curves, and second to employers substituting capital for labour. The premise of activist demand management was that the demand for labour would fluctuate only according to output. This was no longer so. Some Keynesians regarded this as an argument for incomes policy.

What is relevant is that the achievement of full employment depended on a belief that it **could and would be achieved**. This was because investment was much higher as a consequence of the belief in the effectiveness of government policy. Such beliefs, however, also had adverse effects which made the continuation of full employment

much harder to achieve: indeed, perhaps impossible. In summary, belief that governments could achieve and maintain full employment was self-fulfilling in the 1950s, but problems also arose both because this confidence declined and because of the management and trade union movement's response to its belief in full employment.

It was certainly the case that full employment policies encouraged complacency and inefficient management of firms. Firms expected to sell their products irrespective of quality, design or reliability, so they had no incentive to produce reliable, high quality goods. Hence the two aspects of the 'English disease' arose as a consequence: bad management, and aggressive unions which resisted innovation and demanded high wages.

■ *12.12* Freidman's Critique

The most important omission from the elementary Keynesian theory of demand management is **inflationary expectations**. In essence, the idea underlying this concept is very simple: if economic agents expect inflation, they will change their behaviour such that there will be inflation. Although originally introduced into economic analysis by Friedman, the concept is now central to all economic models whether Keynesian, monetarist, post-Keynesian, new classical or anything else.

Let us suppose that the government decides to pursue an expansionary policy which can be represented by an outward shift of the AD curve for the whole economy. Output will rise, and so will inflation. In the Keynesian model this is the end of the story, whereas Friedman argues:

a that the higher rate of inflation will generate higher expectations as to the future rate of inflation;

b that this will cause the AS curve to shift up and to the left;

c that ultimately the AS curve will come to rest such that output falls to its original level and inflation is ongoing at the rate determined by the point of intersection of AD and AS.

If Friedman is right, then obviously activist demand management will work in the short run but not in the long run. However, the reader may very well ask two pertinent questions, namely: (a) Why does a rise in inflationary expectations cause the AS curve to shift upwards? (b) Why is this shift exactly enough such that output reverts to its original level?

The answer to the first question is most easily answered by considering underlying microeconomic behaviour. Firms make decisions about their prices on the basis of costs and demand (marginal and average revenue). However, all of these have to be based on their beliefs about these variables since in the real world they cannot be known with certainty. In many cases, prices are fixed for a period of time so these beliefs are expectations about the future. For example, when Hoover are deciding what price to charge for washing machines, they need to determine the demand for their product. This will depend on such matters as the price of substitutes. If Hoover believe that rivals are going to increase their prices then the demand curve for Hoover's products moves further to the right. So Hoover's expectations about price increases by rivals will thus determine the position of their demand curve and hence their price. If every firm expects every other firm to charge more, the belief is self-fulfilling. Moreover, a higher price for the same output is a definition of an upward shift in a supply curve, aggregate or otherwise.

The argument is even simpler in the labour market. The perceived shift in the demand for goods causes a shift in the demand for the labour which made them. A higher expected level of prices causes a fall in perceived real wages, and so leads to an inward shift in the supply of labour. Supply moves in and demand moves out, hence wages rise at each level of employment. All of these shifts can be represented at an aggregate level by a shift of the AS curve. Higher inflationary expectations thus lead to an upward shift of the AS curve.

Freidman's argument is that higher inflation leads to a higher expected level of inflation and so to an adverse shift of the AS curve. The extent of this shift of the AS curve depends upon how expectations of inflation respond to actual inflation. There can be little doubt that there is some response, since if inflation is high or rising it is unreasonable not to expect it to be higher in future than one would if inflation were low. Friedman's analysis is, however, a special case in that he assumes that the rise in the expected rate of inflation is exactly equal to the current rise in inflation. Thus if inflation rose from 4 to 5 per cent, expected inflation would follow suit (at least in the long run). If this is so, the shift in AS is exactly enough for output to fall to its original level (that is, for AS to shift from AS_1 to AS_2 in **Figure 12.4**) thus answering the second question posed above. Friedman's analysis can be presented in another way:

$$\text{Inflation}_t = \text{Expected inflation}_t + \text{Demand inflation}$$

$$\text{Expected Inflation}_t = \text{Inflation}_{t-1}$$

$$\text{so Inflation}_t = \text{Inflation}_{t-1} + \text{Demand inflation}$$

It is the linkage between **inflation and past inflation** which is one of the achievements of Friedman's model. In linking these items, it explains inflation as a continuing increase in prices,

Figure 12.4 *AD, AS and Inflation*

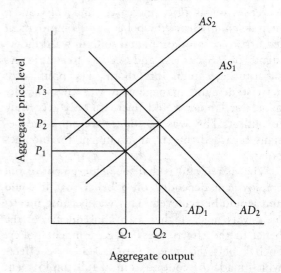

rather than as a once-and-for-all rise in price. In the orthodox model there is an inverse relationship between inflation and unemployment. In Friedman's model the inverse relationship is between **demand** inflation and unemployment. The cost of a lower level of unemployment is demand inflation and hence an accelerating, rising level of total inflation: whenever there is demand inflation, inflation is necessarily higher than in the previous year (inflation falls only when demand inflation is negative). In brief, Friedman's argument is that activist demand management can keep unemployment at a low level only by accepting an accelerating level of inflation. This is likely to be both unacceptable and probably uncontainable.

The other major plank of Friedman's critique has been emphasised since his earliest writings in the late 1940s: that the theory of (Keynesian) activist demand management was based upon an **assumption of omniscience**. Activist demand management assumes that governments know both the entire structure of the economy and the shocks that it will face. Friedman stressed the enormous amount of knowledge of behaviour required to write even the simple consumption function and other relationships discussed in so doing Chapter 3 above. The government is unlikely, in Friedman's view, to know the value of the marginal propensity to save, with the result that it cannot carry out the calculations necessary to manage the economy. Behaviour, Friedman argued, is much more complex and difficult to predict than the activists had assumed.

Similarly, in order to use stabilisation policy to offset shocks as described above, governments must be able to **predict them**. Friedman argued that any government which believed it had such knowledge was living in a fools' paradise. In this respect Friedman was echoing Keynes, who had based his analysis on the threat posed by the 'dark forces of ignorance and uncertainty'. Keynes was, however, by temperament an activist and an optimist who believed that governments could reduce the consequences of the dark forces. Friedman, by nature a pessimist, believed that they could not. Opponents of demand management have continued to stress these Friedmanite argu-

ments. Laidler, for many years the most prominent of UK monetarists, recently described it as 'the bottom line' of his moderate Friedmanite-monetarist position, the foundation on which he rested his opposition to activist policy.

Friedman went on to argue that activist demand management policies would confuse the private sector and introduce an element of unpredictability into private sector decision-making (for example, about tax rates). In Friedman's view this would have two adverse effects.

1   It would render private sector behaviour less efficient: with less knowledge upon which to base their decisions, economic agents would inevitably make worse decisions; hence, the economy would be less efficient (in the terms of the analysis used in this book, the AS curve would shift upwards).
2   It would render private sector behaviour less stable and so contradict the goals of demand management; private sector behaviour would respond to contra-cyclical policy by being more erratic, and so income would vary more than without government action designed to reduce such fluctuations.

To summarise Friedman's argument: activist demand management is possible only with a degree of knowledge and predictive ability that is normally unattainable. However, for a variety of temporary reasons it seemed in the 1950s that such omniscience was the case. The 1960s and 1970s revealed the hollowness of this claim.

12.13 New Classical and Radical Critiques

So far in this chapter, the analysis has concentrated upon Friedman's critique of the theory and practice of Keynesian demand management. The contrast between these is marked when the analysis of the effect of an increase in AD on the economy is considered.

In **Figure 12.5** this is shown using both AD/AS analysis and Phillips Curves. The naive Keynesian model says that the expansionary policy, represented by a shift in the AD curve from AD_1 to AD_2 will move the economy from 1 to 2: that is, it will reduce unemployment, albeit at a cost in terms of inflation. Friedman argues that the result is only a short-run one. The higher inflation will generate expectations of higher inflation which will cause the AS or Phillips Curve to shift such that the economy finishes at point 3. For Friedman, then, acceptance of higher rate of inflation buys only a transient fall in unemployment. The only way to reduce unemployment permanently is to accept accelerating inflation. Sophisticated Keynesians accept the essence of Friedman's analysis, but suggest econometric or theoretical reasons why the AS or Phillips Curve will not shift as far as in Friedman's analysis, so the economy will finally come to rest at K. In this case there is still a long-run trade-off between unemployment and inflation, albeit a much more expensive one than in the naive Keynesian model.

Many economists reject both the Keynesian and Friedmanite analysis. Indeed, they are both regarded as being very similar and open to the same objections. These critics take various positions, but all regard the Keynesian–Friedman model as 'orthodox', or some such similar term which they regard as pejorative. These critiques will now be analysed.

12.13.1 New Classical Macroeconomics

The new classical school focuses upon the formation of inflationary expectations in Friedman's model. He argues that people usually expect inflation to be what it was in the previous period. This is regarded as irrational by the new classical school because it introduces a systematic error. If inflation is rising, then in Friedman's world economic agents **always underpredict**. If inflation is falling, they always **overpredict**. On either statistical or common sense grounds it is easy to see that a better predictor could be devised. For example, if inflation has risen from 4 to 6 per cent, it is more plausible to expect 8 per cent in the following year rather than 6. Once this point is accepted then there is no reason for the 1–2–3 route shown in **Figure 12.5**. Indeed, 4 is just as likely as 2 as a response to an increase in aggregate demand.

The above analysis is often called **rational expectations**. The argument is that a rational efficient prediction is equally likely to be right or wrong in either duration. Constant underprediction can be eliminated merely by adding a constant to the model. There is also another sense of rational expectations, that expectations should be model-consistent. The proposition is

Figure 12.5   *AD, AS and Phillips Curves*

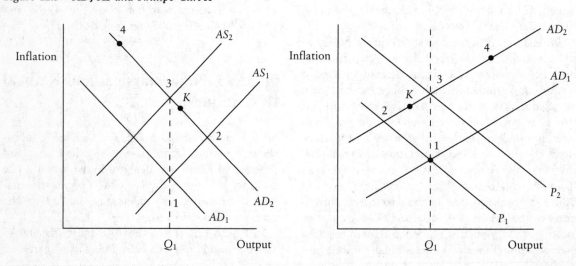

that of economic modellers who believe that the final resting place of the economy in **Figure 12.5** is 3; it is assumed that economic agents will also be able to calculate this.

In its simplest and most plausible form, the new classical critique argues that Friedman's model is just as mechanistic and illogical as the Keynesian analysis. Some new classical economists, however, go on to argue that since it is known that the real wage will not rise even though money wages are being bid up, there is simply an instantaneous movement up the long-run Phillips Curve without the short-run curve coming into play. This would happen only if the government were deliberately to introduce an unpredictable policy change, but this is rarely possible.

☐ 12.13.2 Radical Critiques

Some new classical economists argue for the 'clean kill': that is, an instantaneous reduction in inflation with a minimal cut in unemployment. It should be possible for the government to send out unambiguous signals about its intention to cut the money supply with a view to reducing inflation, causing an instantaneous movement down the AS curve or the long-run Phillips Curve; in other words, reducing inflation without creating unemployment in the process. But such a policy is unlikely to be practicable since it depends upon a government's credibility (economic agents have to believe that the government has both the power and the intention to execute such a policy). Even in 1979–82 the government faced major credibility problems, although its strategy was much less extreme than the 'clean kill' strategy.

Although there are other unorthodox right-wing critiques of the Keynesian–Friedmanite analysis, more attention has been paid to self-styled radical critiques. Radicals draw inspiration from Marx, Kalecki and the 'fundamentalist' interpretation of Keynes advanced by Shackle, Joan Robinson and Paul Davidson. There are many different streams of radical thought. Some radicals – post-Keynesians – stress the significance of speculation and argue that in consequence financial markets are inherently unstable. 'Black Monday'

in October 1987 fitted their theories, but the ease with which the world economy adjusted to the shock came close to refuting this line of thought. Other radicals stress that apparently economic decisions are frequently weapons in a class or sectoral conflict. Inflation may be the by-product of such conflict. If a group of workers wish to increase their share of real income they can do this only by bidding for higher nominal wages. The response by an opposed group will similarly be to raise its prices or to ask for higher wages. Such conflict theories are but some of a whole army of sociological theories of inflation. However, it is the premise of this book that economic models suffice without recourse to sociology.

A less radical but more influential approach emphasises the role of organised labour. It is argued that trade unions bargain for a money wage compatible with their real wage aspirations, after which employers simply add a mark-up to the wage cost in order to cover other costs and to provide an acceptable profit margin. This mark-up is not influenced by the demand for the end-product, hence an increase in demand will not cause money wages and prices to rise or fall relative to their previous levels. In this way of thinking the problem created by raising demand is not that it will fail to be matched by greater supply, thus creating inflation, but rather that UK firms are too uncompetitive to be the preferred source of the things demanded with the result that the excess demand gets side-tracked into imports. This leads to justification for import controls, which were an integral part of the New Cambridge model once favoured by radical Keynesians.

■ 12.14 Financial Policy in the Ascendant

☐ 12.14.1 The Loss of Faith in Incomes Policy

In the 1980s the government relied upon financial policy and largely ignored direct and Keynesian instruments. The argument for an incomes policy is that it can reduce inflationary expectations and so reduce the unemployment cost of fighting inflation caused by the shifting of AS curves upwards. This effect depends upon economic agents having faith in the government achieving its objectives. The Thatcherite view was that, if after 30 years of effort success had not yet been achieved, it was time to abandon the experiment of incomes policy. The essence of the Thatcherite view was that incomes policy has an adverse effect on AS: that is, it causes the AS curve to shift upwards and not downwards as the postwar orthodoxy suggested. The argument is simple:

a   incomes policies interfere with the workings of market forces;
b   market forces ensure efficiency;
c   therefore, incomes policies reduce efficiency; in other words they cause the AS curve to shift upwards.

The full list of postwar incomes policies is set out below. The contrast between Thatcherism and the frequent use of incomes policy during the previous Keynesian era is clear to see.

12.14.2 The Loss of Faith in Fiscal Policy

The Thatcher era also witnessed the (temporary?) end of the use of Keynesian fiscal policy. It has been argued that Keynesian demand management policies carry the seeds of their own destruction because after a while fiscal devices cease to influence AD. The argument is that, once individuals and companies realise that governments are seeking to use the tools of demand management to influence their behaviour, the private sector will change its behaviour. A special and much publicised example of this is the 'rational expectations' model but, in fact, the argument is both more general and more widely accepted.

It is clear that private sector behaviour does depend upon its perceptions of government policy as well as upon objective reality. Sometimes such behaviour can reinforce the workings of policy, as suggested above, because if the business sector believes that governments will maintain a high level of demand they will invest more, which leads to a high level of demand.

1	Cripps–TUC Pact	February 1948–1950
2	Selwyn Lloyd Pay Pause	July 1961–March 1962
3	Guiding Light	April 1962–October 1964

The Labour Government 1964–70 had an incomes policy which changed its name and form:

4	Statement of Intent	December 1964–July 1966
5	The Freeze	July 1966–December 1966
6	Severe restraint	January 1967–July 1967
7	Continued restraint	July 1967–April 1968
8	Reserved restraint	April 1968–June 1970

The Conservative Government (1972–4) had an incomes policy divided into 3 stages:

9	Stage 1	November 1972–January 1973
10	Stage 2	February 1973–October 1973
11	Stage 3	November 1973–February 1974
12	Social Contract	March 1974–July 1975
13	Compulsory non-statutory incomes policy	July 1975–May 1979

Source: Gowland (1989).

However, in most cases the effect on policy is counterproductive. The following example illustrates the use of one tool of fiscal policy: to vary income tax rates so as to vary PDI and hence, given an orthodox Keynesian consumption function, consumers' expenditure. The idea behind this is the manipulation of consumers' expenditure so as to offset fluctuations in investment and exports, and thus maintain a stable, full employment level of output. As a consequence the private sector will have a fluctuating level of consumption. An example of this is shown in **Table 12.8**, in which consumers always have a pre-tax income of 100 and always choose to spend 75 per cent of their post-tax income. The government can then adjust tax rates so as to attain the level of consumers' expenditure necessary for the success of its demand management policy.

In each of three years, consumers' income is 100. The government's stabilisation goals require that consumers' spending be 42, 75 and 60 in the successive years. Believing that the consumption function is such that expenditure is 0.75 of PDI, the government sets taxes at 44 per cent, 0 per cent and 20 per cent. In consequence, PDI is 56, 100 and 80 and so consumers' expenditure is 42, 75 and 60. Stabilisation policy is thus effective. However, the personal sector would prefer a stable path of consumers' expenditure, if only because of the **diminishing marginal utility of consumption.** This principle states that a consumer will obtain less pleasure from consuming a ninth pint of beer than he or she obtained from the eighth. In consequence, **ceteris paribus**, they would rather drink 8 pints of beer on each of two successive nights than 7 on one night and 9 on the other (since the extra benefit – an eighth pint – produces more pleasure than the cost, the forgone ninth).

By extension to the macroeconomic level it is reasonable to assume that, **ceteris paribus**, consumers would like to spend the same amount in real terms each year. Once consumers realise the nature of policy – and the consequent fluctuations in their incomes and consumption that it induces – they will react by adjusting their borrowing and saving plans. The personal sector will maintain a constant path of consumers' expenditure and pay for any extra taxes by drawing upon savings, which will be replenished when taxation is low. Once it is realised how government policy is working, consumers will adjust their behaviour such that if the policy is repeated it will not work, as set out in the lower part of **Table 12.8**: consumers will spend 59 each year – and so maximise their utility – and vary their savings to achieve this.

If necessary they will dissave (borrow) in year 1 so as to achieve their welfare-maximising level of consumption. It is important to realise that consumers do not need to understand how government policy operates, but merely to observe that there are fluctuations in their tax bills which will cause them to adjust their saving. In this case, when the government varies the size of one withdrawal (taxation) it is not income which adjusts (as in the simple model) but another withdrawal

Table 12.8   *Stabilisation Policy*

	Income	Tax	PDI	Consumers' Expenditure	Saving
Initially:					
1	100	44	56	42	14
2	100	0	100	75	25
3	100	20	80	60	20
Once consumers react to policy:					
1	100	44	56	59	−3
2	100	0	100	59	41
3	100	20	80	59	21

(savings), so demand management is ineffective. Hence, in the belief that direct controls and Keynesian instuments are ineffective, the government has relied upon financial policy since 1979.

☐ 12.14.3 *Monetary Targets*

Since Wicksell, in the 1880s, economists have argued that some quantity target, such as money, is necessary as well as a price target, such as the rate of interest. Otherwise, the price level is indeterminate in theory and hyperinflation is possible in practice. However, while the system requires some anchor to avoid this, the institutional structure of the UK provides this without any target. Hence, whilst this argument is both reasonable and theoretically important, it has little practical relevance. Indeed, it was shown above that an exchange rate target ensures that prices grow at the world (German) rate. It is fanciful to imagine that this introduces a serious danger of hyperinflation. It can be demonstrated that a money target is desirable if the economy is subject to shocks in domestic goods markets, and an interest rate target if it is subject to monetary shocks. Similarly, a money target is preferable if shocks come from foreign sources and an exchange rate target if they come from domestic sources. The predominant nature of uncertainty in the UK in the 1980s is probably from the foreign and goods, rather than the domestic and monetary, sectors.

The most interesting argument against monetary targets is the post-Keynesian critique. This argues that money is so powerful in its effects that control of the money supply is likely to have dramatic and unpredictable effects. It is better to let money adjust to shocks, especially to changes in speculative sentiment, than to seek to control it. Money is the best buffer. Milton Friedman argues on similar lines, except that for him the best buffer is no change in money. In other words, post-Keynesians accept Friedman's argument for a neutral financial policy, but disagree with him about the meaning of neutrality. In the UK context the argument is that although the effects of no control have been devastating, the effects of

trying to control money would have been still more destabilising.

Friedman has always argued that excess money growth causes high and variable (nominal) interest rates. Monetary growth raises inflation and inflationary expectations. Both cause interest rates to rise and the monetary authorities, moreover, have to increase rates still further to reduce inflation. Friedman could argue that the period 1984–88 in the UK proves his point.

☐ 12.14.4 *The EMS and Monetary Targets*

Many of the arguments for an exchange rate target closely mirror those for a monetary target. The arguments for the ERM, like monetarism, impose a form of discipline on economic management that is designed to induce lower inflation and greater stability. The statistical data presented above showed that, at least in the short run, the two indicators do present divergent signals about the behaviour of the economy. In 1991, the monetarist Patrick Minford argued that membership of the ERM was forcing the government to pursue a misguided monetary policy. He argued that the consequence was an excessively rapid rise in unemployment. This is a good example of the fact that in recent years arguments in favour of variable exchange rates (and so opposition to the ERM) have been based on domestic macroeconomic grounds. In its negative form, the argument is that exchange rate constraints may inhibit freedom to exercise domestic instruments to combat inflation and unemployment. The German authorities have found that trying to stabilise the DM tends to lead to excess monetary growth, because such intervention leads to a positive overseas impact on the money supply. In the UK the argument is usually more forcefully put: higher exchange rates reduce inflation, lower ones reduce unemployment. Hence a government needs the freedom to adjust exchange rates for domestic reasons.

As previously noted, if the ERM is to survive there must be coordination of monetary policies;

probably a common DCE target. Otherwise, differential macroeconomic policies will produce differential inflation and so mean that ERM rates cease to be in equilibria. Given that the UK's trade pattern is different from that of the rest of the EU, it will be harder for it to maintain ERM membership than for existing other countries. Hence the need for macro coordination is greater. Indeed for good or ill, ERM membership probably implies not only a monetary target but a common one with Germany.

12.15 The Desirability of Intermediate Targets

☐ 12.15.1 The Case for Targets

From 1976 to 1985 UK governments pursued monetary targets. After that, until his resignation, Mr Lawson argued against any effective target. It was his critics who argued for a restoration of some target: either the money supply, or the exchange rate through membership of the ERM.

The most basic case for targets is that they give information about the **future behaviour of objectives**. In the UK, monetary developments in 1986–87 suggested that inflation would accelerate, eventually. It did, in late 1988. Advance knowledge should make it possible to take corrective action. If this is done, less drastic measures will be needed than if action is delayed. The dramatic 5 per cent rise in UK interest rates in May–October 1988 would not have been necessary if a 1 per cent increase in 1986 and a 2 per cent increase in 1987 had been implemented.

In addition, three arguments have been put in favour of targets. The first is that a money supply target acts as an automatic stabiliser: that is, it will reduce the deviation of output from its trend level. This can be accepted by many Keynesians since it is agreed that the action necessary to meet a monetary target will frequently reduce the impact of shocks on output. The difference, of course, is that Milton Friedman and Brunner have argued that this reduction of the impact of

shocks is the most that is attainable, whereas Tobin and other self-styled Keynesians believe that more is possible. However, less emphasis is now given to this aspect of Keynesian beliefs, since the implicit fine-tuning discretionary policy is very hard to implement successfully.

The shock analysed for illustrative purposes is a fall in exports caused, for example, by a world recession. This will reduce the overseas effect below what it would otherwise be. In this case it is necessary to influence one of the other items so that it is larger (or less negative) than it otherwise would be, and thus offset the monetary effects of the fall in exports. Any action that would do this would be expansionary in any model, whether lower interest rates, higher public spending or a relaxation of credit ceilings. Consequently, the reduction in output and employment caused by a fall in exports would be offset. The monetarist argument is that setting the economy on an automatic course is better than letting the authorities use their judgement. Hence, it is universally accepted that observance of a monetary target will be stabilising. However, whereas Brunner and Friedman argue that this is the maximum attainable degree of stability, Keynesian writers would either rely on discretionary action or on automatic stabilisers of a fiscal kind.

The second argument is beguilingly attractive. The private sector needs information about the public sector's behaviour if it is to plan its activities optimally. Information about government monetary policy is the most useful information that private sector agents can have, so a government should commit itself to a specific path of monetary growth. This proposition is very similar to the arguments put forward for indicative planning in the 1960s. The counterarguments of opponents of monetary targets are that more useful information can be given – for example, a commitment to price stability or full employment – or that the benefits of more information are less than the costs imposed by monetary targets.

However, much more attention has been given, at least in the UK, to the more sophisticated argument of the role of the money supply in the formation of inflationary expectations. This argument can range from a purely economic argument to one incorporating a large element of politics. Minford has argued that the function of monetary targets is to show that the government 'means business about inflation'.

The third argument for targets is that they are necessary to constrain or discipline governments. Buchanan has been a frequent proponent of this view, but it is even more closely associated with Friedman. This view can be put in a rather illiberal, undemocratic fashion: governments, left to themselves, will pursue policies that cause inflation, perhaps to buy votes, so it is necessary to find devices which will constrain them. This method of presentation is, however, unfair to its proponents who, to use Buchanan's terminology, want to see the introduction of an 'economic constitution'. Governments have enormous potential political power but accept constraints upon it, either through a written constitution as in the USA, or tacitly as in the UK. Such constraints involve both an acceptance of 'rules of the game' (the opposition is not kept out of power by force) and of rights such as freedom of the press, as well as procedural safeguards, such as trial by jury. Buchanan and Friedman argue that it is equally necessary to constrain the economic power of government by similar devices. In this form the argument is not unreasonable, although one may argue that the majority's right to use economic power is sufficiently is circumscribed by a political constitution. Nevertheless, it is worthy of note that this form of argument is new to monetarism in the twentieth century; traditionally monetarists believed in discretion, not fixed rules (for example, in their contests in the nineteenth century with supporters of the gold standard).

To summarise, monetarists believe that governments should accept a commitment to a monetary target and should be prepared to make sacrifices to achieve it. This is justified because of the impact of monetary targets on expectations and because their adoption constrains governments and tends to stabilise output. None of these is without foundation. The 'automatic stabiliser' proposition is incontestably valid; the dispute is whether discretion or an alternative rule could do better. Monetary targets do convey information

and influence expectations, but it is as easy to overstate as to ignore this case for their introduction.

Nevertheless, an issue which needs to be addressed is 'why money?' Similar arguments could be constructed for interest rate targets, other quantity targets, exchange rate targets or more complex rules. This is seen most clearly in the discipline case. Buchanan acknowledges that a balanced budget rule (or a maximum tax: GDP ratio) or fixed exchange rates may be better constraints on governments. So what are the relative merits of monetary and other targets?

■ 12.16 Broad and Narrow Money

Governments must choose the intermediate target of macroeconomic policy: the money supply, the exchange rate or whatever. It is possible to approach this question in an analytical framework. In this case one must determine which model is most useful in analysing the economy. In this context, the distinction between approximate targets and indicators is crucial. However, it is also possible to approach the question in a pragmatic, indeed eclectic manner. Governments have various instruments at their disposal. They wish to manipulate them so as to influence various ultimate targets, especially inflation and unemployment. The role of intermediate variables is twofold. They must give some indication of the stance of macroeconomic policy: is it deflationary or expansionary? They must also give some indication as to the likely future development of the economy. Is it heading for recession? In this context, it is then a pragmatic question which of the available variables performs these roles best. Even Friedman's views can be presented as a particular case within this framework. Governments should obviously look at a range of such variables. However, monetarism amounts to a statement that the government should concentrate on a single variable: the money supply. Monetarists would argue that economic management would have been better if the government had concentrated on a single measure, money, rather than pursued exchange-rate targetting in various forms. Those who argue for the ERM argue the reverse.

It is interesting to observe the various measures of money. Friedman and Schwartz argued that one should choose between these measures on pragmatic grounds – money is what does the work of money. In other words, the best definition of money is to be selected using the criteria outlined in the preceding paragraph. However, it is very likely that the best definition of money will change from time to time, hence it is something of a problem for monetarism if different definitions of money give different signals. What should a policy maker do if broad money signals a danger of inflation, but narrow money a danger of depression? Indeed, those opposed to monetarism have frequently argued that this was a major practical defect of the creed. Measurement problems exist in all areas of economics. Nevertheless, there is some justice in this criticism.

In a modern economy, narrow definitions of money are likely to grow much more slowly than broader ones. Narrow money is held almost exclusively for transaction purposes. Moreover, it is held largely by the personal sector. Theoretically, it is easy to demonstrate that these balances should grow less quickly than income. Broad income includes balance held for precautionary motives and some savings. Much of broad money is held by the corporate sector. These balances should grow much more rapidly than income, so a 5 per cent growth in narrow money would suggest something very different from a 5 per cent growth in broad money. These differences are reflected in the government's 1993 indicative targets. However, this is not a major problem. In some ways it is similar to converting fahrenheit into centigrade, or vice versa. The government can calculate the monetary growth consistent with its inflation target (2 per cent) and its growth target (3 per cent). These are consistent with about 3 per cent growth in M0 and about 10 per cent growth in broader measures of money. If either definition of money grows less quickly than these figures, then monetary policy is acting in a deflationary manner. Contrawise, if money is growing more rapidly than these figures, then it is intensifying inflationary pressures. One may extend this ana-

lysis somewhat. On the whole, broad money gives signals about economic developments at an earlier stage than narrow money. Broad money gives signals about a wider range of economic activity, including (crucially) house and other asset prices. A rise in interest rates will, on the other hand, produce a more rapid impact on narrow than broad money. All of this is relatively straightforward but would take us far beyond the confines of this book.

■ *12.17* Direct Controls on Credit

The analysis presented above regarding the relationship between the ERM and monetary policy stressed that direct controls on credit were one of the few instruments that might preserve the autonomy of domestic economic policy within a monetary union.

In 1988, with inflation accelerating and a £15 billion BoP deficit, it was clear that either money or credit, or both, needed to be controlled. Moreover, since the PSBR was already in surplus and the government had in 1985 ruled out the use of debt sales as an instrument of monetary policy, it followed that to control money it was necessary to control bank lending. Thus Keynesians and monetarists were agreed about **what** was necessary, but not about **why**. Many critics suggested that it would be either necessary or desirable to use quantity ceilings or other direct controls on credit, but the Chancellor opted for the alternative of control of interest rates. The choices are illustrated in **Figure 12.6**. The authorities wish to reduce credit from Q_1 to Q_2. They can either ration credit and aim for point 2, or raise interest rates to r_2 and aim for point 3.

In general the following considerations apply to the choice of methods:

1 **Direct controls are ineffective:** Any form of rationing creates an incentive to evade it (profitably!), resulting in the classic black market. Direct controls on credit led, during the 1960s, to black markets (called parallel markets) and to disintermediation (see **pp. 125** and **139**). Direct controls on bank depos-

Figure 12.6   *Alternative Approaches to Credit Control*

its (the corset) led similarly to evasion in the 1970s. The simplest form of evasion involves the use of the overseas sector, and involves a loan (or credit card) from, say, the Midland Bank of Paris rather than the Midland Bank of York. Evasion is a serious problem with direct controls, but with personal sector credit they could probably be effective **for a time.**

2   **Direct controls are (Pareto) inefficient:** Direct controls lead to a loss of economic welfare.

3   **Direct controls are inequitable or unfair:** Some lenders and borrowers are far more adversely affected than others.

4   **Direct controls distort official statistics:** This may not seem important, but it is probably one of the two main arguments against direct controls on credit. A direct control will probably be partially effective, but to an unknown extent. Hence it is no longer clear whether policy is too tight or too slack. For example, if the authorities wish the level of credit to be £250 billion and use direct controls, official statistics will understate the size of credit. Black market transactions are never included in official data, and rarely even under official purview in the short term. Hence, if the official data shows £240 billion of credit, it is not clear if official policy is too tight, too

slack or about right; it depends on whether the black market is more or less than £10 billion.

Given these circumstances, the reader may wonder why anyone supports the use of direct controls. There are two main reasons. One is that rationing of any kind leads to a lower price – in this case interest rates – than would otherwise be the case. This may be thought desirable in its own right or as a means to a preferred redistribution. Lower interest rates help the rich, mortgagees, the young and debtors generally at the expense of the poor, the old and creditors generally.

More usually, lower interest rates are welcomed because they lead to a higher ratio of investment to consumers' expenditure. Investment is usually more interest-sensitive than consumers' expenditure in empirical studies, and moreover in theory a rise in interest rates has an ambiguous effect on consumers' expenditure since the income and substitution effects operate in opposition direction.

The other argument is more interesting. It is that direct controls are relatively quick-acting, unlike interest rates. Indeed, their effect may wear off quickly. Nevertheless, for a short period a direct control is likely to work, especially if used skilfully by the authorities. This may be invaluable if the authorities have got policy seriously wrong, as Mr Lawson had in 1988. In similar circumstances direct controls proved useful in 1974 and 1978, whereas their absence made the conduct of monetary policy very difficult in 1979–80. This is the choice concerning direct controls on credit: the fast-acting instrument against the disadvantages of black markets. This choice is probably the most important short-term economic policy issue in the UK at present.

12.18 Are Budget Surpluses Beneficial?

In his 1988 and 1989 Budget speeches, Mr Lawson took considerable pride in large Budget surpluses. Indeed, there was much press comment about the possibility and desirability of running Budget surpluses of sufficient size for sufficient time to pay. The Budget thereafter moved rapidly into deficit, and is expected to reach £50 billion in 1993–94. This revived the issue of whether the size of the budget deficit mattered of itself. Classical authors have always argued that a Budget deficit was undesirable. In support of such a policy one may argue that a surplus will:

a   **benefit** future generations **at the expense of** present ones. After centuries of argument, it has been agreed amongst economists that the national debt is a burden and does impose costs on future generations.

b   **eliminate the danger of crowding-out,** which occurs when government spending or borrowing reduces private spending or borrowing in an undesirable way. There is no evidence that it has ever been a serious problem in the UK, but it is still of some relevance. In particular, the withdrawal by the government from the long-term bond market has led to an upsurge of private corporate bond issues.

c   **raises the saving ratio.** Private sector saving fell in the UK in the 1980s. A Budget deficit – public sector saving – may be a substitute for it (see **p. 25**).

A deficit will have the opposite and, hence, undesirable effect. It imposes burdens on future generations and lowers the overall savings ratio. In some circumstances, it may crowd out private sector expenditure with deleterious effects on the economy. Keynesian authors believe, however, that all these effects are relatively unimportant. They believe that budgetary policy should be used to stabilise the economy. In the UK, some monetarist authors have taken a similar position and, as noted above, they have argued that the Budget balance is an important contribution to monetary growth. They therefore believe that Budget surplus and deficits are unimportant in themselves so long as the money supply is growing at the correct level. In some circumstances, budget deficits might be desirable as a means of increasing monetary growth. However, most monetarists believe that the debt management policy is a better tool of monetary control. Hence most monetarists, Milton Friedman notable among them, believe that Budget balance should be a long-term aim of government policy. In the short term, though, governments should be willing to accept a large deficit or surplus if the means of eliminating it are undesirable. These consequences might either be monetary or supply side. Friedman has frequently emphasised that it is not desirable to increase taxation as a means of eliminating Budget deficits since, in his view, lower taxation is almost certainly preferable to running a Budget surplus.

12.19 An Independent Central Bank

In recent years, there has been a revival of interest in the concept of an independent central bank: that is, one which is not subject to direct political control. In both the USA and Germany, the respective central banks can formulate and execute monetarist policy, whereas in the UK final decision making power rests with the Prime Minister and Chancellor. Mr Lawson argued in favour of an independent central bank in his resignation speech in 1989, and Mr Lamont argued similarly in his resignation speech after his dismissal in 1993. However, the principal stimulus to an independent central bank has come from the Maastricht Treaty which both embodies an independent European central bank and requires that each member country will make its central bank independent by 1997. Most members of the EU, notably France, have introduced legislation to enact this.

Various arguments have been made in favour of an independent central bank. One is the rather negative, but not unreasonable, proposition that politicians have not been very successful with economic policy. It is argued that they are too prone to put short-term considerations first and ignore the longer-term consequences of their policies. This danger arises in particular with expansionary policy. Normally, expansionary policy leads to a rise in output within six months and a fall in unemployment within 18 months. These desirable effects appear before any adverse affect on inflation. Even if inflation rises somewhat, the main effects will not be seen until inflationary expectations have responded (at least two years in the future). This proposition can be restated as saying that the Phillips curve trade-off is much more favourable in the short term than in the long term. Hence electoral exigency means that governments are tempted to expand the economy so as to win an election, knowing that the costs will not be seen until after the election.

In recent years, this argument has been reiterated in a more sophisticated form. Suppose that politicians can in fact, resist the temptations described in the preceding paragraph. Economic agents, especially in financial markets, will be uncertain as to whether or not they will resist temptation, and hence inflationary expectations will remain high. On the other hand, economic agents will have confidence in an independent central bank. They know that it does not have to face the electorate and therefore can pursue a consistent anti-inflationary policy. This is usually referred to as credibility, resulting in lower inflationary expectations (which make low inflation easier to achieve). In general, it is argued that no democratic government will ever possess sufficient credibility. These theoretical musings are reinforced by statistical evidence which seems to suggest that economic performance is better in those countries with an independent central bank.

The case against an independent central bank is partly one of political theory. Mrs Thatcher and many left-wing commentators believe that governments should possess the power to manage the economy, even if they may misuse it. Moreover, it can be argued that an independent central bank may reflect a credible anti-inflationary policy, rather than be the cause of it. The German policy community is committed to fighting inflation for many social and historical reasons; therefore an independent central bank is enshrined in the German constitution. This does not mean that introducing an independent central bank would create a similar consensus and credibility in the UK. Indeed, one might argue that an independent central bank is but the latest of a long series of

gimmicks which have been suggested in the UK. For at least 30 years, commentators and governments have sought a magic cure for the UK economy. Incomes policies (several times), the ERM, floating exchange rates and monetary targets are but a few of the (inconsistent) nostrums that have been suggested.

■ *12.20* Unbalanced Policy

Mr Lawson's boom was marked by a combination of rapid monetary growth and a tight fiscal policy. In the Reagan era, US policy was the exact opposite. In this section, we briefly discuss the impact of unbalanced policy and conclude by emphasising one of the major themes of this chapter: how monetary policy influences the economy.

Governments have usually used monetary and fiscal policy at the same time. For example, during the Barber expansion (1971–73), the money supply grew rapidly and there was a record Budget deficit. During the Jenkins squeeze (1968–69) both monetary and fiscal indicators measured the tightness of policy (the first Budget surplus for 50 years, the smallest money supply growth for 15 years). On occasions, governments used one instrument earlier than another (monetary policy was tightened in 1974, fiscal policy in 1975), or eased one without adjusting the other (monetary policy alone was eased in 1977–78). Nevertheless, the tools were always in approximate balance, whereas since 1980 government policy has been unbalanced. However, it is necessary to examine the impact of an unbalanced policy, combining a loose monetary policy with a tight fiscal policy (it is interesting to note that at the same time the USA pursued an equally unbalanced policy but the other way around). The effects of this lack of balance mean that the basic assumptions of macroeconomics must be relaxed: the economy can no longer be treated as if it were producing a single good. Instead, it is both necessary and possible to examine the form and duration that the stimulus to demand takes.

Monetary policy operates through **changing the demand for assets**. For an expansionary policy:

a   an increase in the money supply creates an excess of supply over demand in the money market;

b   some of the excess money is switched to those assets which are substitutes for money (say, houses, antiques and Spanish villas);

c   this extra demand means that there is excess demand for these assets. Hence either their price rises (antiques), or their quantity (Spanish villas), depending on the elasticity of supply. The two examples cited are unusual examples of (almost) perfectly inelastic and elastic supply respectively, and rather more often both price and output rise (houses).

Some monetarists argue that supply is virtually inelastic (classical monetarism); others, including French monetarists, that it is perfectly elastic. Milton Friedman takes the compromise position: output responds in the short run but price in the long run. Hence, to examine the effects of the imbalance, one must seek to list the assets that private sector economic agents, companies and persons wish to purchase with their excess money holdings:

a   foreign assets: factories, shares, property.

b   consumer durables: (in particular) cars and electrical goods. Most of these came from abroad, so there was little effect on prices, but an enormous BoP deficit was created.

c   shares and financial assets: one reason why, in the boom prior to October 1979, share prices rose faster in the UK than elsewhere.

d   houses.

Undoubtedly, the monetary expansion caused the explosion in house prices. This generated a rise in housebuilding but it also caused serious social problems as well as impeding labour mobility. More generally unbalanced demand management led to the concentration of growth in a few sectors of the economy and a few regions, notably the South-East.

Bibliography

Allsop, C. and D. Mayes (1985) Chapter 13 in D. Morris (ed.) *The Economic System in the UK* (Oxford University Press) 3rd edn.

Bank of England (1971) 'Competition and Credit Control. The New Approach', *Bank of England Quarterly Bulletin* (December).

Bank of England (1990a) 'Monetary Aggregates in a Changing Environment: a Statistical Discussion Paper', *Discussion Paper*, 47 (March).

Bank of England (1990b) 'The Determination of the Monetary Aggregates', *Bank of England Quarterly Bulletin* (August).

Bank of England (1991) 'Liquid Assets Outside M4', *Bank of England Quarterly Bulletin* (May).

Blackaby, F. (ed.) (1978) *British Economic Policy 1960–74* (London: Heinemann).

Cmnd 7858 (1980) *Monetary Control* (London: HMSO).

Dornbusch, R. and R. Layard (1987) *The Performance of the British Economy* (Oxford University Press).

Gowland, D.H. (1984) *Controlling the Money Supply* (London: Croom Helm) 2nd edn.

Gowland, D.H. (1989) *Whatever Happened to Demand Management?* (London: RJA Books).

Lawson, N. (1988) *The State of the Market* (London: Institute of Economic Affairs).

Minford, P. (1989) *The Sunday Telegraph*, 5 March.

Shields, J. 'Controlling Household Credit', *National Institute Economic Review* (August).

Walters, A. (1986) *Britain's Economic Renaissance* (Oxford University Press).

Index